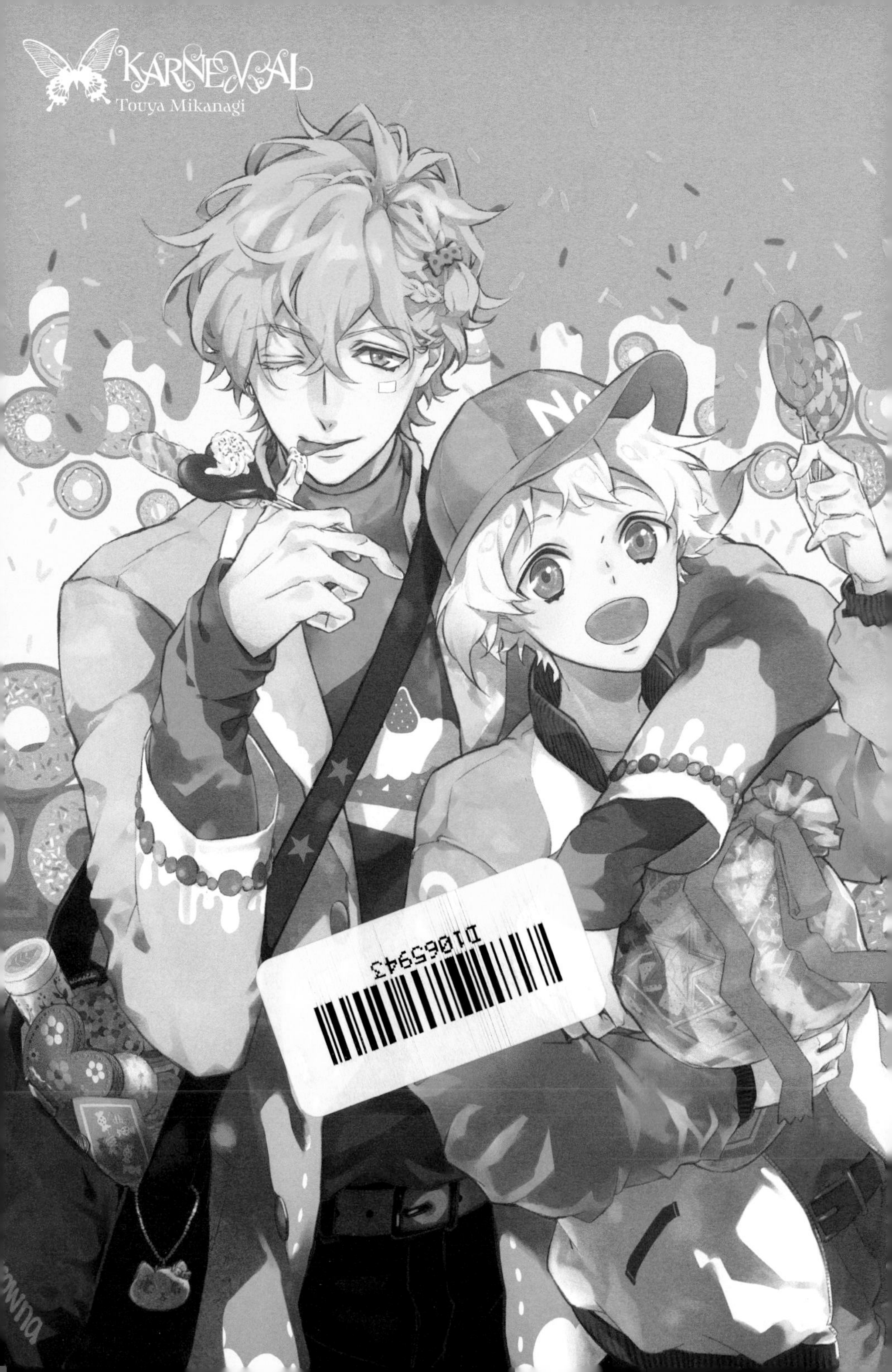
KARNEVAL
Touya Mikanagi

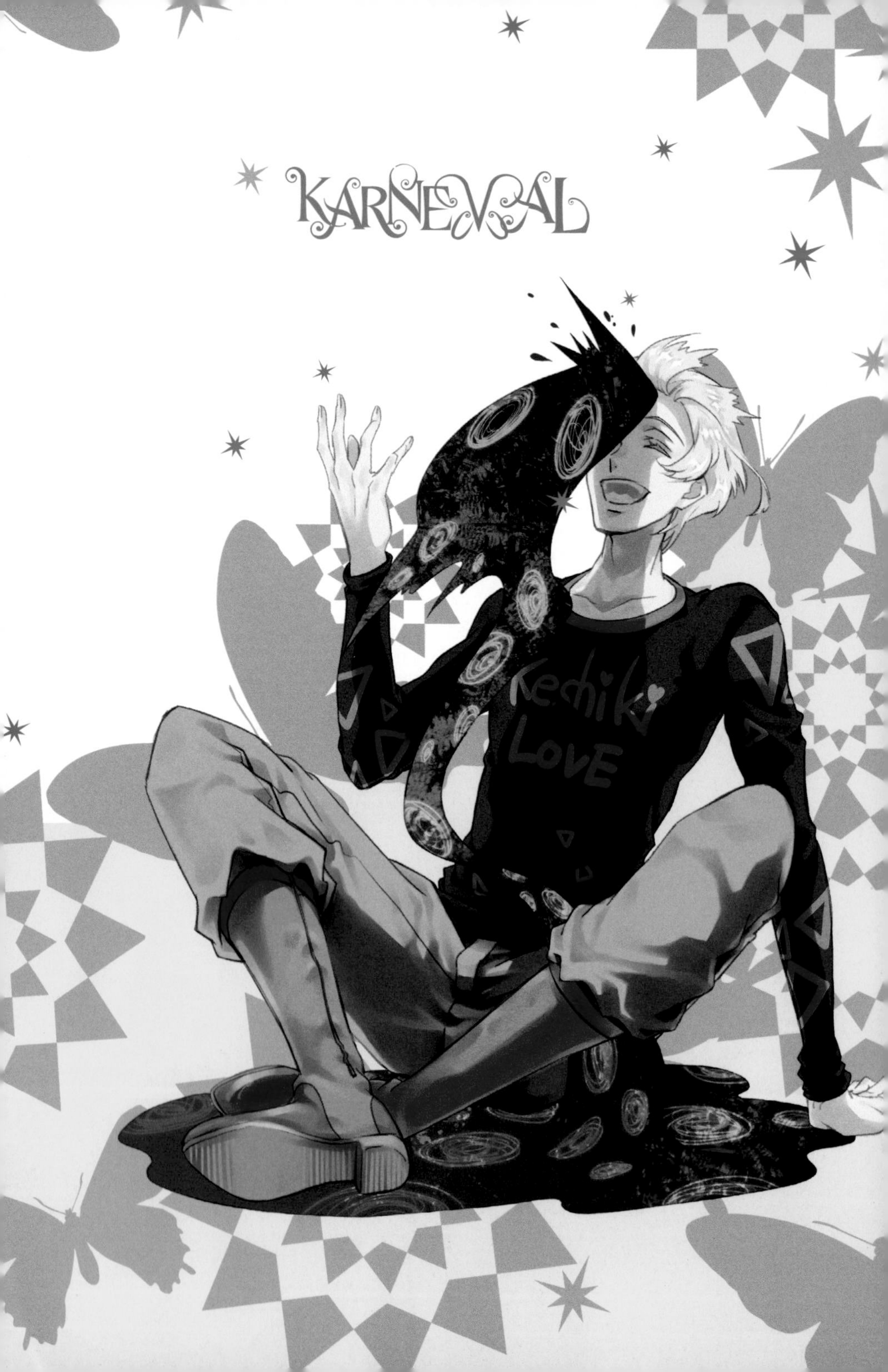
KARNEVAL
Kechiki
LOVE

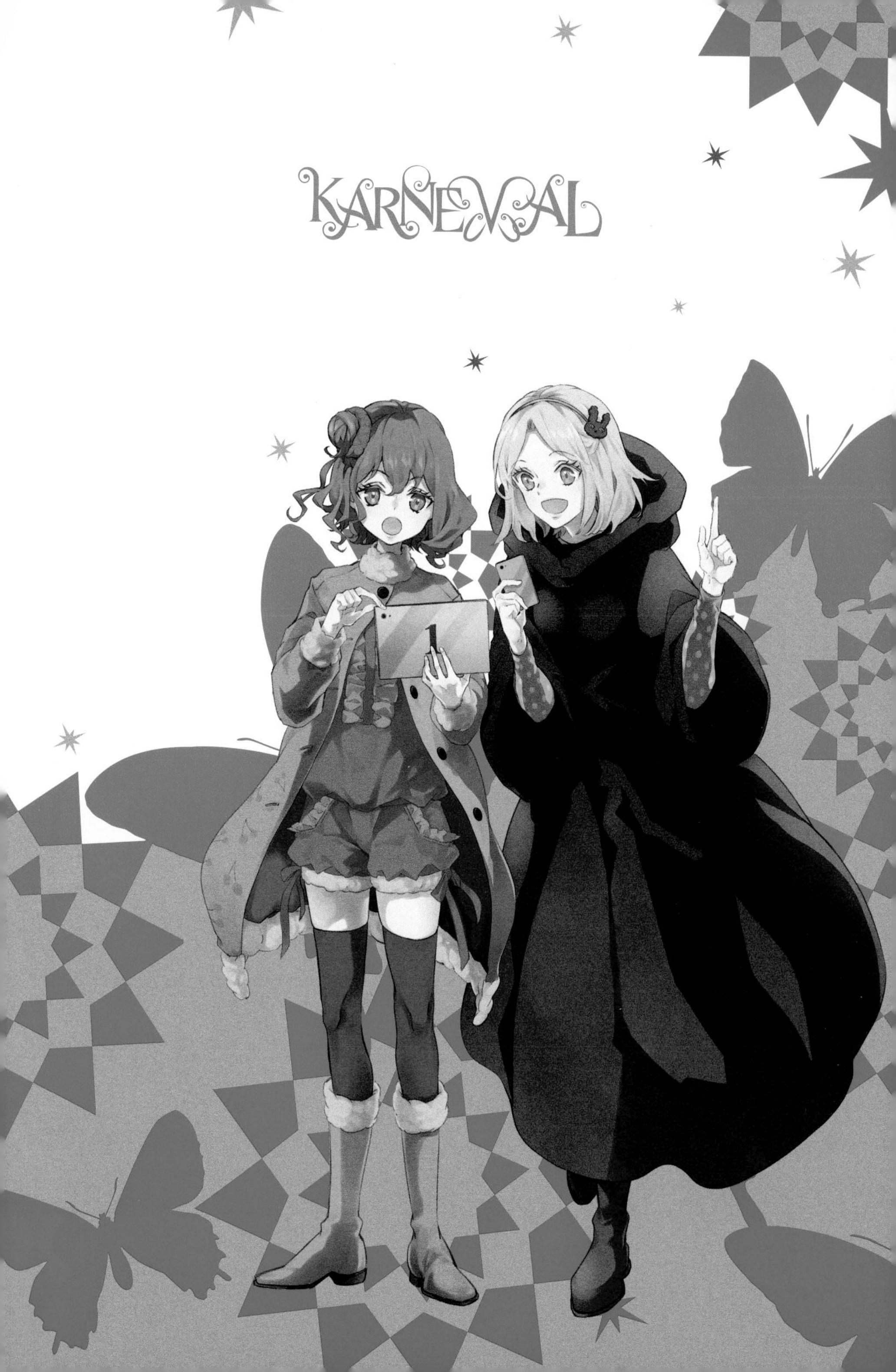
KARNEVAL
1

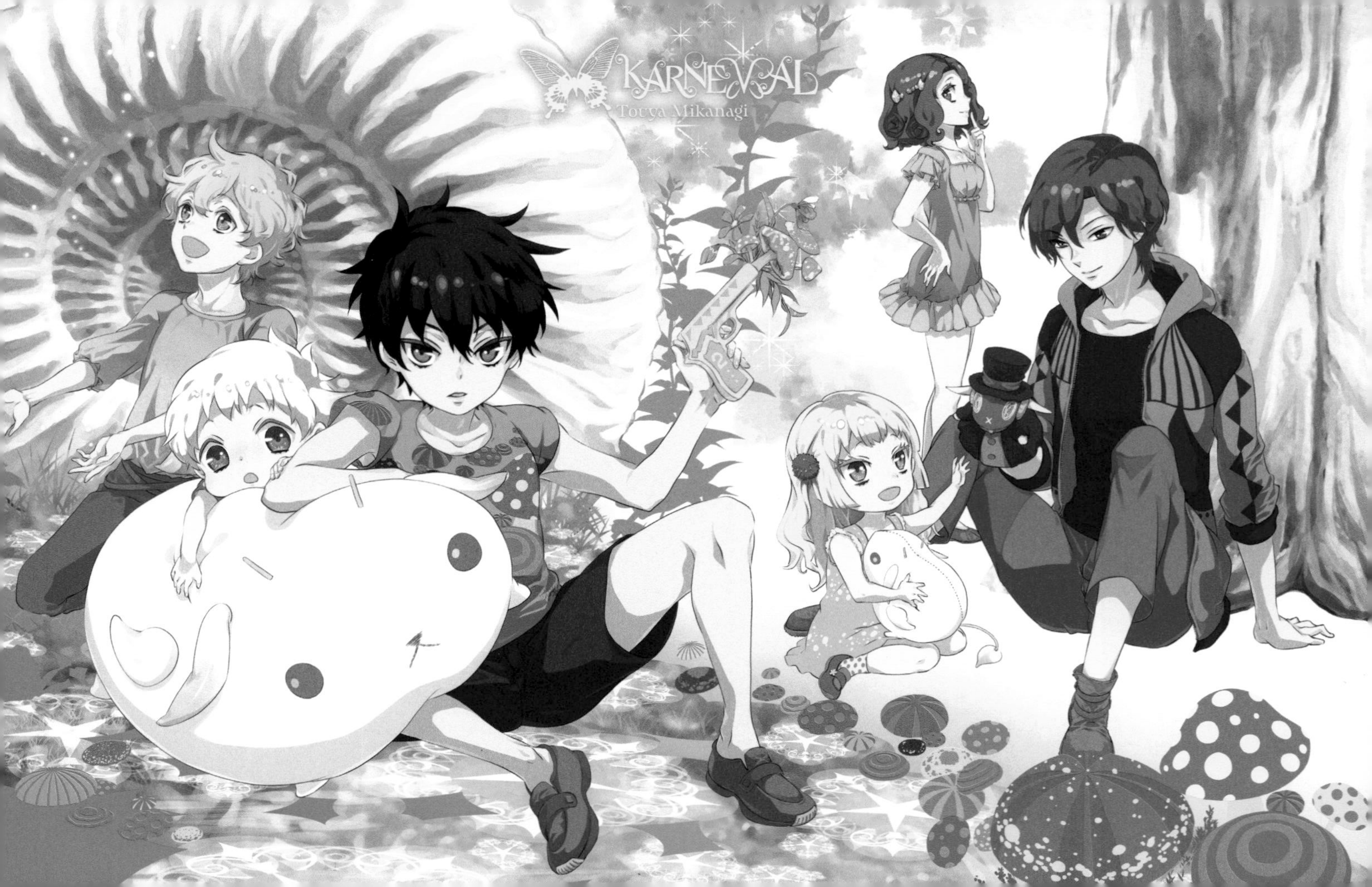
KARNEVAL
Touya Mikanagi

KARNEVAL 13

Touya Mikanagi

STORY

FROM THE DEPTHS OF NAI'S MIND, A VOICE CALLS OUT TO HIM REMINDING HIM OF HIS ROLE AS "THE REGULATOR." THE VOICE...IS HIS OWN CONSCIOUSNESS. IN THE MEANTIME, CIRCUS CONTINUES GATHERING CLUES ABOUT KAFKA—AND GAINS AN UNEXPECTED LEAD WHEN VERANOCHKA REQUESTS WITH HER DYING BREATH THAT AGENTS PERFORM AN AUTOPSY ON HER PERSON. INSIDE HER BODY, THEY FIND A MESSAGE SHE LEFT BEHIND, LAMENTING THE MANY LIVES SHE STOLE AFTER HER VARUGA TRANSFORMATION...ALONG WITH A PET VARUGA WHO BELONGS TO A KAFKA EXECUTIVE! AND WHILE ON A SEPARATE MISSION EXPLORING THE ALLONGAN VILLAGE OF THE GHAGATAR MOUNTAIN RANGE, HIRATO DISCOVERS AZANA—A TRAITOR WHO FORMERLY WORKED IN THE RESEARCH TOWER. AT THE SAME TIME, GAREKI UNEXPECTEDLY RUNS INTO NAI BACK IN KARASUNA AND...!?

CHARACTERS OF KARNEVAL

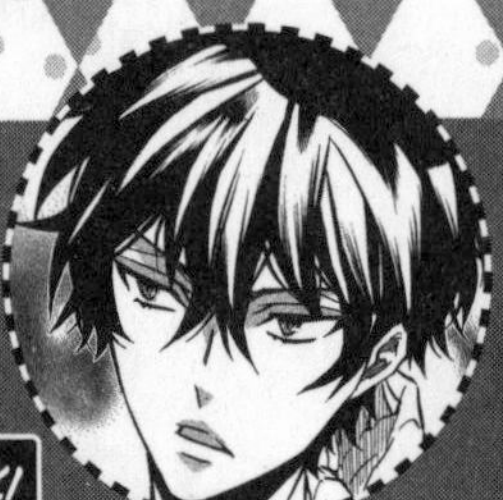

GAREKI

HE MET NAI INSIDE AN EERIE MANSION THAT HE HAD INTENDED TO BURGLARIZE. HE IS CURRENTLY STUDYING AT THE RESEARCH TOWER IN ORDER TO BECOME CIRCUS'S FIRST COMBAT MEDIC.

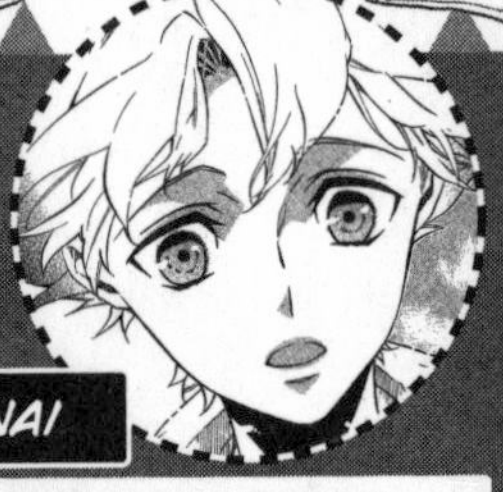

NAI

A BOY WHO POSSESSES EXTRAORDINARY HEARING AND HAS A SOMEWHAT LIMITED UNDERSTANDING OF HOW THE WORLD WORKS. DISAPPEARED FROM THE RESEARCH TOWER DURING AN INSPECTION.

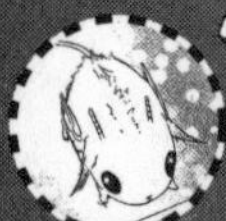

NIJI

THE ANIMAL FROM WHICH NAI WAS CREATED. THEY EXIST ONLY IN THE RAINBOW FOREST, A HIGHLY UNUSUAL ECOSYSTEM THAT ALLOWED THE NIJI TO EVOLVE AS THEY DID.

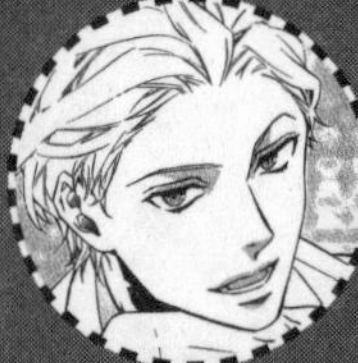

AKARI

A BRILLIANT DOCTOR AND RESEARCHER IN THE NATIONAL DEFENSE'S RESEARCH TOWER. HE TERRIFIES YOGI, AND HE AND HIRATO FIGHT LIKE CATS AND DOGS.

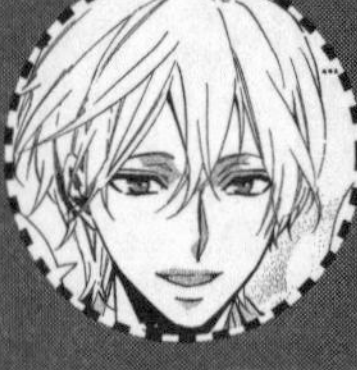

KAROKU

HE FIRST MET NAI AFTER HE FLED FROM AN ORGANIZATION CALLED "KAFKA." HE HAS RECOVERED HIS MEMORIES AND IS NOW ASSISTING THE GOVERNMENT.

NATIONAL SUPREME DEFENSE FORCE "CIRCUS" 2ND SHIP

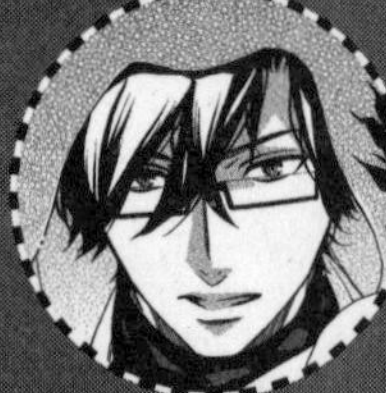

HIRATO

CAPTAIN OF CIRCUS'S 2ND SHIP. NAI, WHO BROUGHT HIM A BRACELET BELONGING TO CIRCUS, AND GAREKI ARE CURRENTLY UNDER HIS PROTECTION. HE AND TSUKITACHI, CAPTAIN OF CIRCUS'S 1ST SHIP, ARE FORMER CLASSMATES.

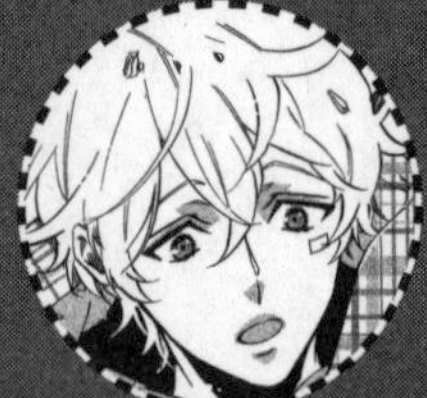

YOGI

CIRCUS'S 2ND SHIP COMBAT SPECIALIST. HE HAS A CHEERFUL, FRIENDLY PERSONALITY. HE WAS BORN THE CROWN PRINCE OF RIMHAKKA, A KINGDOM THAT WAS DESTROYED IN A VARUGA ATTACK.

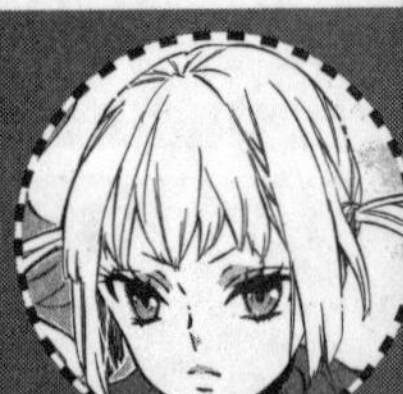

TSUKUMO

CIRCUS'S 2ND SHIP COMBAT SPECIALIST. A BEAUTIFUL GIRL WITH A COOL, SERIOUS PERSONALITY. RECENTLY, SHE SEEMS TO HAVE TAKEN UP SEWING STUFFED TOYS AS A PASTIME. SHE HATES BUGS.

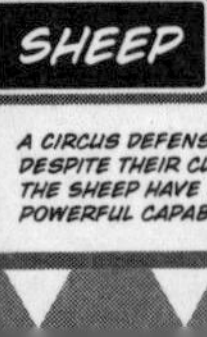

SHEEP

A CIRCUS DEFENSE SYSTEM. DESPITE THEIR CUTE APPEARANCE, THE SHEEP HAVE SOME VERY POWERFUL CAPABILITIES.

Q: WHAT IS CIRCUS?

A: THE EQUIVALENT OF THE REAL-WORLD POLICE. THEY CONDUCT THEIR LARGE-SCALE "OPERATIONS" UTILIZING COORDINATED, POWERFUL ATTACKS WITHOUT FOREWARNING TO ENSURE THEIR TARGETS WILL NOT ESCAPE ARREST!! AFTER SUCH AN OPERATION, CIRCUS PERFORMS A "SHOW" FOR THE PEOPLE OF THE CITY AS AN APOLOGY FOR THE FEAR AND INCONVENIENCE THEIR WORK MAY HAVE CAUSED. IN SHORT, "CIRCUS" IS A CHEERFUL(?) AGENCY THAT CARRIES OUT THEIR MISSION DAY AND NIGHT TO APPREHEND EVIL AND PROTECT THE PEACE OF THE LAND.

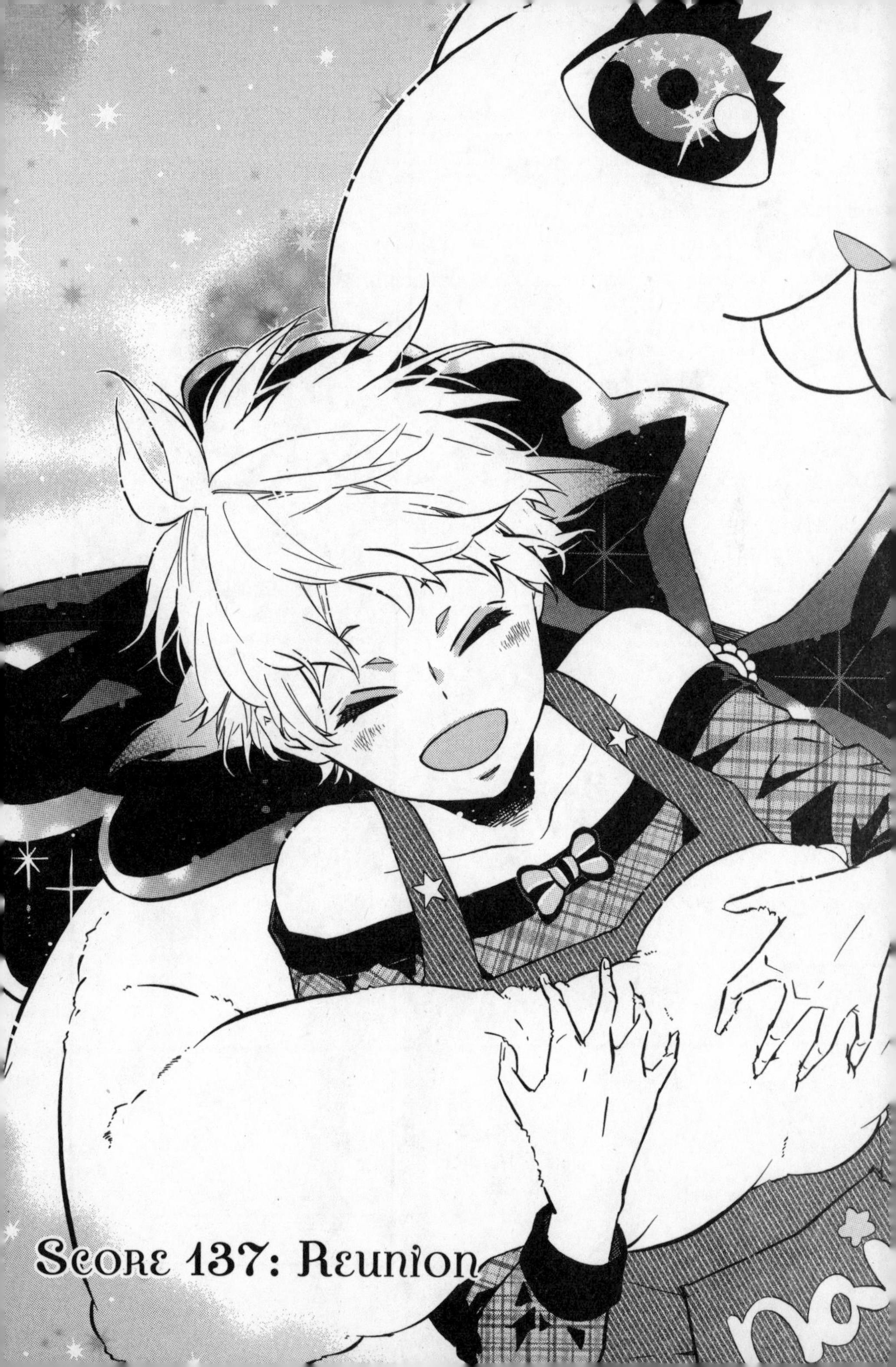
Score 137: Reunion

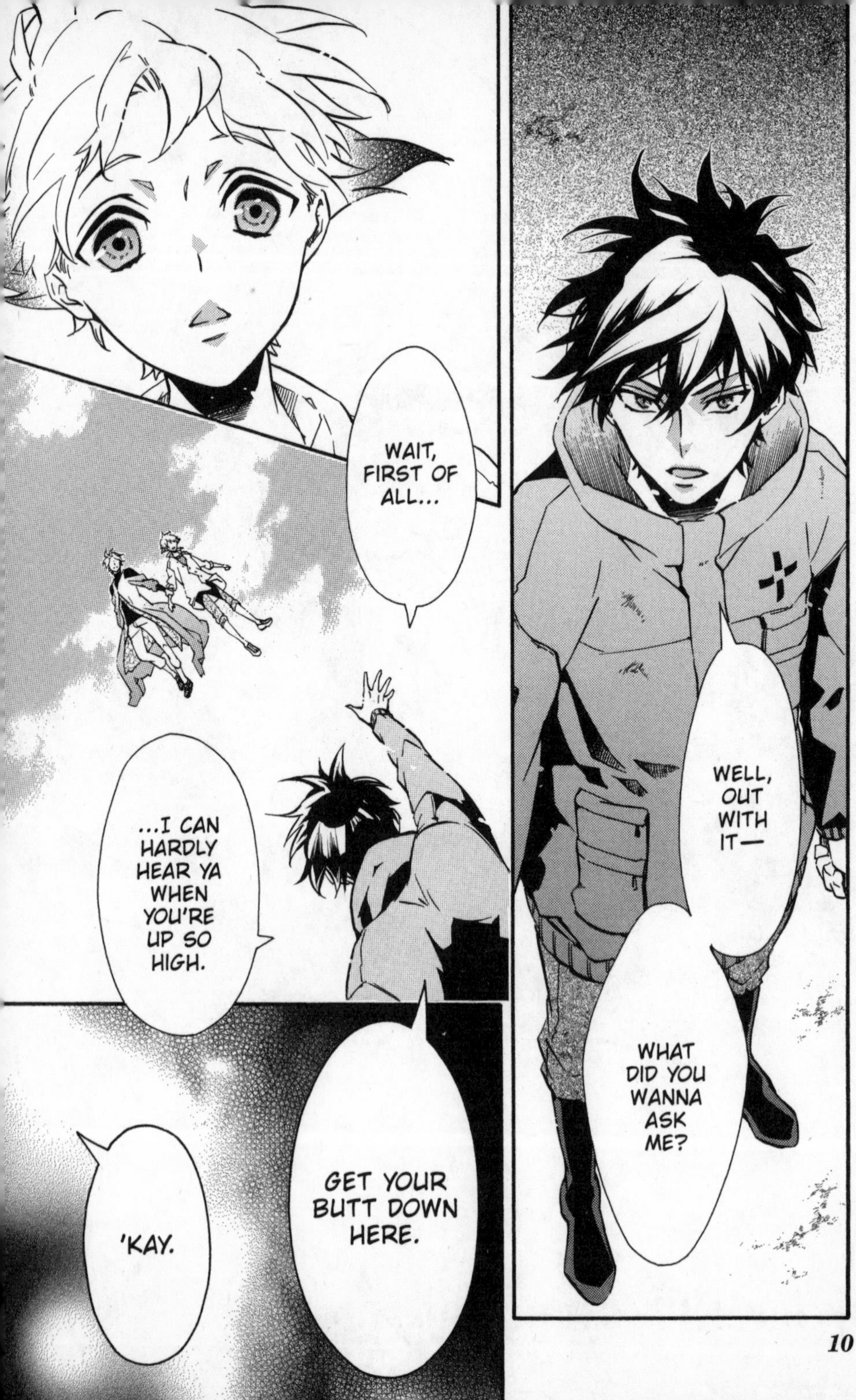
WELL, OUT WITH IT—
WHAT DID YOU WANNA ASK ME?
WAIT, FIRST OF ALL...
...I CAN HARDLY HEAR YA WHEN YOU'RE UP SO HIGH.
GET YOUR BUTT DOWN HERE.
'KAY.

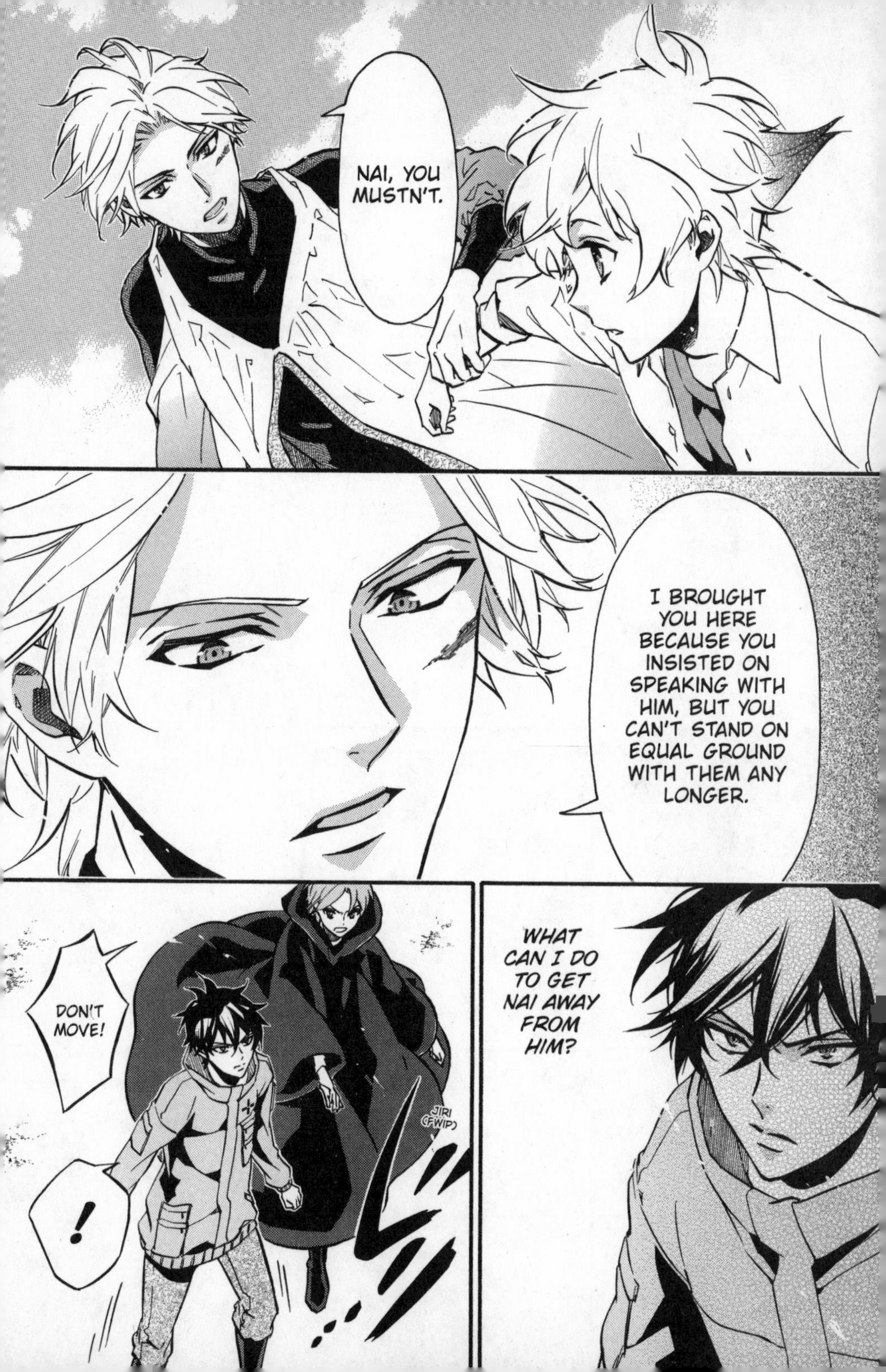
NAI, YOU MUSTN'T.
I BROUGHT YOU HERE BECAUSE YOU INSISTED ON SPEAKING WITH HIM, BUT YOU CAN'T STAND ON EQUAL GROUND WITH THEM ANY LONGER.
WHAT CAN I DO TO GET NAI AWAY FROM HIM?
DON'T MOVE!
!
JIRI (FWIP)

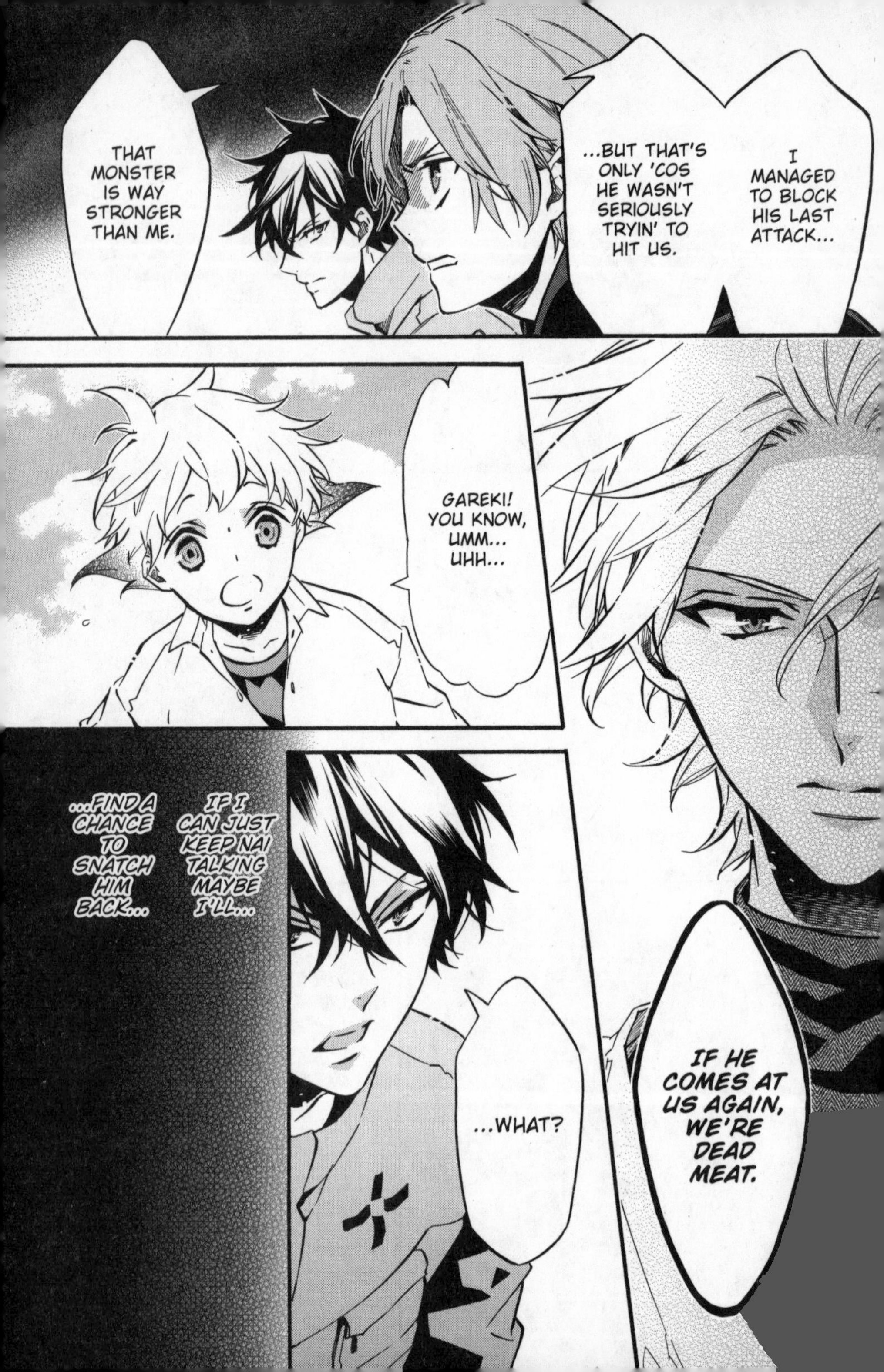
I MANAGED TO BLOCK HIS LAST ATTACK...
...BUT THAT'S ONLY 'COS HE WASN'T SERIOUSLY TRYIN' TO HIT US.
THAT MONSTER IS WAY STRONGER THAN ME.
IF HE COMES AT US AGAIN, WE'RE DEAD MEAT.
GAREKI! YOU KNOW, UMM... UHH...
...WHAT?
IF I CAN JUST KEEP NAI TALKING MAYBE I'LL...
...FIND A CHANCE TO SNATCH HIM BACK...

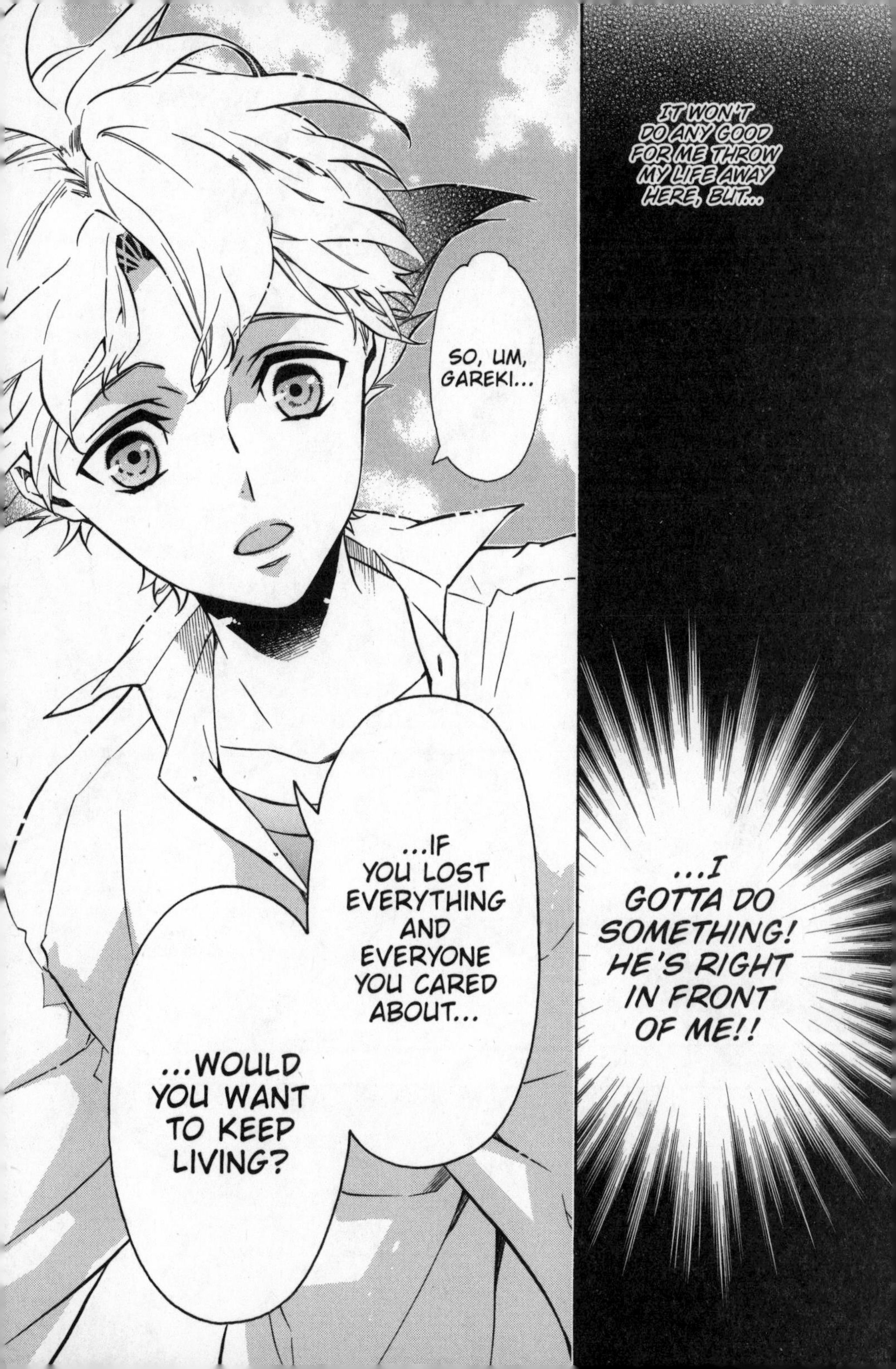
IT WON'T DO ANY GOOD FOR ME THROW MY LIFE AWAY HERE, BUT...
...I GOTTA DO SOMETHING! HE'S RIGHT IN FRONT OF ME!!
SO, UM, GAREKI...
...IF YOU LOST EVERYTHING AND EVERYONE YOU CARED ABOUT...
...WOULD YOU WANT TO KEEP LIVING?

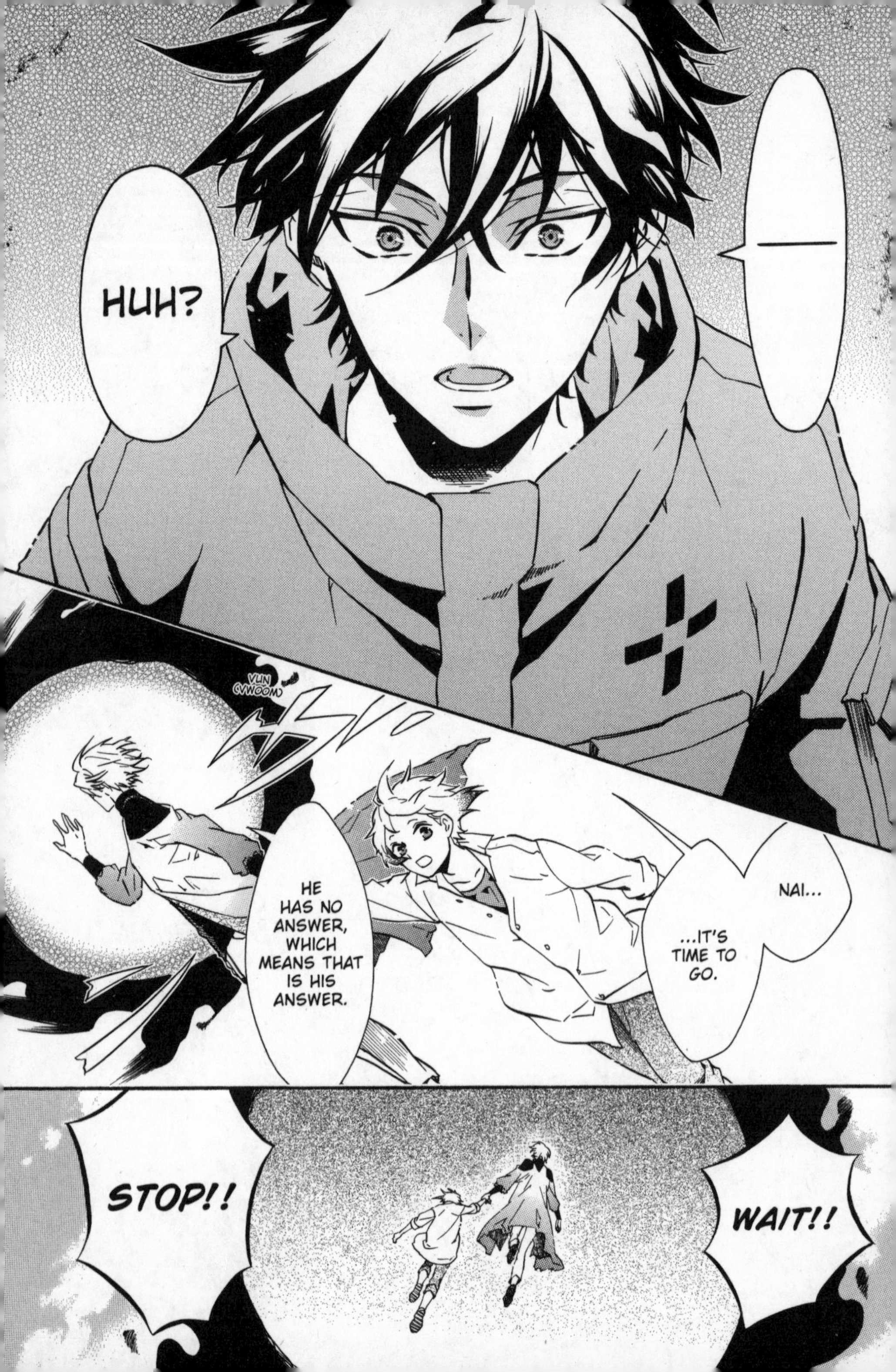
——
HUH?
NAI...
...IT'S TIME TO GO.
HE HAS NO ANSWER, WHICH MEANS THAT IS HIS ANSWER.
VUN (VWOOM)
WAIT!!
STOP!!

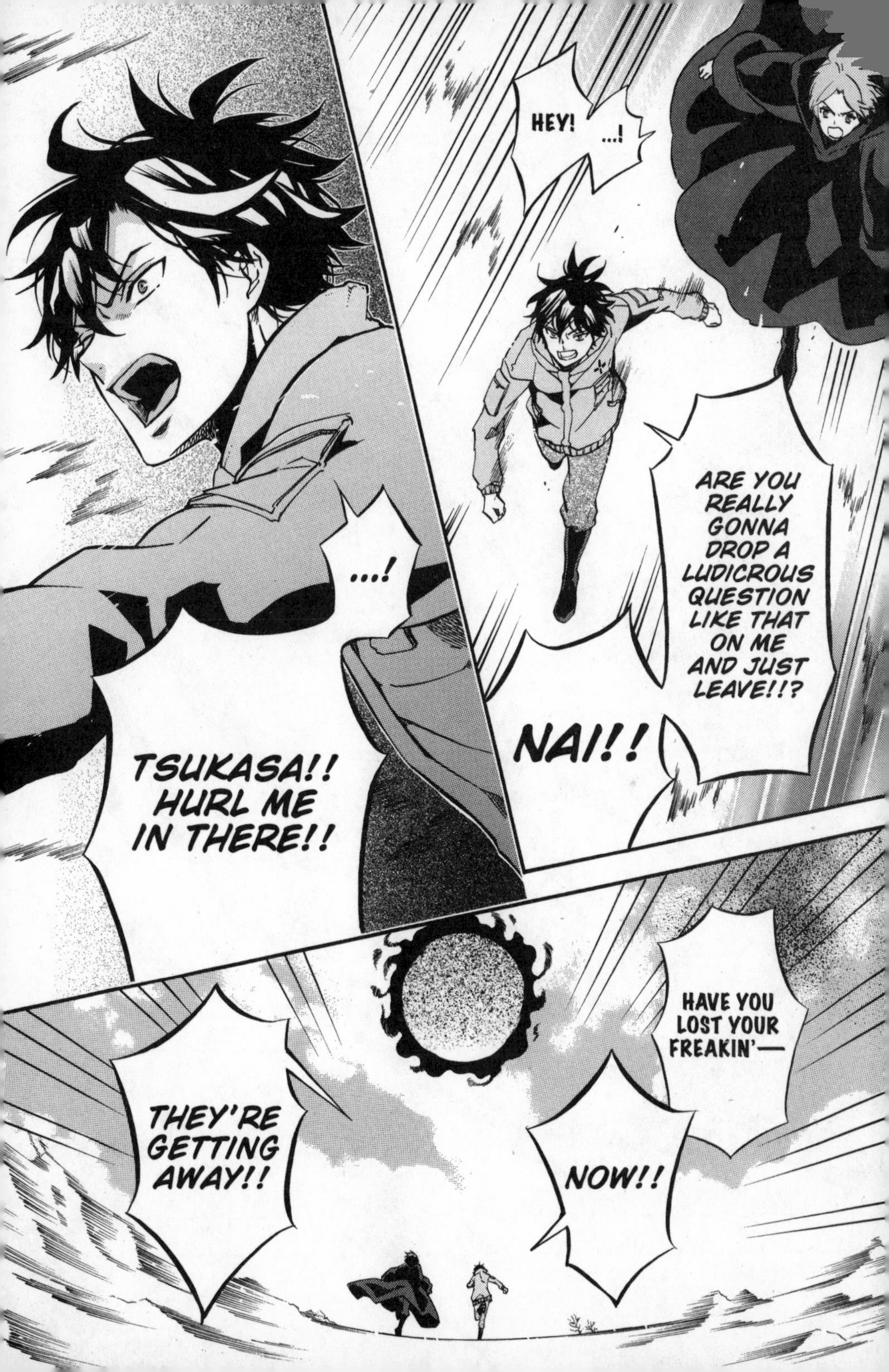
HEY! ...!
ARE YOU REALLY GONNA DROP A LUDICROUS QUESTION LIKE THAT ON ME AND JUST LEAVE!!?
NAI!!
...!
TSUKASA!! HURL ME IN THERE!!
HAVE YOU LOST YOUR FREAKIN'—
NOW!!
THEY'RE GETTING AWAY!!

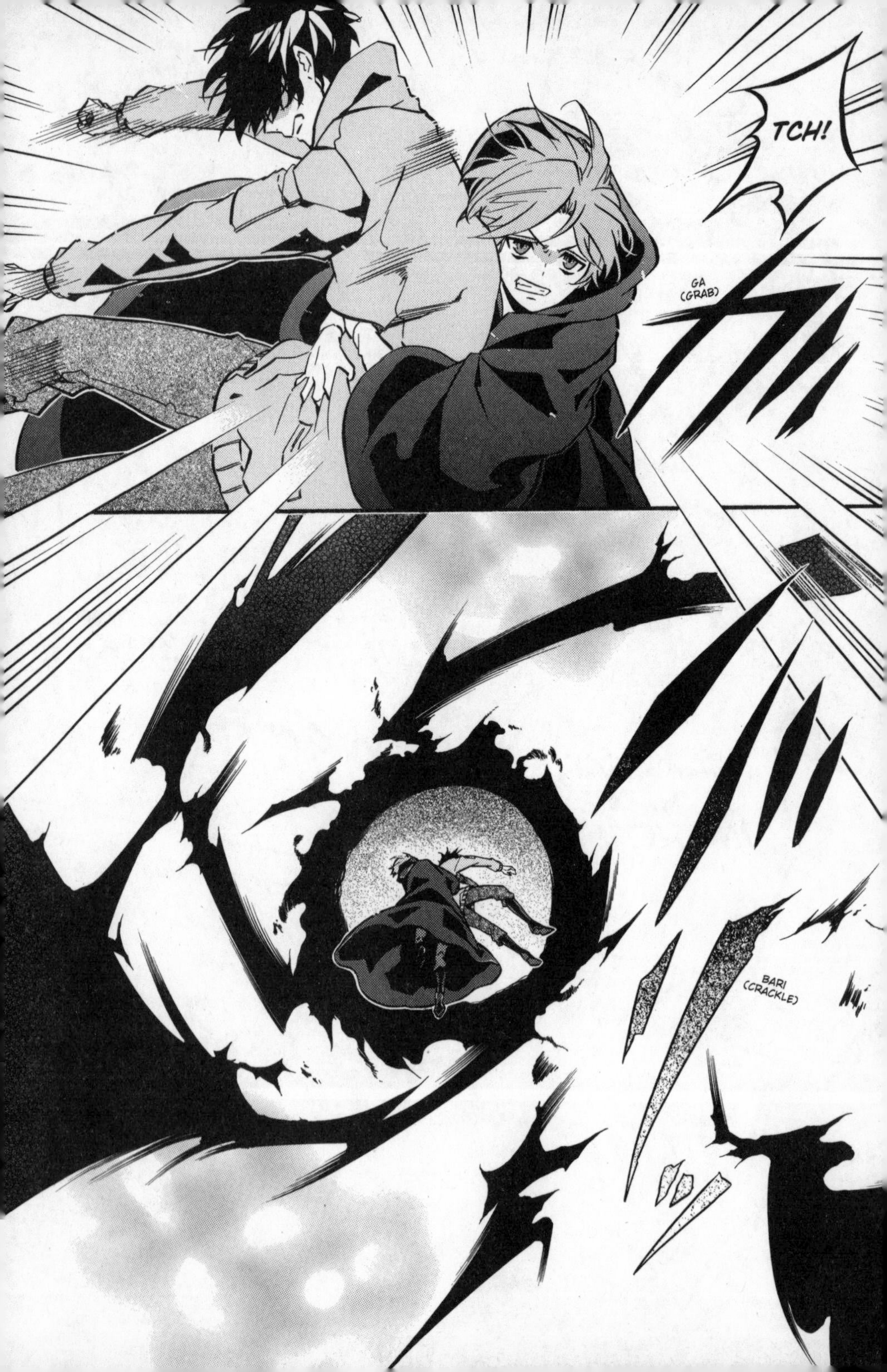
TCH!
GA
(GRAB)
BARI
(CRACKLE)

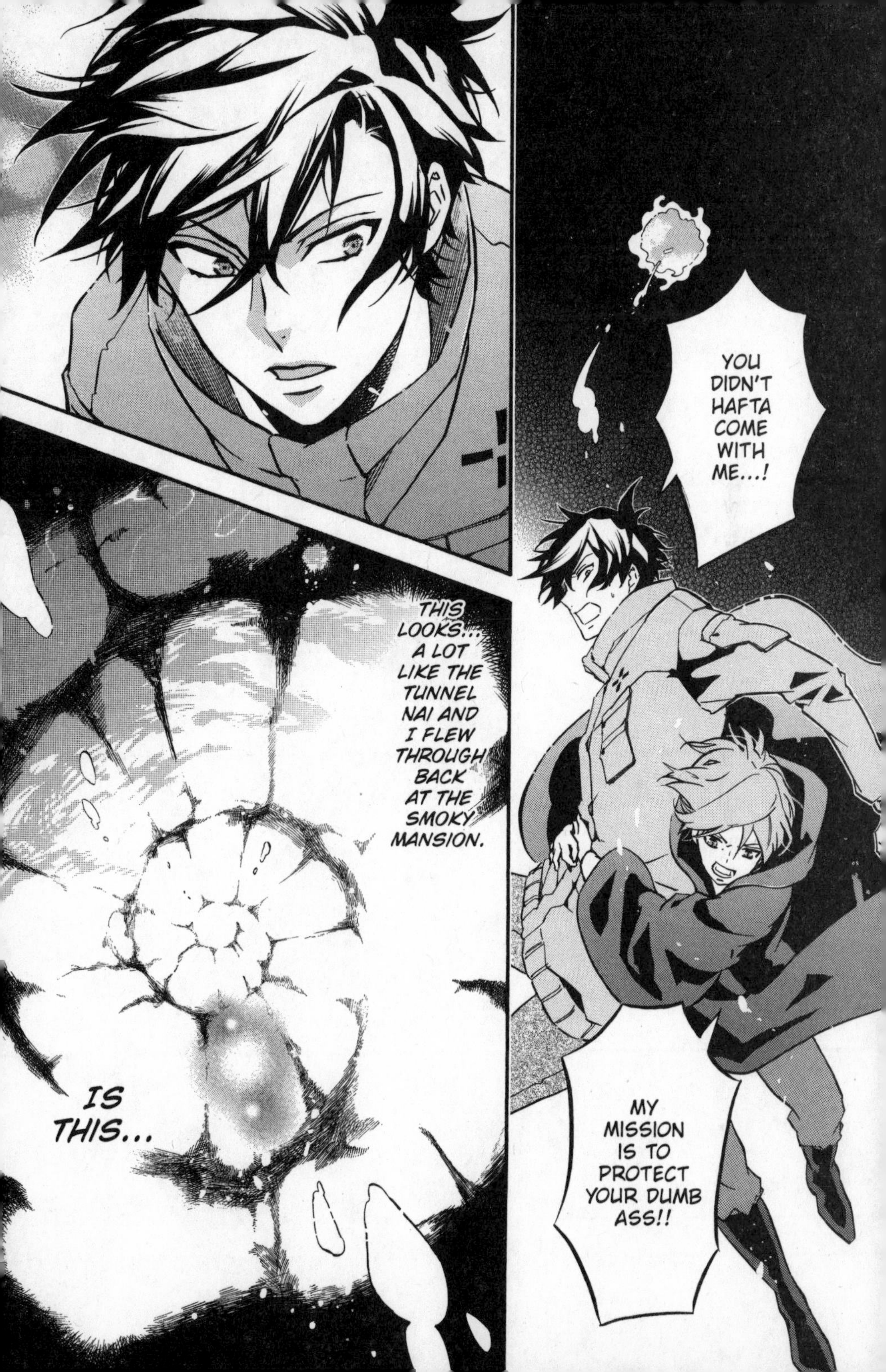
YOU DIDN'T HAFTA COME WITH ME...!
MY MISSION IS TO PROTECT YOUR DUMB ASS!!
THIS LOOKS... A LOT LIKE THE TUNNEL NAI AND I FLEW THROUGH BACK AT THE SMOKY MANSION.
IS THIS...

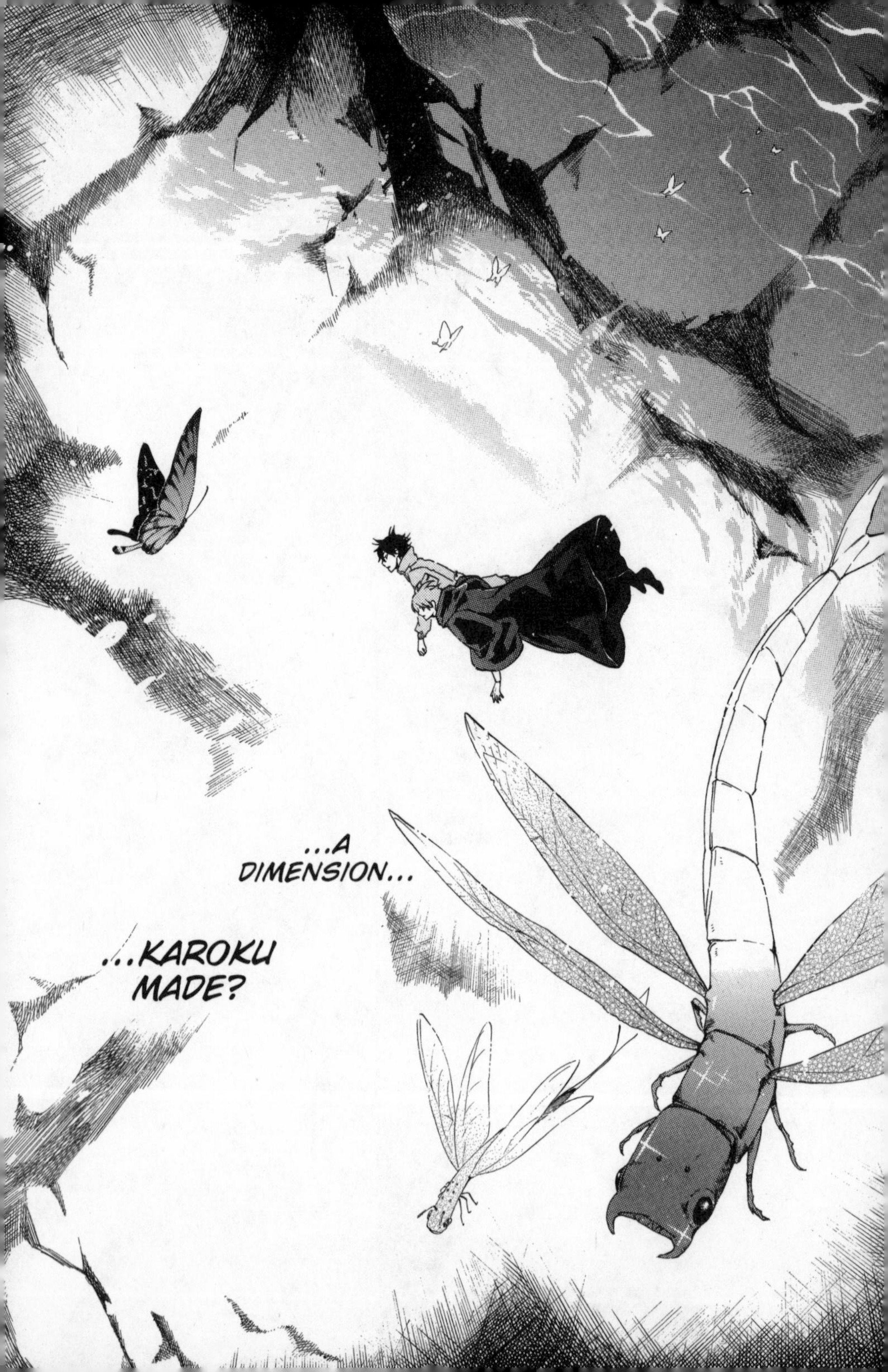
...A DIMENSION...
...KAROKU MADE?

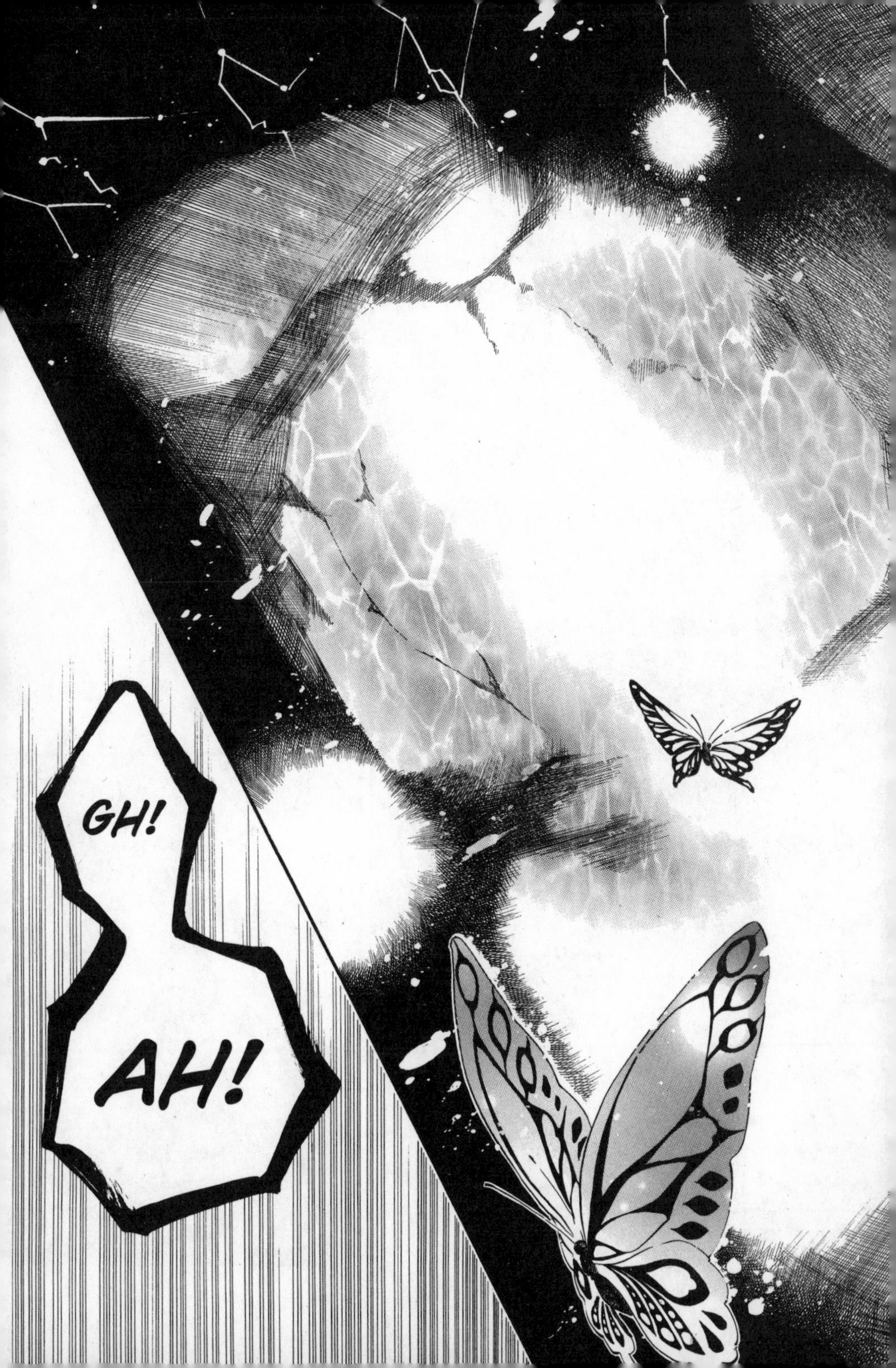
GH!
AH!

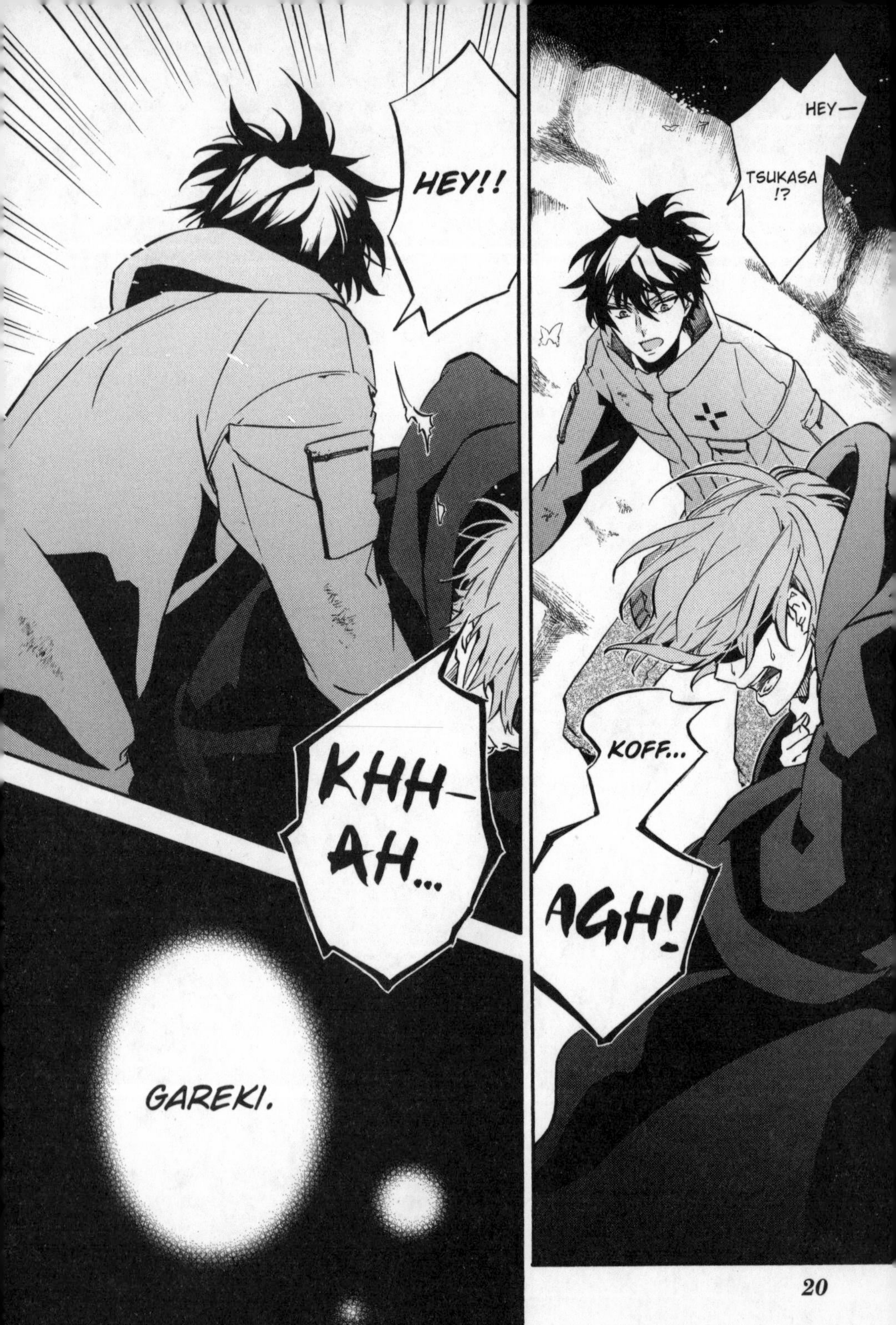
HEY—
TSUKASA!?
KOFF...
AGH!
HEY!!
KHH-AH...
GAREKI.

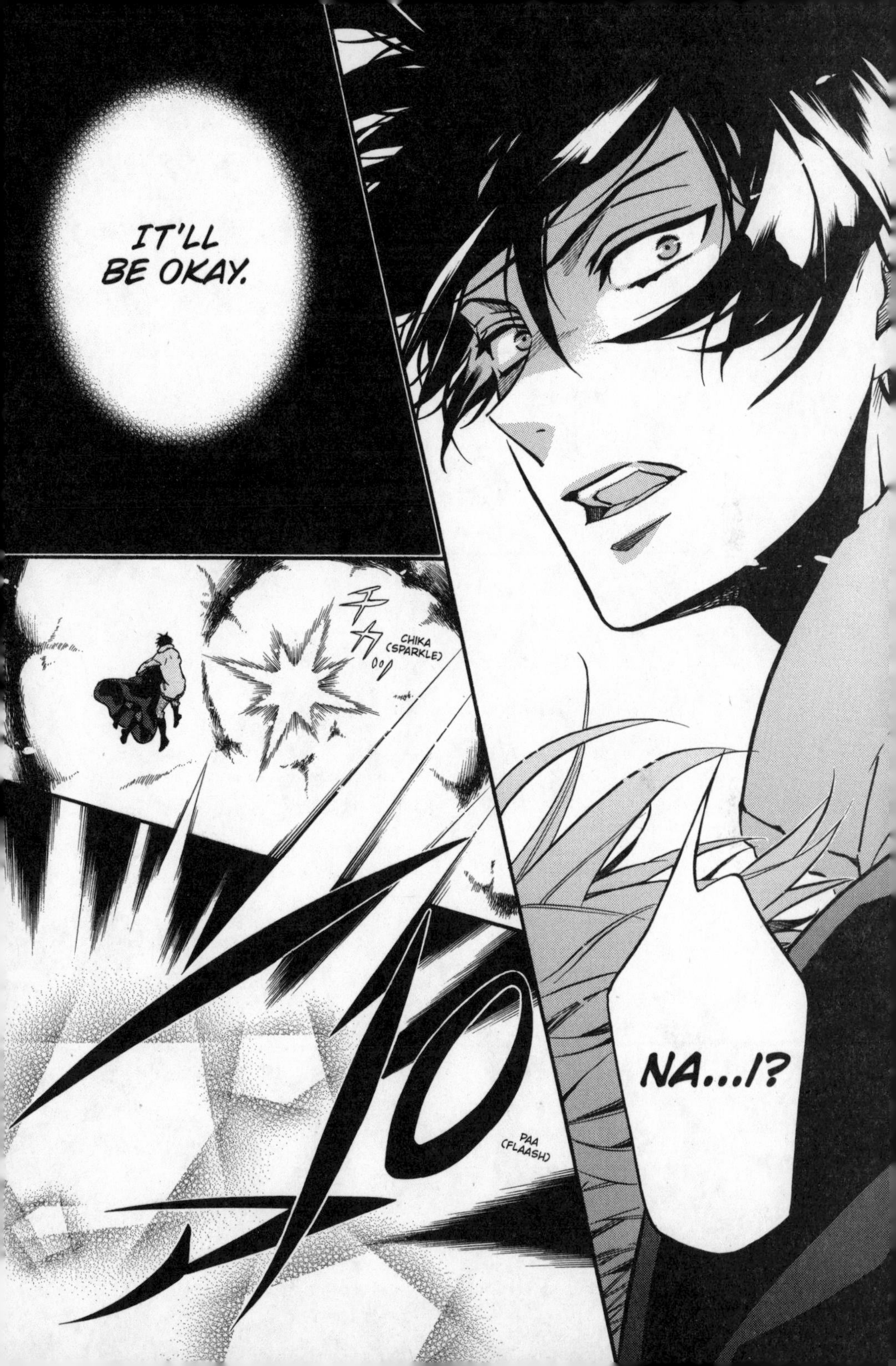
NA...!?
IT'LL BE OKAY.
CHIKA (SPARKLE)
PAA (FLAASH)

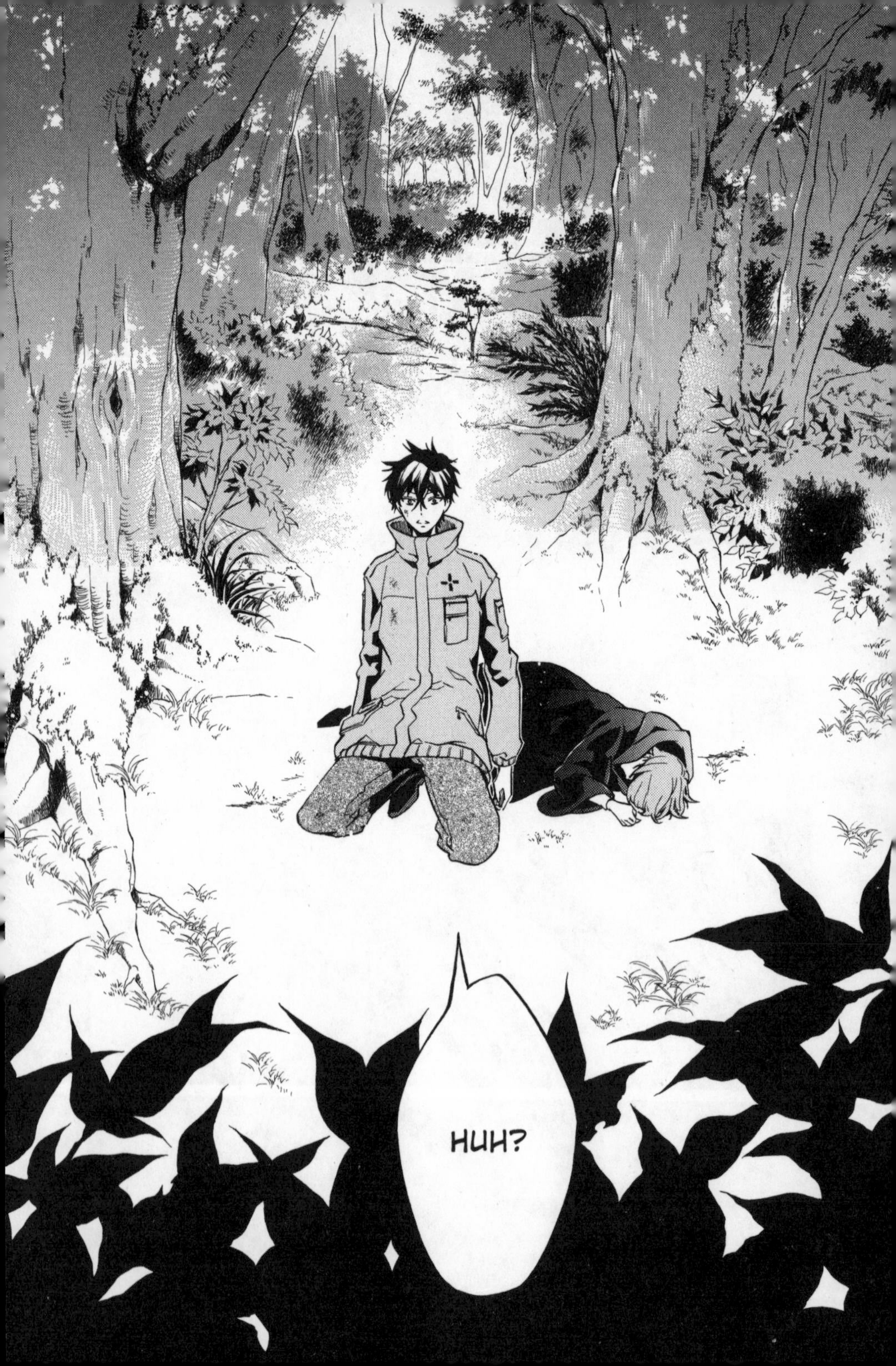
HUH?

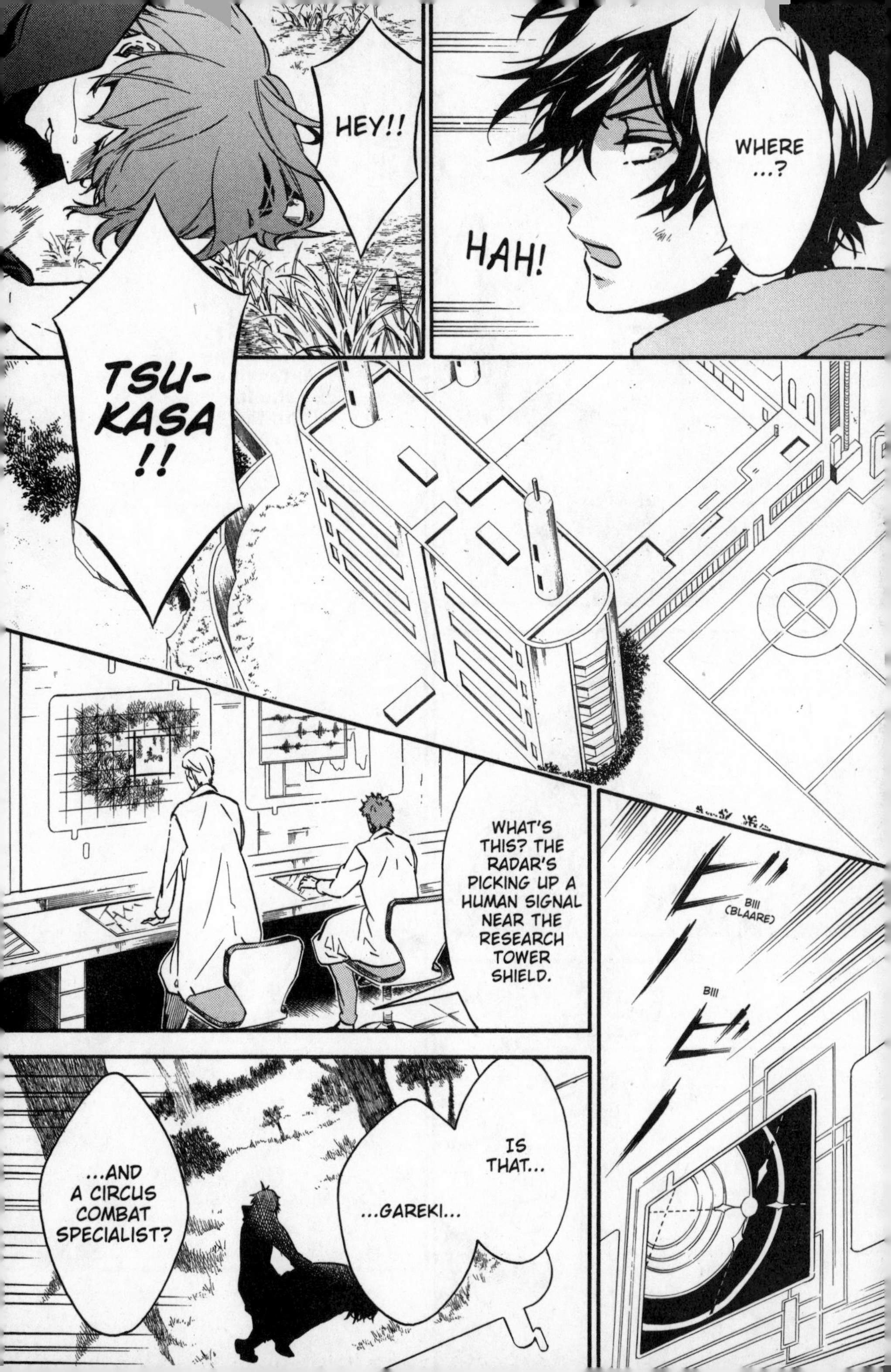
WHERE ...?
HAH!
HEY!!
TSU-KASA !!
BIII (BLAARE)
BIII
WHAT'S THIS? THE RADAR'S PICKING UP A HUMAN SIGNAL NEAR THE RESEARCH TOWER SHIELD.
IS THAT...
...GAREKI...
...AND A CIRCUS COMBAT SPECIALIST?

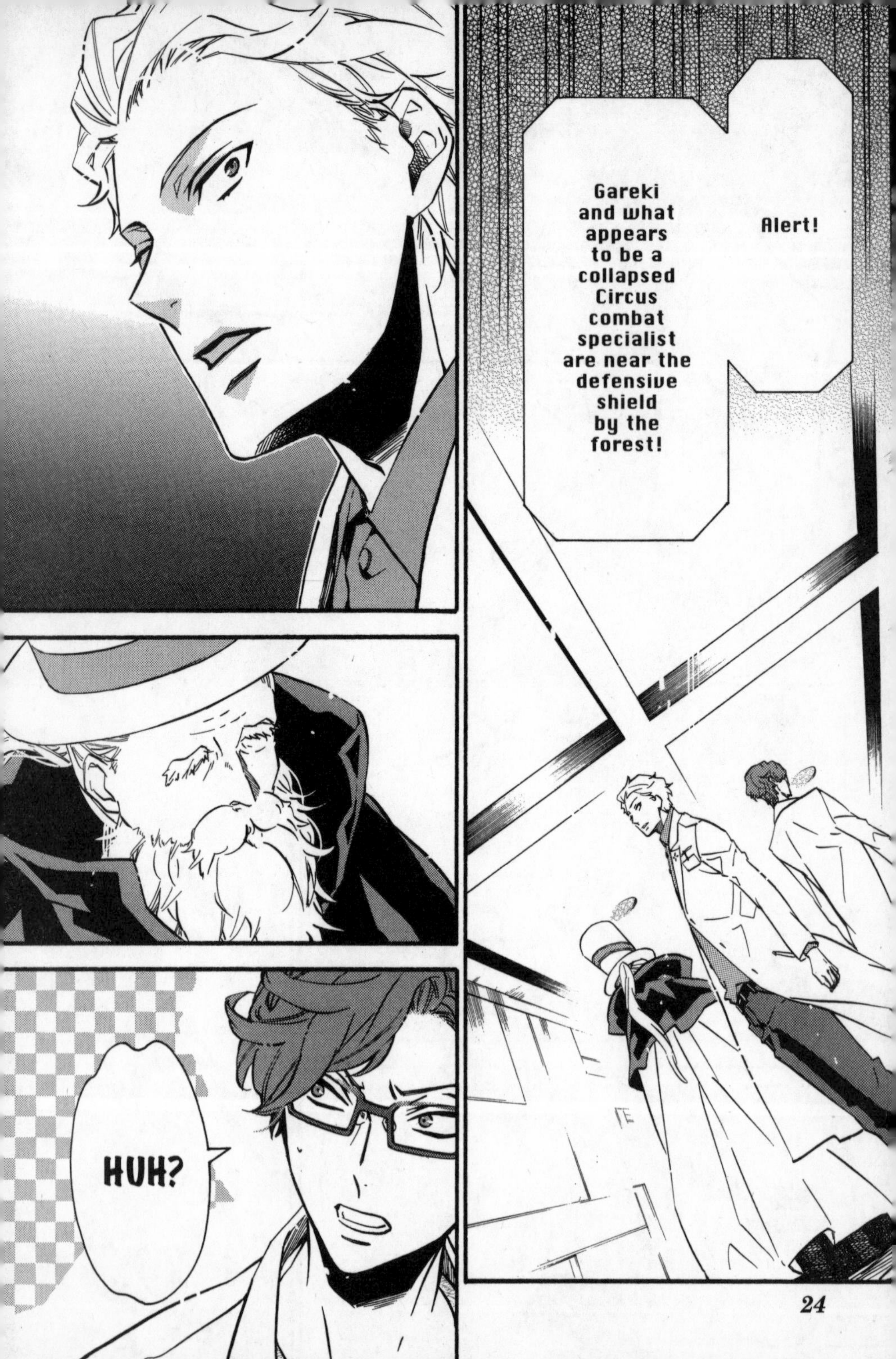
Alert!
Gareki and what appears to be a collapsed Circus combat specialist are near the defensive shield by the forest!
HUH?

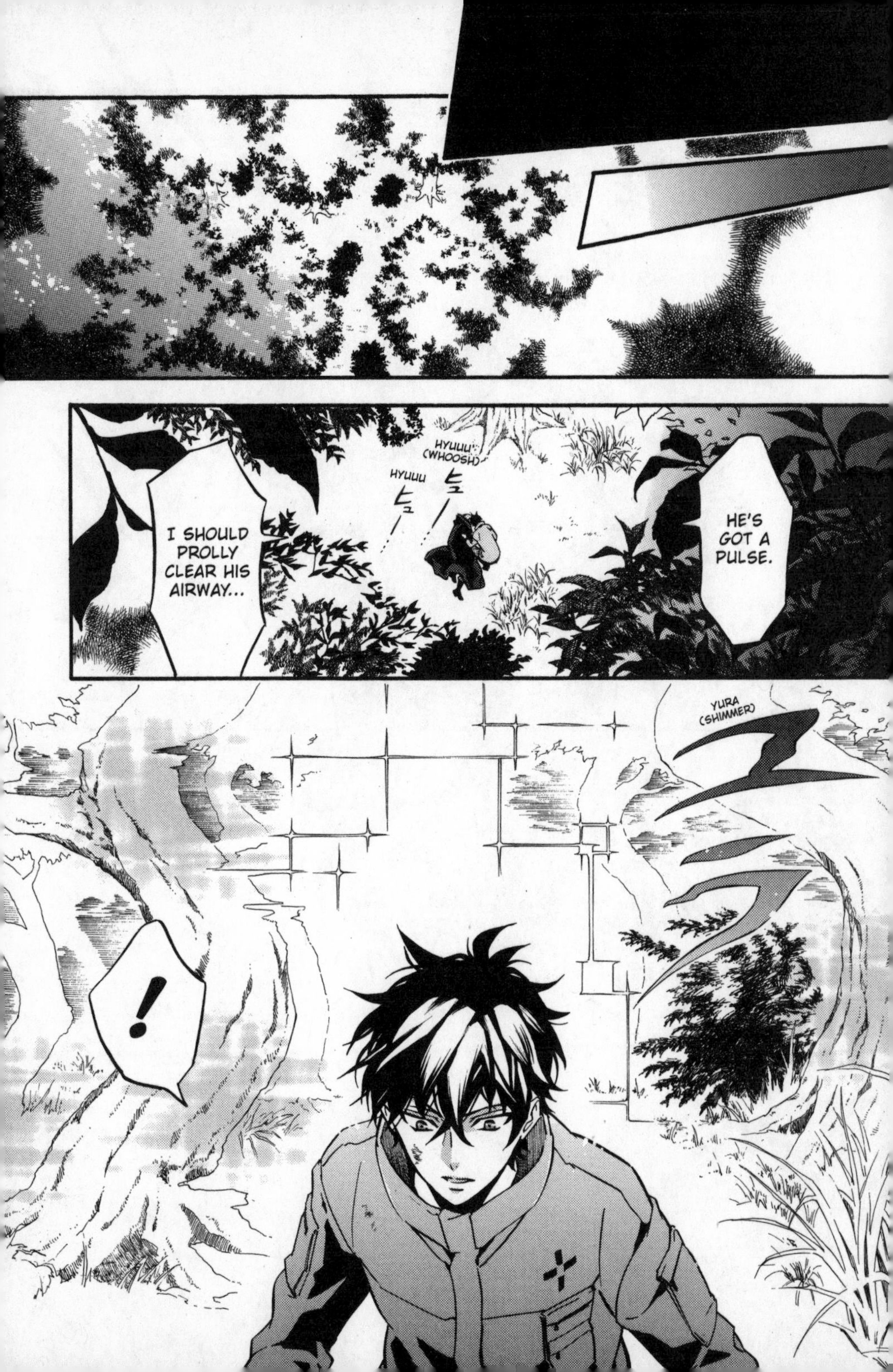
HE'S GOT A PULSE.
HYUUU (WHOOSH)
ヒュ
HYUUU
ヒュ
I SHOULD PROLLY CLEAR HIS AIRWAY...
YURA (SHIMMER)
!

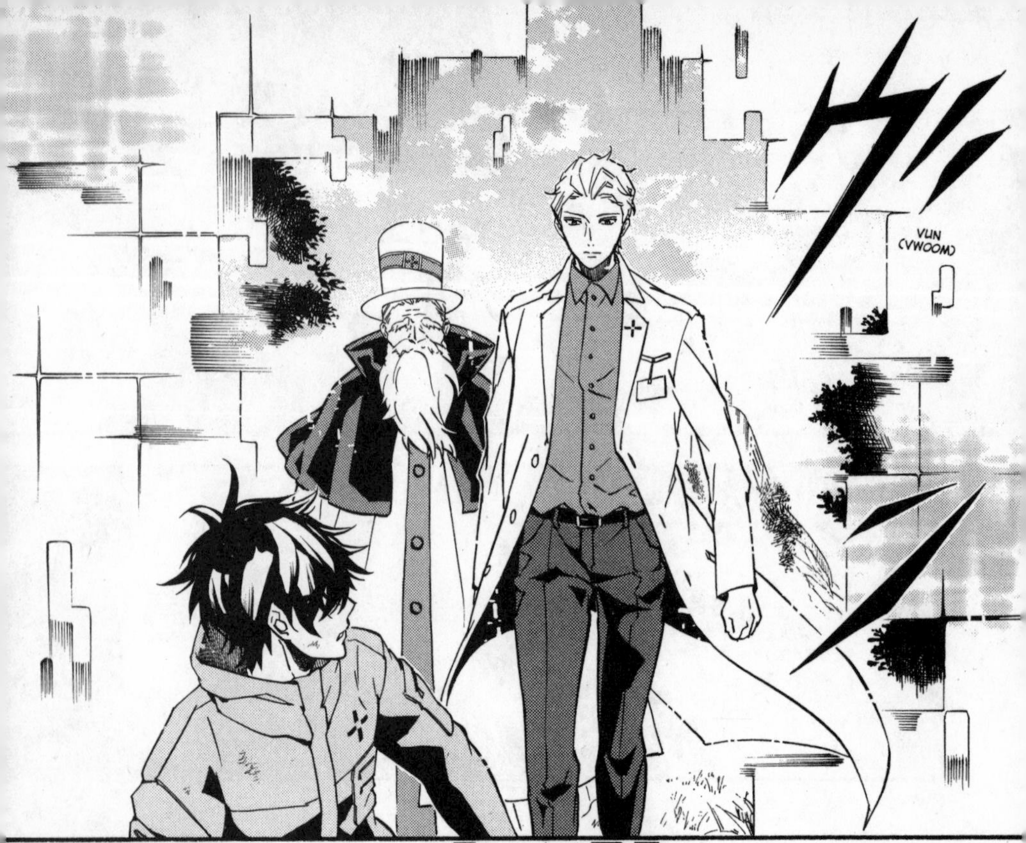
VUN
(VWOOM)

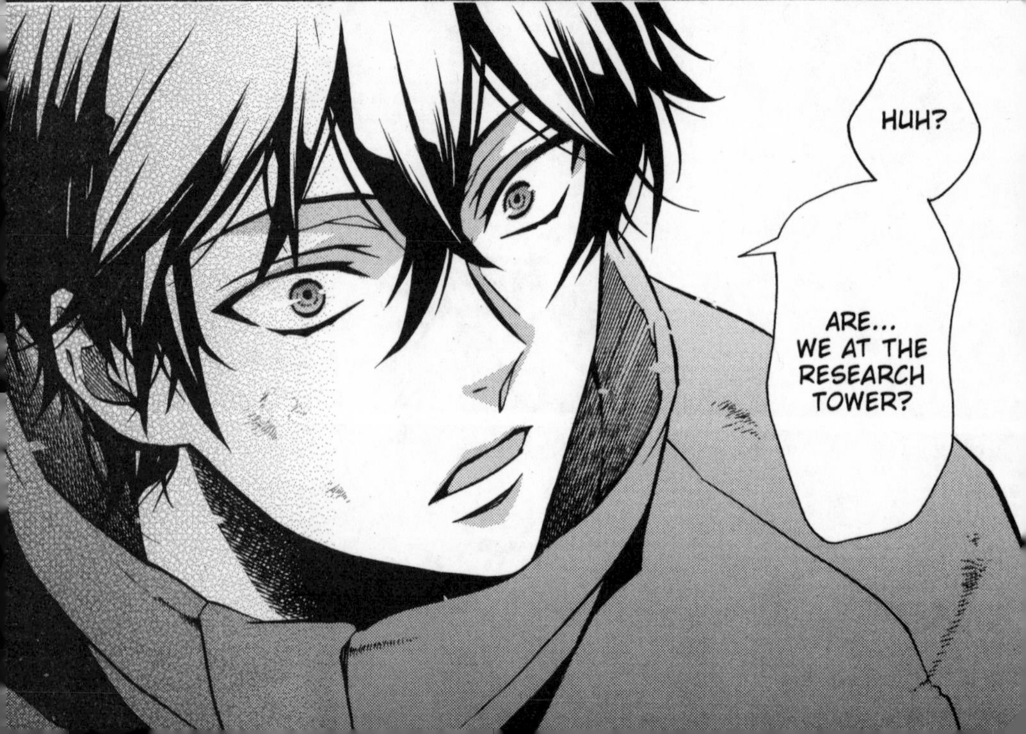
HUH?
ARE... WE AT THE RESEARCH TOWER?

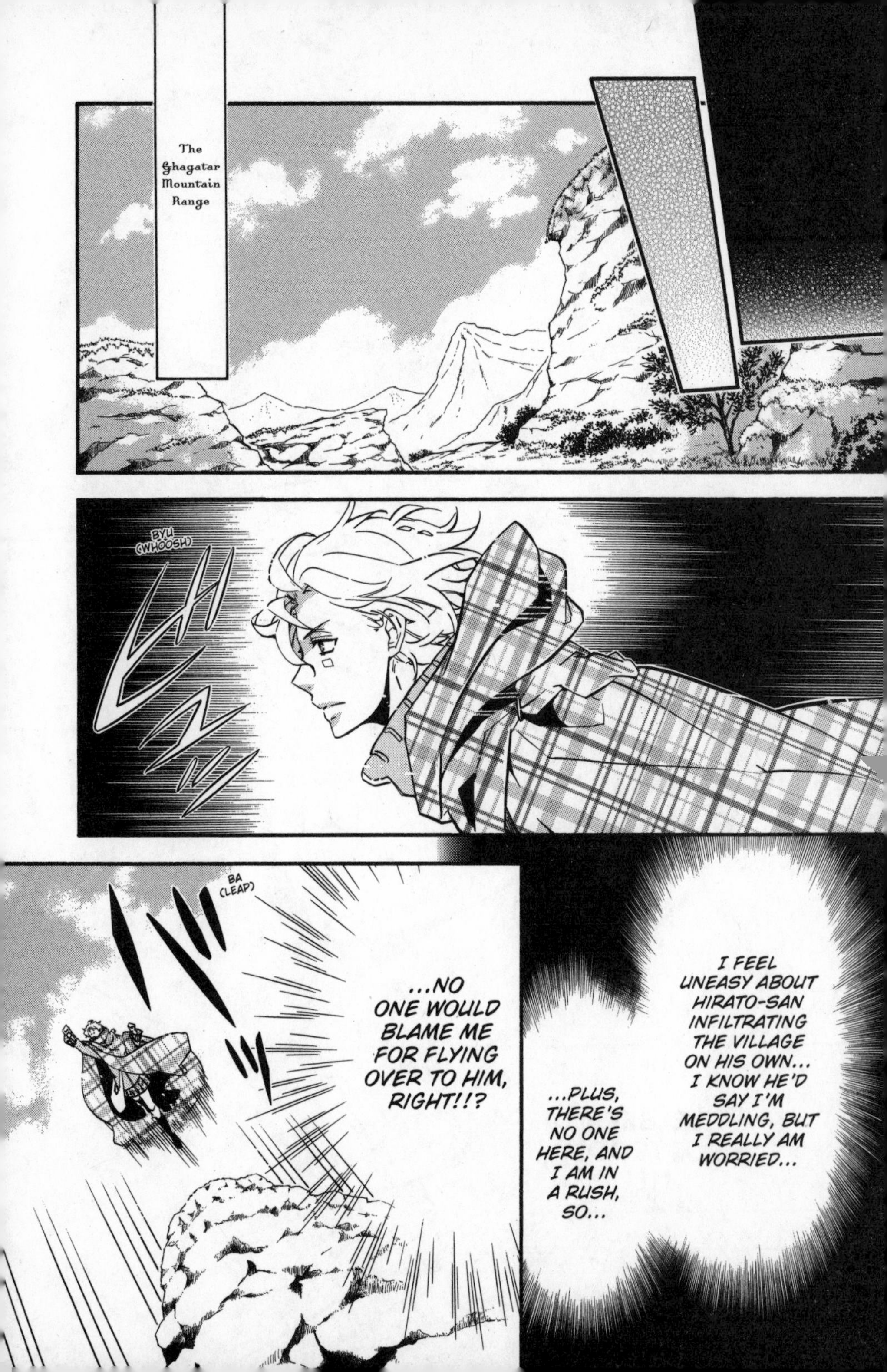
The Ghagatar Mountain Range
BYU (WHOOSH)
I FEEL UNEASY ABOUT HIRATO-SAN INFILTRATING THE VILLAGE ON HIS OWN... I KNOW HE'D SAY I'M MEDDLING, BUT I REALLY AM WORRIED...
...PLUS, THERE'S NO ONE HERE, AND I AM IN A RUSH, SO...
BA (LEAP)
...NO ONE WOULD BLAME ME FOR FLYING OVER TO HIM, RIGHT!!?

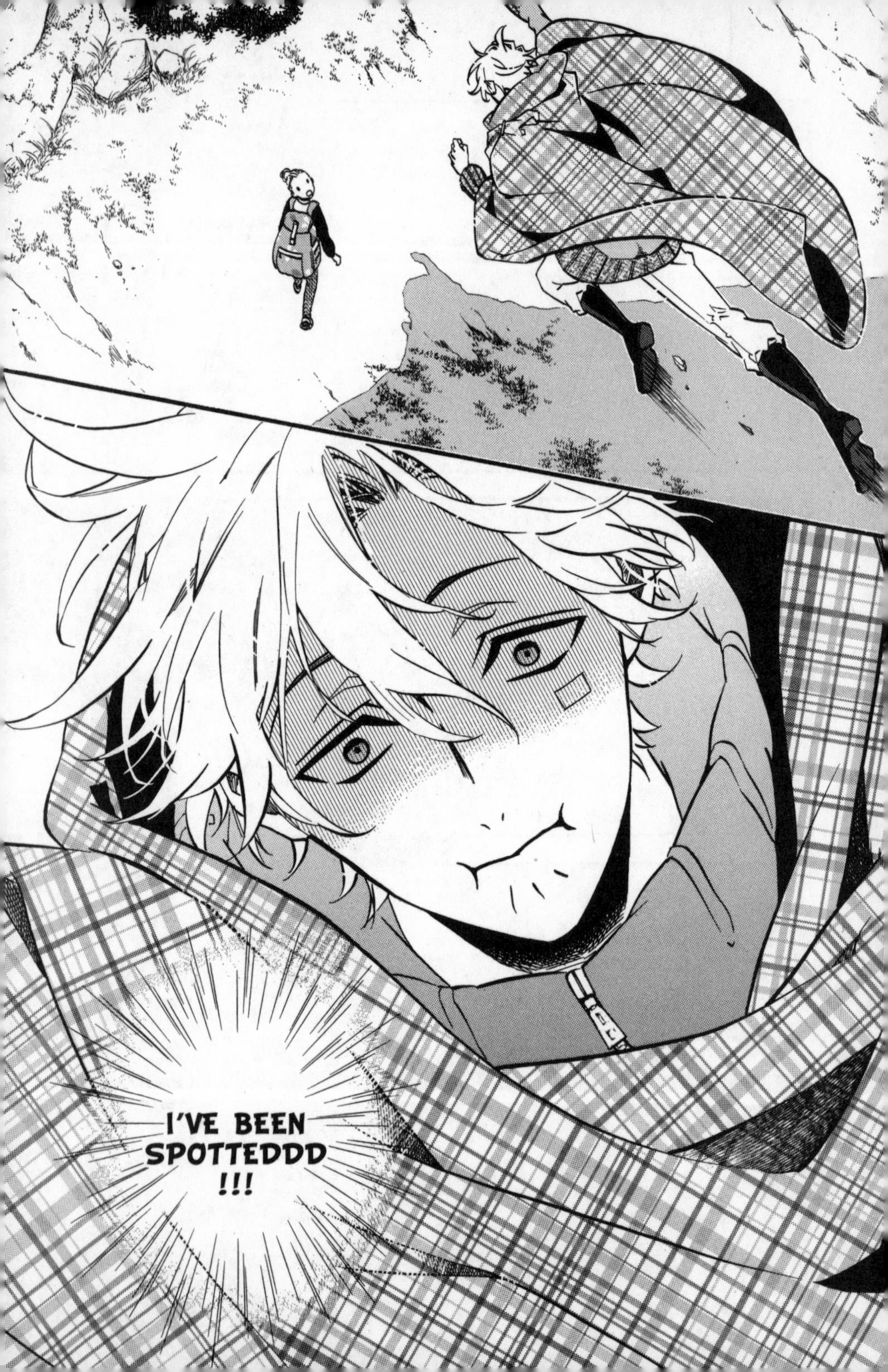
I'VE BEEN SPOTTEDDD !!!

KARNEVAL

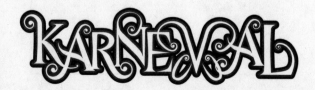

KARNEVÁL

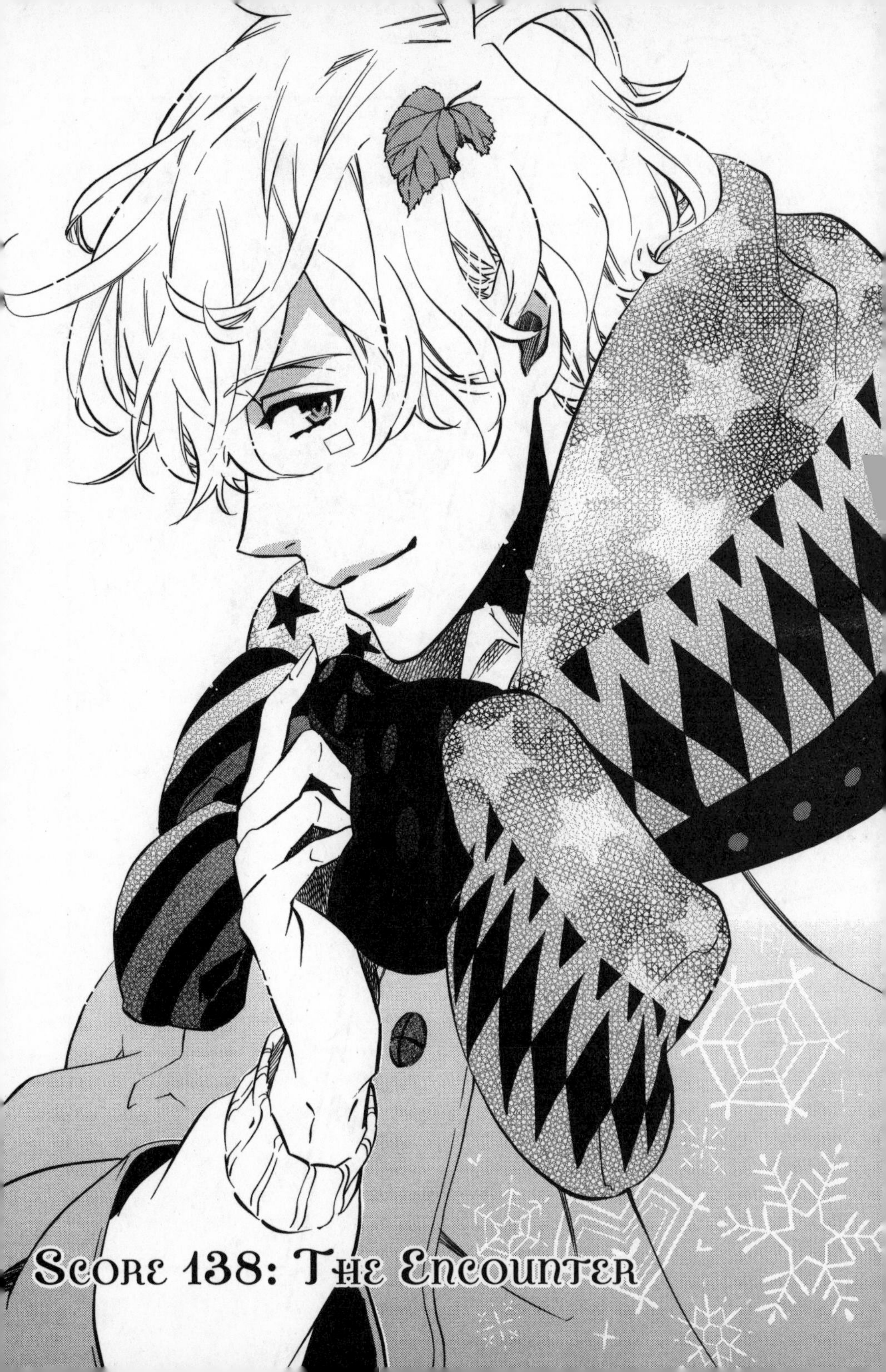
Score 138: The Encounter

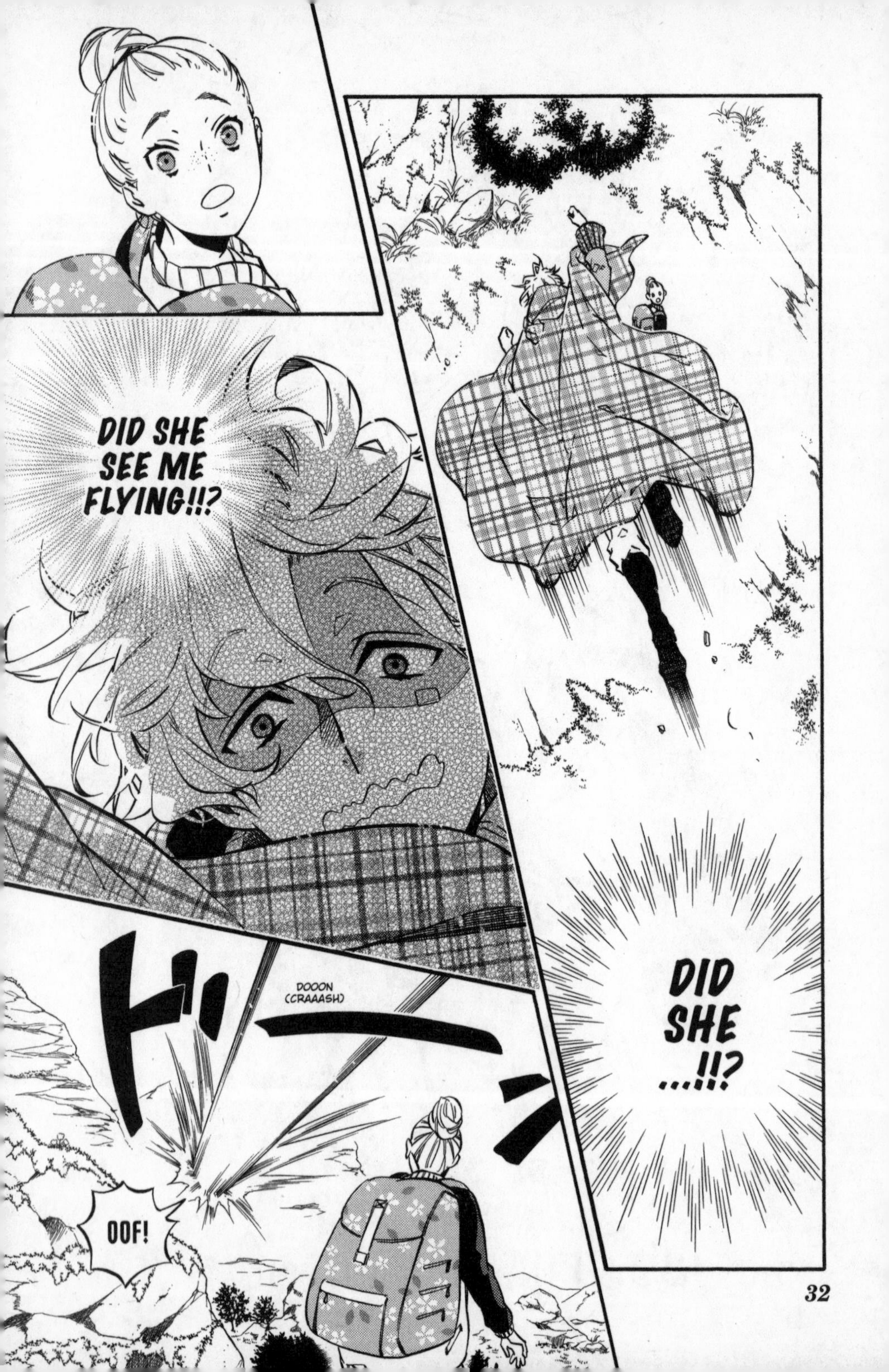
DID SHE ...!!?
DID SHE SEE ME FLYING!!?
ドーン
DOOON (CRAAASH)
OOF!

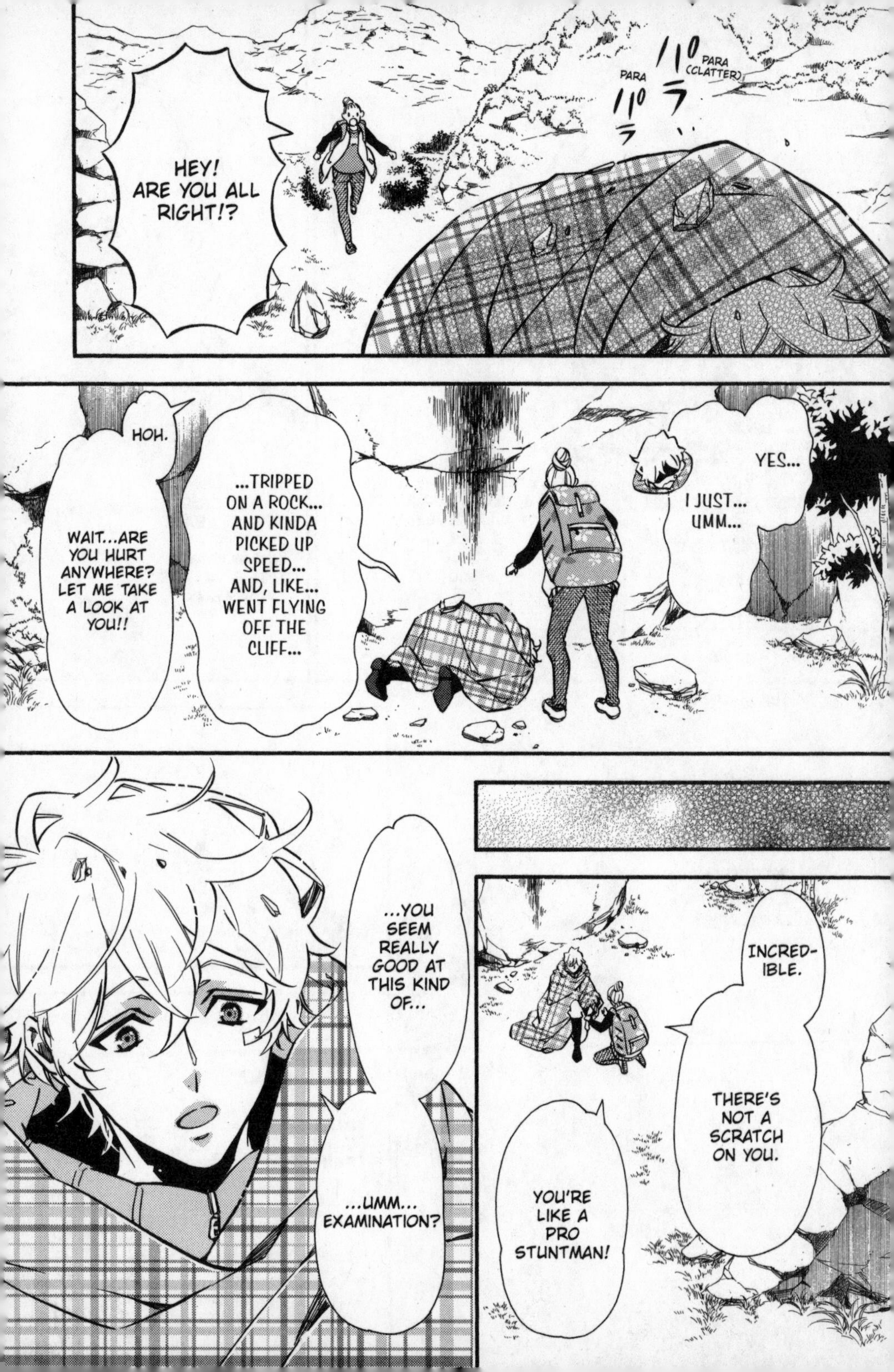
PARA (CLATTER)
PARA
HEY! ARE YOU ALL RIGHT!?
YES... I JUST... UMM...
...TRIPPED ON A ROCK... AND KINDA PICKED UP SPEED... AND, LIKE... WENT FLYING OFF THE CLIFF...
HOH.
WAIT...ARE YOU HURT ANYWHERE? LET ME TAKE A LOOK AT YOU!!
INCRED-IBLE.
THERE'S NOT A SCRATCH ON YOU.
YOU'RE LIKE A PRO STUNTMAN!
...YOU SEEM REALLY GOOD AT THIS KIND OF...
...UMM... EXAMINATION?

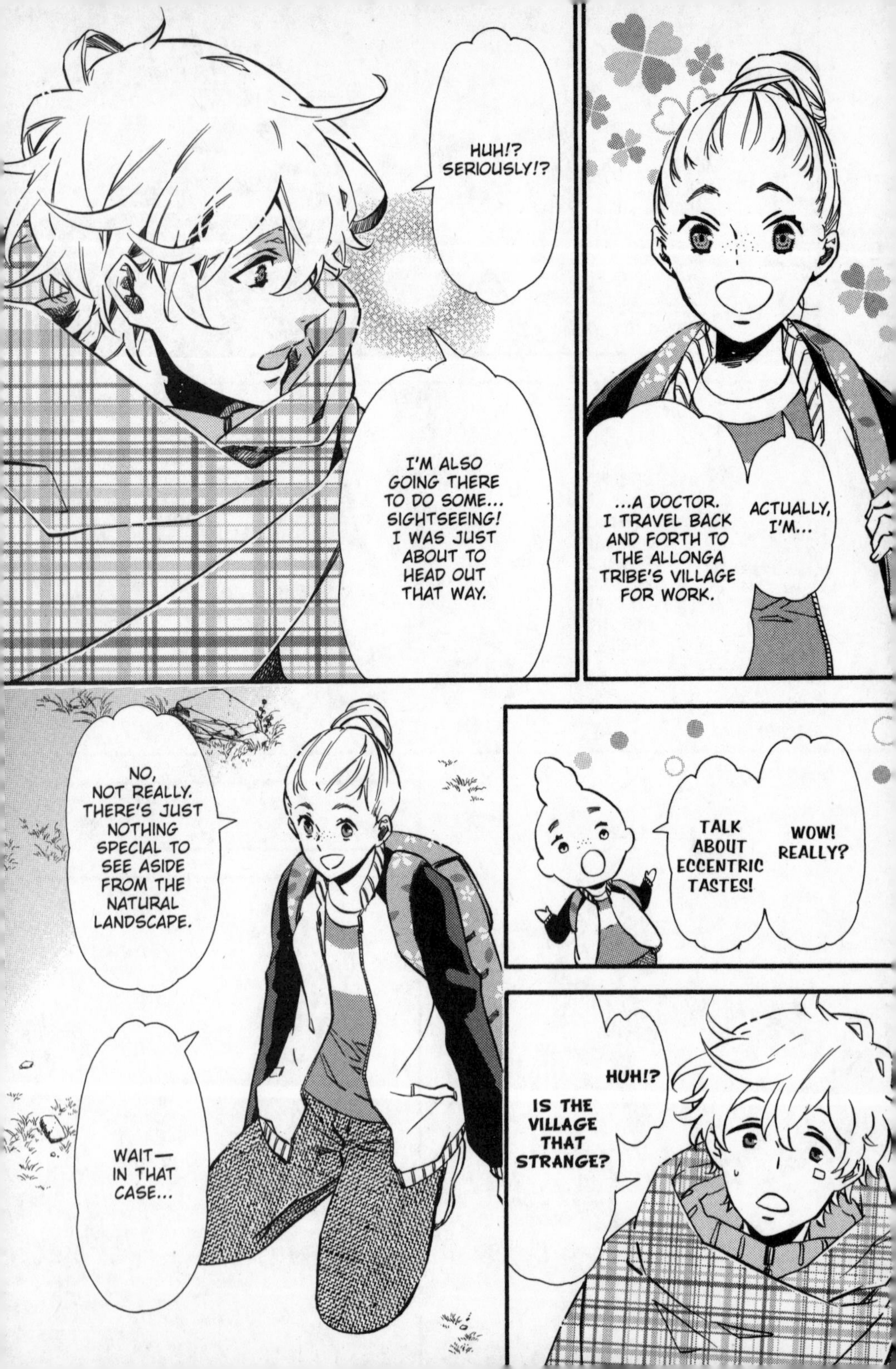
ACTUALLY, I'M...
...A DOCTOR. I TRAVEL BACK AND FORTH TO THE ALLONGA TRIBE'S VILLAGE FOR WORK.
HUH!? SERIOUSLY!?
I'M ALSO GOING THERE TO DO SOME... SIGHTSEEING! I WAS JUST ABOUT TO HEAD OUT THAT WAY.
WOW! REALLY?
TALK ABOUT ECCENTRIC TASTES!
HUH!?
IS THE VILLAGE THAT STRANGE?
NO, NOT REALLY. THERE'S JUST NOTHING SPECIAL TO SEE ASIDE FROM THE NATURAL LANDSCAPE.
WAIT— IN THAT CASE...

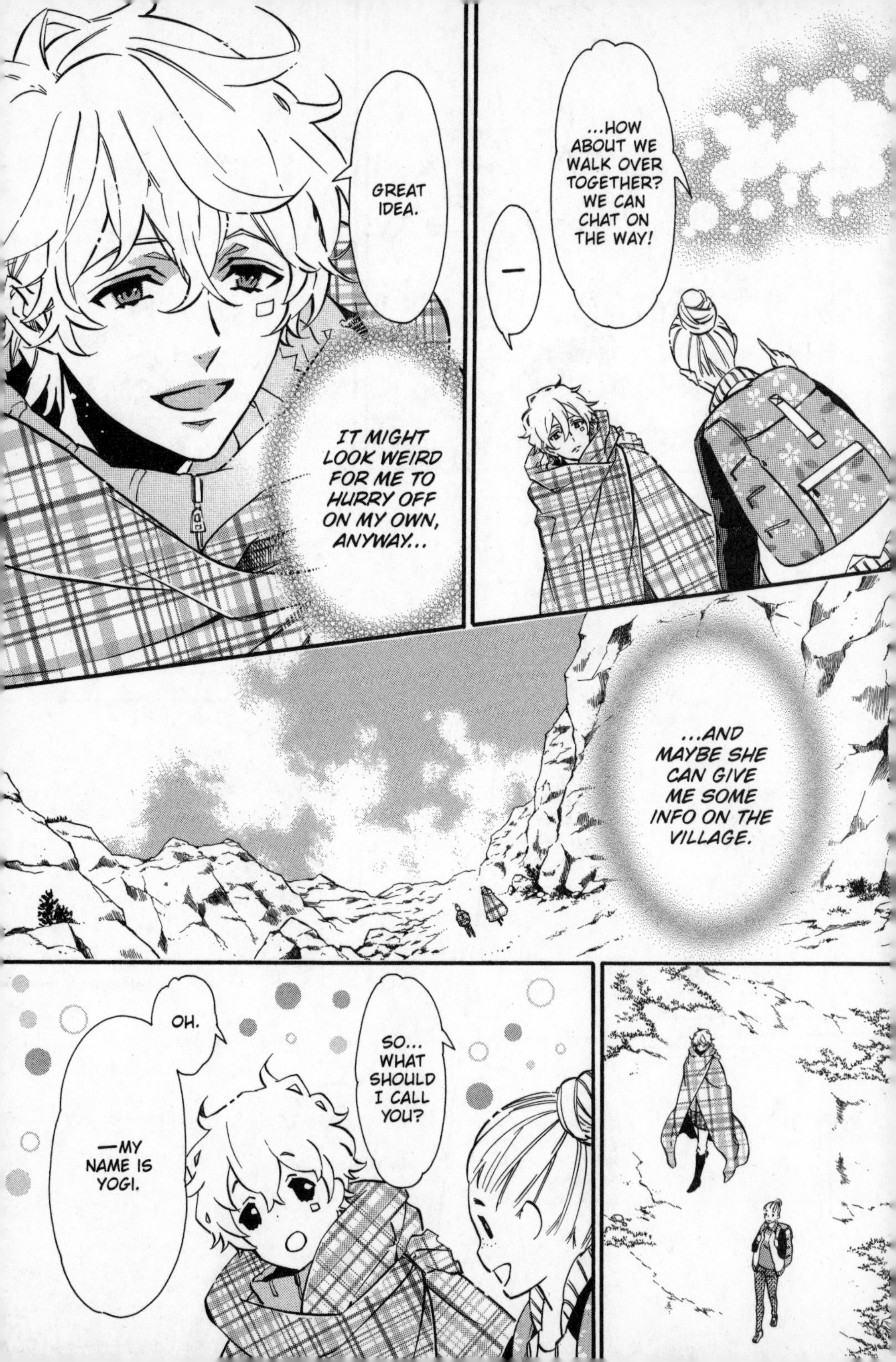
...HOW ABOUT WE WALK OVER TOGETHER? WE CAN CHAT ON THE WAY!
—
GREAT IDEA.
IT MIGHT LOOK WEIRD FOR ME TO HURRY OFF ON MY OWN, ANYWAY...
...AND MAYBE SHE CAN GIVE ME SOME INFO ON THE VILLAGE.
SO... WHAT SHOULD I CALL YOU?
OH.
—MY NAME IS YOGI.

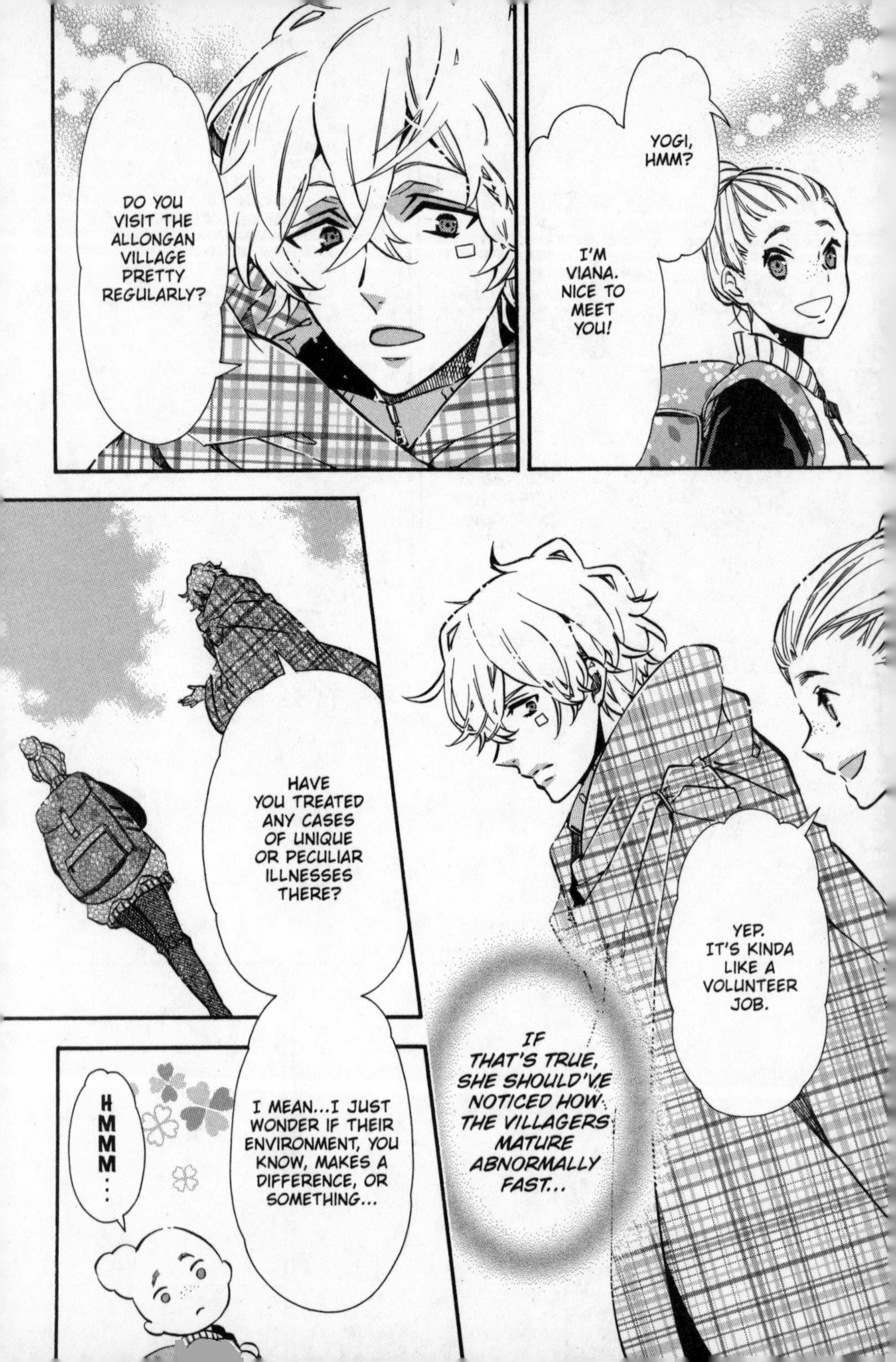
YOGI, HMM?
I'M VIANA. NICE TO MEET YOU!
DO YOU VISIT THE ALLONGAN VILLAGE PRETTY REGULARLY?
YEP. IT'S KINDA LIKE A VOLUNTEER JOB.
IF THAT'S TRUE, SHE SHOULD'VE NOTICED HOW THE VILLAGERS MATURE ABNORMALLY FAST...
HAVE YOU TREATED ANY CASES OF UNIQUE OR PECULIAR ILLNESSES THERE?
I MEAN...I JUST WONDER IF THEIR ENVIRONMENT, YOU KNOW, MAKES A DIFFERENCE, OR SOMETHING...
HMMM...

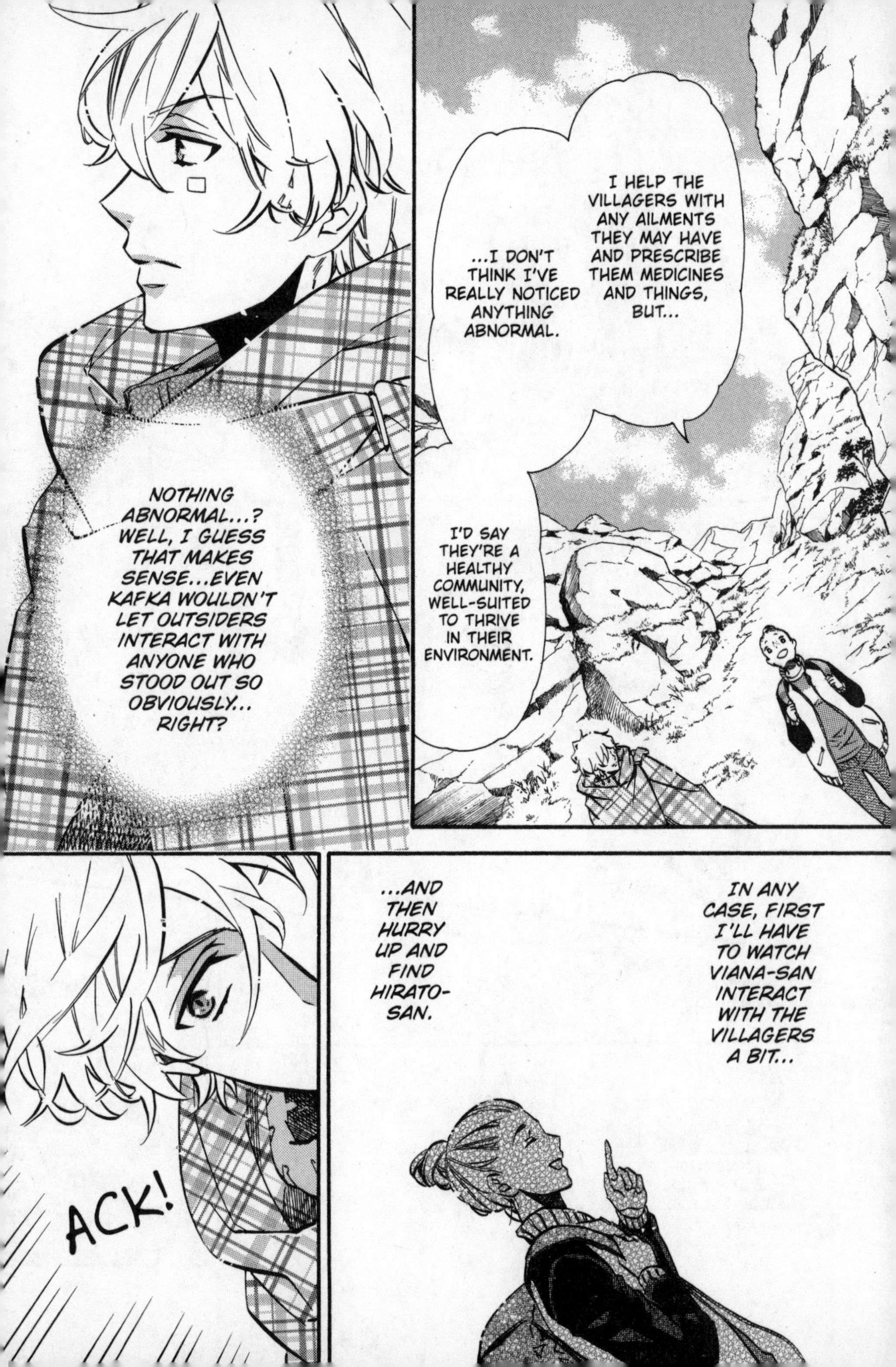
I HELP THE VILLAGERS WITH ANY AILMENTS THEY MAY HAVE AND PRESCRIBE THEM MEDICINES AND THINGS, BUT...
...I DON'T THINK I'VE REALLY NOTICED ANYTHING ABNORMAL.
I'D SAY THEY'RE A HEALTHY COMMUNITY, WELL-SUITED TO THRIVE IN THEIR ENVIRONMENT.
NOTHING ABNORMAL...? WELL, I GUESS THAT MAKES SENSE...EVEN KAFKA WOULDN'T LET OUTSIDERS INTERACT WITH ANYONE WHO STOOD OUT SO OBVIOUSLY... RIGHT?
IN ANY CASE, FIRST I'LL HAVE TO WATCH VIANA-SAN INTERACT WITH THE VILLAGERS A BIT...
...AND THEN HURRY UP AND FIND HIRATO-SAN.
ACK!

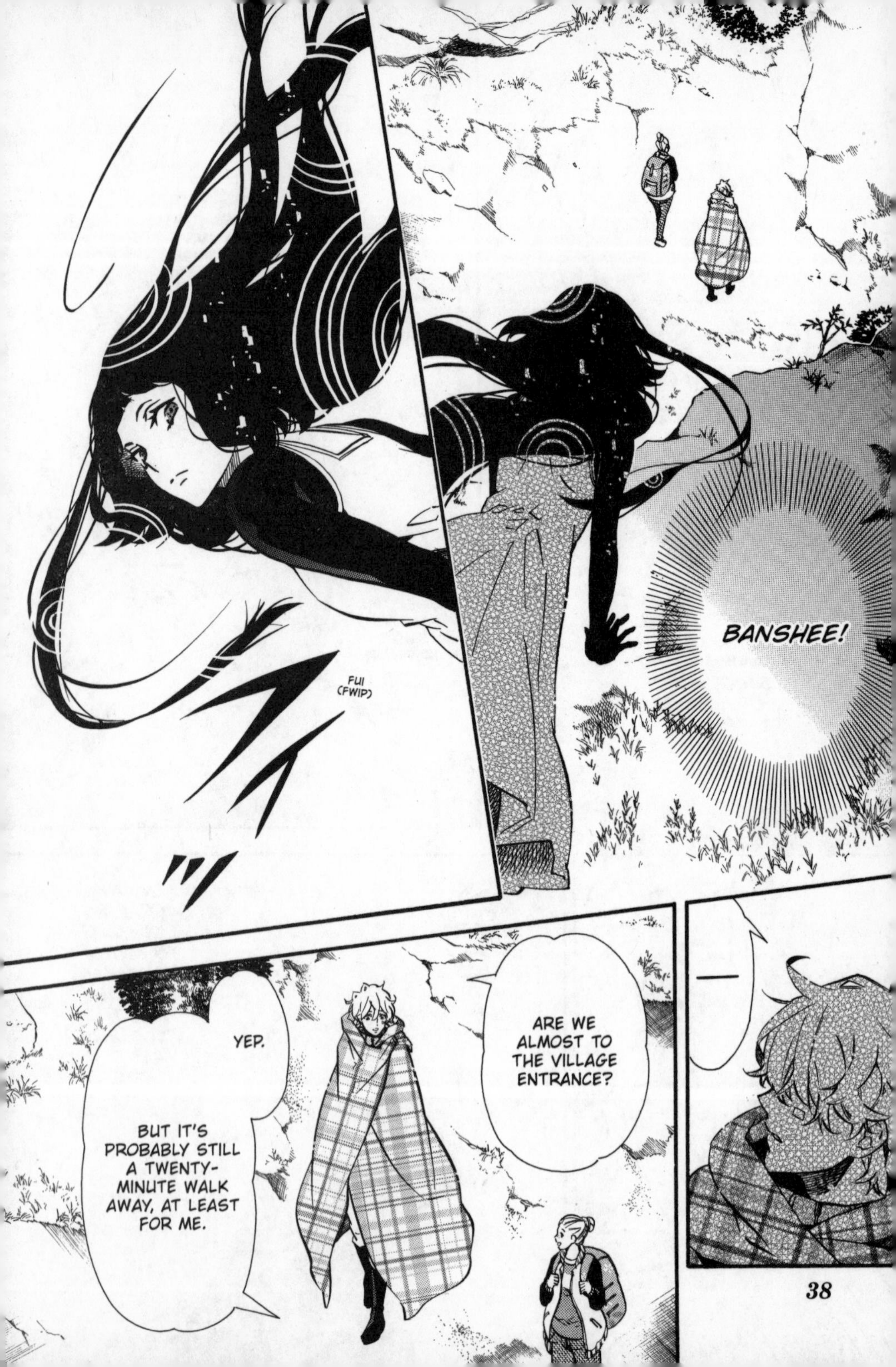
BANSHEE!
FUI (FWIP)
—
ARE WE ALMOST TO THE VILLAGE ENTRANCE?
YEP.
BUT IT'S PROBABLY STILL A TWENTY-MINUTE WALK AWAY, AT LEAST FOR ME.

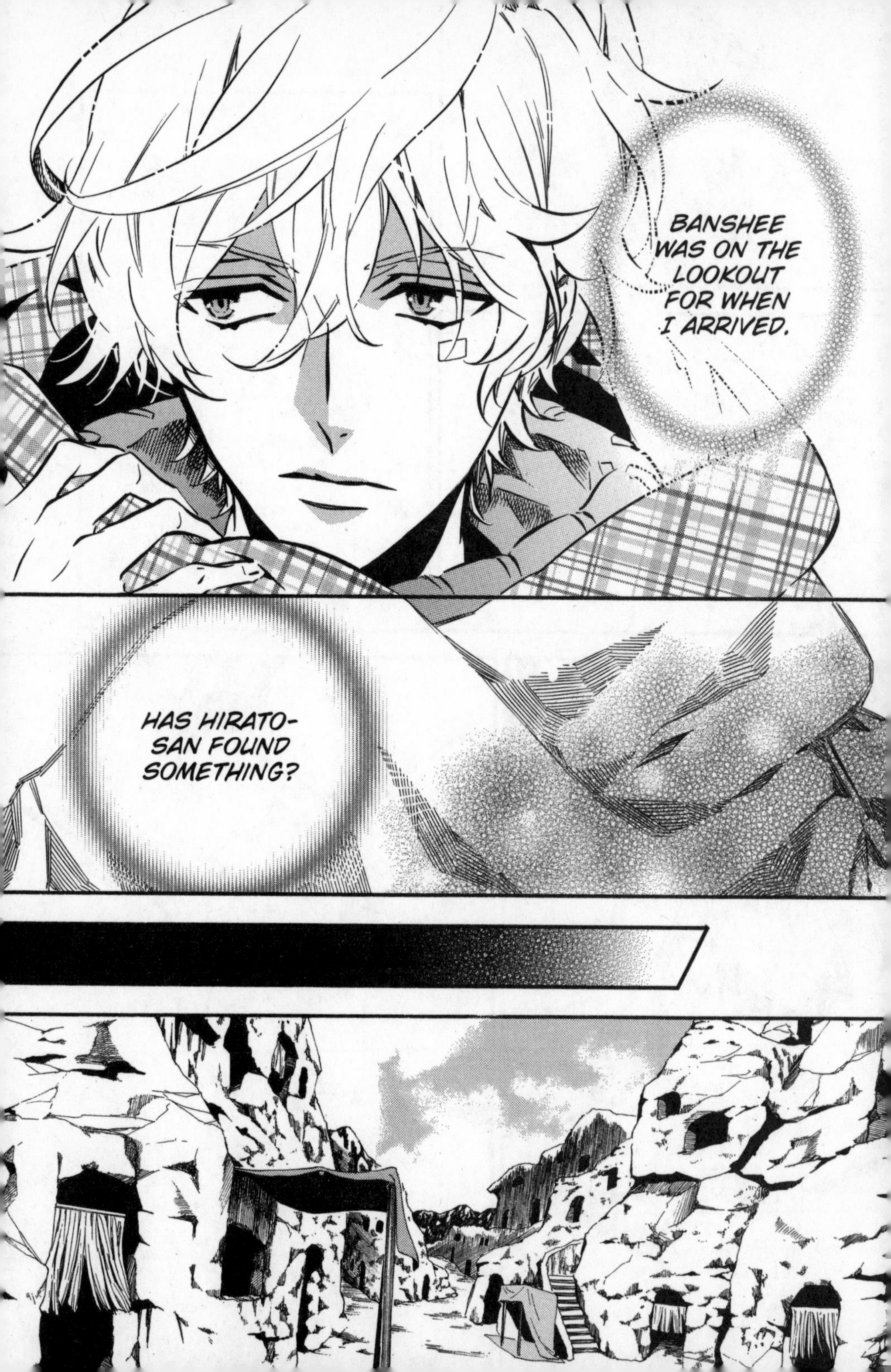
BANSHEE WAS ON THE LOOKOUT FOR WHEN I ARRIVED.
HAS HIRATO-SAN FOUND SOMETHING?

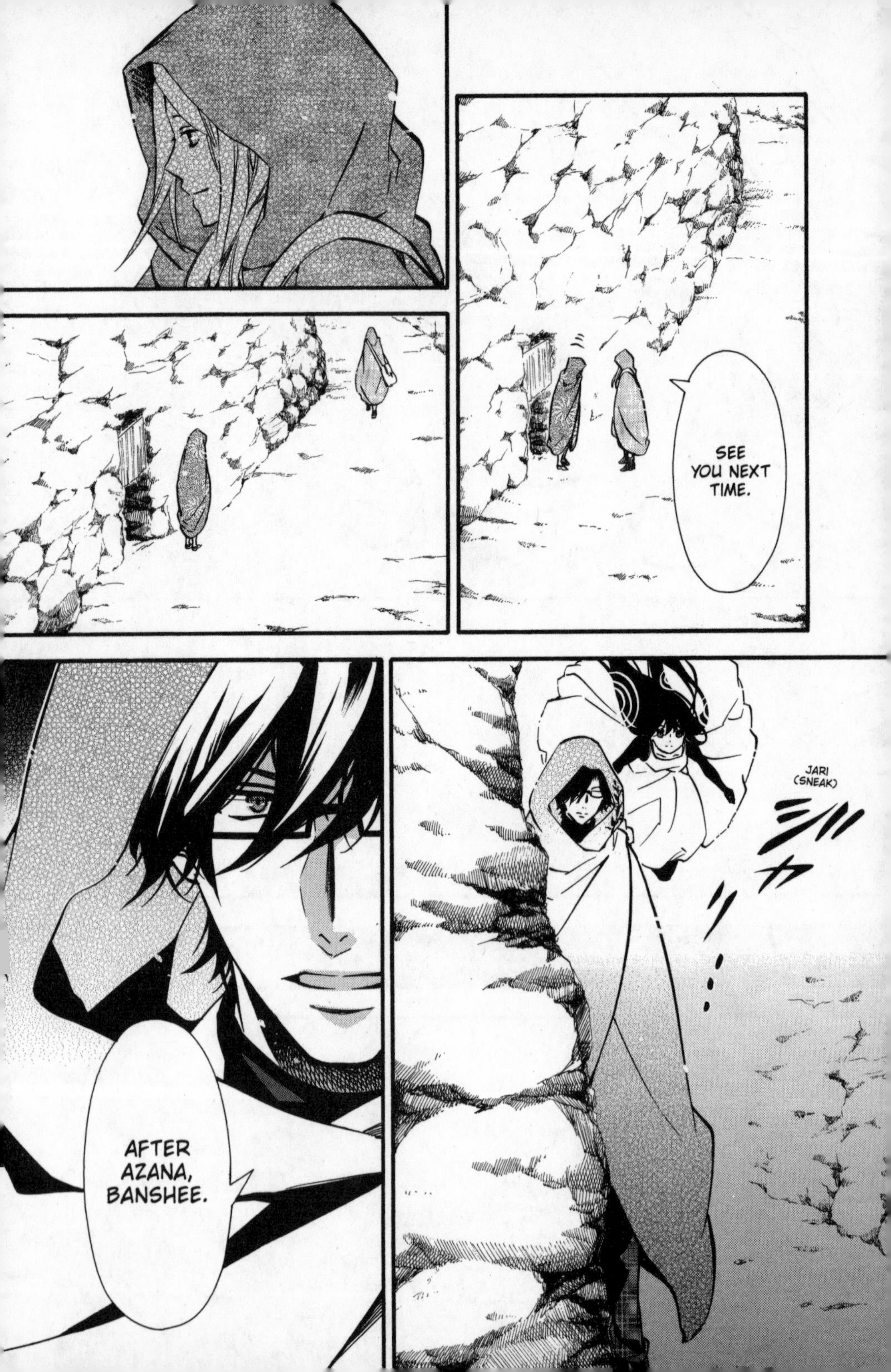
SEE YOU NEXT TIME.
JARI (SNEAK)
AFTER AZANA, BANSHEE.

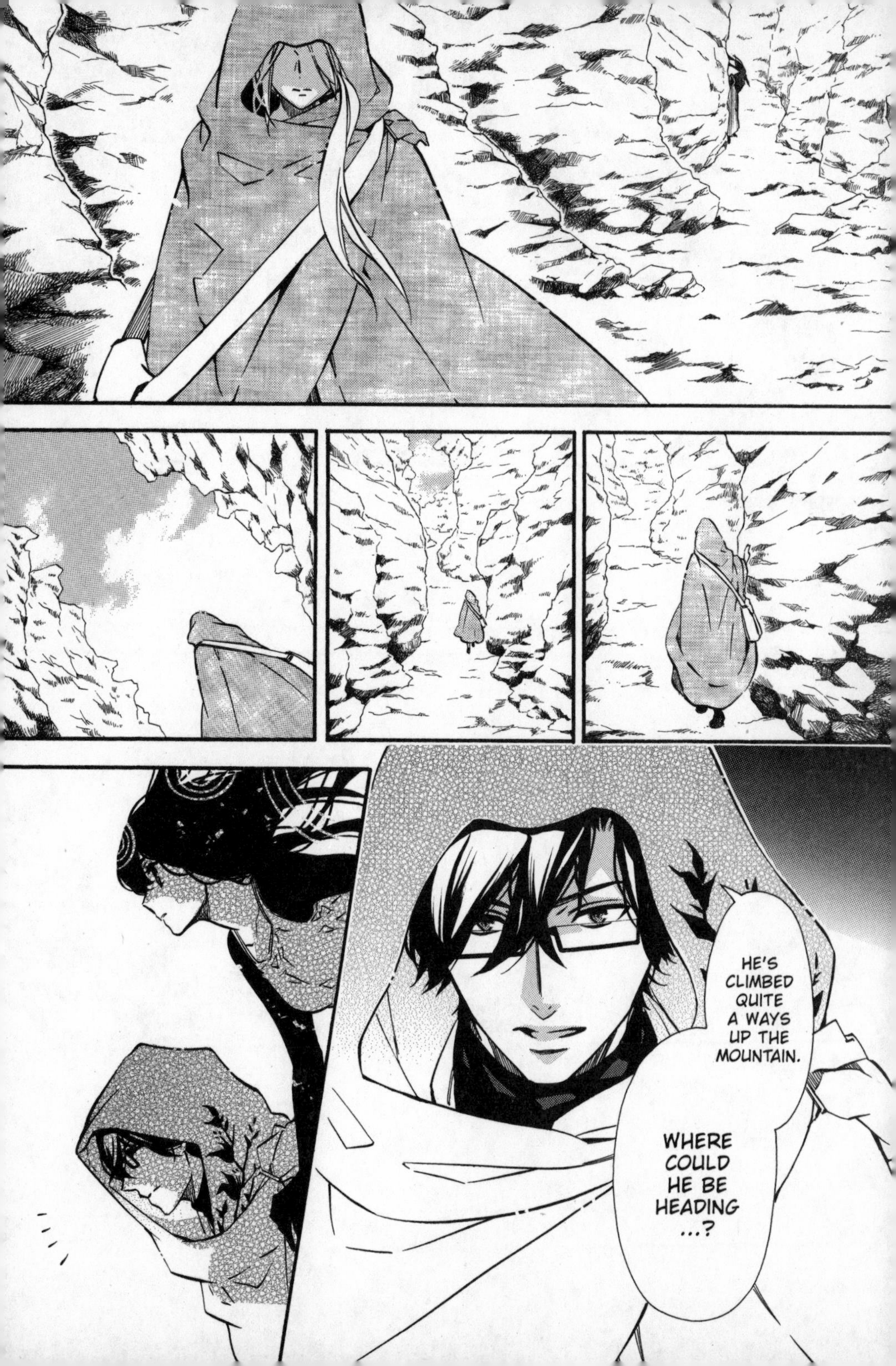

HE'S CLIMBED QUITE A WAYS UP THE MOUNTAIN.
WHERE COULD HE BE HEADING ...?

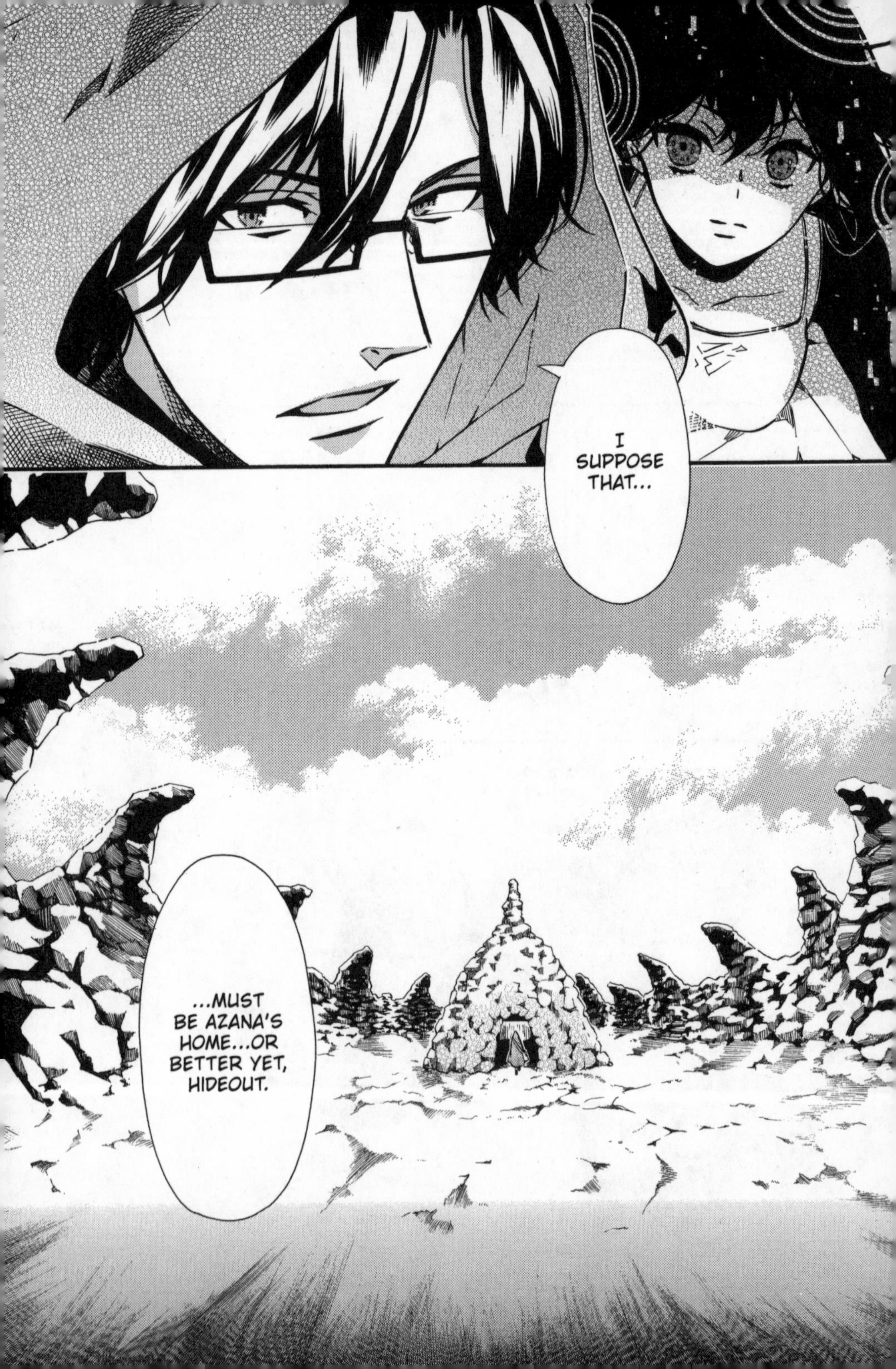
I SUPPOSE THAT...
...MUST BE AZANA'S HOME...OR BETTER YET, HIDEOUT.

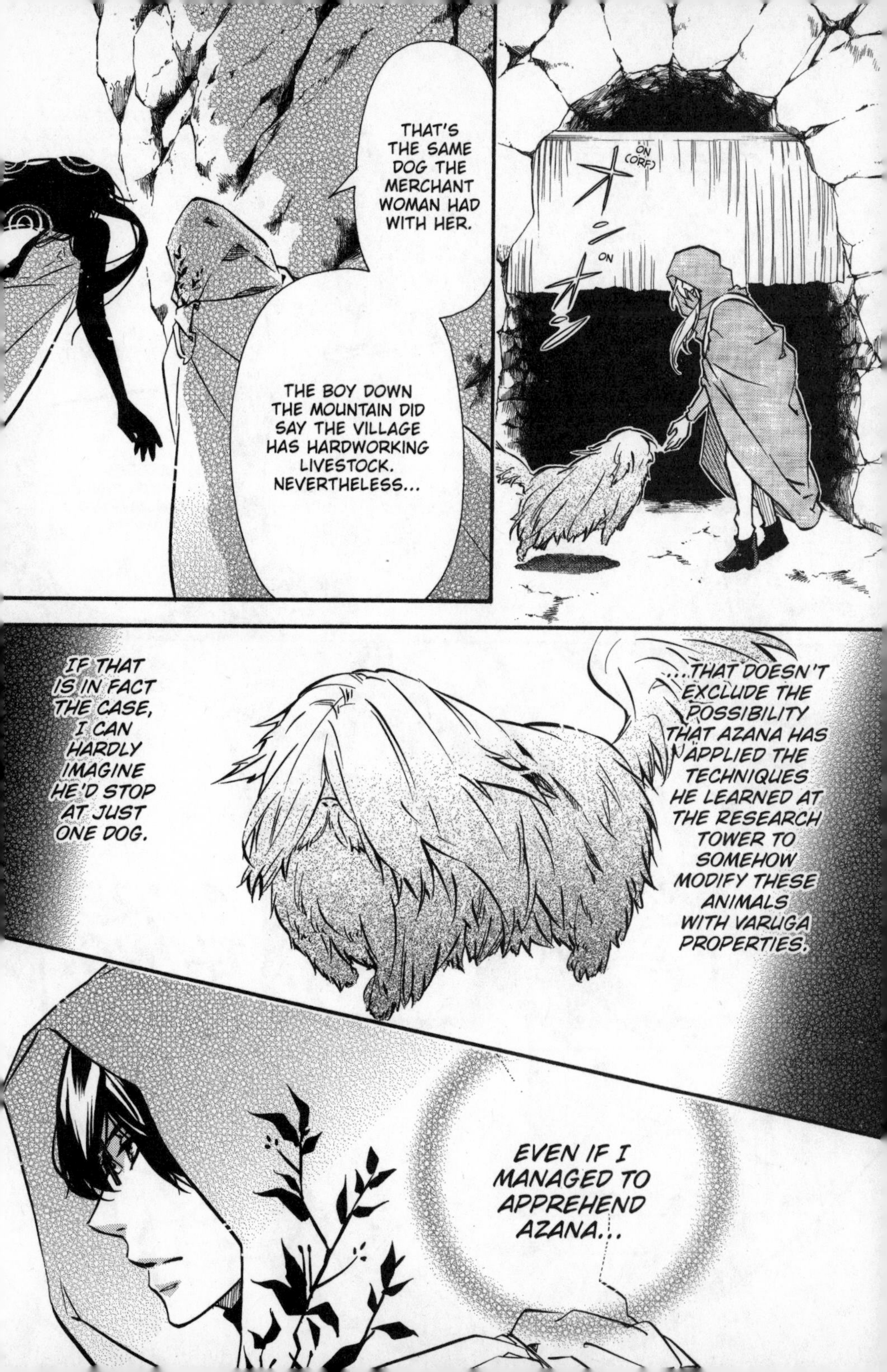
ON
(ORF)
ON
THAT'S THE SAME DOG THE MERCHANT WOMAN HAD WITH HER.
THE BOY DOWN THE MOUNTAIN DID SAY THE VILLAGE HAS HARDWORKING LIVESTOCK. NEVERTHELESS...
...THAT DOESN'T EXCLUDE THE POSSIBILITY THAT AZANA HAS APPLIED THE TECHNIQUES HE LEARNED AT THE RESEARCH TOWER TO SOMEHOW MODIFY THESE ANIMALS WITH VARUGA PROPERTIES.
IF THAT IS IN FACT THE CASE, I CAN HARDLY IMAGINE HE'D STOP AT JUST ONE DOG.
EVEN IF I MANAGED TO APPREHEND AZANA...

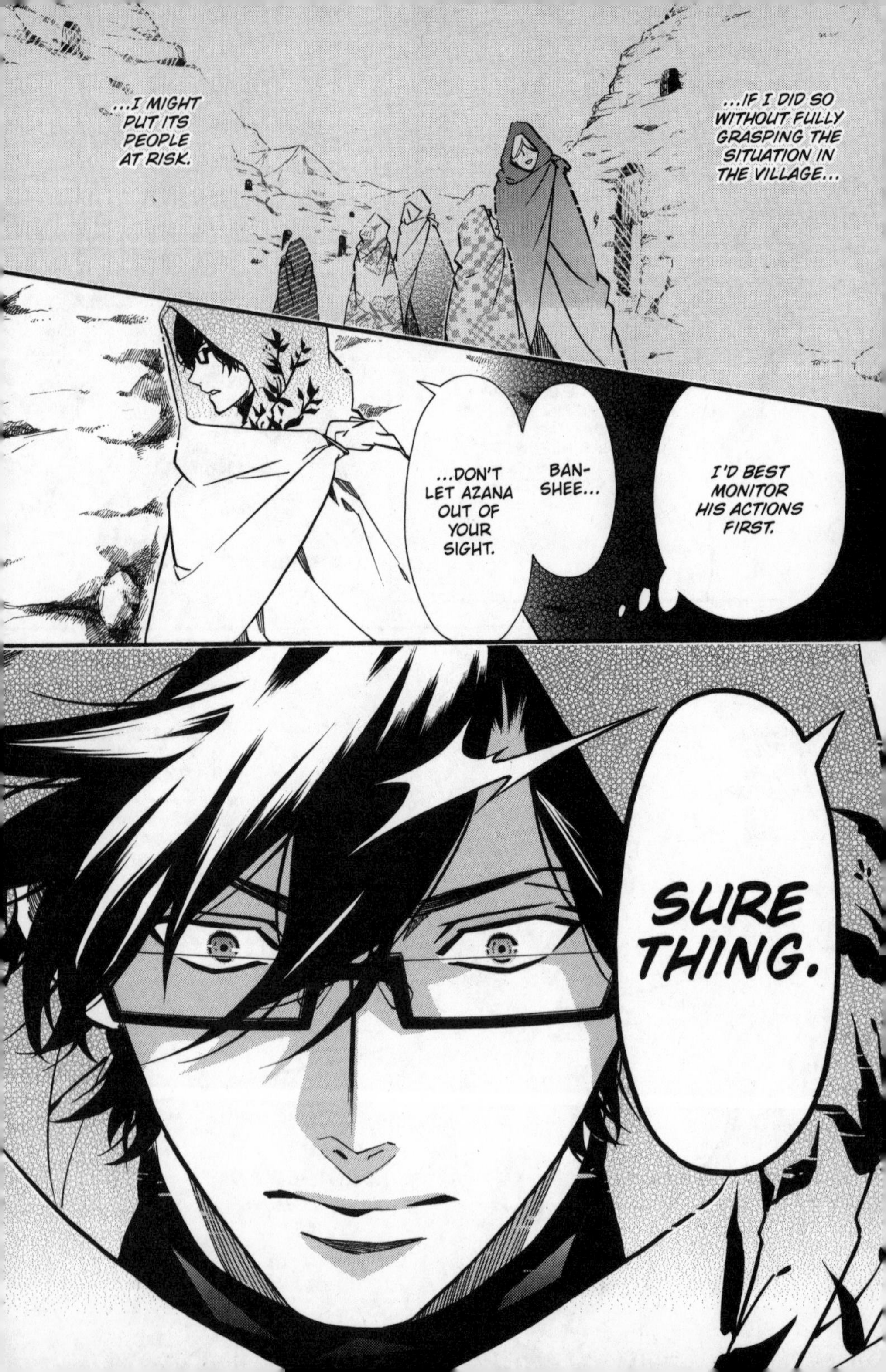
...IF I DID SO WITHOUT FULLY GRASPING THE SITUATION IN THE VILLAGE...
...I MIGHT PUT ITS PEOPLE AT RISK.
I'D BEST MONITOR HIS ACTIONS FIRST.
BAN-SHEE...
...DON'T LET AZANA OUT OF YOUR SIGHT.
SURE THING.

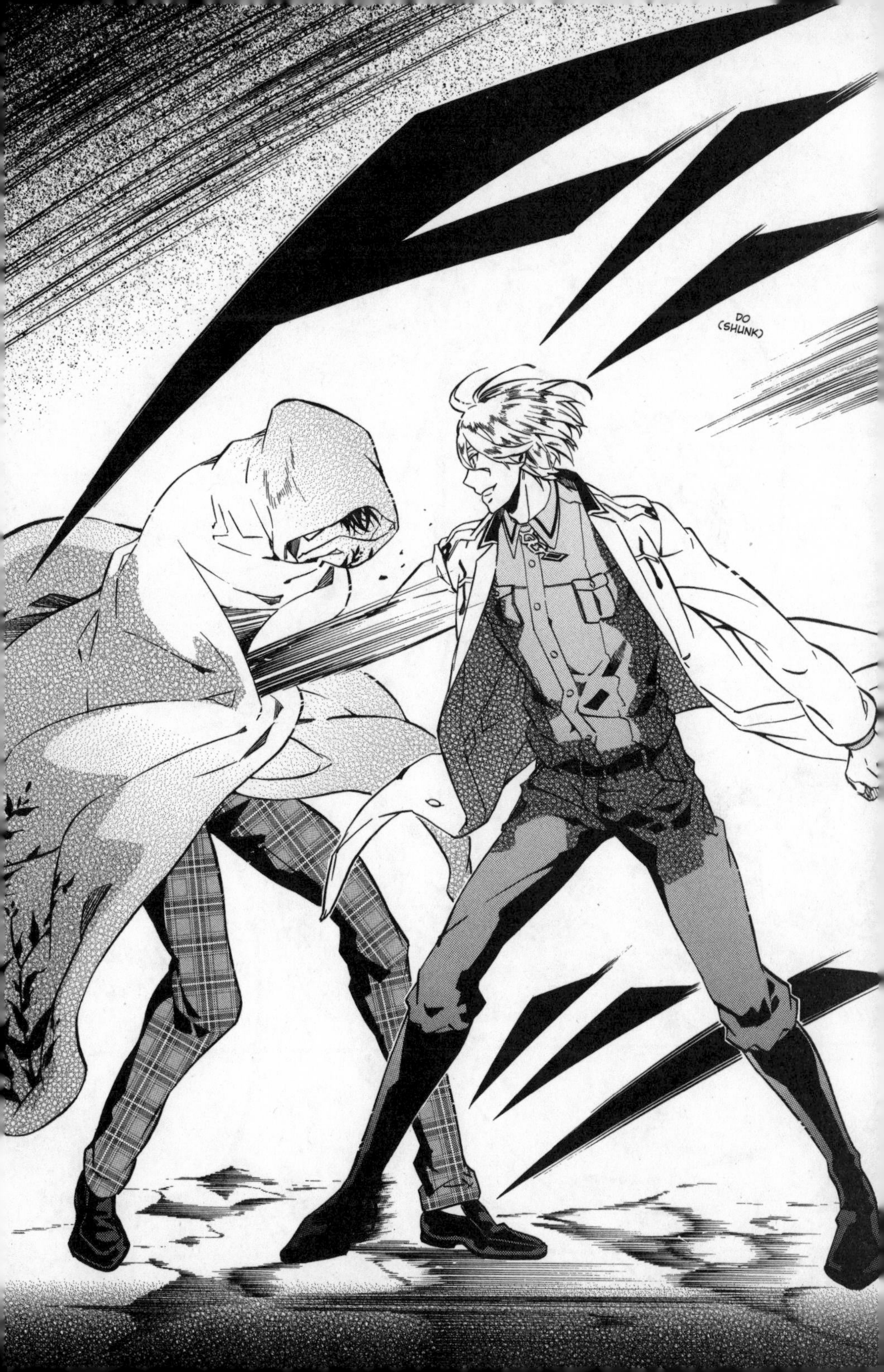
DO
(SHUNK)

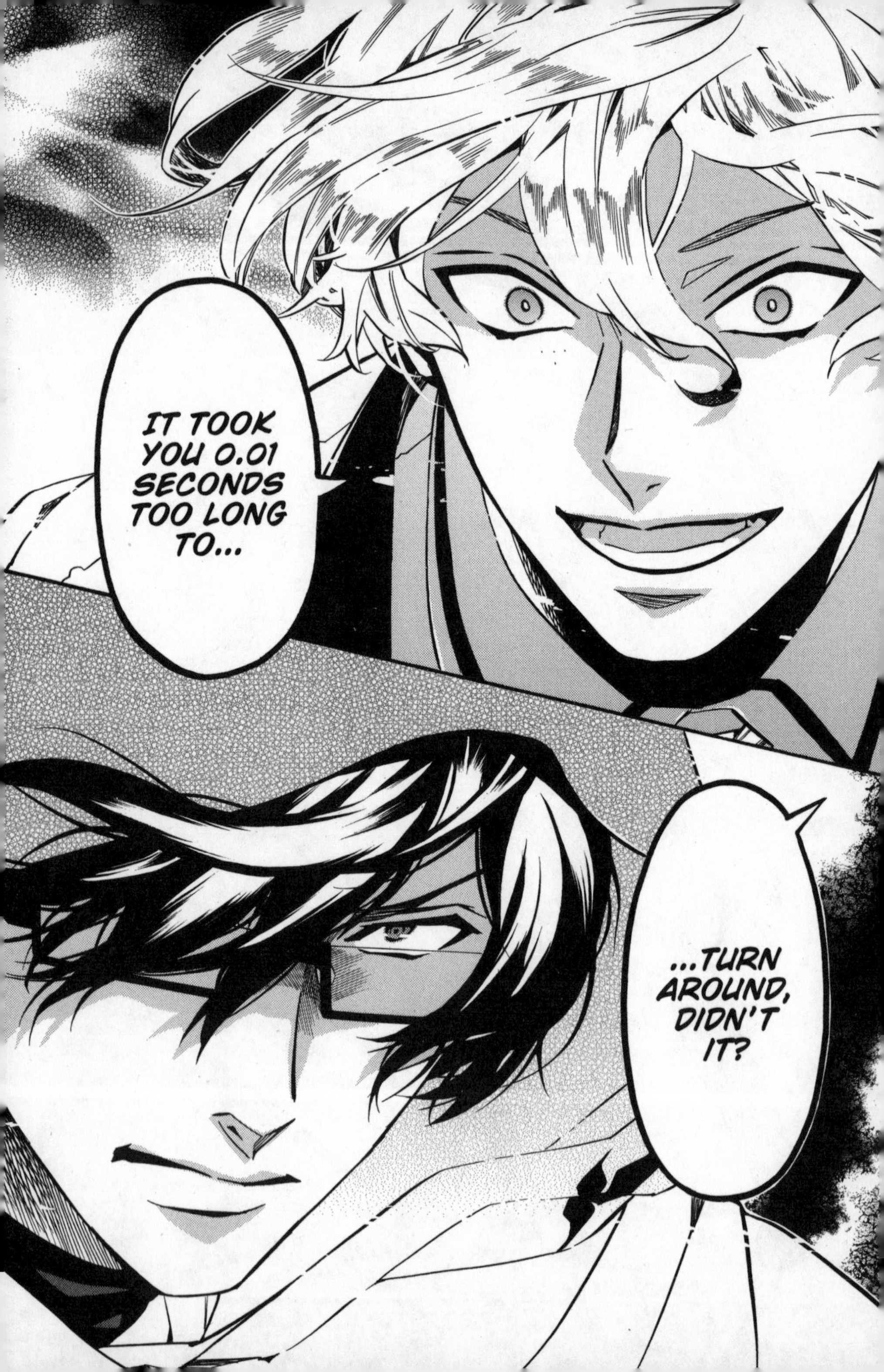
IT TOOK YOU 0.01 SECONDS TOO LONG TO...
...TURN AROUND, DIDN'T IT?

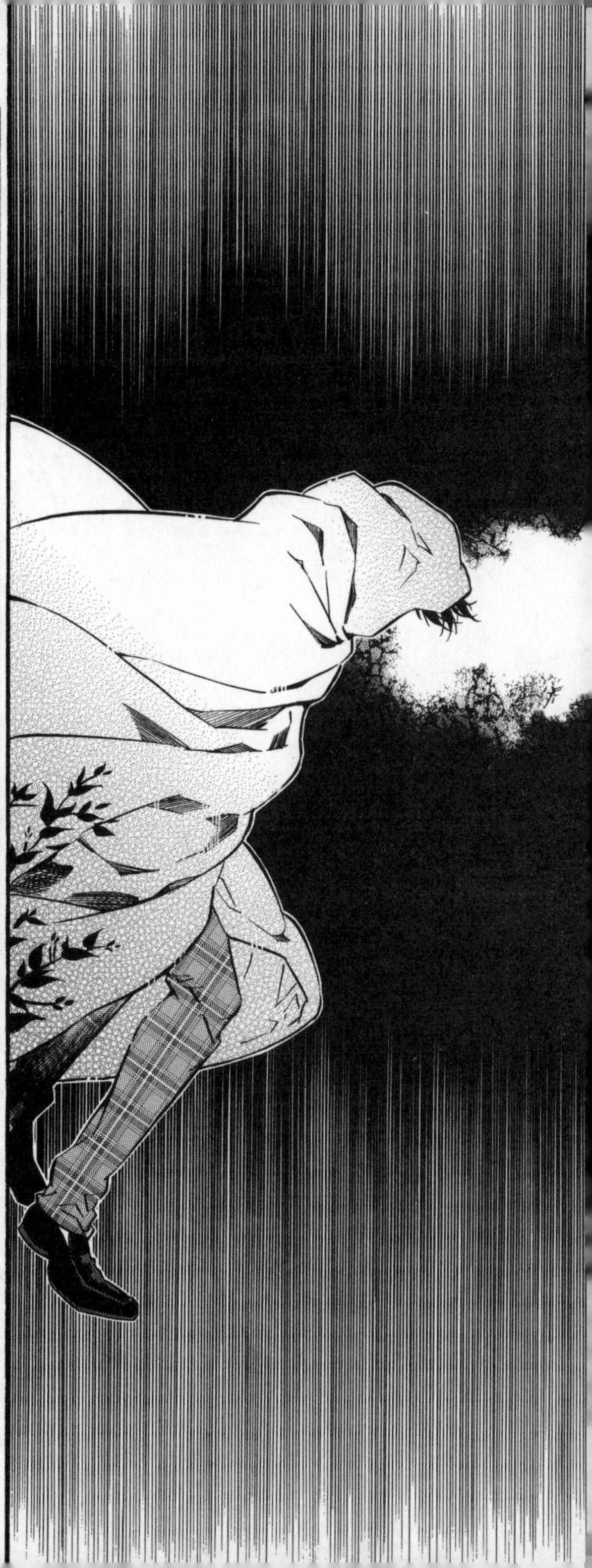

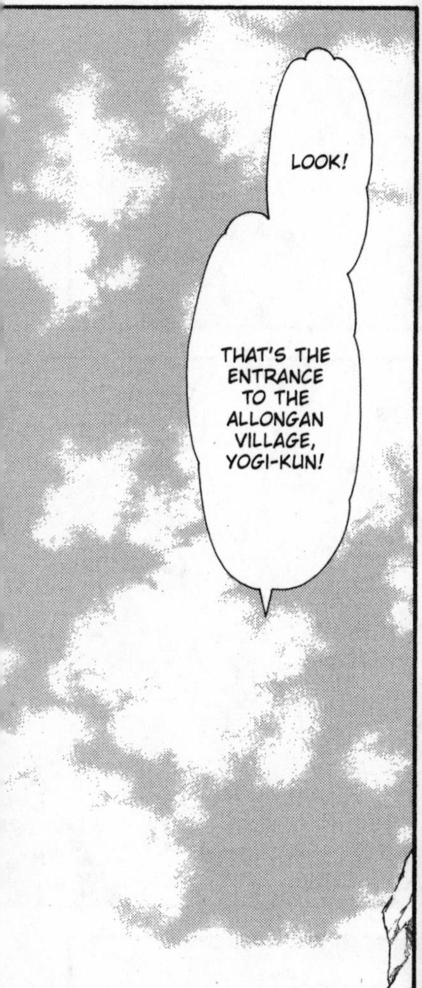
LOOK!
THAT'S THE ENTRANCE TO THE ALLONGAN VILLAGE, YOGI-KUN!

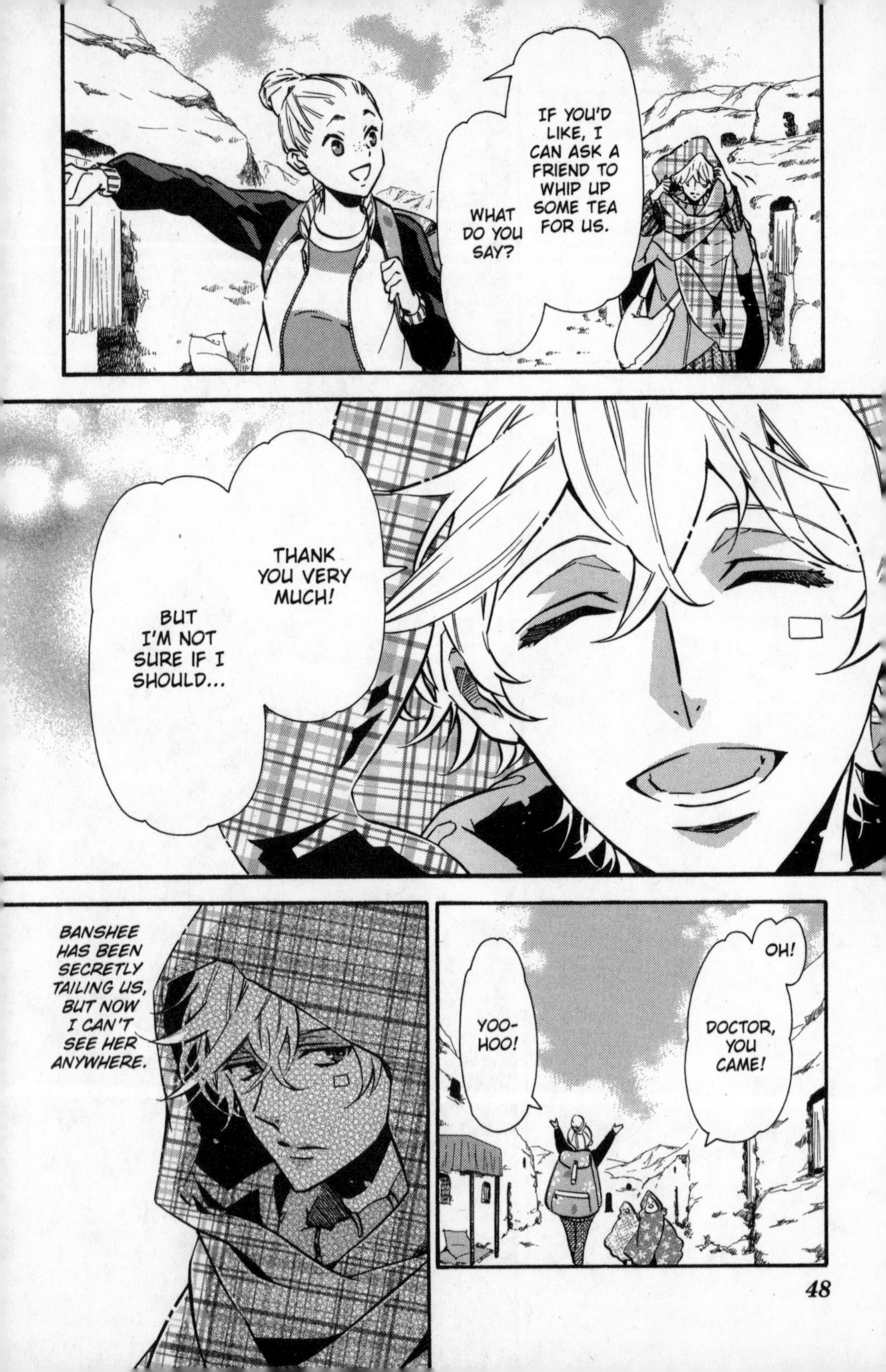
IF YOU'D LIKE, I CAN ASK A FRIEND TO WHIP UP SOME TEA FOR US.
WHAT DO YOU SAY?
THANK YOU VERY MUCH!
BUT I'M NOT SURE IF I SHOULD...
OH!
DOCTOR, YOU CAME!
YOO-HOO!
BANSHEE HAS BEEN SECRETLY TAILING US, BUT NOW I CAN'T SEE HER ANYWHERE.

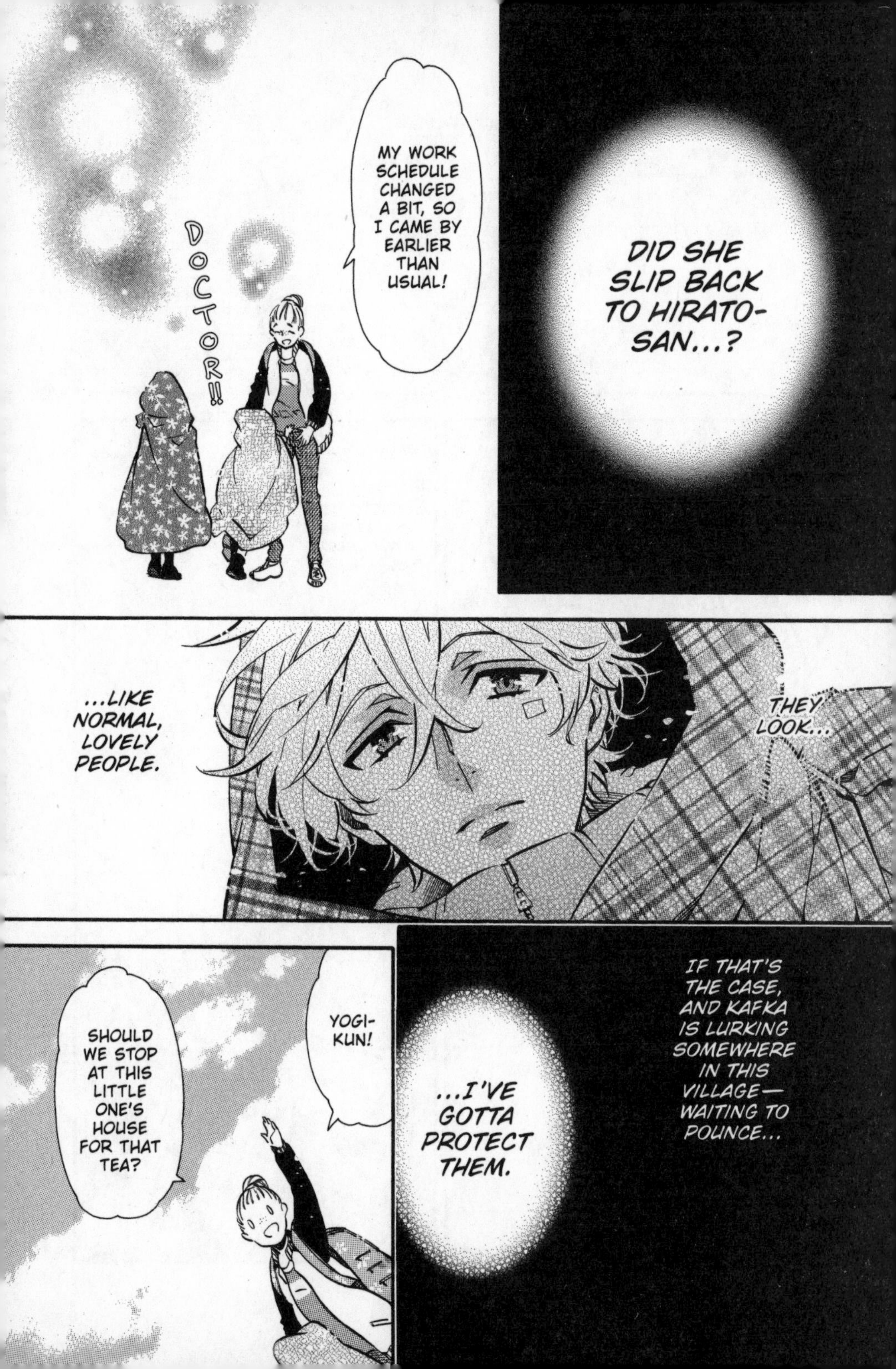
DID SHE SLIP BACK TO HIRATO-SAN...?
MY WORK SCHEDULE CHANGED A BIT, SO I CAME BY EARLIER THAN USUAL!
DOCTOR!!
THEY LOOK...
...LIKE NORMAL, LOVELY PEOPLE.
IF THAT'S THE CASE, AND KAFKA IS LURKING SOMEWHERE IN THIS VILLAGE—WAITING TO POUNCE...
...I'VE GOTTA PROTECT THEM.
YOGI-KUN!
SHOULD WE STOP AT THIS LITTLE ONE'S HOUSE FOR THAT TEA?

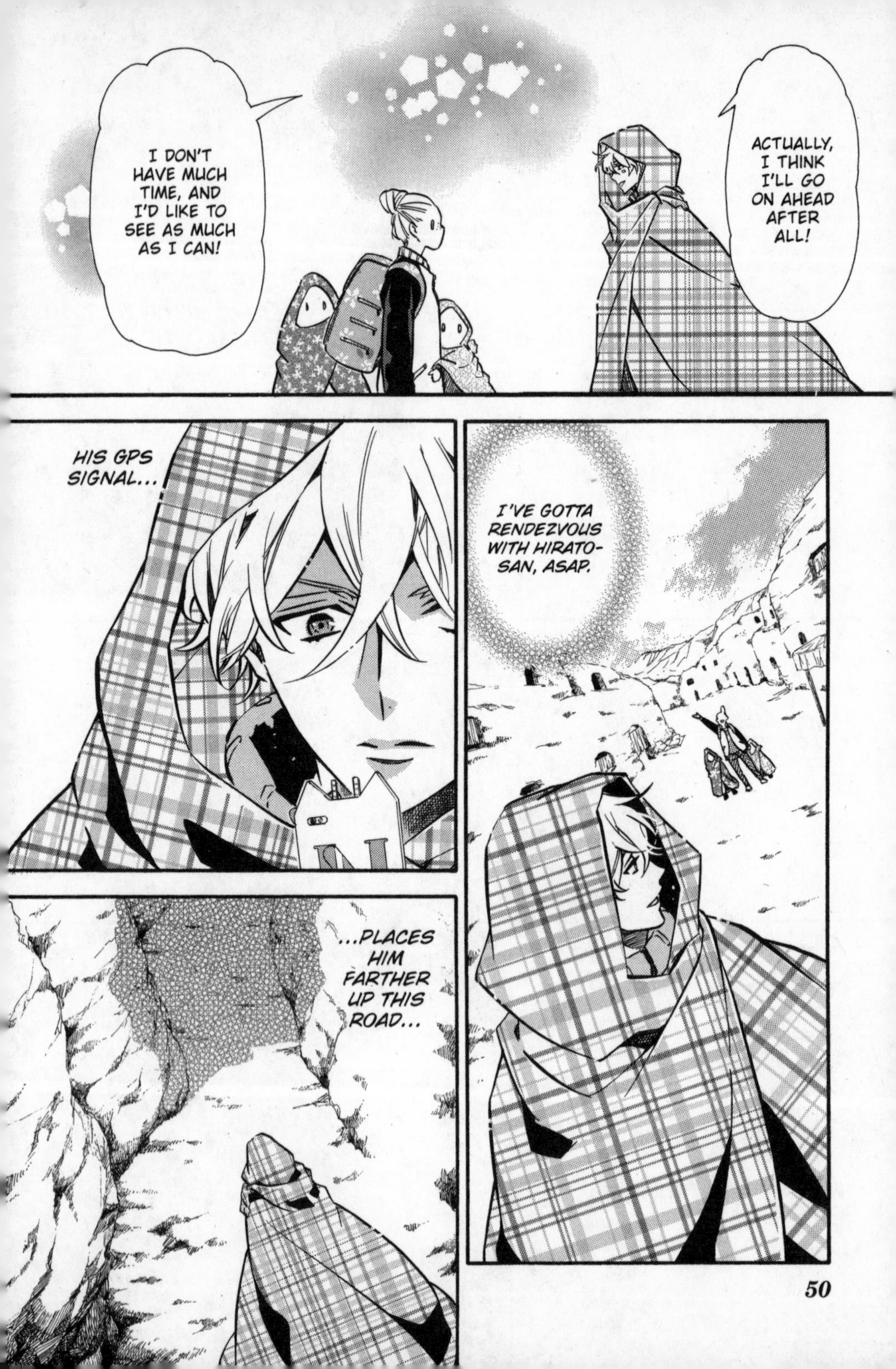
ACTUALLY, I THINK I'LL GO ON AHEAD AFTER ALL!
I DON'T HAVE MUCH TIME, AND I'D LIKE TO SEE AS MUCH AS I CAN!
I'VE GOTTA RENDEZVOUS WITH HIRATO-SAN, ASAP.
HIS GPS SIGNAL...
...PLACES HIM FARTHER UP THIS ROAD...

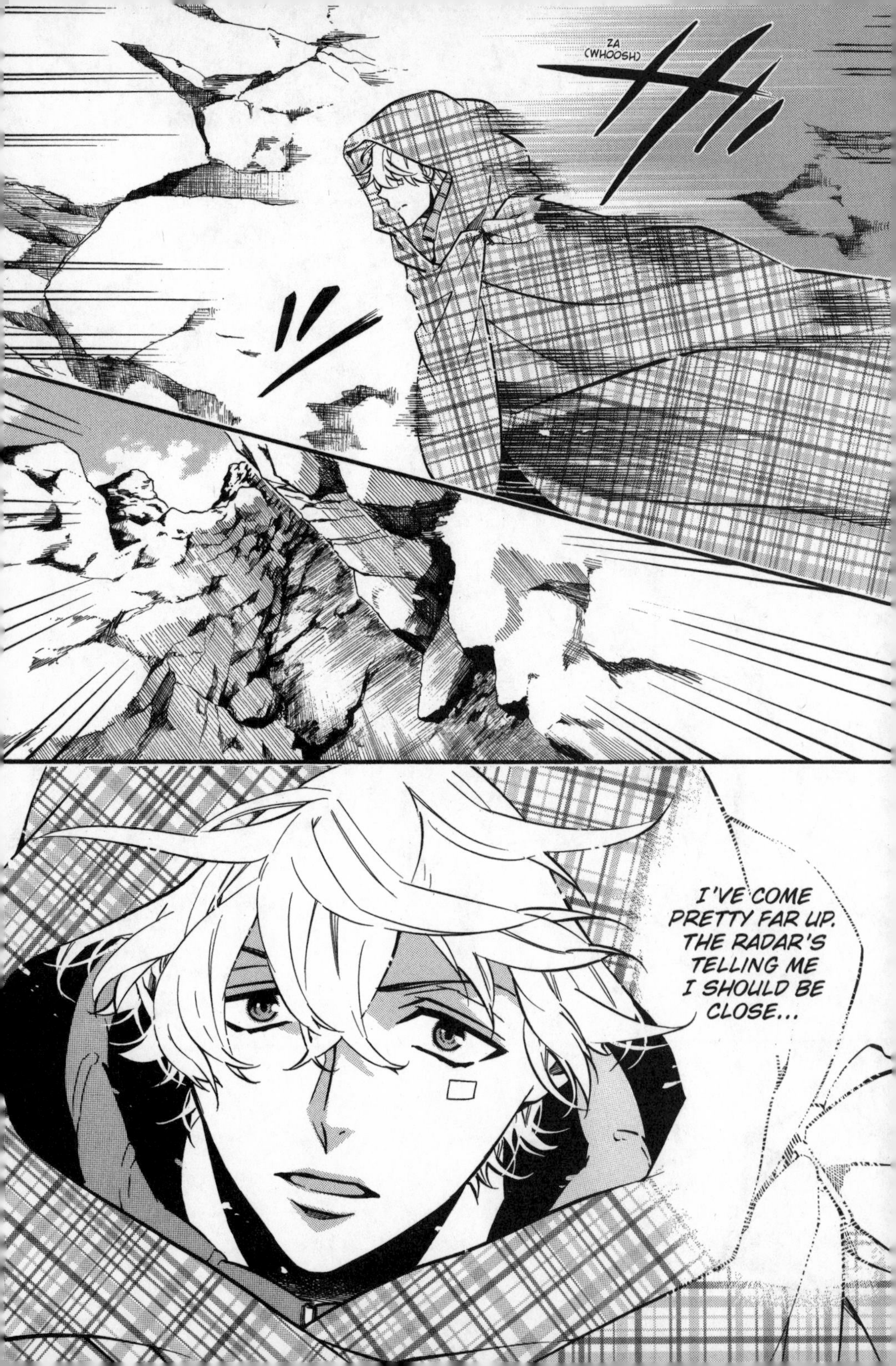
ZA (WHOOSH)
I'VE COME PRETTY FAR UP. THE RADAR'S TELLING ME I SHOULD BE CLOSE...

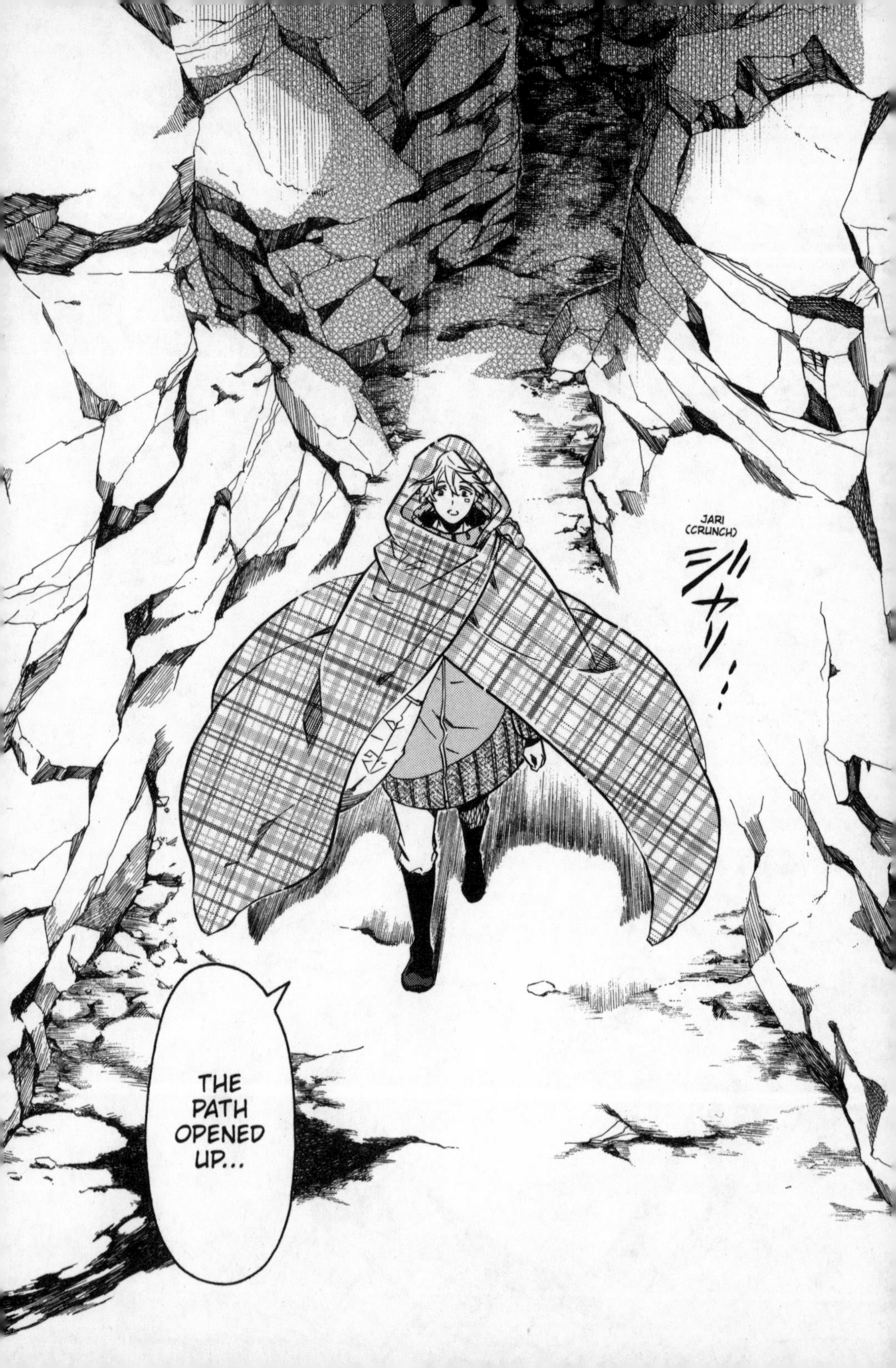
JARI (CRUNCH)
ジャリ…
THE PATH OPENED UP...

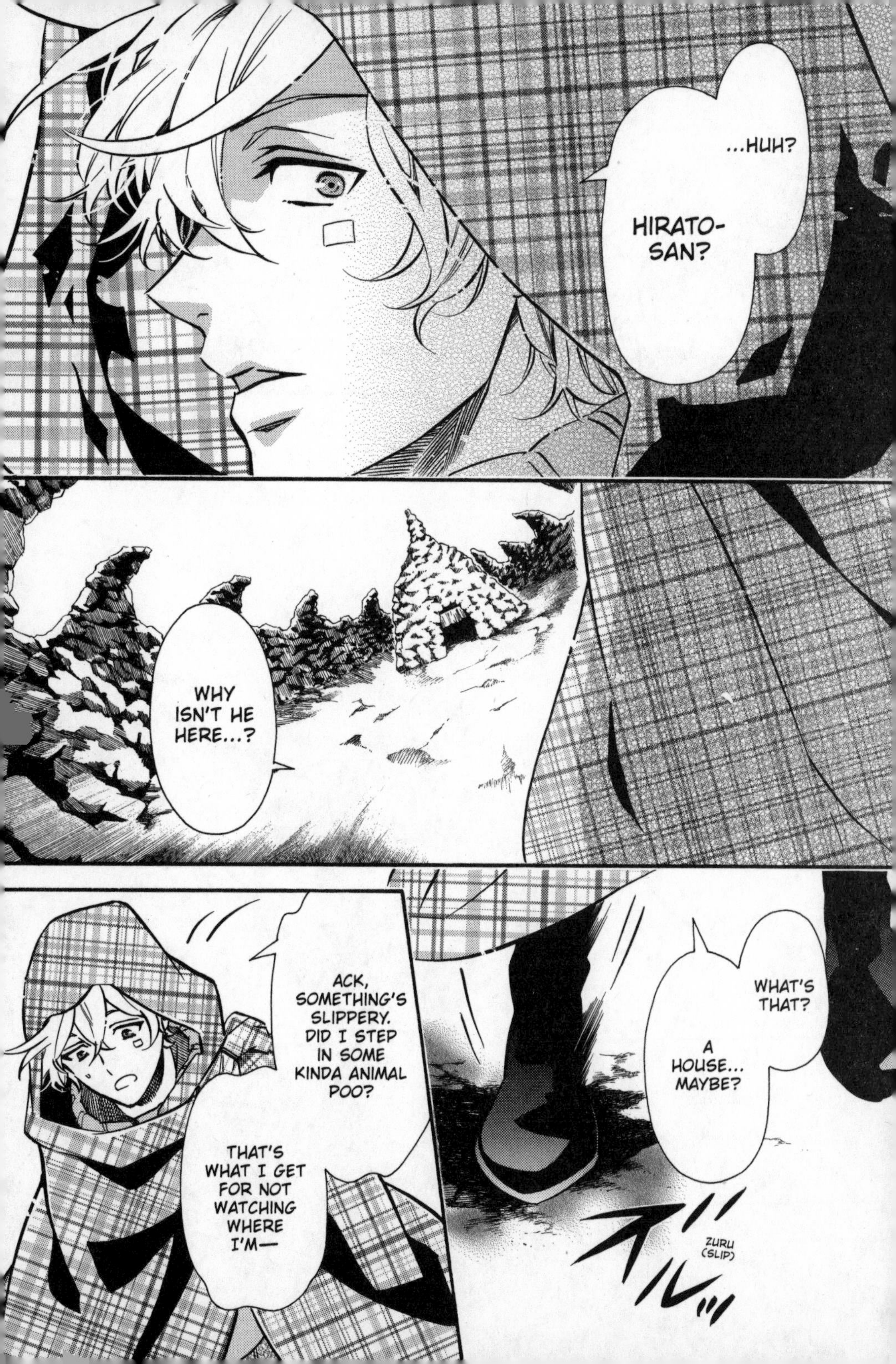

...HUH?
HIRATO-SAN?
WHY ISN'T HE HERE...?
WHAT'S THAT?
A HOUSE... MAYBE?
ACK, SOMETHING'S SLIPPERY. DID I STEP IN SOME KINDA ANIMAL POO?
ZURU (SLIP)
THAT'S WHAT I GET FOR NOT WATCHING WHERE I'M—

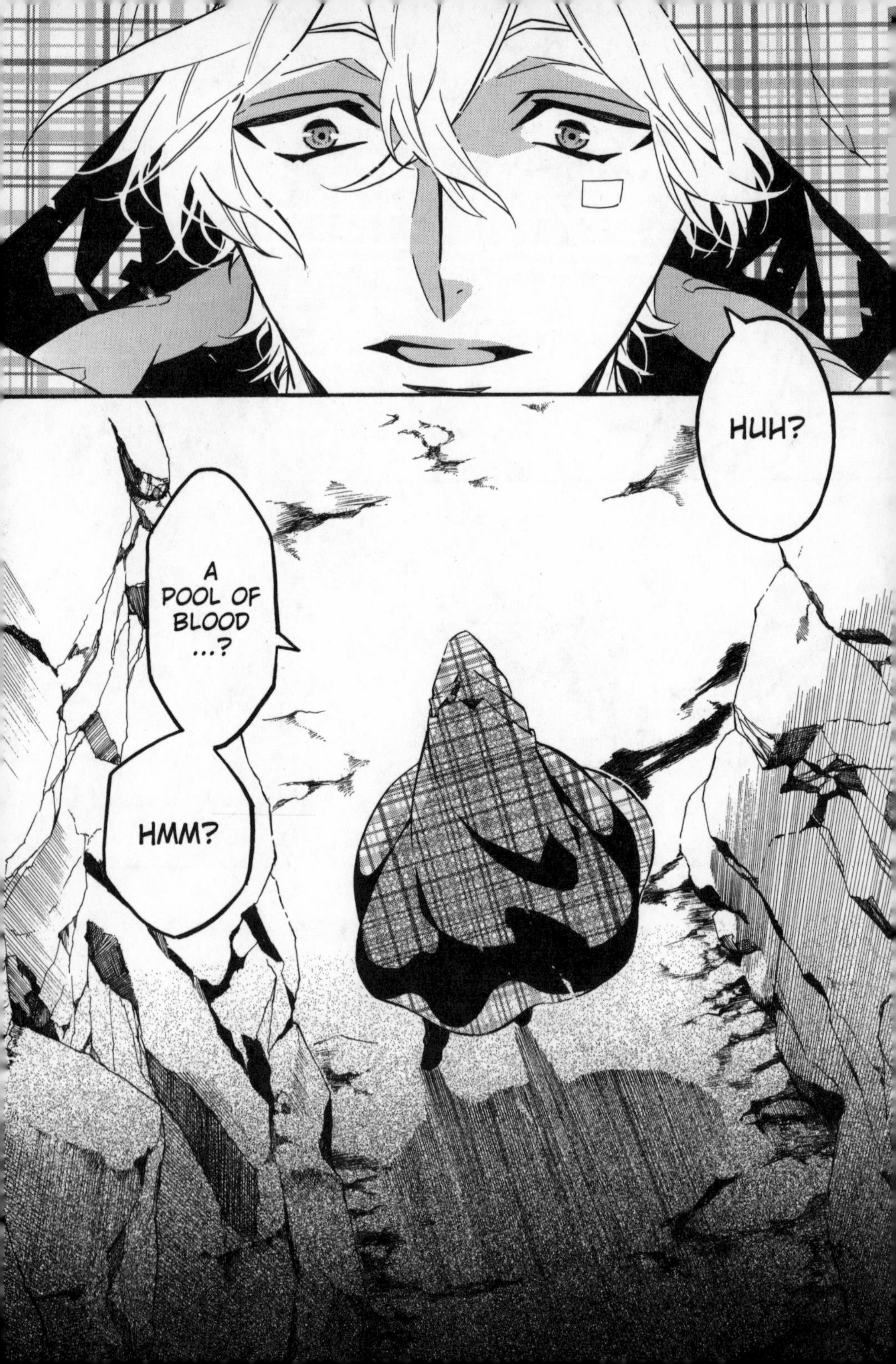
HUH?
A POOL OF BLOOD ...?
HMM?

KARNEVAL

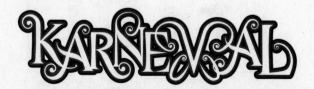

KARNEVAL

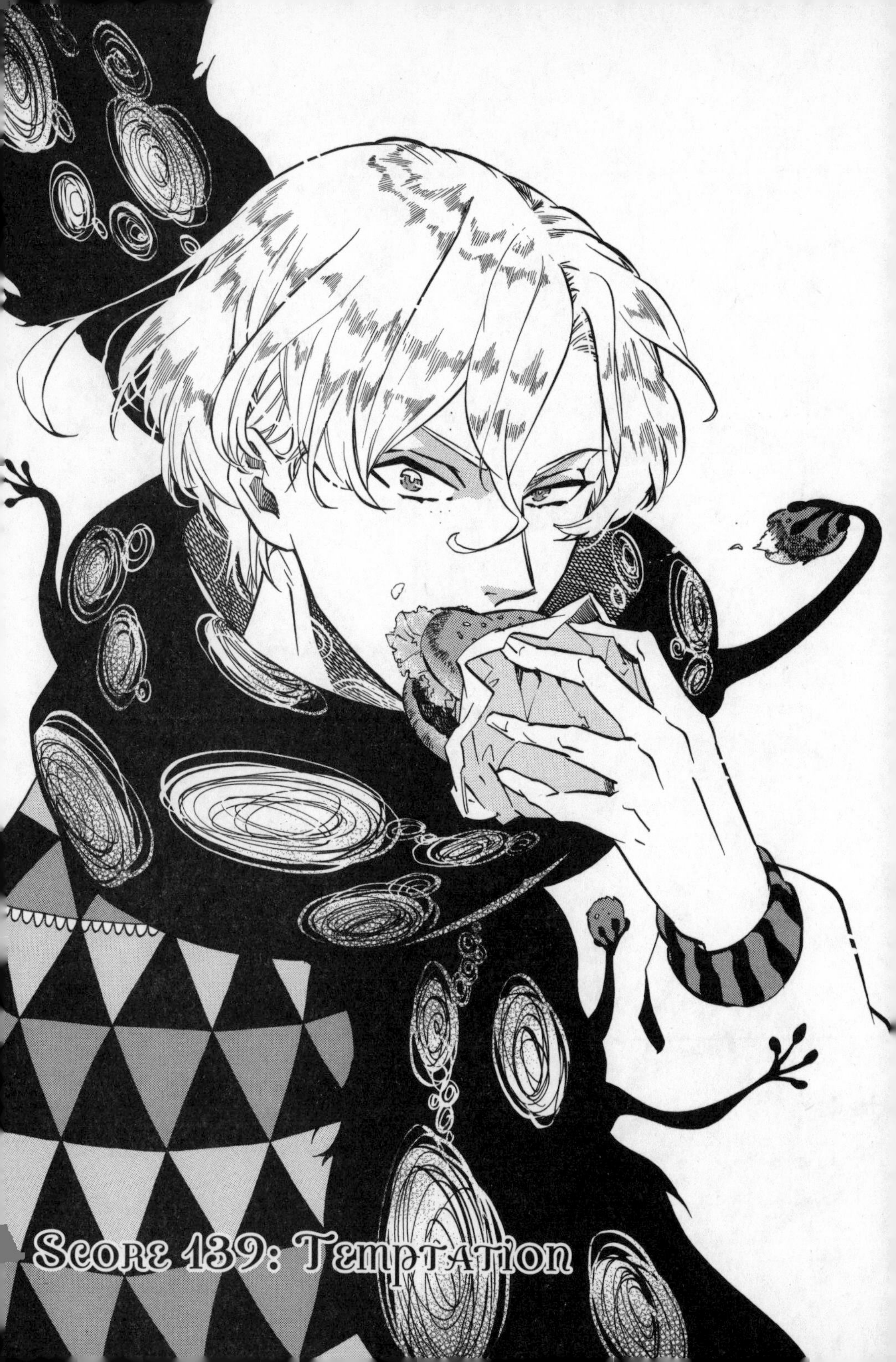
Score 139: Temptation

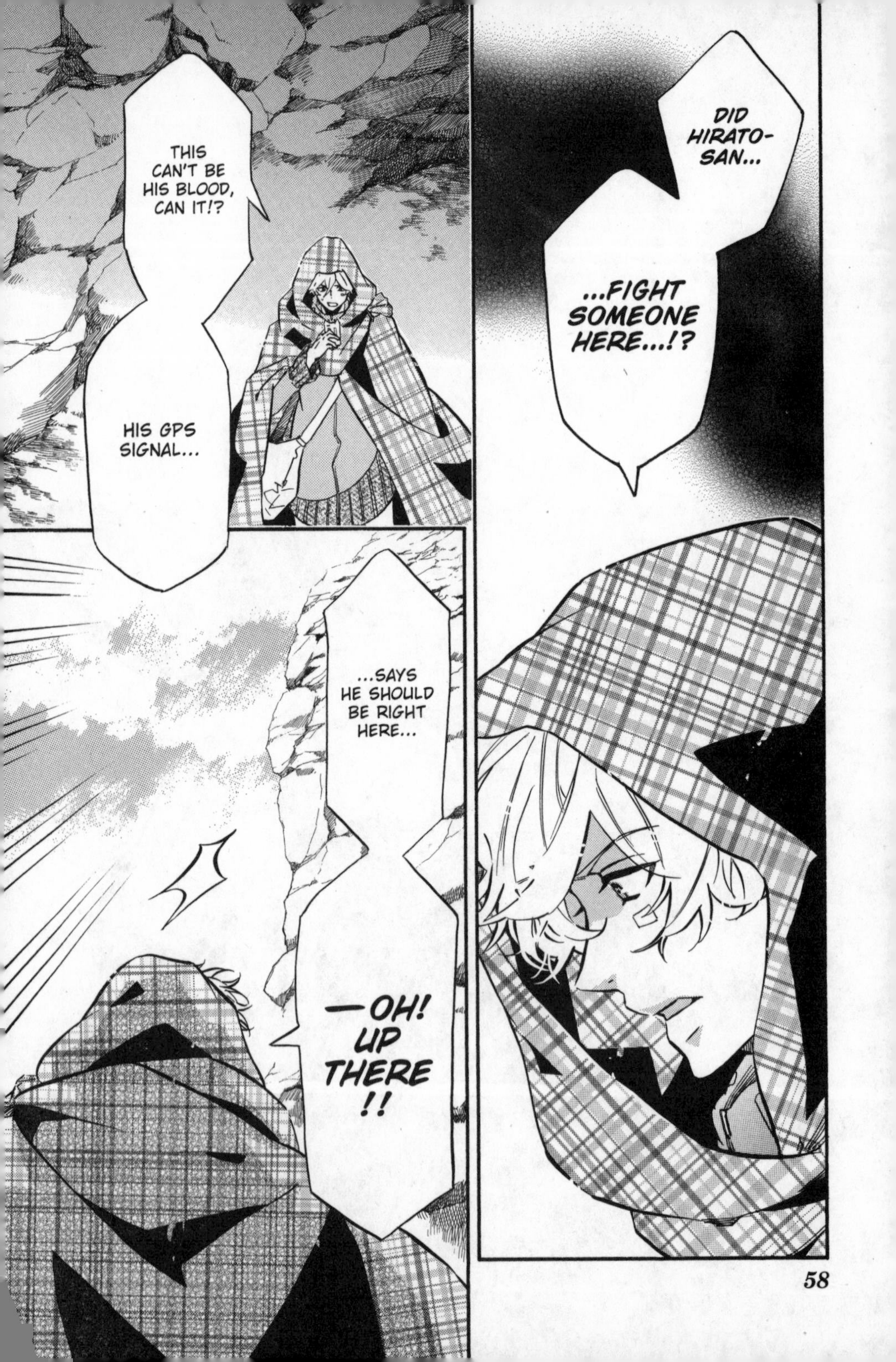
DID HIRATO-SAN...
...FIGHT SOMEONE HERE...!?
THIS CAN'T BE HIS BLOOD, CAN IT!?
HIS GPS SIGNAL...
...SAYS HE SHOULD BE RIGHT HERE...
—OH! UP THERE!!

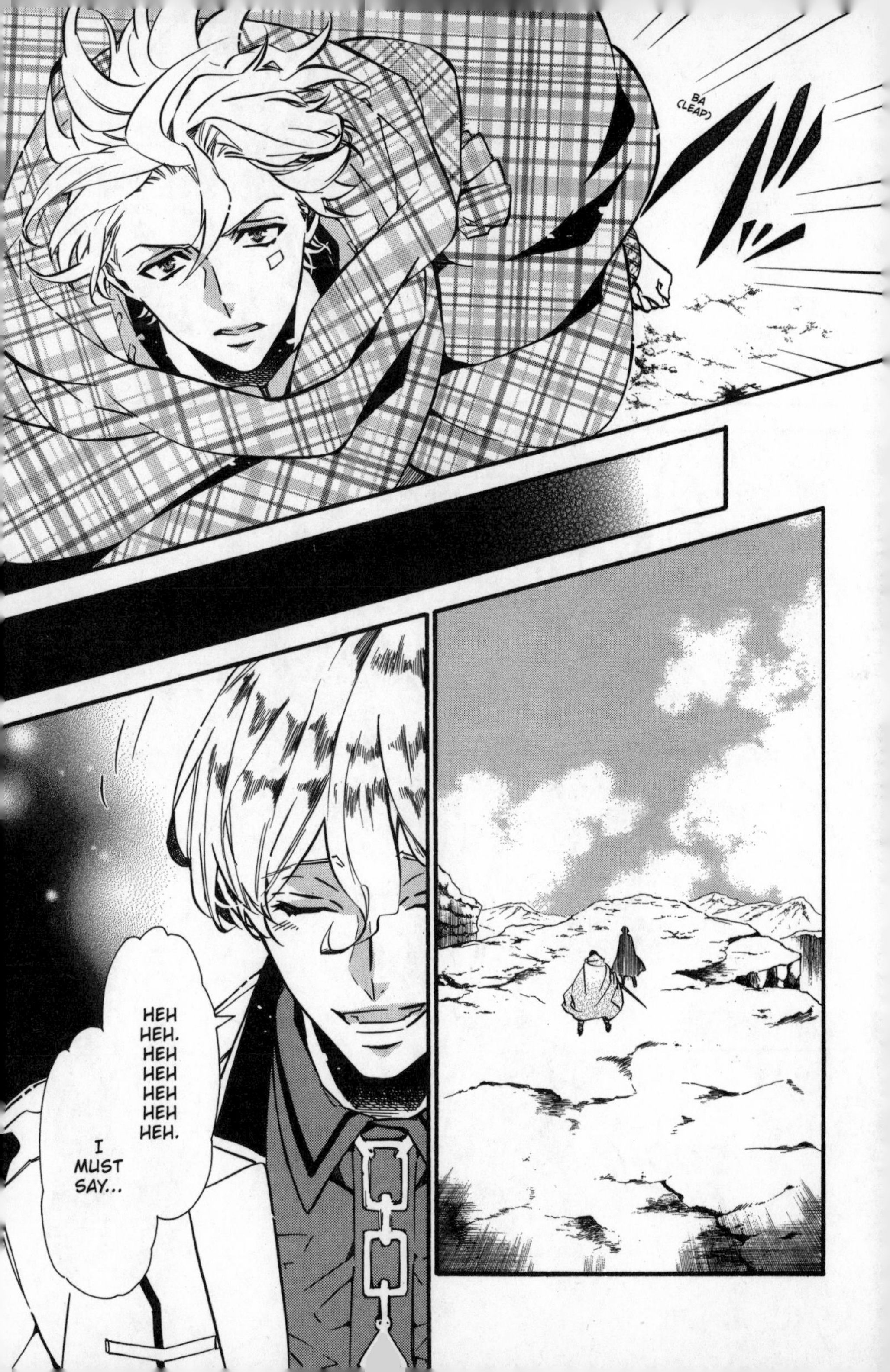
BA (LEAP)
HEH HEH. HEH HEH HEH HEH HEH.
I MUST SAY...

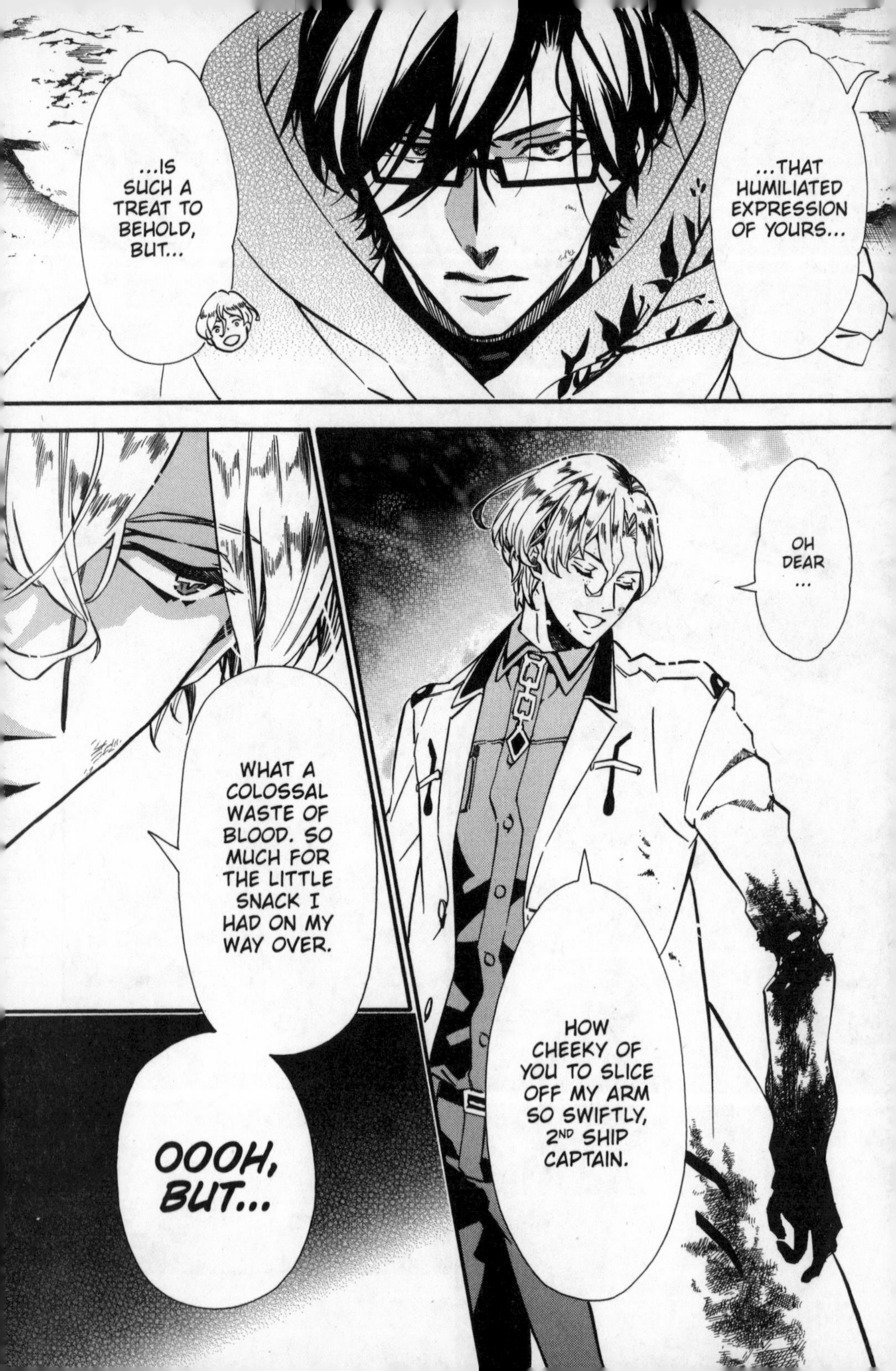
...THAT HUMILIATED EXPRESSION OF YOURS...
...IS SUCH A TREAT TO BEHOLD, BUT...
OH DEAR ...
HOW CHEEKY OF YOU TO SLICE OFF MY ARM SO SWIFTLY, 2ND SHIP CAPTAIN.
WHAT A COLOSSAL WASTE OF BLOOD. SO MUCH FOR THE LITTLE SNACK I HAD ON MY WAY OVER.
OOOH, BUT...

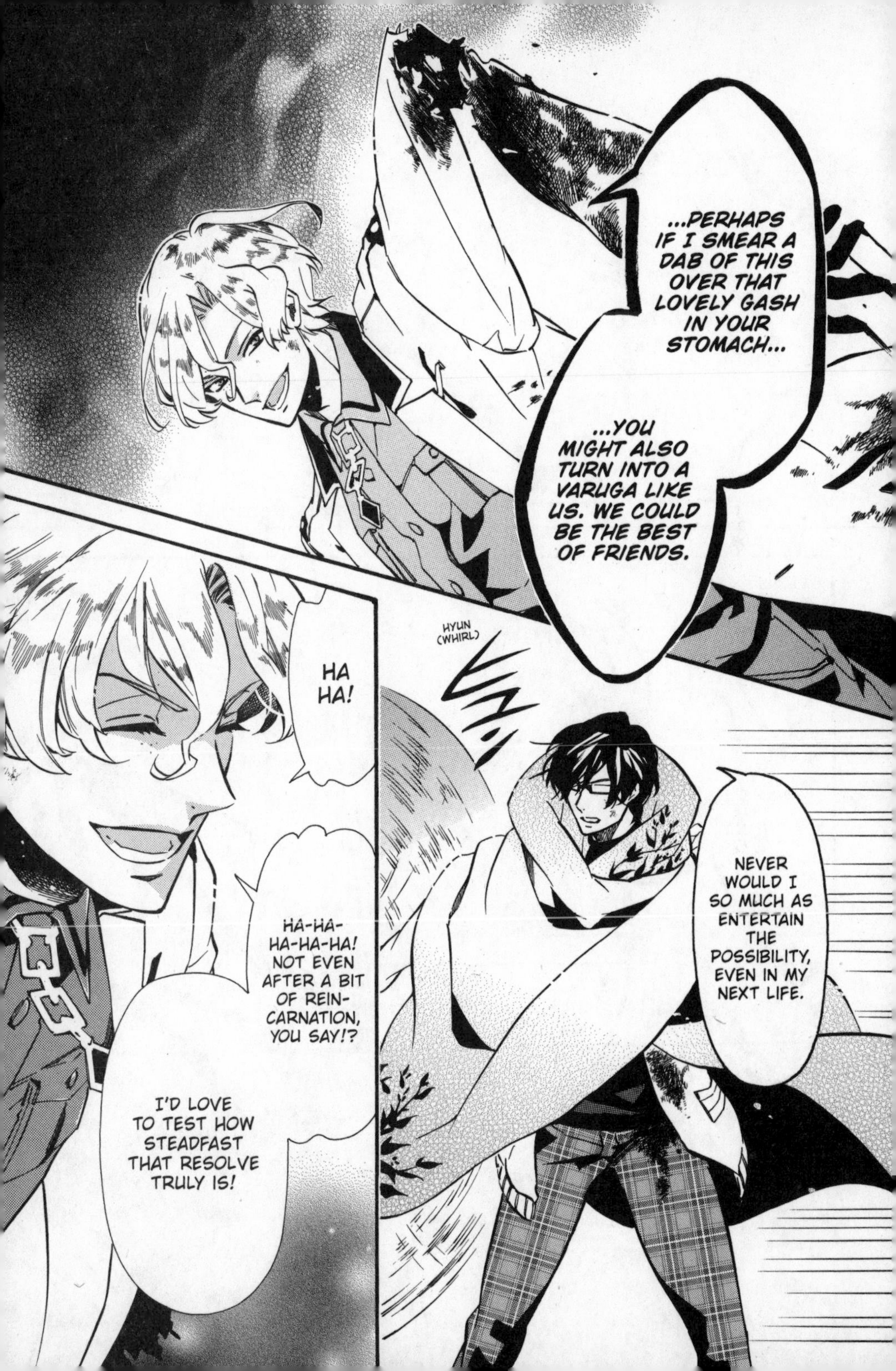
...PERHAPS IF I SMEAR A DAB OF THIS OVER THAT LOVELY GASH IN YOUR STOMACH...
...YOU MIGHT ALSO TURN INTO A VARUGA LIKE US. WE COULD BE THE BEST OF FRIENDS.
HYUN (WHIRL)
NEVER WOULD I SO MUCH AS ENTERTAIN THE POSSIBILITY, EVEN IN MY NEXT LIFE.
HA HA!
HA-HA-HA-HA-HA! NOT EVEN AFTER A BIT OF REIN-CARNATION, YOU SAY!?
I'D LOVE TO TEST HOW STEADFAST THAT RESOLVE TRULY IS!

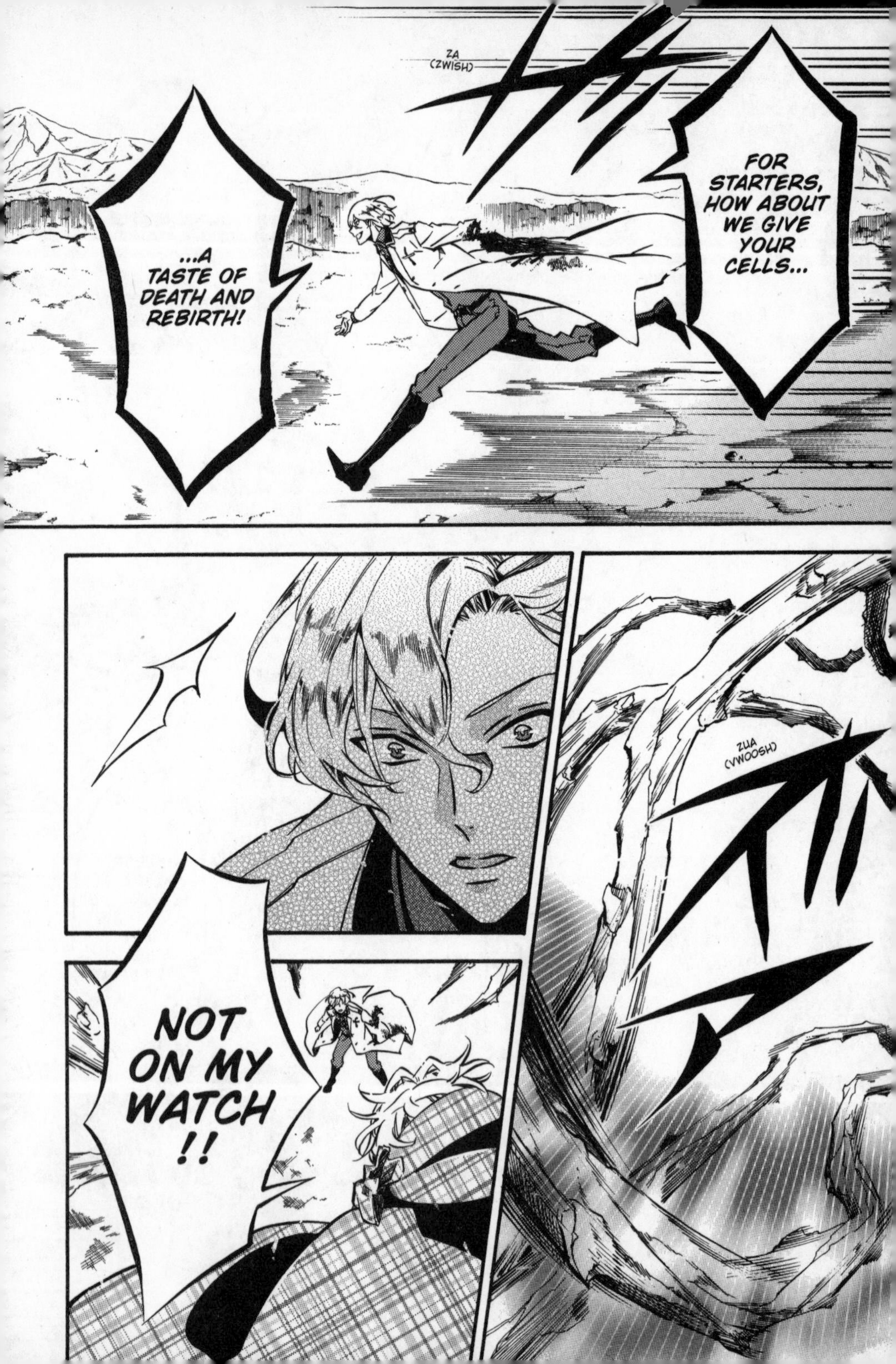
FOR STARTERS, HOW ABOUT WE GIVE YOUR CELLS...
ZA (ZWISH)
...A TASTE OF DEATH AND REBIRTH!
ZUA (VWOOSH)
NOT ON MY WATCH!!

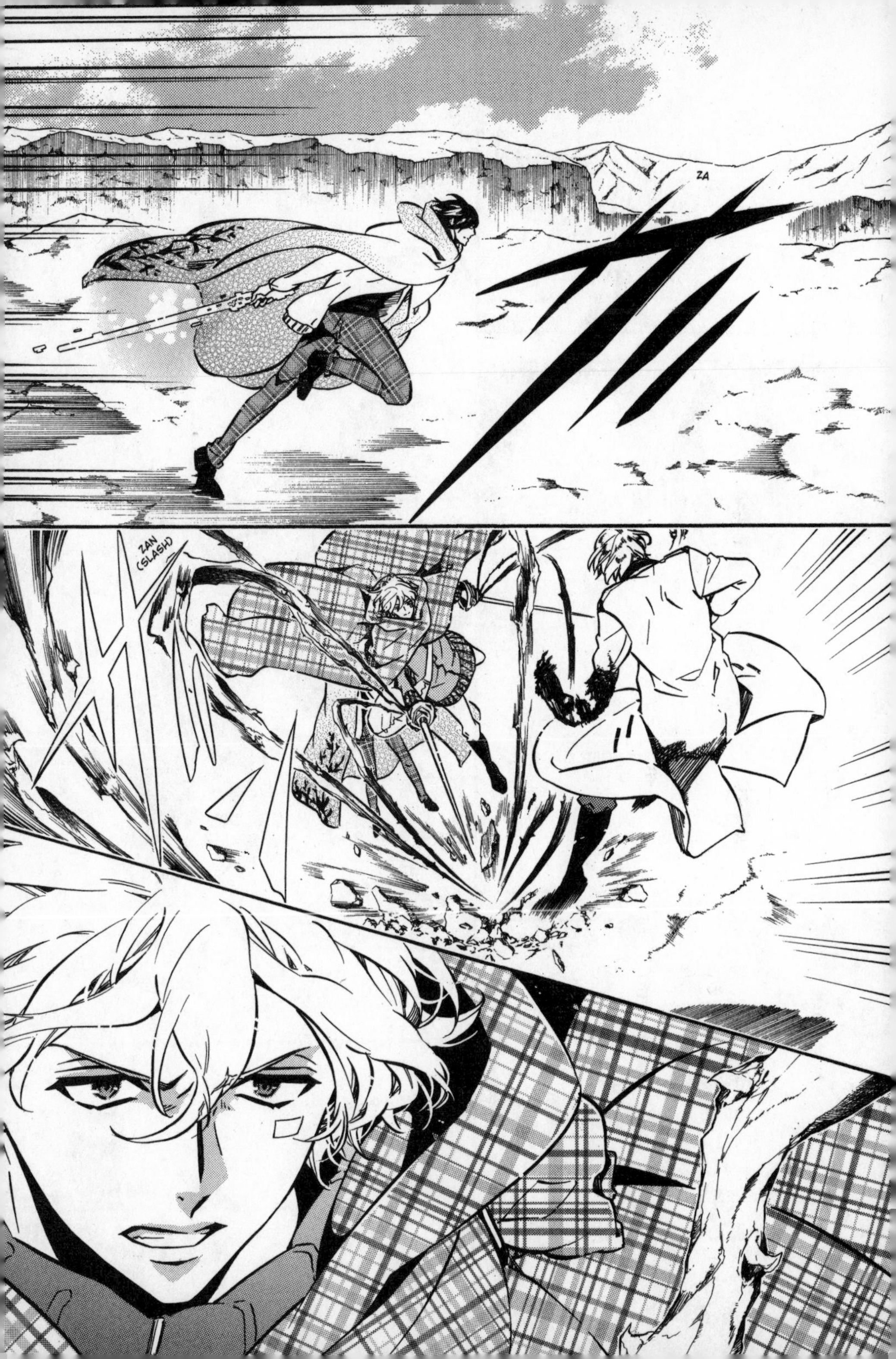
ZA
ZAN (SLASH)

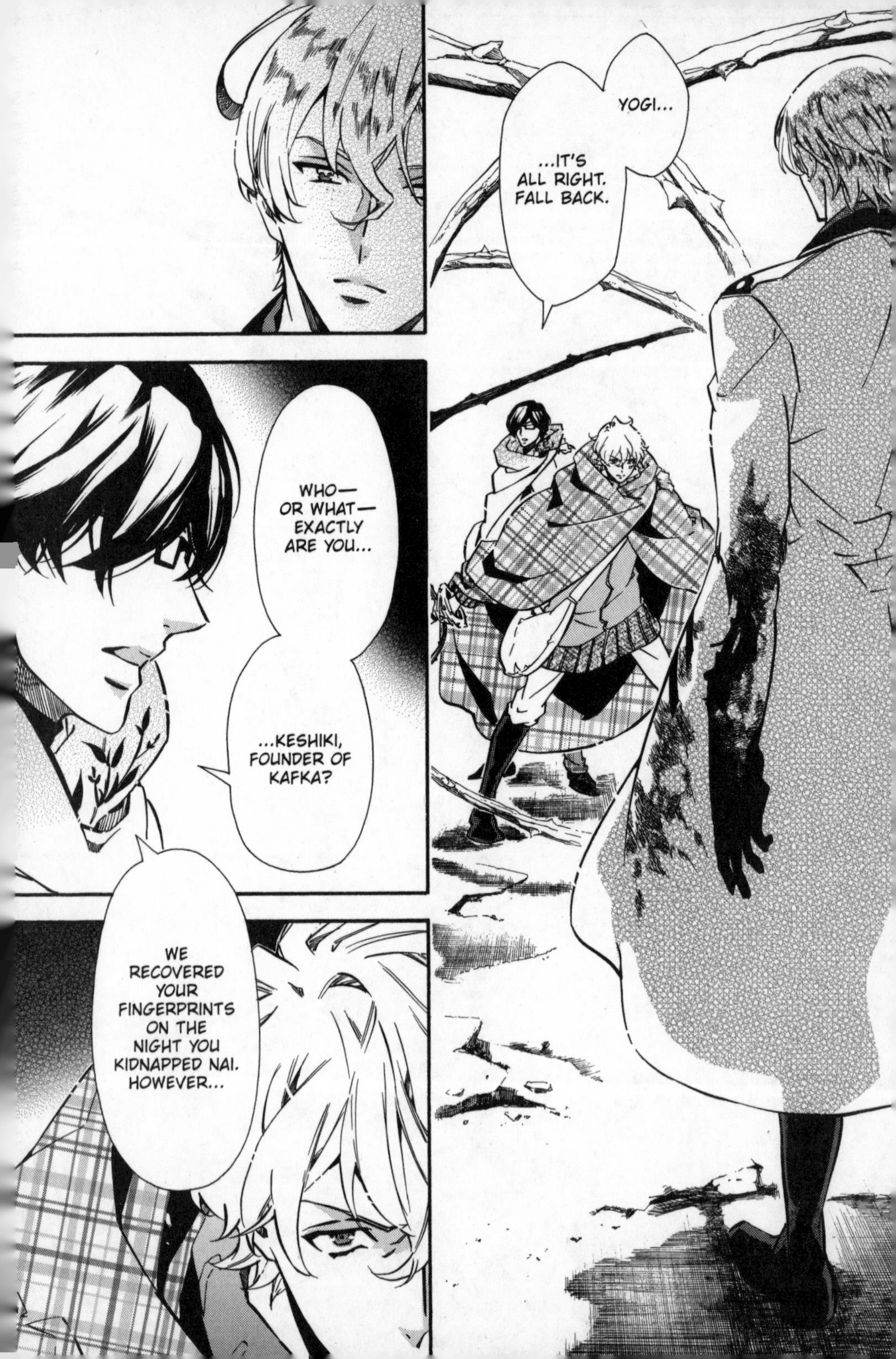
YOGI...
...IT'S ALL RIGHT. FALL BACK.
WHO—OR WHAT—EXACTLY ARE YOU...
...KESHIKI, FOUNDER OF KAFKA?
WE RECOVERED YOUR FINGERPRINTS ON THE NIGHT YOU KIDNAPPED NAI. HOWEVER...

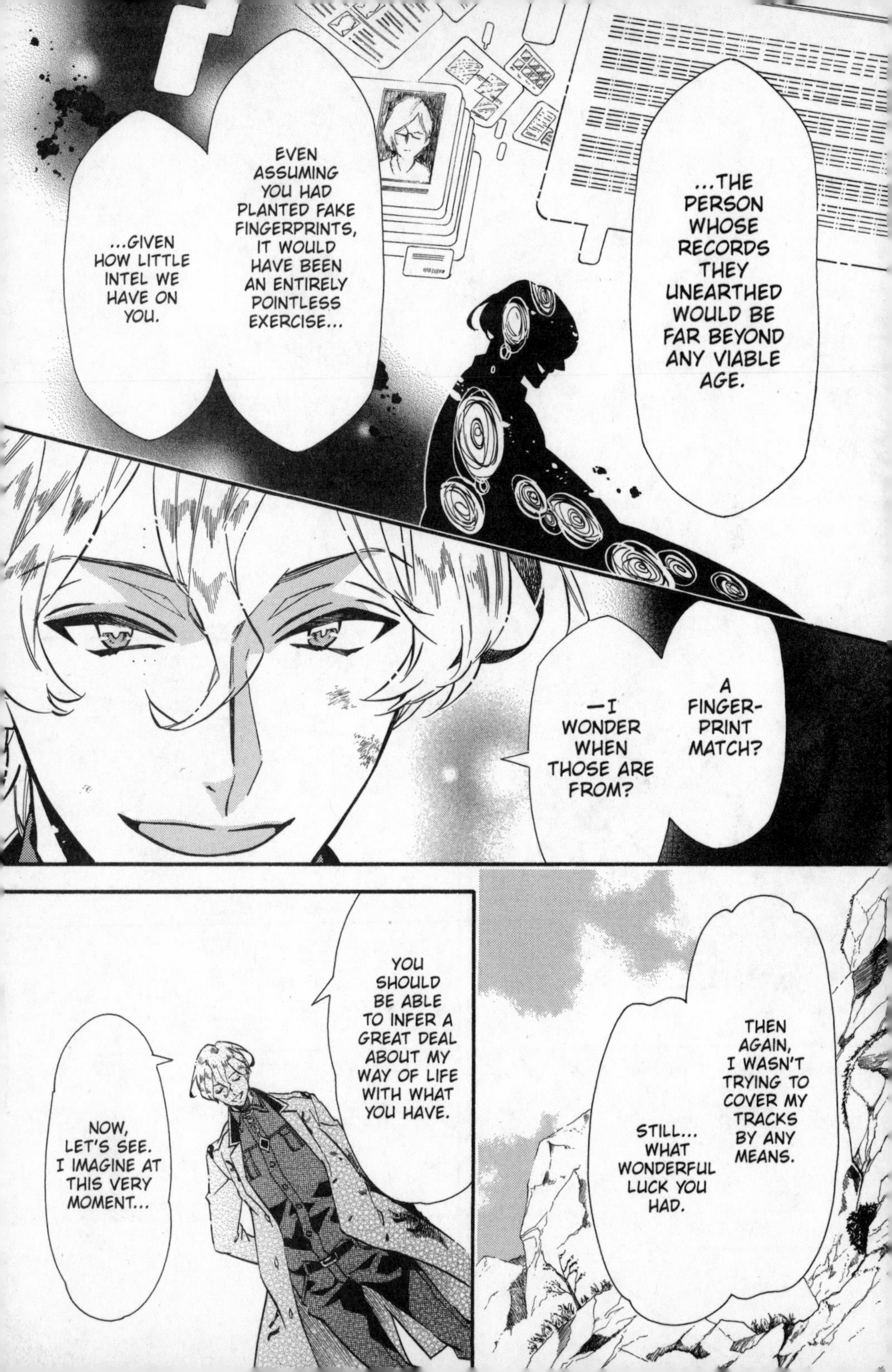

...THE PERSON WHOSE RECORDS THEY UNEARTHED WOULD BE FAR BEYOND ANY VIABLE AGE.
EVEN ASSUMING YOU HAD PLANTED FAKE FINGERPRINTS, IT WOULD HAVE BEEN AN ENTIRELY POINTLESS EXERCISE...
...GIVEN HOW LITTLE INTEL WE HAVE ON YOU.
A FINGER-PRINT MATCH?
—I WONDER WHEN THOSE ARE FROM?
THEN AGAIN, I WASN'T TRYING TO COVER MY TRACKS BY ANY MEANS.
STILL... WHAT WONDERFUL LUCK YOU HAD.
YOU SHOULD BE ABLE TO INFER A GREAT DEAL ABOUT MY WAY OF LIFE WITH WHAT YOU HAVE.
NOW, LET'S SEE. I IMAGINE AT THIS VERY MOMENT...

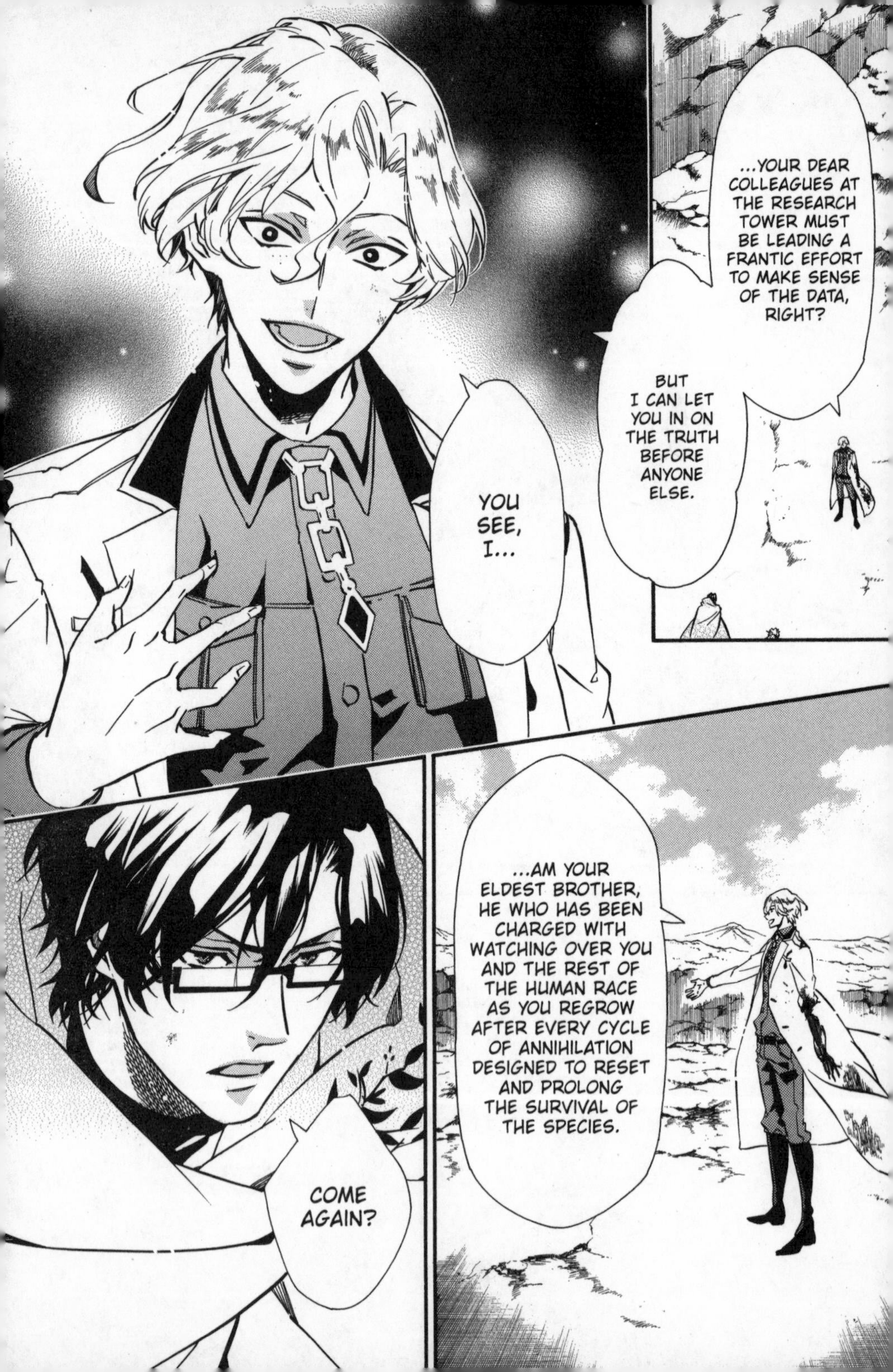
...YOUR DEAR COLLEAGUES AT THE RESEARCH TOWER MUST BE LEADING A FRANTIC EFFORT TO MAKE SENSE OF THE DATA, RIGHT?
BUT I CAN LET YOU IN ON THE TRUTH BEFORE ANYONE ELSE.
YOU SEE, I...
...AM YOUR ELDEST BROTHER, HE WHO HAS BEEN CHARGED WITH WATCHING OVER YOU AND THE REST OF THE HUMAN RACE AS YOU REGROW AFTER EVERY CYCLE OF ANNIHILATION DESIGNED TO RESET AND PROLONG THE SURVIVAL OF THE SPECIES.
COME AGAIN?

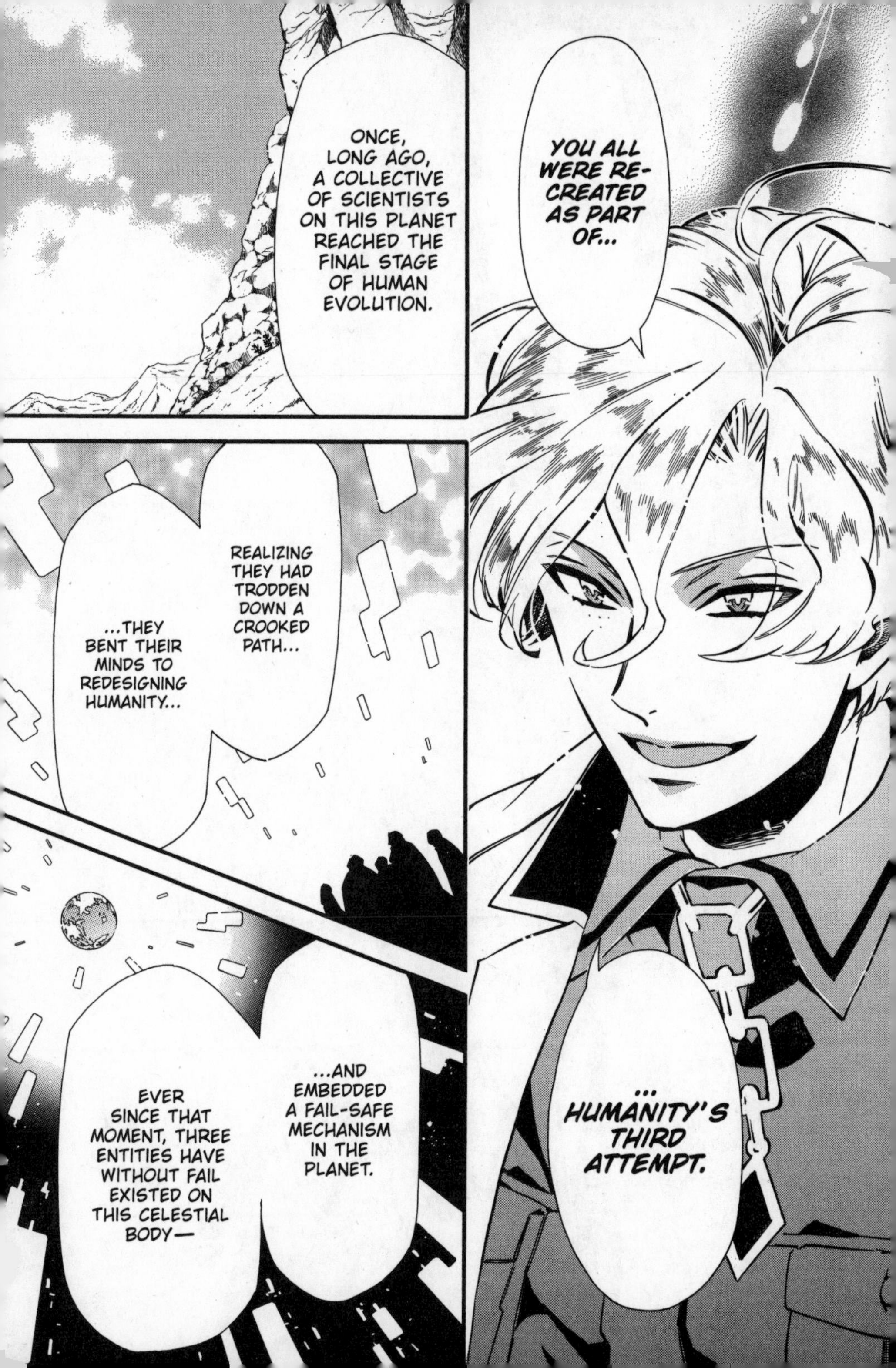
YOU ALL WERE RE-CREATED AS PART OF...
...HUMANITY'S THIRD ATTEMPT.
ONCE, LONG AGO, A COLLECTIVE OF SCIENTISTS ON THIS PLANET REACHED THE FINAL STAGE OF HUMAN EVOLUTION.
REALIZING THEY HAD TRODDEN DOWN A CROOKED PATH...
...THEY BENT THEIR MINDS TO REDESIGNING HUMANITY...
...AND EMBEDDED A FAIL-SAFE MECHANISM IN THE PLANET.
EVER SINCE THAT MOMENT, THREE ENTITIES HAVE WITHOUT FAIL EXISTED ON THIS CELESTIAL BODY—

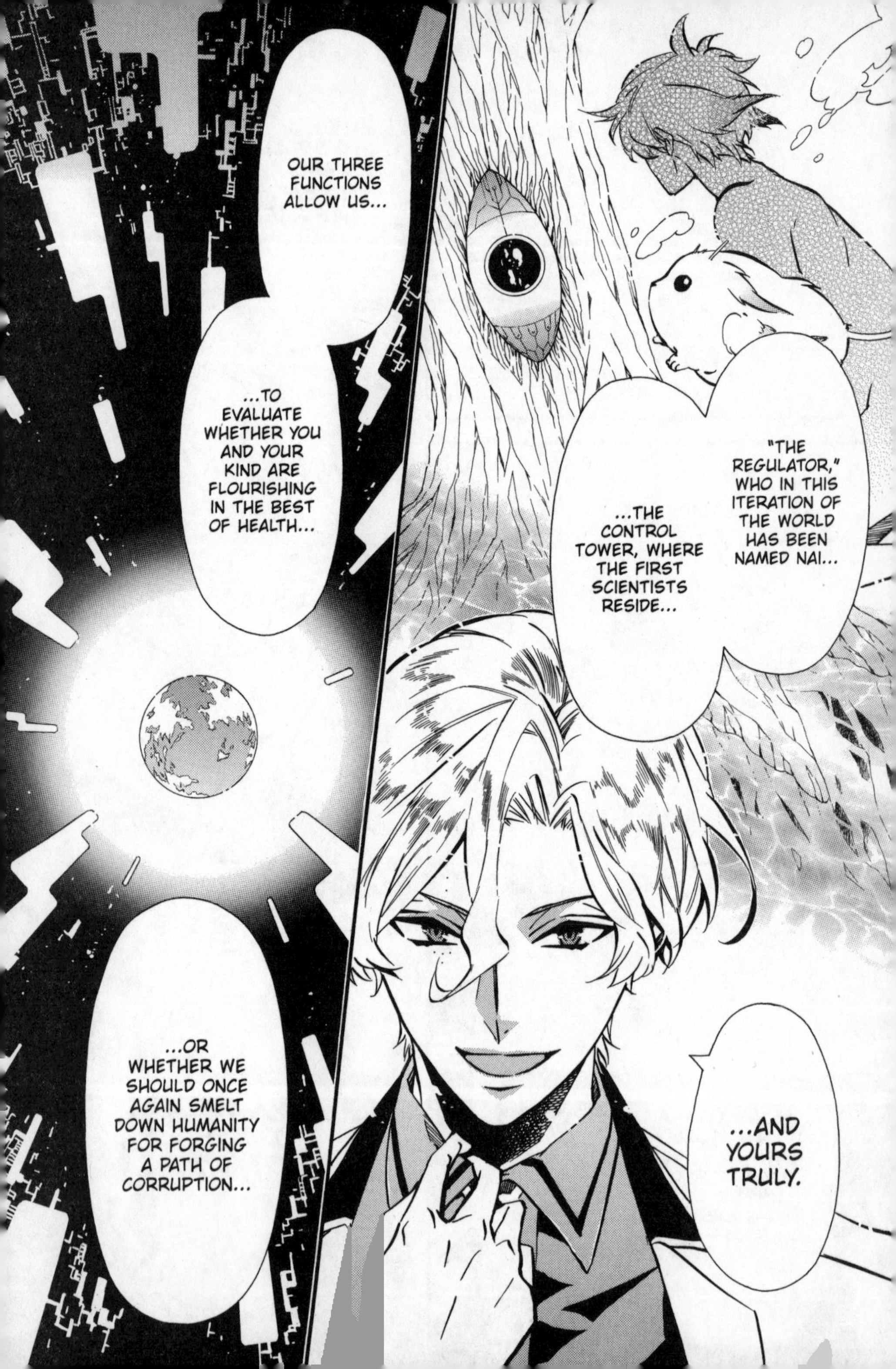
"THE REGULATOR," WHO IN THIS ITERATION OF THE WORLD HAS BEEN NAMED NAI...
...THE CONTROL TOWER, WHERE THE FIRST SCIENTISTS RESIDE...
...AND YOURS TRULY.
OUR THREE FUNCTIONS ALLOW US...
...TO EVALUATE WHETHER YOU AND YOUR KIND ARE FLOURISHING IN THE BEST OF HEALTH...
...OR WHETHER WE SHOULD ONCE AGAIN SMELT DOWN HUMANITY FOR FORGING A PATH OF CORRUPTION...

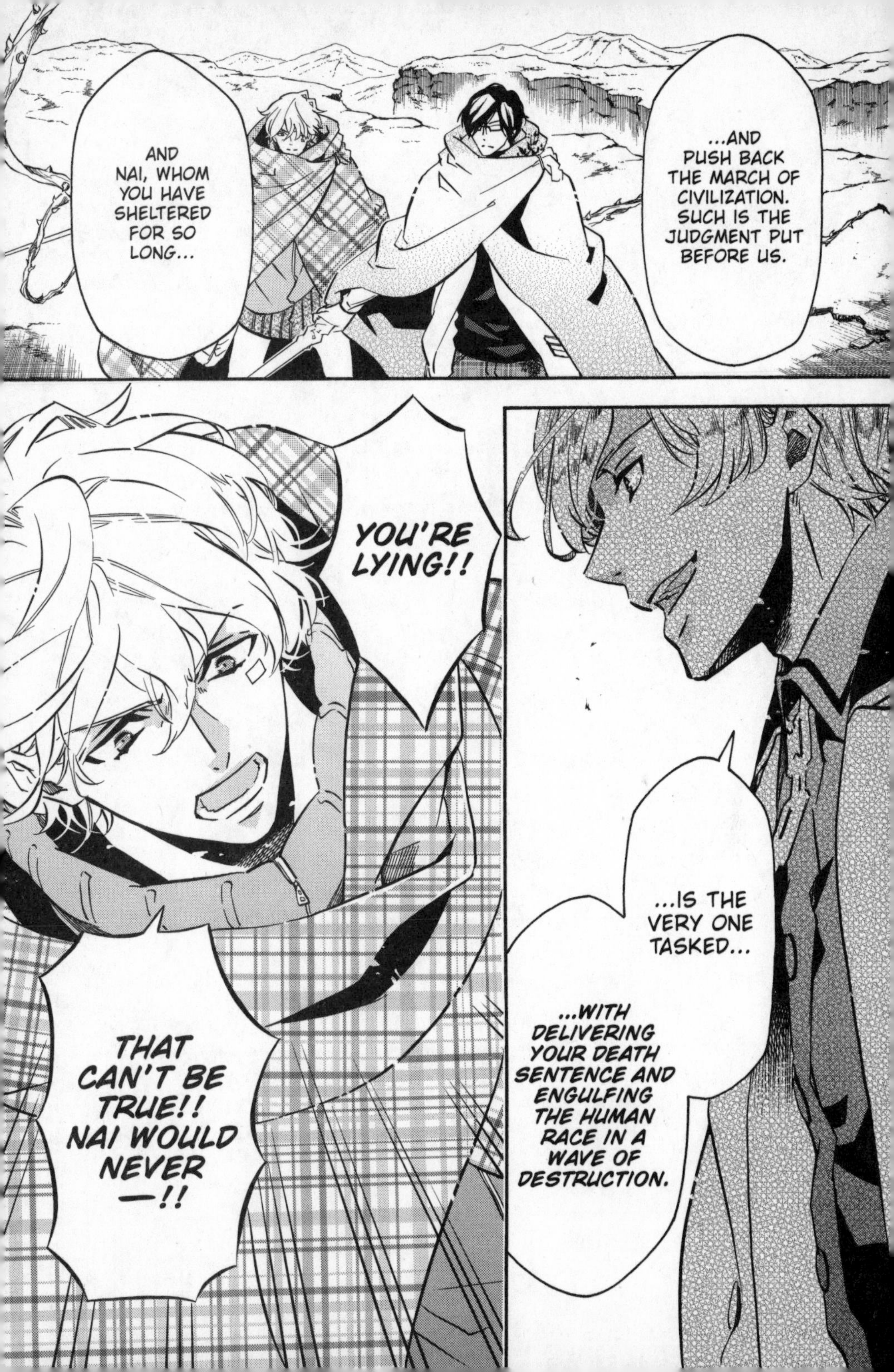
...AND PUSH BACK THE MARCH OF CIVILIZATION. SUCH IS THE JUDGMENT PUT BEFORE US.
AND NAI, WHOM YOU HAVE SHELTERED FOR SO LONG...
...IS THE VERY ONE TASKED...
...WITH DELIVERING YOUR DEATH SENTENCE AND ENGULFING THE HUMAN RACE IN A WAVE OF DESTRUCTION.
YOU'RE LYING!!
THAT CAN'T BE TRUE!! NAI WOULD NEVER—!!

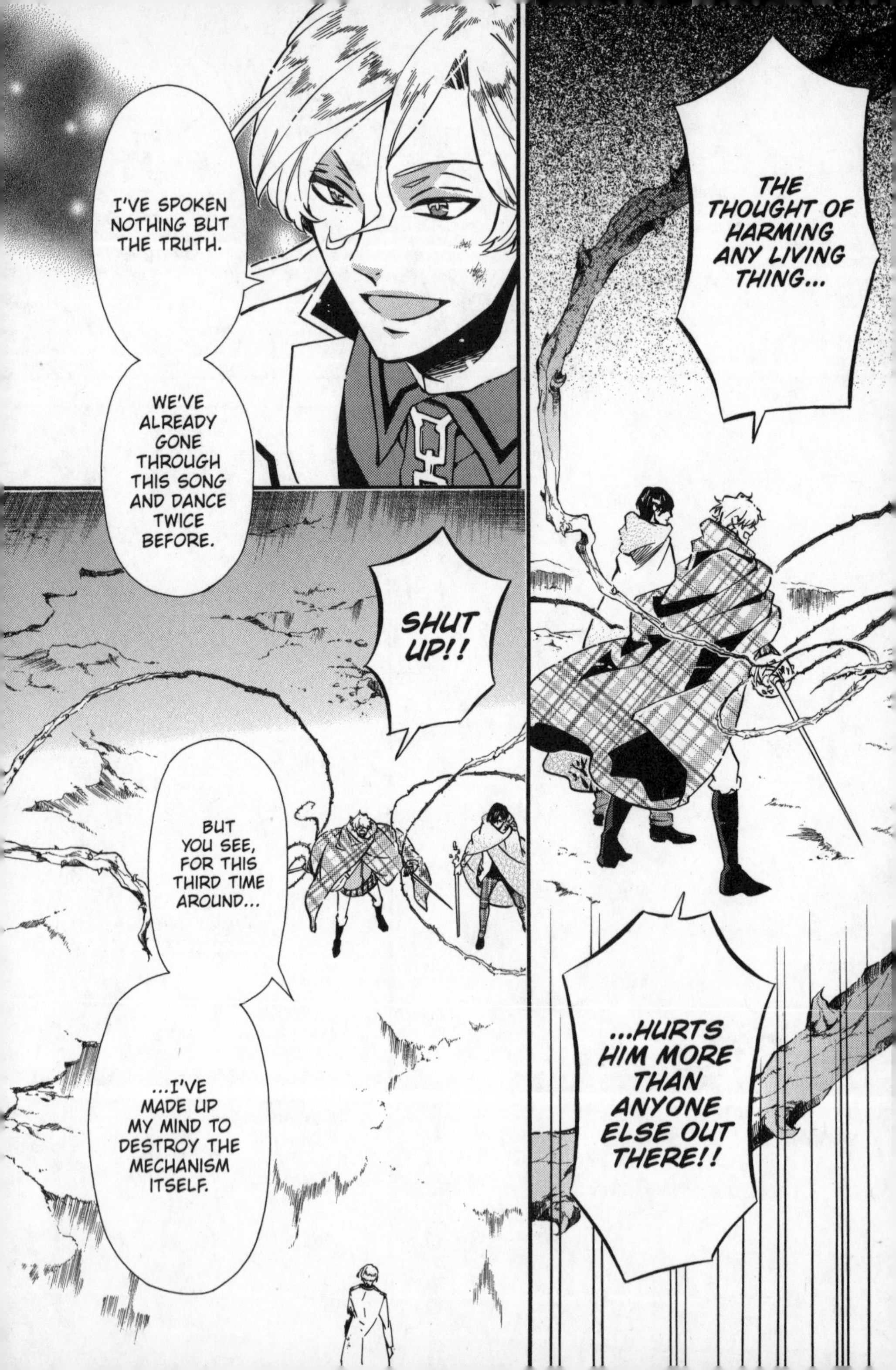
THE THOUGHT OF HARMING ANY LIVING THING...
...HURTS HIM MORE THAN ANYONE ELSE OUT THERE!!
I'VE SPOKEN NOTHING BUT THE TRUTH.
WE'VE ALREADY GONE THROUGH THIS SONG AND DANCE TWICE BEFORE.
SHUT UP!!
BUT YOU SEE, FOR THIS THIRD TIME AROUND...
...I'VE MADE UP MY MIND TO DESTROY THE MECHANISM ITSELF.

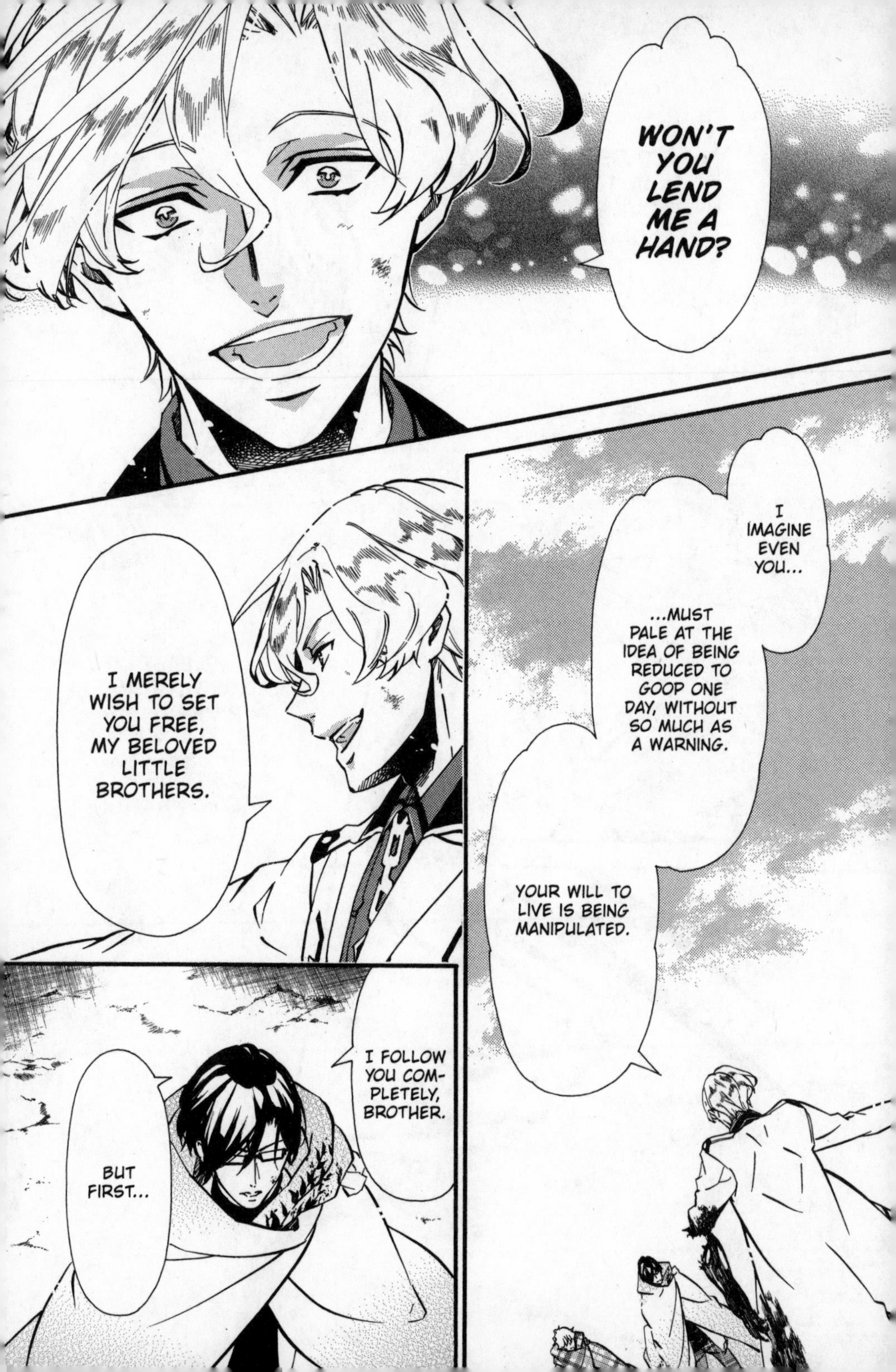
WON'T YOU LEND ME A HAND?
I IMAGINE EVEN YOU...
...MUST PALE AT THE IDEA OF BEING REDUCED TO GOOP ONE DAY, WITHOUT SO MUCH AS A WARNING.
YOUR WILL TO LIVE IS BEING MANIPULATED.
I MERELY WISH TO SET YOU FREE, MY BELOVED LITTLE BROTHERS.
I FOLLOW YOU COM-PLETELY, BROTHER.
BUT FIRST...

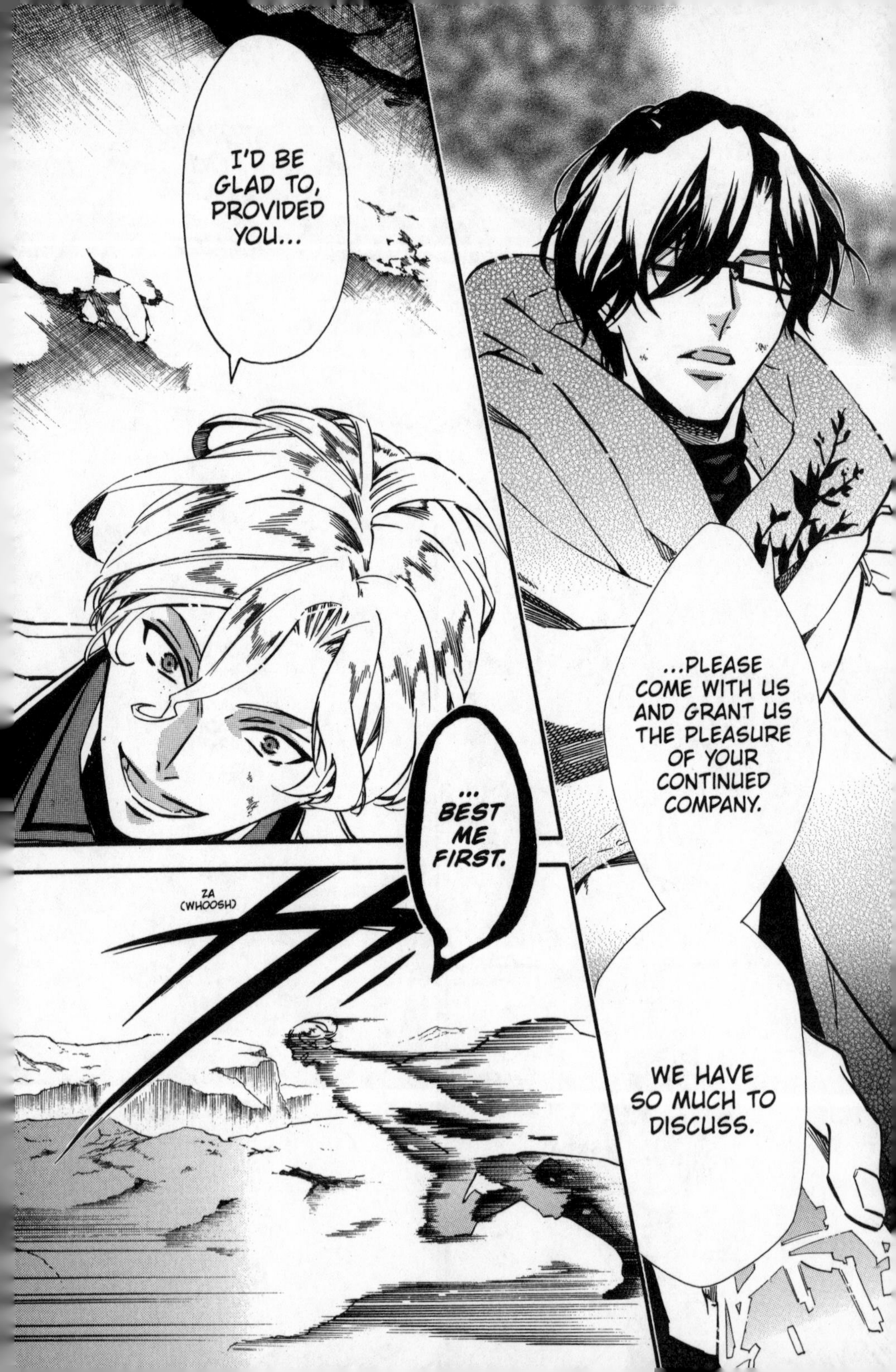
...PLEASE COME WITH US AND GRANT US THE PLEASURE OF YOUR CONTINUED COMPANY.
WE HAVE SO MUCH TO DISCUSS.
I'D BE GLAD TO, PROVIDED YOU...
...BEST ME FIRST.
ZA (WHOOSH)

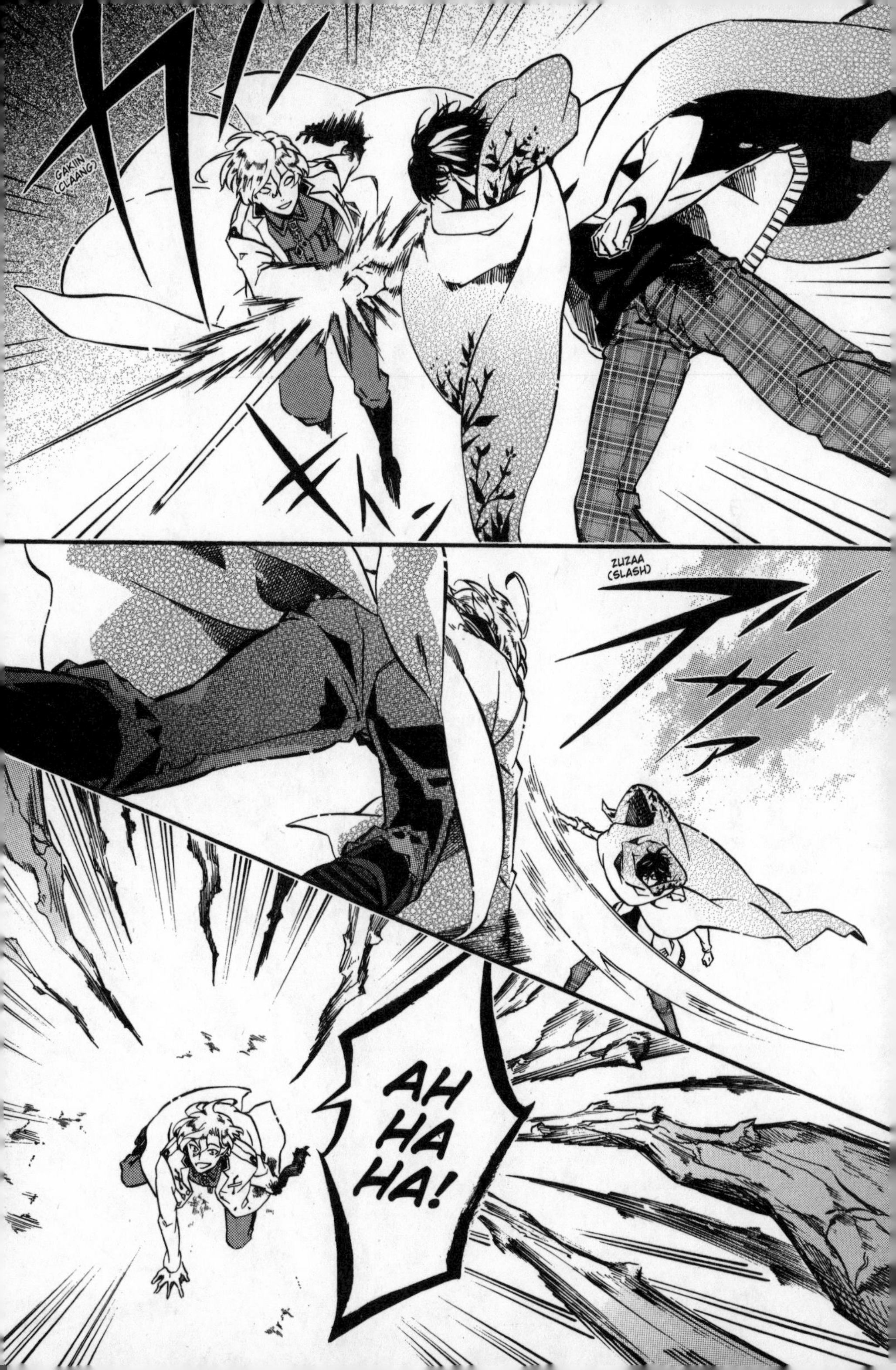
GAKIIN (CLAANG)
ZUZAA (SLASH)
AH HA HA!

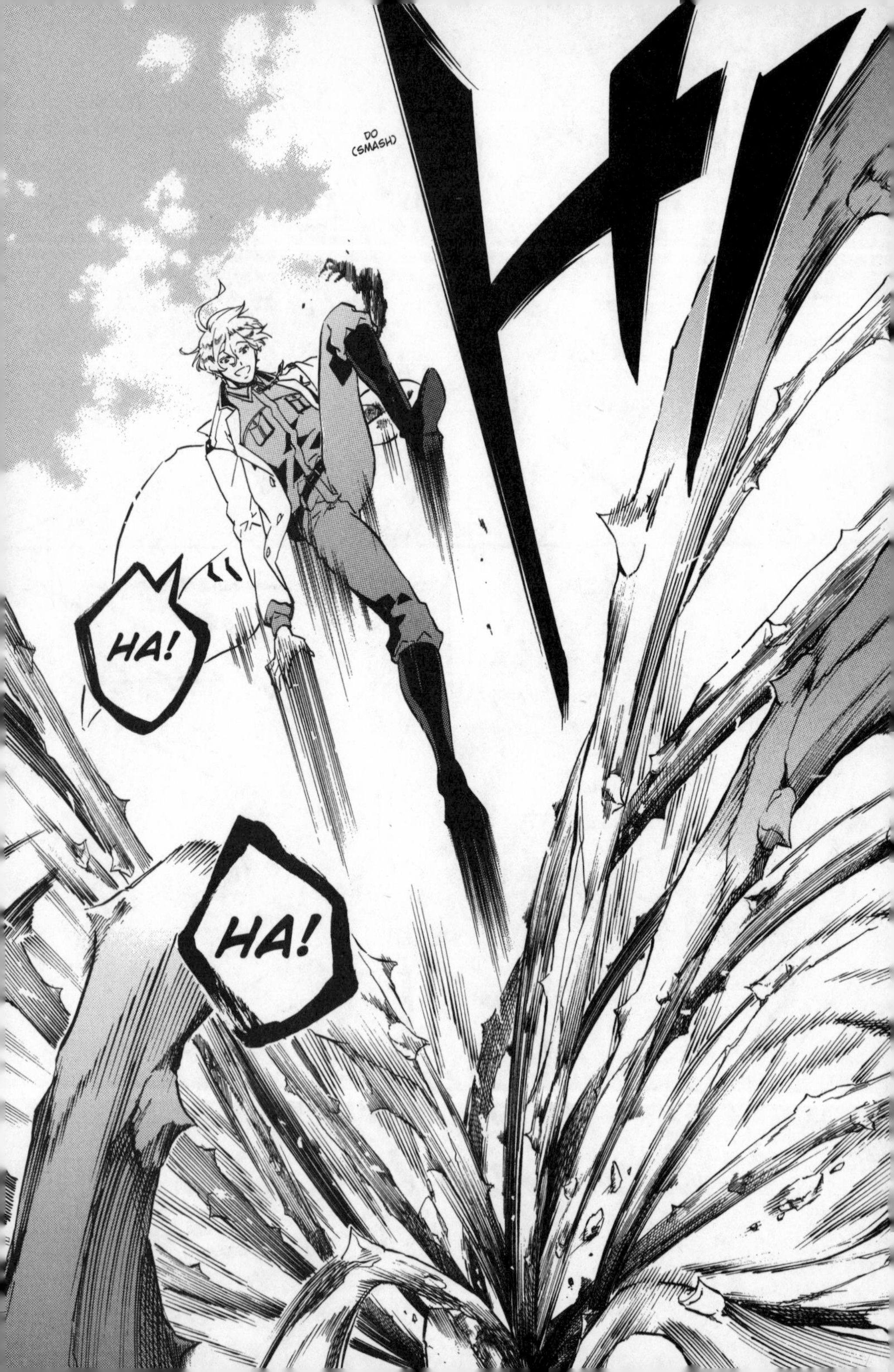
DO
(SMASH)
HA!
HA!

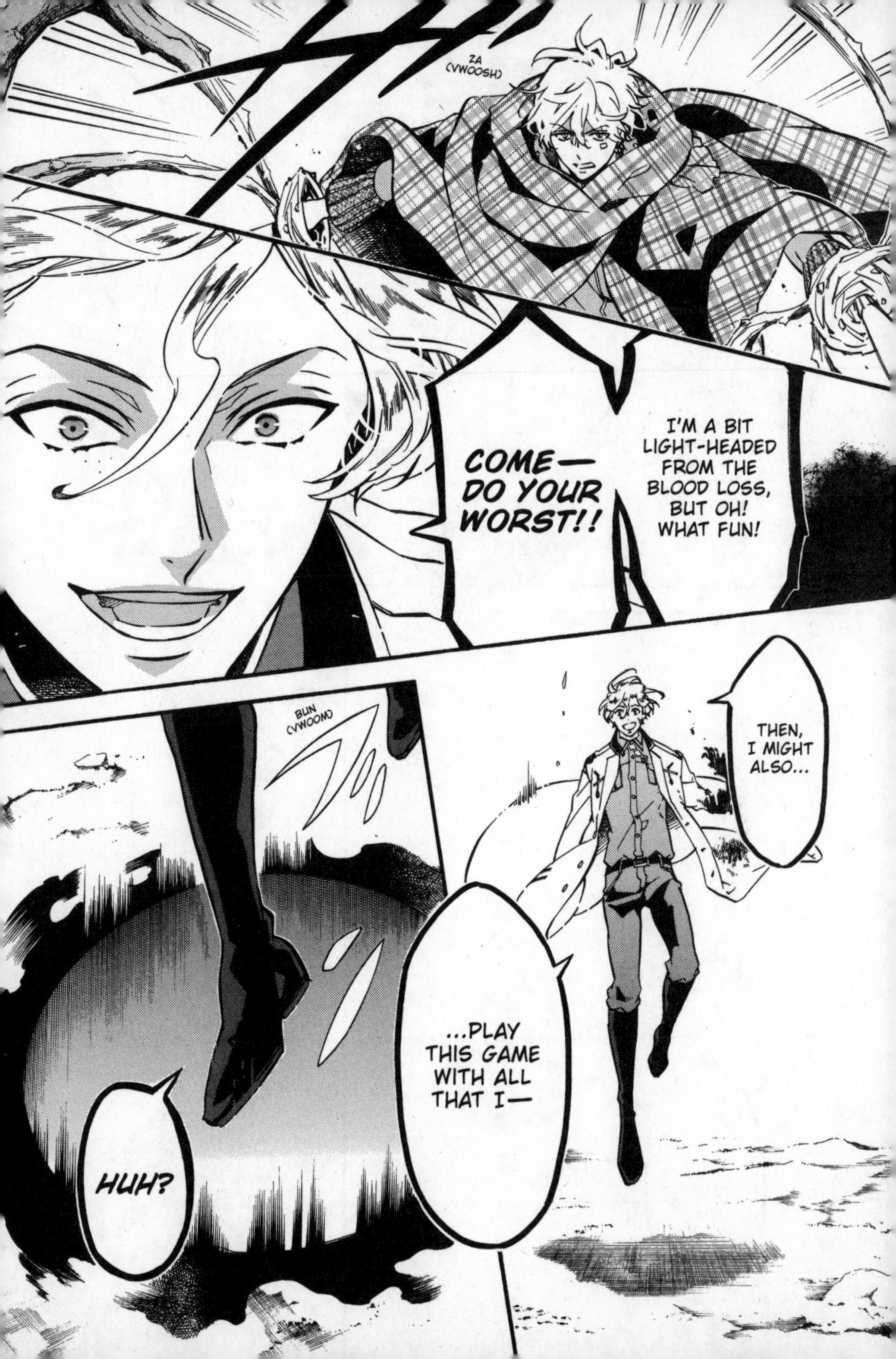
ZA
(VWOOSH)
I'M A BIT LIGHT-HEADED FROM THE BLOOD LOSS, BUT OH! WHAT FUN!
COME— DO YOUR WORST!!
THEN, I MIGHT ALSO...
...PLAY THIS GAME WITH ALL THAT I—
BUN
(VWOOM)
HUH?

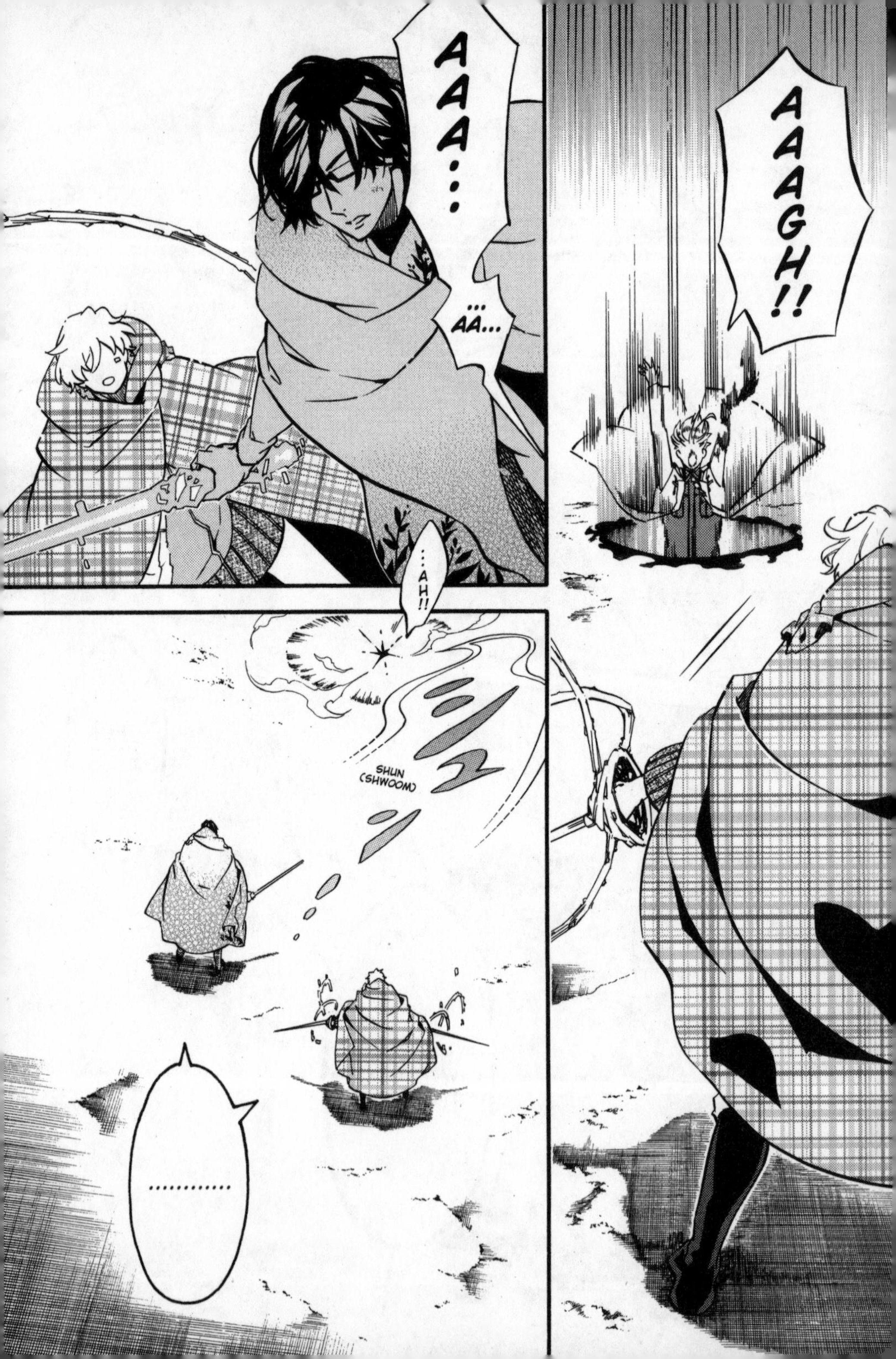
AAAAGH!!
AAA...
...AA...
...AH!!
SHUN (SHWOOM)
....

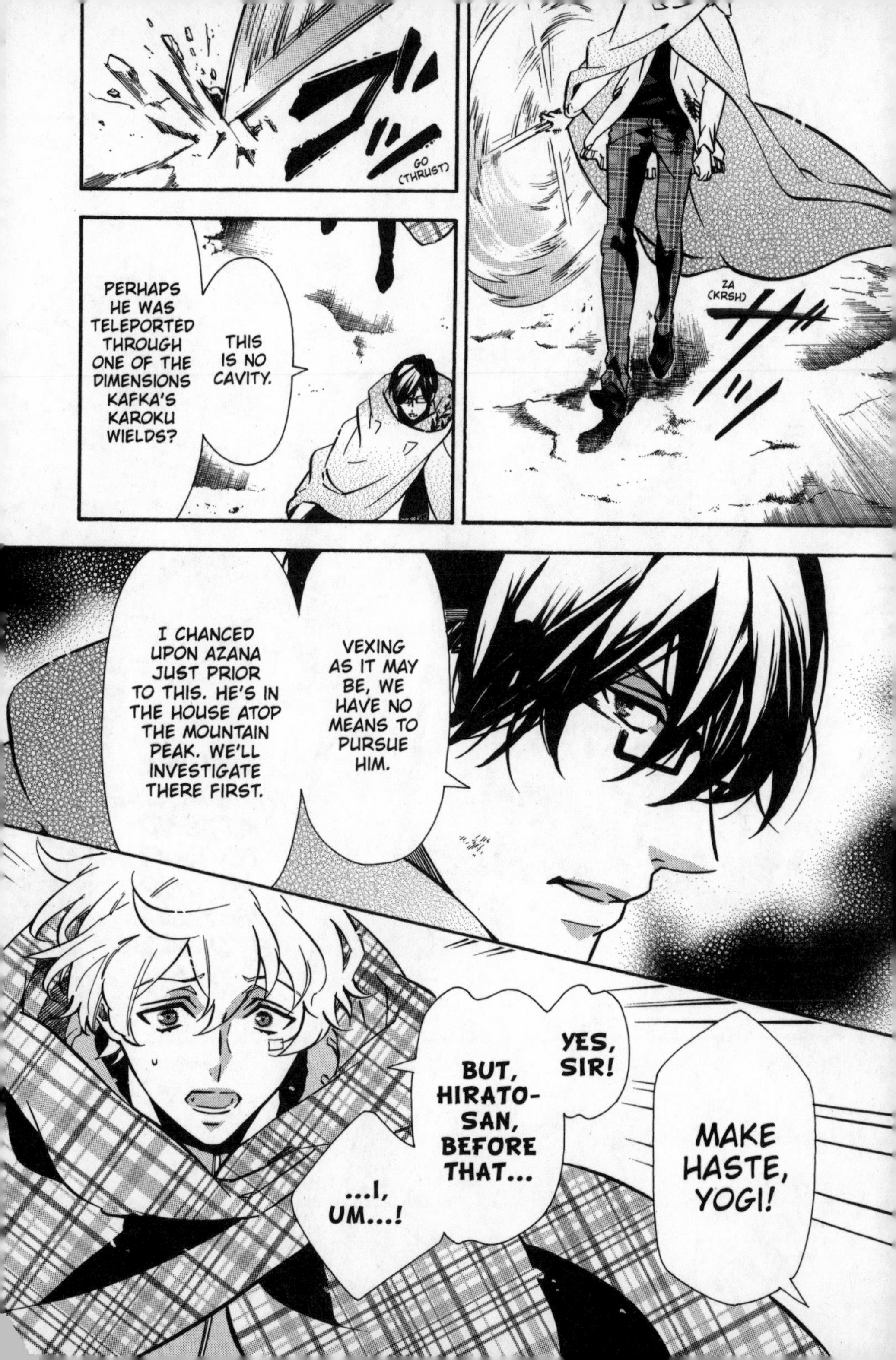
ZA (KRSH)
GO (THRUST)
THIS IS NO CAVITY.
PERHAPS HE WAS TELEPORTED THROUGH ONE OF THE DIMENSIONS KAFKA'S KAROKU WIELDS?
VEXING AS IT MAY BE, WE HAVE NO MEANS TO PURSUE HIM.
I CHANCED UPON AZANA JUST PRIOR TO THIS. HE'S IN THE HOUSE ATOP THE MOUNTAIN PEAK. WE'LL INVESTIGATE THERE FIRST.
MAKE HASTE, YOGI!
YES, SIR!
BUT, HIRATO-SAN, BEFORE THAT...
...I, UM...!

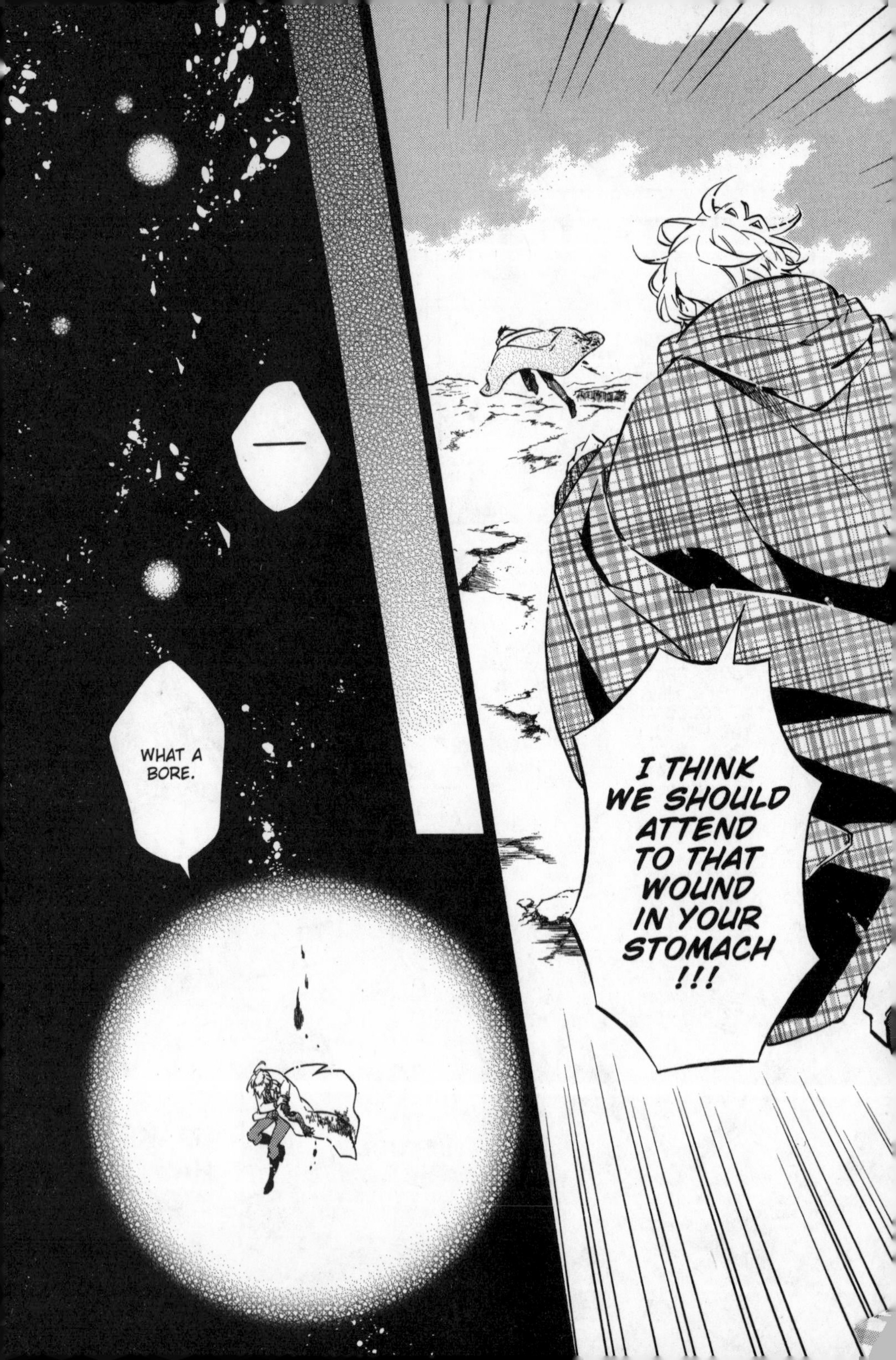
I THINK WE SHOULD ATTEND TO THAT WOUND IN YOUR STOMACH !!!
—
WHAT A BORE.

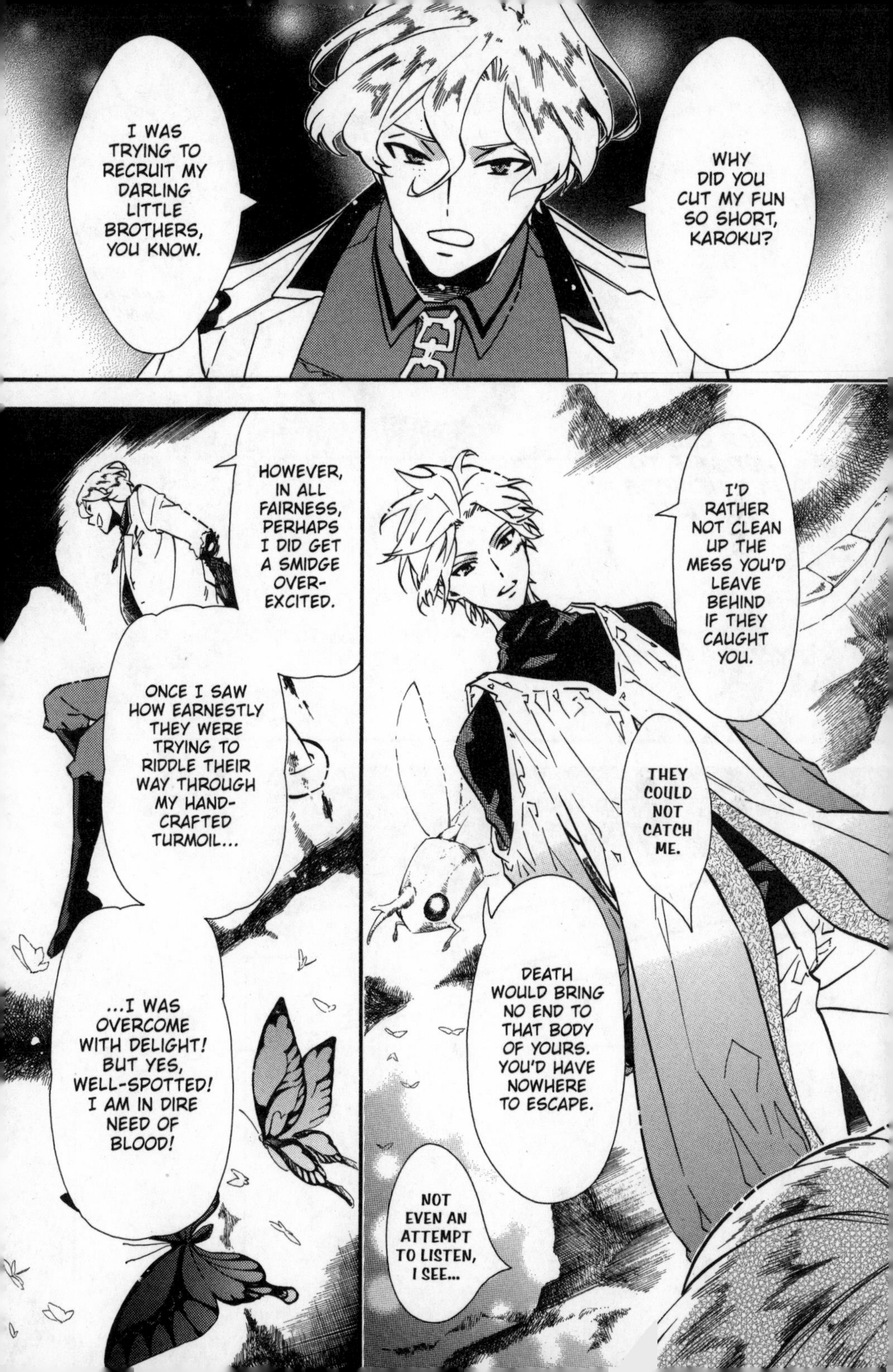
WHY DID YOU CUT MY FUN SO SHORT, KAROKU?
I WAS TRYING TO RECRUIT MY DARLING LITTLE BROTHERS, YOU KNOW.
I'D RATHER NOT CLEAN UP THE MESS YOU'D LEAVE BEHIND IF THEY CAUGHT YOU.
THEY COULD NOT CATCH ME.
DEATH WOULD BRING NO END TO THAT BODY OF YOURS. YOU'D HAVE NOWHERE TO ESCAPE.
NOT EVEN AN ATTEMPT TO LISTEN, I SEE...
HOWEVER, IN ALL FAIRNESS, PERHAPS I DID GET A SMIDGE OVER-EXCITED.
ONCE I SAW HOW EARNESTLY THEY WERE TRYING TO RIDDLE THEIR WAY THROUGH MY HAND-CRAFTED TURMOIL...
...I WAS OVERCOME WITH DELIGHT! BUT YES, WELL-SPOTTED! I AM IN DIRE NEED OF BLOOD!

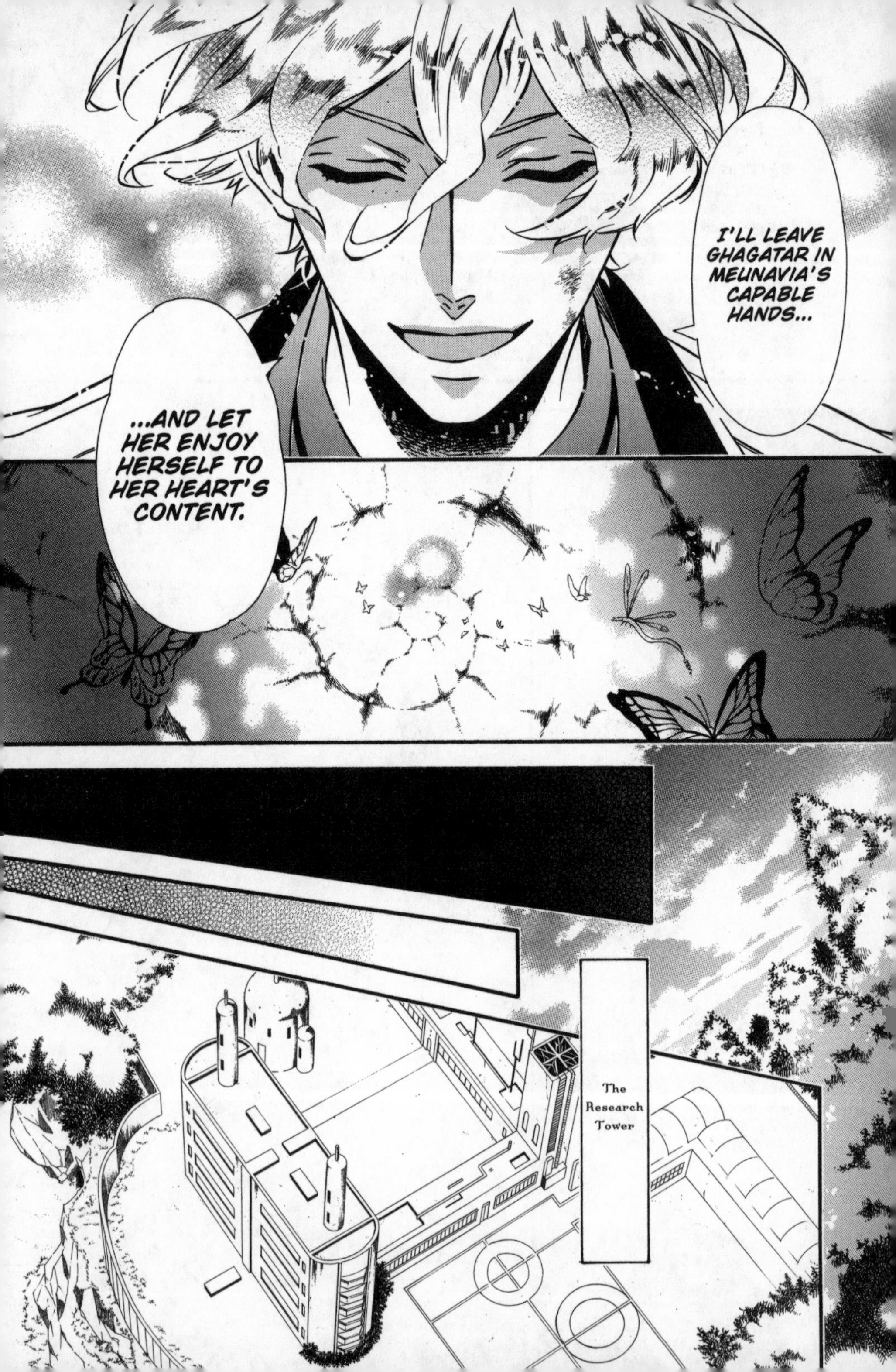
I'LL LEAVE GHAGATAR IN MEUNAVIA'S CAPABLE HANDS...
...AND LET HER ENJOY HERSELF TO HER HEART'S CONTENT.
The Research Tower

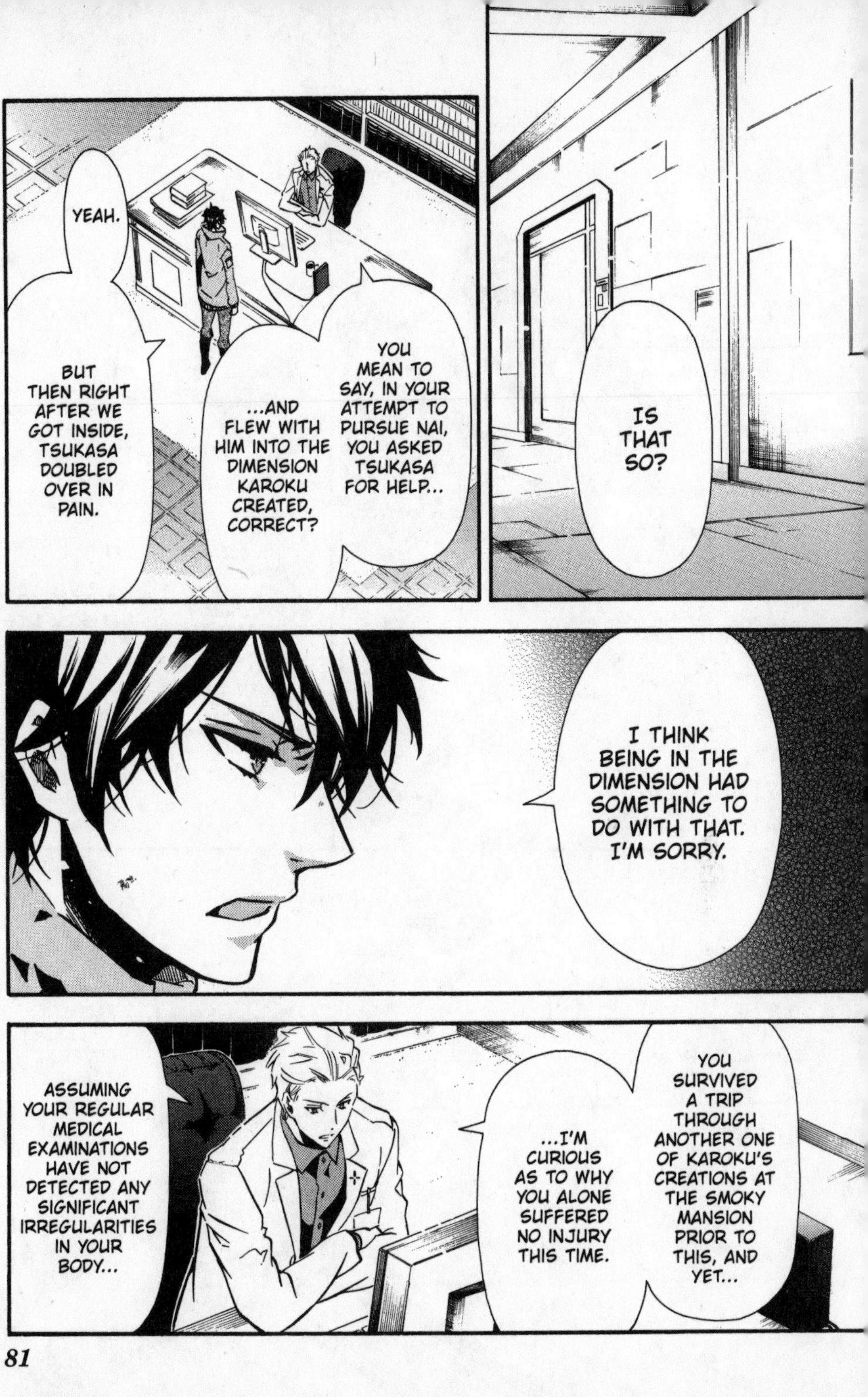
IS THAT SO?
YOU MEAN TO SAY, IN YOUR ATTEMPT TO PURSUE NAI, YOU ASKED TSUKASA FOR HELP...
...AND FLEW WITH HIM INTO THE DIMENSION KAROKU CREATED, CORRECT?
YEAH.
BUT THEN RIGHT AFTER WE GOT INSIDE, TSUKASA DOUBLED OVER IN PAIN.
I THINK BEING IN THE DIMENSION HAD SOMETHING TO DO WITH THAT. I'M SORRY.
YOU SURVIVED A TRIP THROUGH ANOTHER ONE OF KAROKU'S CREATIONS AT THE SMOKY MANSION PRIOR TO THIS, AND YET...
...I'M CURIOUS AS TO WHY YOU ALONE SUFFERED NO INJURY THIS TIME.
ASSUMING YOUR REGULAR MEDICAL EXAMINATIONS HAVE NOT DETECTED ANY SIGNIFICANT IRREGULARITIES IN YOUR BODY...

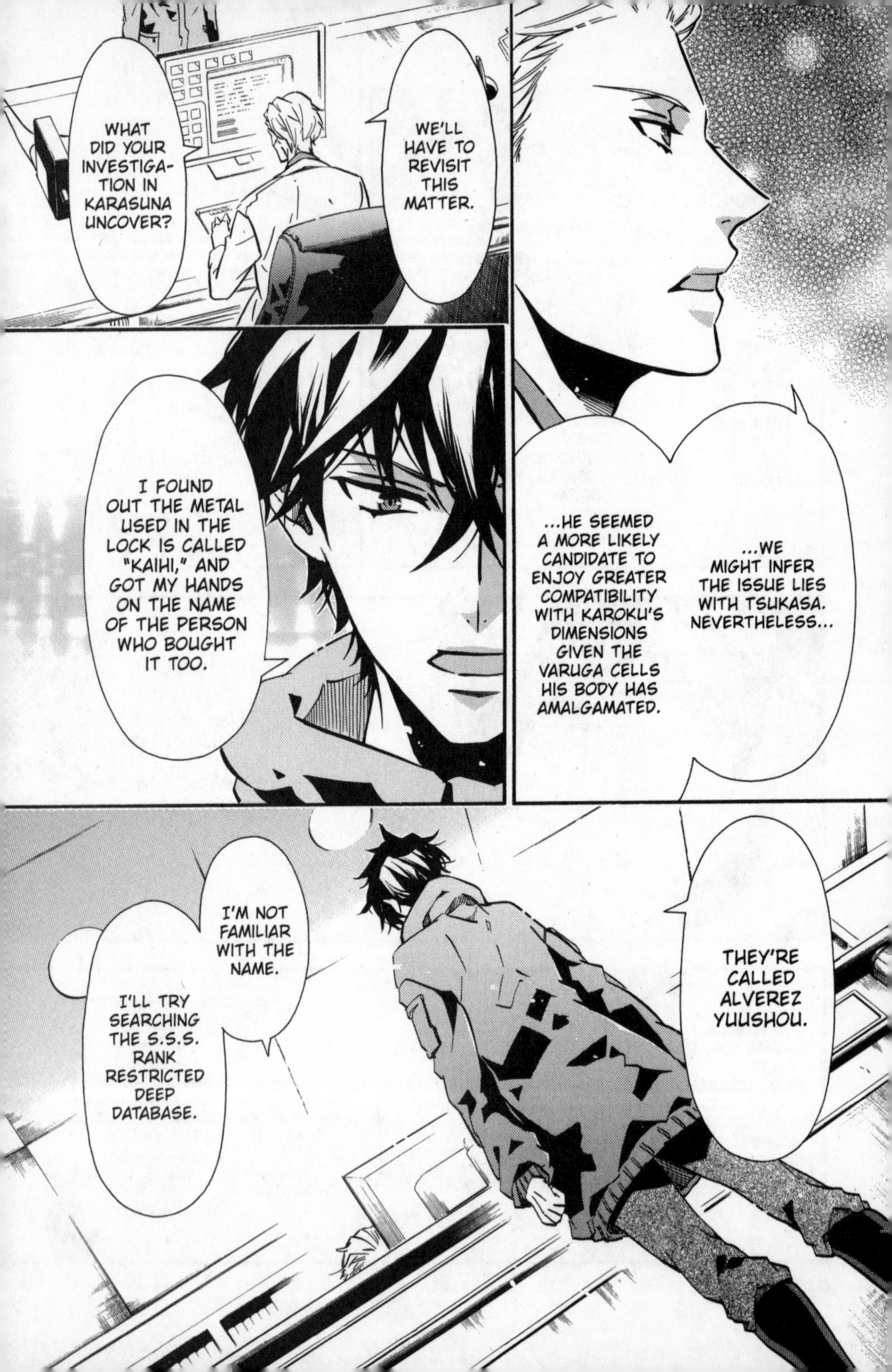
...WE MIGHT INFER THE ISSUE LIES WITH TSUKASA. NEVERTHELESS...
...HE SEEMED A MORE LIKELY CANDIDATE TO ENJOY GREATER COMPATIBILITY WITH KAROKU'S DIMENSIONS GIVEN THE VARUGA CELLS HIS BODY HAS AMALGAMATED.
WE'LL HAVE TO REVISIT THIS MATTER.
WHAT DID YOUR INVESTIGATION IN KARASUNA UNCOVER?
I FOUND OUT THE METAL USED IN THE LOCK IS CALLED "KAIHI," AND GOT MY HANDS ON THE NAME OF THE PERSON WHO BOUGHT IT TOO.
THEY'RE CALLED ALVEREZ YUUSHOU.
I'M NOT FAMILIAR WITH THE NAME.
I'LL TRY SEARCHING THE S.S.S. RANK RESTRICTED DEEP DATABASE.

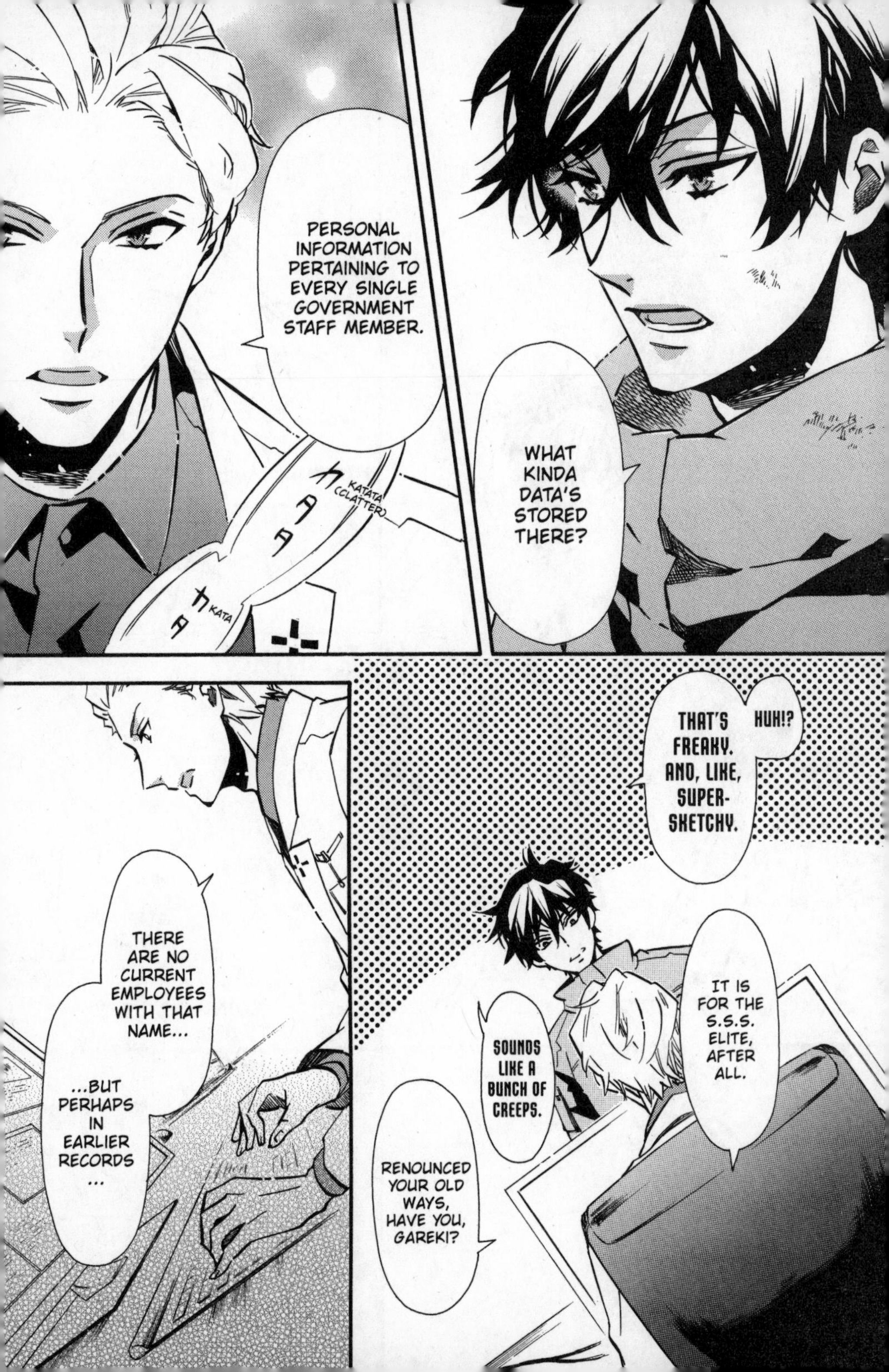

WHAT KINDA DATA'S STORED THERE?
PERSONAL INFORMATION PERTAINING TO EVERY SINGLE GOVERNMENT STAFF MEMBER.
KATATA (CLATTER)
KATA
HUH!?
THAT'S FREAKY. AND, LIKE, SUPER-SKETCHY.
IT IS FOR THE S.S.S. ELITE, AFTER ALL.
SOUNDS LIKE A BUNCH OF CREEPS.
RENOUNCED YOUR OLD WAYS, HAVE YOU, GAREKI?
THERE ARE NO CURRENT EMPLOYEES WITH THAT NAME...
...BUT PERHAPS IN EARLIER RECORDS...

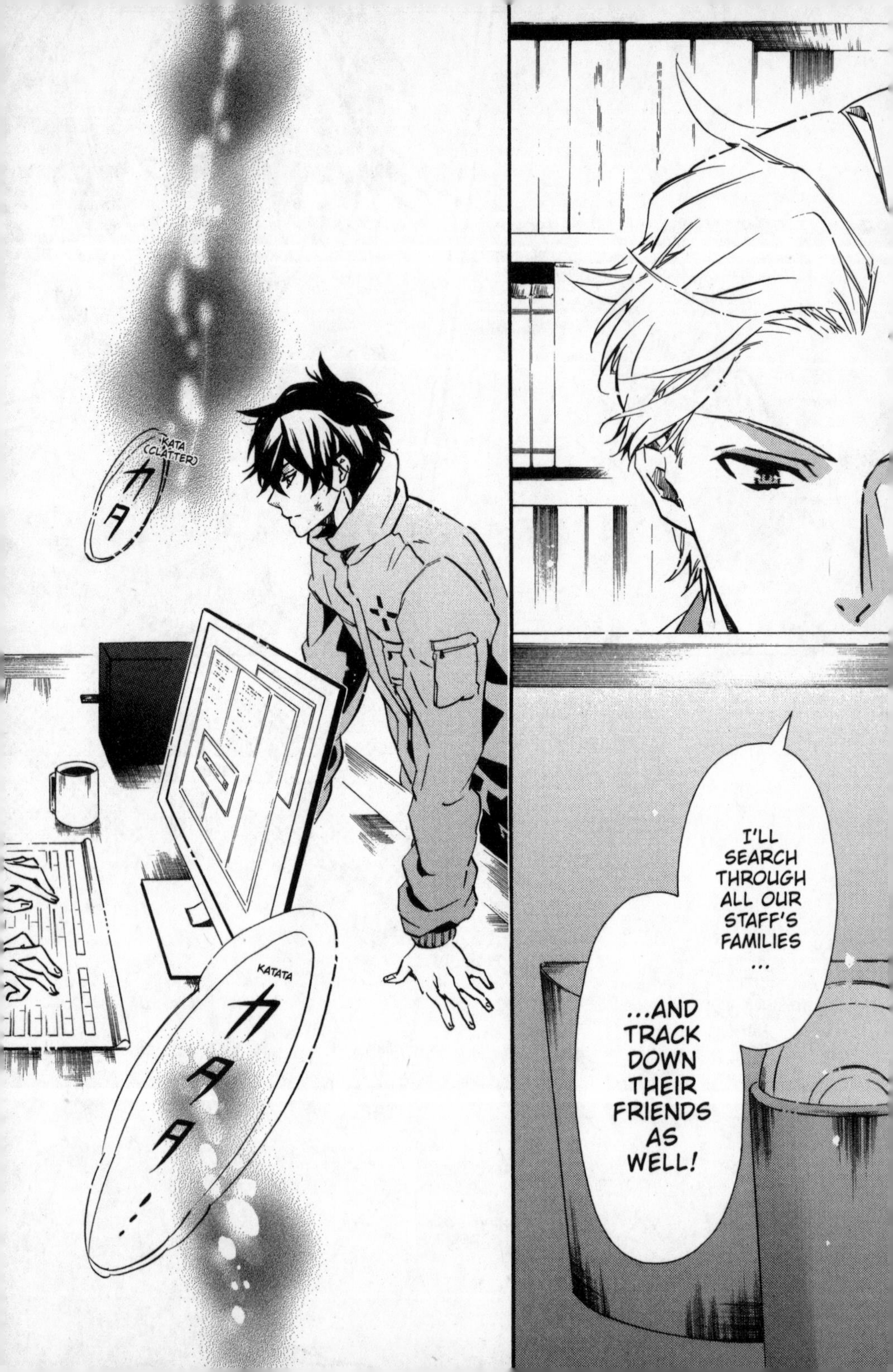
I'LL SEARCH THROUGH ALL OUR STAFF'S FAMILIES ...
...AND TRACK DOWN THEIR FRIENDS AS WELL!
KATA (CLATTER)
カタ
KATATA
カタタタ…!

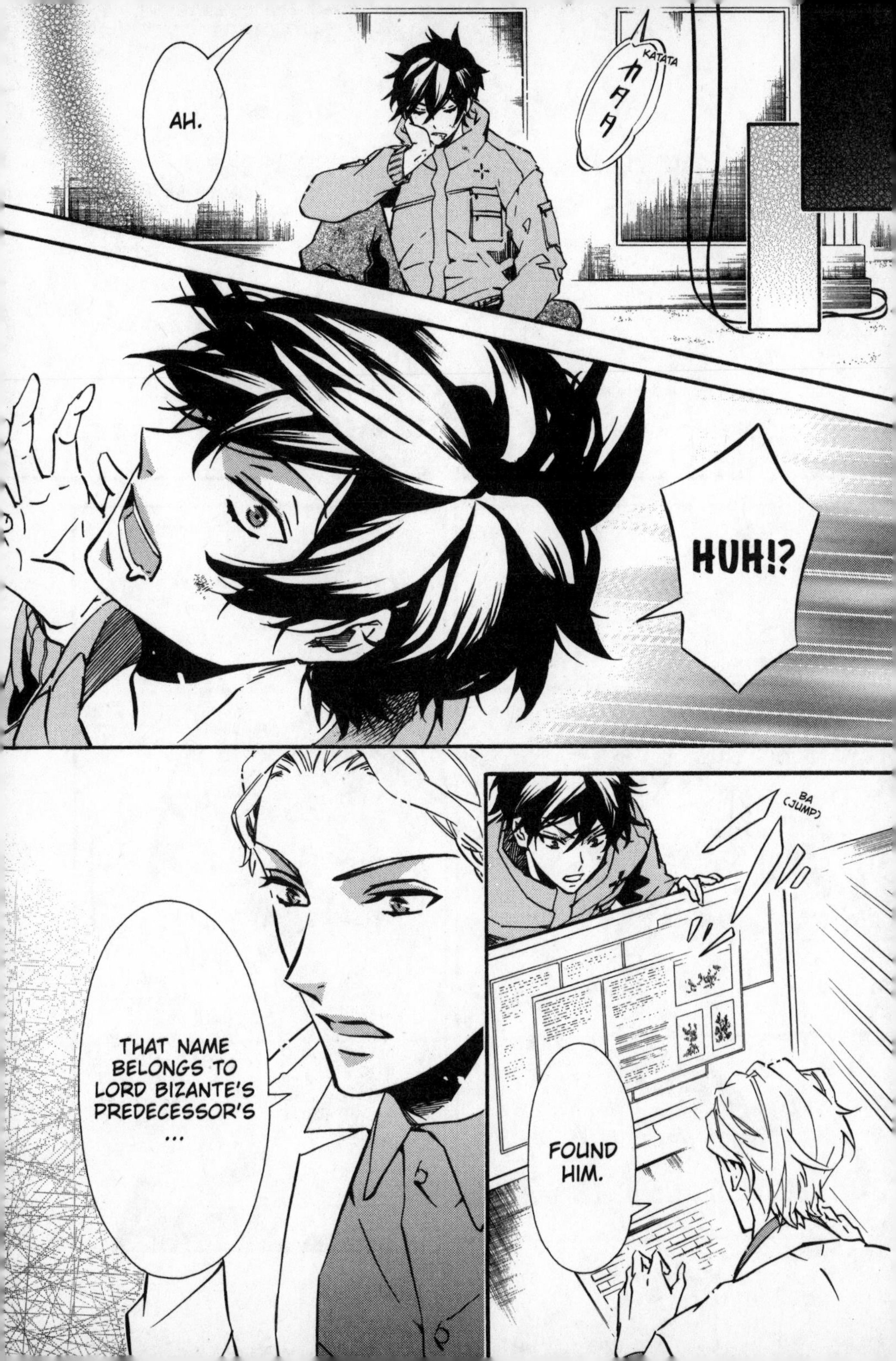
KATATA
カタタ
AH.
HUH!?
BA (JUMP)
FOUND HIM.
THAT NAME BELONGS TO LORD BIZANTE'S PREDECESSOR'S ...

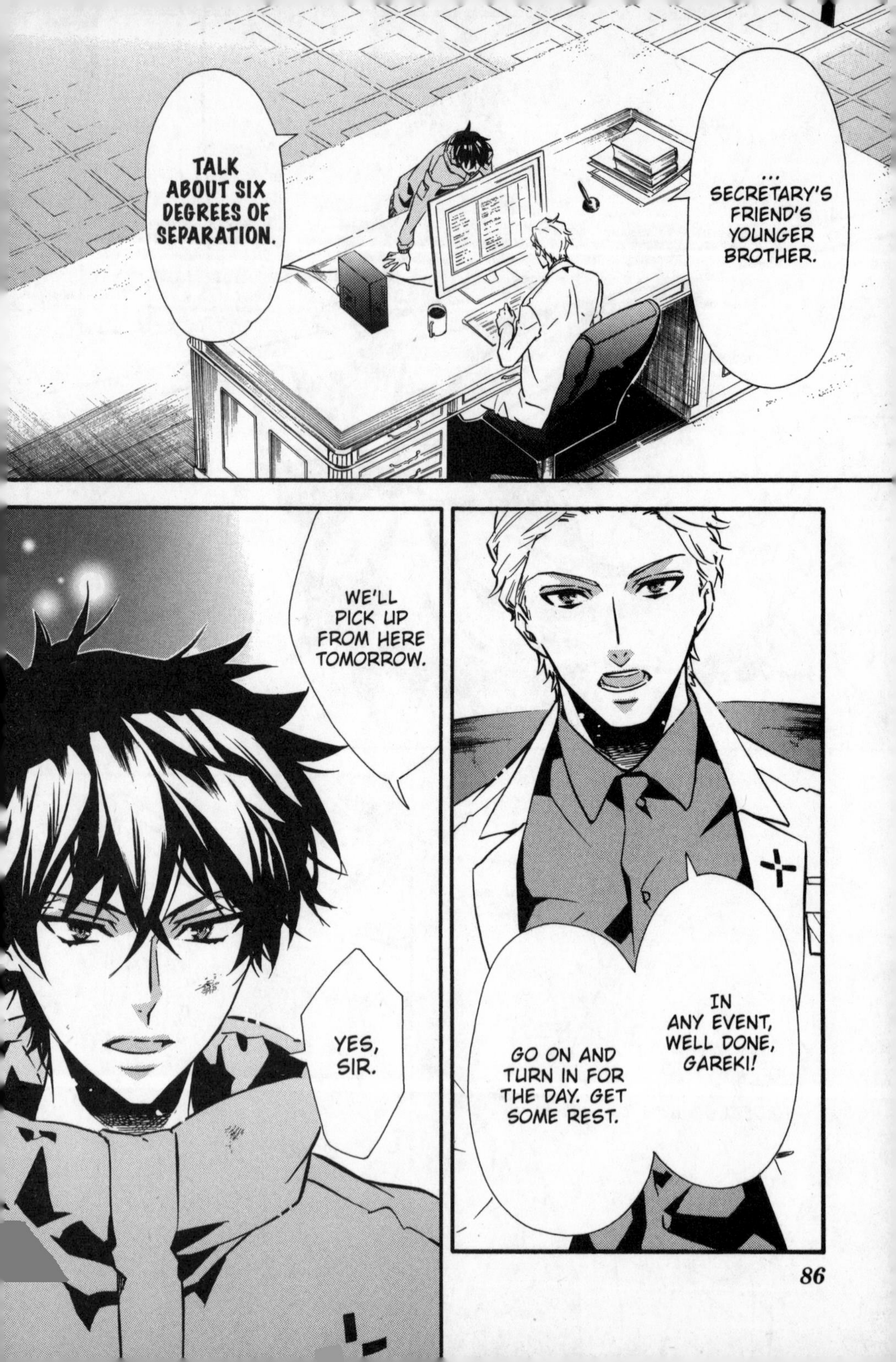
...SECRETARY'S FRIEND'S YOUNGER BROTHER.
TALK ABOUT SIX DEGREES OF SEPARATION.
IN ANY EVENT, WELL DONE, GAREKI!
GO ON AND TURN IN FOR THE DAY. GET SOME REST.
WE'LL PICK UP FROM HERE TOMORROW.
YES, SIR.

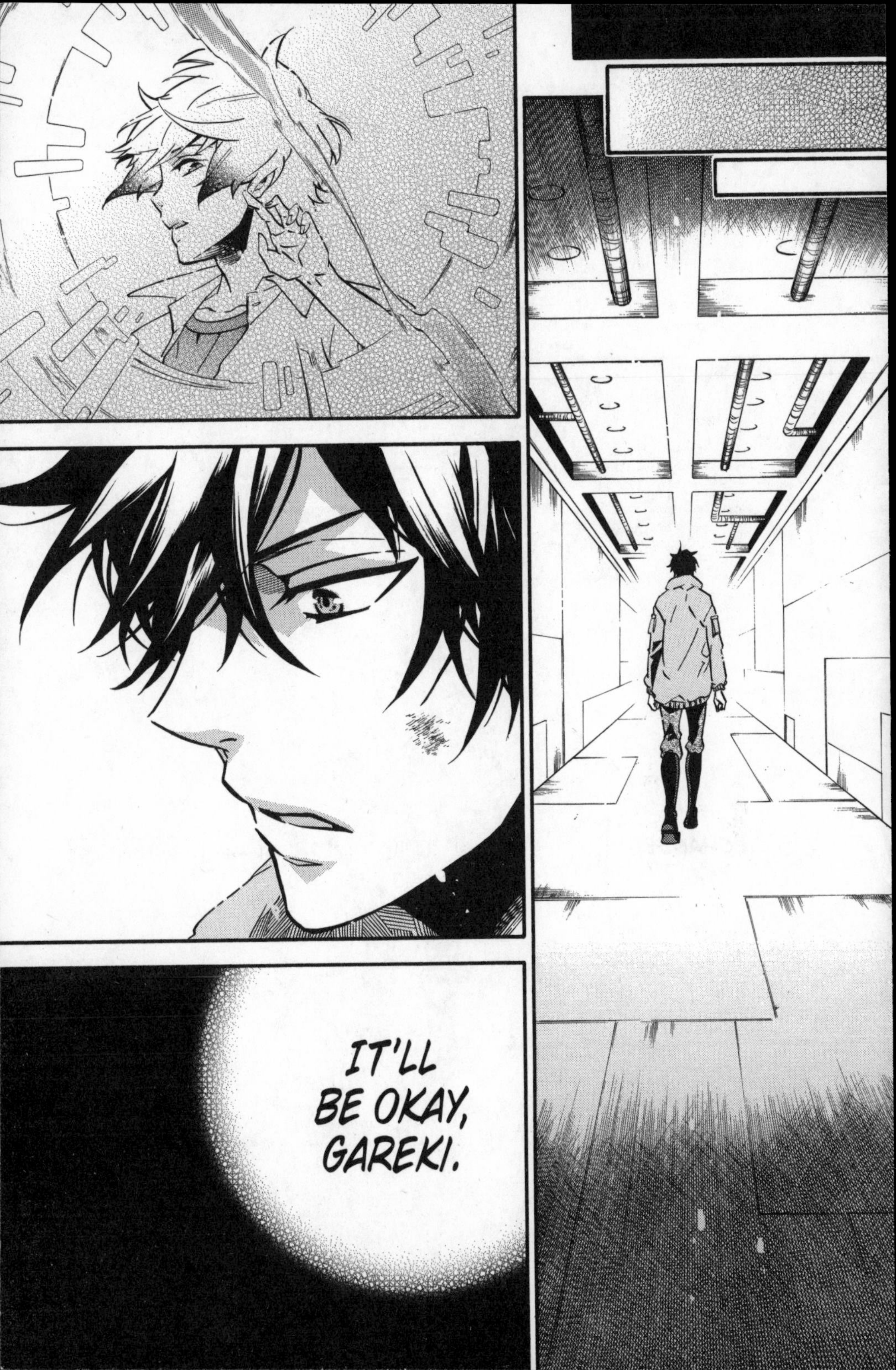
IT'LL BE OKAY, GAREKI.

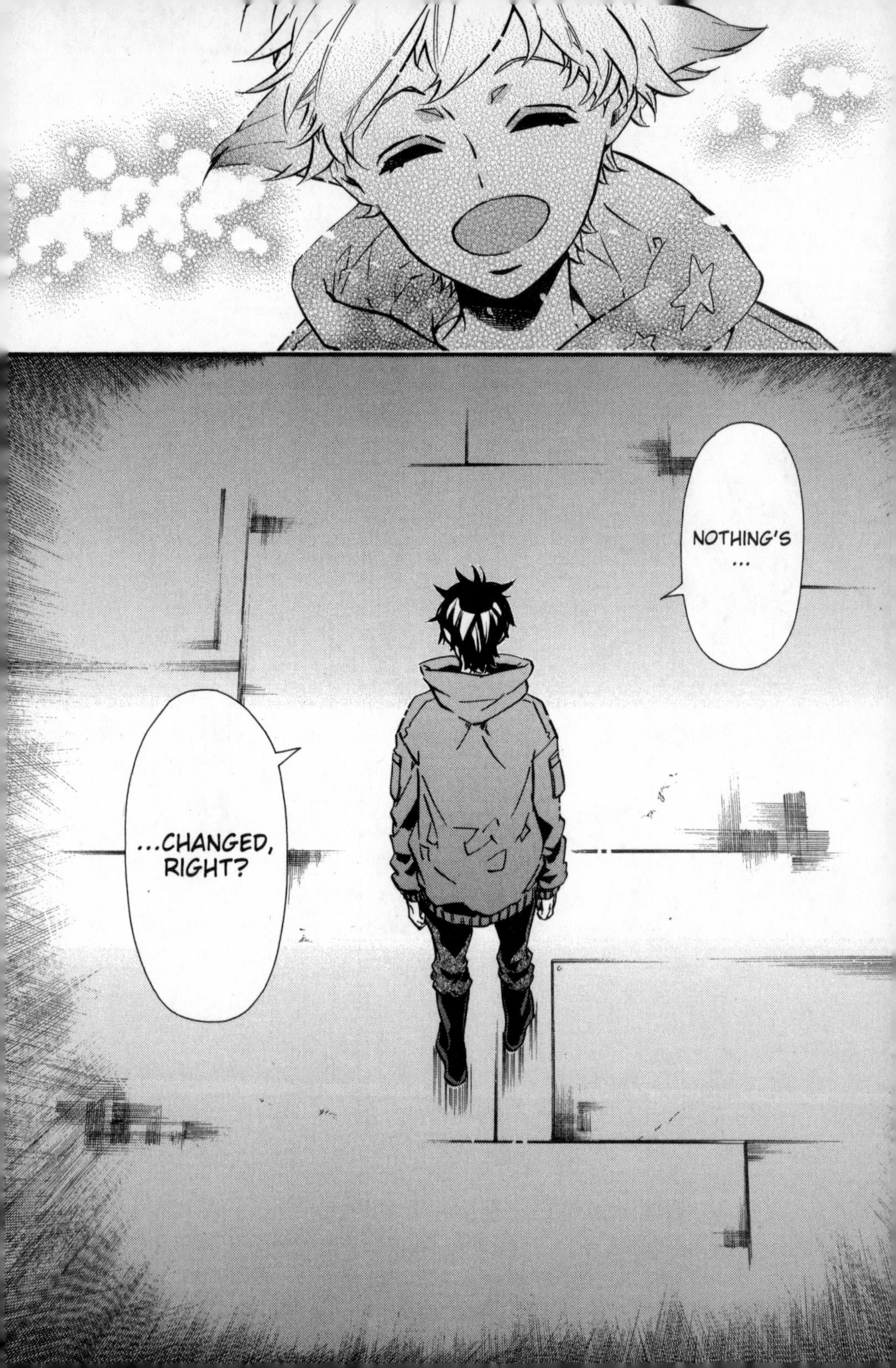
NOTHING'S ...
...CHANGED, RIGHT?

KARNEVAL

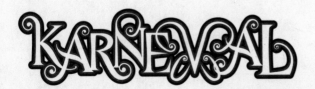

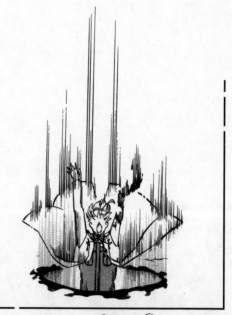

KARNEVAL

Score 140: The Allongan Village

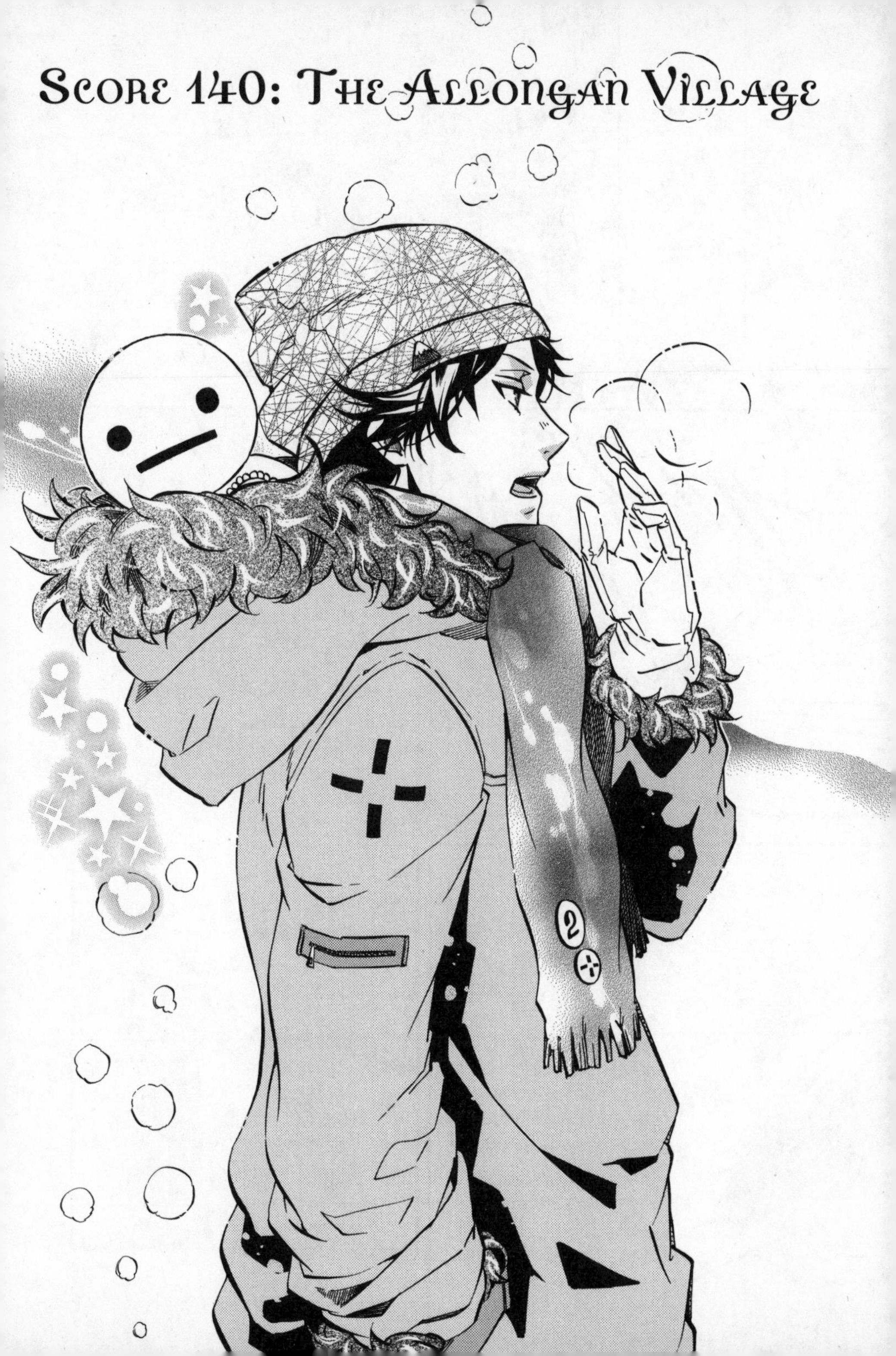

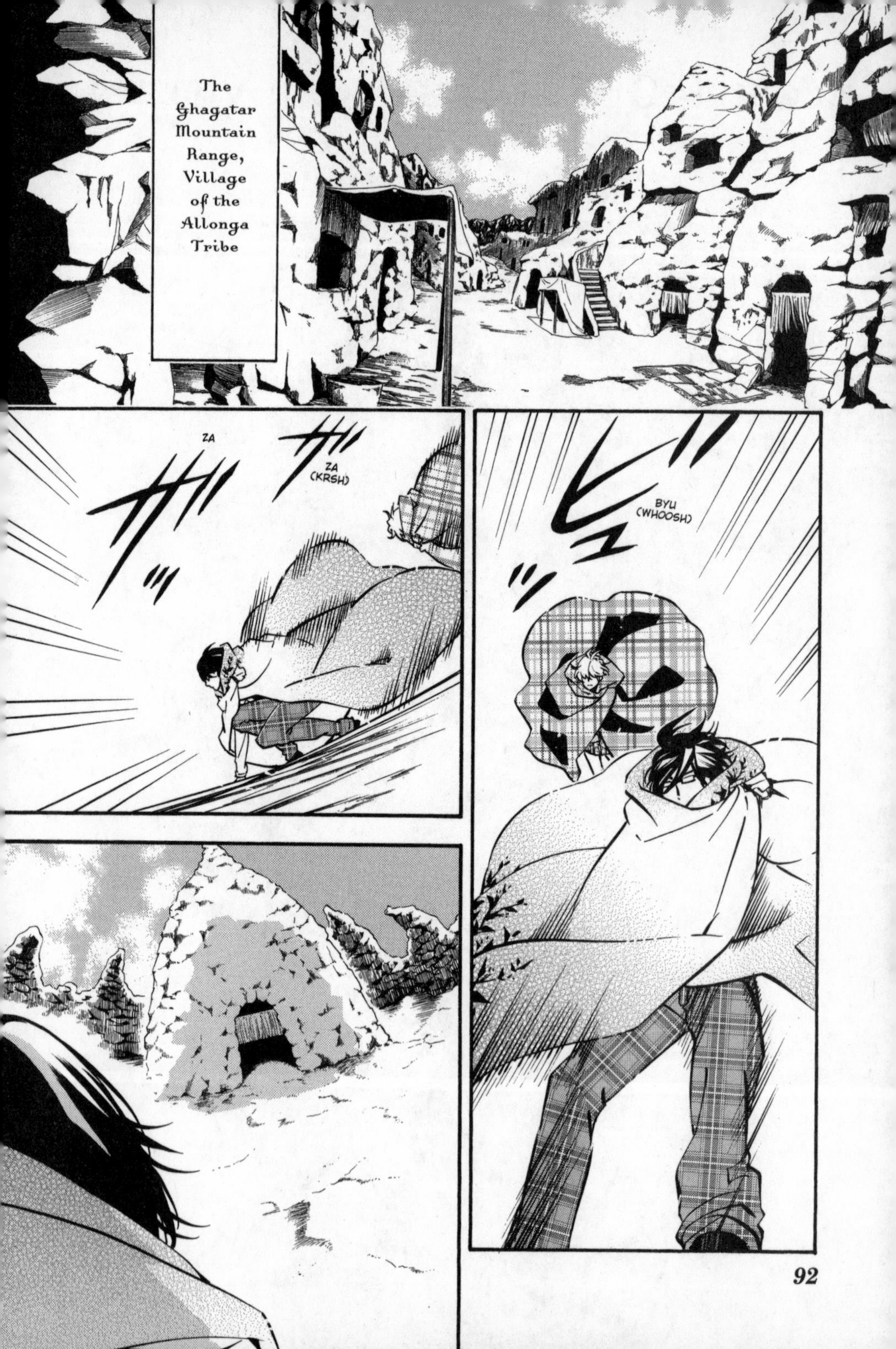
The Ghagatar Mountain Range, Village of the Allonga Tribe
BYU (WHOOSH)
ZA
ZA (KRSH)

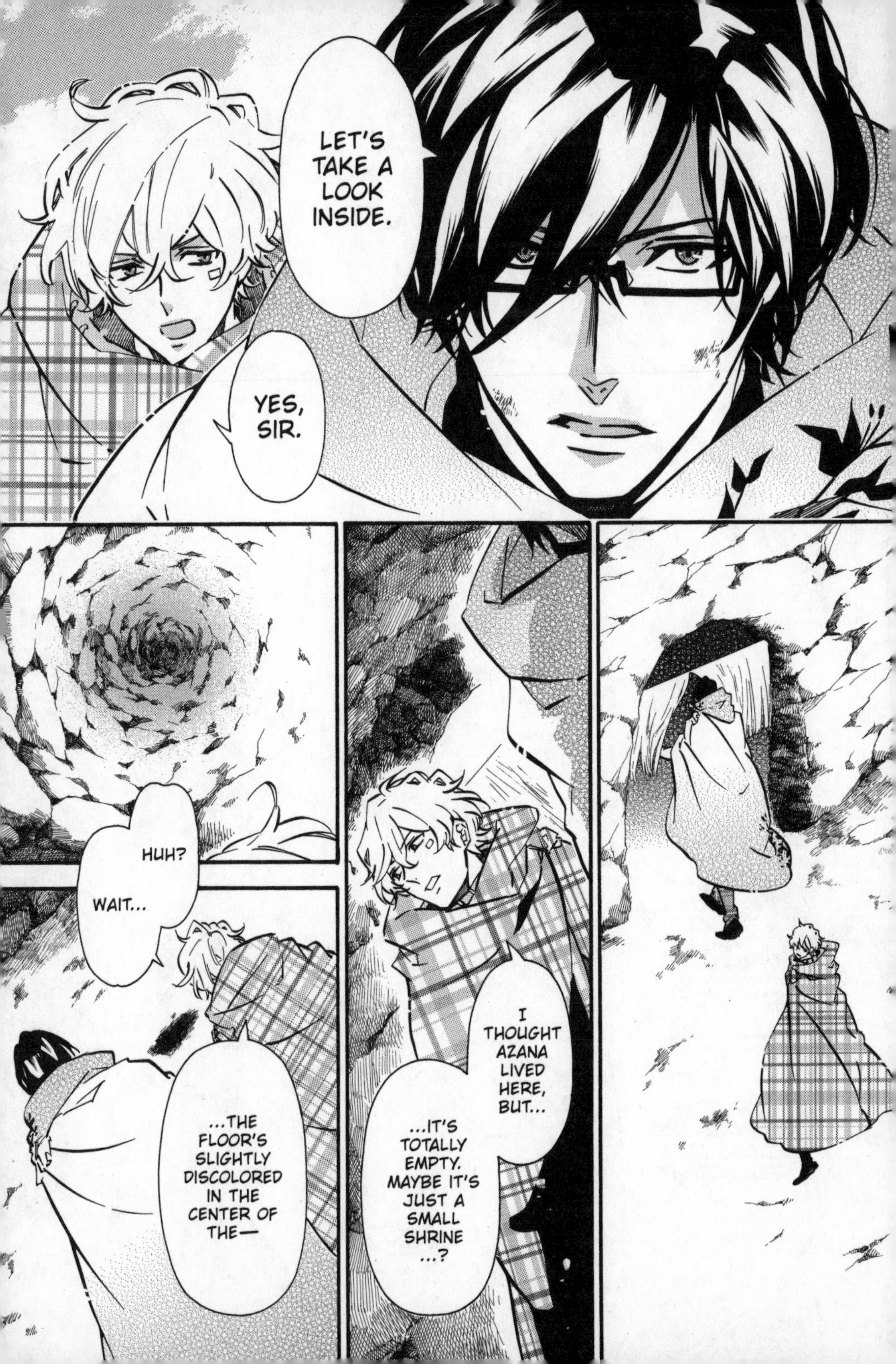
LET'S TAKE A LOOK INSIDE.
YES, SIR.
I THOUGHT AZANA LIVED HERE, BUT...
...IT'S TOTALLY EMPTY. MAYBE IT'S JUST A SMALL SHRINE ...?
HUH?
WAIT...
...THE FLOOR'S SLIGHTLY DISCOLORED IN THE CENTER OF THE—

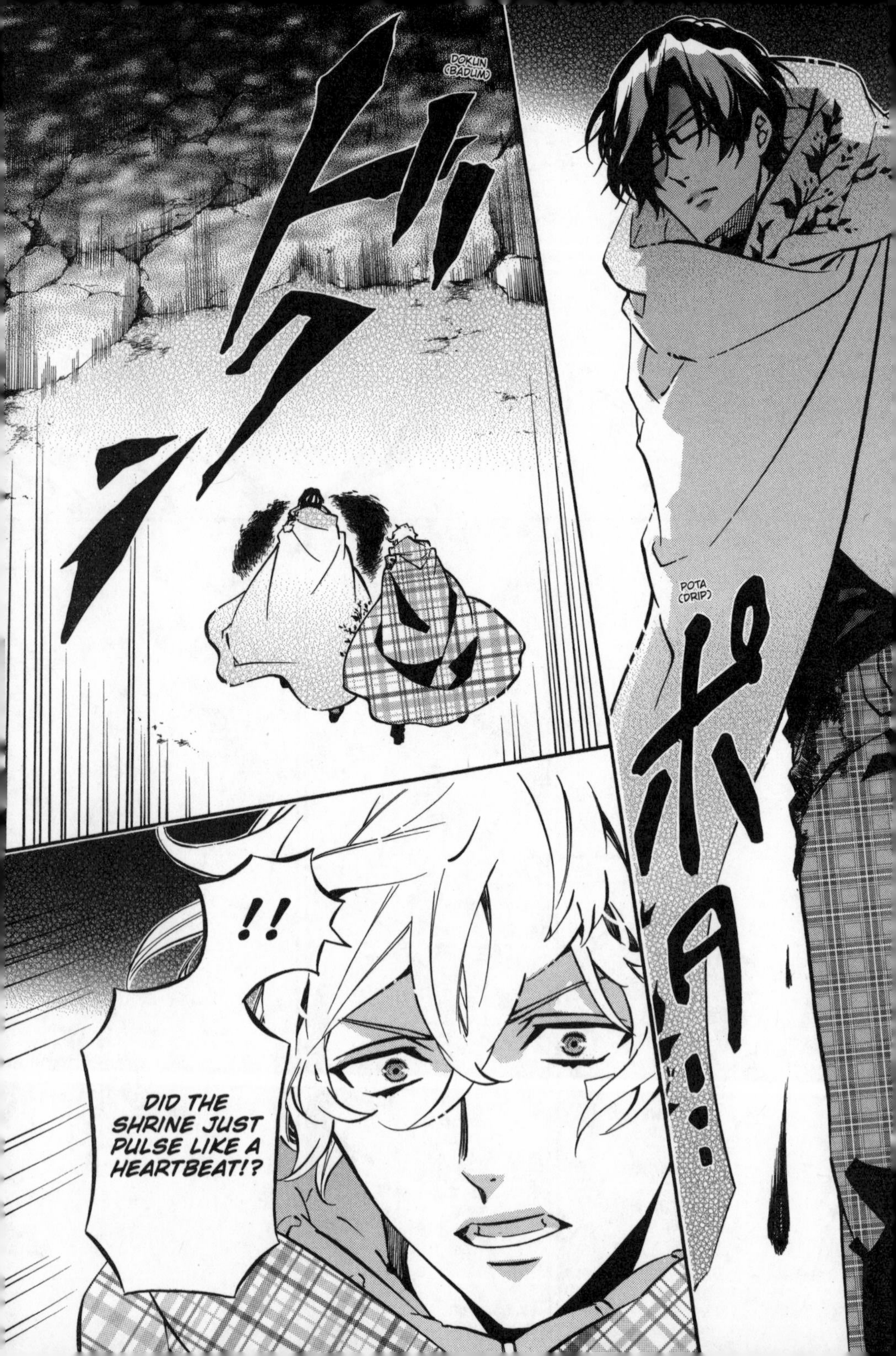
POTA (DRIP)
ポタ
DOKUN (BADUM)
ドクン
!!
DID THE SHRINE JUST PULSE LIKE A HEARTBEAT!?

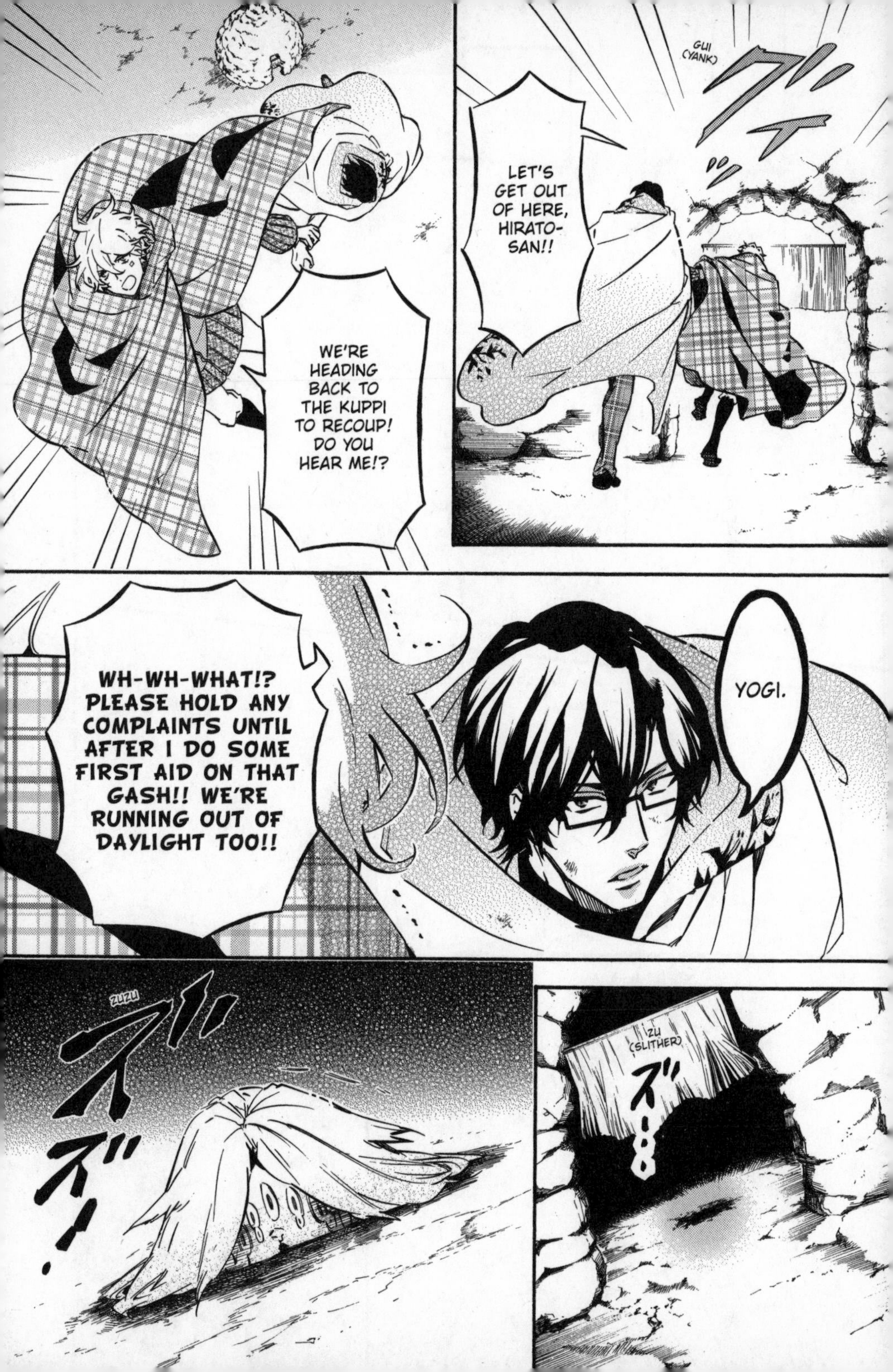
GUI (YANK)
LET'S GET OUT OF HERE, HIRATO-SAN!!
WE'RE HEADING BACK TO THE KUPPI TO RECOUP! DO YOU HEAR ME!?
YOGI.
WH-WH-WHAT!? PLEASE HOLD ANY COMPLAINTS UNTIL AFTER I DO SOME FIRST AID ON THAT GASH!! WE'RE RUNNING OUT OF DAYLIGHT TOO!!
ZU (SLITHER)
ZUZU

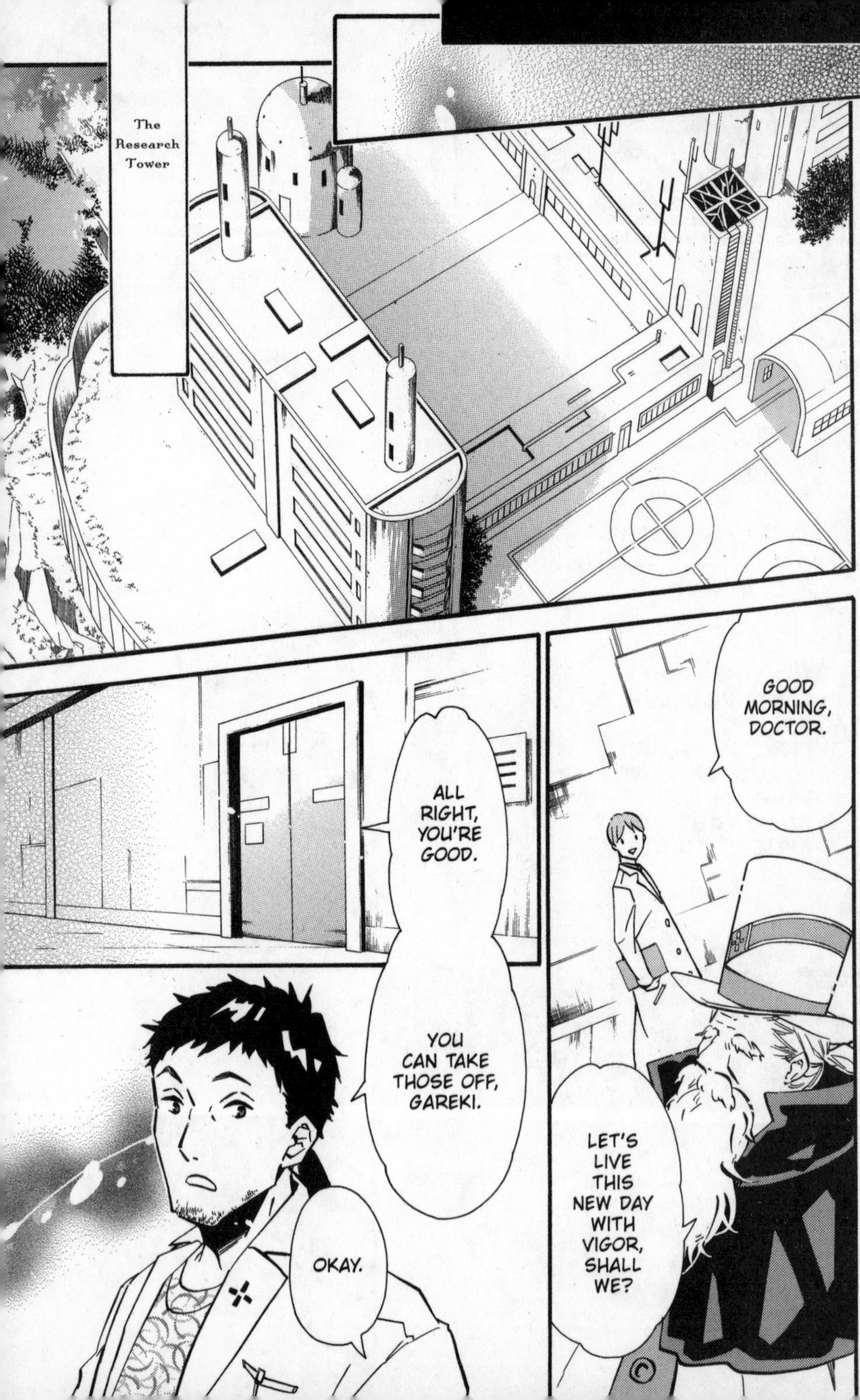

The Research Tower
GOOD MORNING, DOCTOR.
LET'S LIVE THIS NEW DAY WITH VIGOR, SHALL WE?
ALL RIGHT, YOU'RE GOOD.
YOU CAN TAKE THOSE OFF, GAREKI.
OKAY.

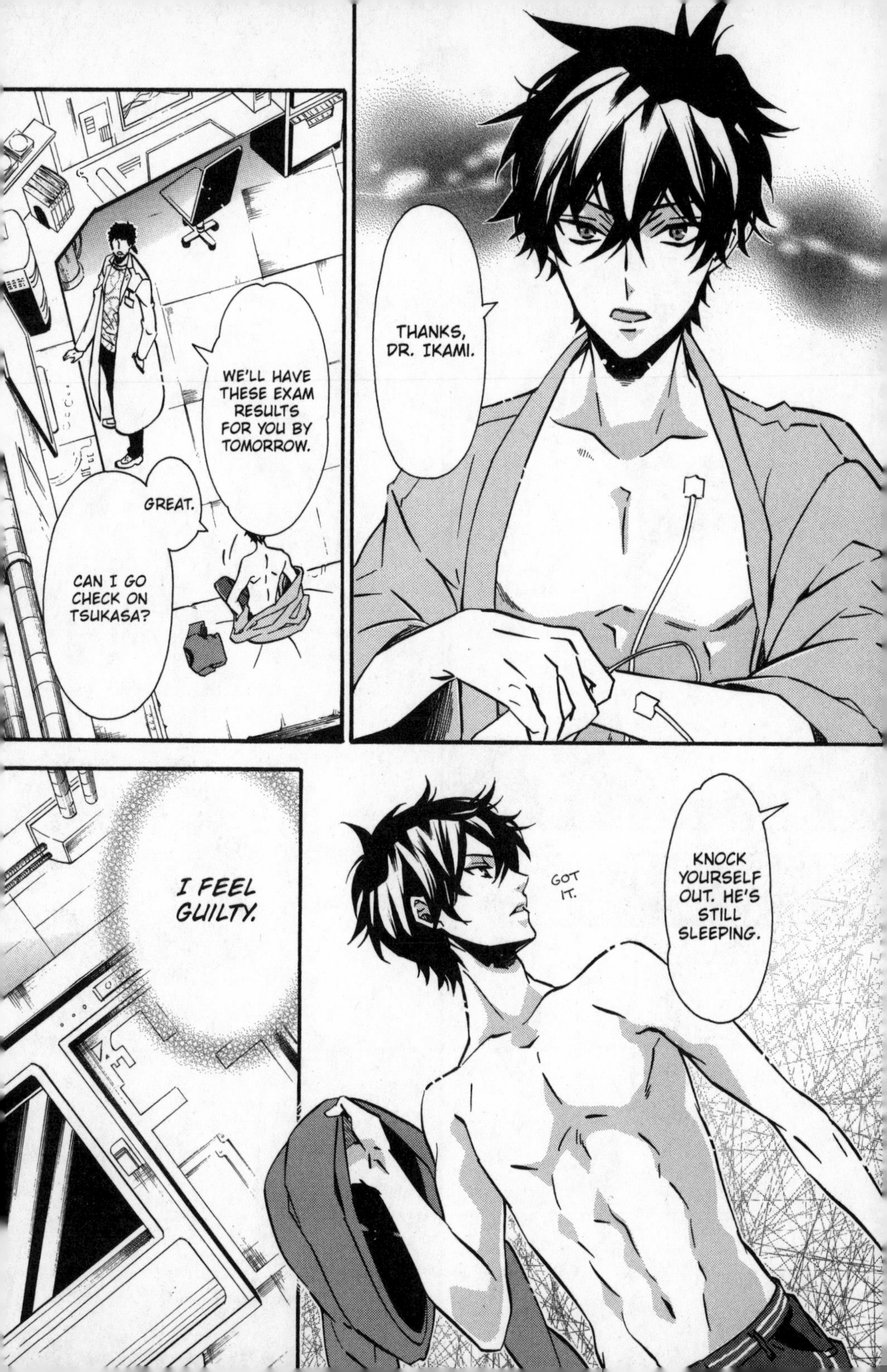
THANKS, DR. IKAMI.
WE'LL HAVE THESE EXAM RESULTS FOR YOU BY TOMORROW.
GREAT.
CAN I GO CHECK ON TSUKASA?
KNOCK YOURSELF OUT. HE'S STILL SLEEPING.
GOT IT.
I FEEL GUILTY.

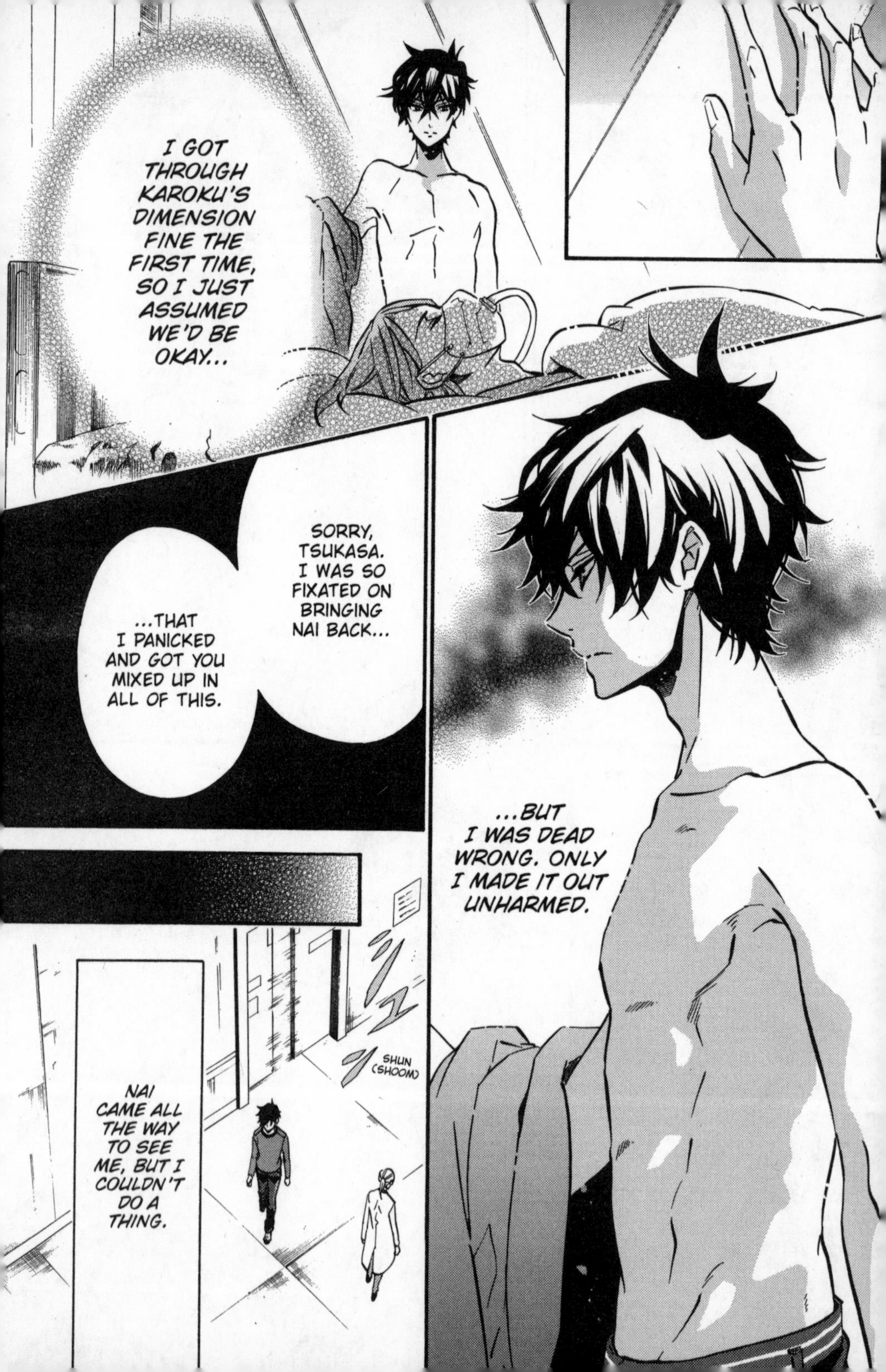
I GOT THROUGH KAROKU'S DIMENSION FINE THE FIRST TIME, SO I JUST ASSUMED WE'D BE OKAY...
...BUT I WAS DEAD WRONG. ONLY I MADE IT OUT UNHARMED.
SORRY, TSUKASA. I WAS SO FIXATED ON BRINGING NAI BACK...
...THAT I PANICKED AND GOT YOU MIXED UP IN ALL OF THIS.
SHUN (SHOOM)
NAI CAME ALL THE WAY TO SEE ME, BUT I COULDN'T DO A THING.

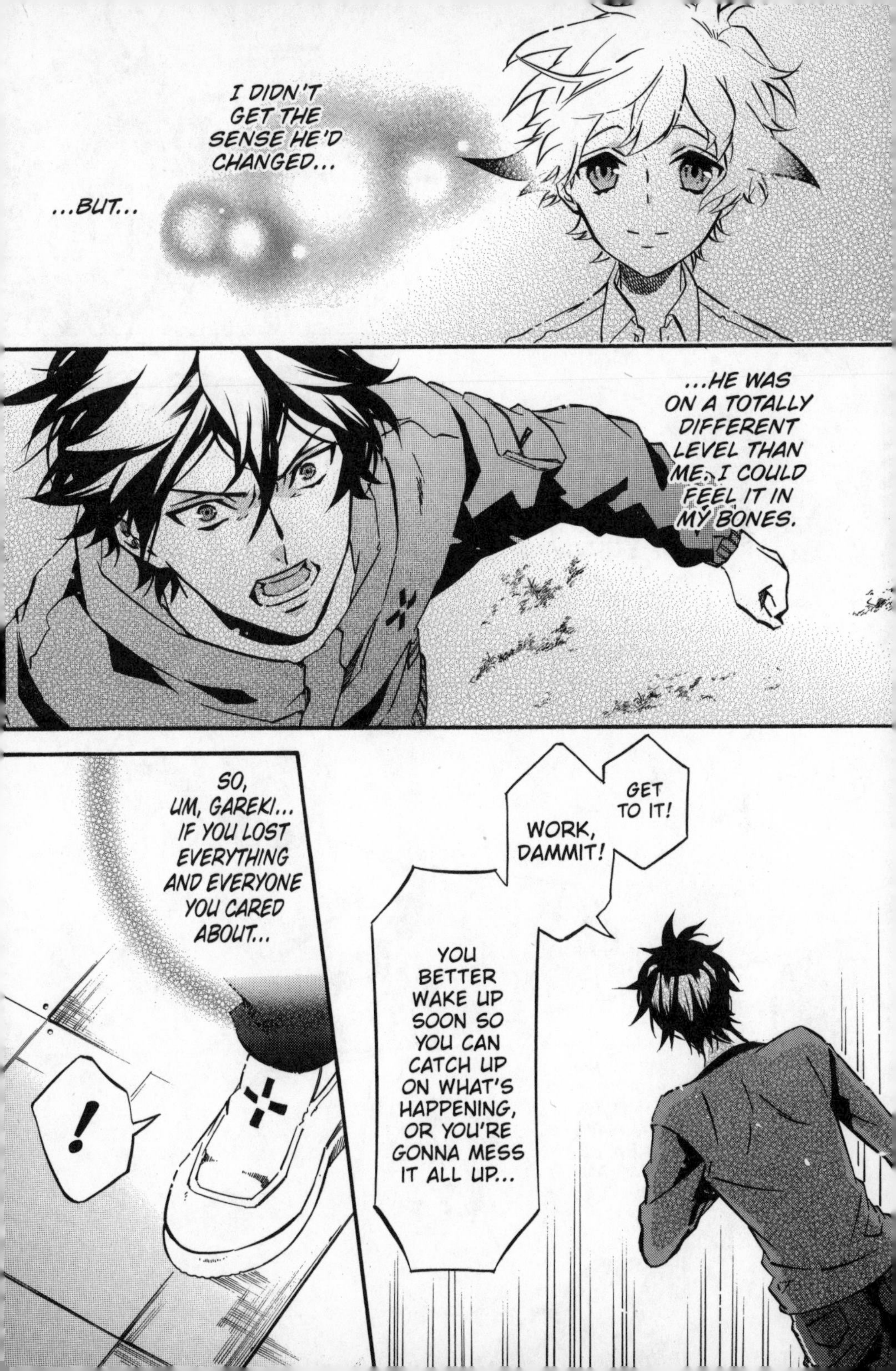
I DIDN'T GET THE SENSE HE'D CHANGED...
...BUT...
...HE WAS ON A TOTALLY DIFFERENT LEVEL THAN ME. I COULD FEEL IT IN MY BONES.
GET TO IT!
WORK, DAMMIT!
YOU BETTER WAKE UP SOON SO YOU CAN CATCH UP ON WHAT'S HAPPENING, OR YOU'RE GONNA MESS IT ALL UP...
SO, UM, GAREKI... IF YOU LOST EVERYTHING AND EVERYONE YOU CARED ABOUT...
!

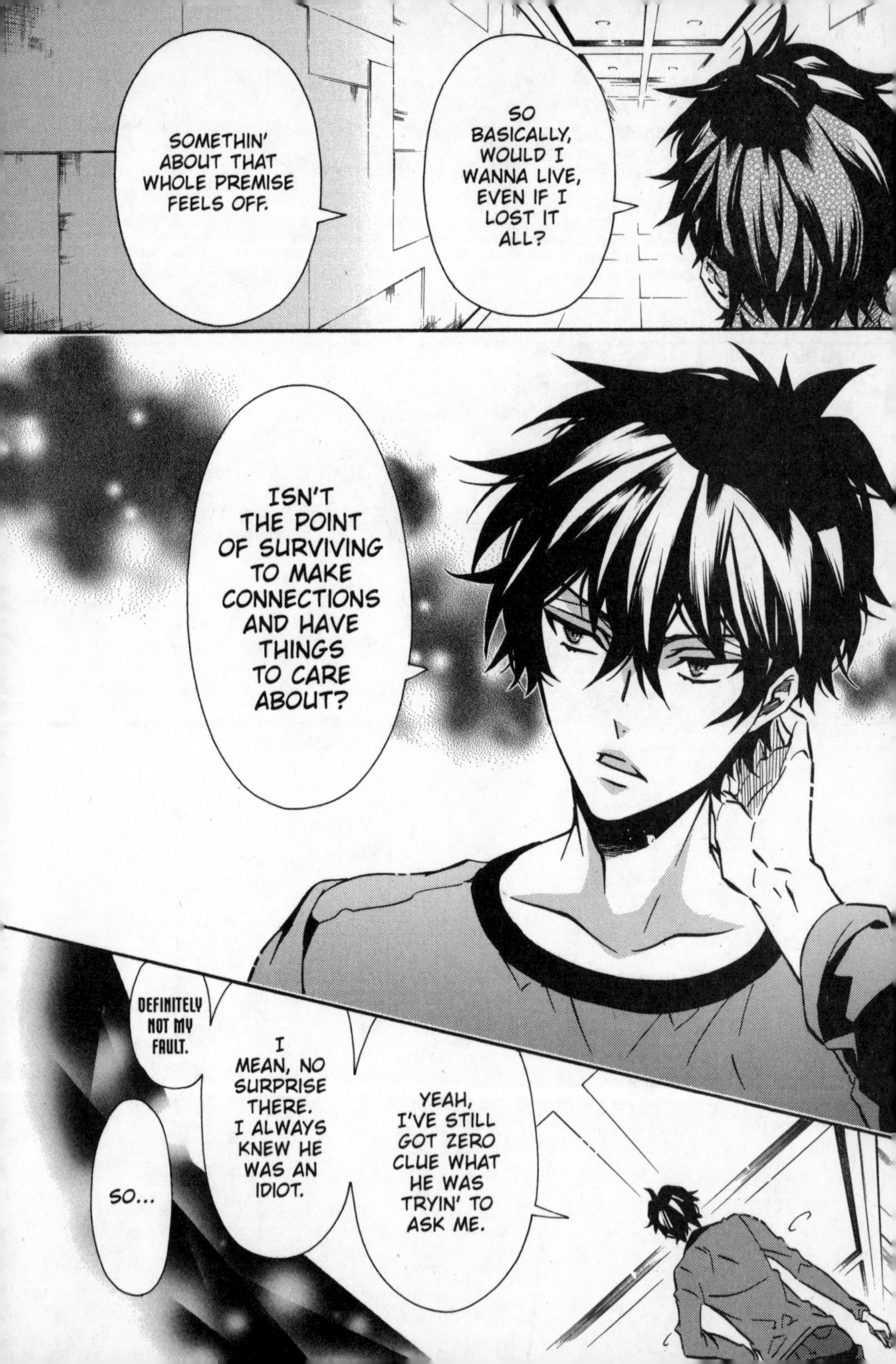
SO BASICALLY, WOULD I WANNA LIVE, EVEN IF I LOST IT ALL?
SOMETHIN' ABOUT THAT WHOLE PREMISE FEELS OFF.
ISN'T THE POINT OF SURVIVING TO MAKE CONNECTIONS AND HAVE THINGS TO CARE ABOUT?
YEAH, I'VE STILL GOT ZERO CLUE WHAT HE WAS TRYIN' TO ASK ME.
I MEAN, NO SURPRISE THERE. I ALWAYS KNEW HE WAS AN IDIOT.
DEFINITELY NOT MY FAULT.
SO...

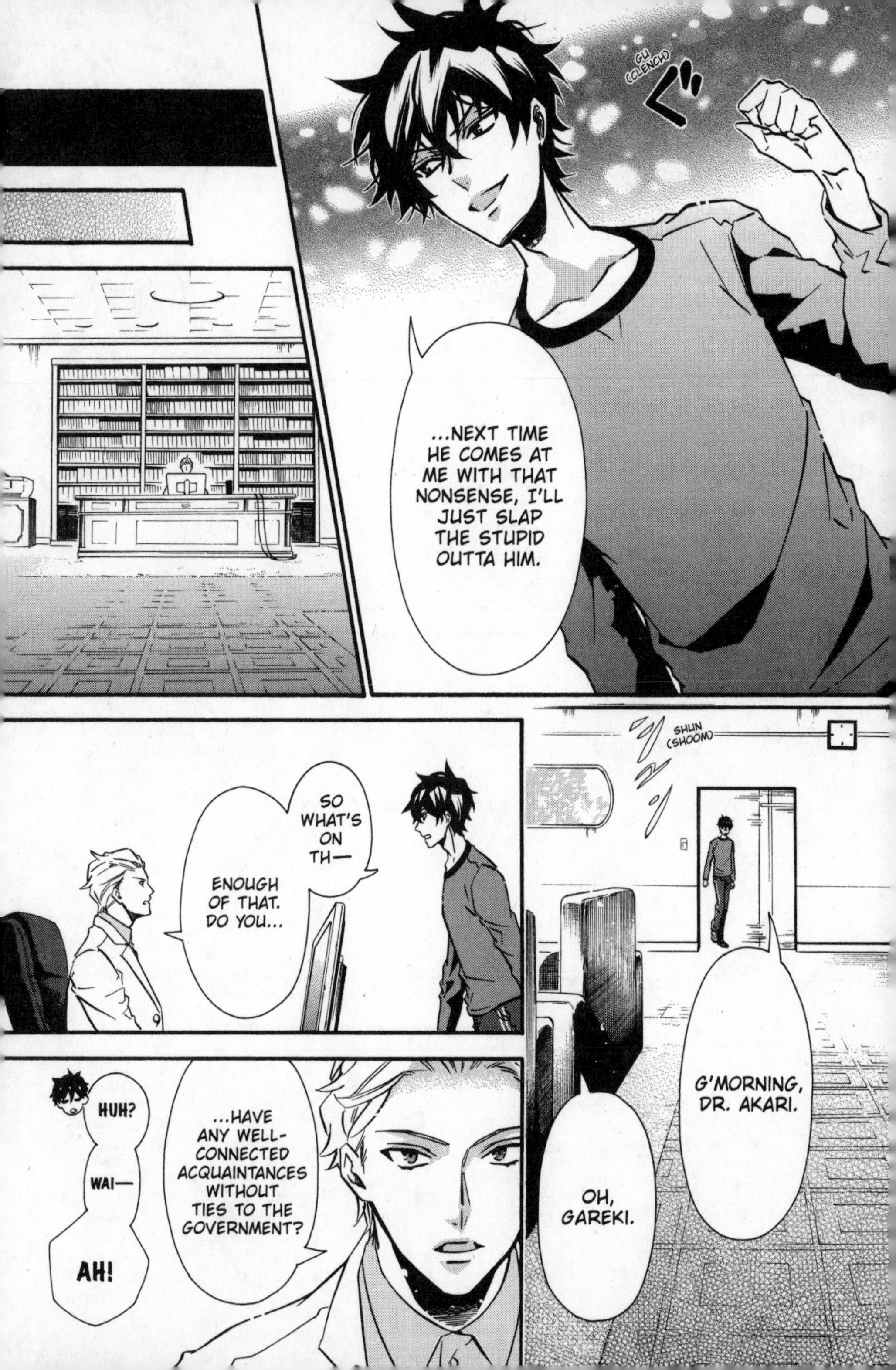
GU (CLENCH)
…NEXT TIME HE COMES AT ME WITH THAT NONSENSE, I'LL JUST SLAP THE STUPID OUTTA HIM.
SHUN (SHOOM)
G'MORNING, DR. AKARI.
OH, GAREKI.
SO WHAT'S ON TH—
ENOUGH OF THAT. DO YOU…
…HAVE ANY WELL-CONNECTED ACQUAINTANCES WITHOUT TIES TO THE GOVERNMENT?
HUH?
WAI—
AH!

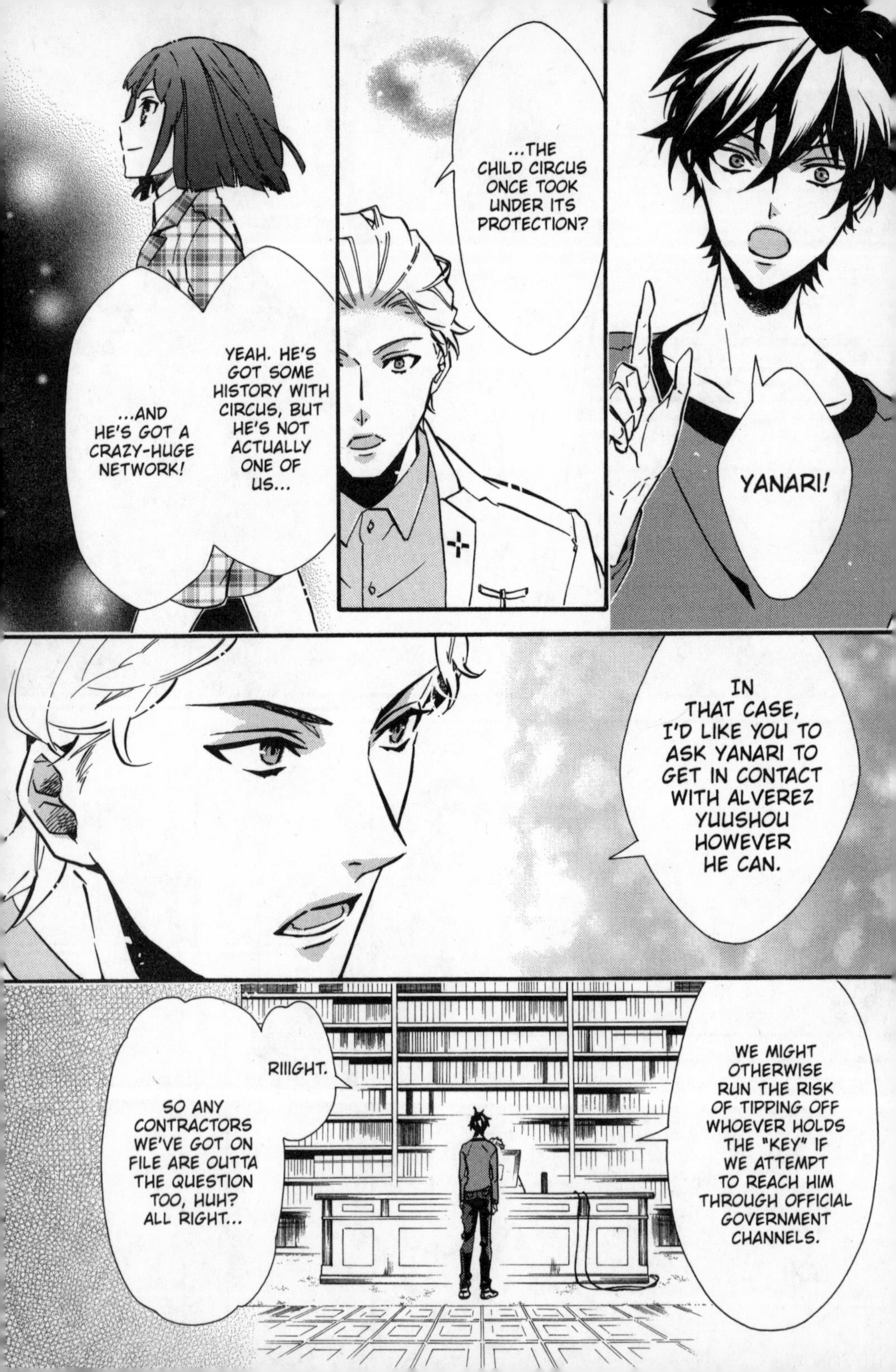
YANARI!
...THE CHILD CIRCUS ONCE TOOK UNDER ITS PROTECTION?
YEAH. HE'S GOT SOME HISTORY WITH CIRCUS, BUT HE'S NOT ACTUALLY ONE OF US...
...AND HE'S GOT A CRAZY-HUGE NETWORK!
IN THAT CASE, I'D LIKE YOU TO ASK YANARI TO GET IN CONTACT WITH ALVEREZ YUUSHOU HOWEVER HE CAN.
WE MIGHT OTHERWISE RUN THE RISK OF TIPPING OFF WHOEVER HOLDS THE "KEY" IF WE ATTEMPT TO REACH HIM THROUGH OFFICIAL GOVERNMENT CHANNELS.
RIIIGHT.
SO ANY CONTRACTORS WE'VE GOT ON FILE ARE OUTTA THE QUESTION TOO, HUH? ALL RIGHT...

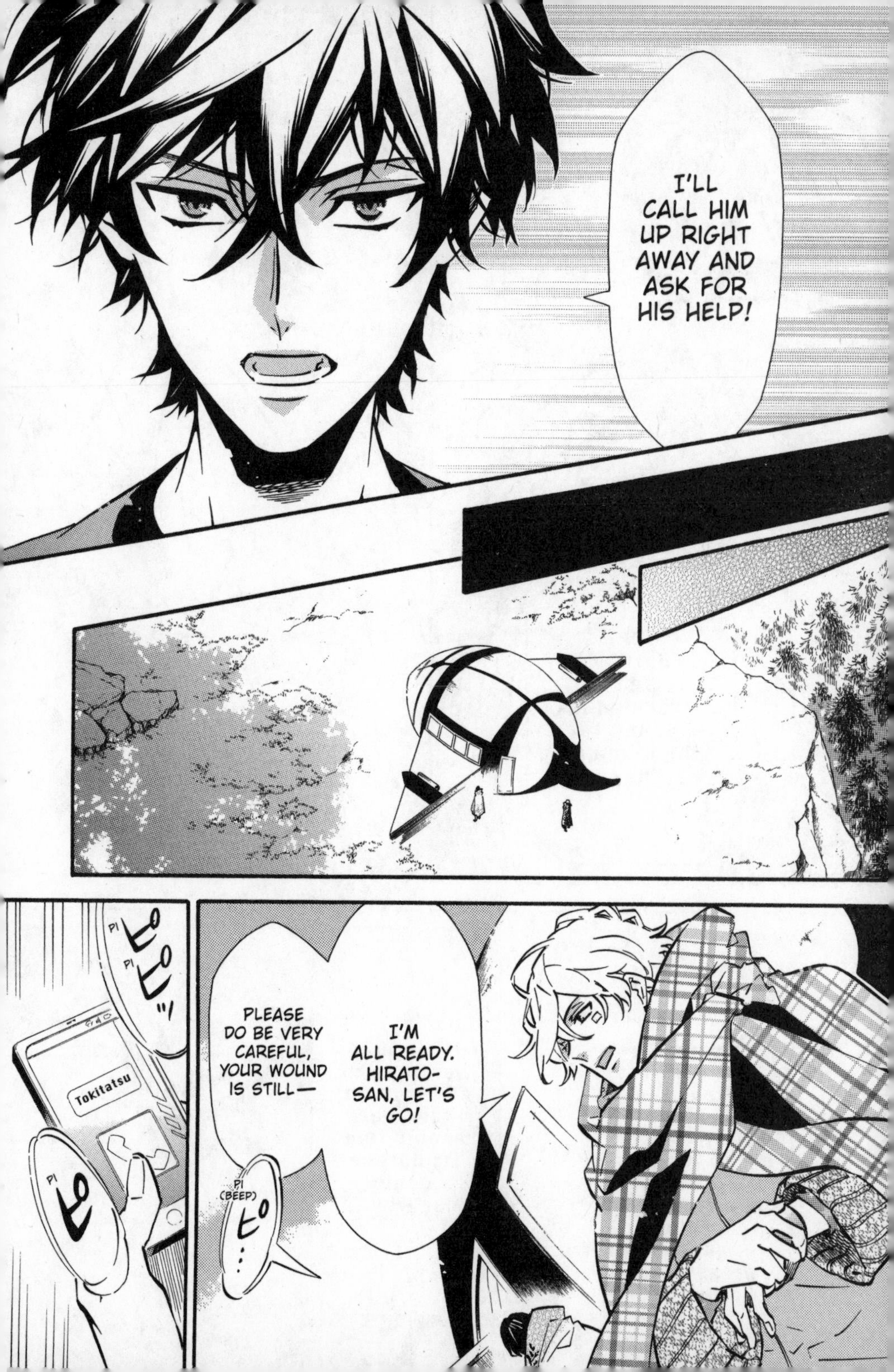
I'LL CALL HIM UP RIGHT AWAY AND ASK FOR HIS HELP!
I'M ALL READY. HIRATO-SAN, LET'S GO!
PLEASE DO BE VERY CAREFUL, YOUR WOUND IS STILL—
PI (BEEP)
PI PI
Tokitatsu
PI

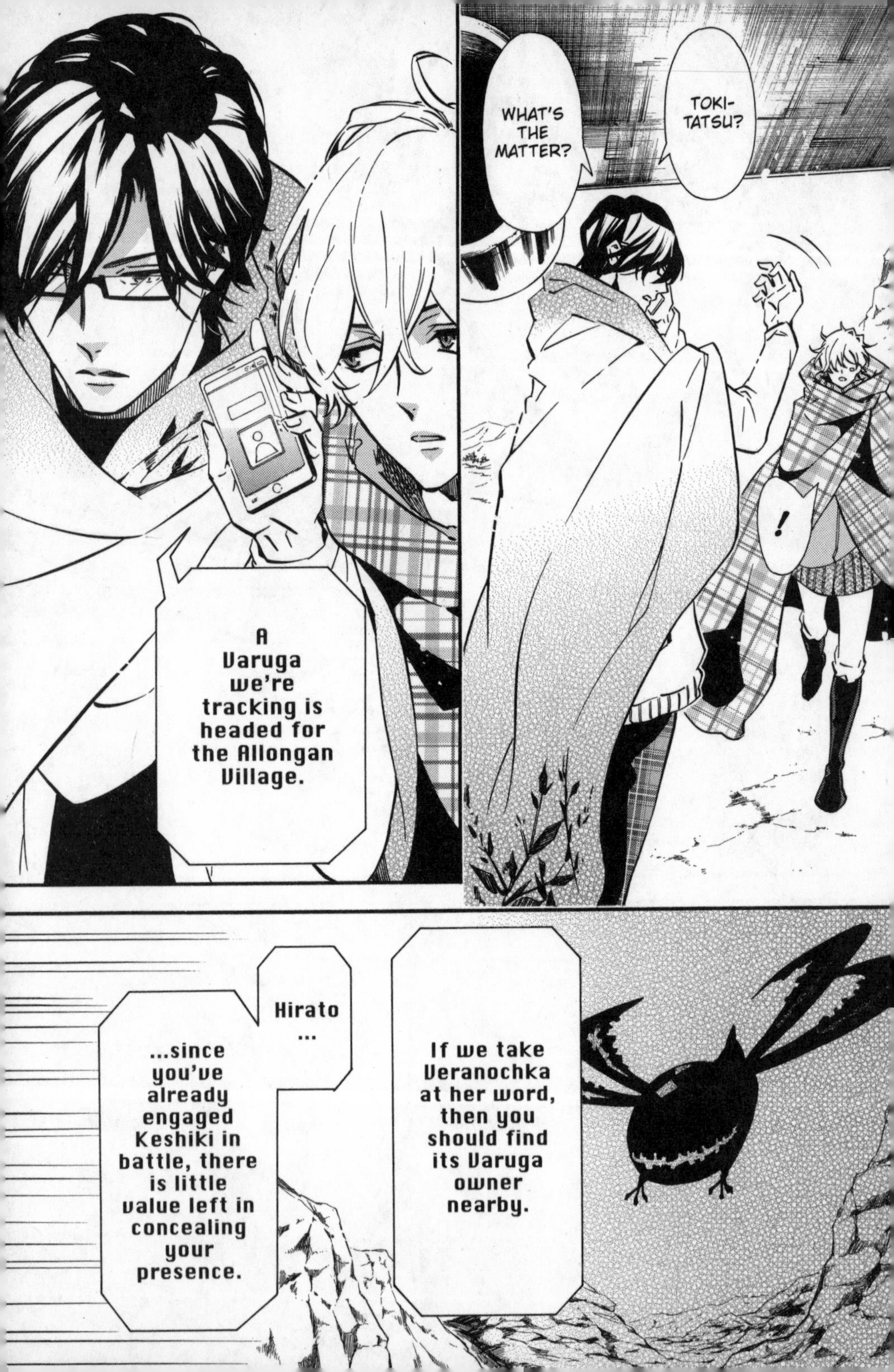
TOKI-TATSU?
WHAT'S THE MATTER?
!
A Varuga we're tracking is headed for the Allongan Village.
If we take Veranochka at her word, then you should find its Varuga owner nearby.
Hirato ...
...since you've already engaged Keshiki in battle, there is little value left in concealing your presence.

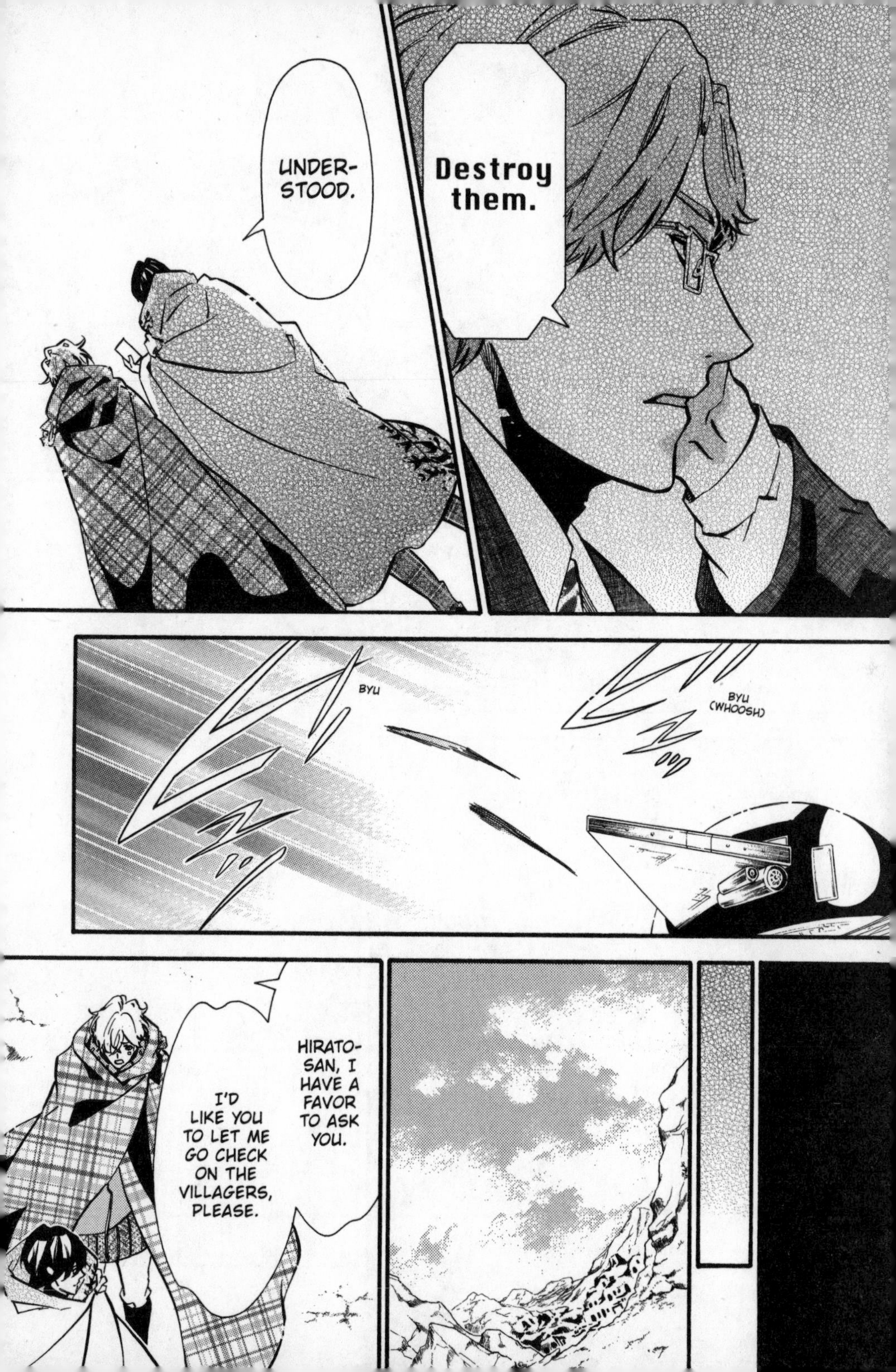
Destroy them.
UNDER-STOOD.
BYU (WHOOSH)
BYU
HIRATO-SAN, I HAVE A FAVOR TO ASK YOU.
I'D LIKE YOU TO LET ME GO CHECK ON THE VILLAGERS, PLEASE.

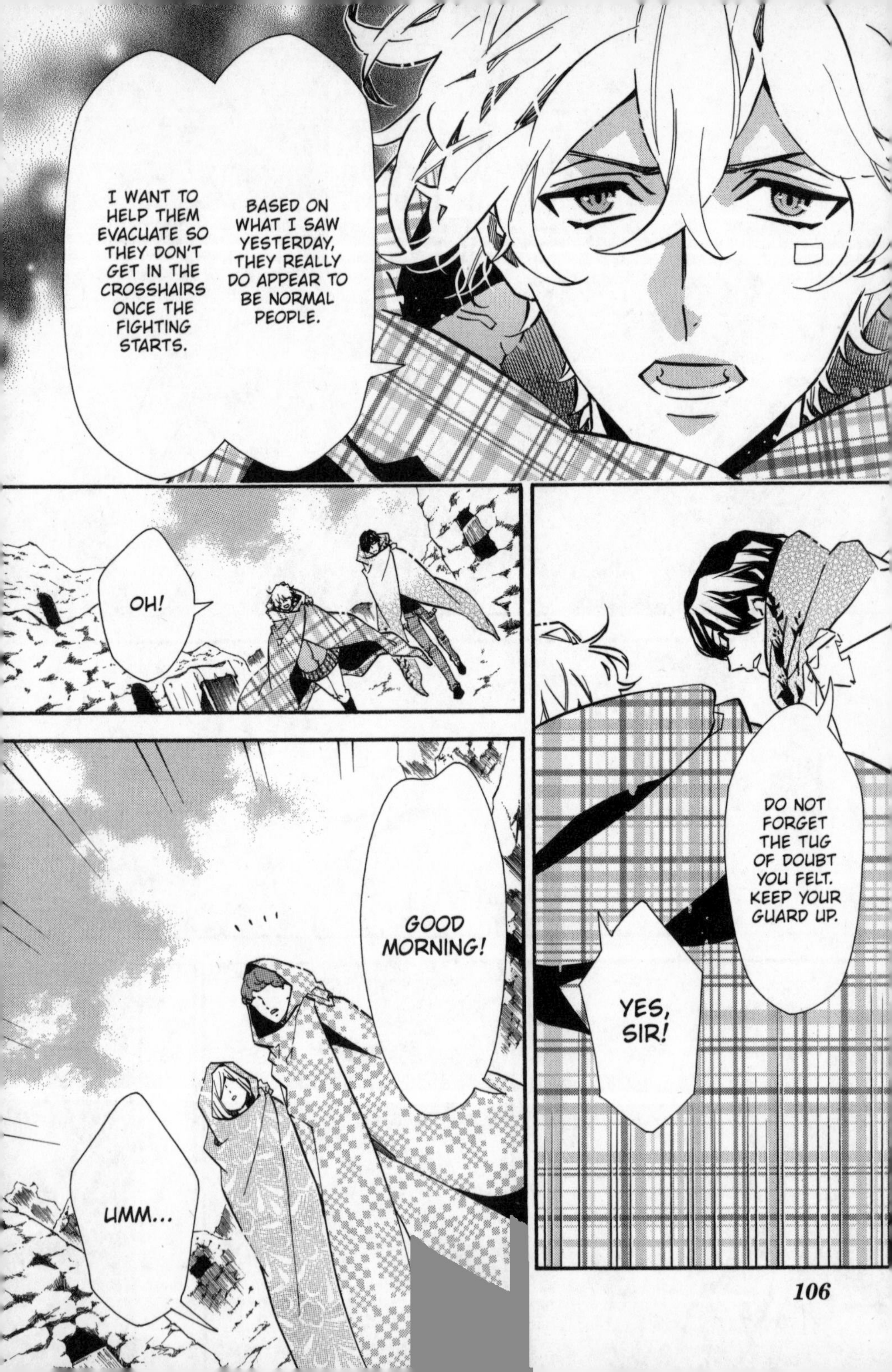
BASED ON WHAT I SAW YESTERDAY, THEY REALLY DO APPEAR TO BE NORMAL PEOPLE.
I WANT TO HELP THEM EVACUATE SO THEY DON'T GET IN THE CROSSHAIRS ONCE THE FIGHTING STARTS.
DO NOT FORGET THE TUG OF DOUBT YOU FELT. KEEP YOUR GUARD UP.
YES, SIR!
OH!
GOOD MORNING!
UMM...

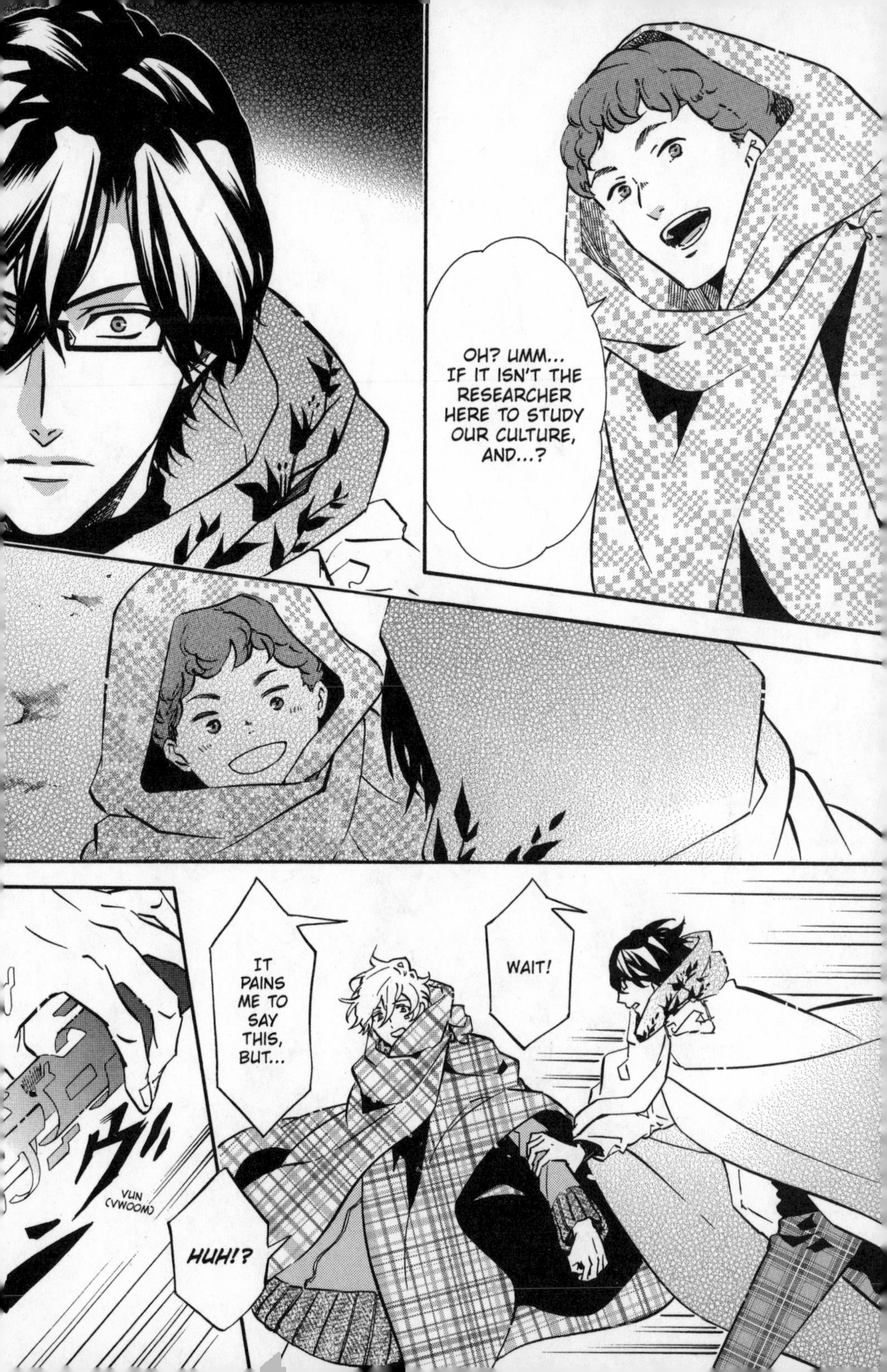
OH? UMM... IF IT ISN'T THE RESEARCHER HERE TO STUDY OUR CULTURE, AND...?
WAIT!
IT PAINS ME TO SAY THIS, BUT...
VUN (VWOOM)
HUH!?

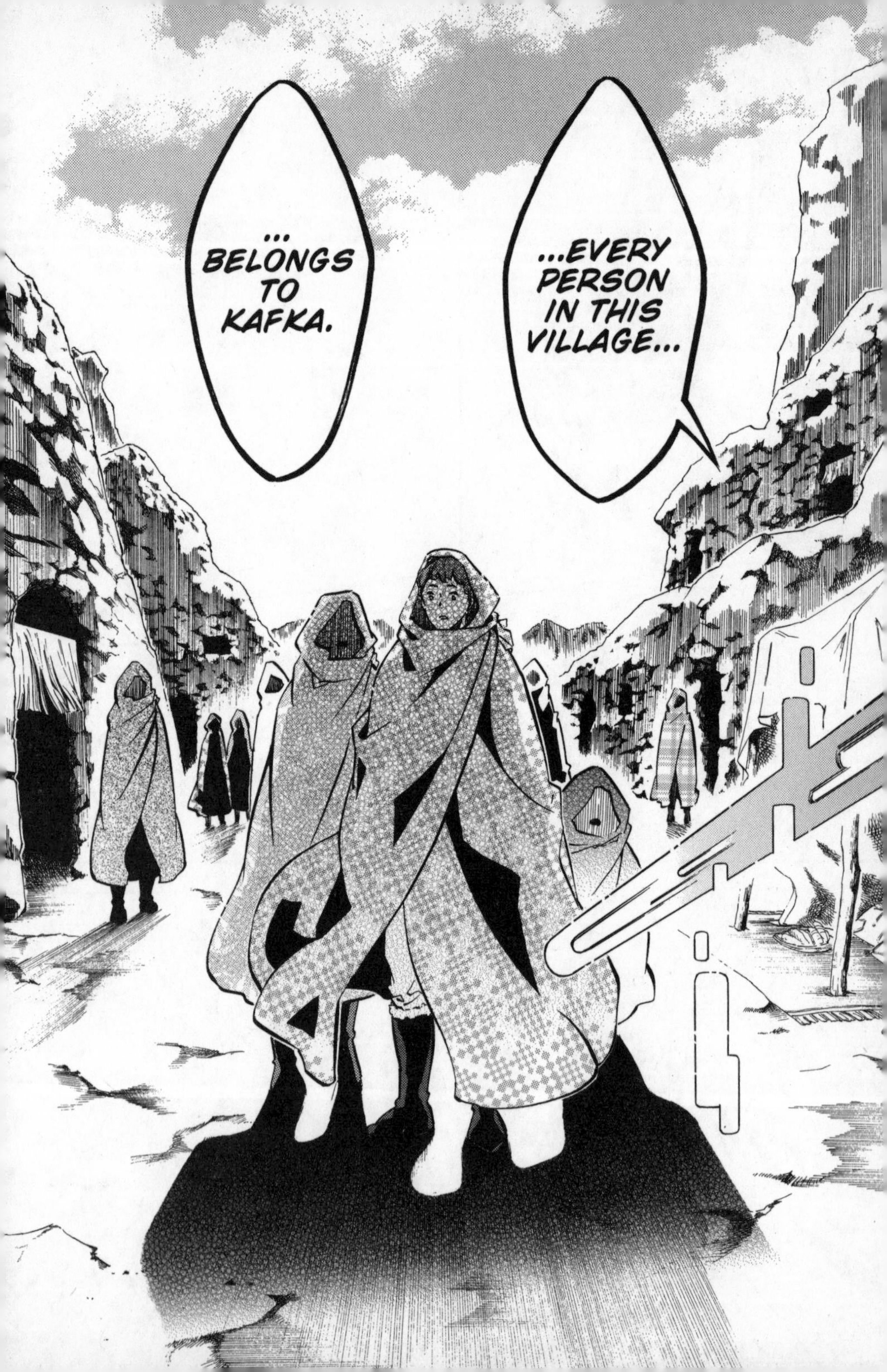
...EVERY PERSON IN THIS VILLAGE...
... BELONGS TO KAFKA.

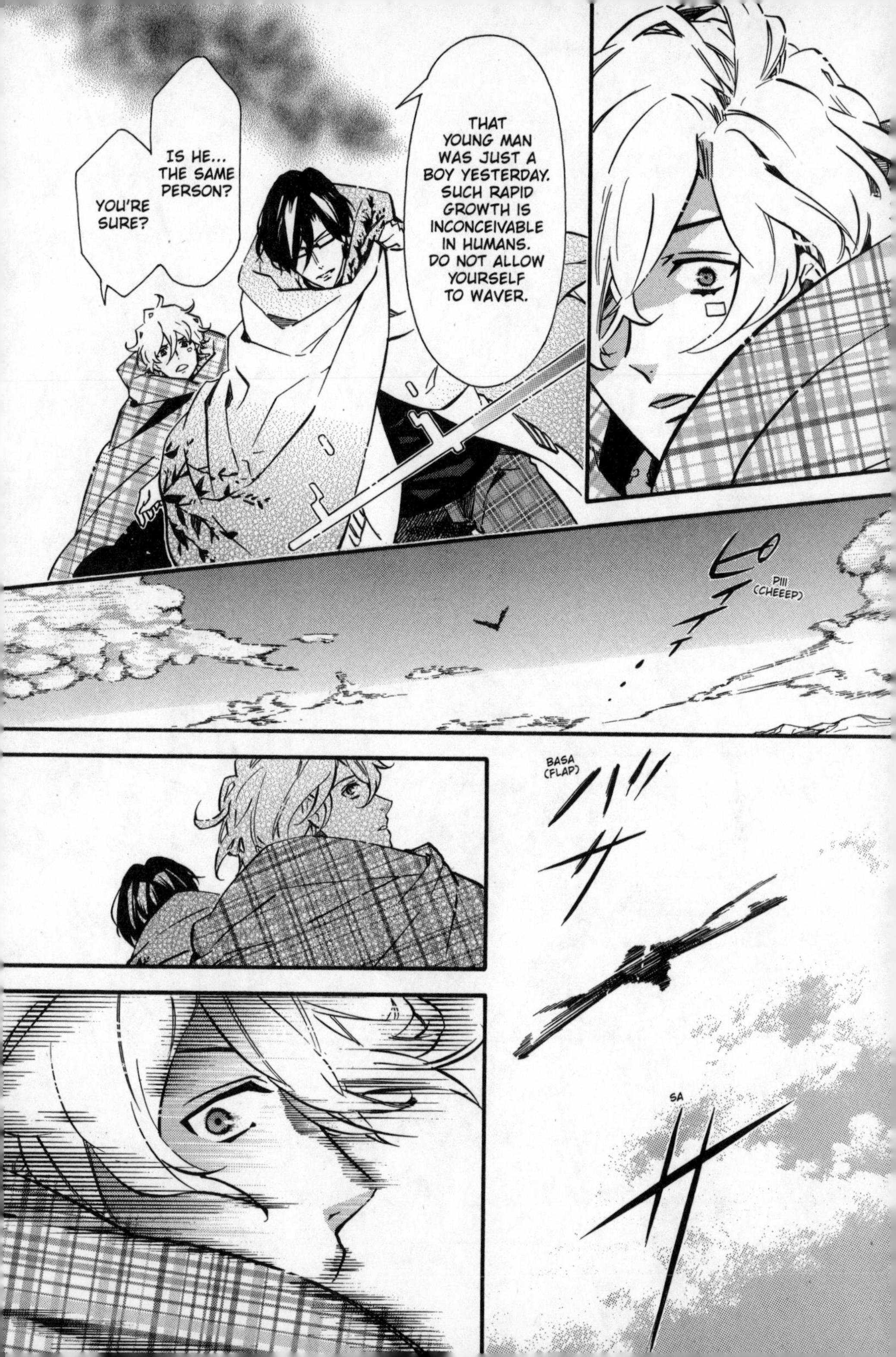
THAT YOUNG MAN WAS JUST A BOY YESTERDAY. SUCH RAPID GROWTH IS INCONCEIVABLE IN HUMANS. DO NOT ALLOW YOURSELF TO WAVER.
IS HE... THE SAME PERSON?
YOU'RE SURE?
PIII (CHEEEP)
BASA (FLAP)
SA

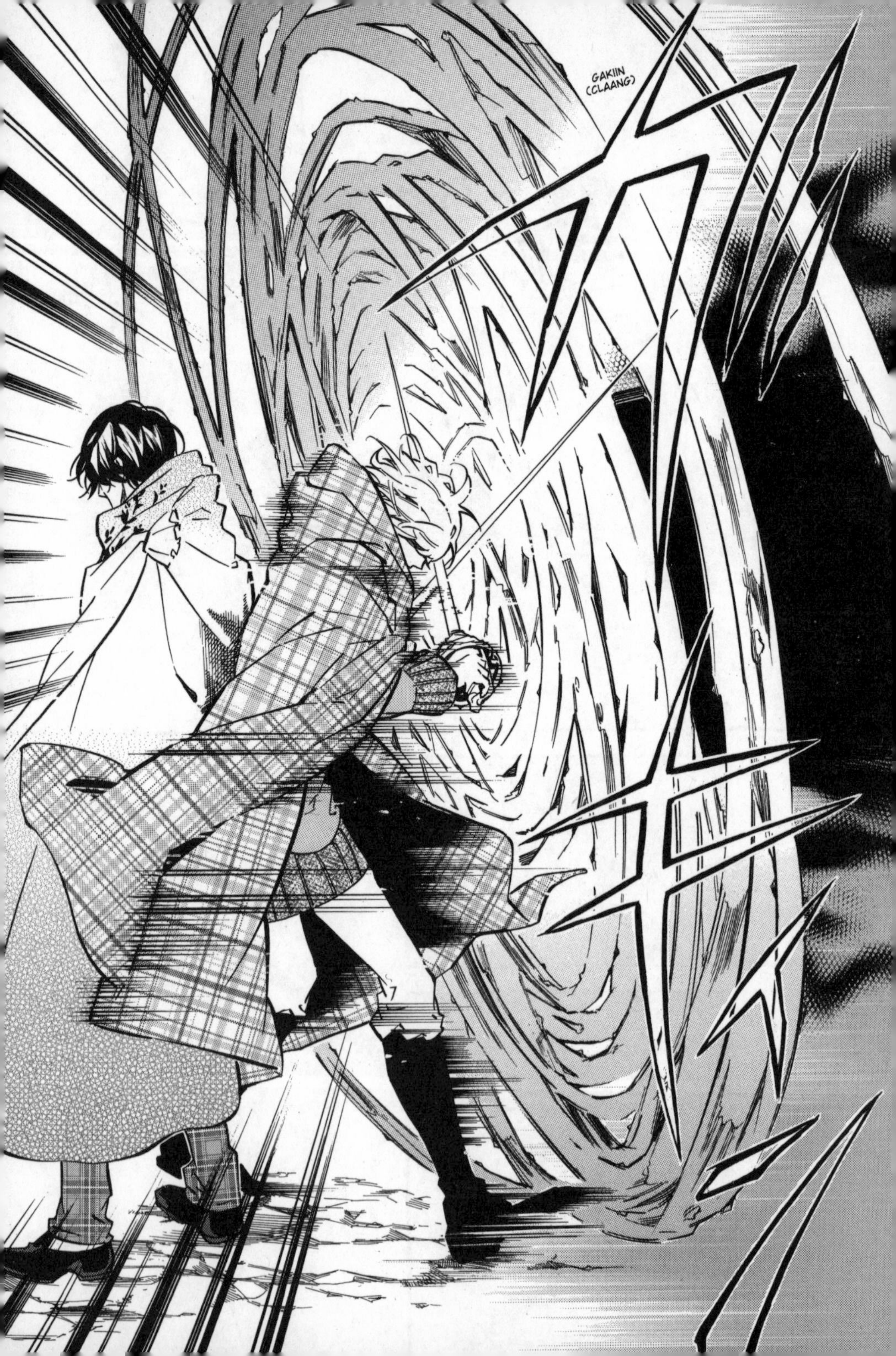
GAKIIN (CLAANG)

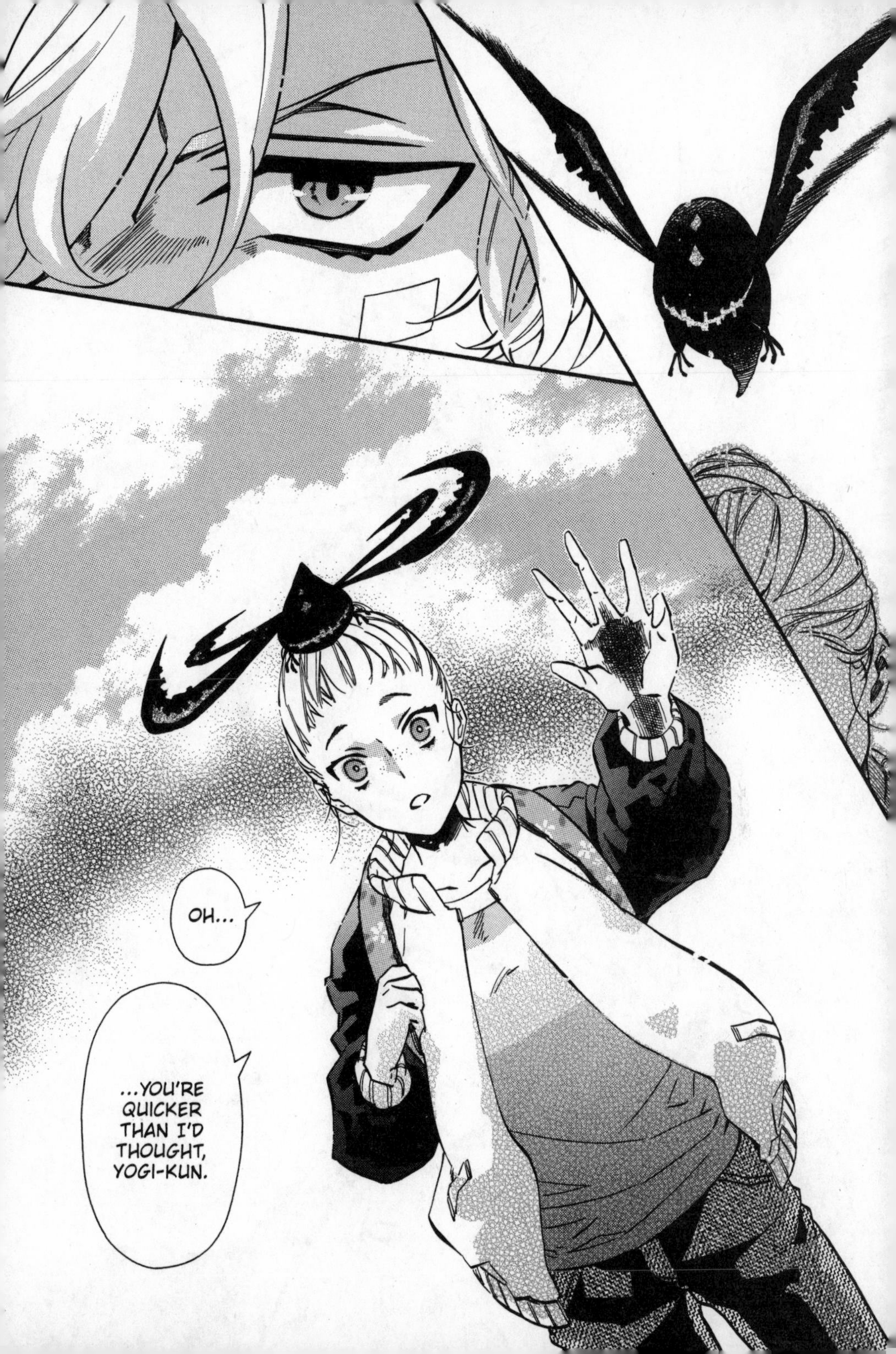
OH...
...YOU'RE QUICKER THAN I'D THOUGHT, YOGI-KUN.

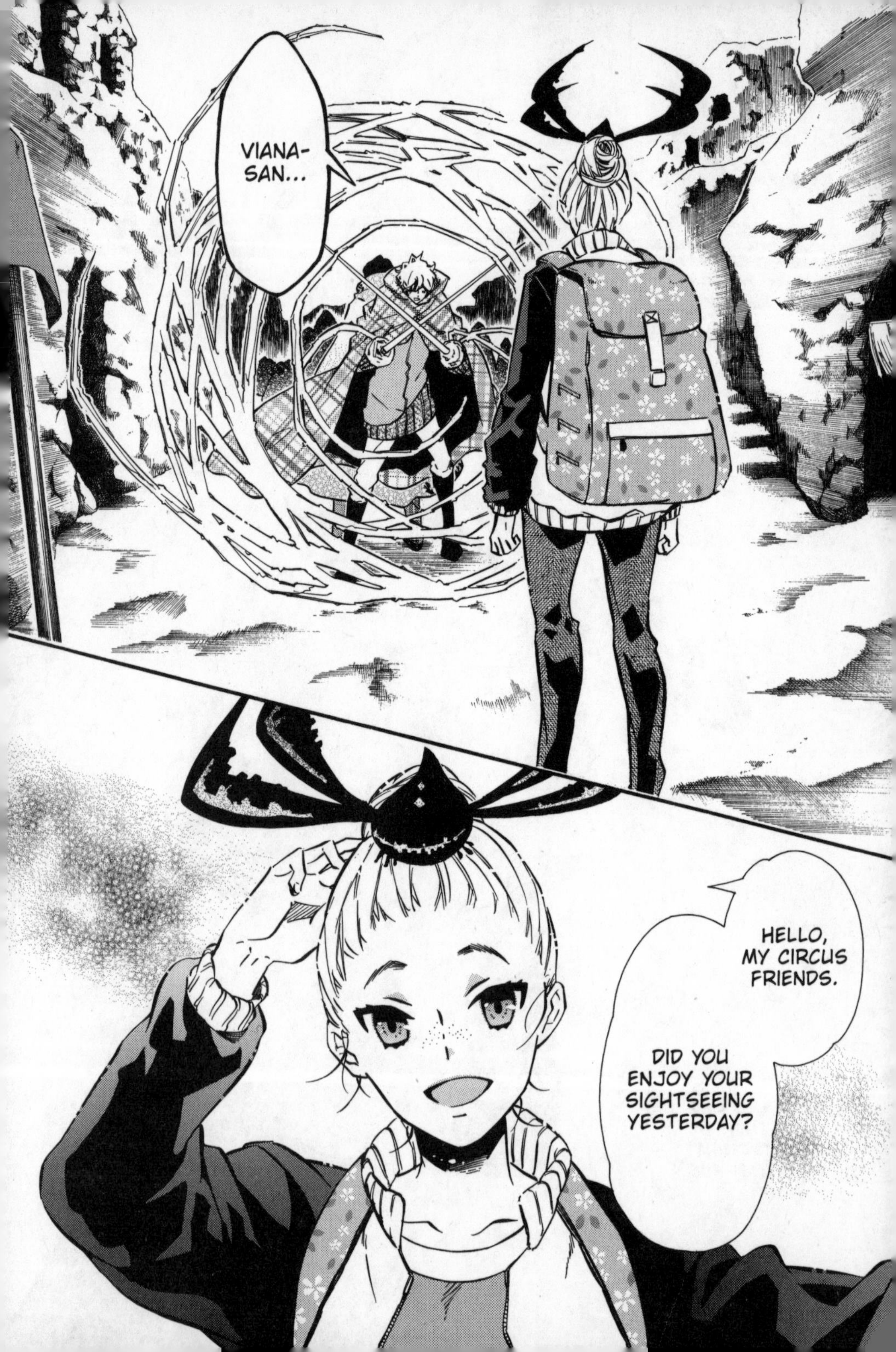
VIANA-
SAN...
HELLO,
MY CIRCUS
FRIENDS.
DID YOU
ENJOY YOUR
SIGHTSEEING
YESTERDAY?

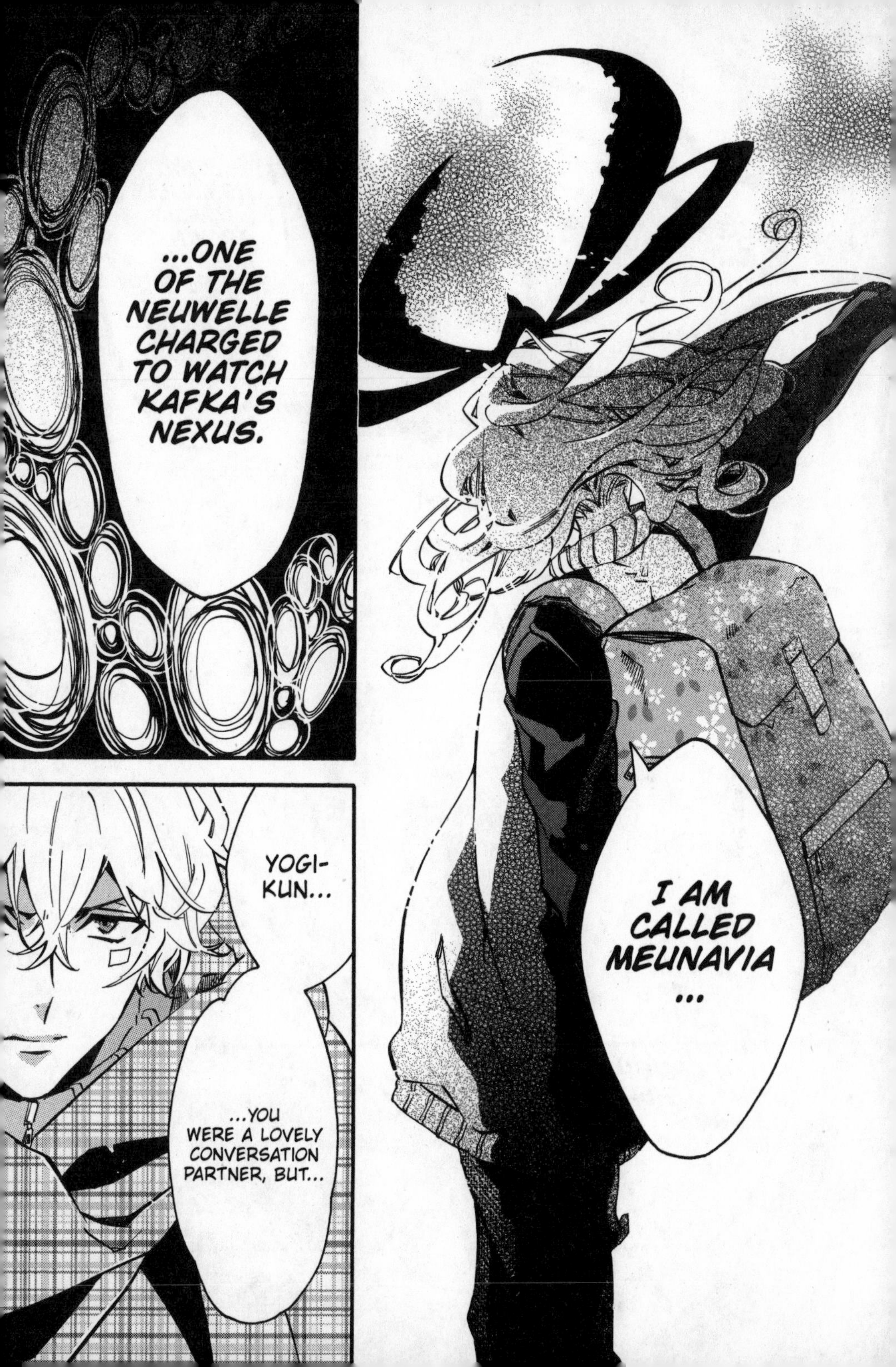
I AM CALLED MEUNAVIA ...
...ONE OF THE NEUWELLE CHARGED TO WATCH KAFKA'S NEXUS.
YOGI-KUN...
...YOU WERE A LOVELY CONVERSATION PARTNER, BUT...

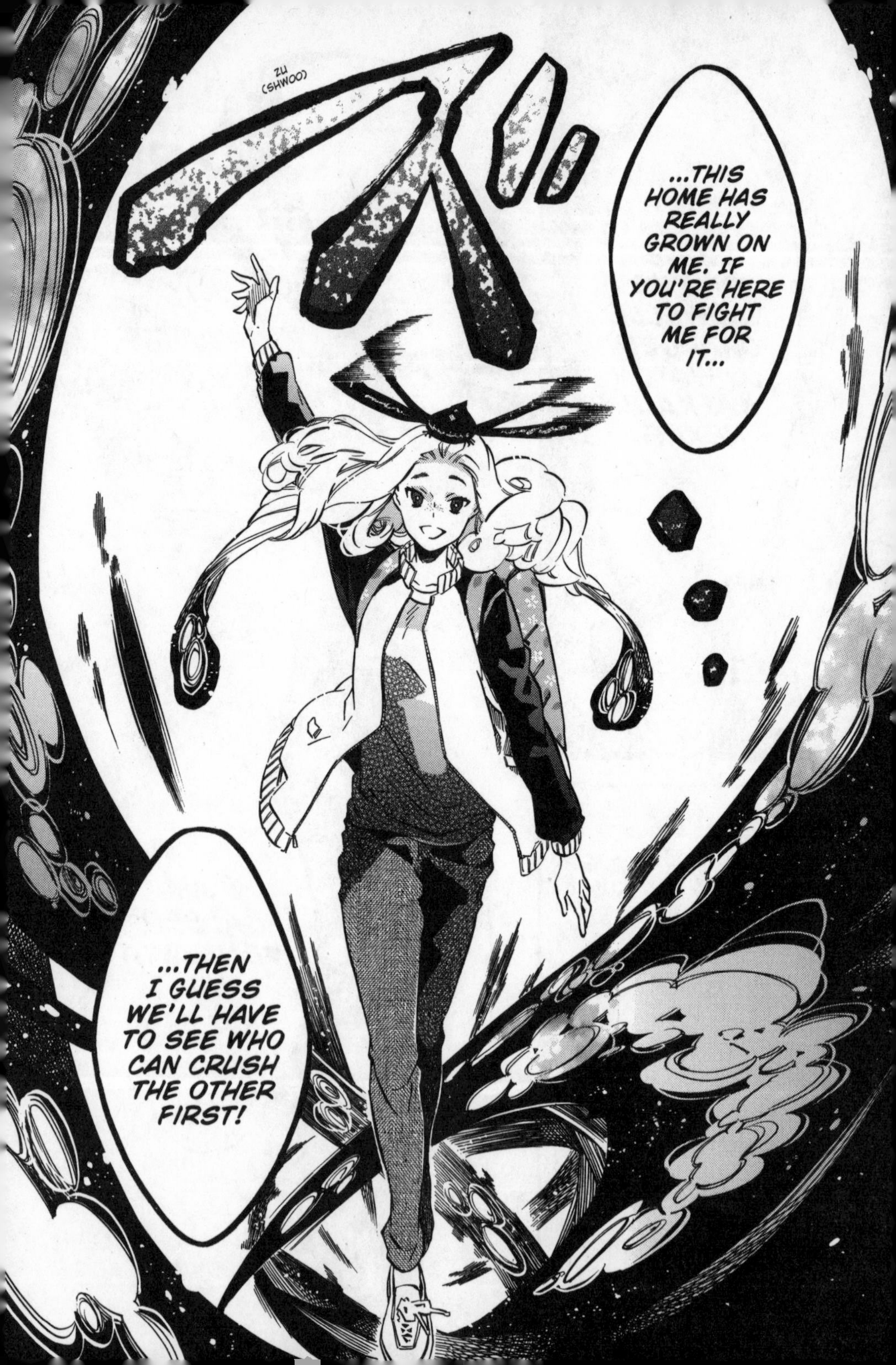
ZU (SHWOO)
...THIS HOME HAS REALLY GROWN ON ME. IF YOU'RE HERE TO FIGHT ME FOR IT...
...THEN I GUESS WE'LL HAVE TO SEE WHO CAN CRUSH THE OTHER FIRST!

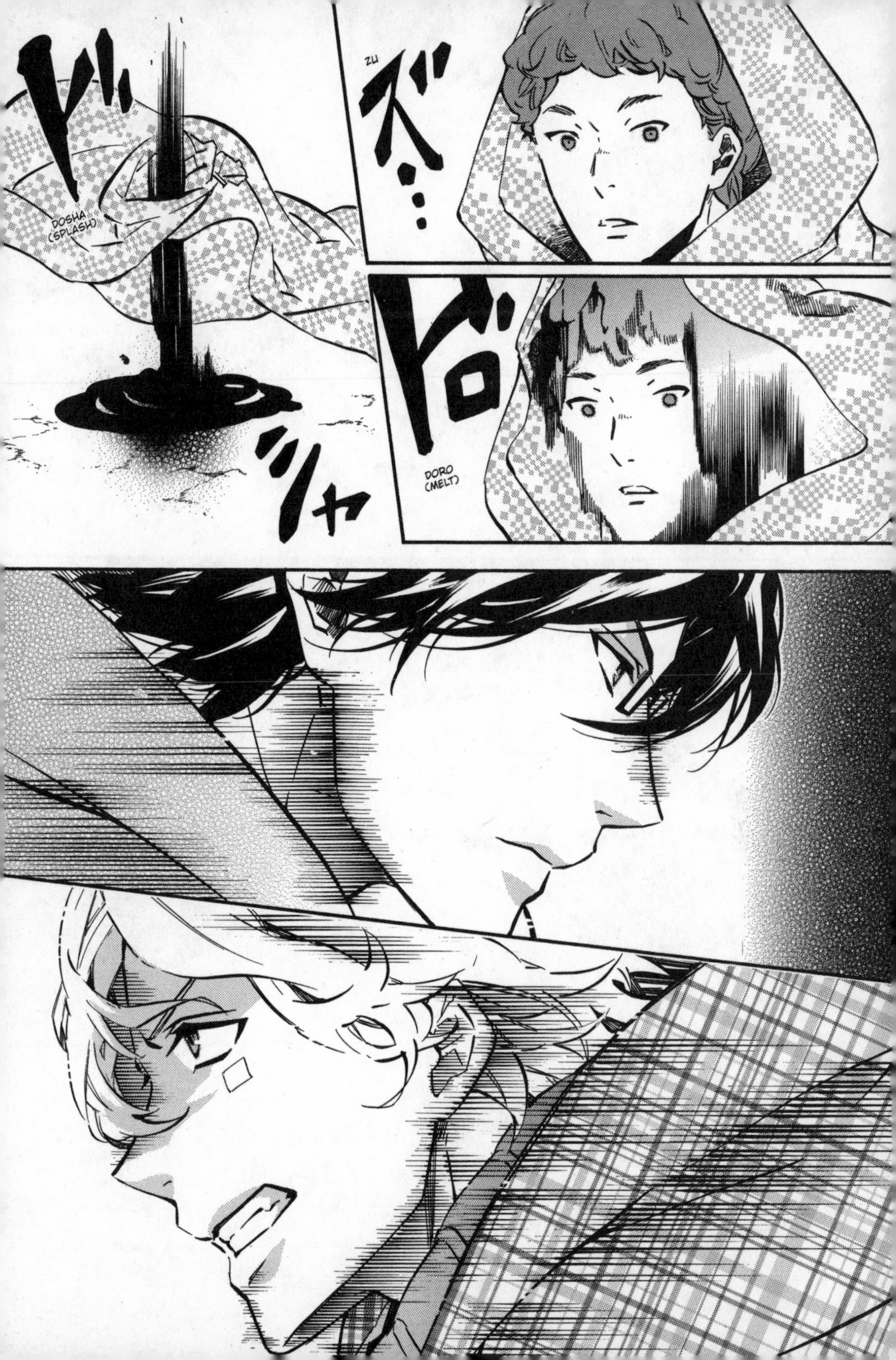
ズ…
ZU
ドロ
DORO (MELT)
ドシャ
DOSHA (SPLASH)

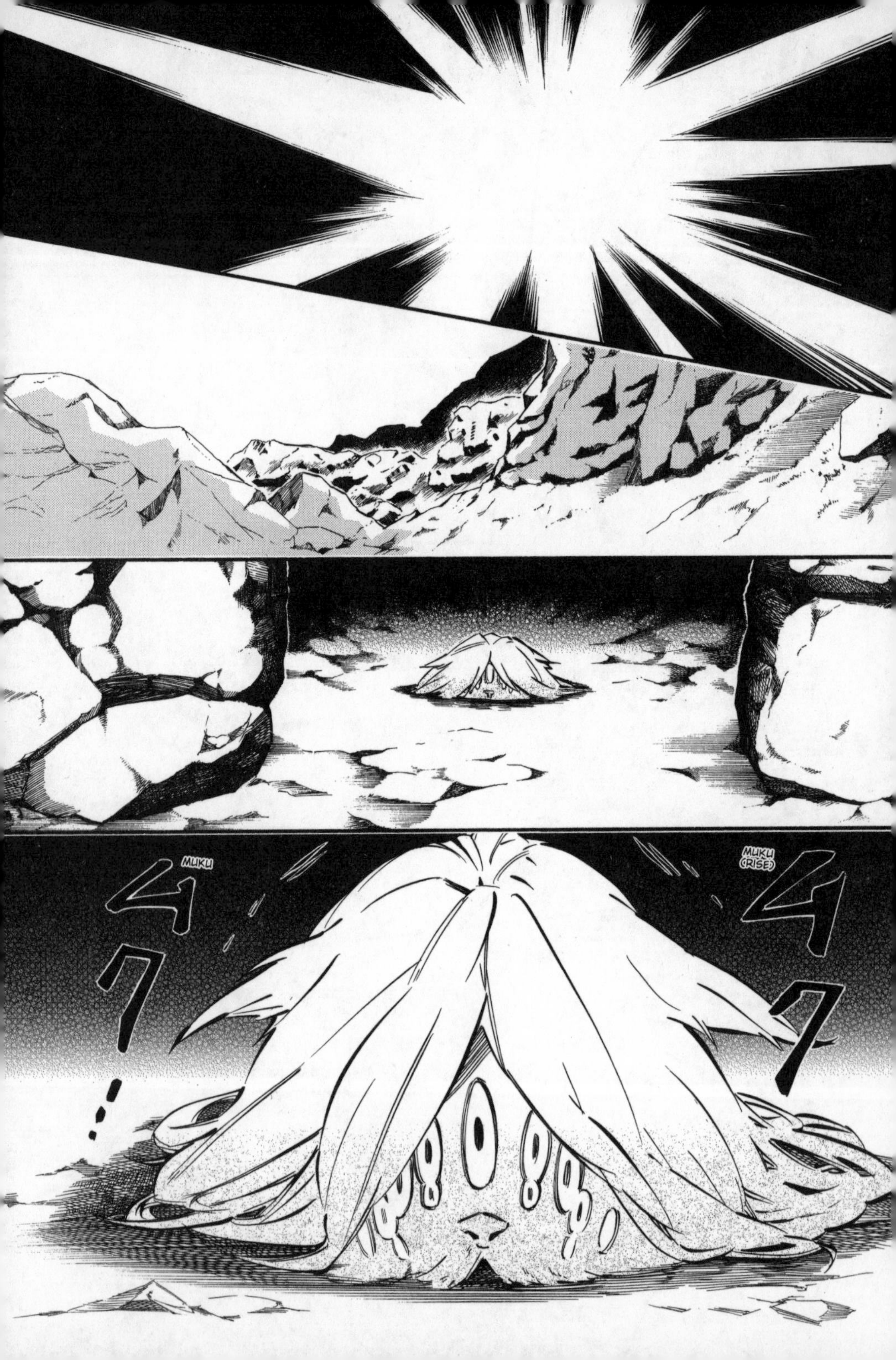
MUKU (RISE)
ムク
MUKU
ムク…

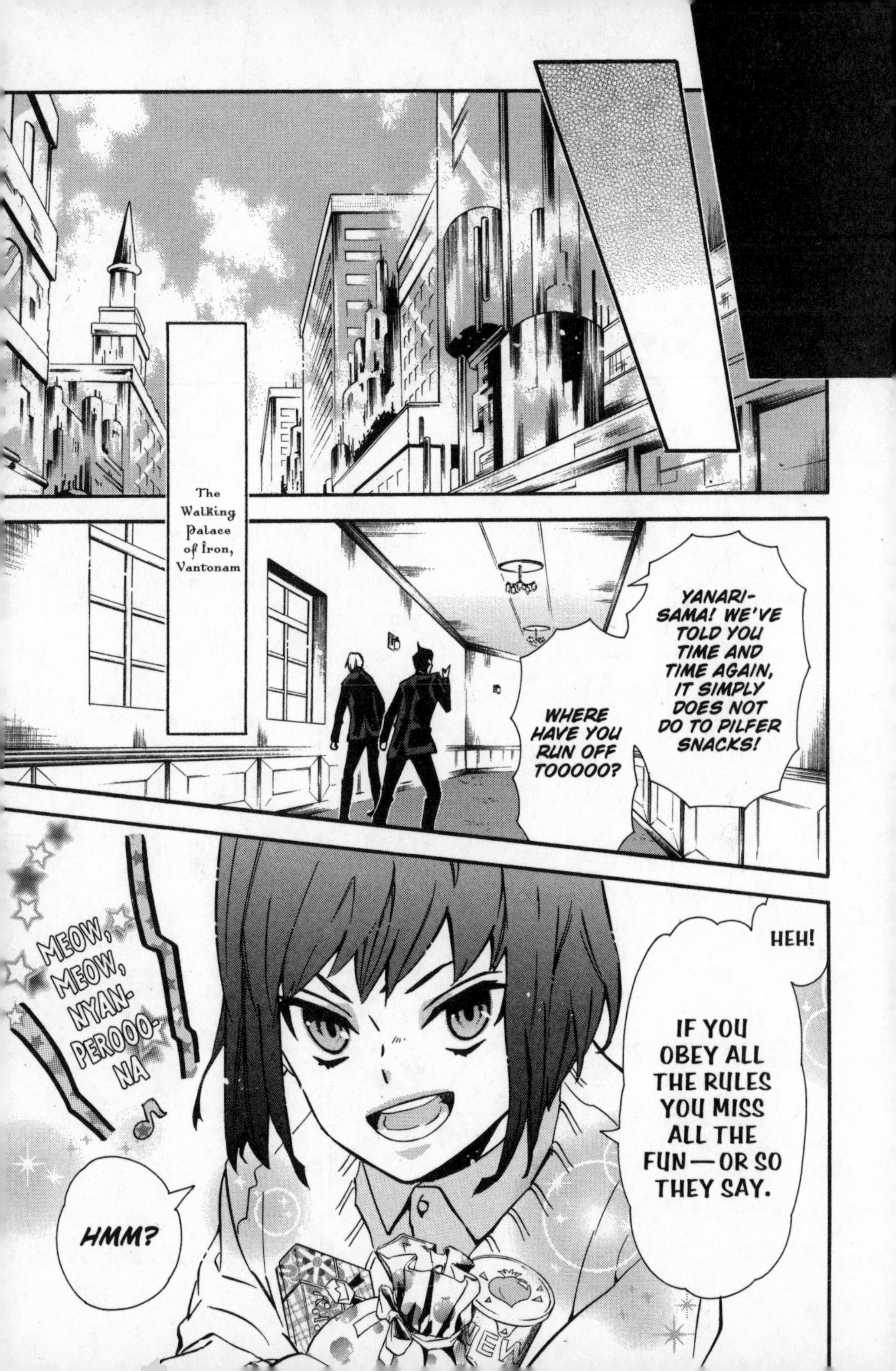
The Walking Palace of Iron, Vantonam
YANARI-SAMA! WE'VE TOLD YOU TIME AND TIME AGAIN, IT SIMPLY DOES NOT DO TO PILFER SNACKS!
WHERE HAVE YOU RUN OFF TOOOOO?
HEH!
IF YOU OBEY ALL THE RULES YOU MISS ALL THE FUN—OR SO THEY SAY.
MEOW, MEOW, NYAN-PEROOO-NA
HMM?

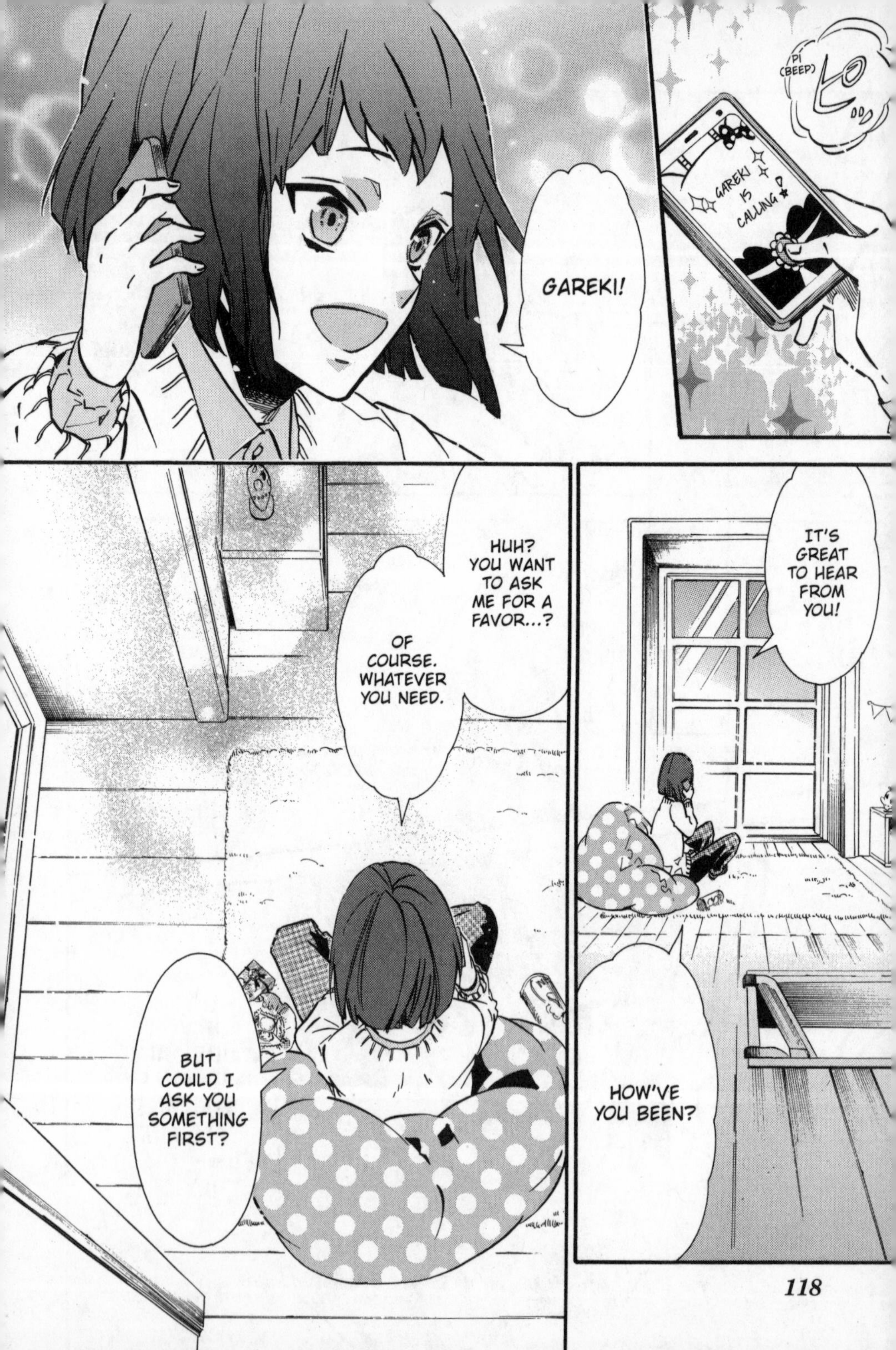
PI (BEEP)
GAREKI IS CALLING
GAREKI!
IT'S GREAT TO HEAR FROM YOU!
HOW'VE YOU BEEN?
HUH? YOU WANT TO ASK ME FOR A FAVOR...?
OF COURSE. WHATEVER YOU NEED.
BUT COULD I ASK YOU SOMETHING FIRST?

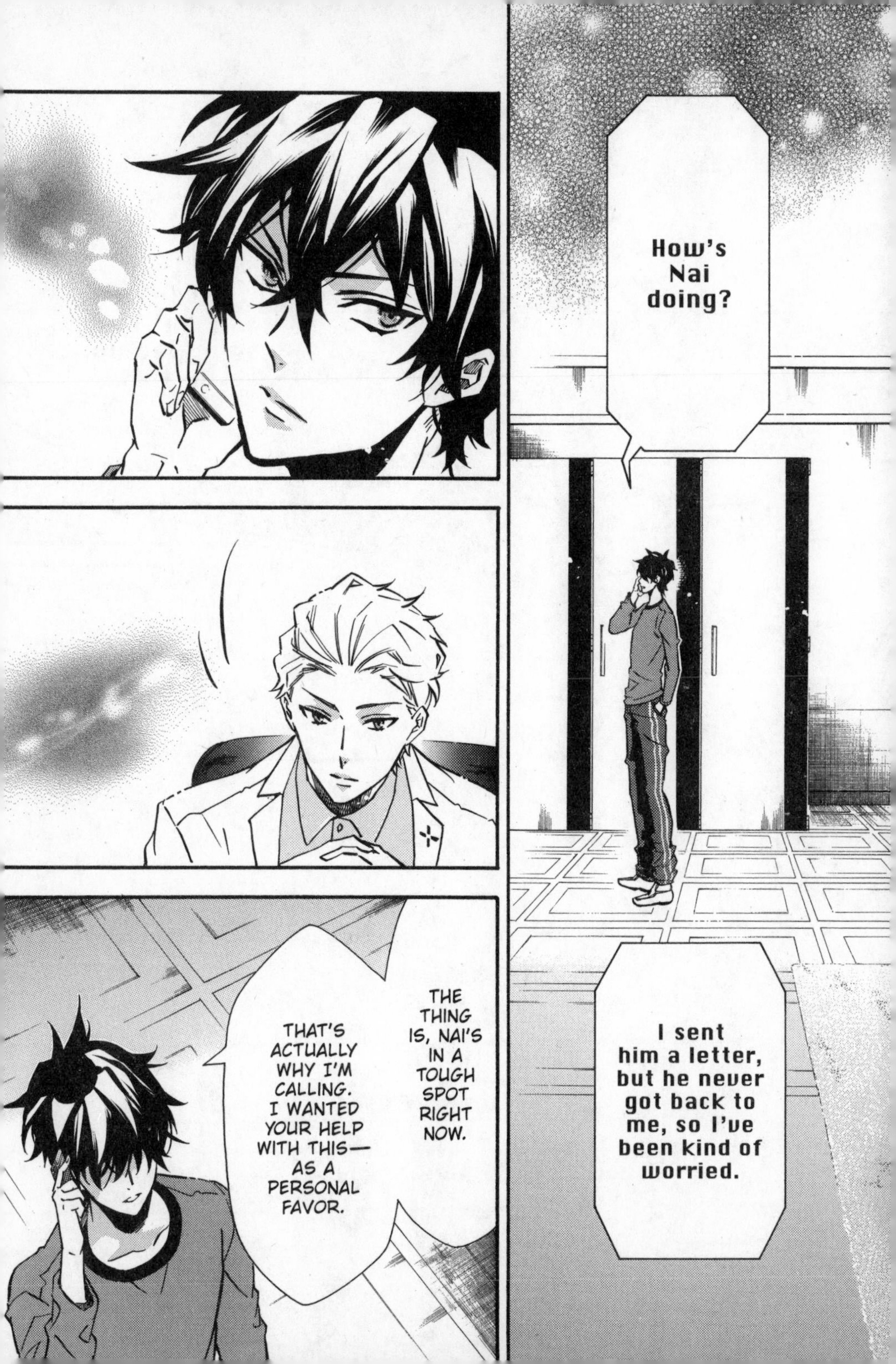
How's Nai doing?
I sent him a letter, but he never got back to me, so I've been kind of worried.
THE THING IS, NAI'S IN A TOUGH SPOT RIGHT NOW.
THAT'S ACTUALLY WHY I'M CALLING. I WANTED YOUR HELP WITH THIS— AS A PERSONAL FAVOR.

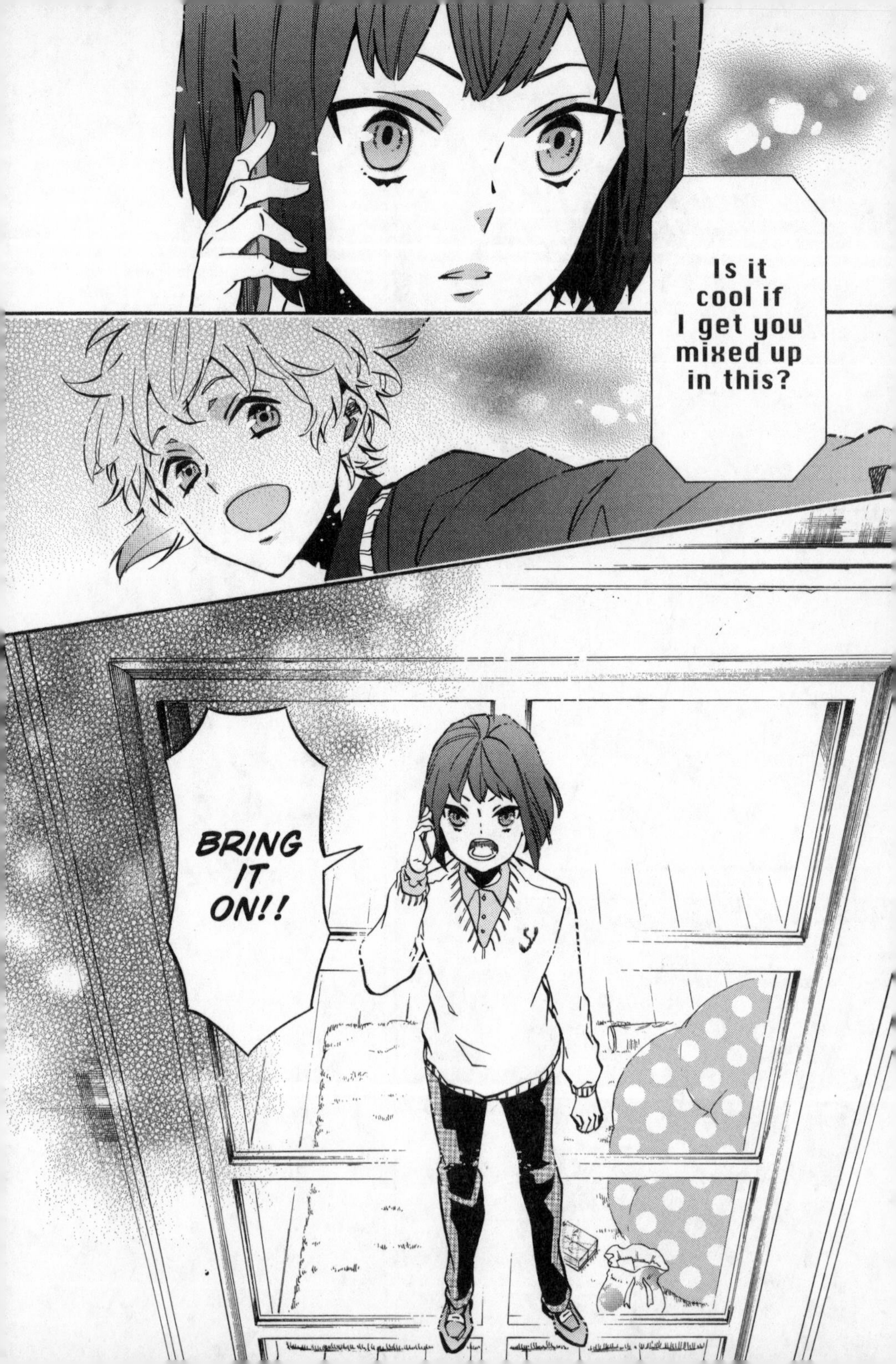
Is it cool if I get you mixed up in this?
BRING IT ON!!

KARNEVAL

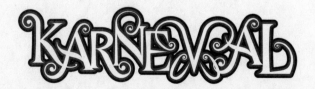

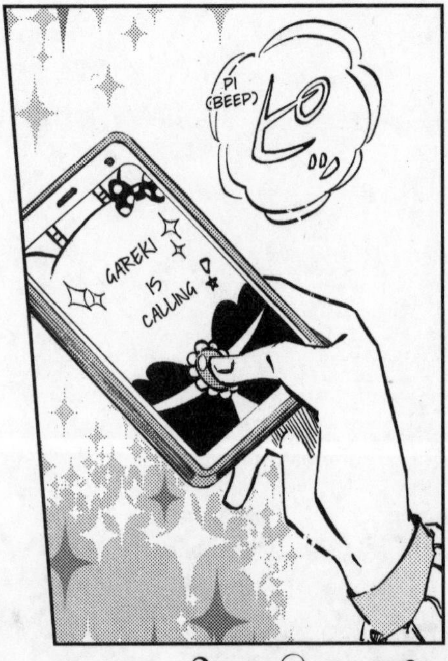
PI
(BEEP)
GAREKI IS CALLING

KARNEVAL

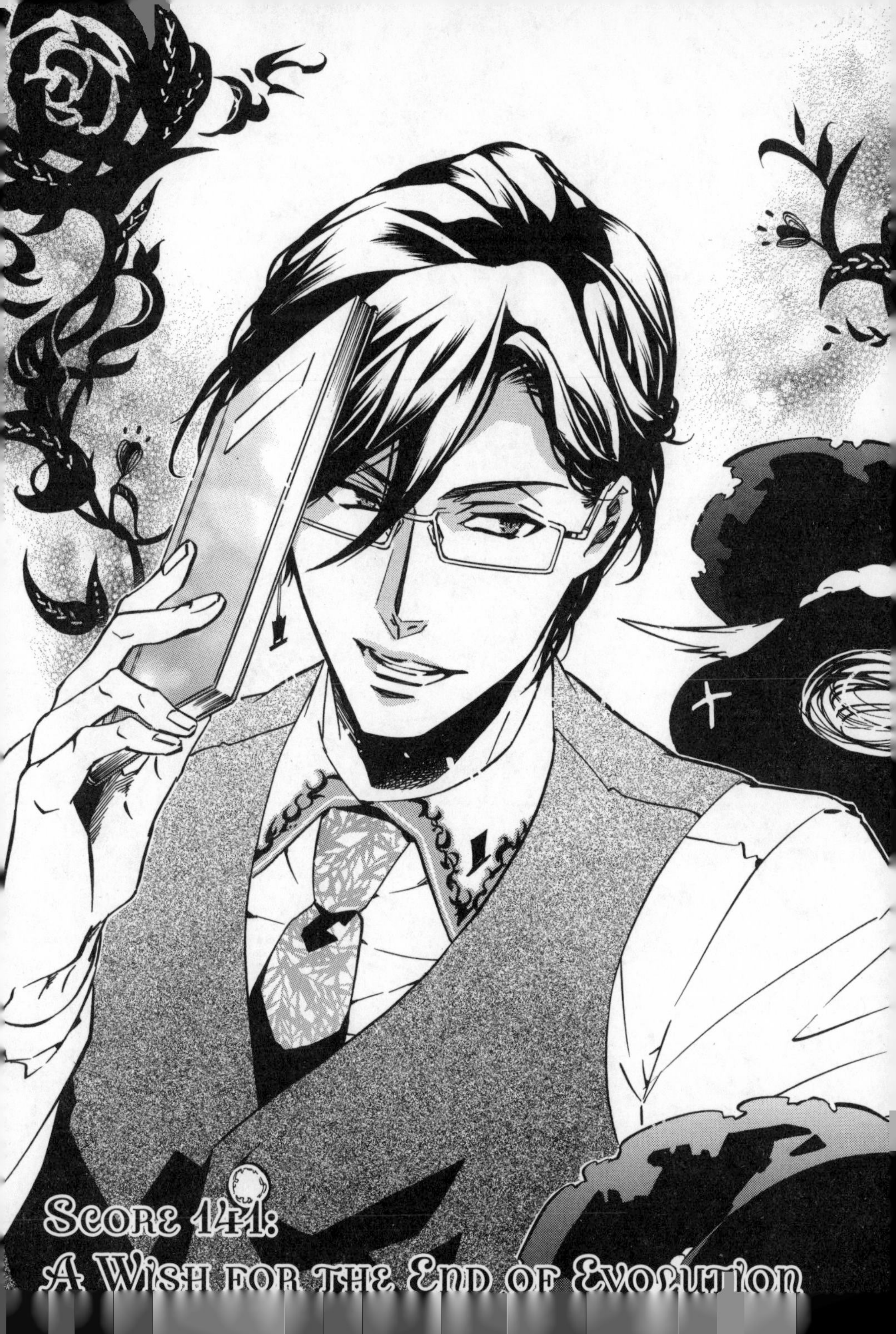

Score 141: A Wish for the End of Evolution

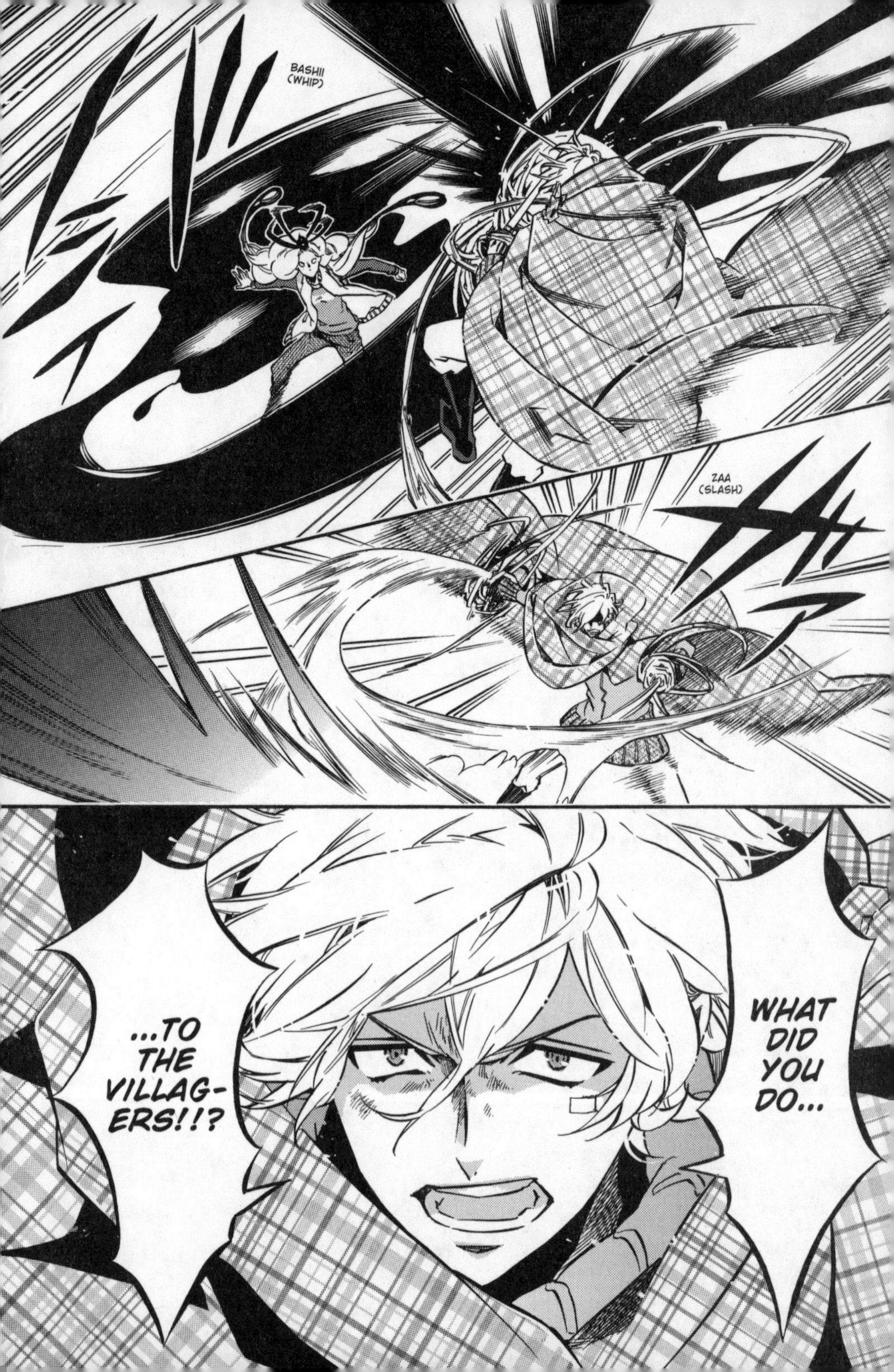
BASHII (WHIP)
ZAA (SLASH)
WHAT DID YOU DO...
...TO THE VILLAGERS!!?

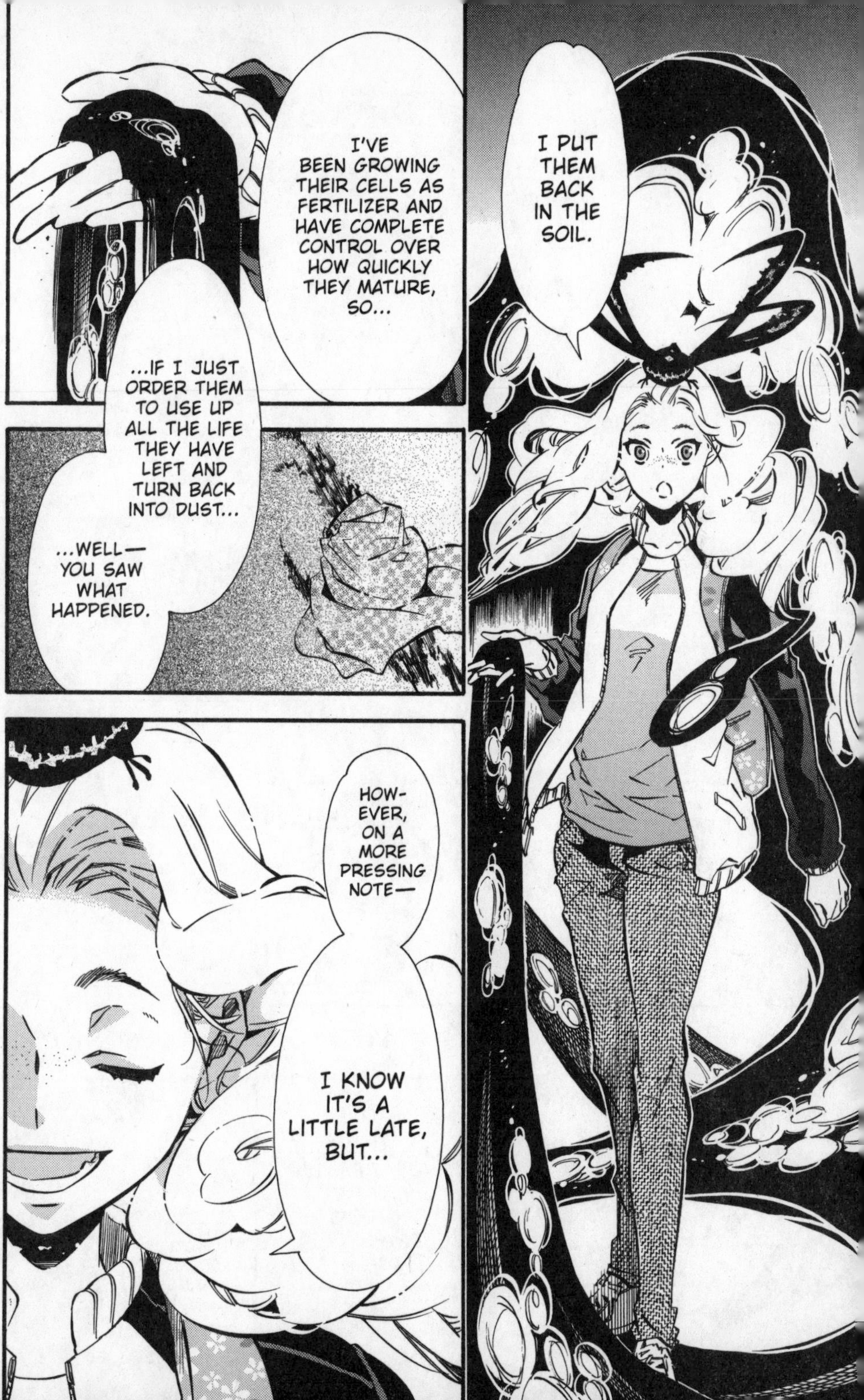
I PUT THEM BACK IN THE SOIL.
I'VE BEEN GROWING THEIR CELLS AS FERTILIZER AND HAVE COMPLETE CONTROL OVER HOW QUICKLY THEY MATURE, SO...
...IF I JUST ORDER THEM TO USE UP ALL THE LIFE THEY HAVE LEFT AND TURN BACK INTO DUST...
...WELL— YOU SAW WHAT HAPPENED.
HOW-EVER, ON A MORE PRESSING NOTE—
I KNOW IT'S A LITTLE LATE, BUT...

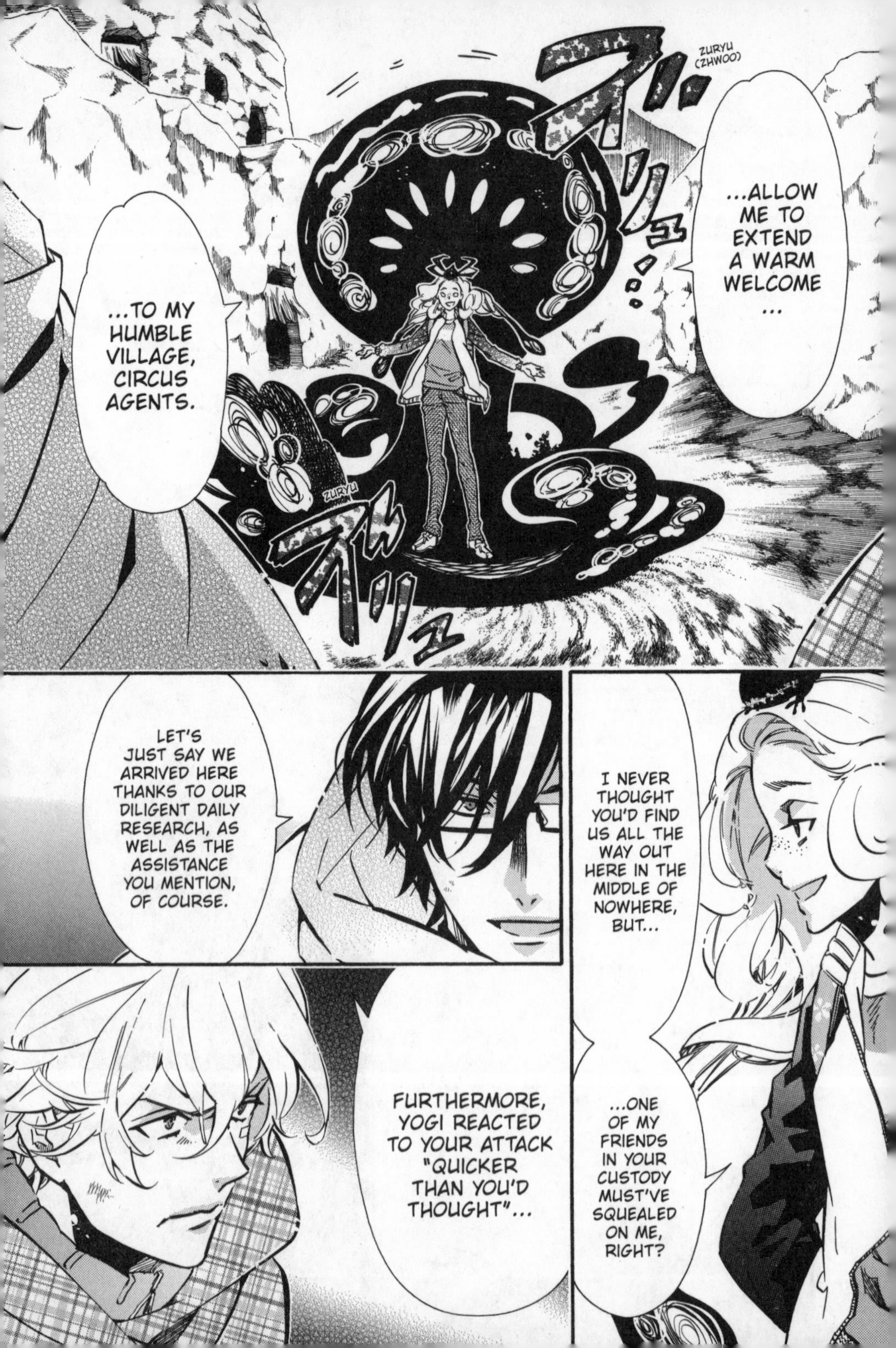
ZURYU (ZHWOO)
...ALLOW ME TO EXTEND A WARM WELCOME...
...TO MY HUMBLE VILLAGE, CIRCUS AGENTS.
ZURYU
I NEVER THOUGHT YOU'D FIND US ALL THE WAY OUT HERE IN THE MIDDLE OF NOWHERE, BUT...
...ONE OF MY FRIENDS IN YOUR CUSTODY MUST'VE SQUEALED ON ME, RIGHT?
LET'S JUST SAY WE ARRIVED HERE THANKS TO OUR DILIGENT DAILY RESEARCH, AS WELL AS THE ASSISTANCE YOU MENTION, OF COURSE.
FURTHERMORE, YOGI REACTED TO YOUR ATTACK "QUICKER THAN YOU'D THOUGHT"...

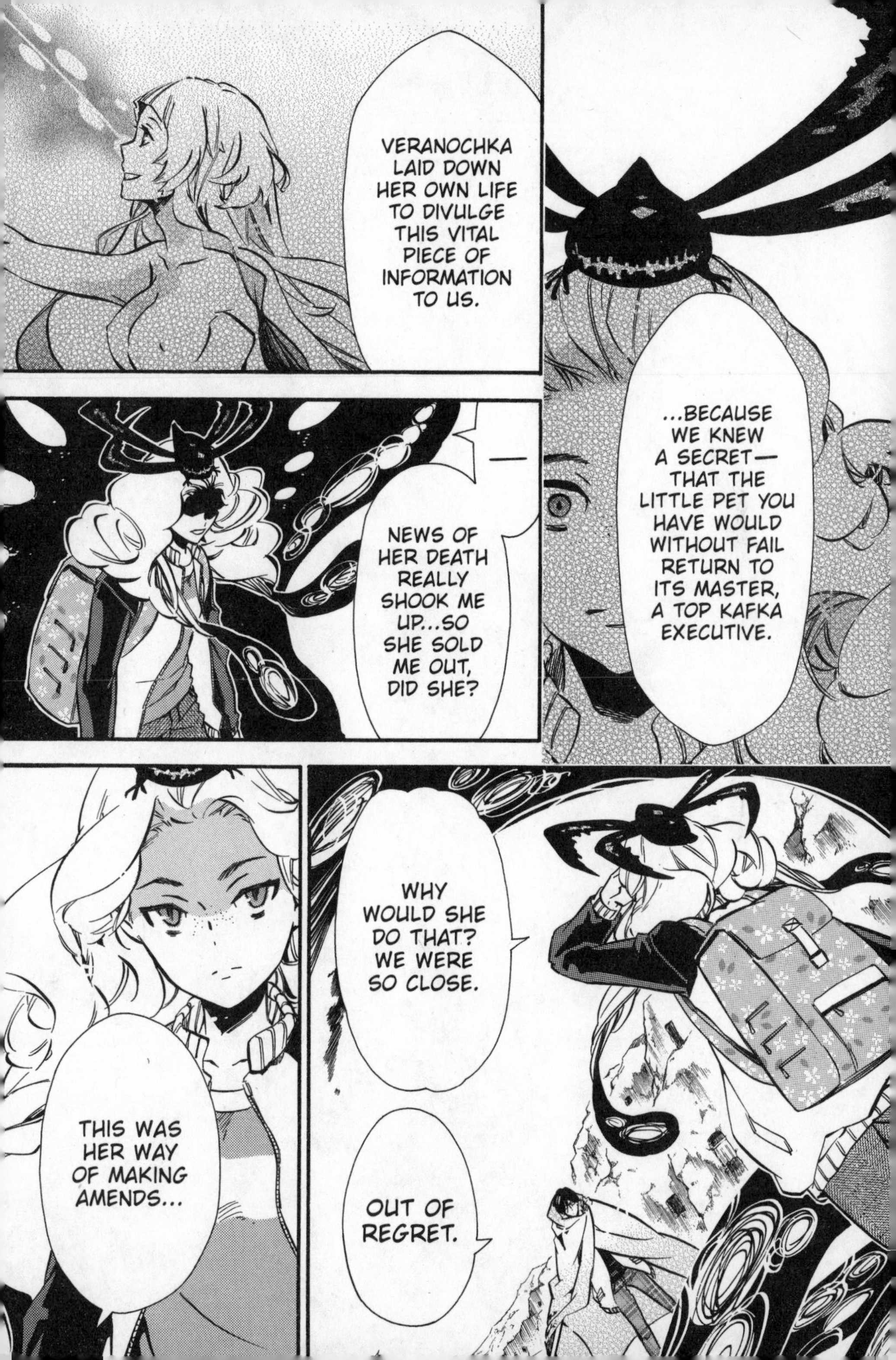

...BECAUSE WE KNEW A SECRET—THAT THE LITTLE PET YOU HAVE WOULD WITHOUT FAIL RETURN TO ITS MASTER, A TOP KAFKA EXECUTIVE.
VERANOCHKA LAID DOWN HER OWN LIFE TO DIVULGE THIS VITAL PIECE OF INFORMATION TO US.
—
NEWS OF HER DEATH REALLY SHOOK ME UP...SO SHE SOLD ME OUT, DID SHE?
WHY WOULD SHE DO THAT? WE WERE SO CLOSE.
OUT OF REGRET.
THIS WAS HER WAY OF MAKING AMENDS...

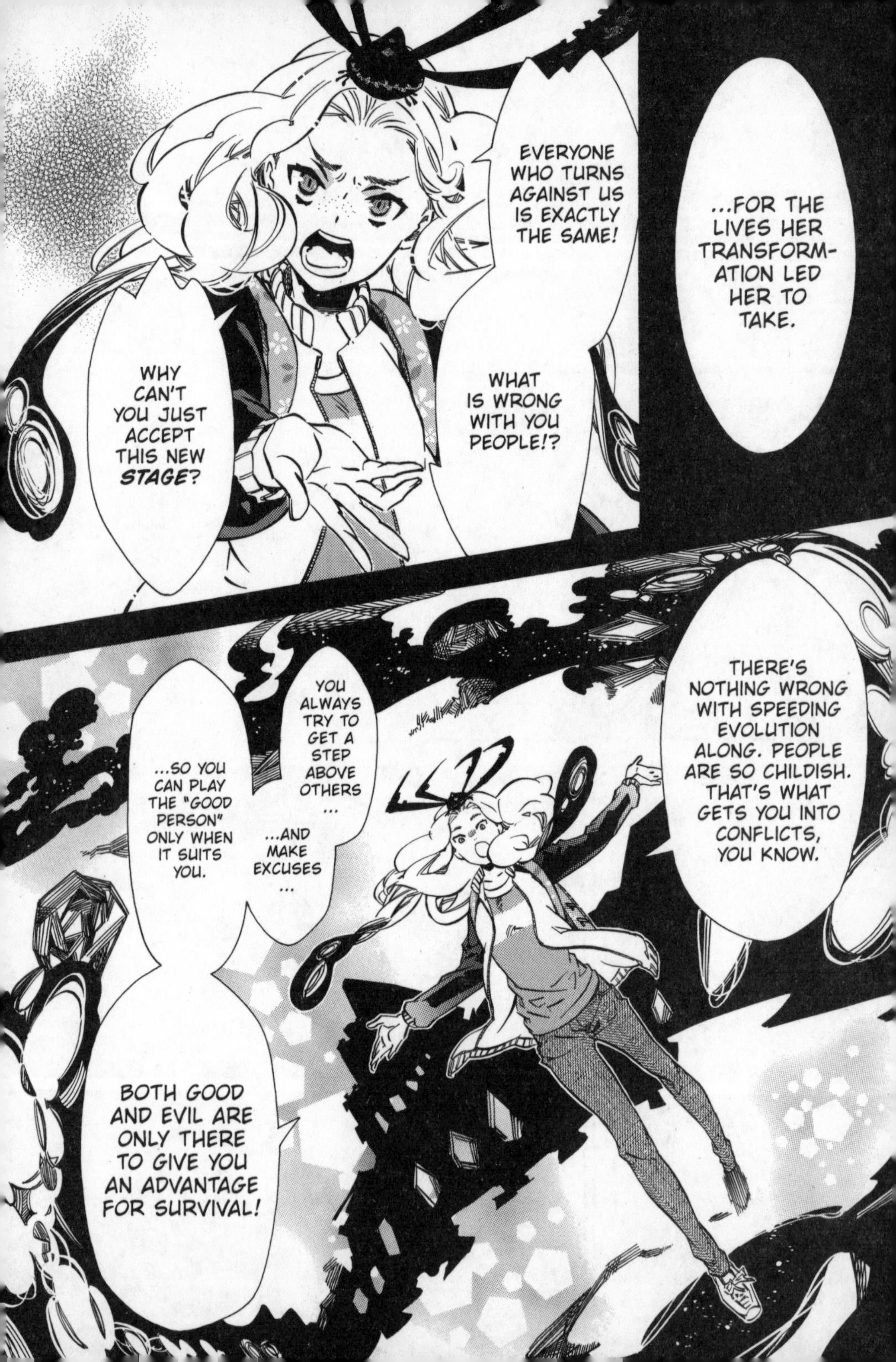
...FOR THE LIVES HER TRANSFORMATION LED HER TO TAKE.
EVERYONE WHO TURNS AGAINST US IS EXACTLY THE SAME!
WHAT IS WRONG WITH YOU PEOPLE!?
WHY CAN'T YOU JUST ACCEPT THIS NEW *STAGE*?
THERE'S NOTHING WRONG WITH SPEEDING EVOLUTION ALONG. PEOPLE ARE SO CHILDISH. THAT'S WHAT GETS YOU INTO CONFLICTS, YOU KNOW.
YOU ALWAYS TRY TO GET A STEP ABOVE OTHERS ...
...AND MAKE EXCUSES ...
...SO YOU CAN PLAY THE "GOOD PERSON" ONLY WHEN IT SUITS YOU.
BOTH GOOD AND EVIL ARE ONLY THERE TO GIVE YOU AN ADVANTAGE FOR SURVIVAL!

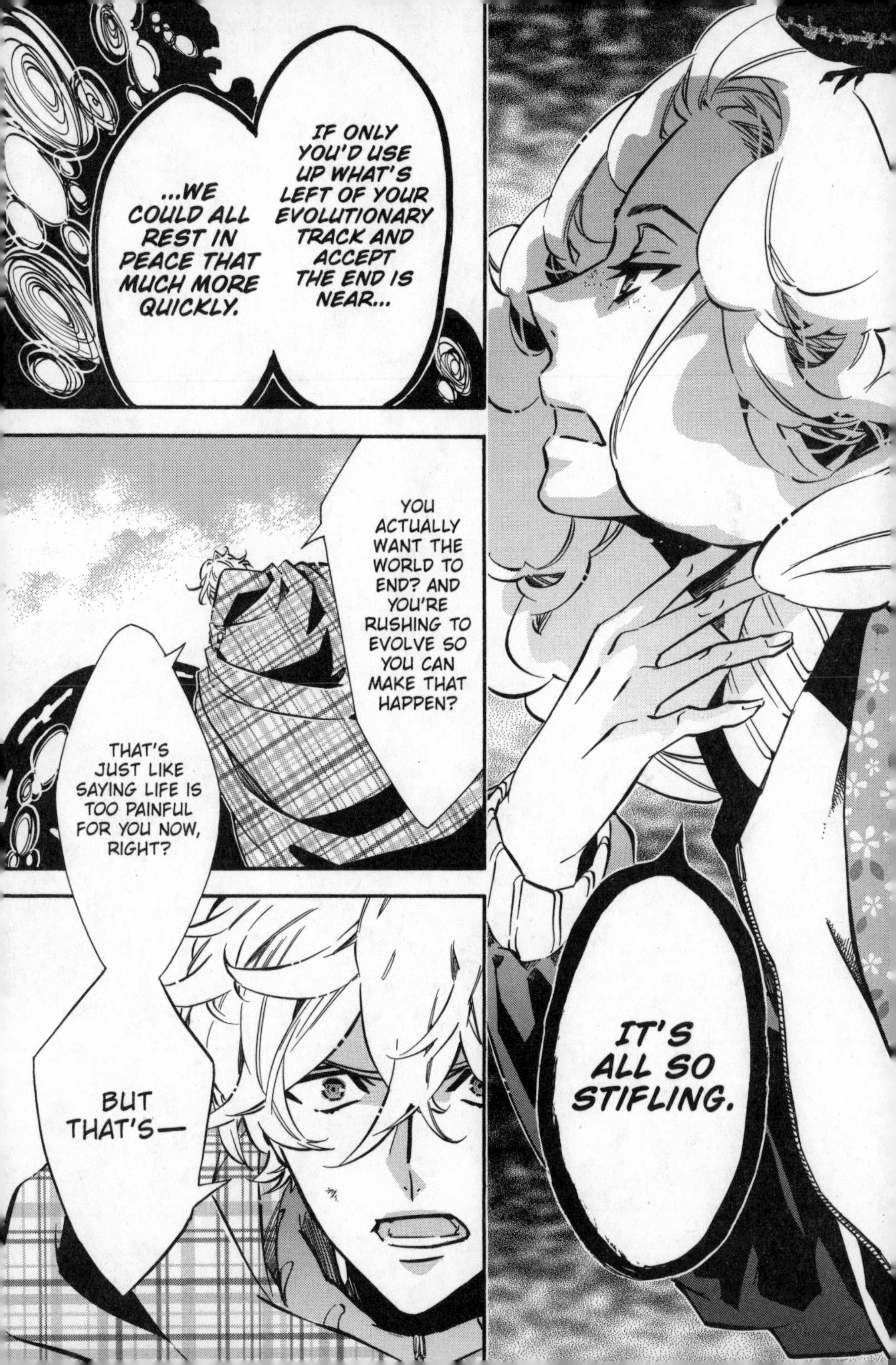
IT'S ALL SO STIFLING.
IF ONLY YOU'D USE UP WHAT'S LEFT OF YOUR EVOLUTIONARY TRACK AND ACCEPT THE END IS NEAR...
...WE COULD ALL REST IN PEACE THAT MUCH MORE QUICKLY.
YOU ACTUALLY WANT THE WORLD TO END? AND YOU'RE RUSHING TO EVOLVE SO YOU CAN MAKE THAT HAPPEN?
THAT'S JUST LIKE SAYING LIFE IS TOO PAINFUL FOR YOU NOW, RIGHT?
BUT THAT'S—

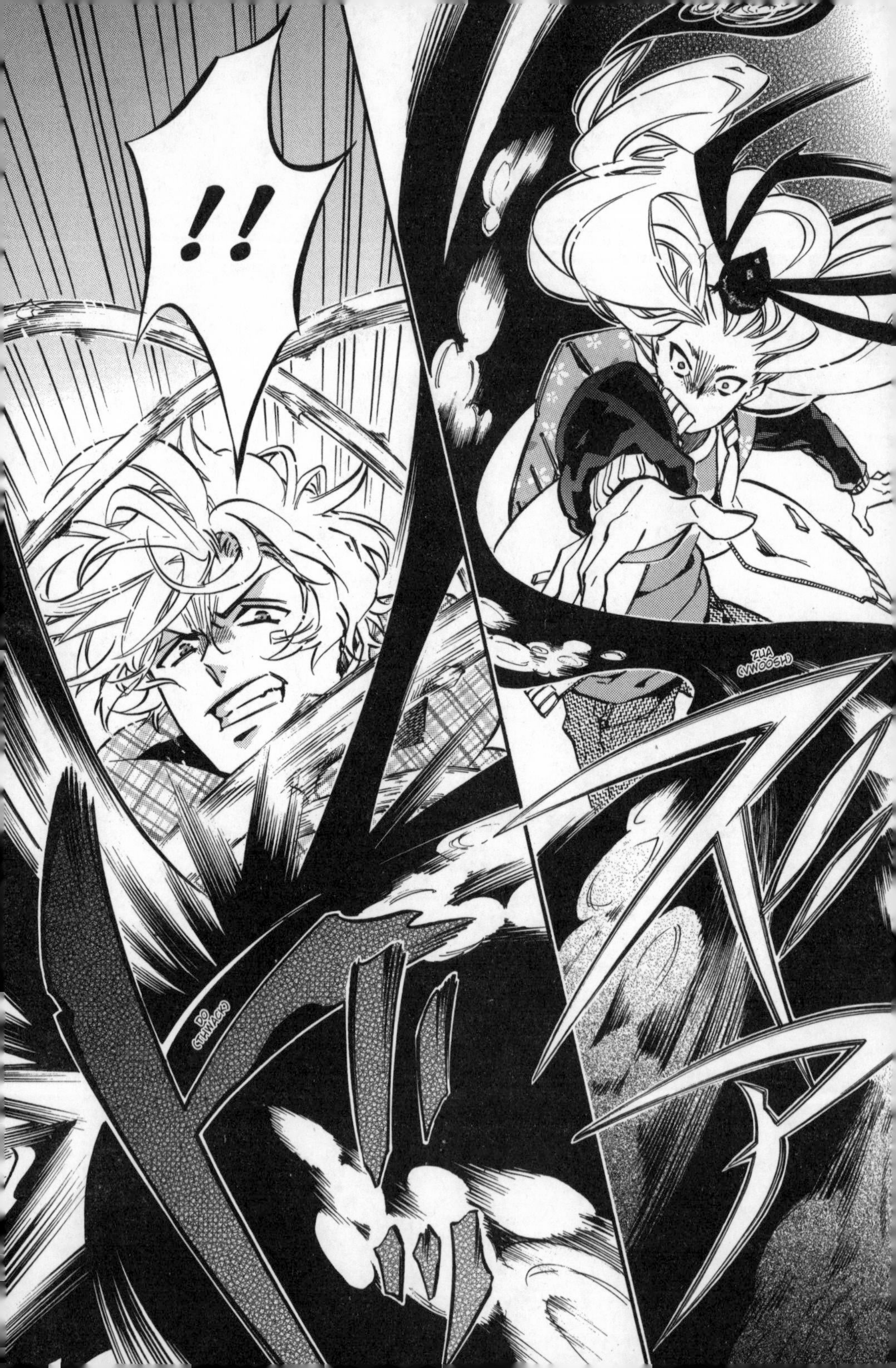
ZUA
(VWOOSH)
!!
DO
(THWACK)

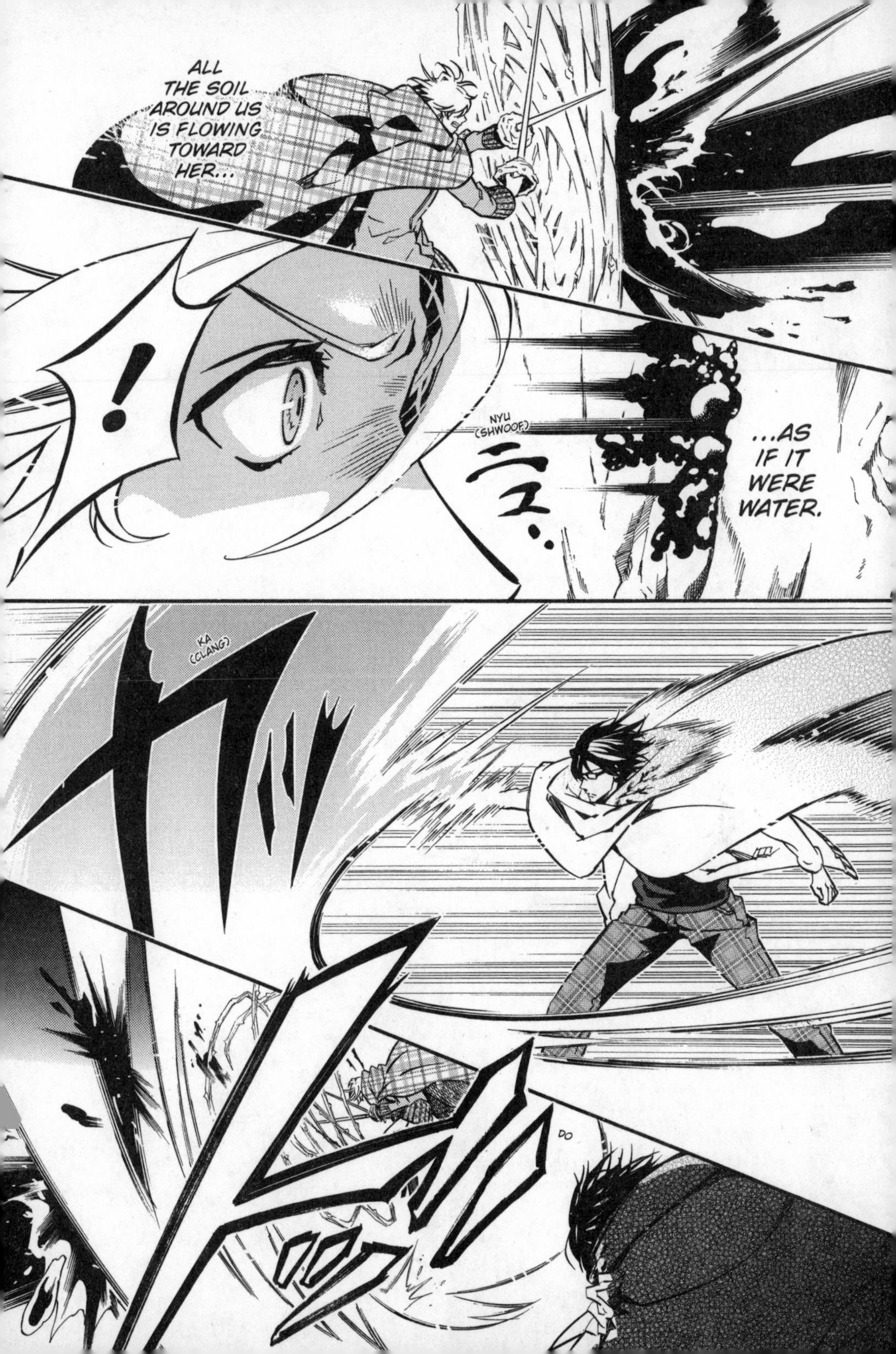

ALL THE SOIL AROUND US IS FLOWING TOWARD HER...
!
NYU (SHWOOF)
ニュ
...AS IF IT WERE WATER.
KA (CLANG)
DO

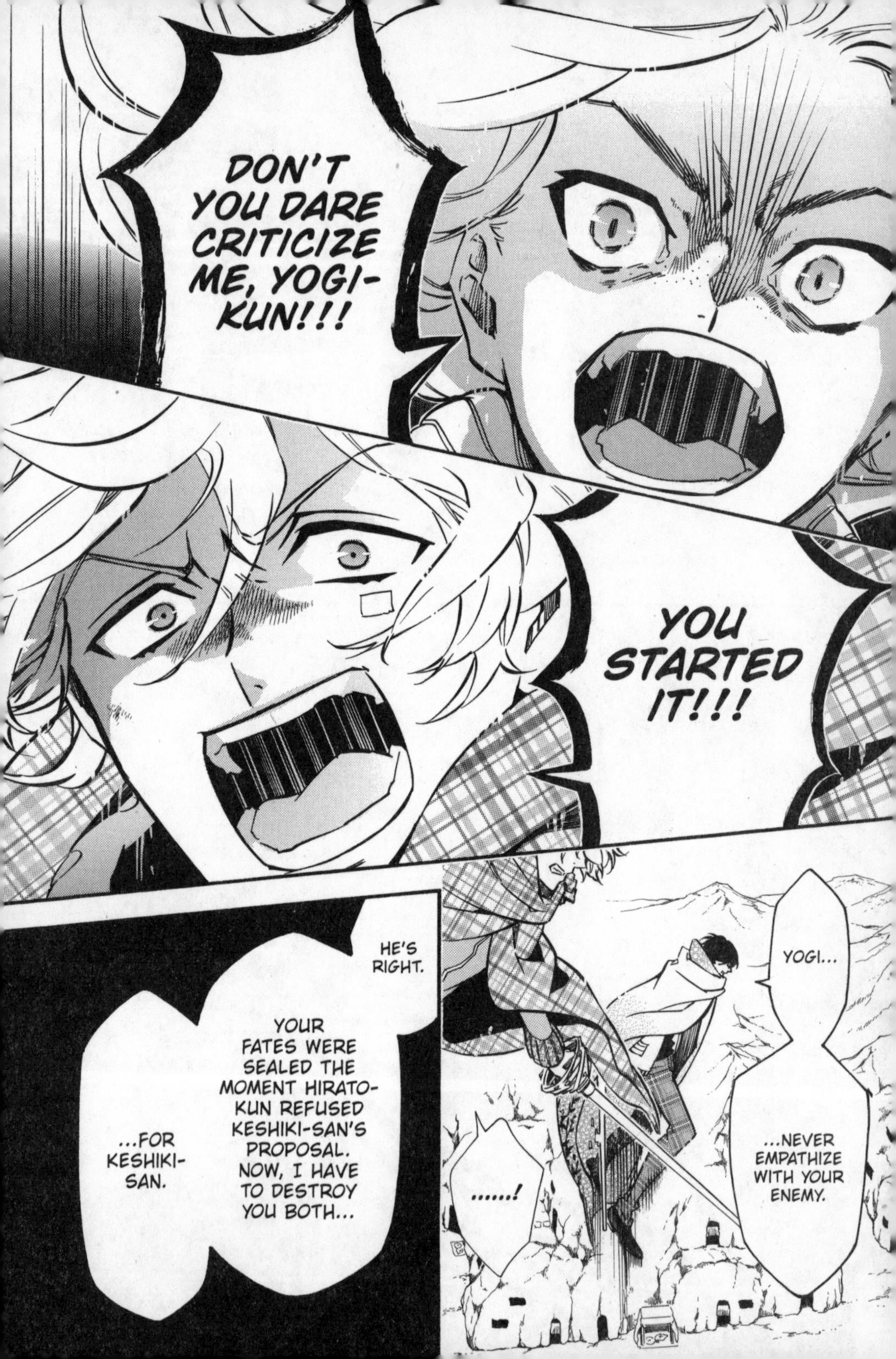
DON'T YOU DARE CRITICIZE ME, YOGI-KUN!!!
YOU STARTED IT!!!
YOGI...
...NEVER EMPATHIZE WITH YOUR ENEMY.
......!
HE'S RIGHT.
YOUR FATES WERE SEALED THE MOMENT HIRATO-KUN REFUSED KESHIKI-SAN'S PROPOSAL. NOW, I HAVE TO DESTROY YOU BOTH...
...FOR KESHIKI-SAN.

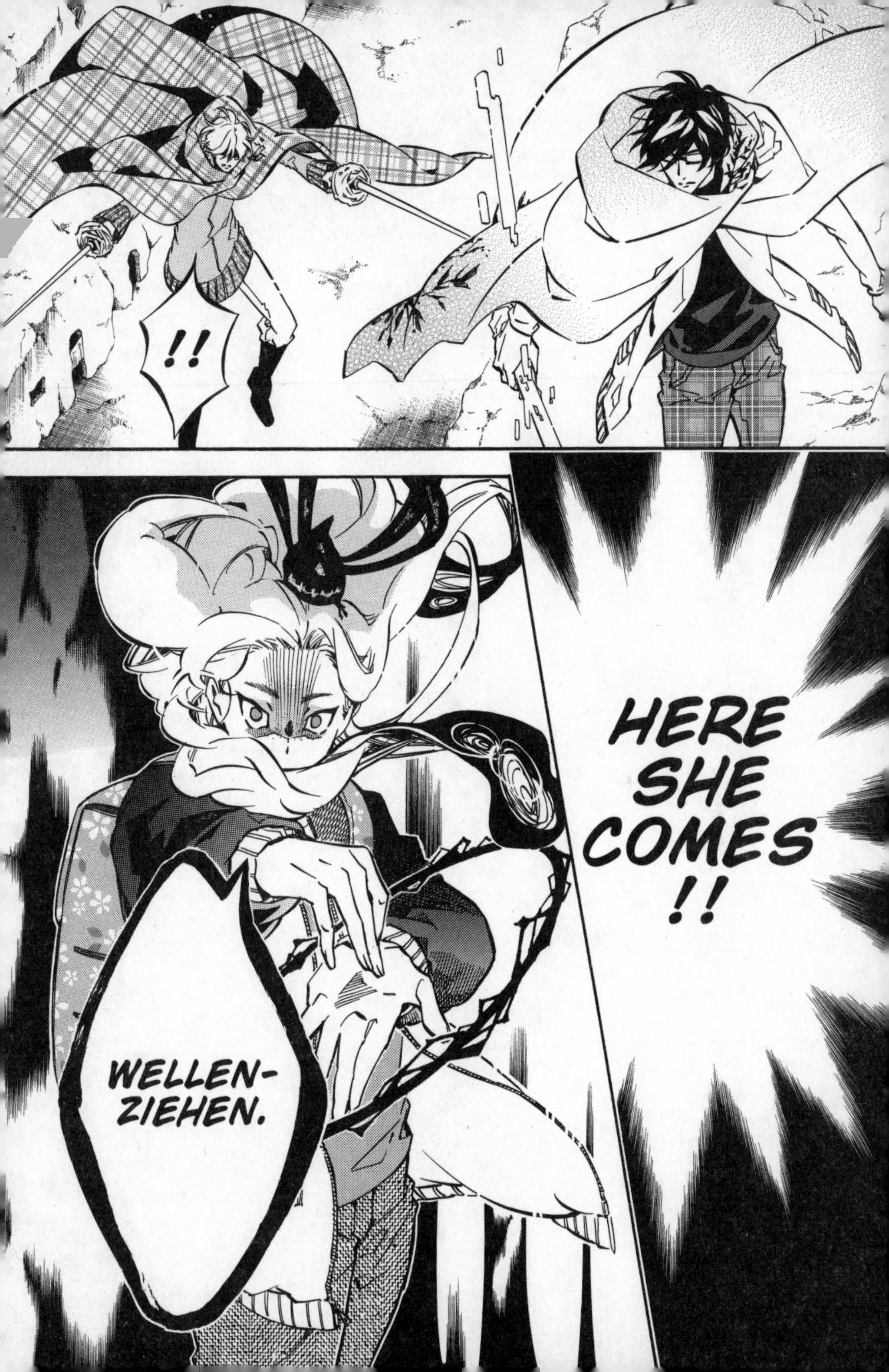
!!
HERE SHE COMES!!
WELLEN-ZIEHEN.

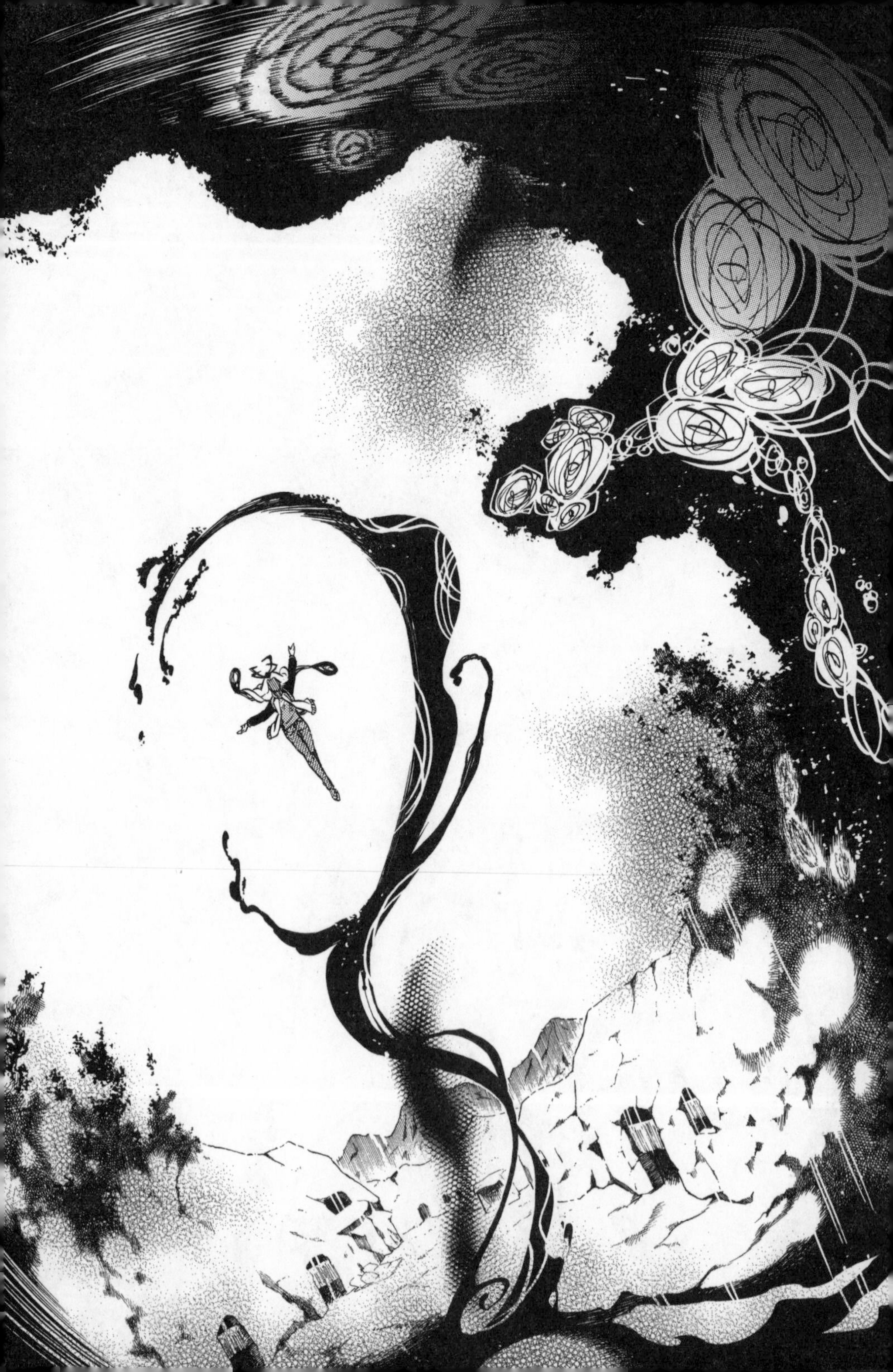

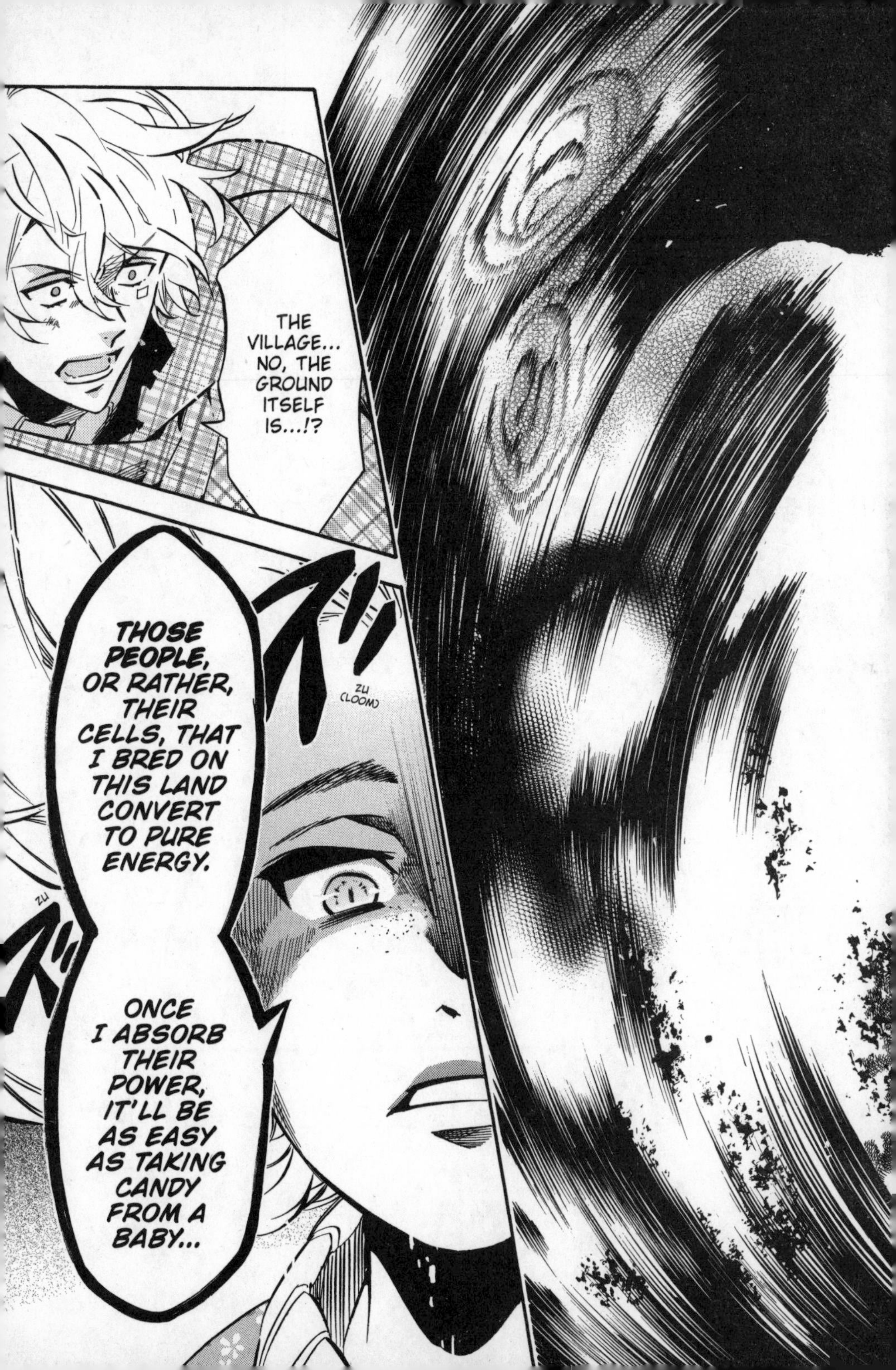
THE VILLAGE... NO, THE GROUND ITSELF IS...!?
ZU (LOOM)
THOSE PEOPLE, OR RATHER, THEIR CELLS, THAT I BRED ON THIS LAND CONVERT TO PURE ENERGY.
ONCE I ABSORB THEIR POWER, IT'LL BE AS EASY AS TAKING CANDY FROM A BABY...
ZU

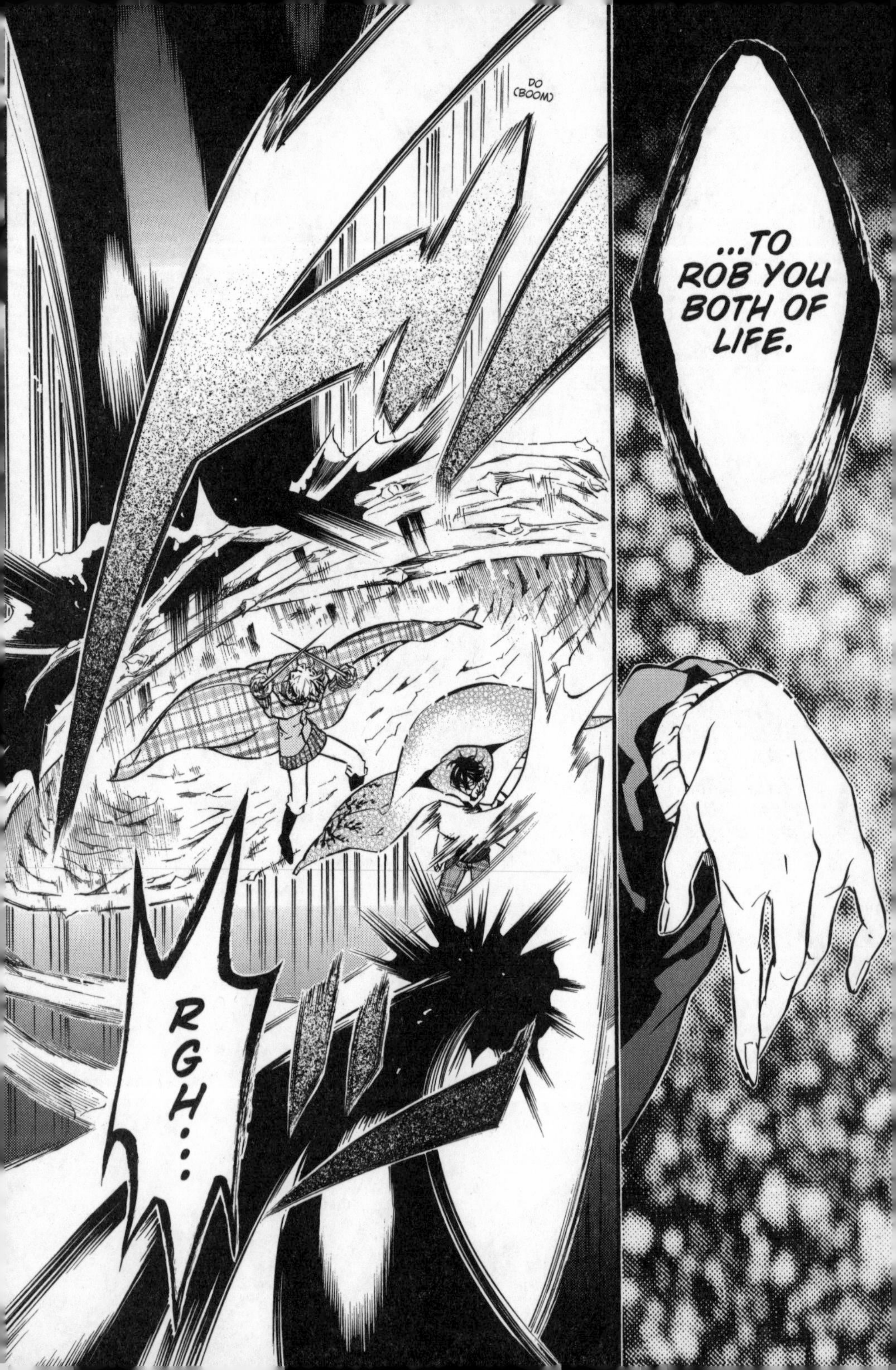
...TO ROB YOU BOTH OF LIFE.
DO (BOOM)
RGH...

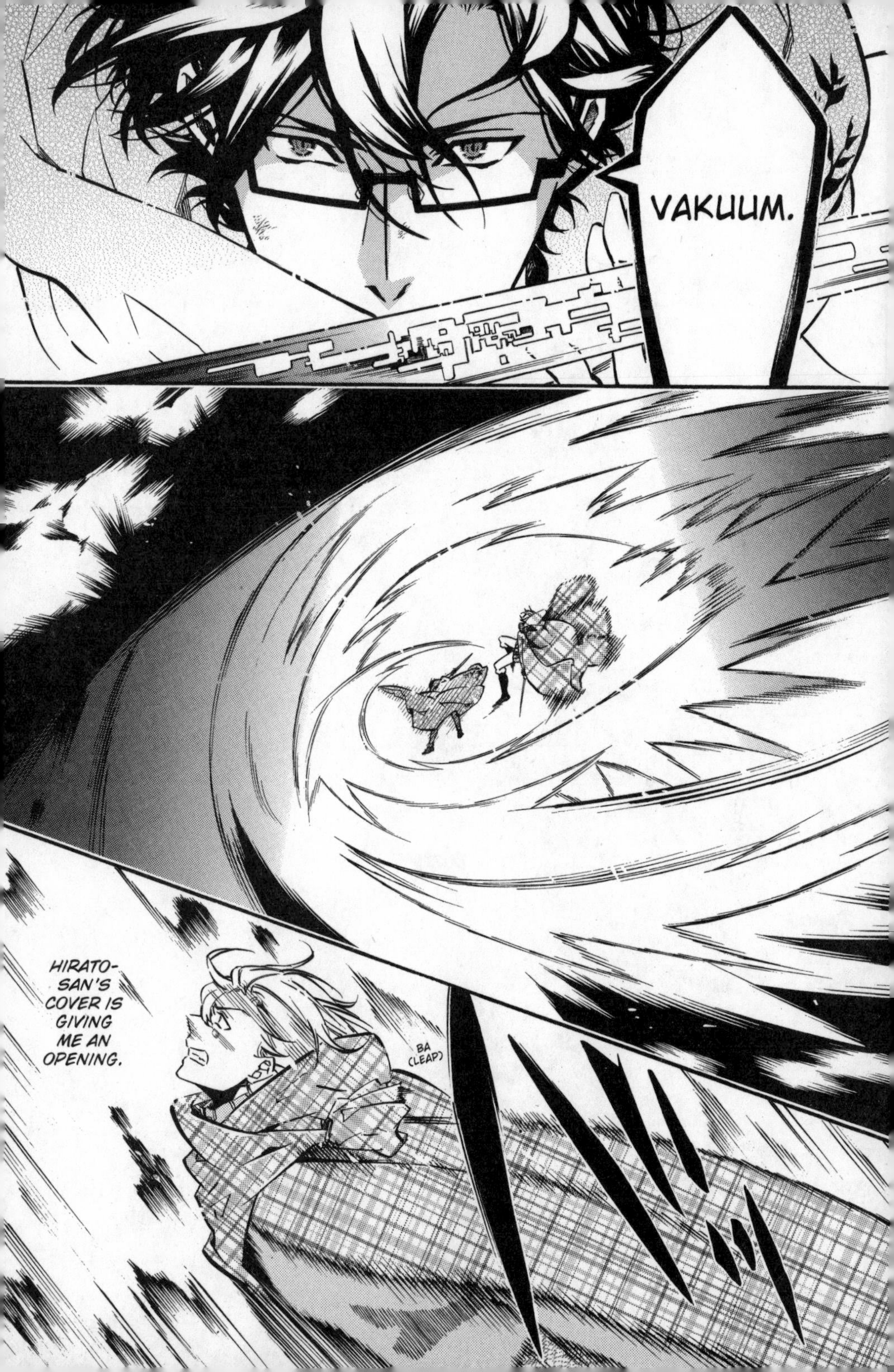
VAKUUM.
HIRATO-SAN'S COVER IS GIVING ME AN OPENING.
BA (LEAP)

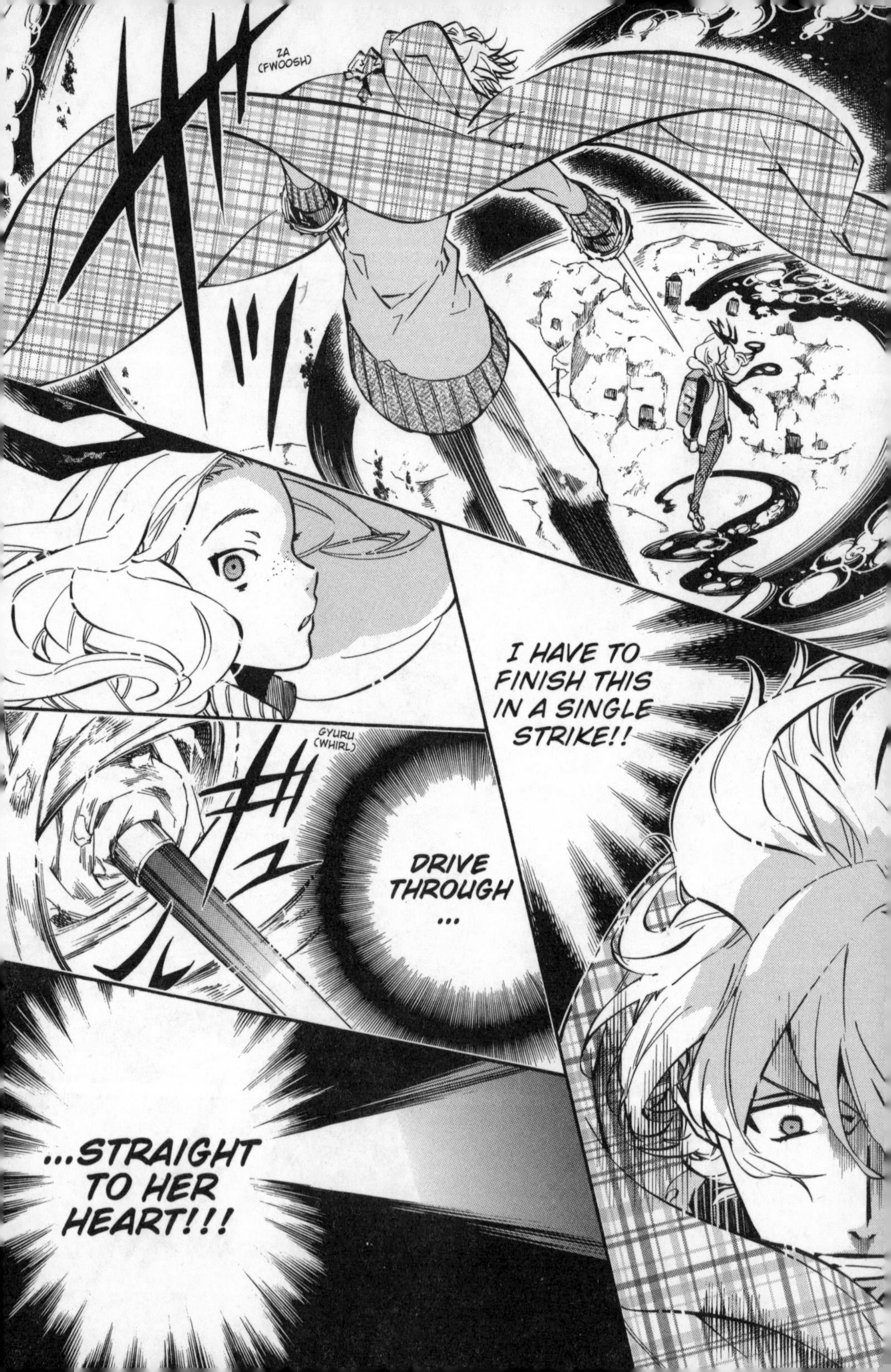
ZA
(FWOOSH)
I HAVE TO FINISH THIS IN A SINGLE STRIKE!!
GYURU
(WHIRL)
DRIVE THROUGH ...
...STRAIGHT TO HER HEART!!!

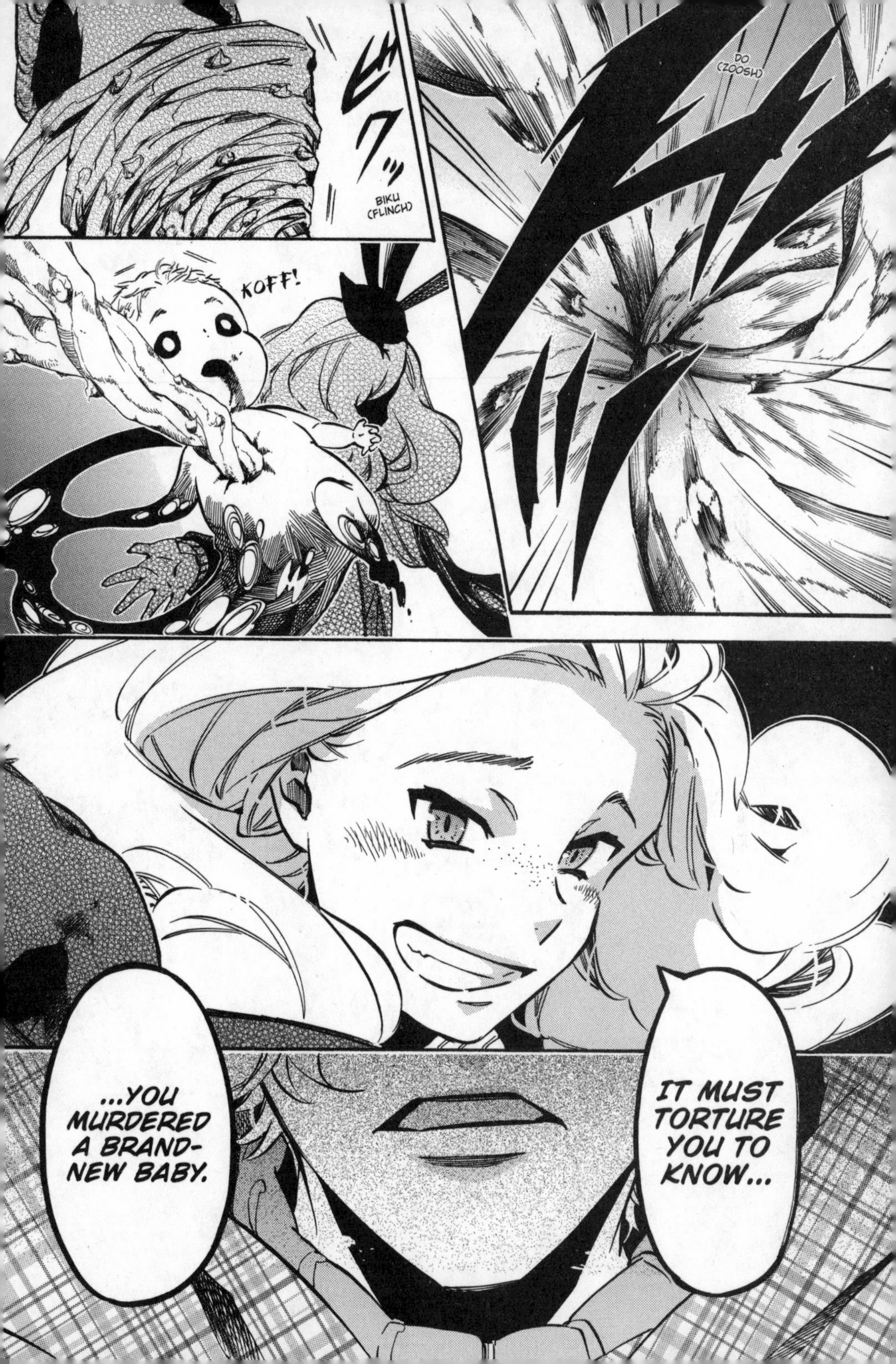
DO (ZOOSH)
BIKU (FLINCH)
KOFF!
IT MUST TORTURE YOU TO KNOW...
...YOU MURDERED A BRAND-NEW BABY.

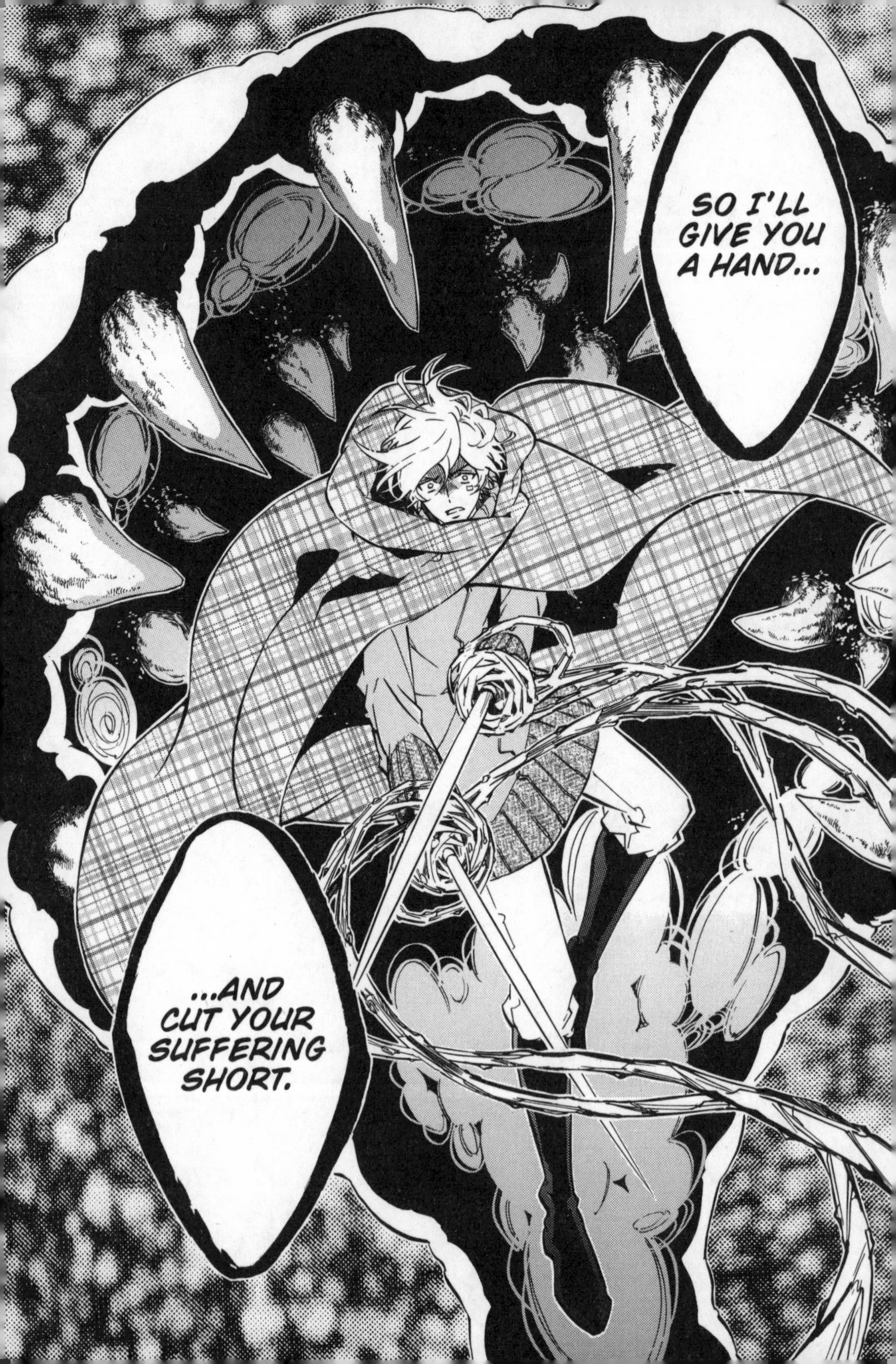
SO I'LL GIVE YOU A HAND...
...AND CUT YOUR SUFFERING SHORT.

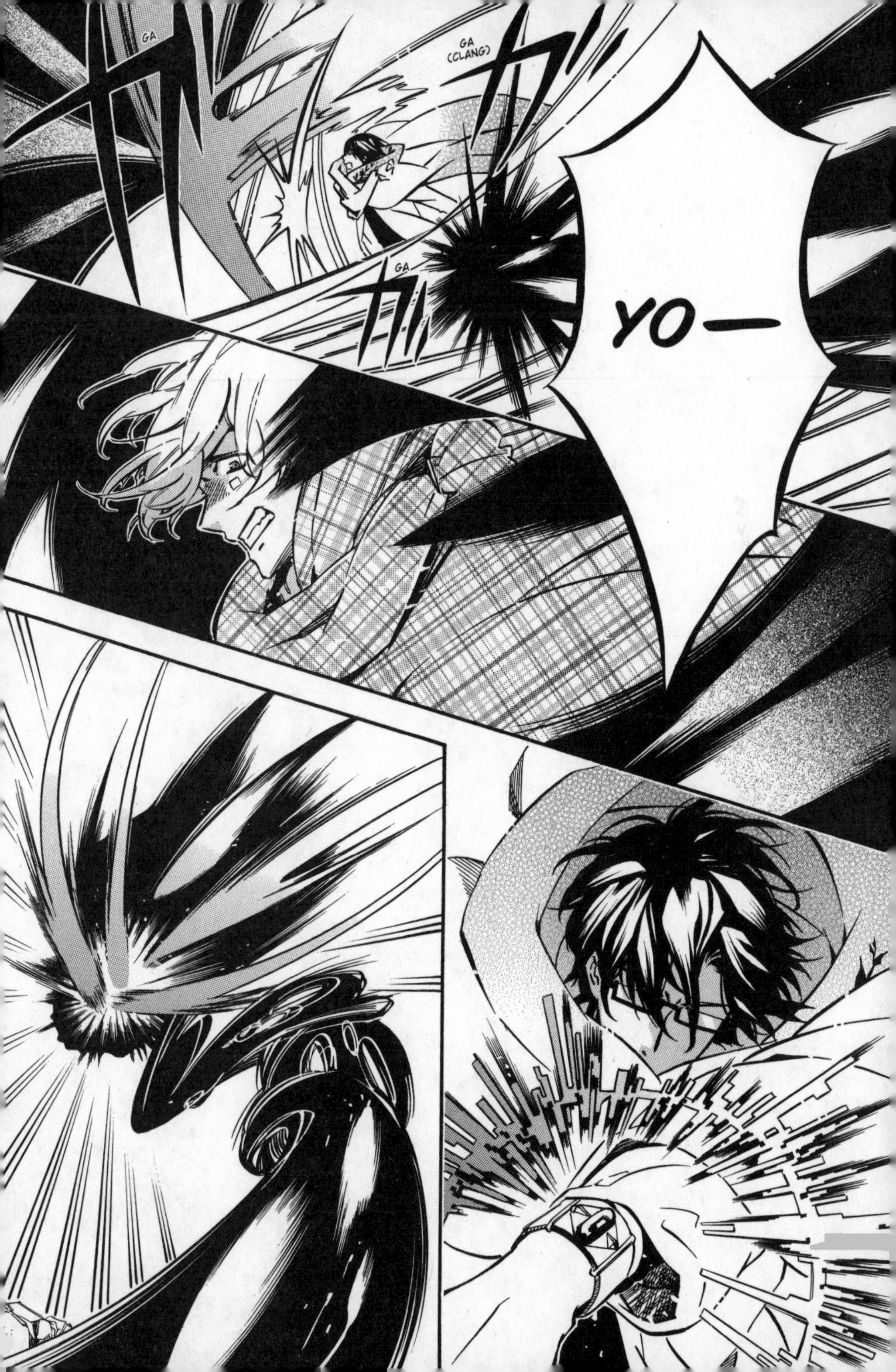
GA (CLANG)
GA
GA
YO—

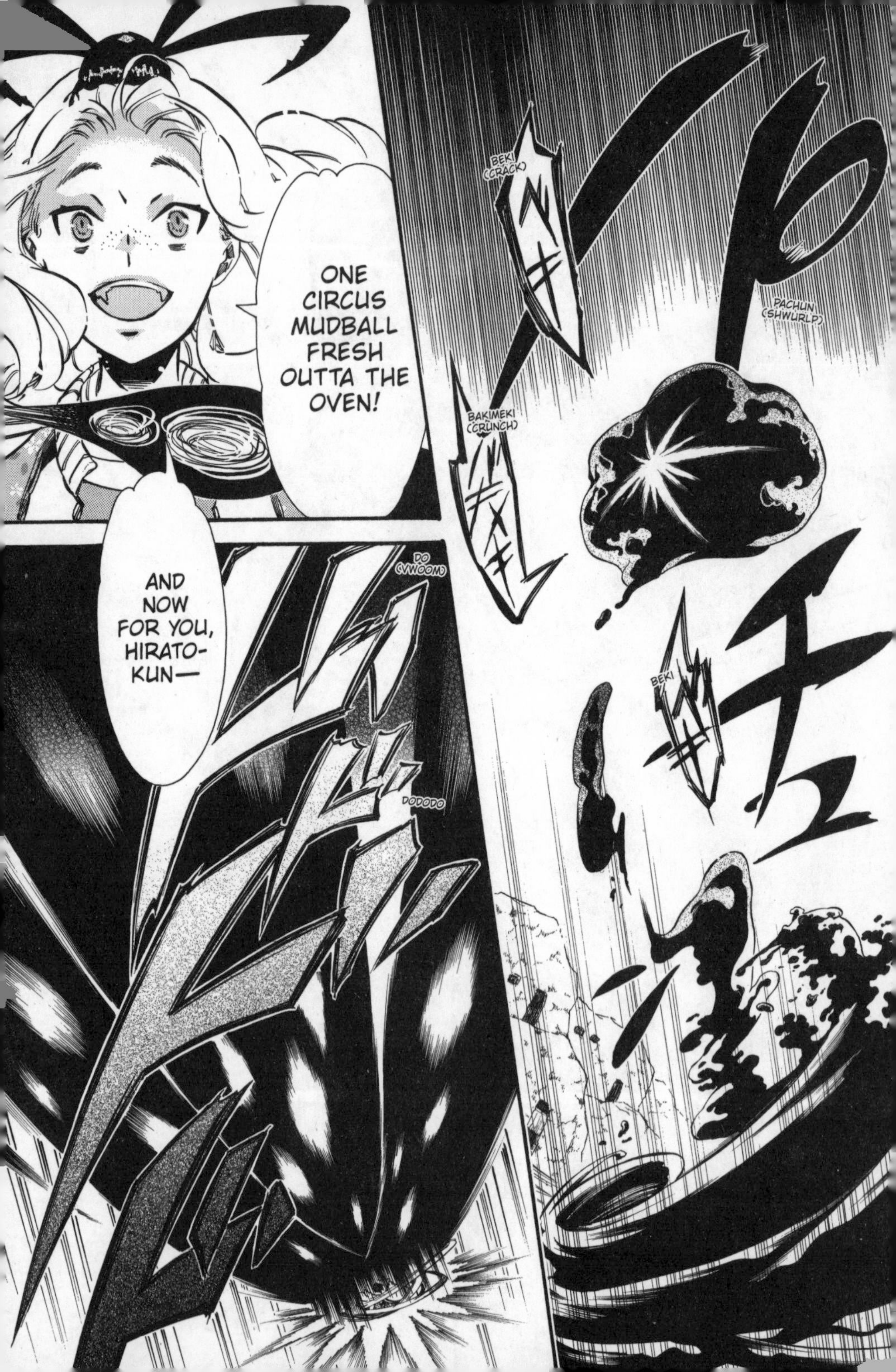
BEKI (CRACK)
PACHUN (SHWURLP)
BAKIMEKI (CRUNCH)
BEKI
ONE CIRCUS MUDBALL FRESH OUTTA THE OVEN!
AND NOW FOR YOU, HIRATO-KUN—
DO (VWOOM)
DODODO

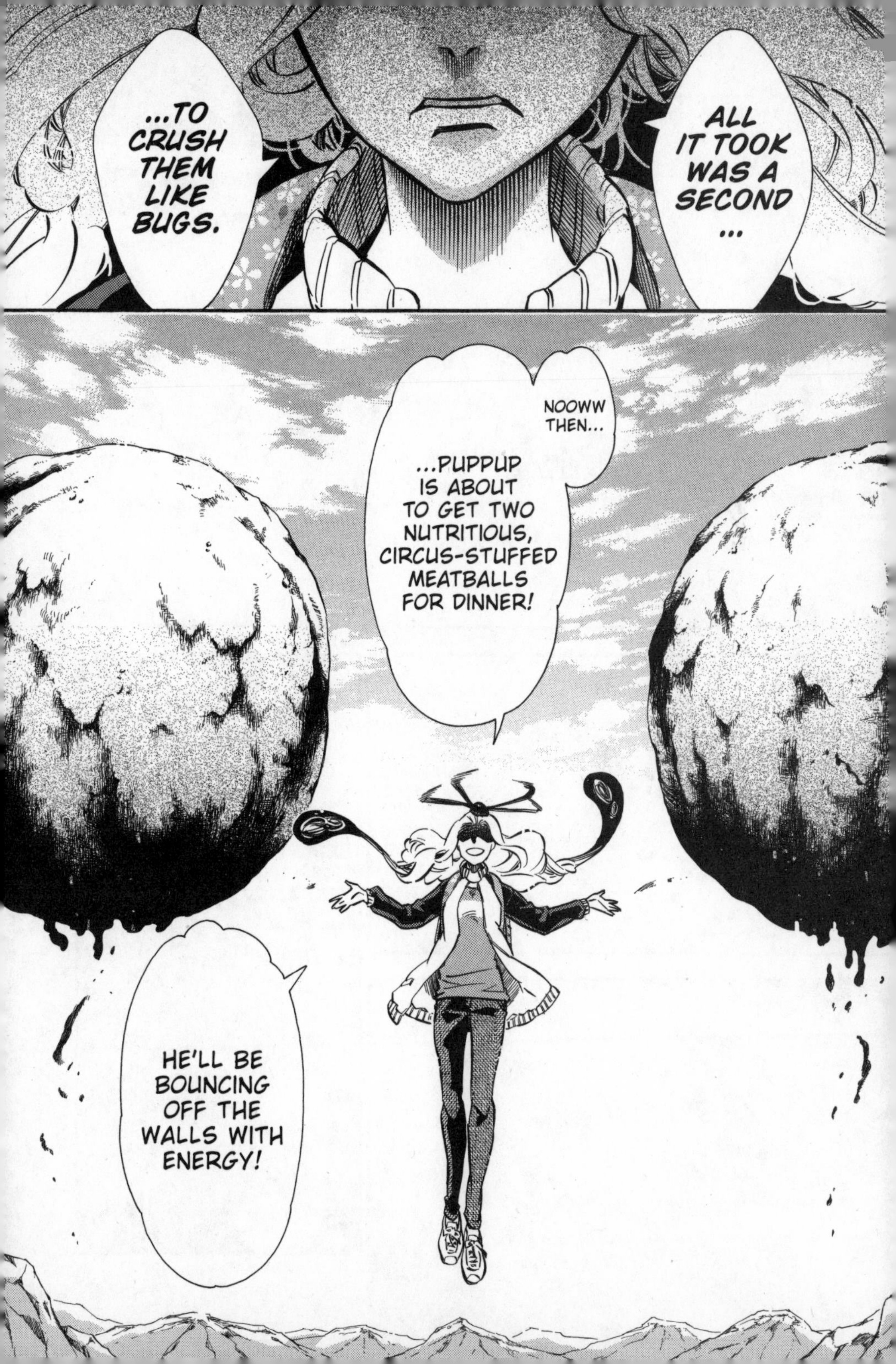
ALL IT TOOK WAS A SECOND...
...TO CRUSH THEM LIKE BUGS.
NOOWW THEN...
...PUPPUP IS ABOUT TO GET TWO NUTRITIOUS, CIRCUS-STUFFED MEATBALLS FOR DINNER!
HE'LL BE BOUNCING OFF THE WALLS WITH ENERGY!

I GOT YOU AN EXTRA-SPECIAL DINNER TODAY, FULL OF MELTED CIRCUS FLESH AND BLOOD.

PUP-PUP!

ORF! ORF!

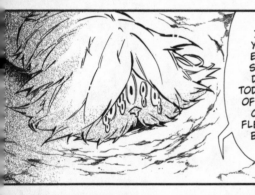

ZU

ZU

ZU (DRAG)

ZU

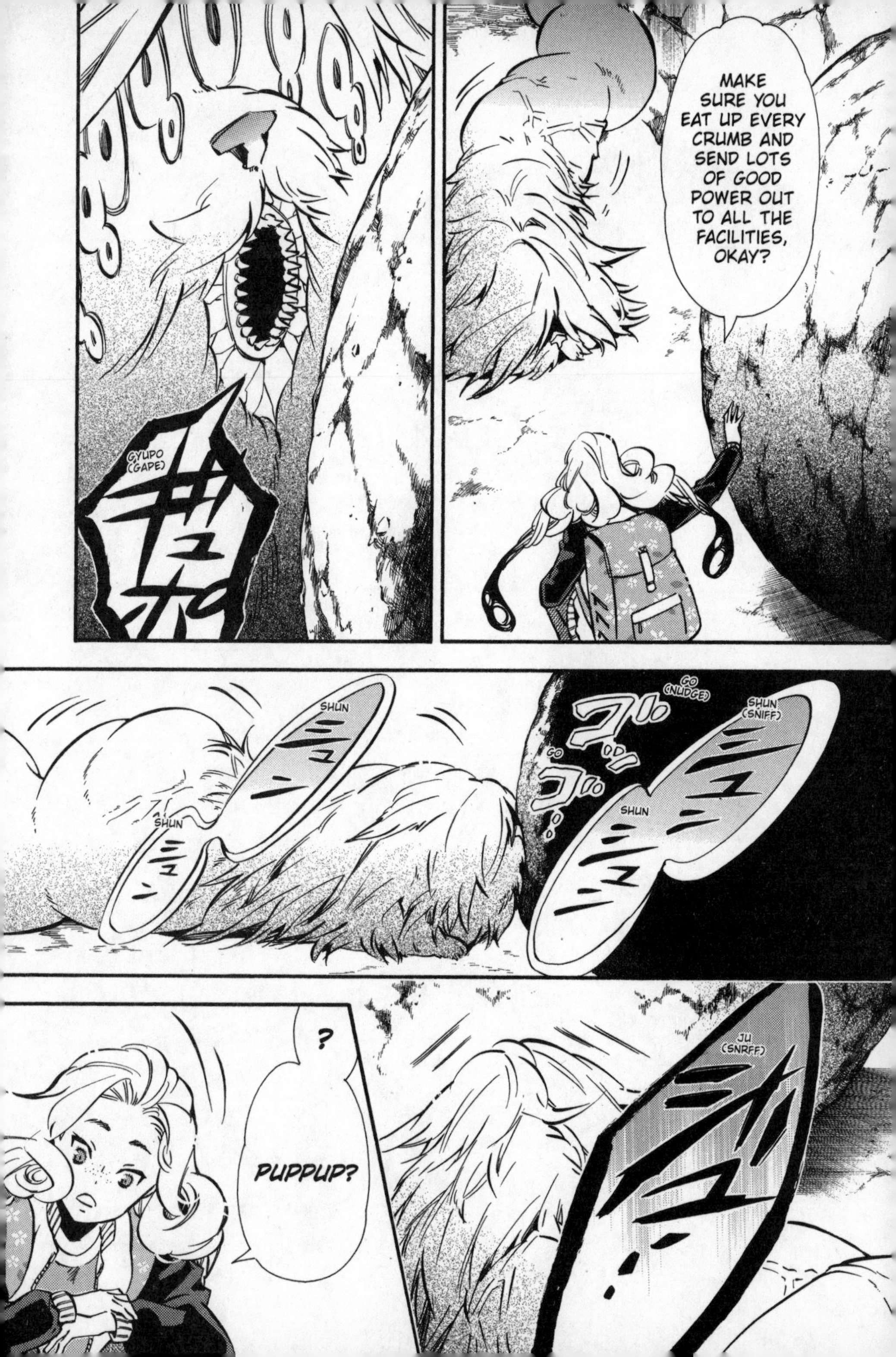
MAKE SURE YOU EAT UP EVERY CRUMB AND SEND LOTS OF GOOD POWER OUT TO ALL THE FACILITIES, OKAY?
GYUPO (GAPE)
GO (NUDGE)
SHUN (SNIFF)
GO
SHUN
SHUN
SHUN
JU (SNRFF)
?
PUPPUP?

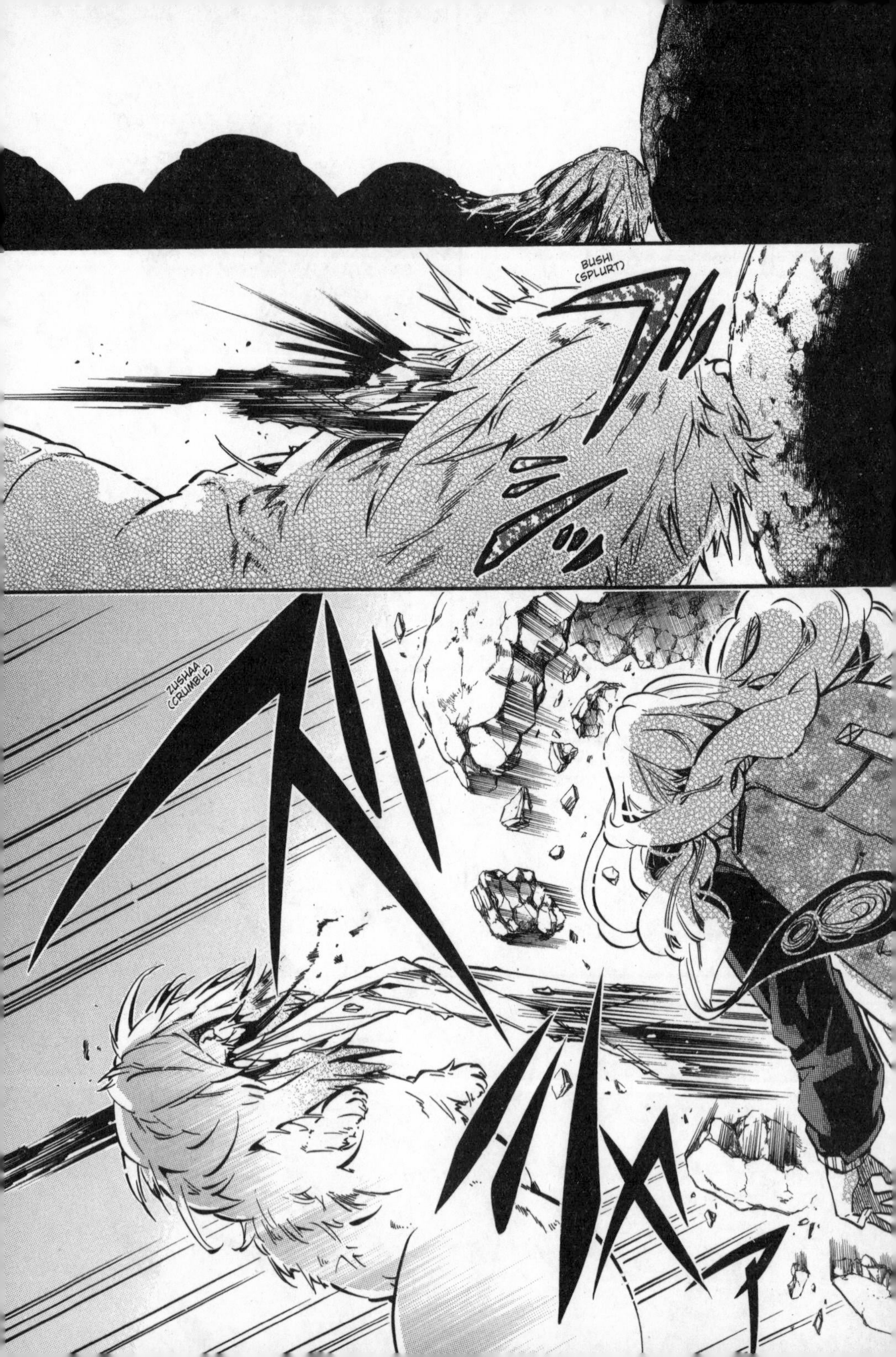
BUSHI (SPLURT)
ZUSHAA (CRUMBLE)

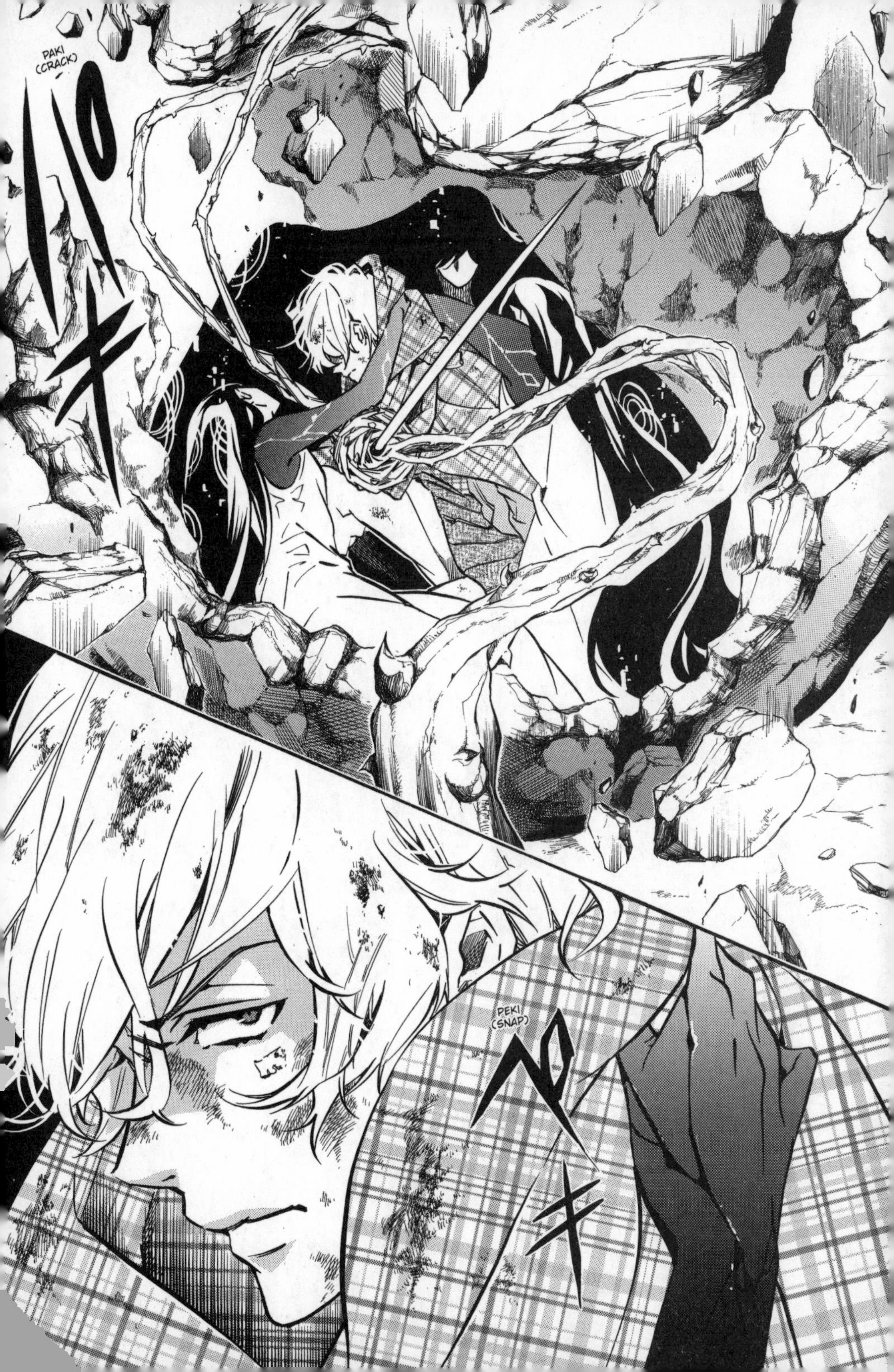
PAKI (CRACK)
PEKI (SNAP)

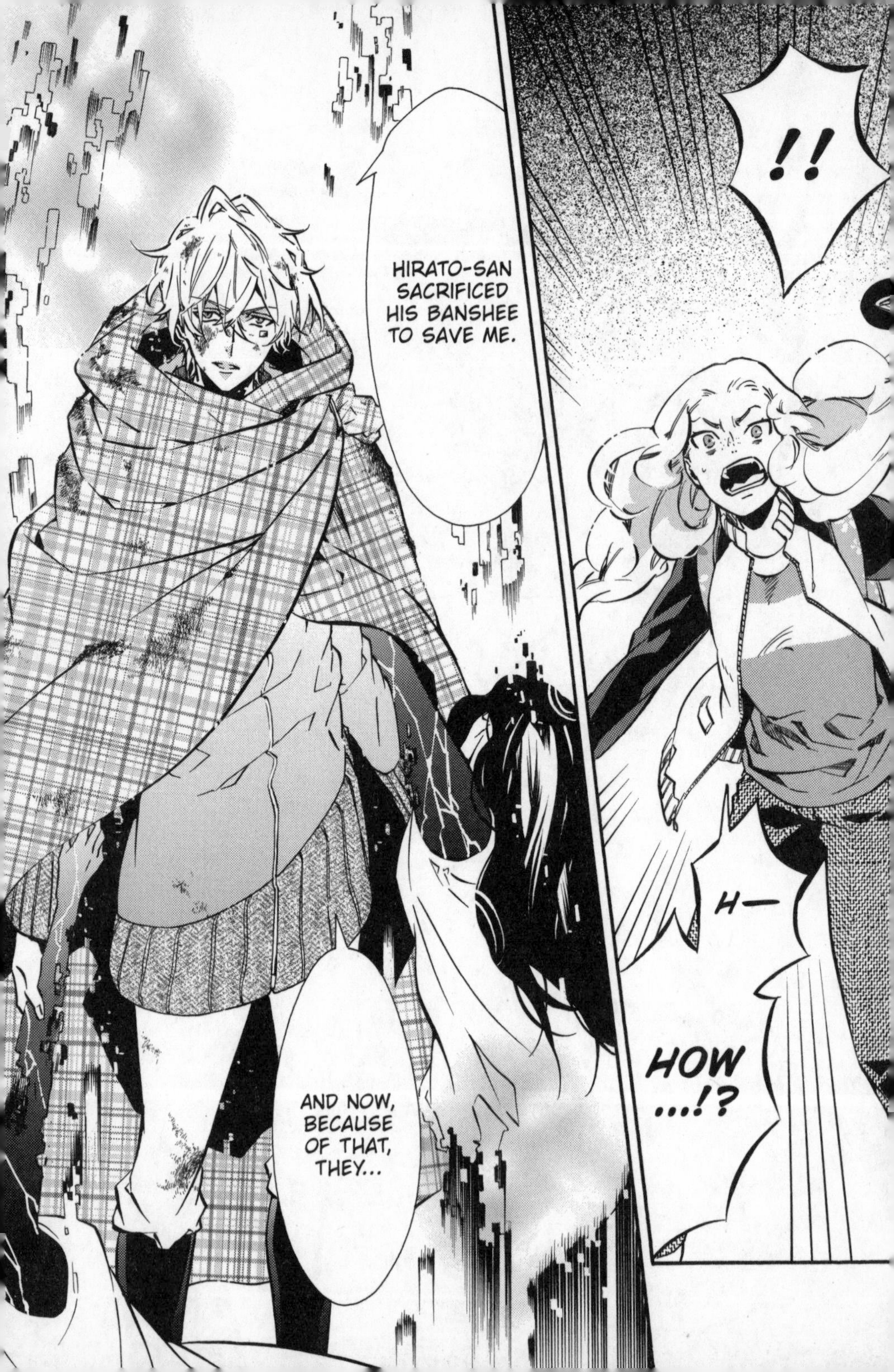
!!
H—
HOW ...!?
HIRATO-SAN SACRIFICED HIS BANSHEE TO SAVE ME.
AND NOW, BECAUSE OF THAT, THEY...

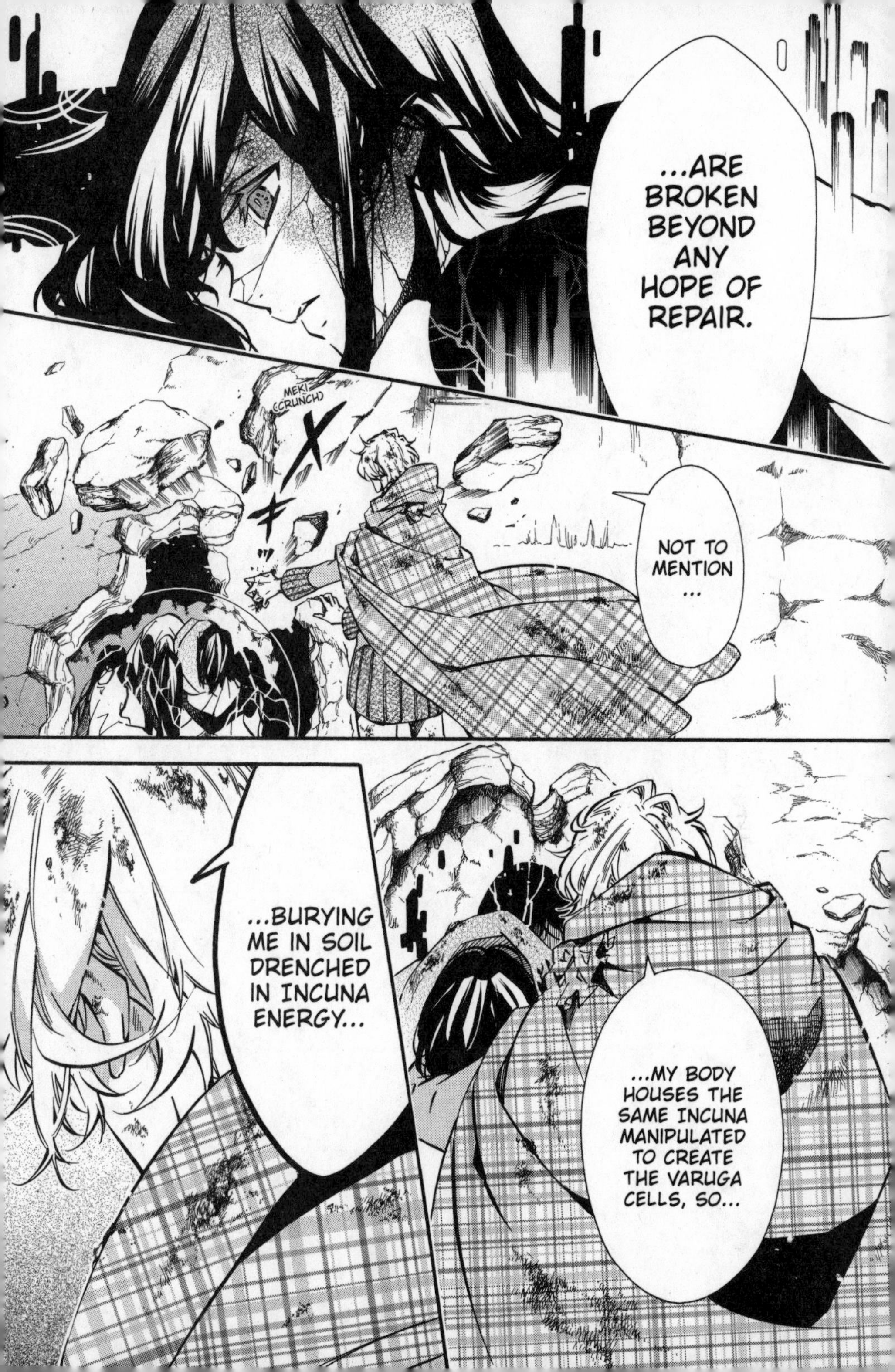
...ARE BROKEN BEYOND ANY HOPE OF REPAIR.
MEKI (CRUNCH)
NOT TO MENTION ...
...BURYING ME IN SOIL DRENCHED IN INCUNA ENERGY...
...MY BODY HOUSES THE SAME INCUNA MANIPULATED TO CREATE THE VARUGA CELLS, SO...

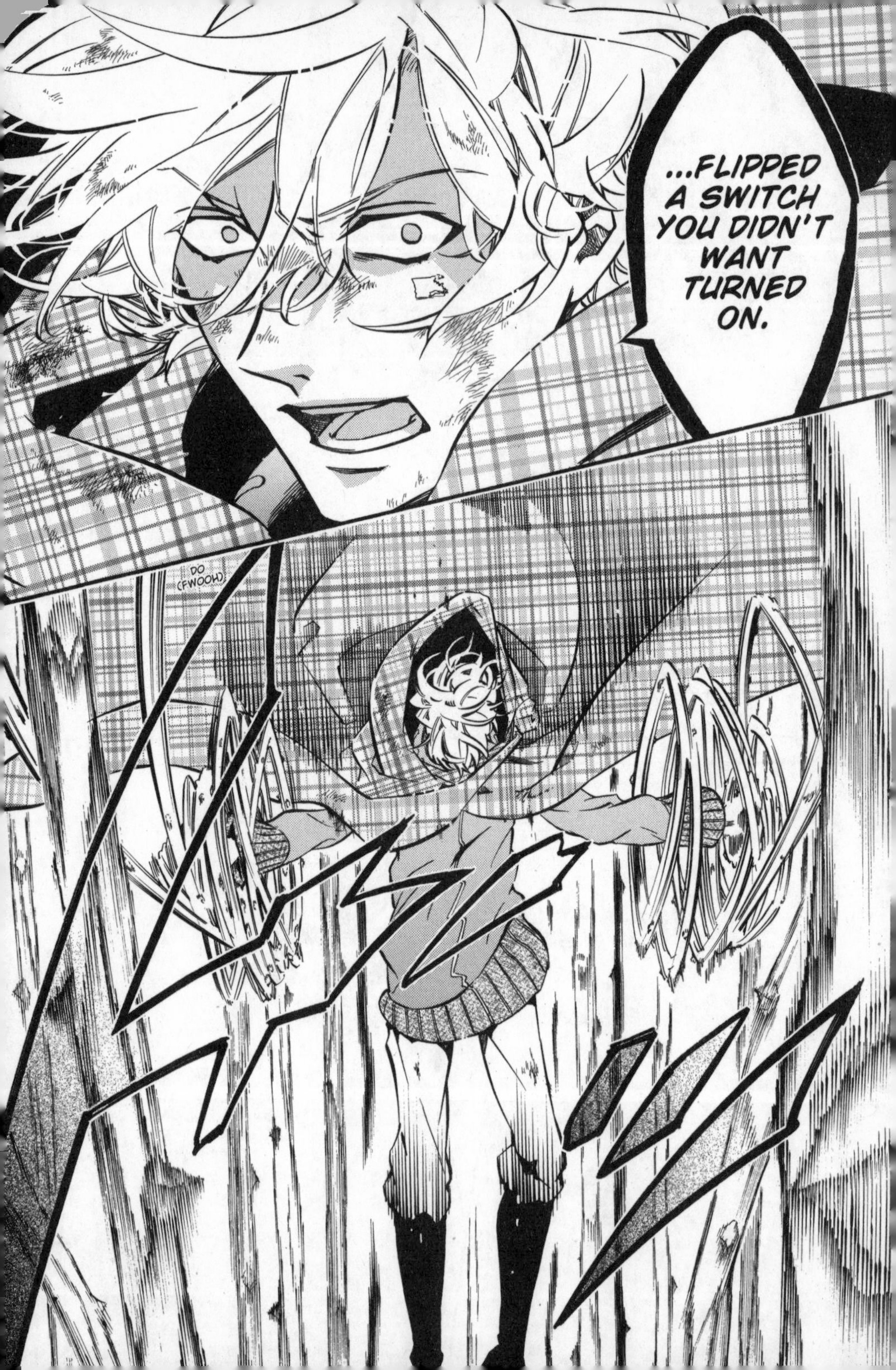
...FLIPPED A SWITCH YOU DIDN'T WANT TURNED ON.
DO (FWOOH)

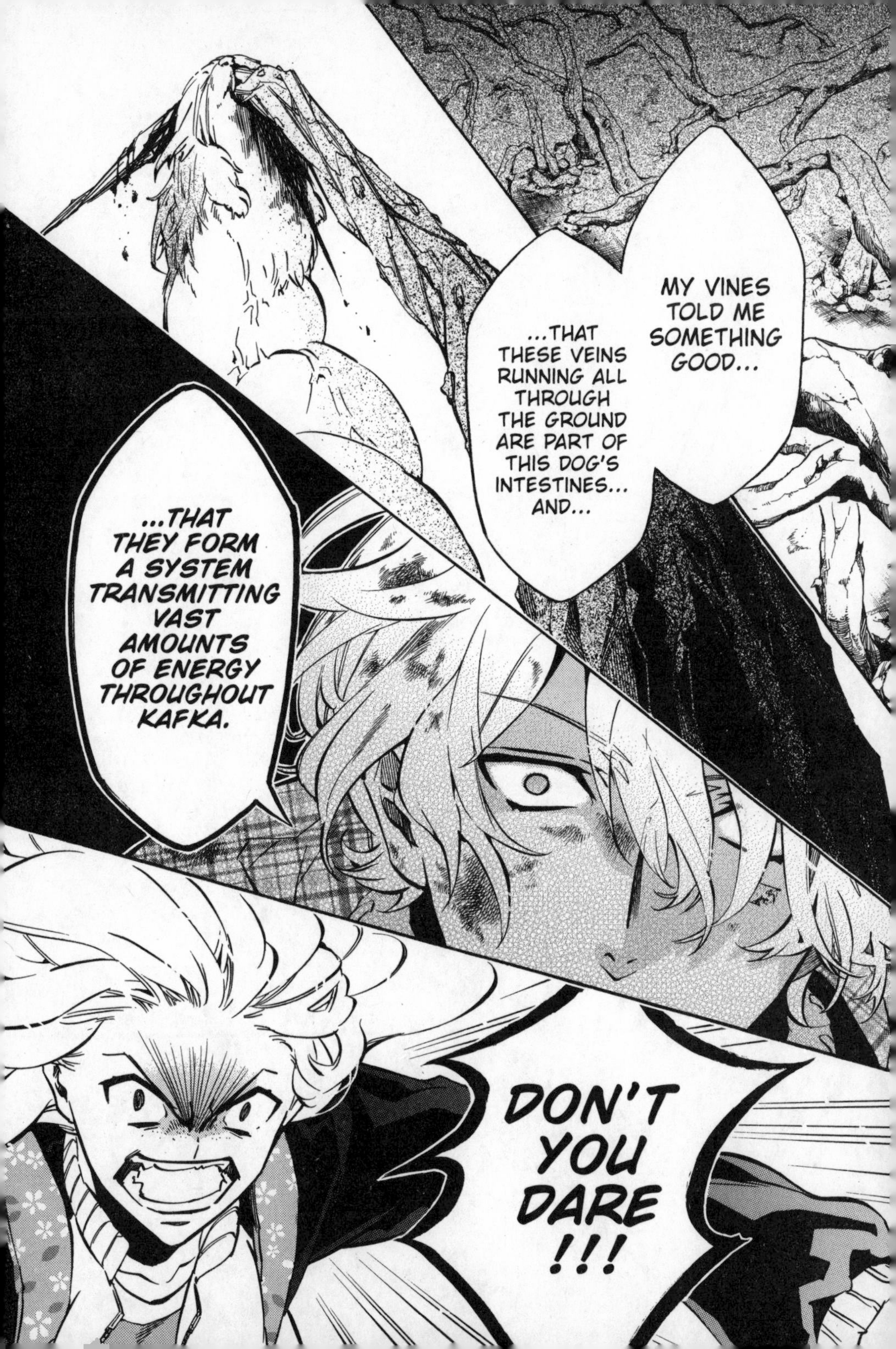
MY VINES TOLD ME SOMETHING GOOD...
...THAT THESE VEINS RUNNING ALL THROUGH THE GROUND ARE PART OF THIS DOG'S INTESTINES... AND...
...THAT THEY FORM A SYSTEM TRANSMITTING VAST AMOUNTS OF ENERGY THROUGHOUT KAFKA.
DON'T YOU DARE!!!

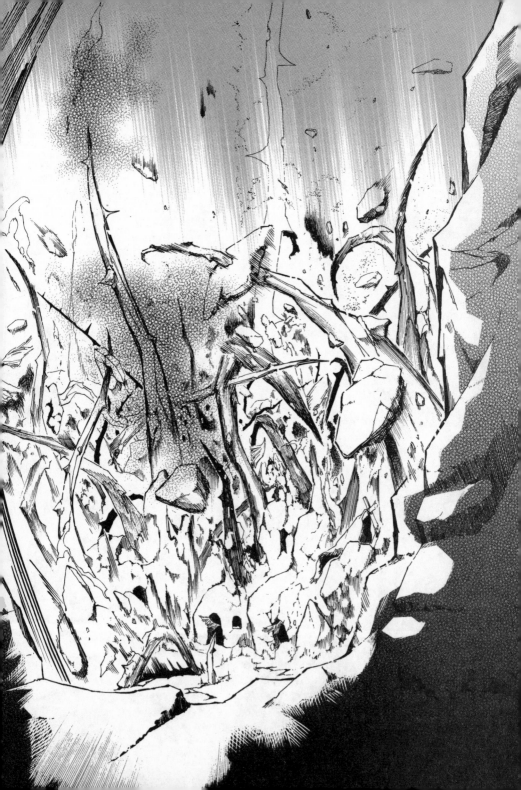

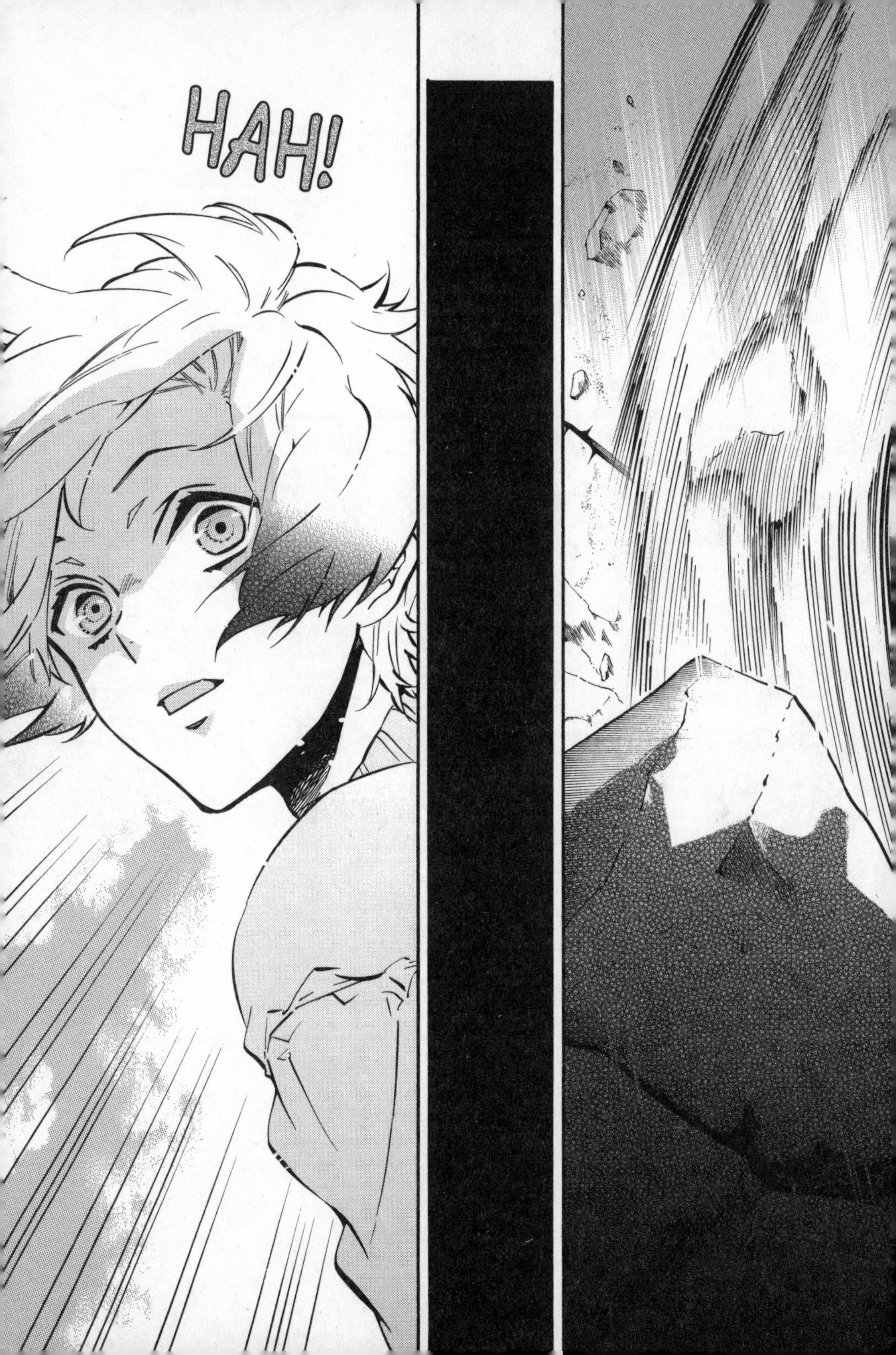
HAH!

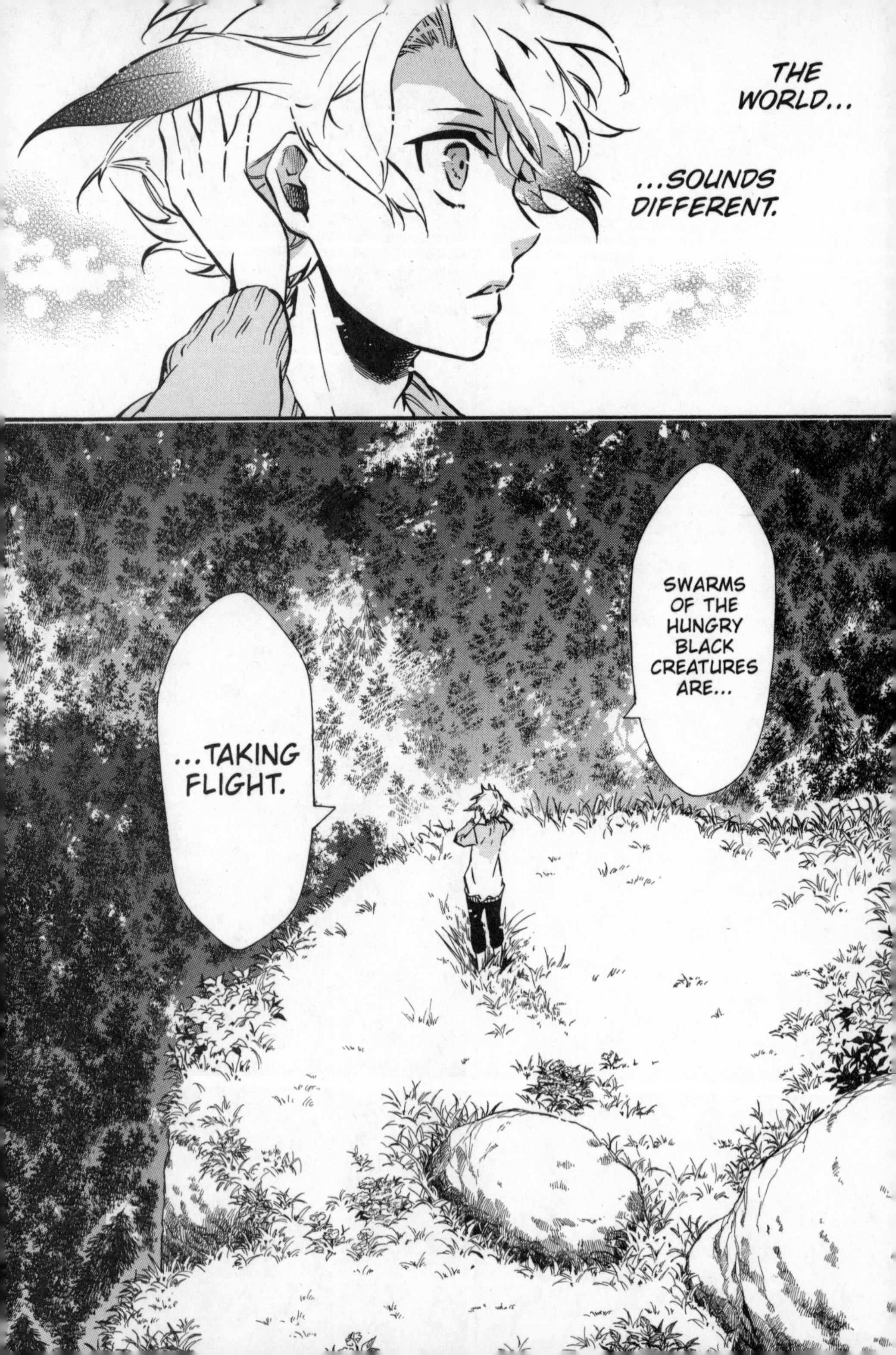
THE WORLD...
...SOUNDS DIFFERENT.
SWARMS OF THE HUNGRY BLACK CREATURES ARE...
...TAKING FLIGHT.

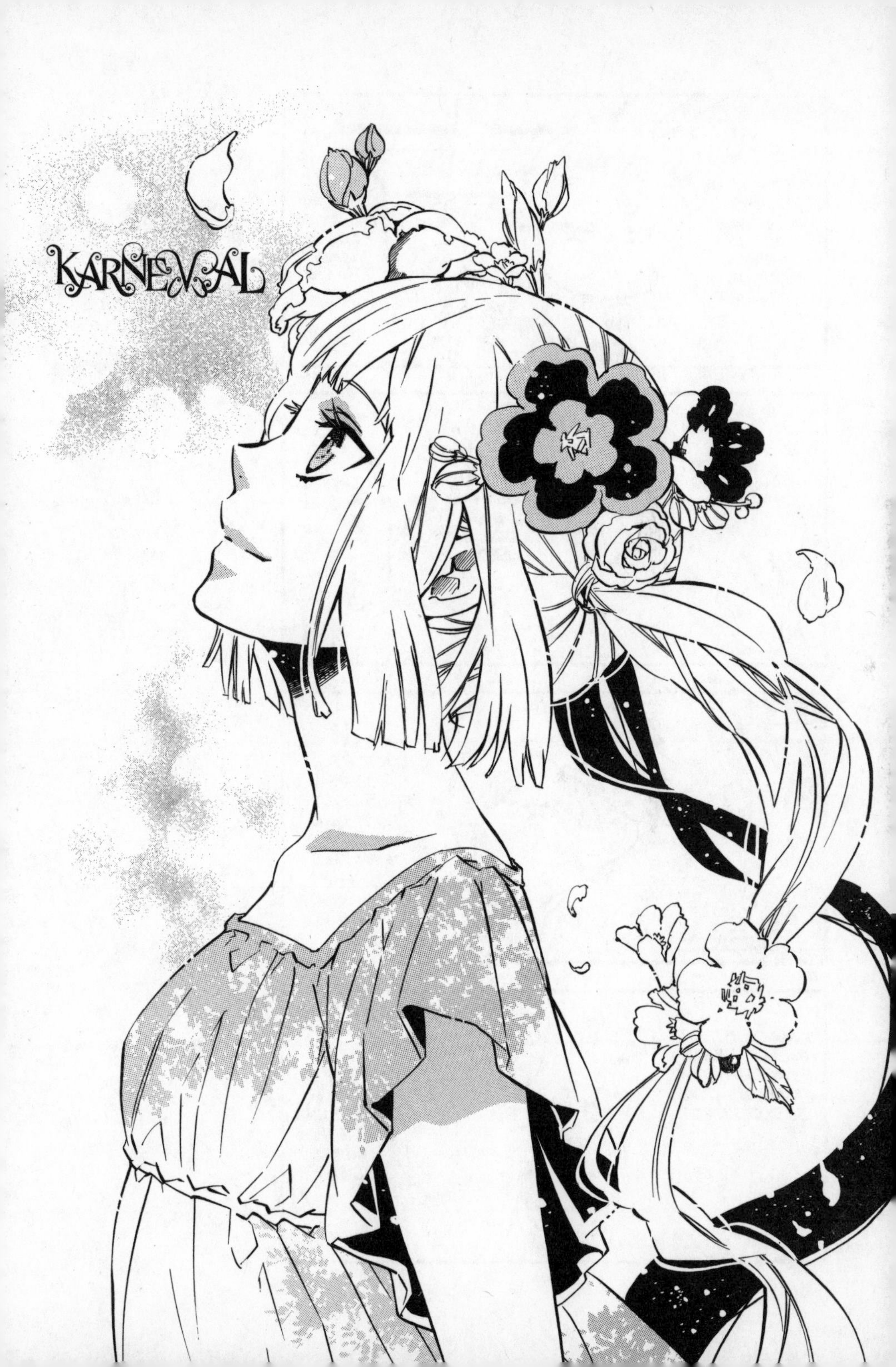
KARNEVAL

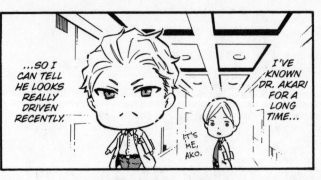

Bonus Comic 1

Reading the Boss

I'VE KNOWN DR. AKARI FOR A LONG TIME...
IT'S ME, AKO.
...SO I CAN TELL HE LOOKS REALLY DRIVEN RECENTLY.
I MEAN, HE'S ALWAYS LIKE THAT, BUT IT'S EVEN MORE THAN USUAL...
DR. AKARI, DID YOU PICK UP A NEW HOBBY OR SOMETHING?
!!
AKO, IT CAN'T BE... HAS HE FOUND OUT ABOUT OUR PLANS TO OPEN THE VAULT—!?
OH!!
I KNOW! YOU MUST BE TEACHING HATTIE NEW TRICKS, RIGHT!?
I'VE NEVER TAUGHT HIM ANYTHING. HE JUST PICKS THEM UP ON HIS OWN.
NOPE. STILL JUST A HIGHLY PERCEPTIVE, IF UNIMAGINATIVE, SUBORDINATE.

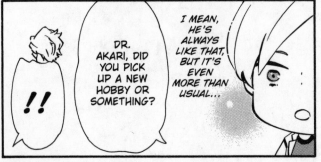

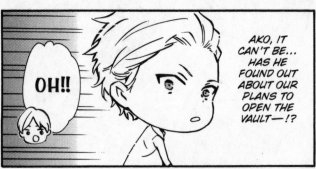

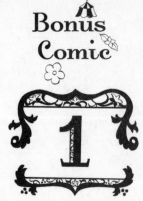

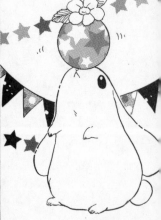

Bonus Comic 2

Leave Your Mark

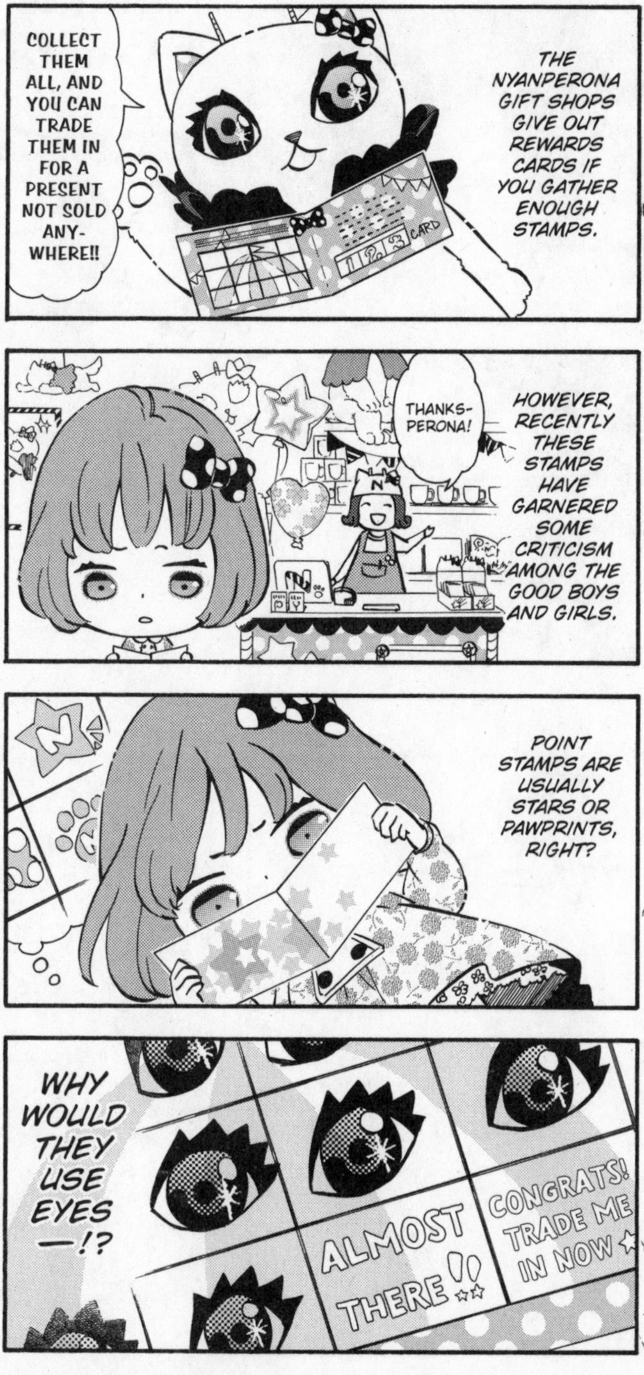

THE NYANPERONA GIFT SHOPS GIVE OUT REWARDS CARDS IF YOU GATHER ENOUGH STAMPS.
CARD
COLLECT THEM ALL, AND YOU CAN TRADE THEM IN FOR A PRESENT NOT SOLD ANYWHERE!!
HOWEVER, RECENTLY THESE STAMPS HAVE GARNERED SOME CRITICISM AMONG THE GOOD BOYS AND GIRLS.
THANKS-PERONA!
POINT STAMPS ARE USUALLY STARS OR PAWPRINTS, RIGHT?
CONGRATS! TRADE ME IN NOW ☆
ALMOST THERE!! ☆☆
WHY WOULD THEY USE EYES—!?

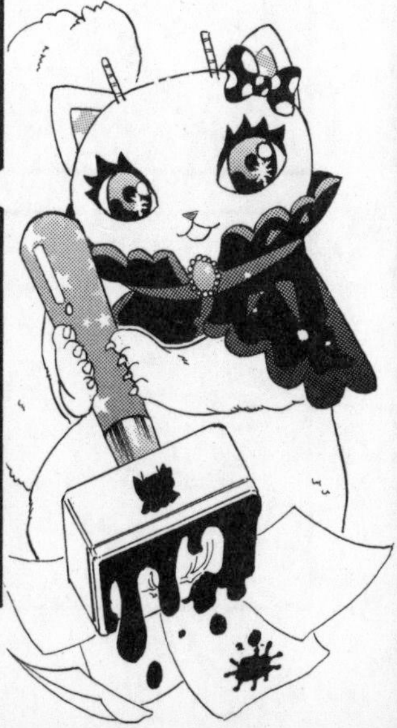

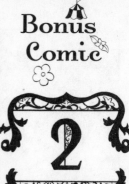

Bonus Comic 3

Memories of Love

UNTIL WE MEET AGAIN NEXT FALL, RIBBIT!

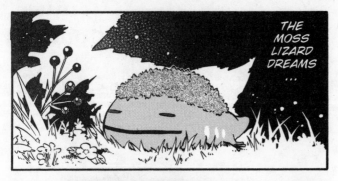

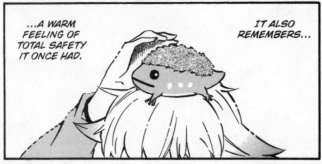

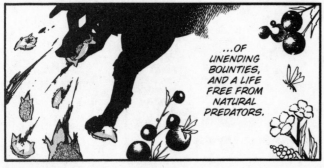

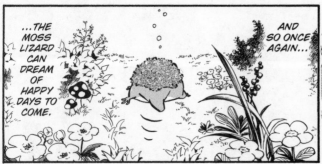

THE MOSS LIZARD DREAMS...
...OF UNENDING BOUNTIES, AND A LIFE FREE FROM NATURAL PREDATORS.
IT ALSO REMEMBERS...
...A WARM FEELING OF TOTAL SAFETY IT ONCE HAD.
AND SO ONCE AGAIN...
...THE MOSS LIZARD CAN DREAM OF HAPPY DAYS TO COME.

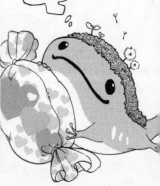

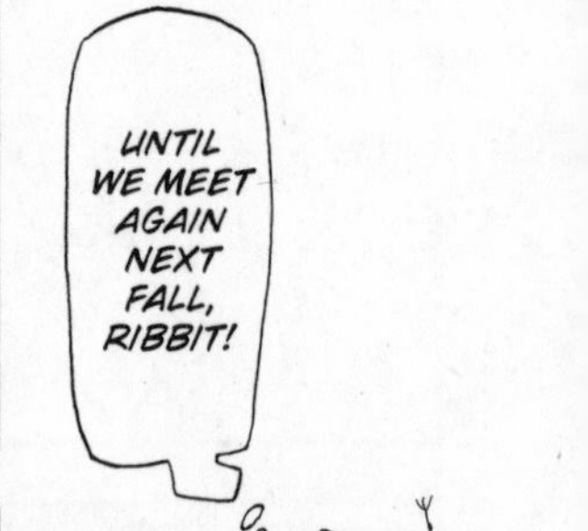

AFTERWORD

THANK YOU SO MUCH FOR READING THE FIRST HALF OF *KARNEVAL* OMNIBUS 13! IT'D MAKE ME SO HAPPY IF YOU ENJOYED IT. I HAD KESHIKI APPEAR ON THE BOOK COVERS THIS TIME, SINCE I WAS PRETTY SURE YOU'RE ALL FAMILIAR ENOUGH WITH HIM BY NOW. MY ASSISTANTS ONCE STARTED TALKING ABOUT POOF WHILE WORKING ON A BATTLE SCENE, SAYING THINGS LIKE, "I DON'T THINK POOF IS ACTUALLY THAT EVIL," AND, "BUT DIDN'T HE EAT SOMEONE?" WHEN I SHOWED THEM THIS COVER, THEIR MAIN TAKEAWAYS WERE "SHARPSHOOTER" AND "PHYSICS." THANK YOU...I THINK. I'M WRITING THIS AFTERWORD IN THE MIDST OF A BIG SNOWSTORM, BUT I IMAGINE SPRING WILL HAVE WARMED THE WORLD BY THE TIME YOU READ IT. MAY YOU ALL FIND YOUR HAPPINESS!

Touya Mikanagi

Special Thanks

MOTSU-SAN, SUAMA-SAN, (ﾟ)-SAN, MY EDITOR OOHASHI-SAN, EVERYONE AT ICHIJINSHA PUBLISHING, ALL THE COLLABORATORS AND EVERYONE AT OUR AFFILIATED COMPANIES, MY FRIENDS, MY FAMILY, and to you!

KARNEVAL

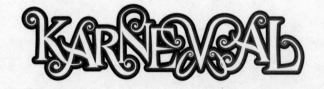

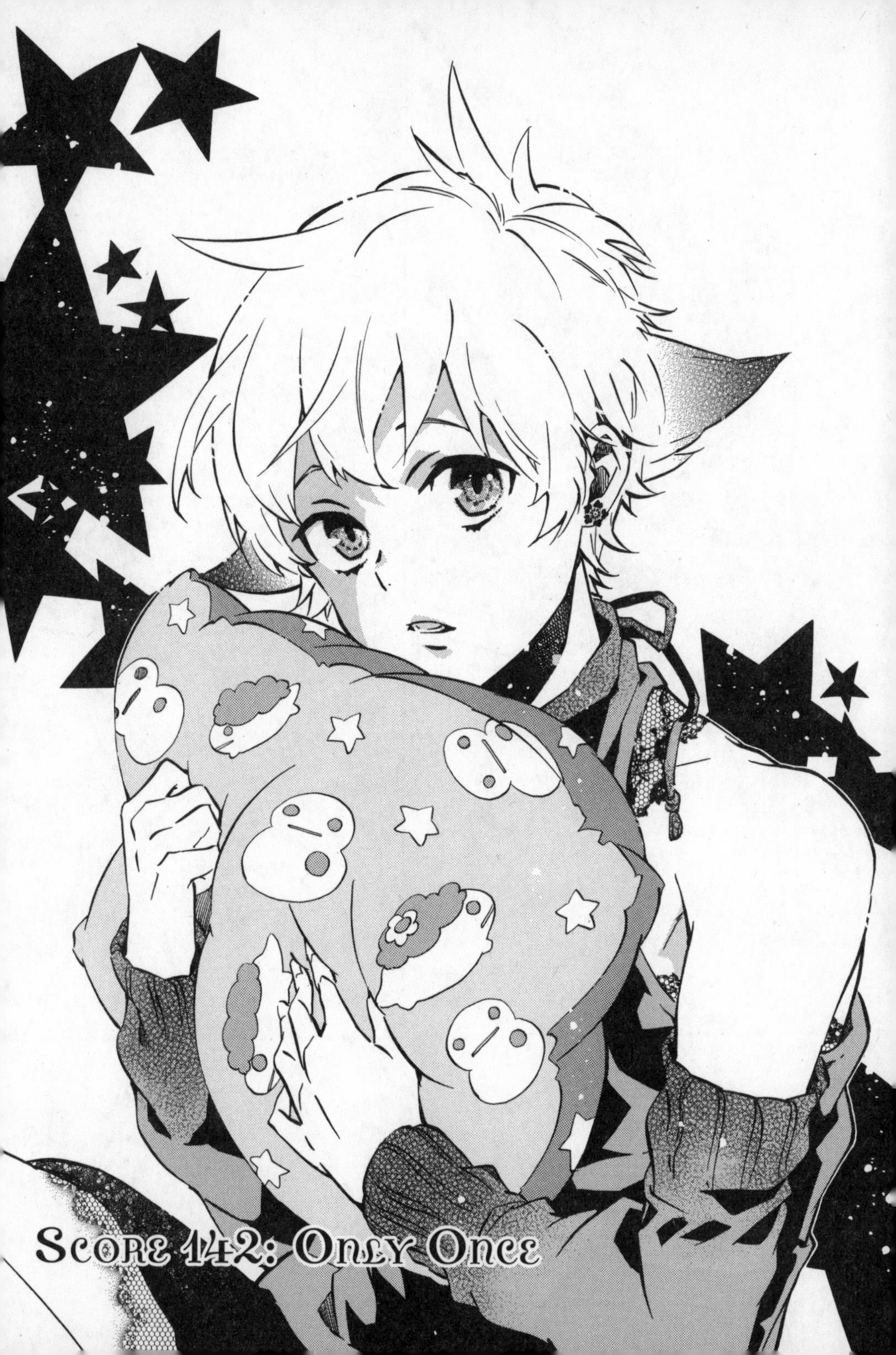
Score 142: Only Once

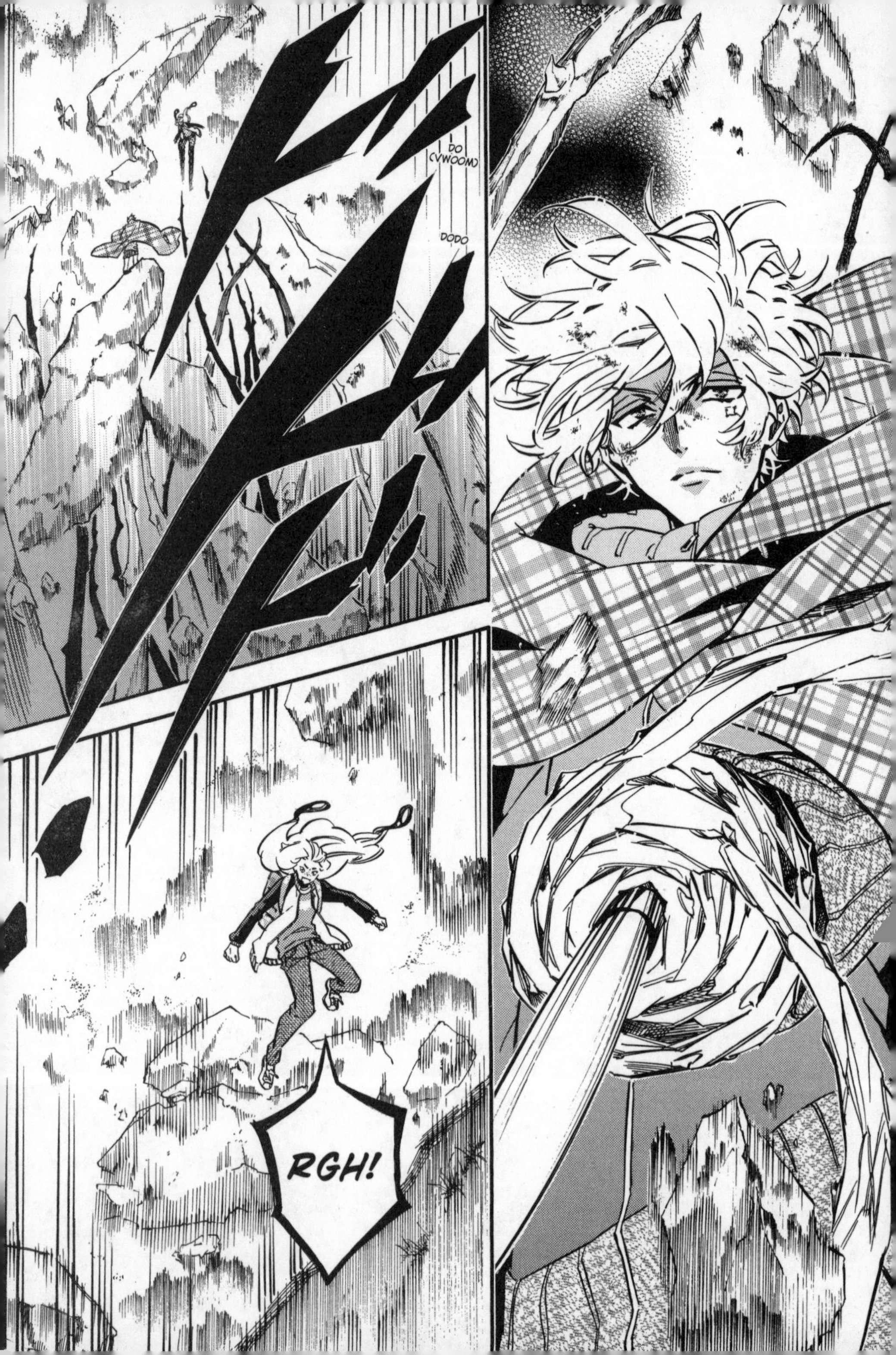
DO
(VWOOM)
DODO
RGH!

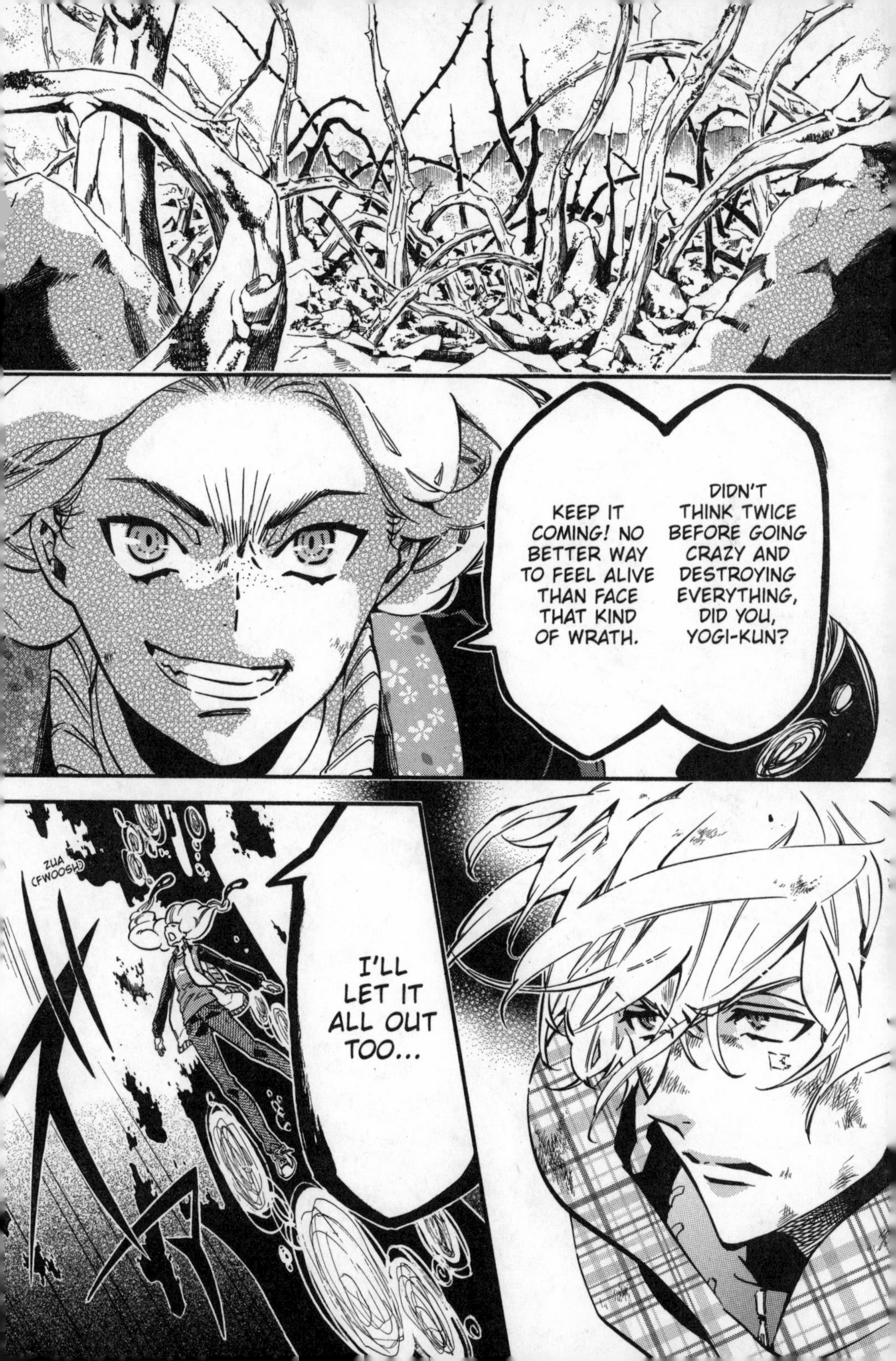
DIDN'T THINK TWICE BEFORE GOING CRAZY AND DESTROYING EVERYTHING, DID YOU, YOGI-KUN?
KEEP IT COMING! NO BETTER WAY TO FEEL ALIVE THAN FACE THAT KIND OF WRATH.
I'LL LET IT ALL OUT TOO...
ZUA (FWOOSH)

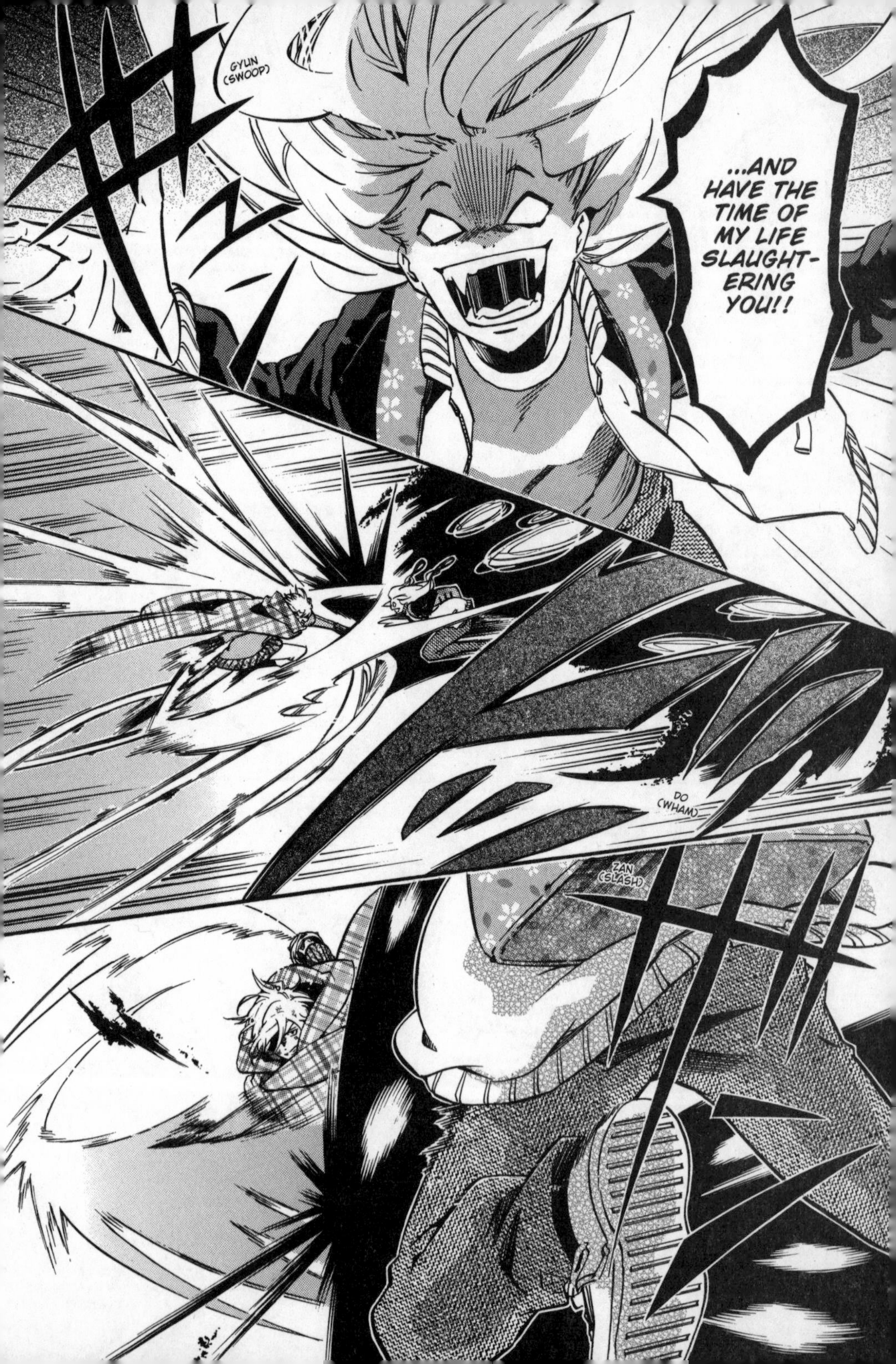
...AND HAVE THE TIME OF MY LIFE SLAUGHTERING YOU!!
GYUN (SWOOP)
DO (WHAM)
ZAN (SLASH)

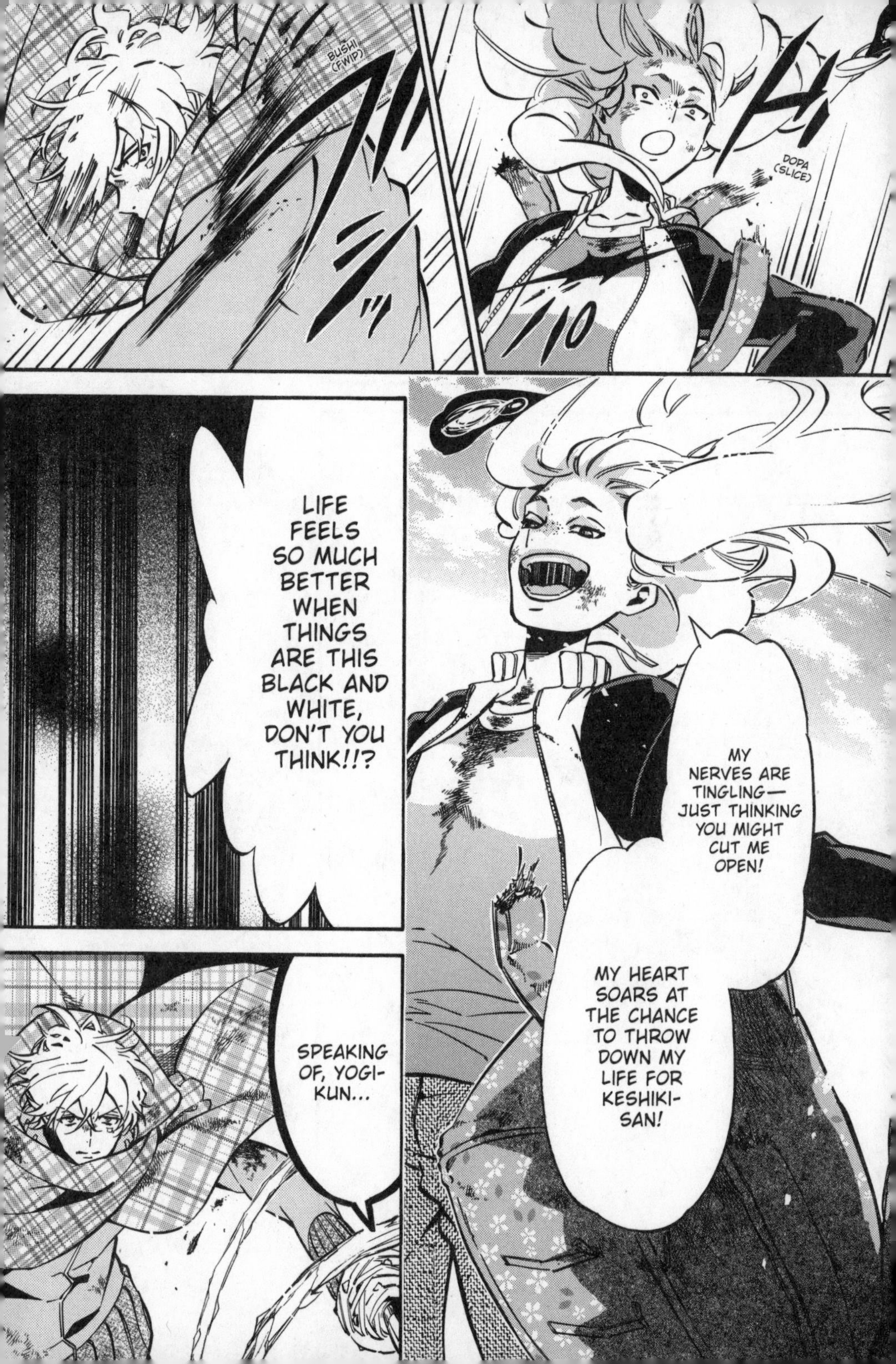
DOPA (SLICE)
BUSHI (FWIP)
MY NERVES ARE TINGLING—JUST THINKING YOU MIGHT CUT ME OPEN!
MY HEART SOARS AT THE CHANCE TO THROW DOWN MY LIFE FOR KESHIKI-SAN!
LIFE FEELS SO MUCH BETTER WHEN THINGS ARE THIS BLACK AND WHITE, DON'T YOU THINK!!?
SPEAKING OF, YOGI-KUN...

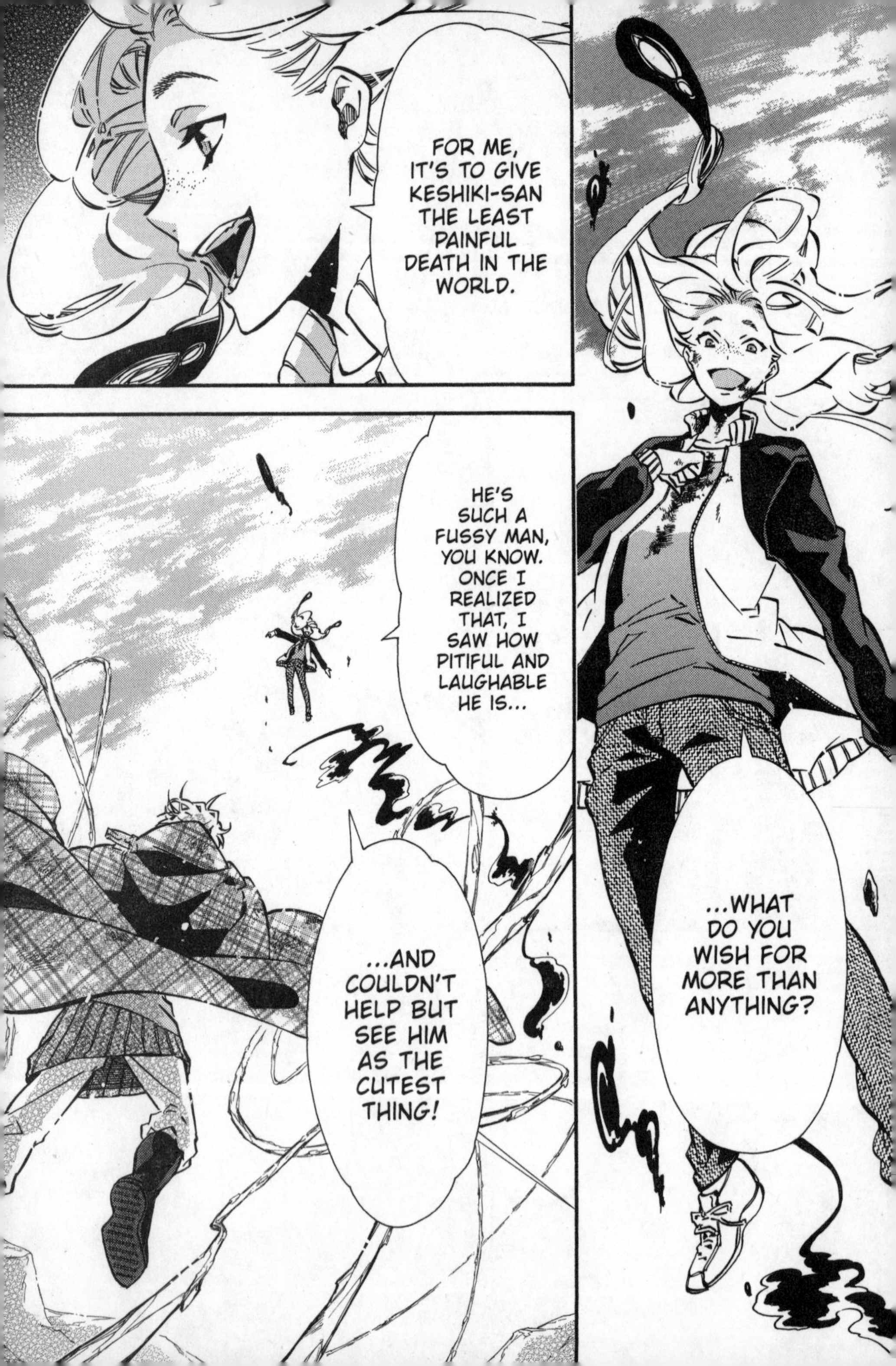
...WHAT DO YOU WISH FOR MORE THAN ANYTHING?
FOR ME, IT'S TO GIVE KESHIKI-SAN THE LEAST PAINFUL DEATH IN THE WORLD.
HE'S SUCH A FUSSY MAN, YOU KNOW. ONCE I REALIZED THAT, I SAW HOW PITIFUL AND LAUGHABLE HE IS...
...AND COULDN'T HELP BUT SEE HIM AS THE CUTEST THING!

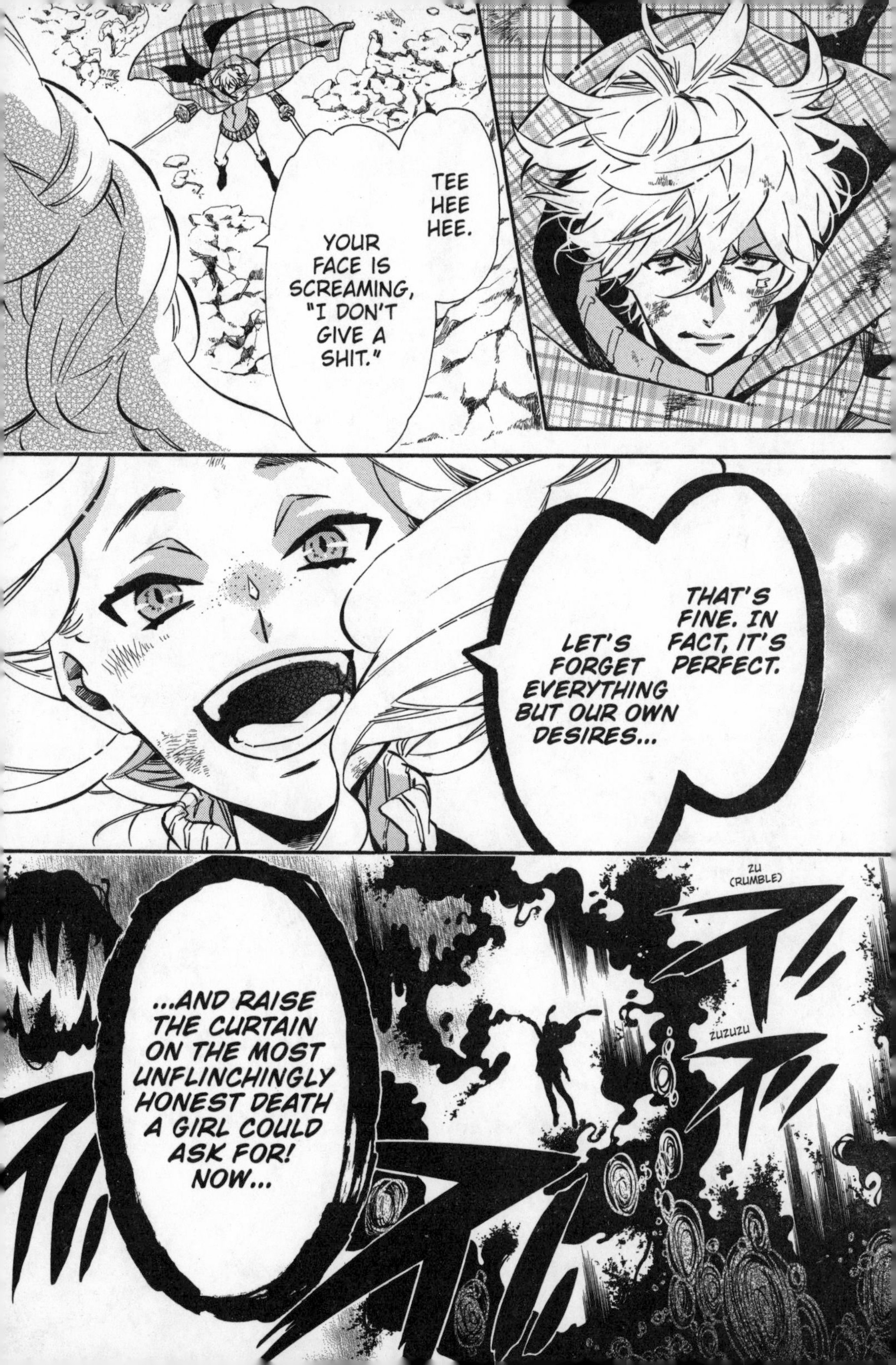
TEE HEE HEE.
YOUR FACE IS SCREAMING, "I DON'T GIVE A SHIT."
THAT'S FINE. IN FACT, IT'S PERFECT.
LET'S FORGET EVERYTHING BUT OUR OWN DESIRES...
ZU (RUMBLE)
ZUZUZU
...AND RAISE THE CURTAIN ON THE MOST UNFLINCHINGLY HONEST DEATH A GIRL COULD ASK FOR! NOW...

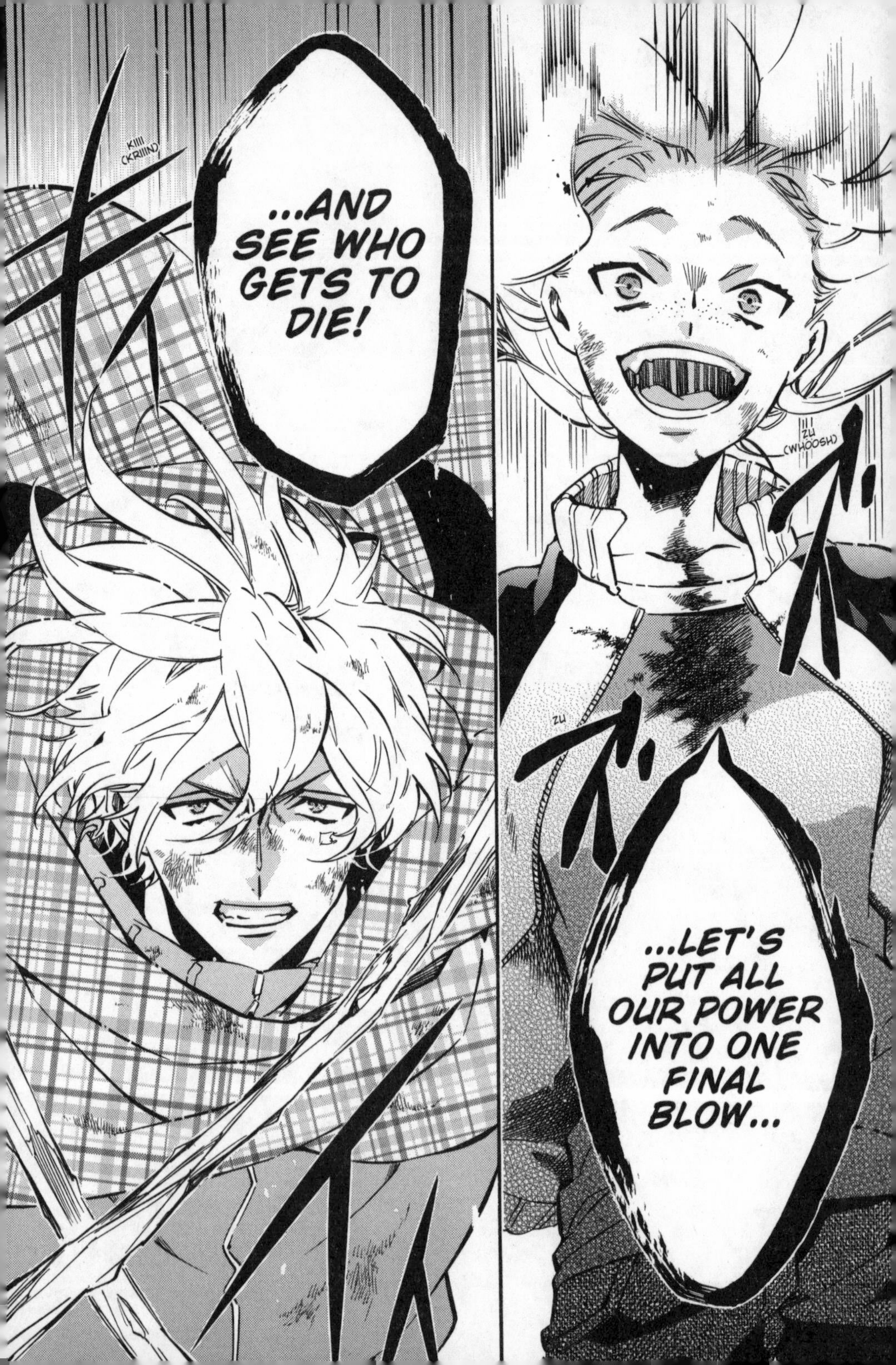
ZU (WHOOSH)
ZU
...LET'S PUT ALL OUR POWER INTO ONE FINAL BLOW...
...AND SEE WHO GETS TO DIE!
KIIII (KRIIIN)

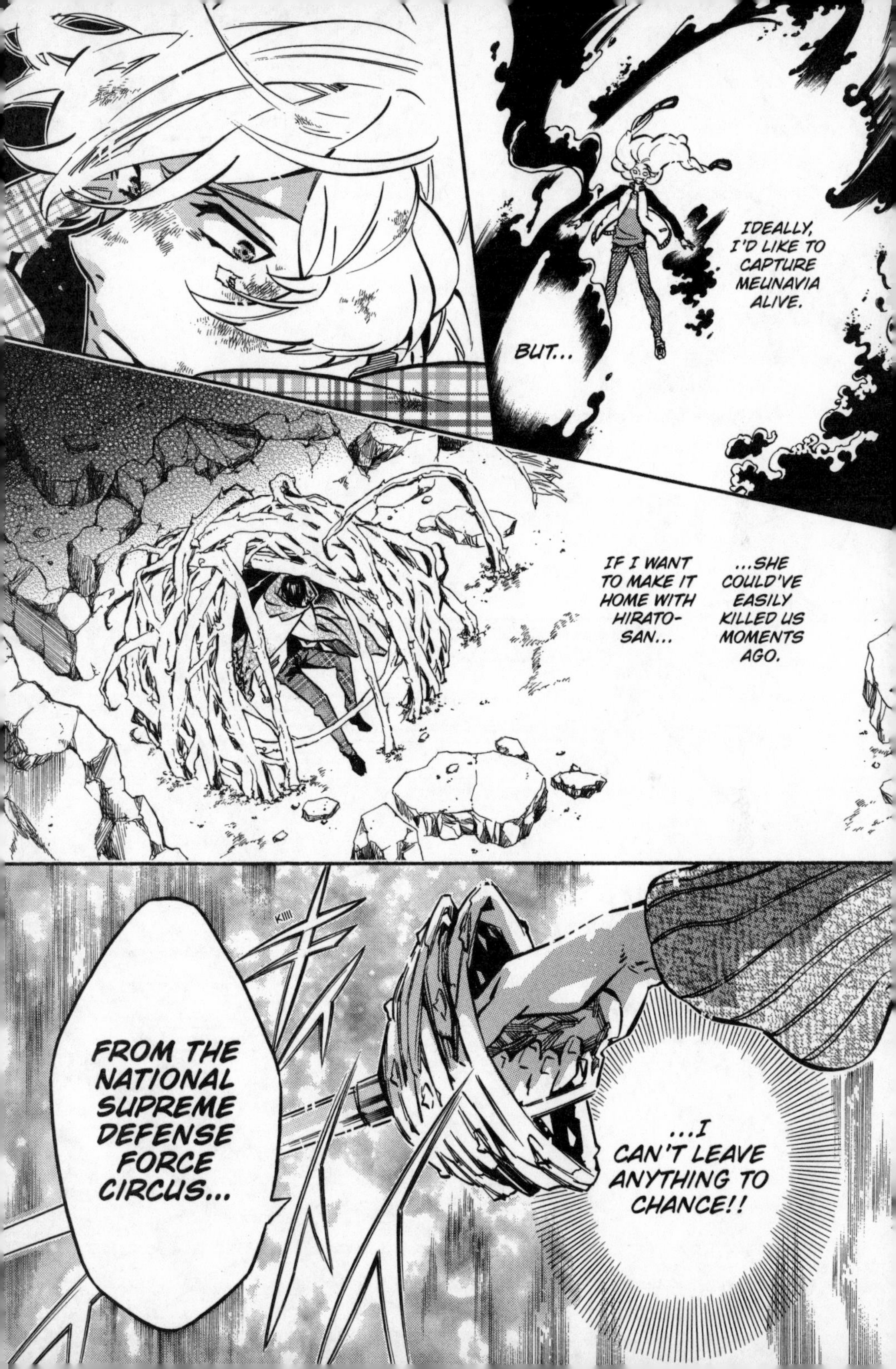
IDEALLY, I'D LIKE TO CAPTURE MEUNAVIA ALIVE.
BUT...
...SHE COULD'VE EASILY KILLED US MOMENTS AGO.
IF I WANT TO MAKE IT HOME WITH HIRATO-SAN...
...I CAN'T LEAVE ANYTHING TO CHANCE!!
FROM THE NATIONAL SUPREME DEFENSE FORCE CIRCUS...

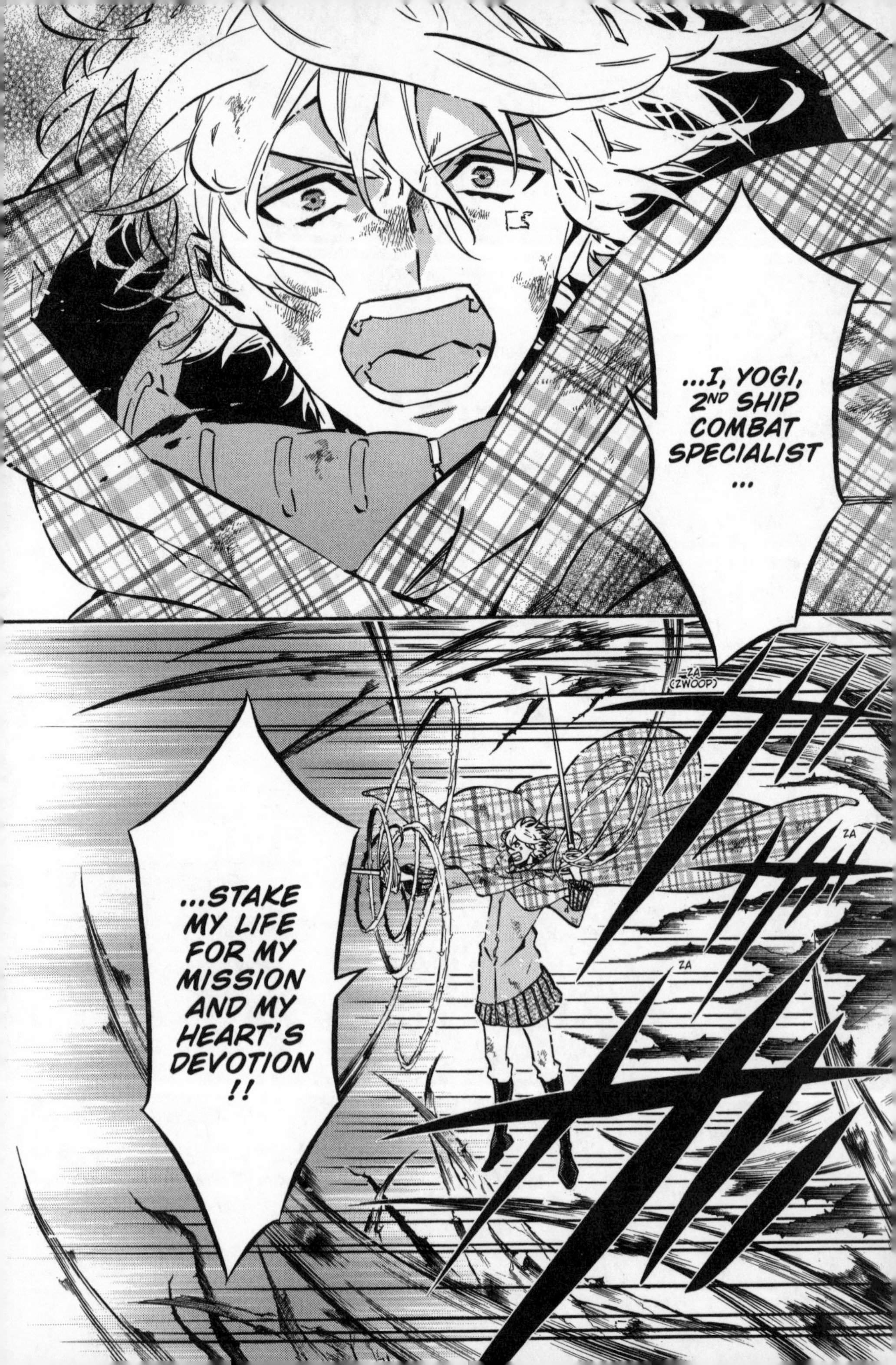
...I, YOGI, 2ND SHIP COMBAT SPECIALIST ...
ZA (ZWOOP)
ZA
ZA
...STAKE MY LIFE FOR MY MISSION AND MY HEART'S DEVOTION !!

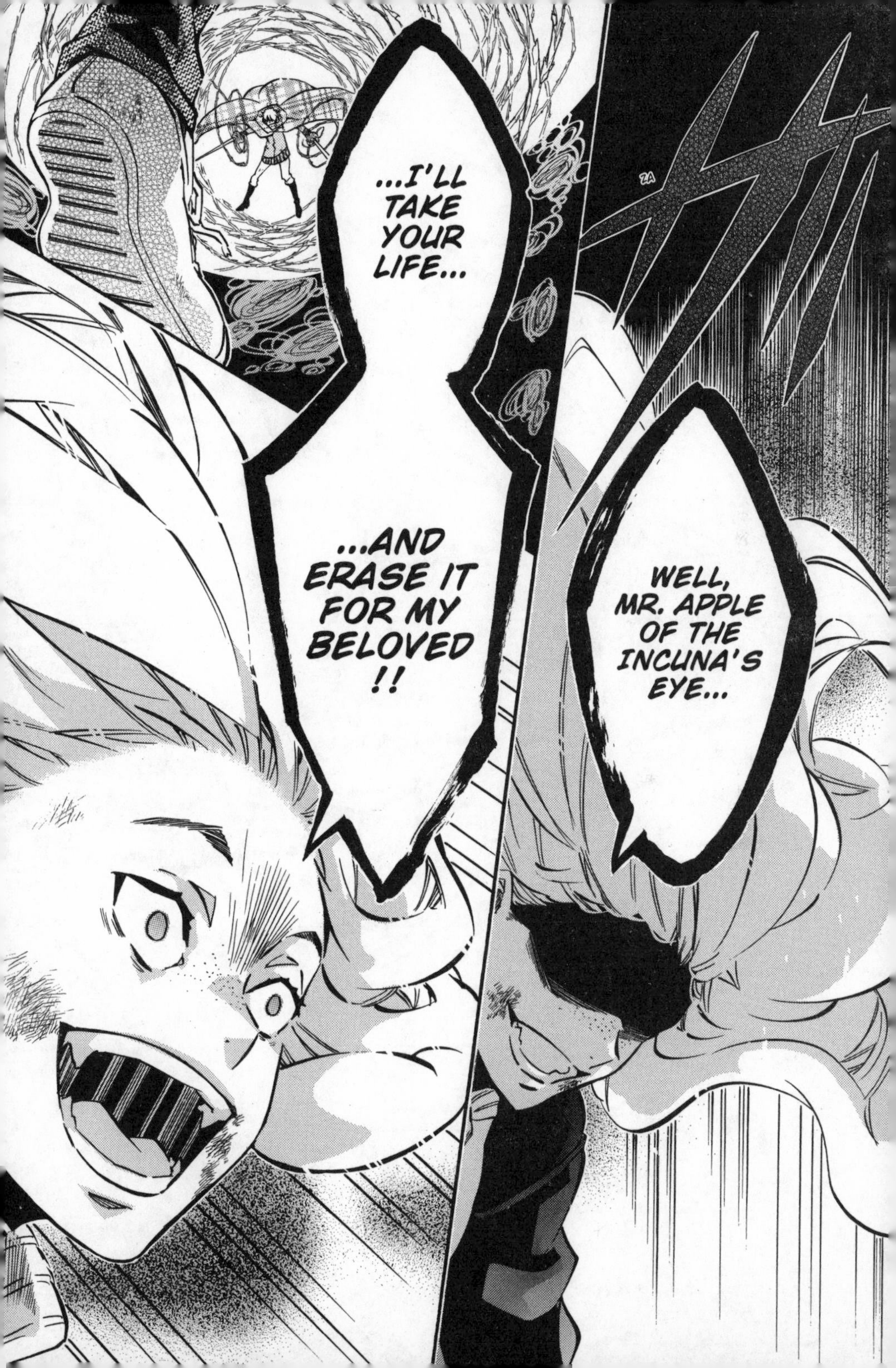
ZA
WELL, MR. APPLE OF THE INCUNA'S EYE...
...I'LL TAKE YOUR LIFE...
...AND ERASE IT FOR MY BELOVED!!

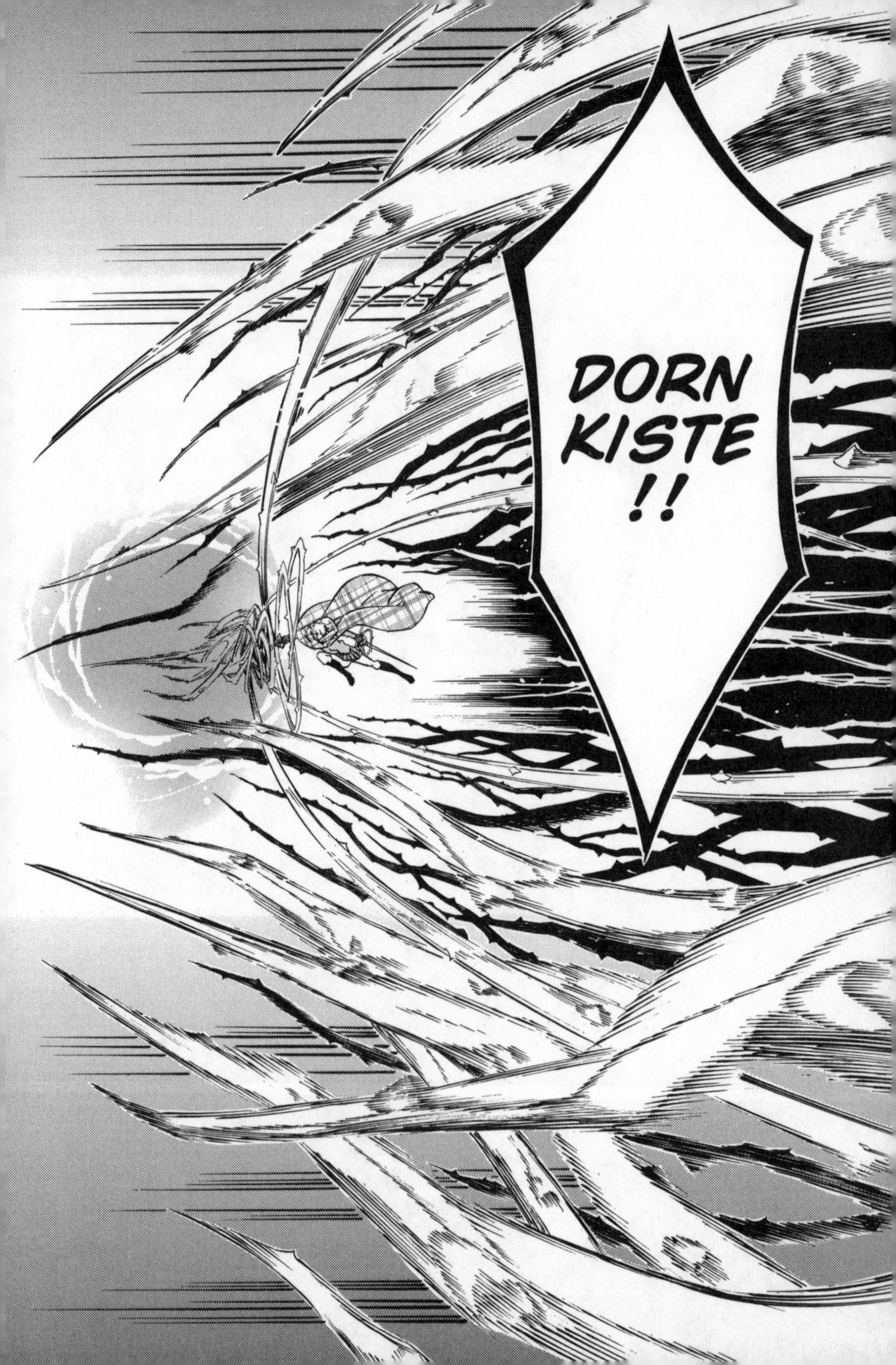
DORN KISTE !!

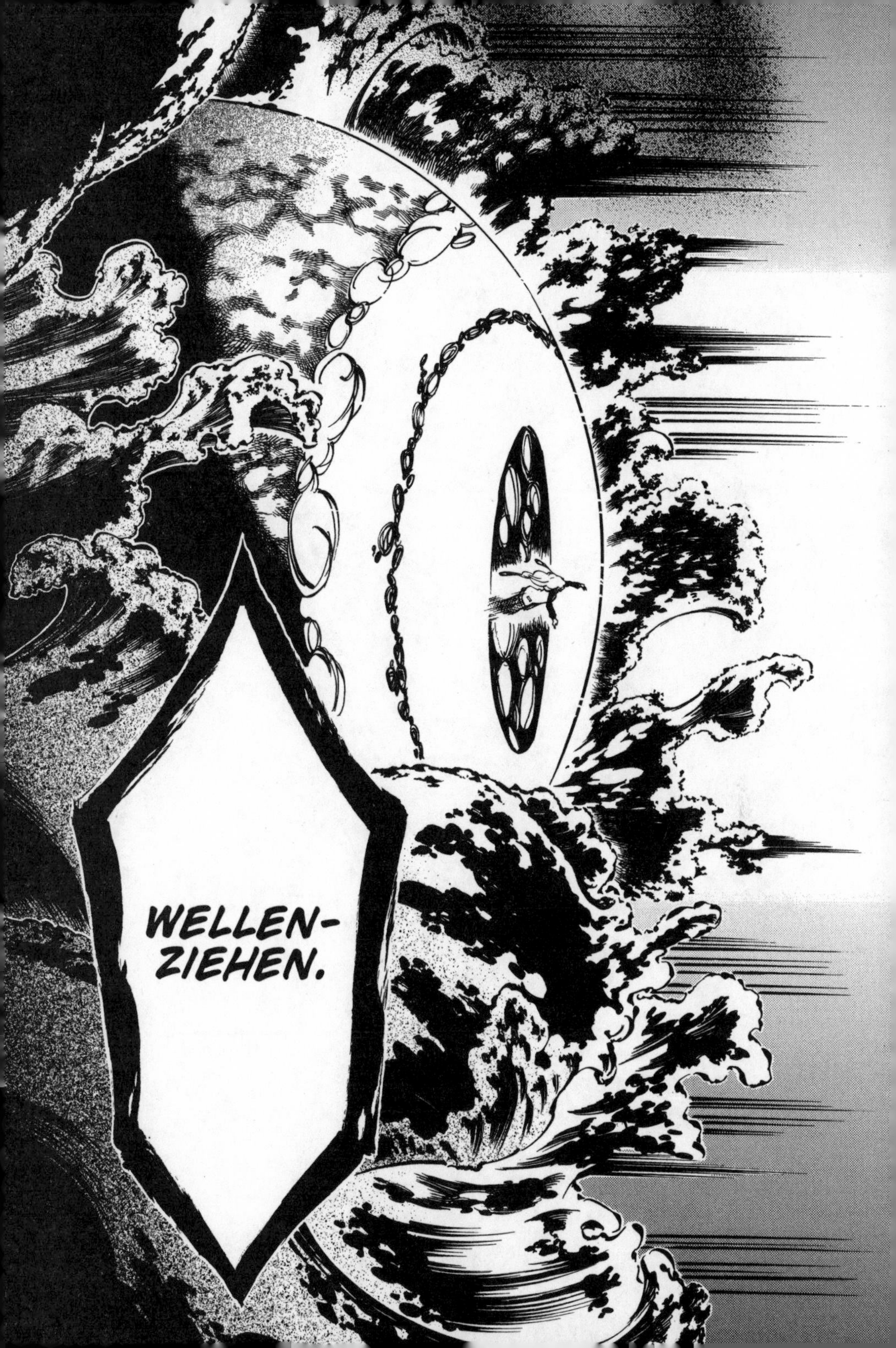
WELLEN-
ZIEHEN.

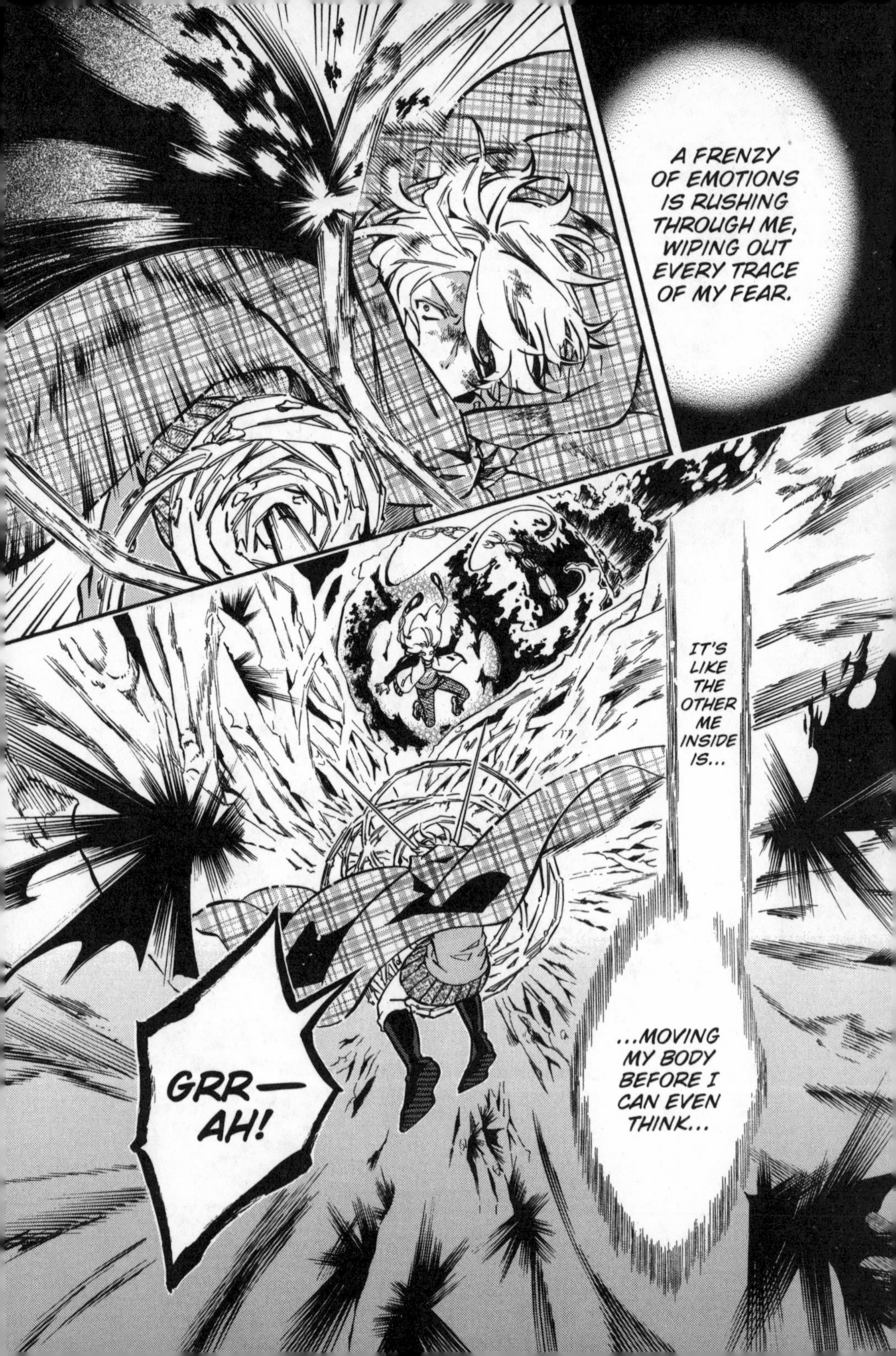
A FRENZY OF EMOTIONS IS RUSHING THROUGH ME, WIPING OUT EVERY TRACE OF MY FEAR.
IT'S LIKE THE OTHER ME INSIDE IS...
...MOVING MY BODY BEFORE I CAN EVEN THINK...
GRR—AH!

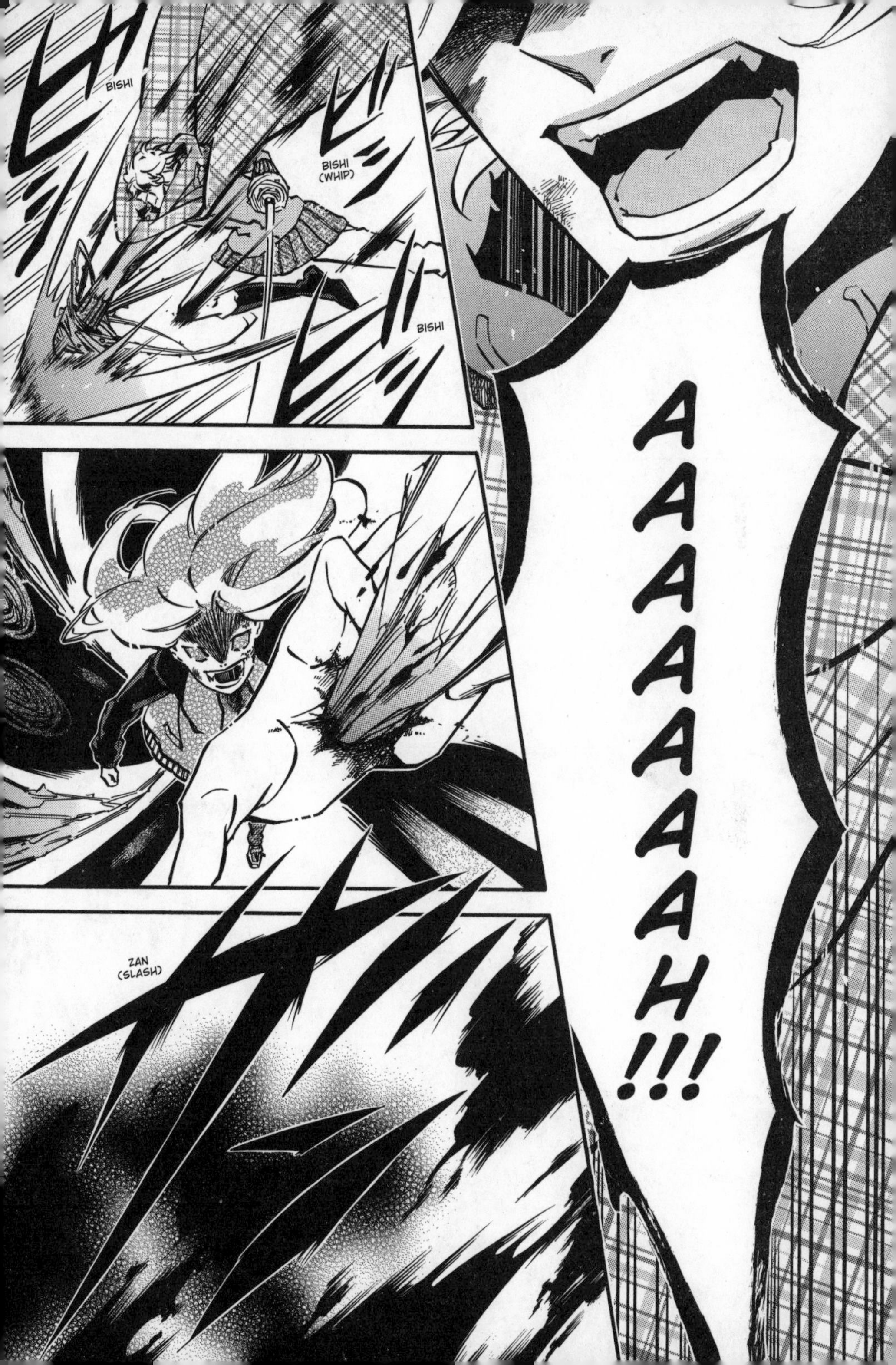
AAAAAAAH!!!
BISHI (WHIP)
BISHI
BISHI
ZAN (SLASH)

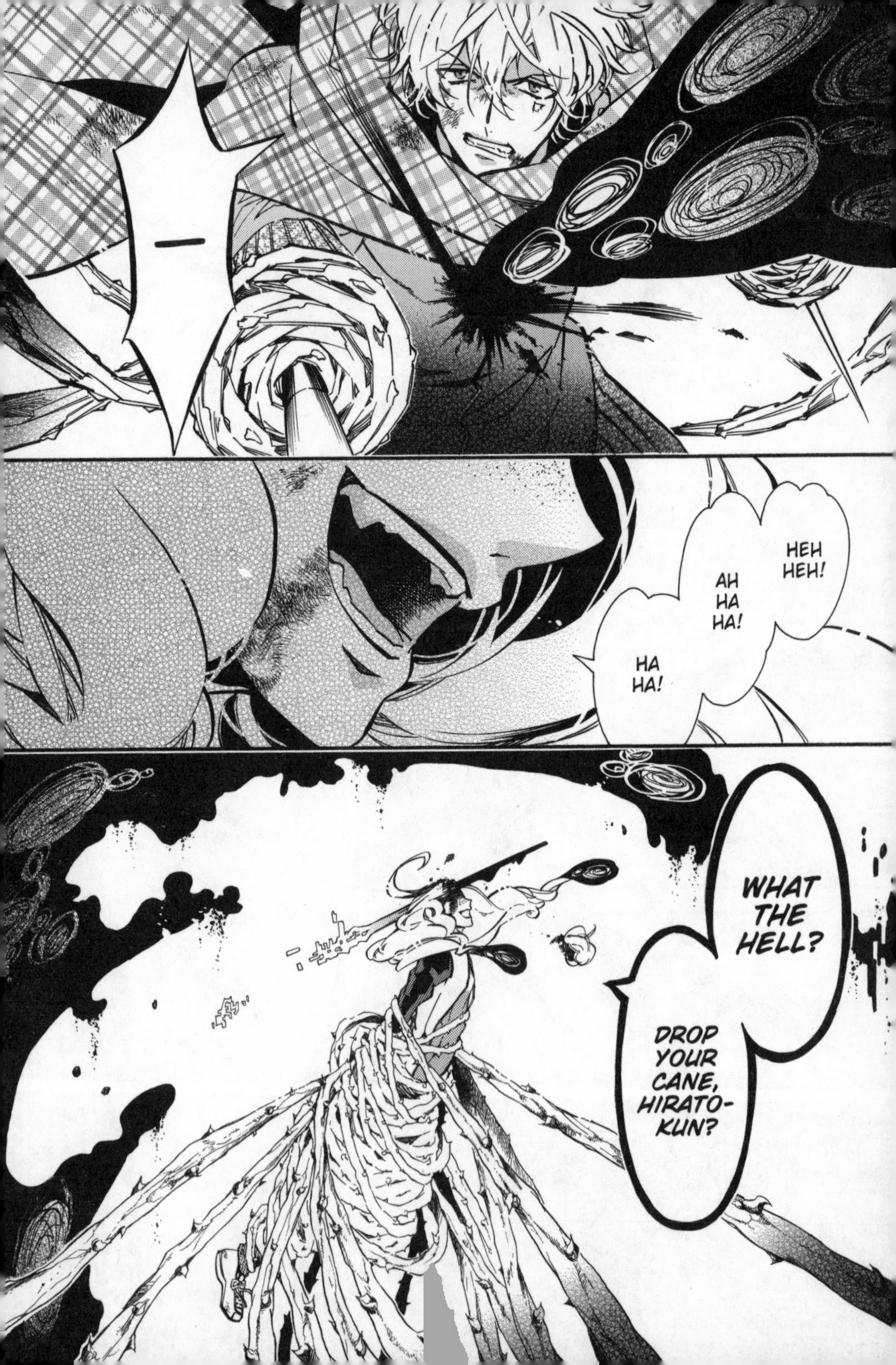
—
HEH HEH!
AH HA HA!
HA HA!
WHAT THE HELL?
DROP YOUR CANE, HIRATO-KUN?

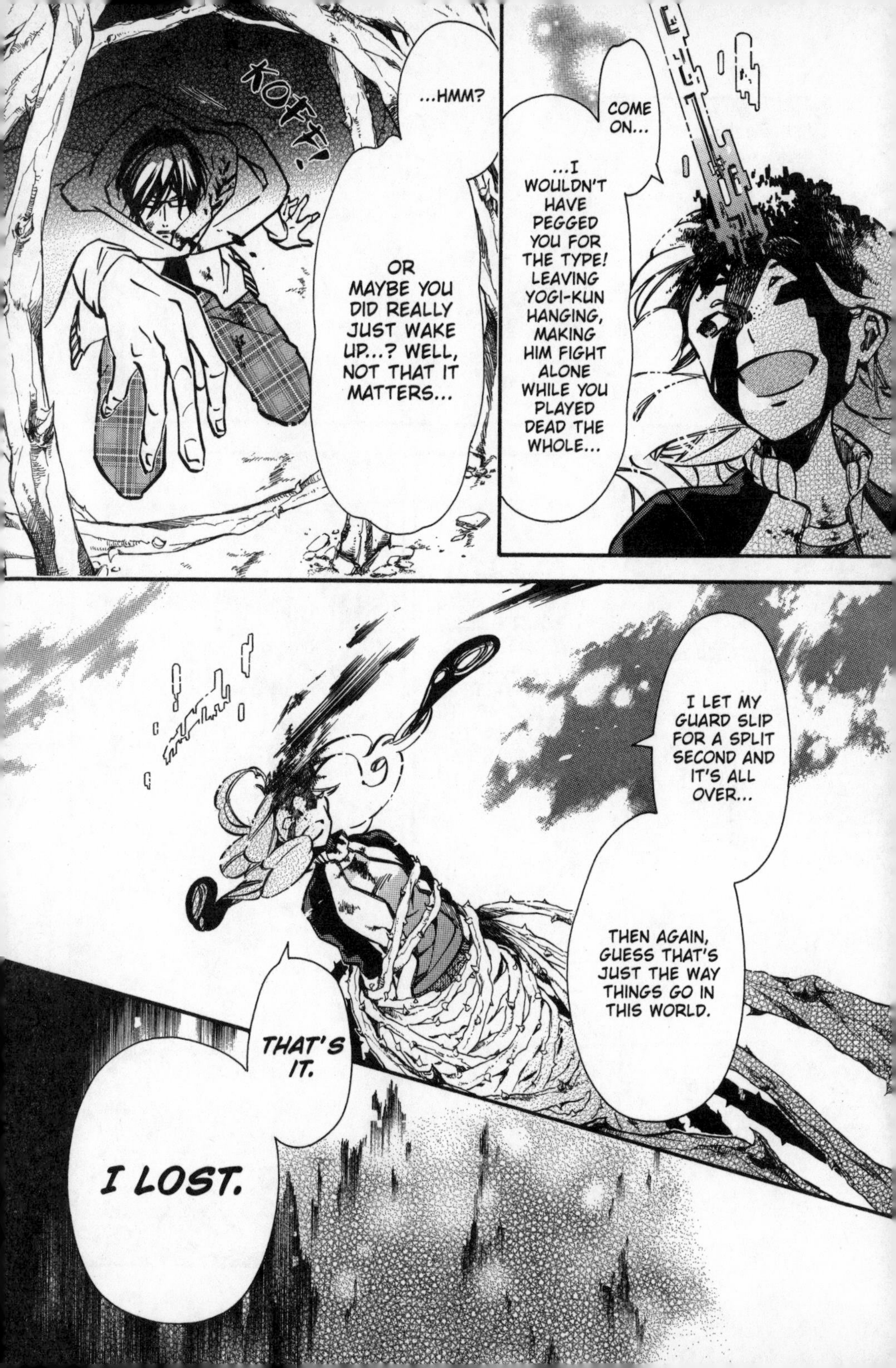
COME ON...
...I WOULDN'T HAVE PEGGED YOU FOR THE TYPE! LEAVING YOGI-KUN HANGING, MAKING HIM FIGHT ALONE WHILE YOU PLAYED DEAD THE WHOLE...
...HMM?
OR MAYBE YOU DID REALLY JUST WAKE UP...? WELL, NOT THAT IT MATTERS...
KOFF!
I LET MY GUARD SLIP FOR A SPLIT SECOND AND IT'S ALL OVER...
THEN AGAIN, GUESS THAT'S JUST THE WAY THINGS GO IN THIS WORLD.
THAT'S IT.
I LOST.

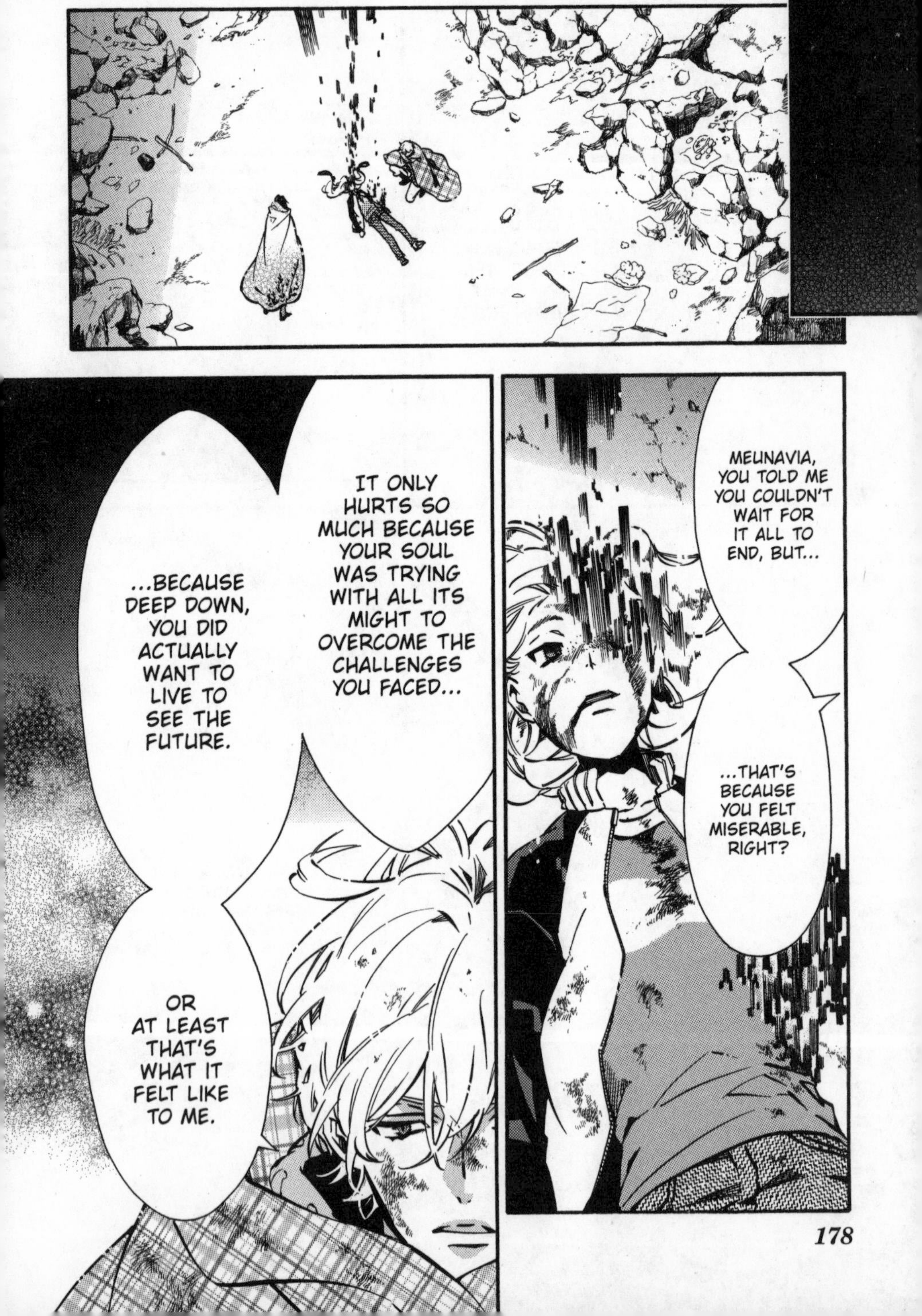
MEUNAVIA, YOU TOLD ME YOU COULDN'T WAIT FOR IT ALL TO END, BUT...
...THAT'S BECAUSE YOU FELT MISERABLE, RIGHT?
IT ONLY HURTS SO MUCH BECAUSE YOUR SOUL WAS TRYING WITH ALL ITS MIGHT TO OVERCOME THE CHALLENGES YOU FACED...
...BECAUSE DEEP DOWN, YOU DID ACTUALLY WANT TO LIVE TO SEE THE FUTURE.
OR AT LEAST THAT'S WHAT IT FELT LIKE TO ME.

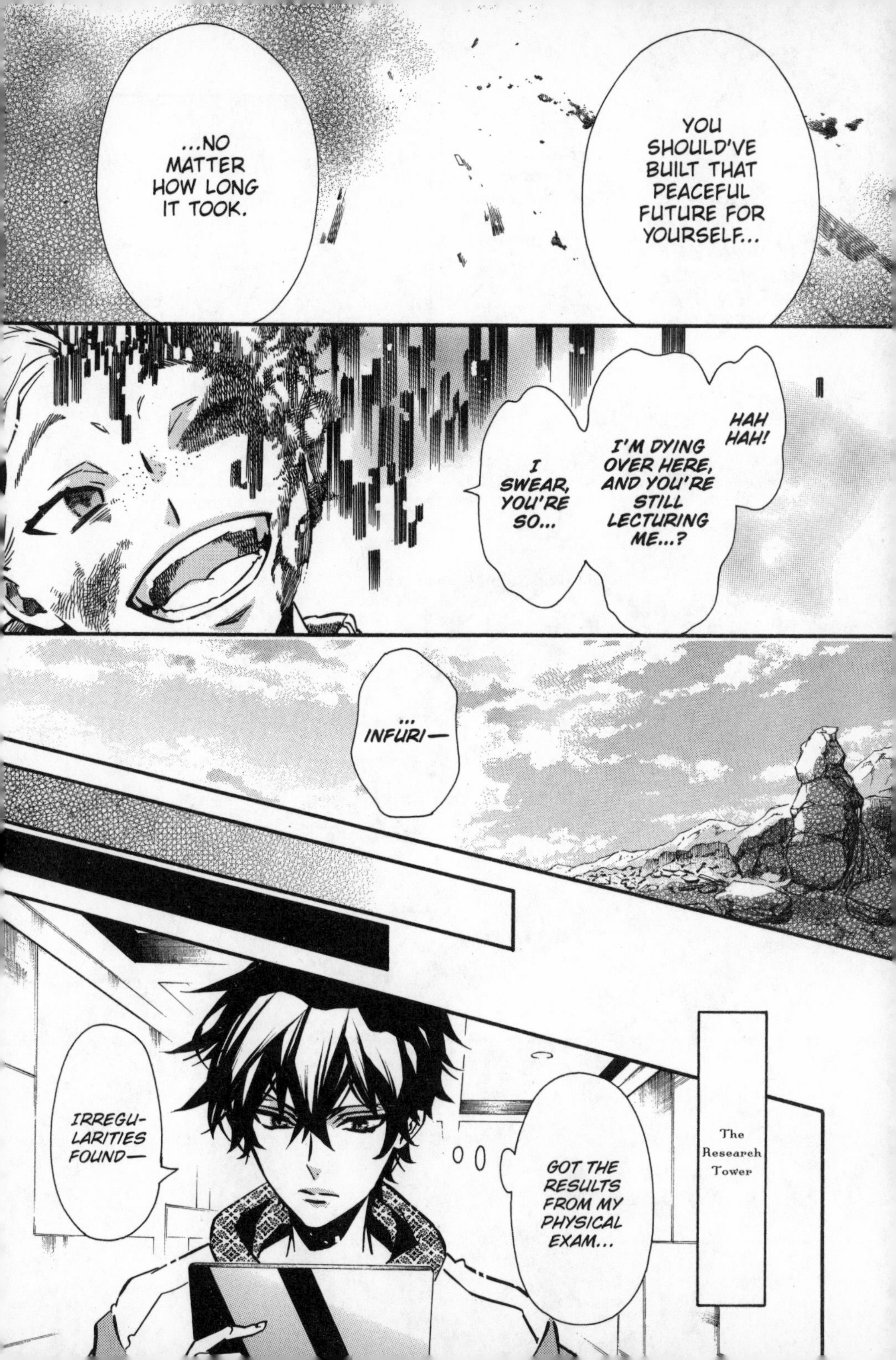
YOU SHOULD'VE BUILT THAT PEACEFUL FUTURE FOR YOURSELF...
...NO MATTER HOW LONG IT TOOK.
HAH HAH!
I'M DYING OVER HERE, AND YOU'RE STILL LECTURING ME...?
I SWEAR, YOU'RE SO...
... INFÜRI—
The Research Tower
GOT THE RESULTS FROM MY PHYSICAL EXAM...
IRREGU-LARITIES FOUND—

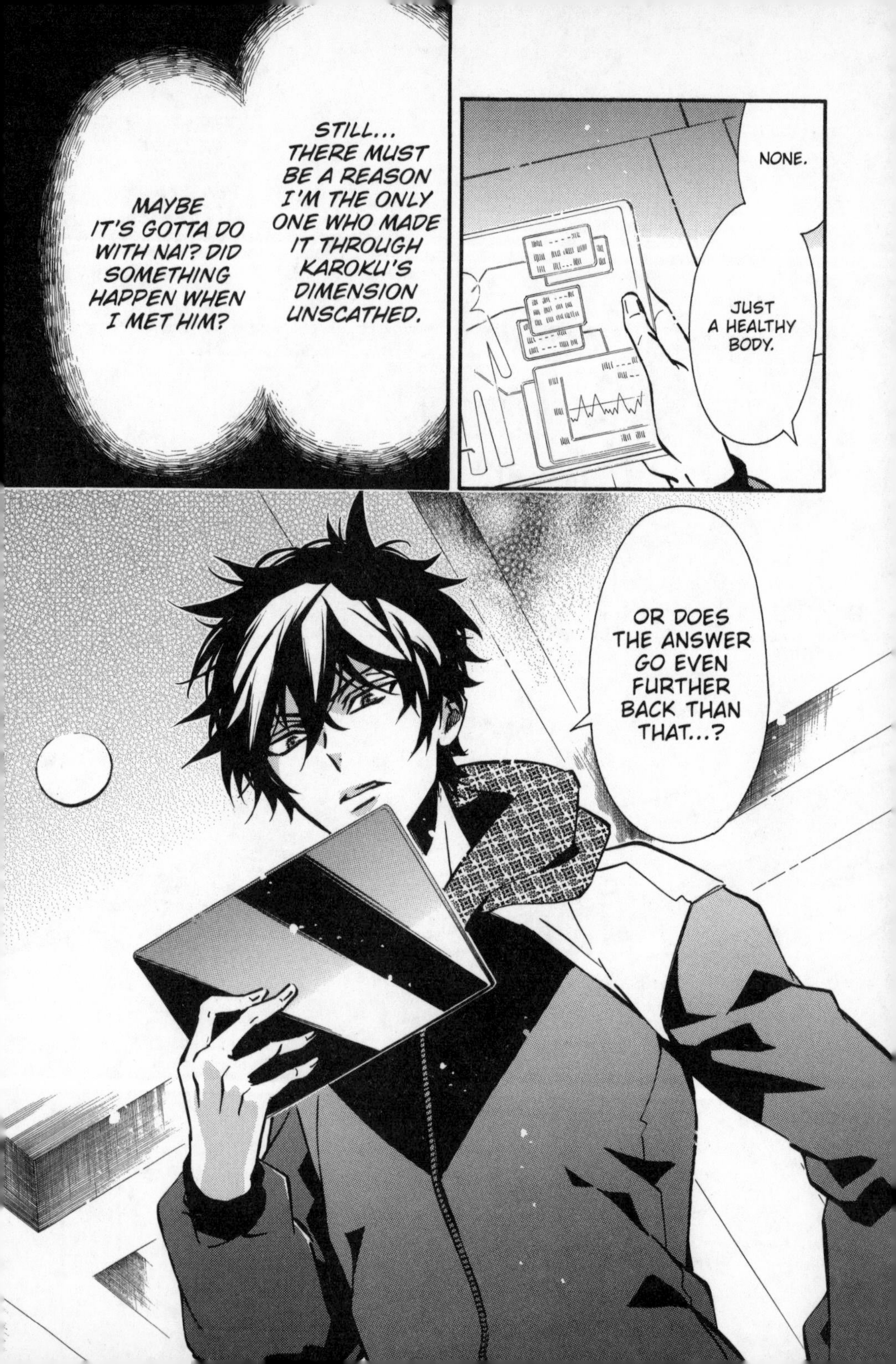
NONE.
JUST A HEALTHY BODY.
STILL... THERE MUST BE A REASON I'M THE ONLY ONE WHO MADE IT THROUGH KAROKU'S DIMENSION UNSCATHED.
MAYBE IT'S GOTTA DO WITH NAI? DID SOMETHING HAPPEN WHEN I MET HIM?
OR DOES THE ANSWER GO EVEN FURTHER BACK THAN THAT...?

KARNEVAL

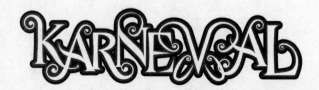

KARNEVAL

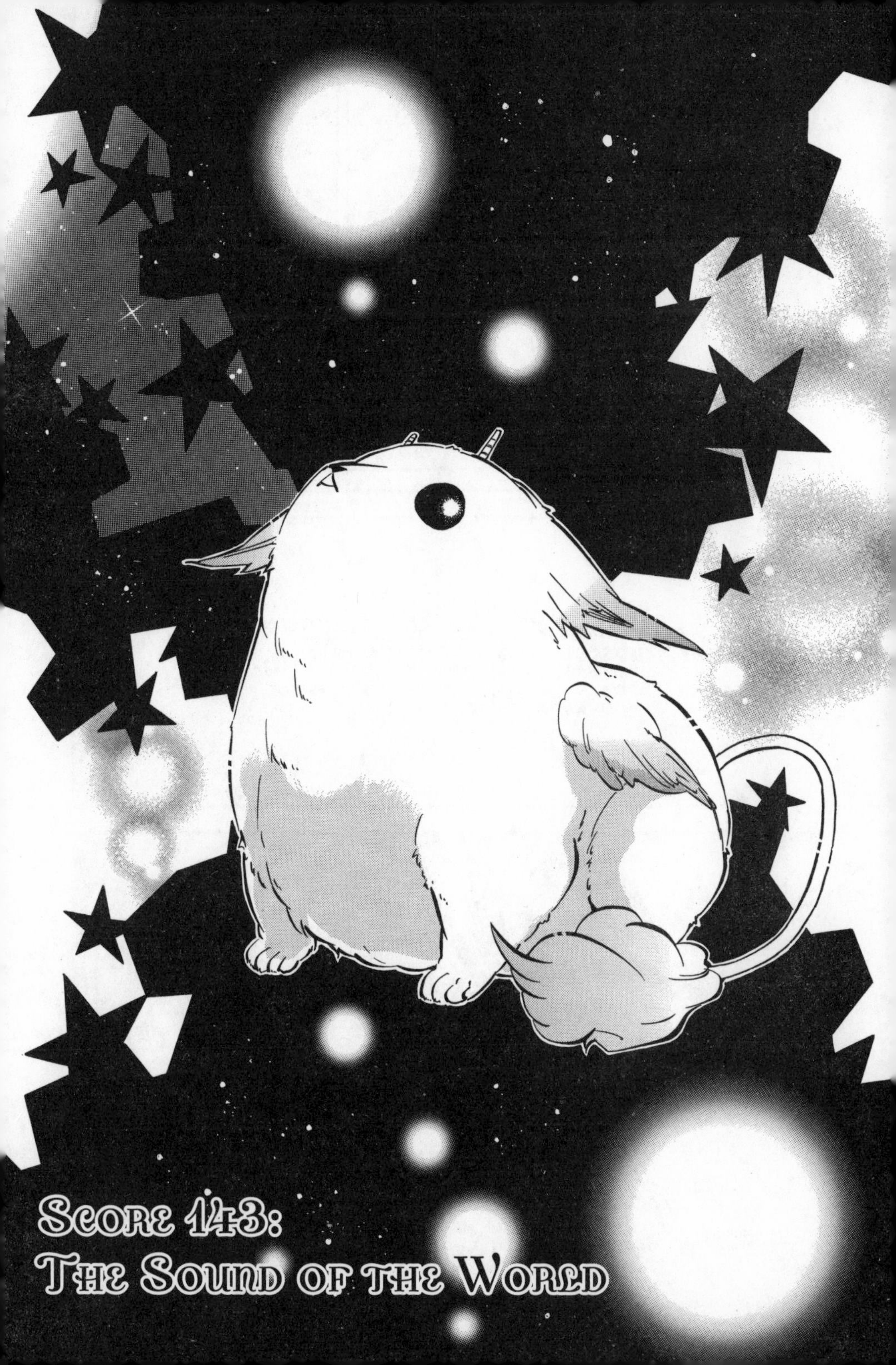
Score 143:
The Sound of the World

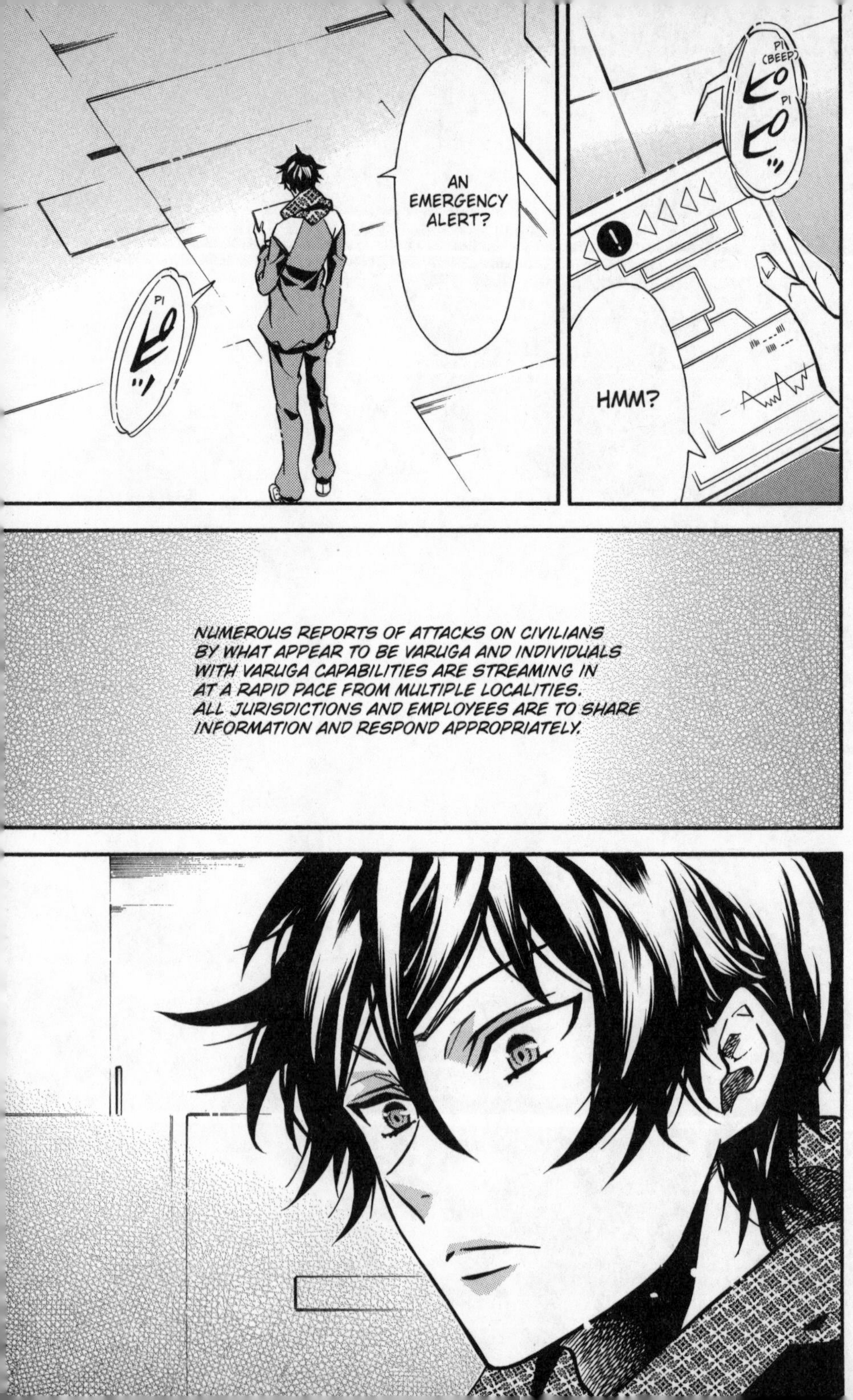
PI (BEEP)
PI
HMM?
PI
AN EMERGENCY ALERT?
NUMEROUS REPORTS OF ATTACKS ON CIVILIANS BY WHAT APPEAR TO BE VARUGA AND INDIVIDUALS WITH VARUGA CAPABILITIES ARE STREAMING IN AT A RAPID PACE FROM MULTIPLE LOCALITIES. ALL JURISDICTIONS AND EMPLOYEES ARE TO SHARE INFORMATION AND RESPOND APPROPRIATELY.

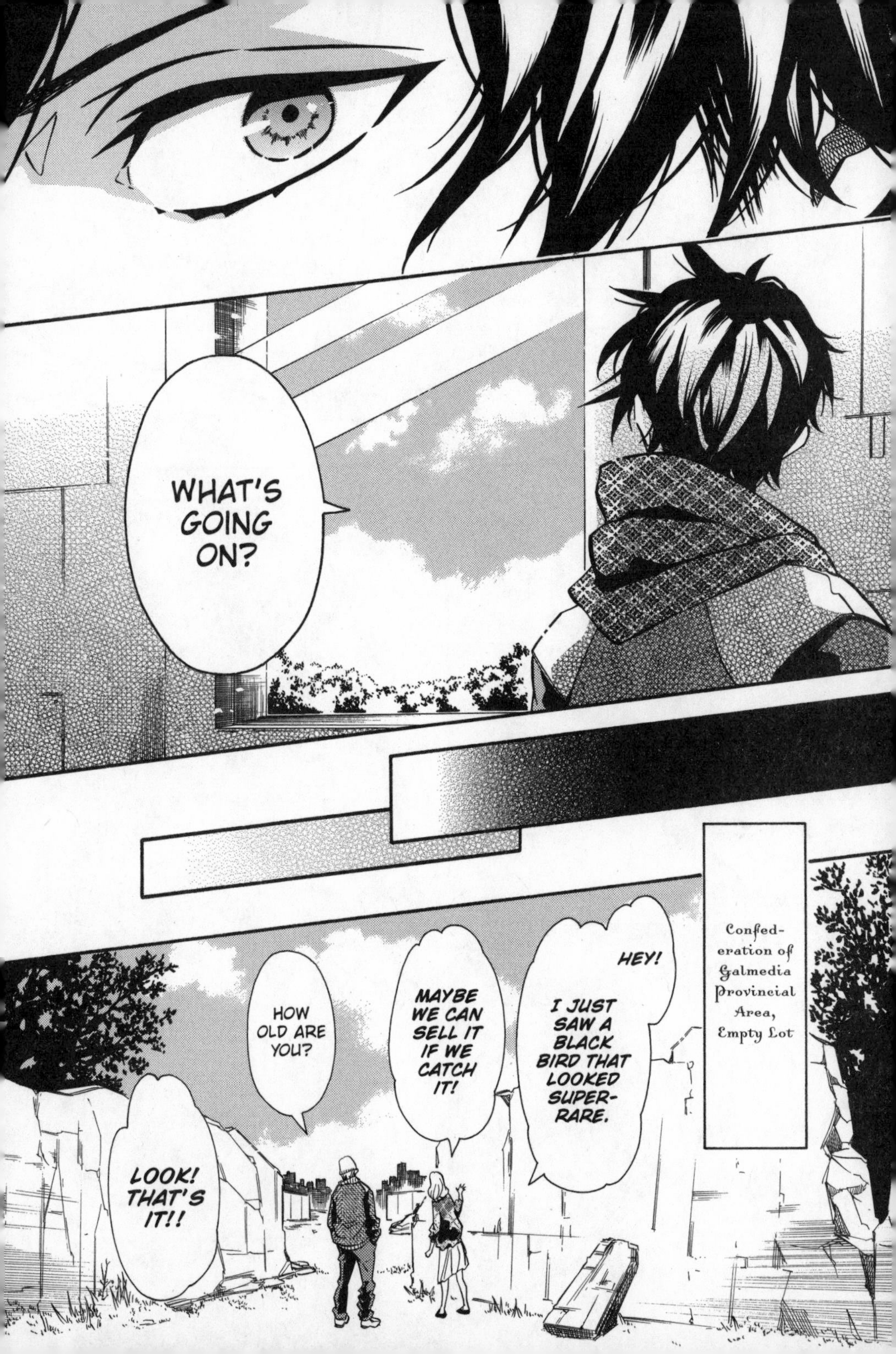
WHAT'S GOING ON?
Confederation of Galmedia Provincial Area, Empty Lot
HEY! I JUST SAW A BLACK BIRD THAT LOOKED SUPERRARE.
MAYBE WE CAN SELL IT IF WE CATCH IT!
HOW OLD ARE YOU?
LOOK! THAT'S IT!!

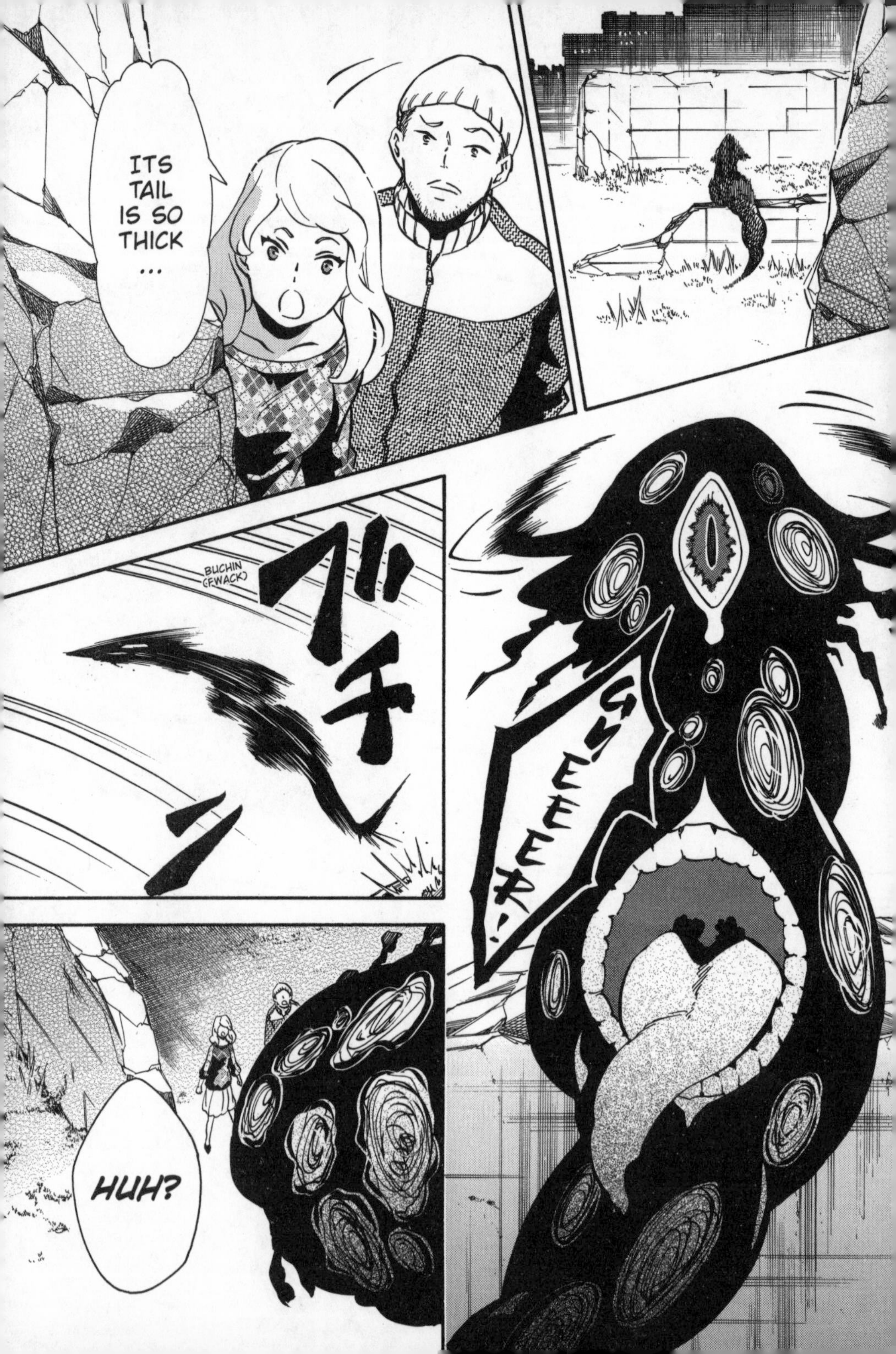
ITS TAIL IS SO THICK ...
SWEEEER!
ブチッ
BUCHIN (FWACK)
HUH?

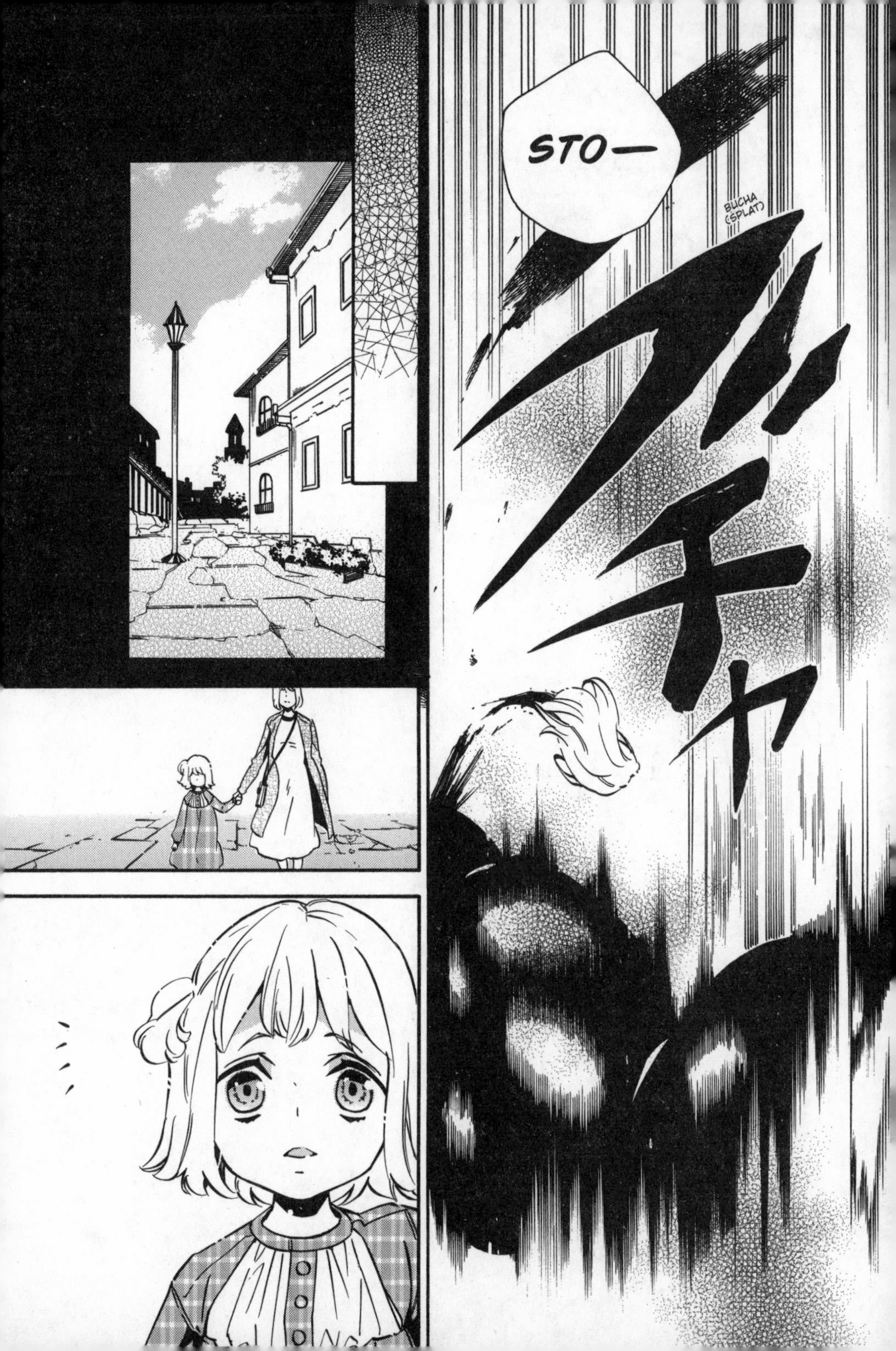
STO—
BUCHA
(SPLAT)
ブチャ

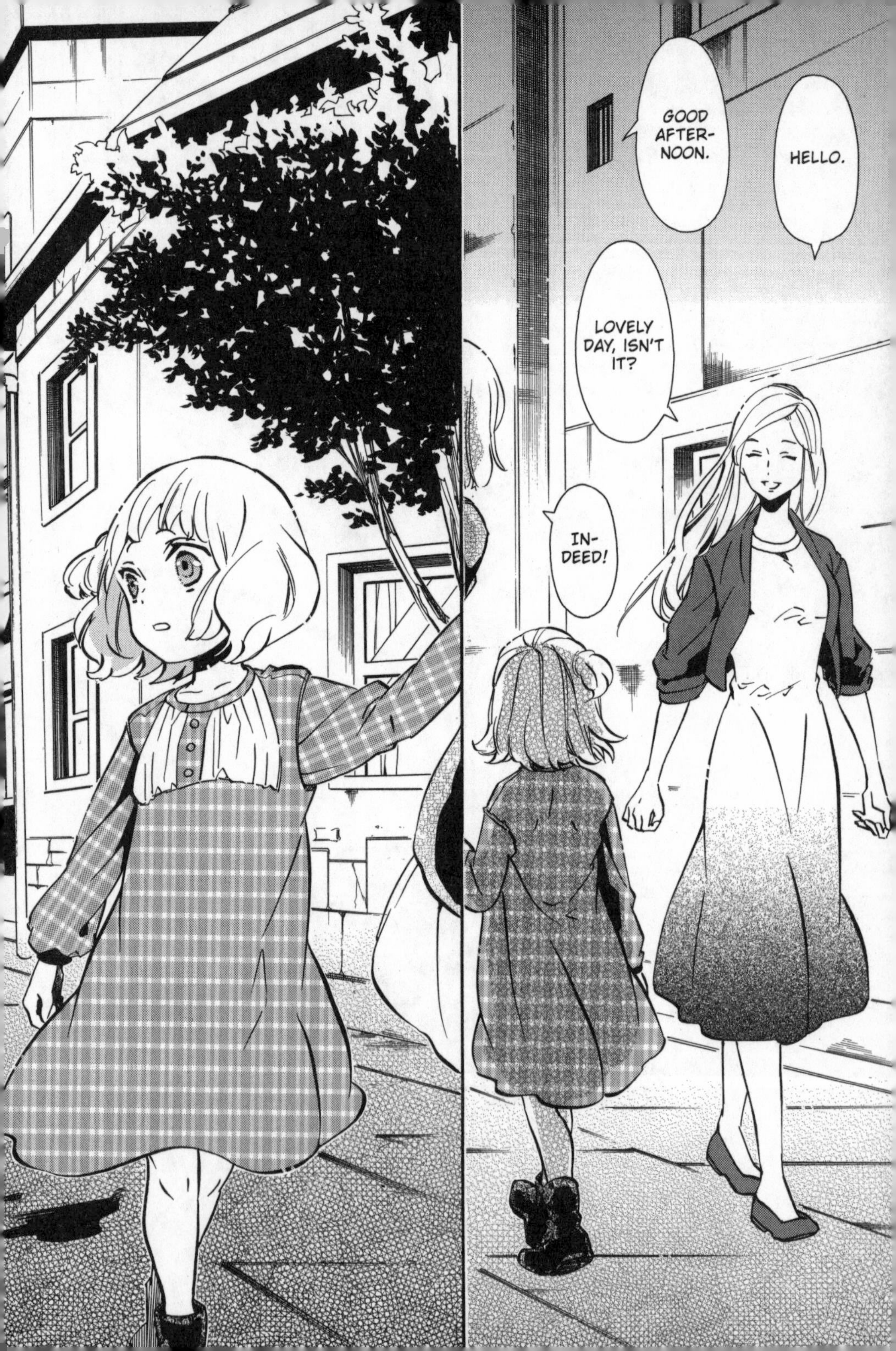
HELLO.
GOOD AFTER-NOON.
LOVELY DAY, ISN'T IT?
IN-DEED!

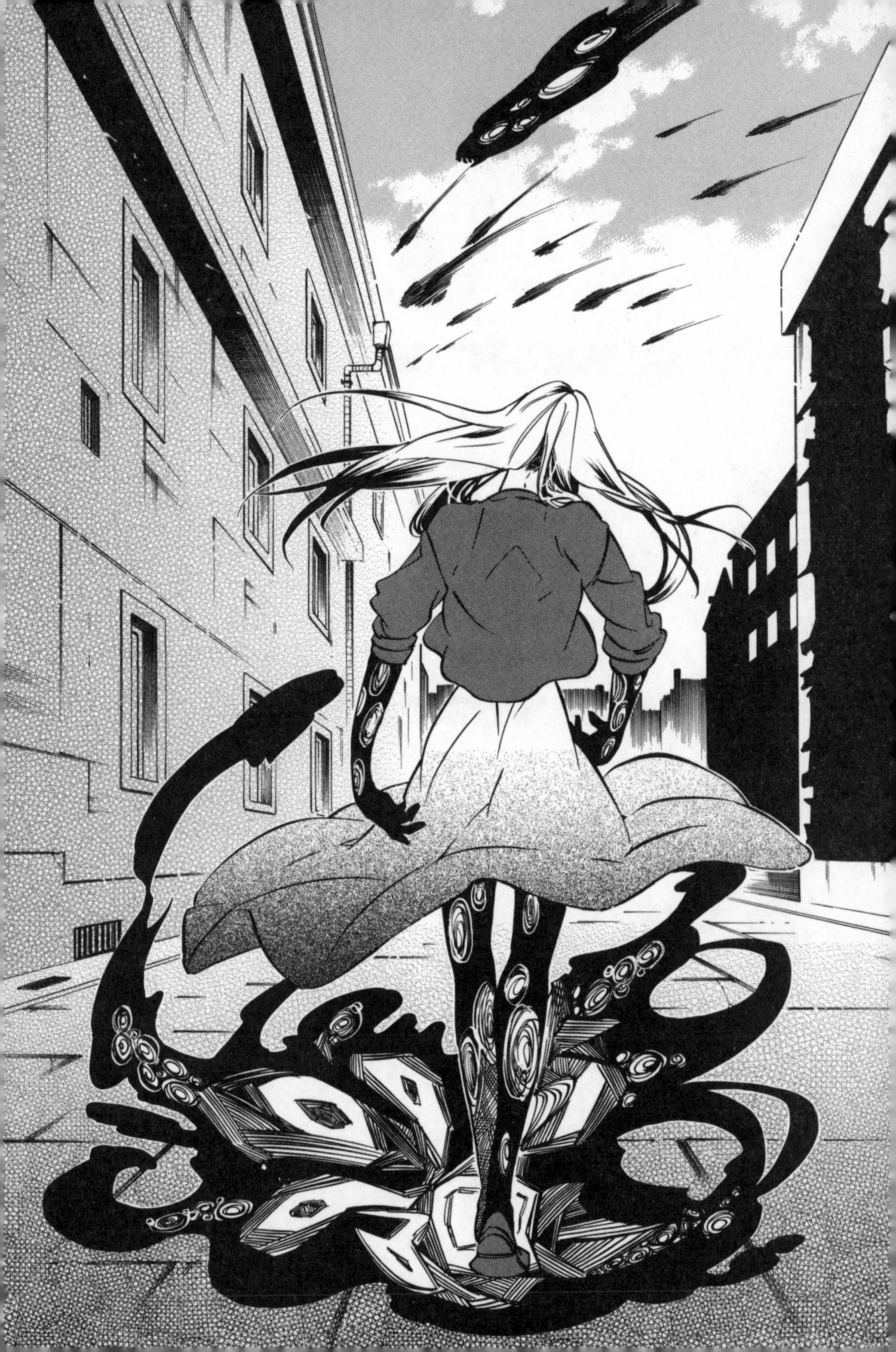

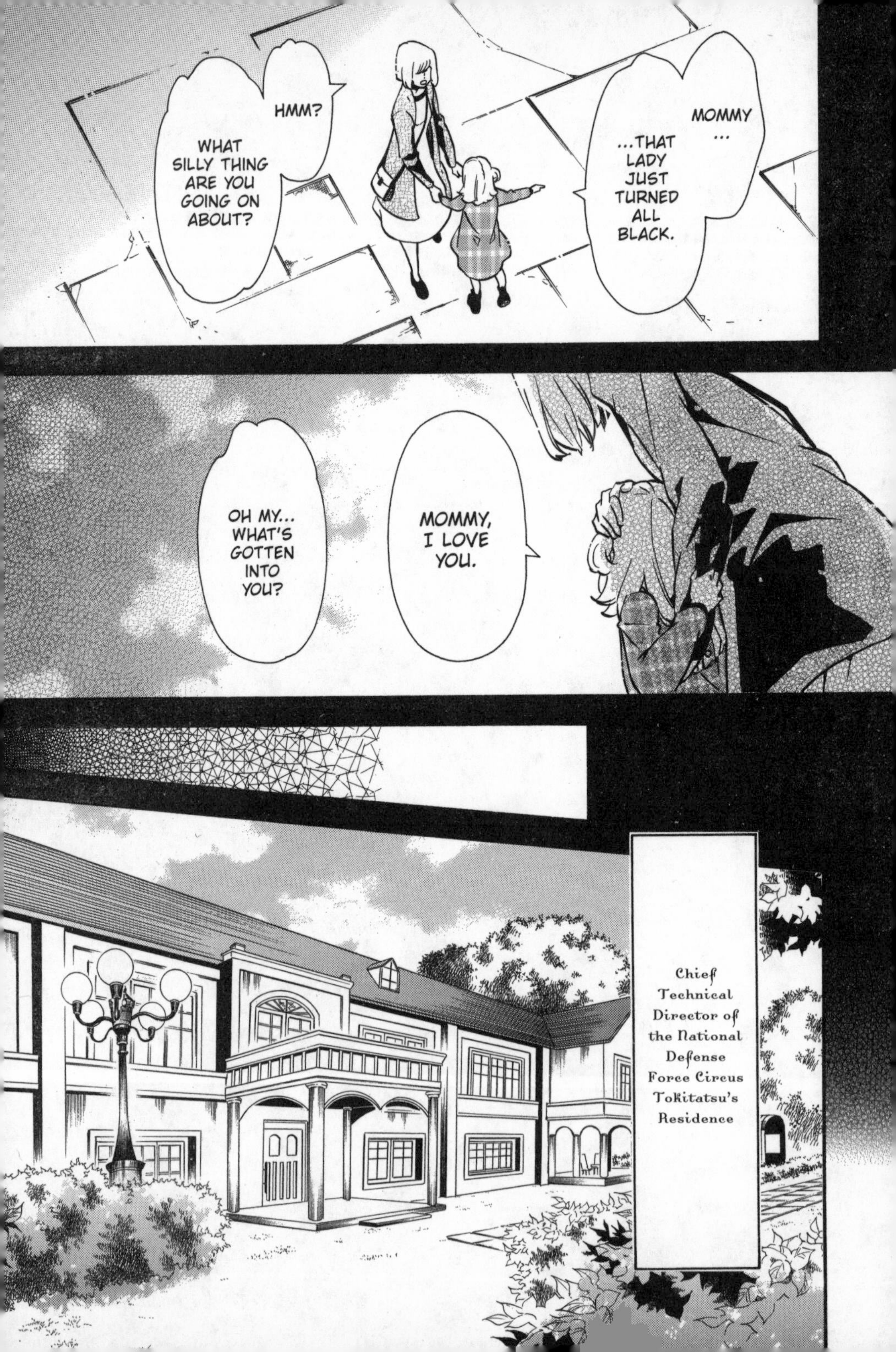
MOMMY...
...THAT LADY JUST TURNED ALL BLACK.
HMM?
WHAT SILLY THING ARE YOU GOING ON ABOUT?
MOMMY, I LOVE YOU.
OH MY... WHAT'S GOTTEN INTO YOU?
Chief Technical Director of the National Defense Force Circus Tokitatsu's Residence

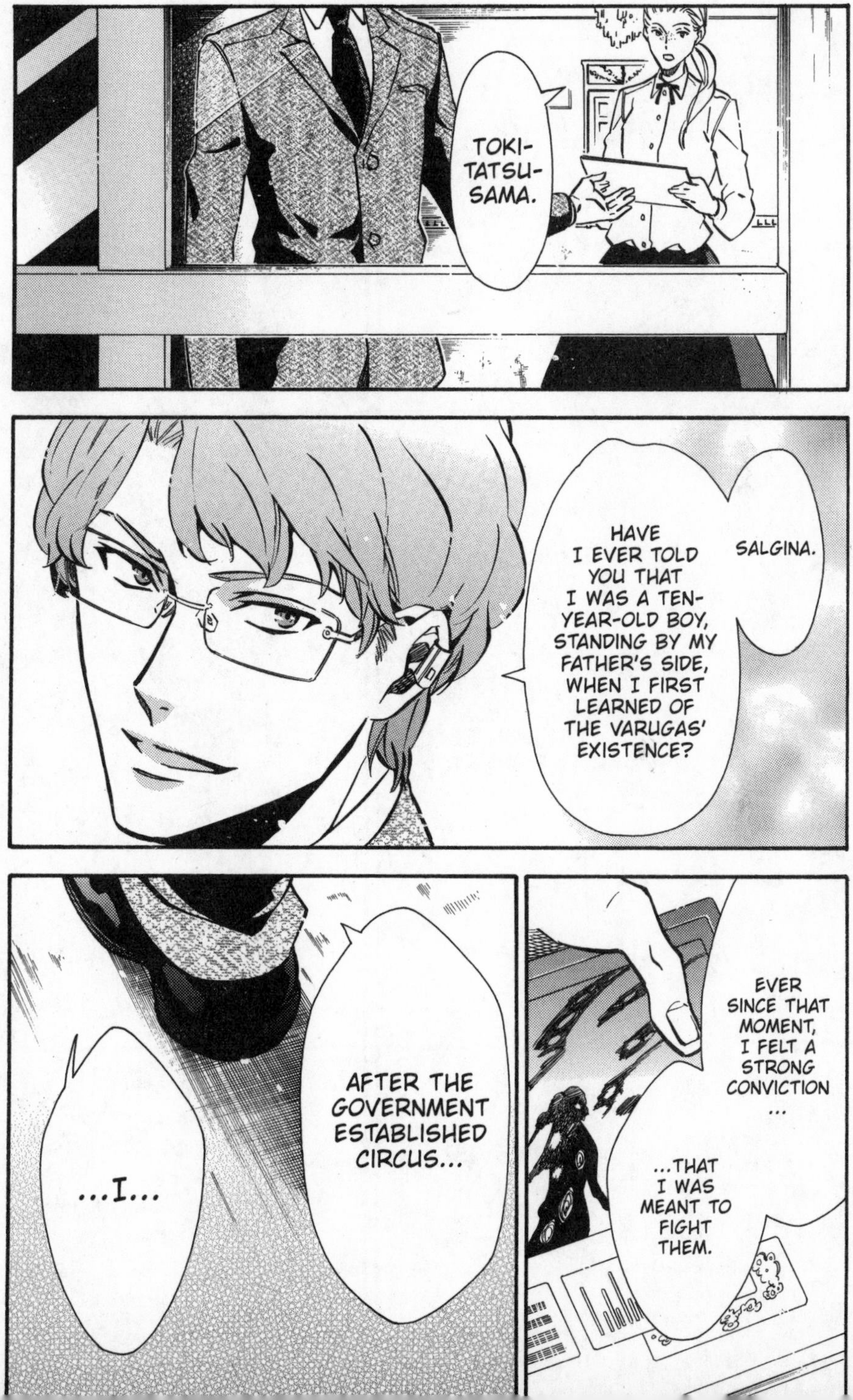
TOKI-TATSU-SAMA.
SALGINA.
HAVE I EVER TOLD YOU THAT I WAS A TEN-YEAR-OLD BOY, STANDING BY MY FATHER'S SIDE, WHEN I FIRST LEARNED OF THE VARUGAS' EXISTENCE?
EVER SINCE THAT MOMENT, I FELT A STRONG CONVICTION...
...THAT I WAS MEANT TO FIGHT THEM.
AFTER THE GOVERNMENT ESTABLISHED CIRCUS...
...I...

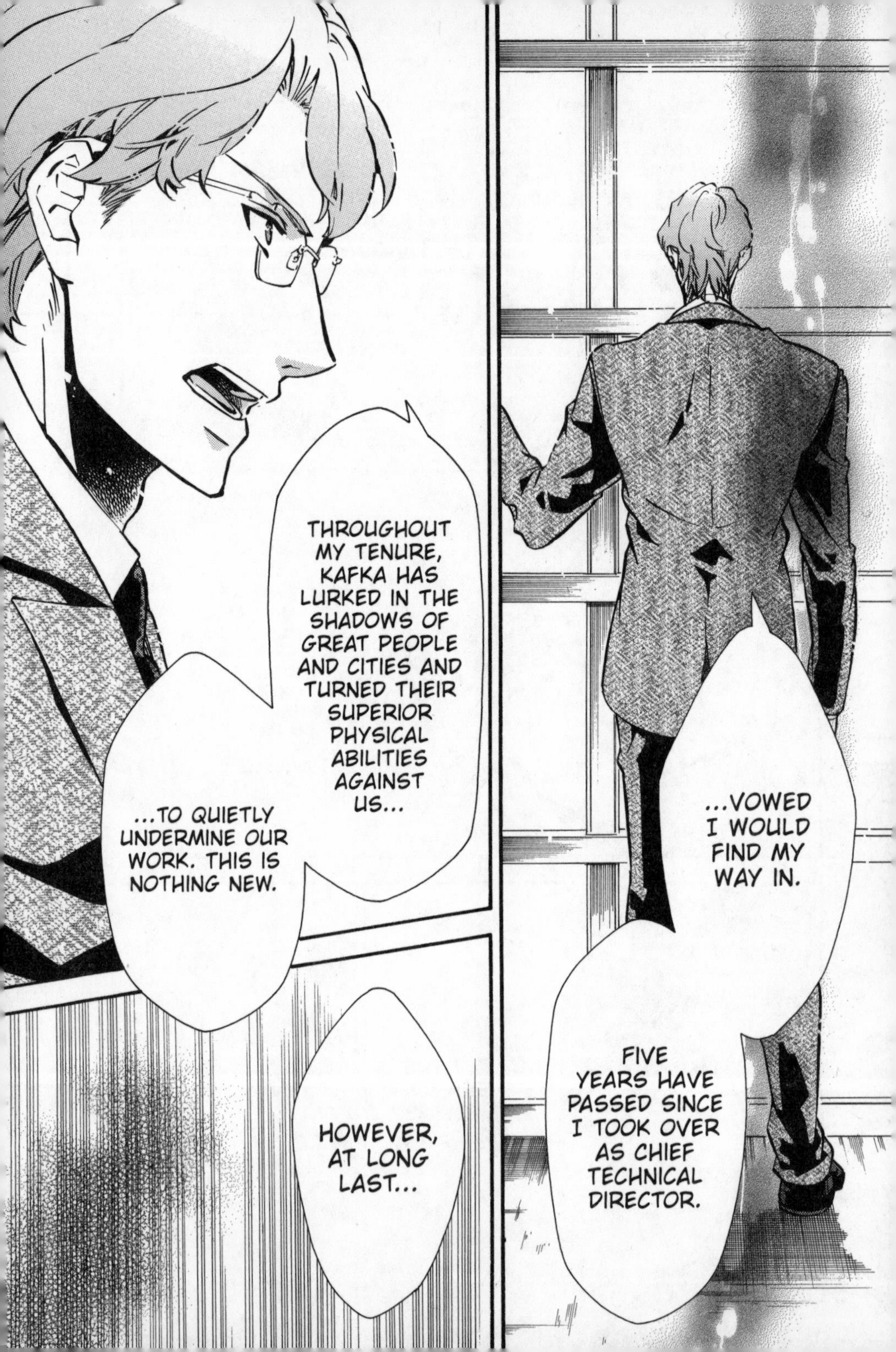
...VOWED I WOULD FIND MY WAY IN.
FIVE YEARS HAVE PASSED SINCE I TOOK OVER AS CHIEF TECHNICAL DIRECTOR.
THROUGHOUT MY TENURE, KAFKA HAS LURKED IN THE SHADOWS OF GREAT PEOPLE AND CITIES AND TURNED THEIR SUPERIOR PHYSICAL ABILITIES AGAINST US...
...TO QUIETLY UNDERMINE OUR WORK. THIS IS NOTHING NEW.
HOWEVER, AT LONG LAST...

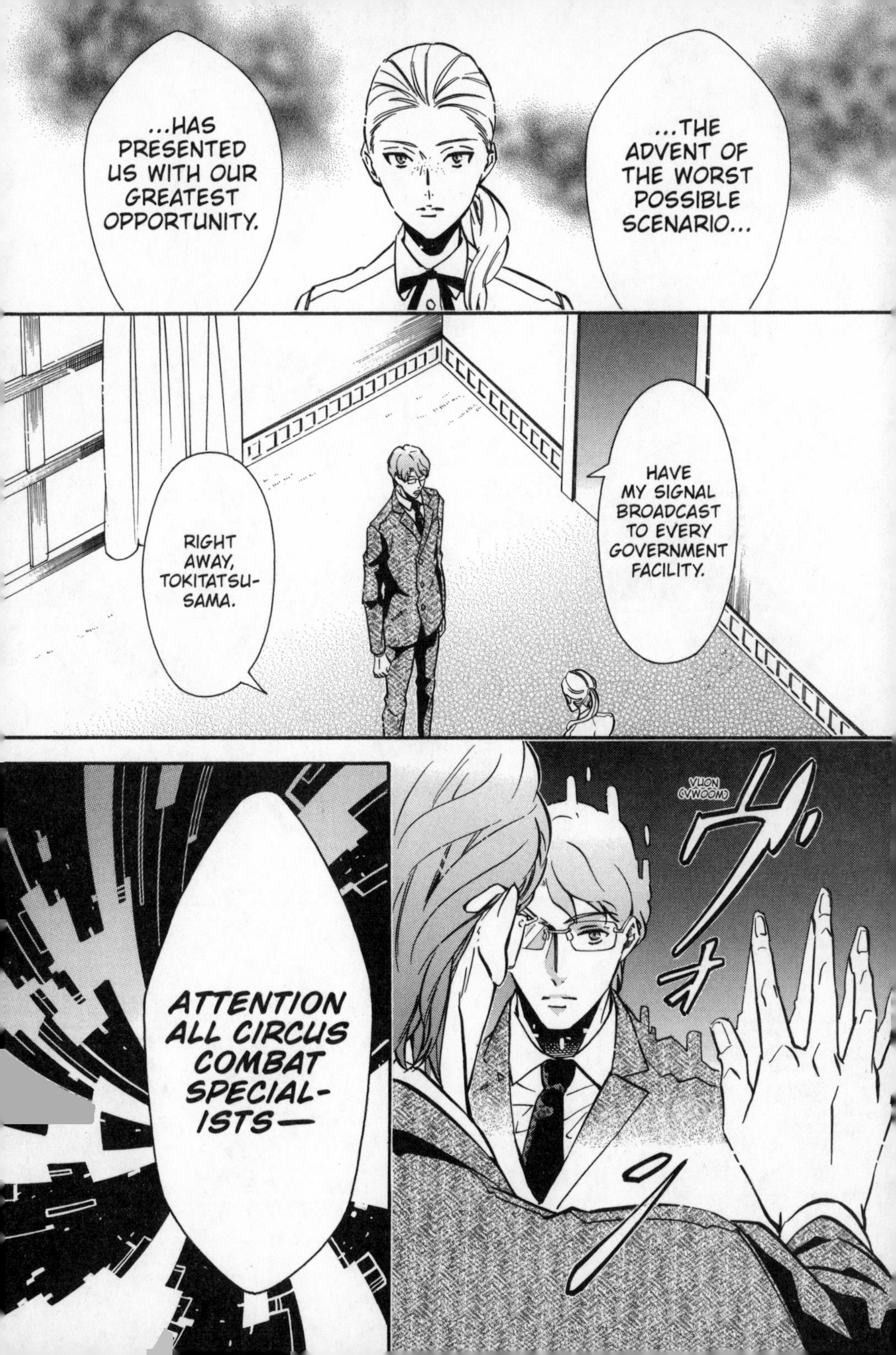
...THE ADVENT OF THE WORST POSSIBLE SCENARIO...
...HAS PRESENTED US WITH OUR GREATEST OPPORTUNITY.
HAVE MY SIGNAL BROADCAST TO EVERY GOVERNMENT FACILITY.
RIGHT AWAY, TOKITATSU-SAMA.
VUON (VWOOM)
ATTENTION ALL CIRCUS COMBAT SPECIAL-ISTS—

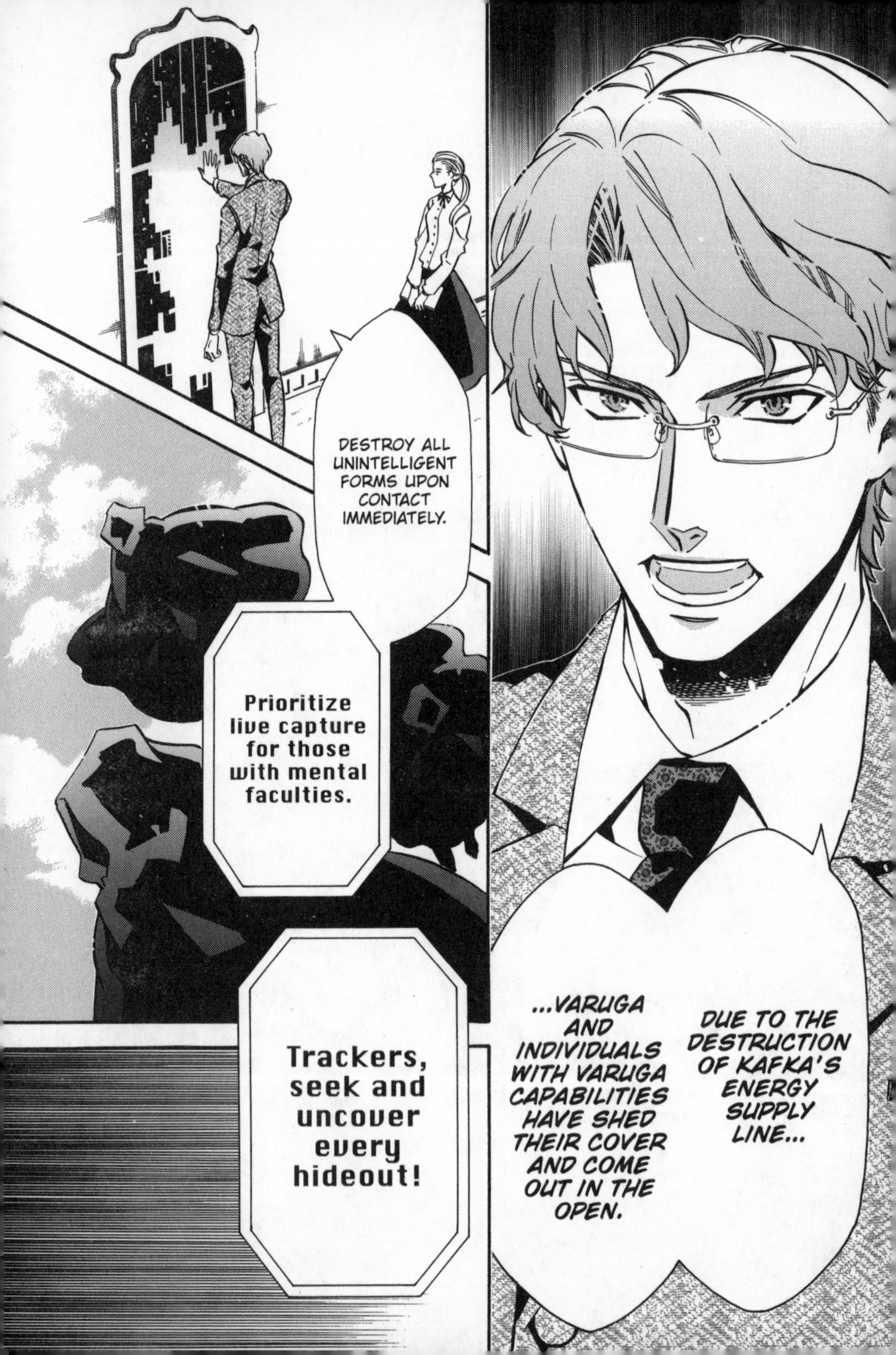
DUE TO THE DESTRUCTION OF KAFKA'S ENERGY SUPPLY LINE...
...VARUGA AND INDIVIDUALS WITH VARUGA CAPABILITIES HAVE SHED THEIR COVER AND COME OUT IN THE OPEN.
DESTROY ALL UNINTELLIGENT FORMS UPON CONTACT IMMEDIATELY.
Prioritize live capture for those with mental faculties.
Trackers, seek and uncover every hideout!

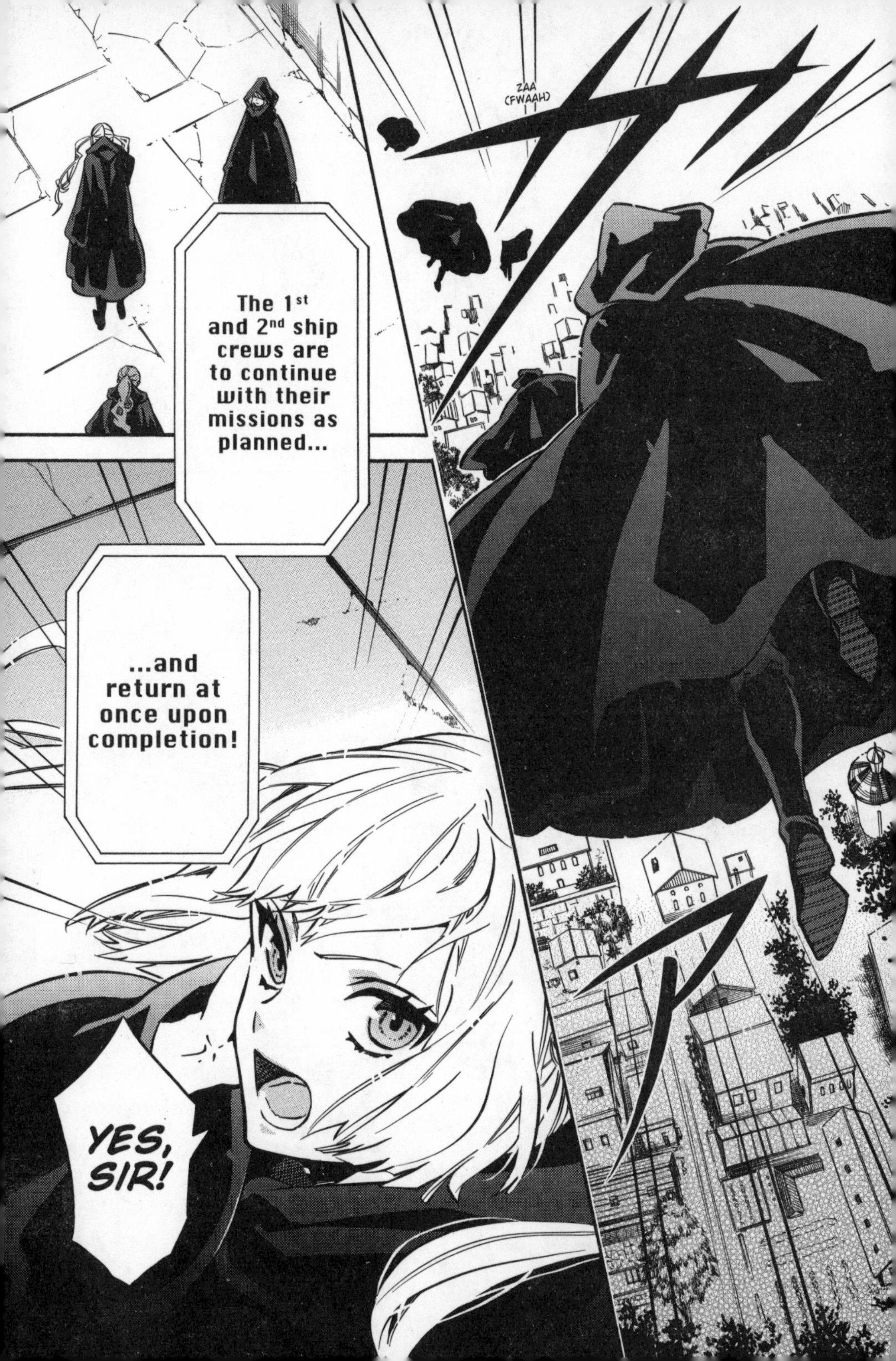
ZAA
(FWAAH)
The 1st and 2nd ship crews are to continue with their missions as planned...
...and return at once upon completion!
YES, SIR!

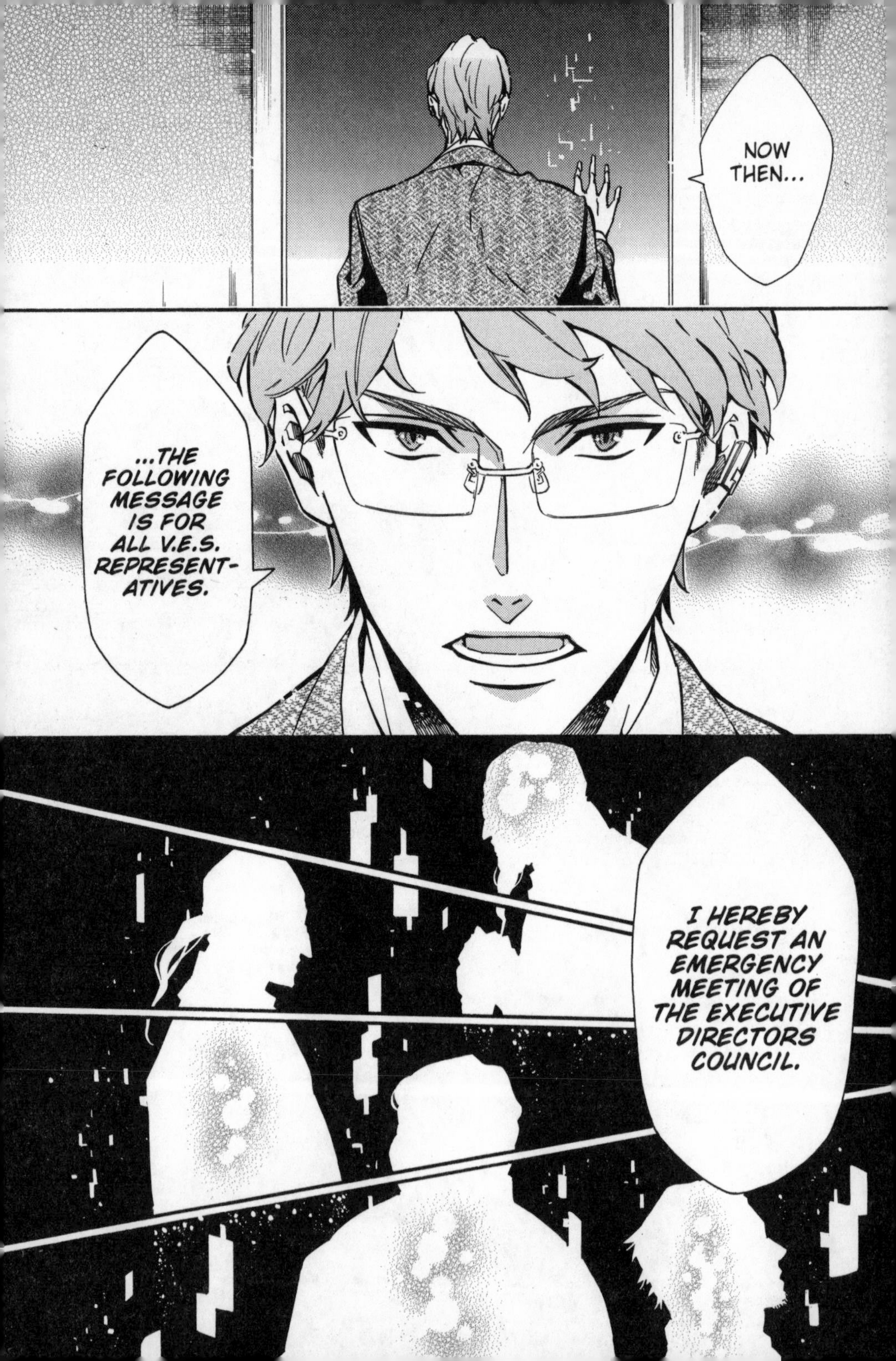
NOW THEN...
...THE FOLLOWING MESSAGE IS FOR ALL V.E.S. REPRESENT-ATIVES.
I HEREBY REQUEST AN EMERGENCY MEETING OF THE EXECUTIVE DIRECTORS COUNCIL.

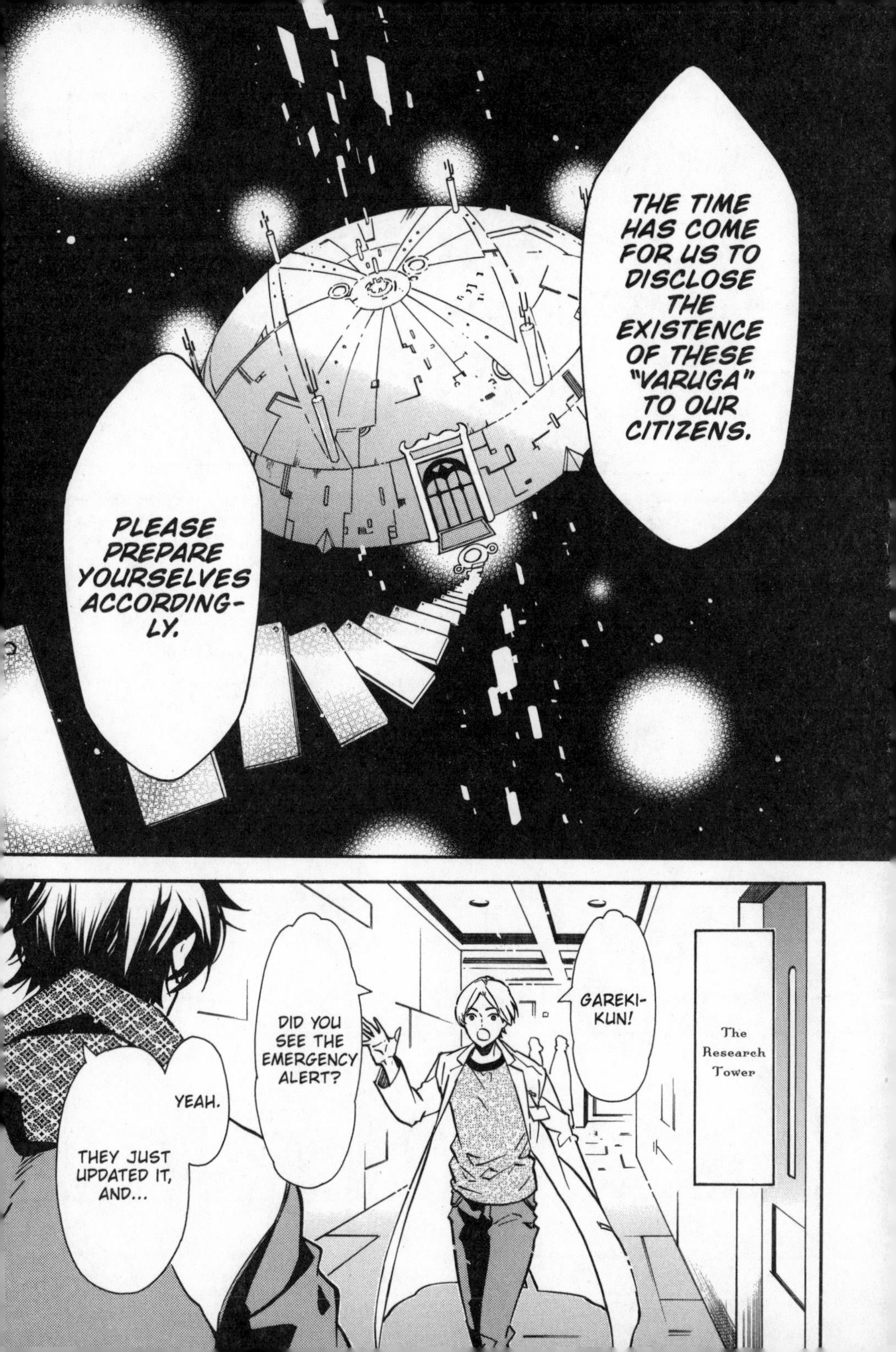
THE TIME HAS COME FOR US TO DISCLOSE THE EXISTENCE OF THESE "VARUGA" TO OUR CITIZENS.
PLEASE PREPARE YOURSELVES ACCORDING-LY.
The Research Tower
GAREKI-KUN!
DID YOU SEE THE EMERGENCY ALERT?
YEAH.
THEY JUST UPDATED IT, AND...

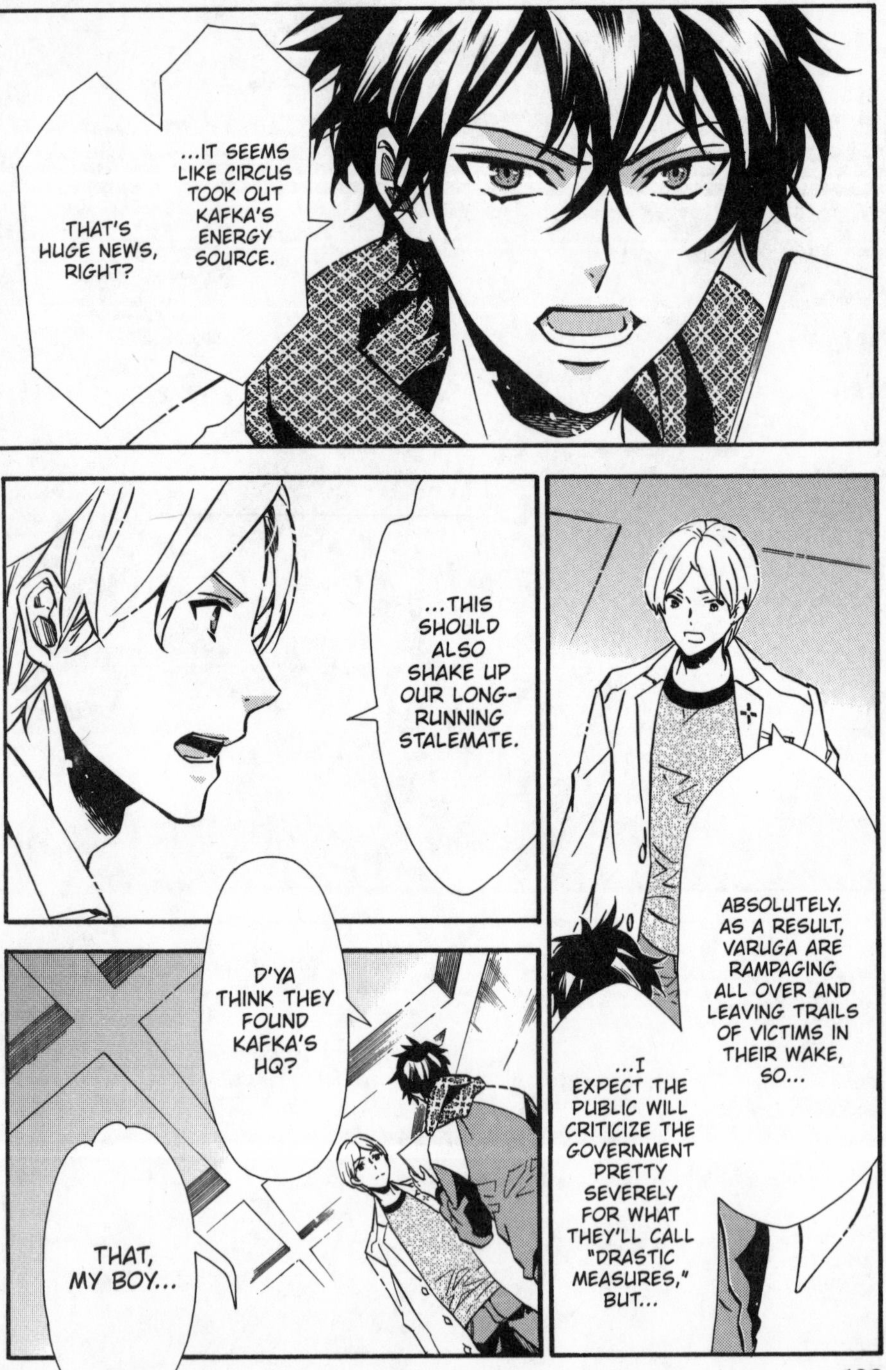
...IT SEEMS LIKE CIRCUS TOOK OUT KAFKA'S ENERGY SOURCE.
THAT'S HUGE NEWS, RIGHT?
ABSOLUTELY. AS A RESULT, VARUGA ARE RAMPAGING ALL OVER AND LEAVING TRAILS OF VICTIMS IN THEIR WAKE, SO...
...I EXPECT THE PUBLIC WILL CRITICIZE THE GOVERNMENT PRETTY SEVERELY FOR WHAT THEY'LL CALL "DRASTIC MEASURES," BUT...
...THIS SHOULD ALSO SHAKE UP OUR LONG-RUNNING STALEMATE.
D'YA THINK THEY FOUND KAFKA'S HQ?
THAT, MY BOY...

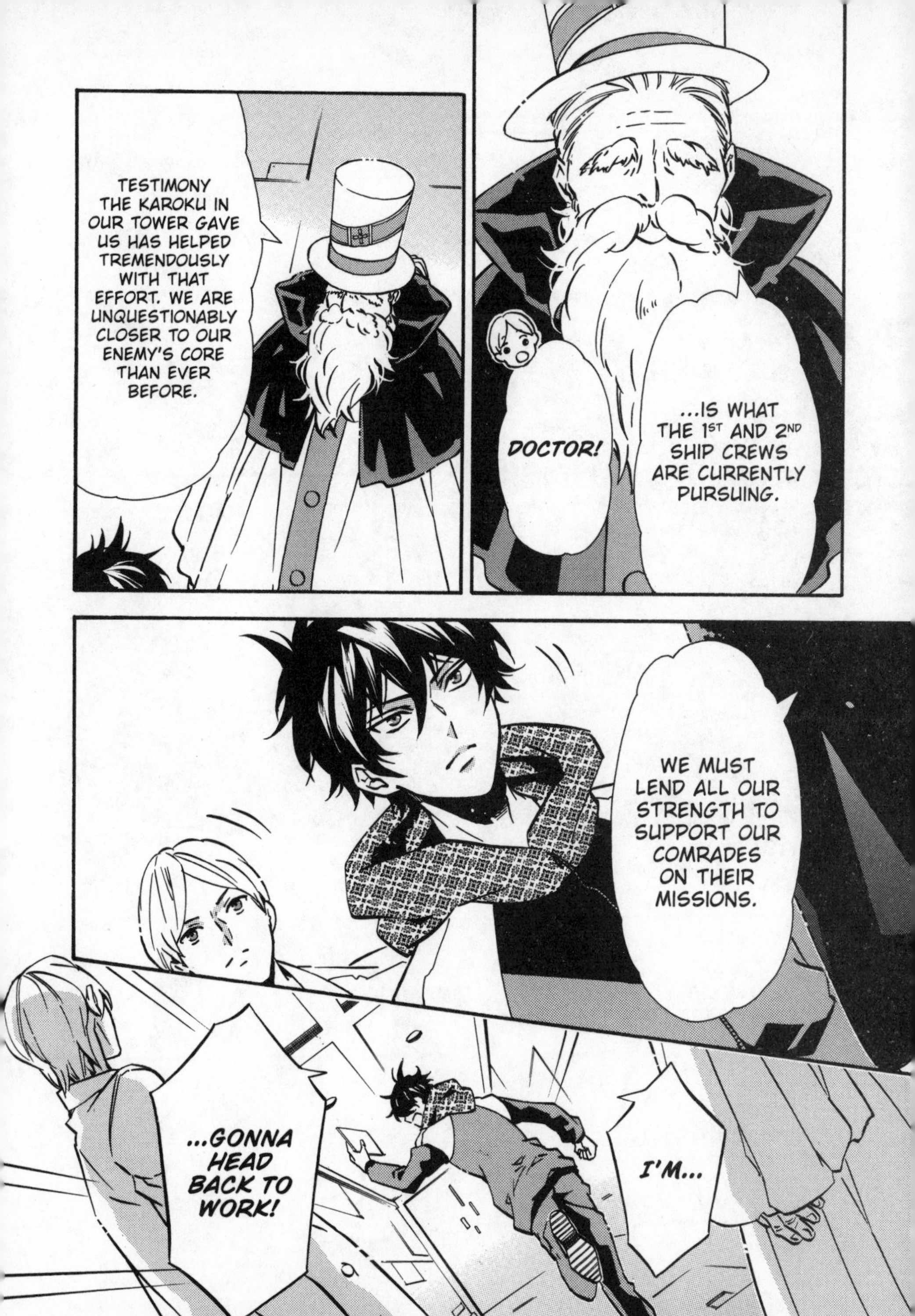
...IS WHAT THE 1ST AND 2ND SHIP CREWS ARE CURRENTLY PURSUING.
DOCTOR!
TESTIMONY THE KAROKU IN OUR TOWER GAVE US HAS HELPED TREMENDOUSLY WITH THAT EFFORT. WE ARE UNQUESTIONABLY CLOSER TO OUR ENEMY'S CORE THAN EVER BEFORE.
WE MUST LEND ALL OUR STRENGTH TO SUPPORT OUR COMRADES ON THEIR MISSIONS.
I'M...
...GONNA HEAD BACK TO WORK!

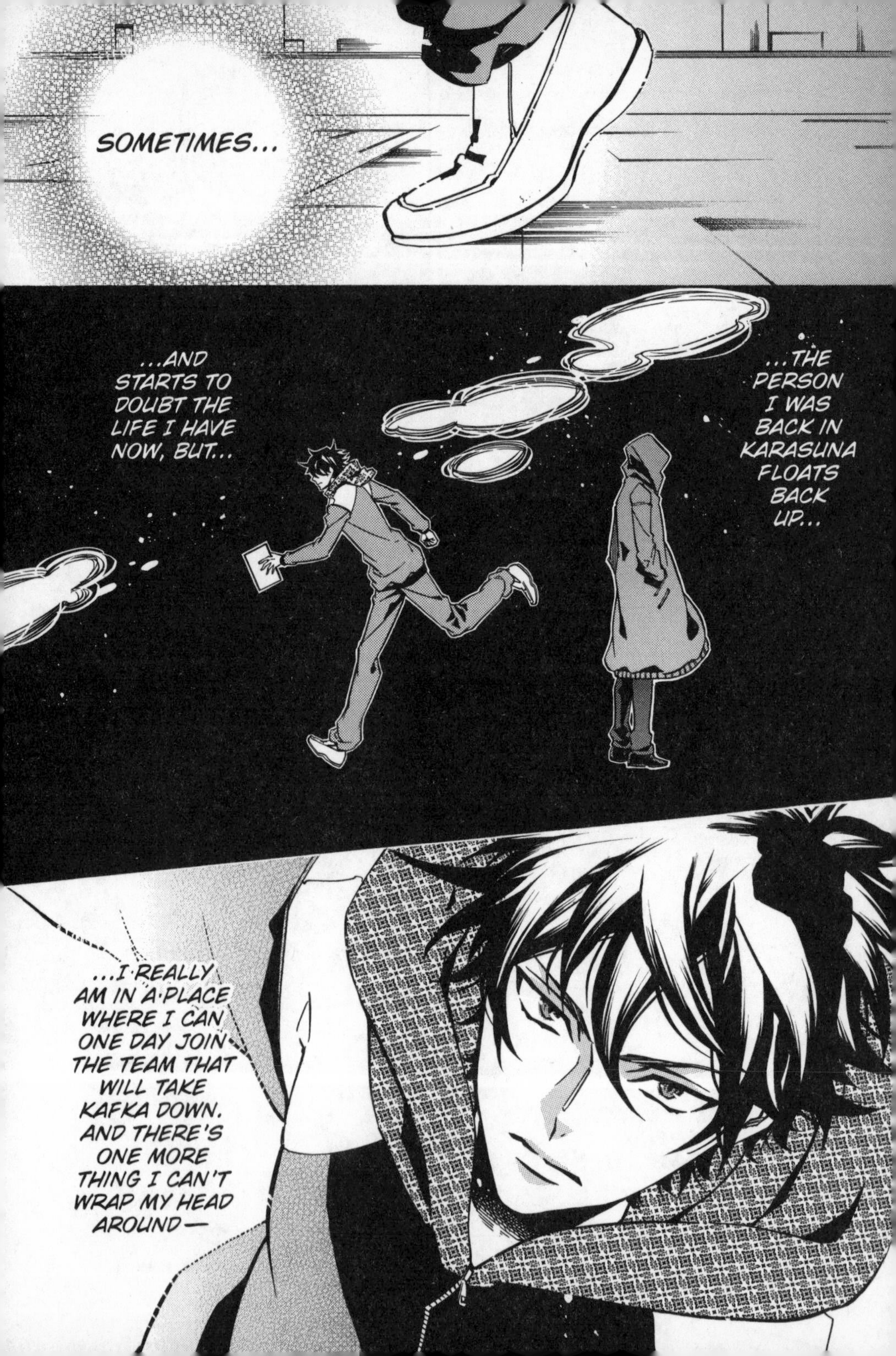
SOMETIMES...
...THE PERSON I WAS BACK IN KARASUNA FLOATS BACK UP...
...AND STARTS TO DOUBT THE LIFE I HAVE NOW, BUT...
...I REALLY AM IN A PLACE WHERE I CAN ONE DAY JOIN THE TEAM THAT WILL TAKE KAFKA DOWN. AND THERE'S ONE MORE THING I CAN'T WRAP MY HEAD AROUND—

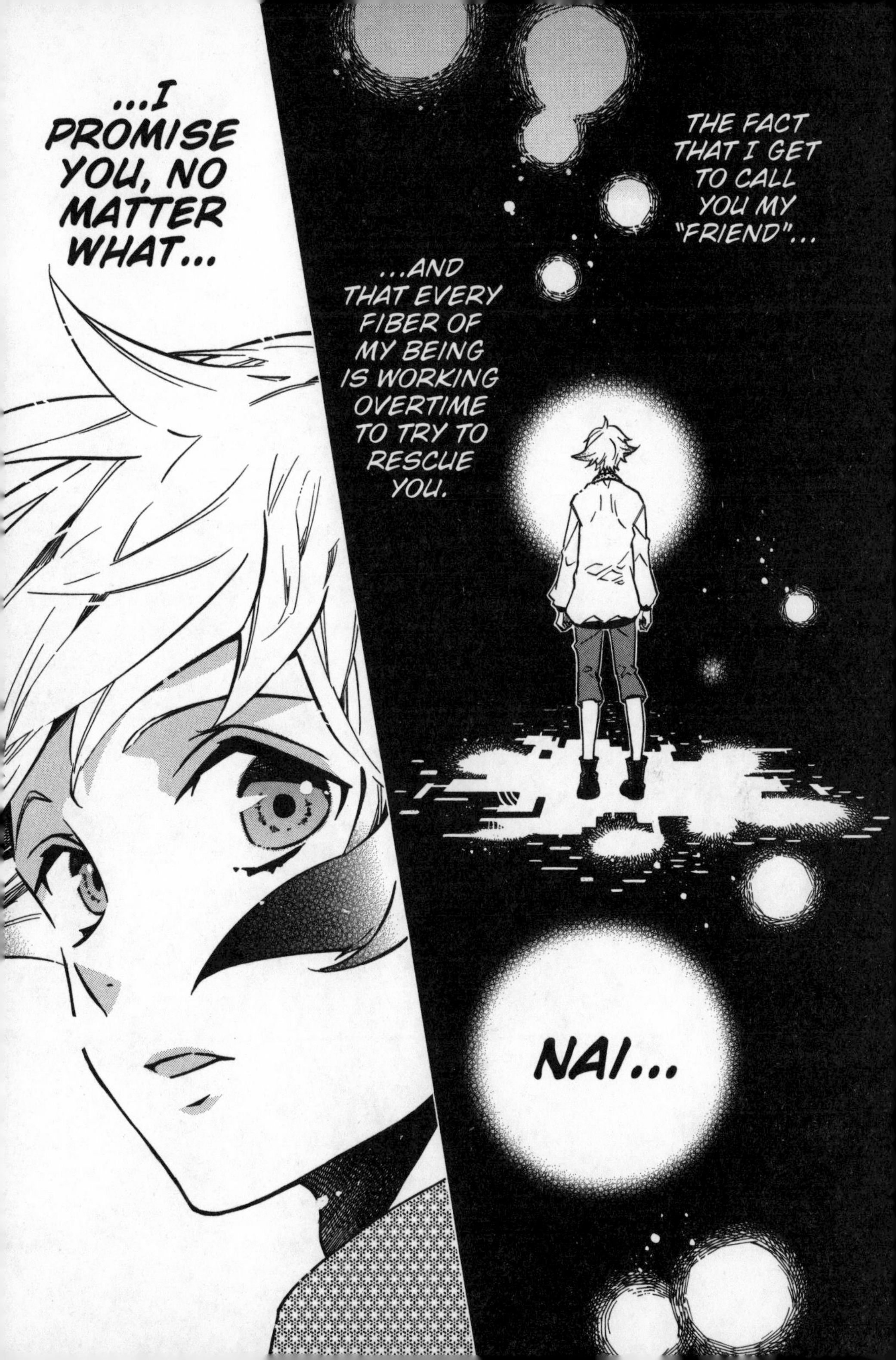
THE FACT THAT I GET TO CALL YOU MY "FRIEND"...
...AND THAT EVERY FIBER OF MY BEING IS WORKING OVERTIME TO TRY TO RESCUE YOU.
NAI...
...I PROMISE YOU, NO MATTER WHAT...

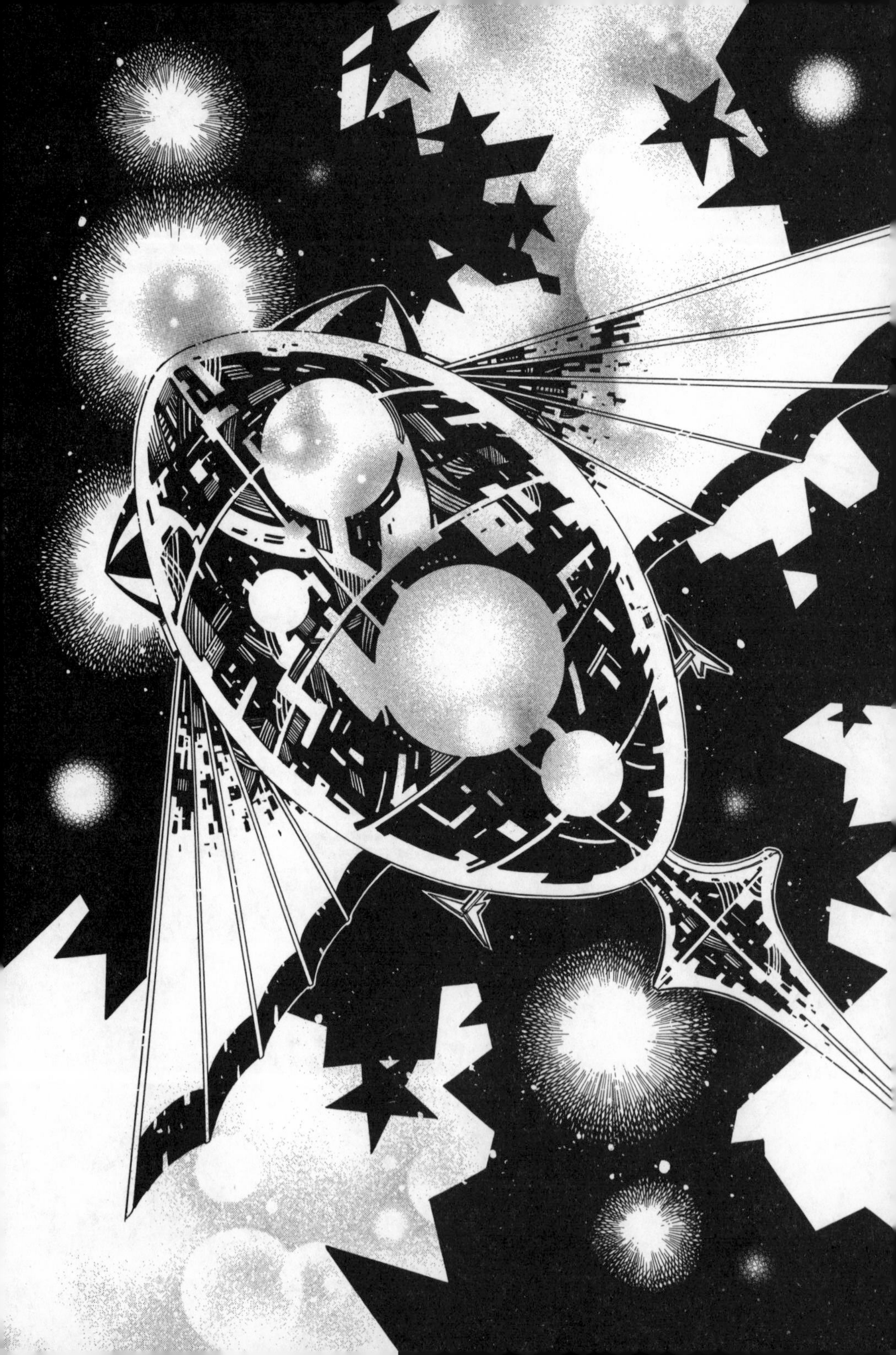

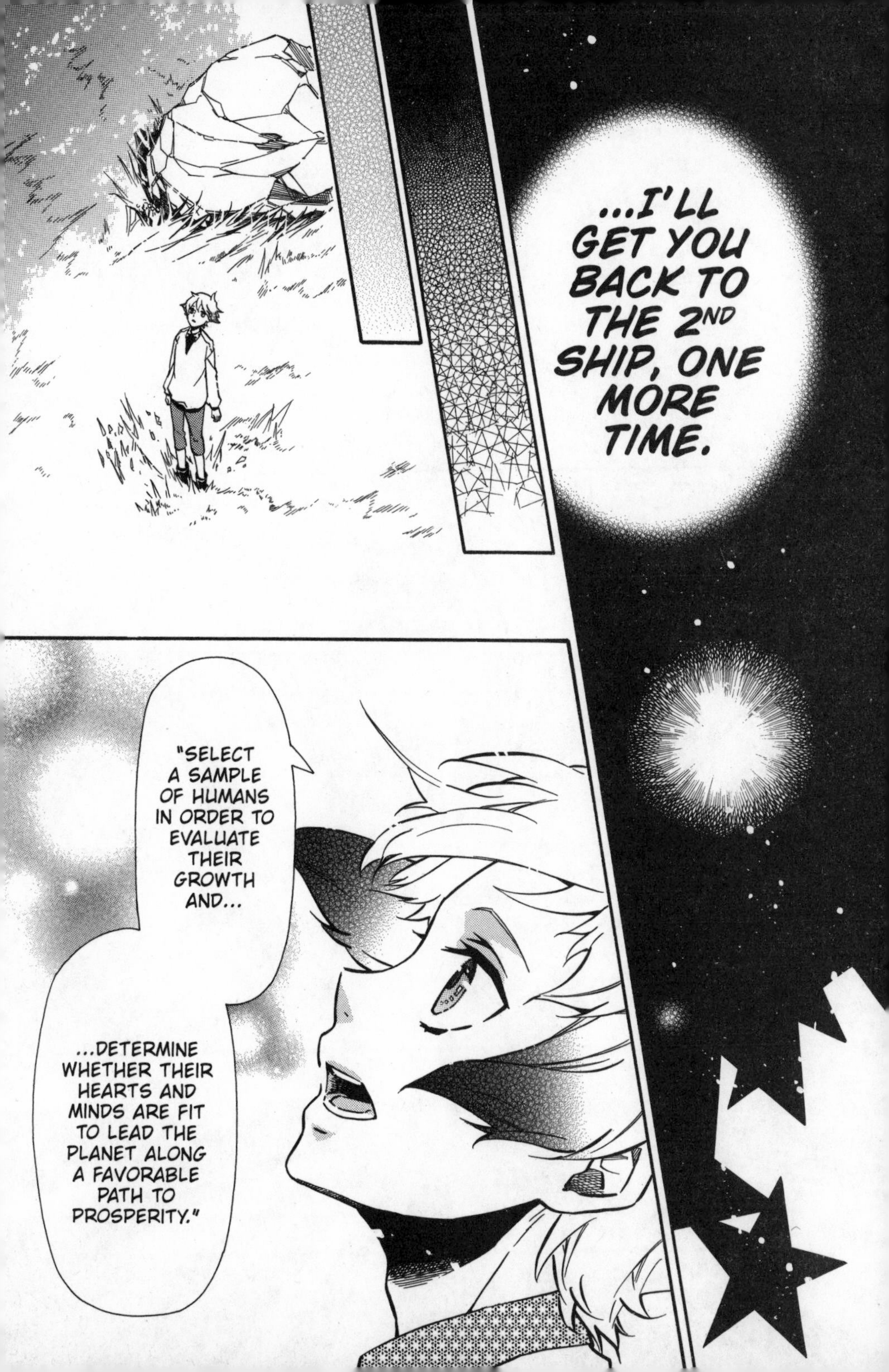
...I'LL GET YOU BACK TO THE 2ND SHIP, ONE MORE TIME.
"SELECT A SAMPLE OF HUMANS IN ORDER TO EVALUATE THEIR GROWTH AND...
...DETERMINE WHETHER THEIR HEARTS AND MINDS ARE FIT TO LEAD THE PLANET ALONG A FAVORABLE PATH TO PROSPERITY."

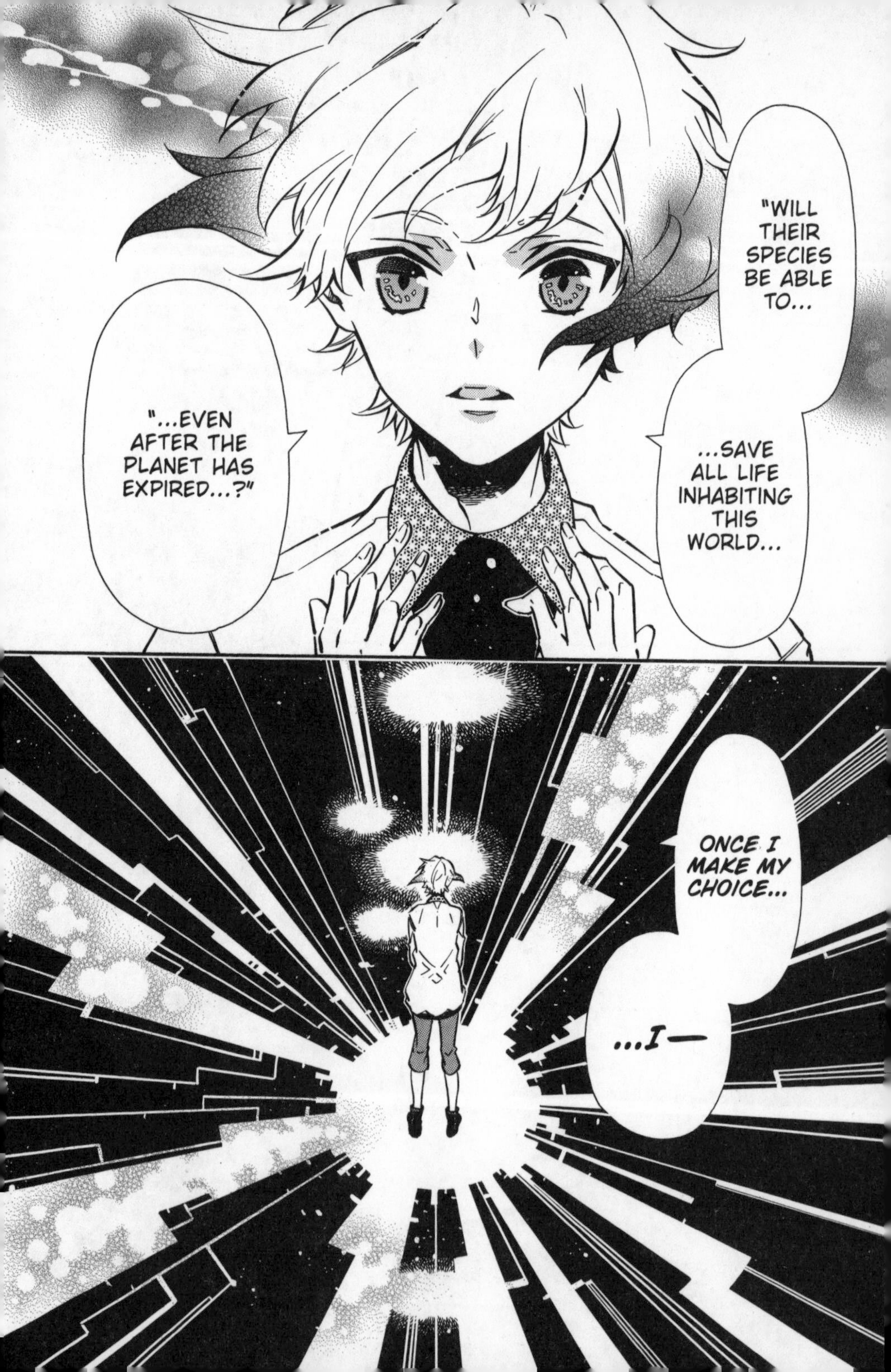
"WILL THEIR SPECIES BE ABLE TO...
...SAVE ALL LIFE INHABITING THIS WORLD...
"...EVEN AFTER THE PLANET HAS EXPIRED...?"
ONCE I MAKE MY CHOICE...
...I—

KARNEVAL

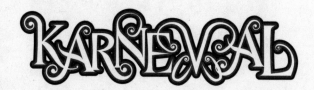

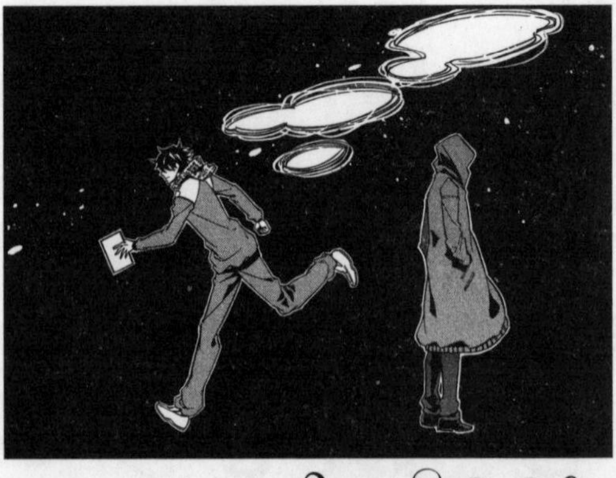

KARNEVAL

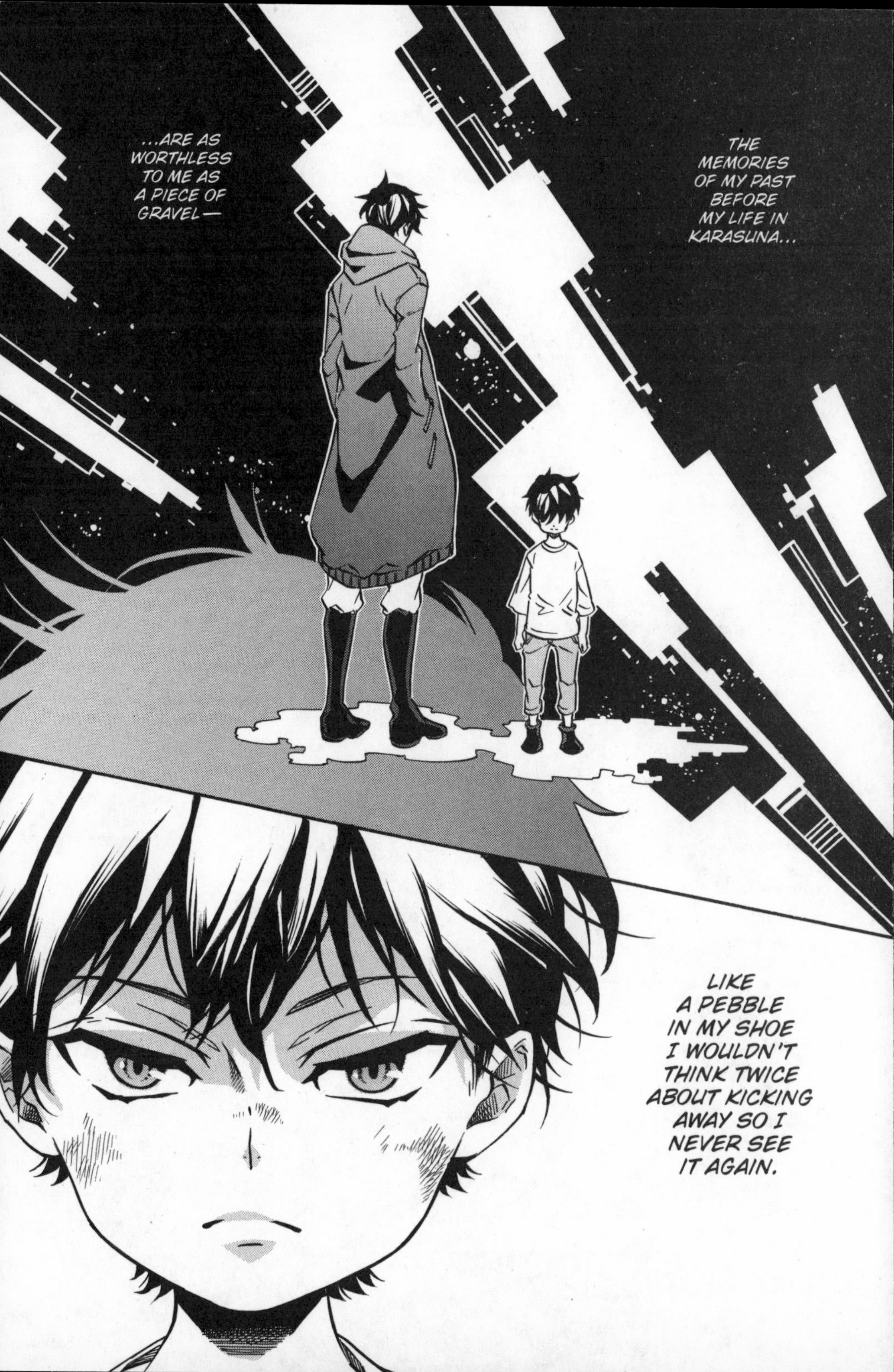
THE MEMORIES OF MY PAST BEFORE MY LIFE IN KARASUNA...
...ARE AS WORTHLESS TO ME AS A PIECE OF GRAVEL—
LIKE A PEBBLE IN MY SHOE I WOULDN'T THINK TWICE ABOUT KICKING AWAY SO I NEVER SEE IT AGAIN.

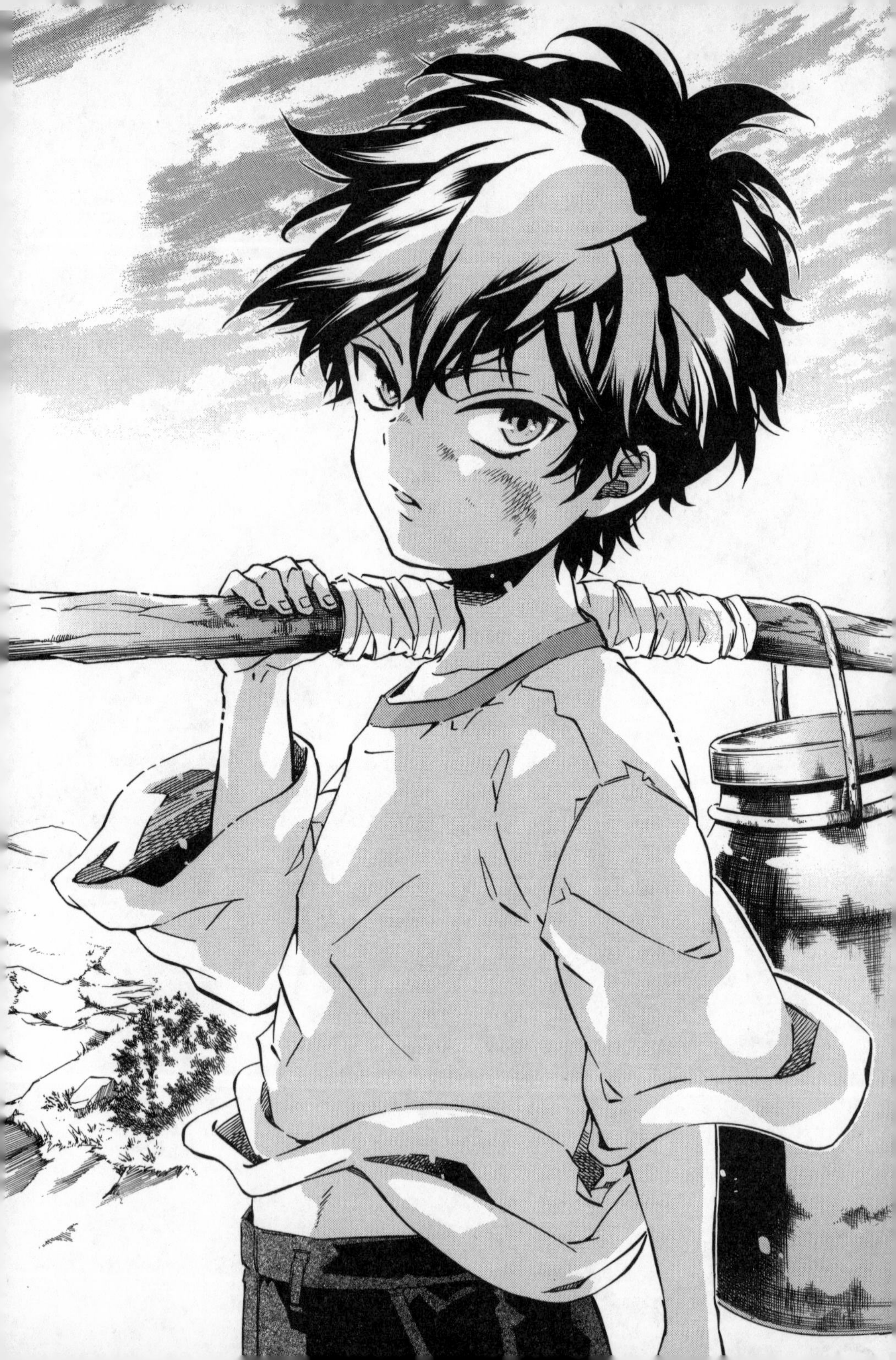

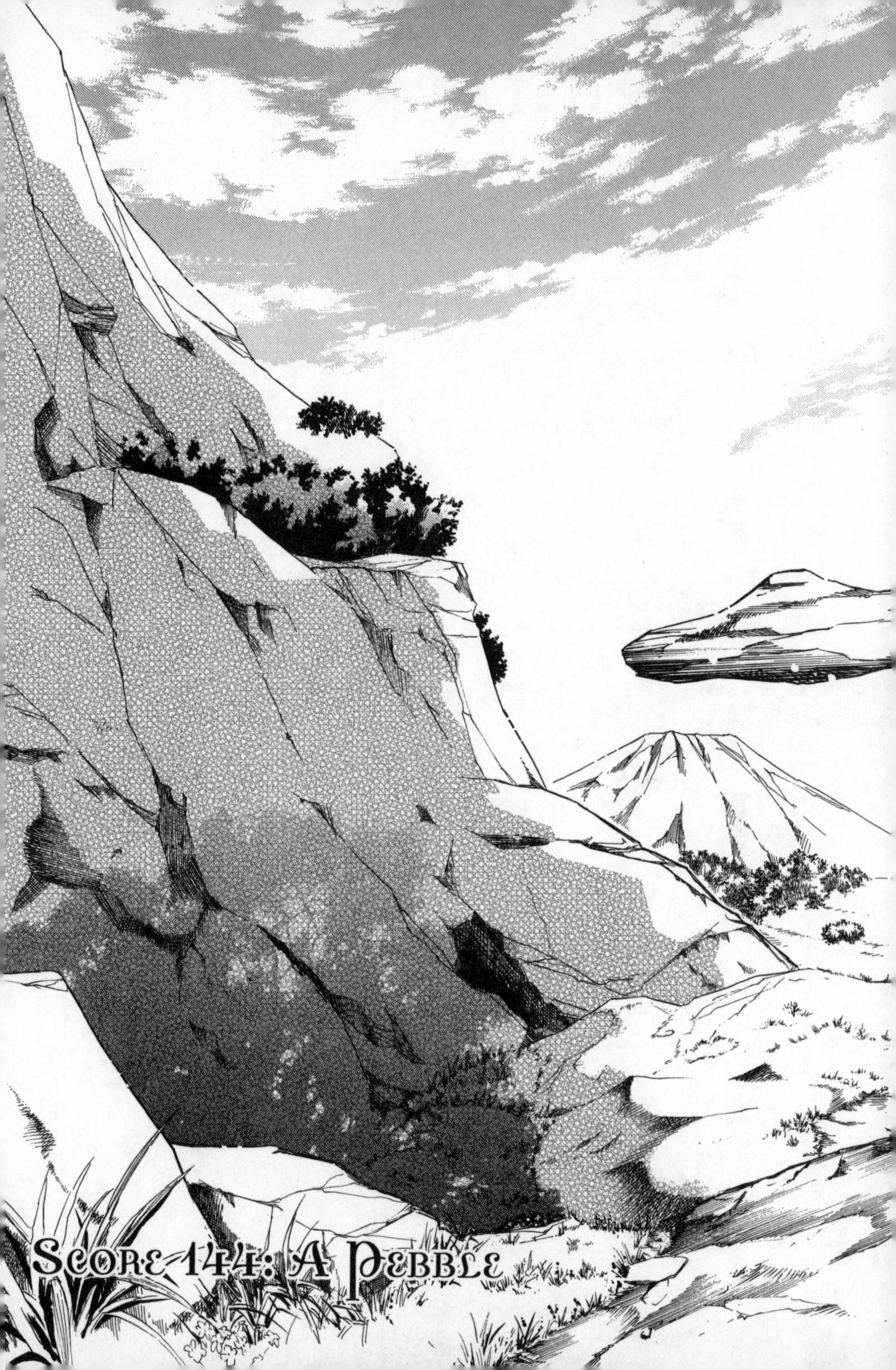
Score 144: A Pebble

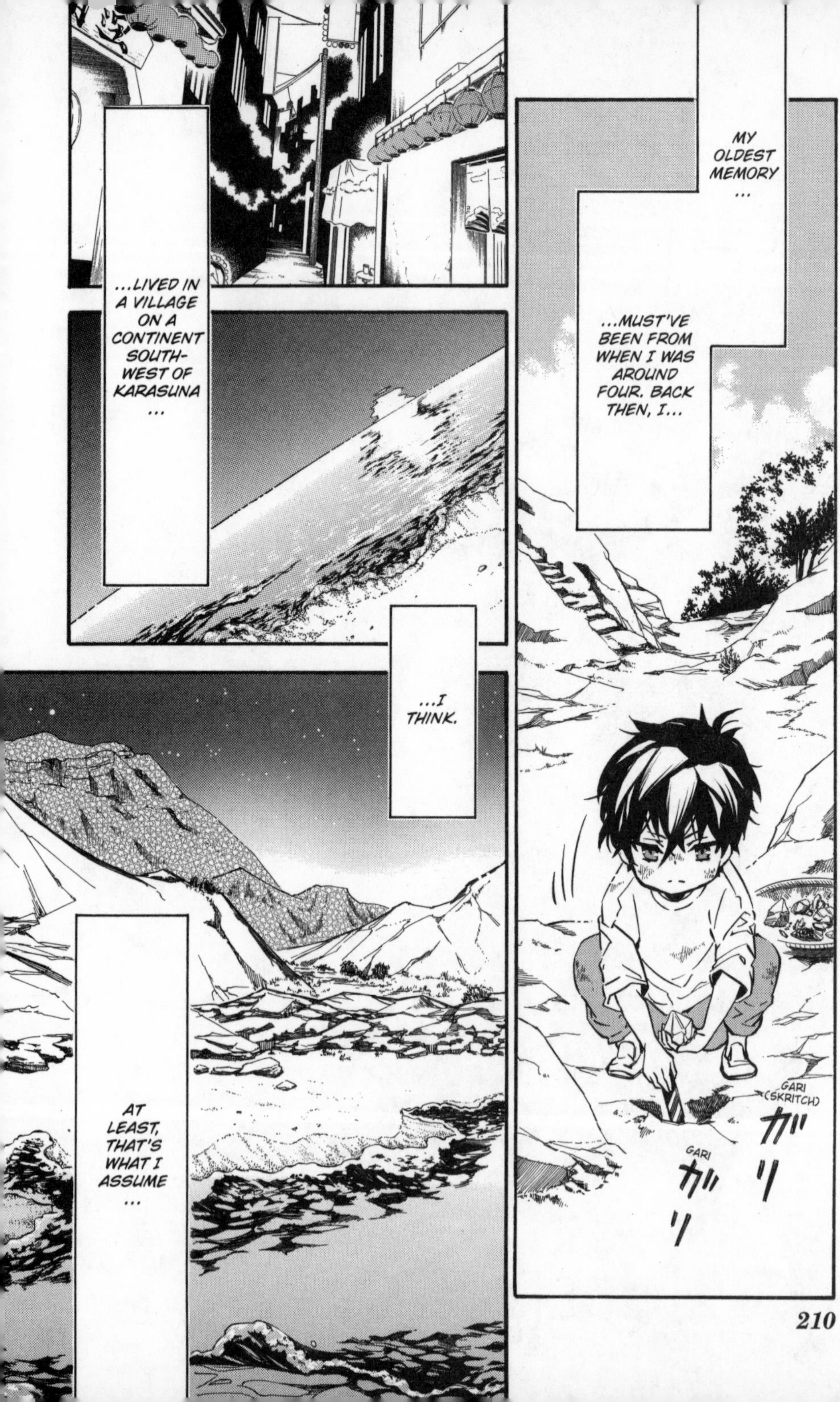
MY OLDEST MEMORY ...
...MUST'VE BEEN FROM WHEN I WAS AROUND FOUR. BACK THEN, I...
GARI (SKRITCH)
ガリ
GARI
ガリ
...LIVED IN A VILLAGE ON A CONTINENT SOUTH-WEST OF KARASUNA ...
...I THINK.
AT LEAST, THAT'S WHAT I ASSUME ...

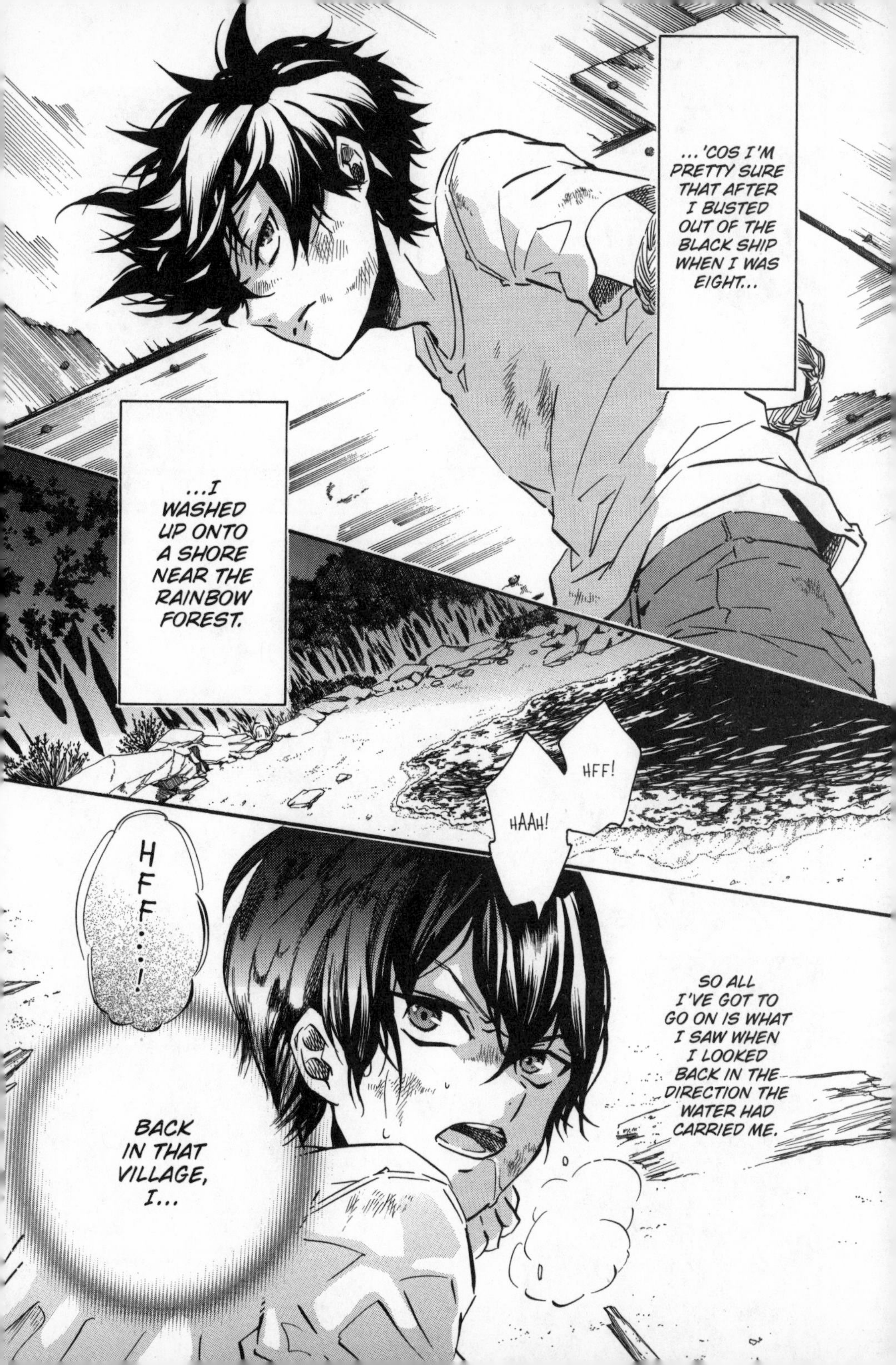
...'COS I'M PRETTY SURE THAT AFTER I BUSTED OUT OF THE BLACK SHIP WHEN I WAS EIGHT...
...I WASHED UP ONTO A SHORE NEAR THE RAINBOW FOREST.
HFF!
HAAH!
SO ALL I'VE GOT TO GO ON IS WHAT I SAW WHEN I LOOKED BACK IN THE DIRECTION THE WATER HAD CARRIED ME.
HFF...!
BACK IN THAT VILLAGE, I...

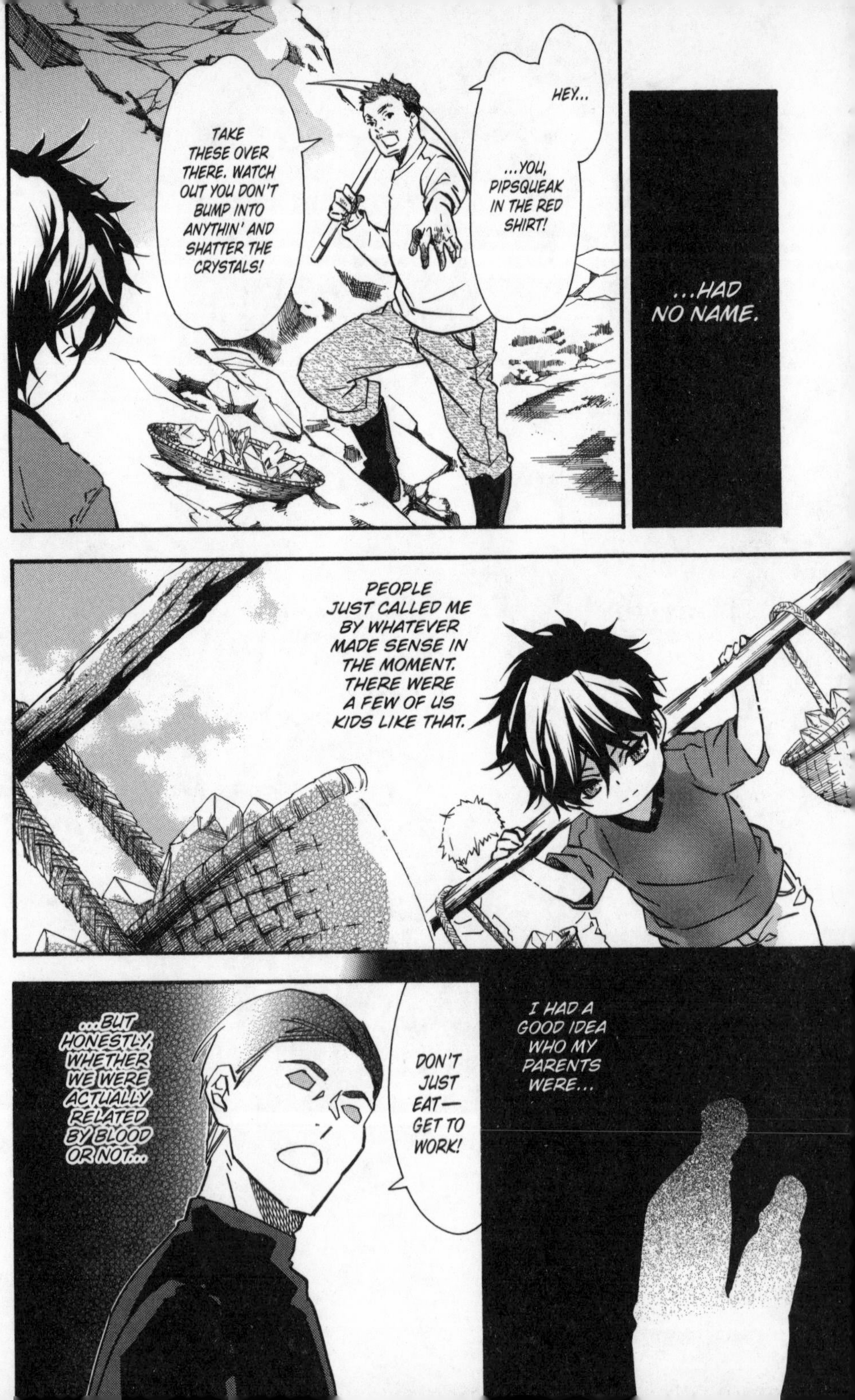
...HAD NO NAME.
HEY...
...YOU, PIPSQUEAK IN THE RED SHIRT!
TAKE THESE OVER THERE. WATCH OUT YOU DON'T BUMP INTO ANYTHIN' AND SHATTER THE CRYSTALS!
PEOPLE JUST CALLED ME BY WHATEVER MADE SENSE IN THE MOMENT. THERE WERE A FEW OF US KIDS LIKE THAT.
I HAD A GOOD IDEA WHO MY PARENTS WERE...
DON'T JUST EAT—GET TO WORK!
...BUT HONESTLY, WHETHER WE WERE ACTUALLY RELATED BY BLOOD OR NOT...

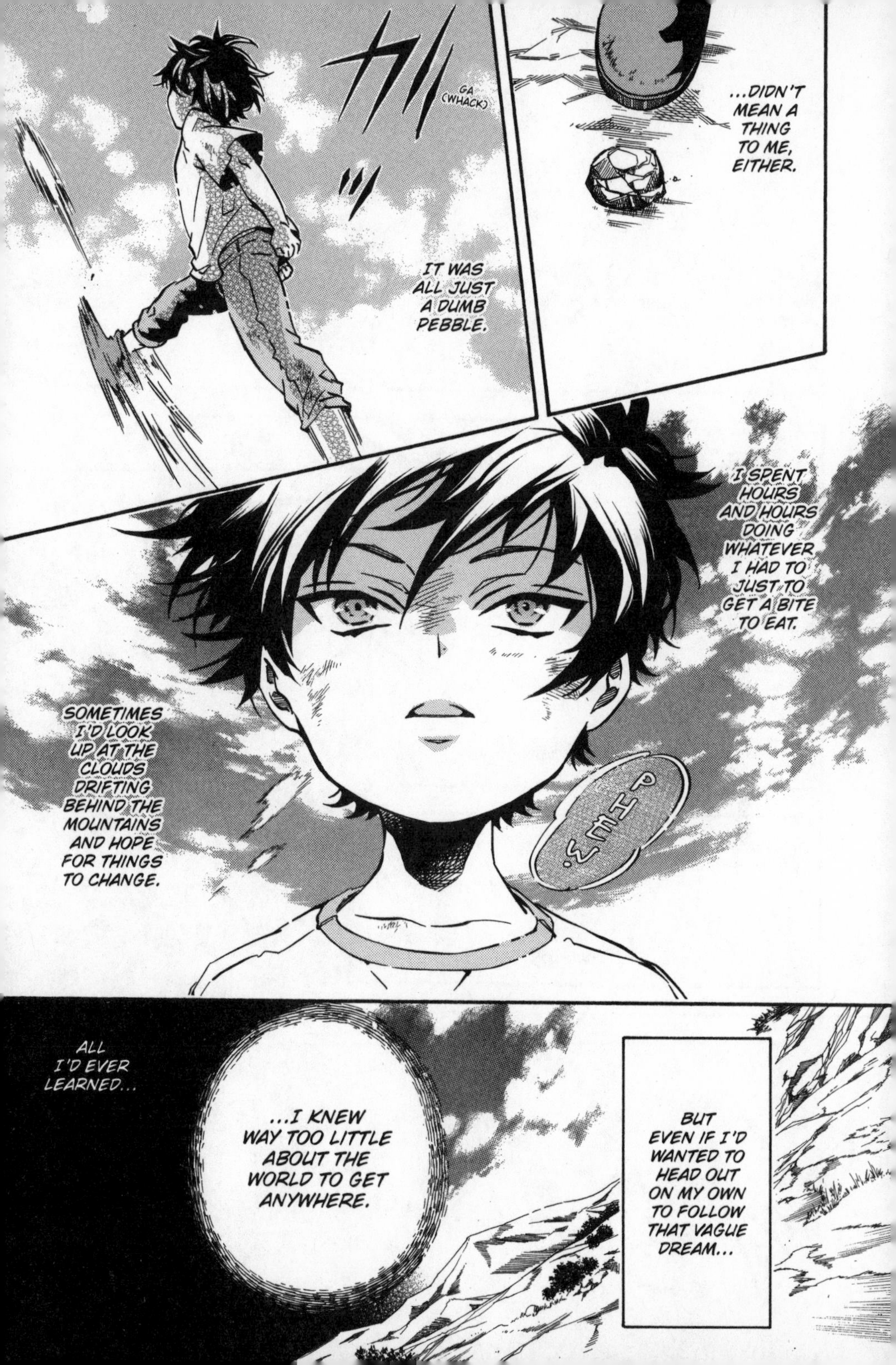
...DIDN'T MEAN A THING TO ME, EITHER.
GA (WHACK)
IT WAS ALL JUST A DUMB PEBBLE.
I SPENT HOURS AND HOURS DOING WHATEVER I HAD TO JUST TO GET A BITE TO EAT.
PHEW.
SOMETIMES I'D LOOK UP AT THE CLOUDS DRIFTING BEHIND THE MOUNTAINS AND HOPE FOR THINGS TO CHANGE.
BUT EVEN IF I'D WANTED TO HEAD OUT ON MY OWN TO FOLLOW THAT VAGUE DREAM...
ALL I'D EVER LEARNED...
...I KNEW WAY TOO LITTLE ABOUT THE WORLD TO GET ANYWHERE.

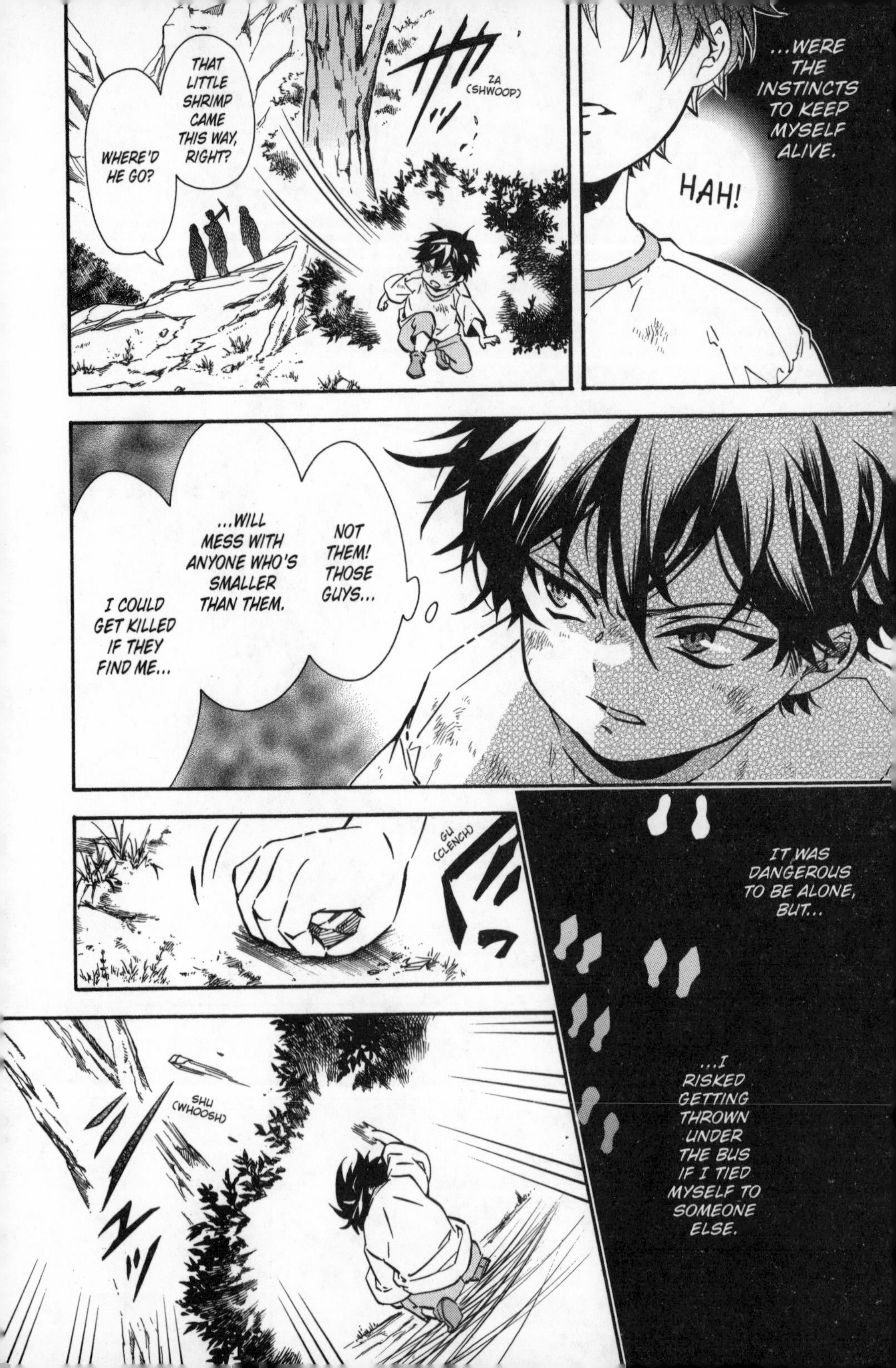
...WERE THE INSTINCTS TO KEEP MYSELF ALIVE.
HAH!
ZA (SHWOOP)
THAT LITTLE SHRIMP CAME THIS WAY, RIGHT?
WHERE'D HE GO?
NOT THEM! THOSE GUYS...
...WILL MESS WITH ANYONE WHO'S SMALLER THAN THEM.
I COULD GET KILLED IF THEY FIND ME...
IT WAS DANGEROUS TO BE ALONE, BUT...
...I RISKED GETTING THROWN UNDER THE BUS IF I TIED MYSELF TO SOMEONE ELSE.
GU (CLENCH)
SHU (WHOOSH)

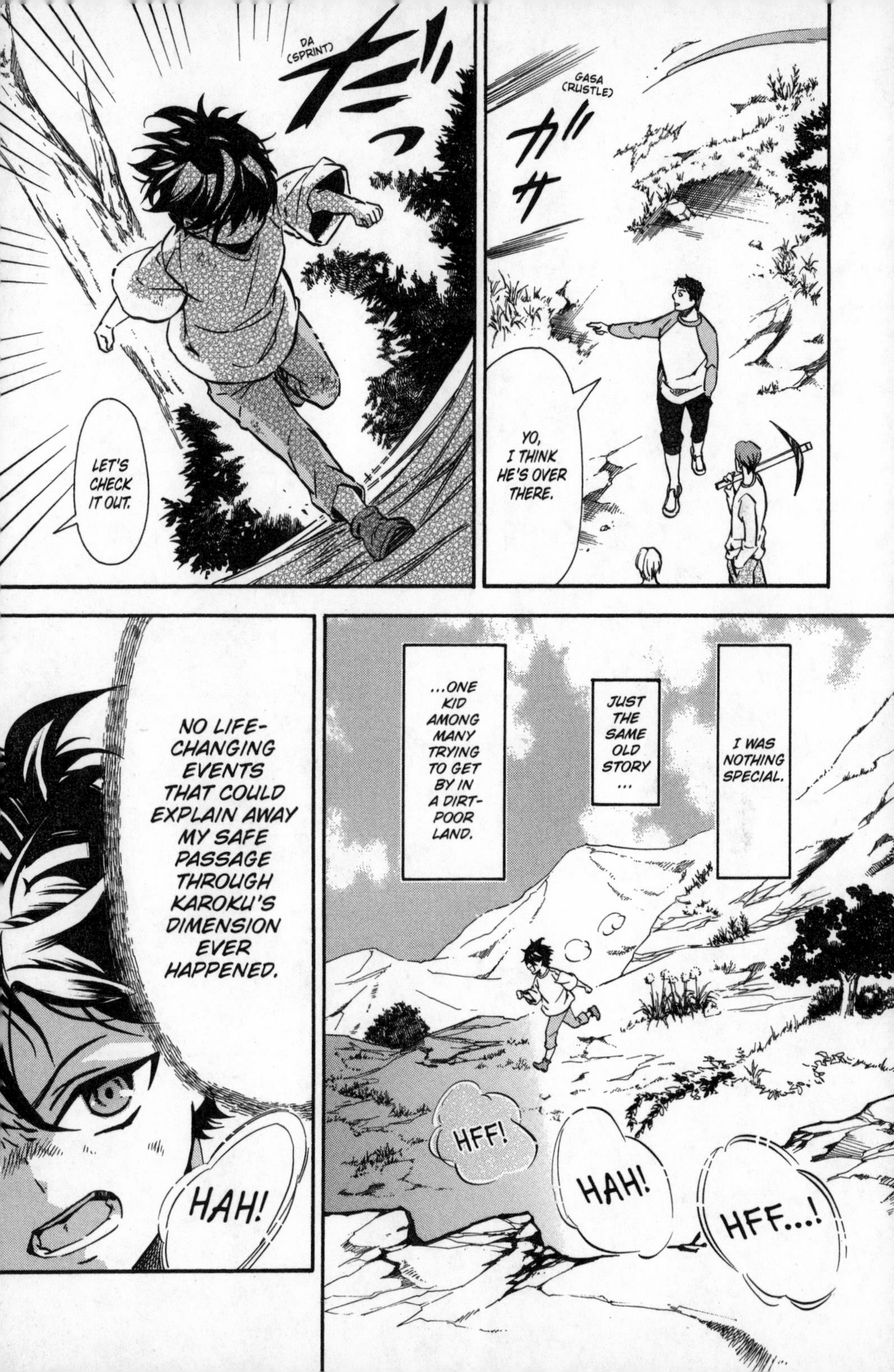
GASA (RUSTLE)
YO, I THINK HE'S OVER THERE.
DA (SPRINT)
LET'S CHECK IT OUT.
I WAS NOTHING SPECIAL.
JUST THE SAME OLD STORY ...
...ONE KID AMONG MANY TRYING TO GET BY IN A DIRT-POOR LAND.
HFF!
HAH!
HFF...!
NO LIFE-CHANGING EVENTS THAT COULD EXPLAIN AWAY MY SAFE PASSAGE THROUGH KAROKU'S DIMENSION EVER HAPPENED.
HAH!

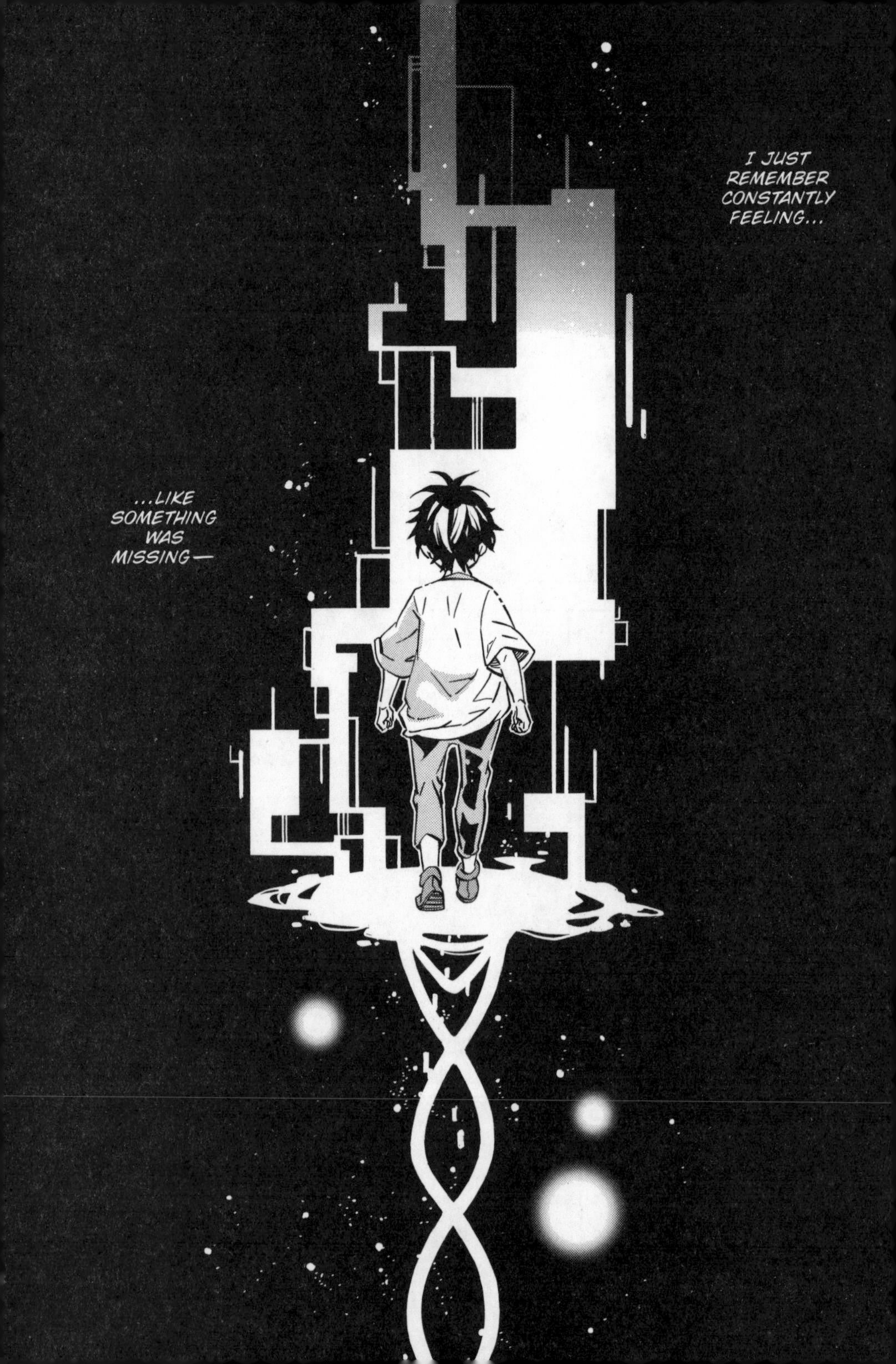
I JUST REMEMBER CONSTANTLY FEELING...
...LIKE SOMETHING WAS MISSING—

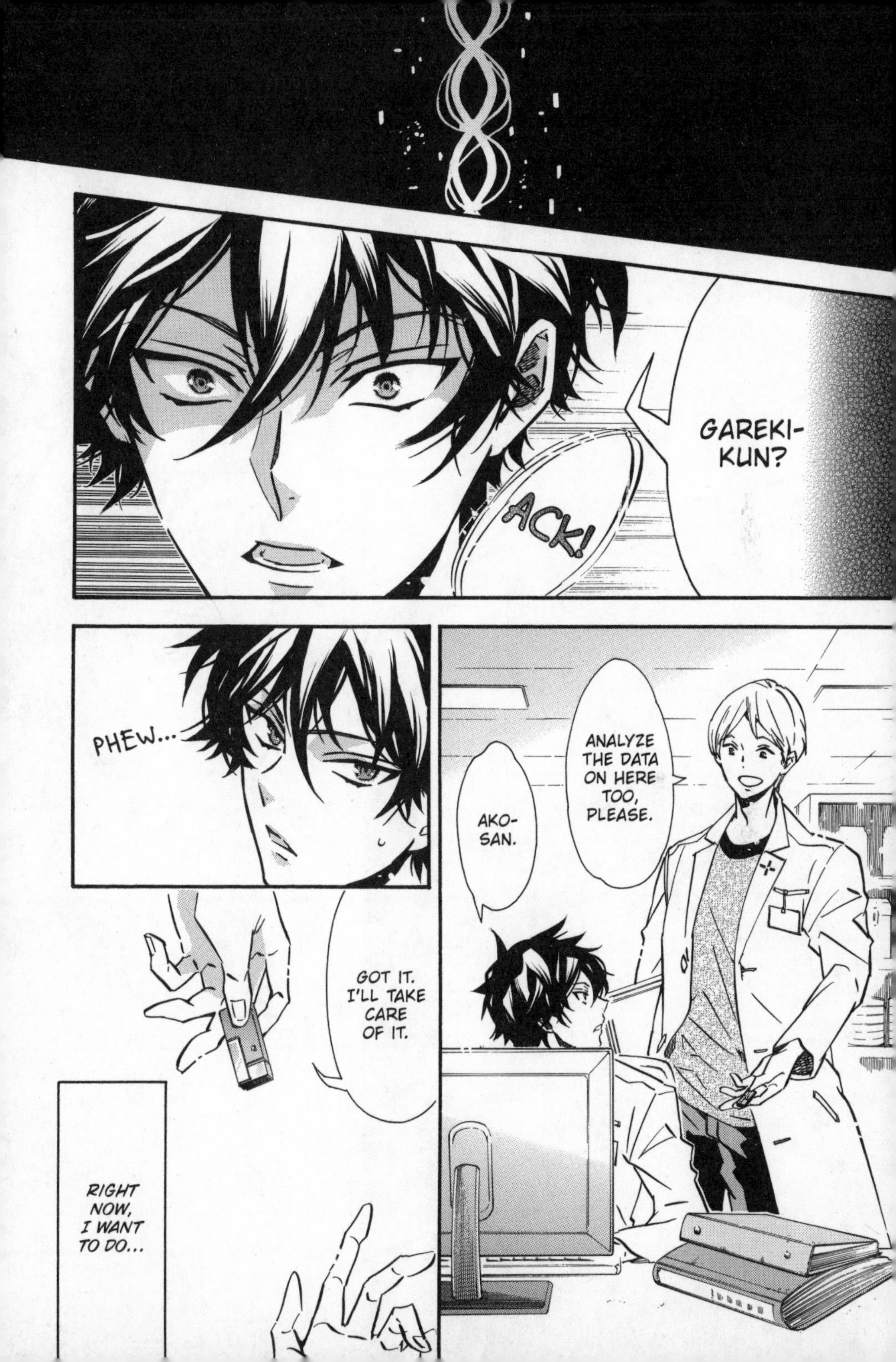
GAREKI-KUN?
ACK!
ANALYZE THE DATA ON HERE TOO, PLEASE.
AKO-SAN.
PHEW...
GOT IT. I'LL TAKE CARE OF IT.
RIGHT NOW, I WANT TO DO...

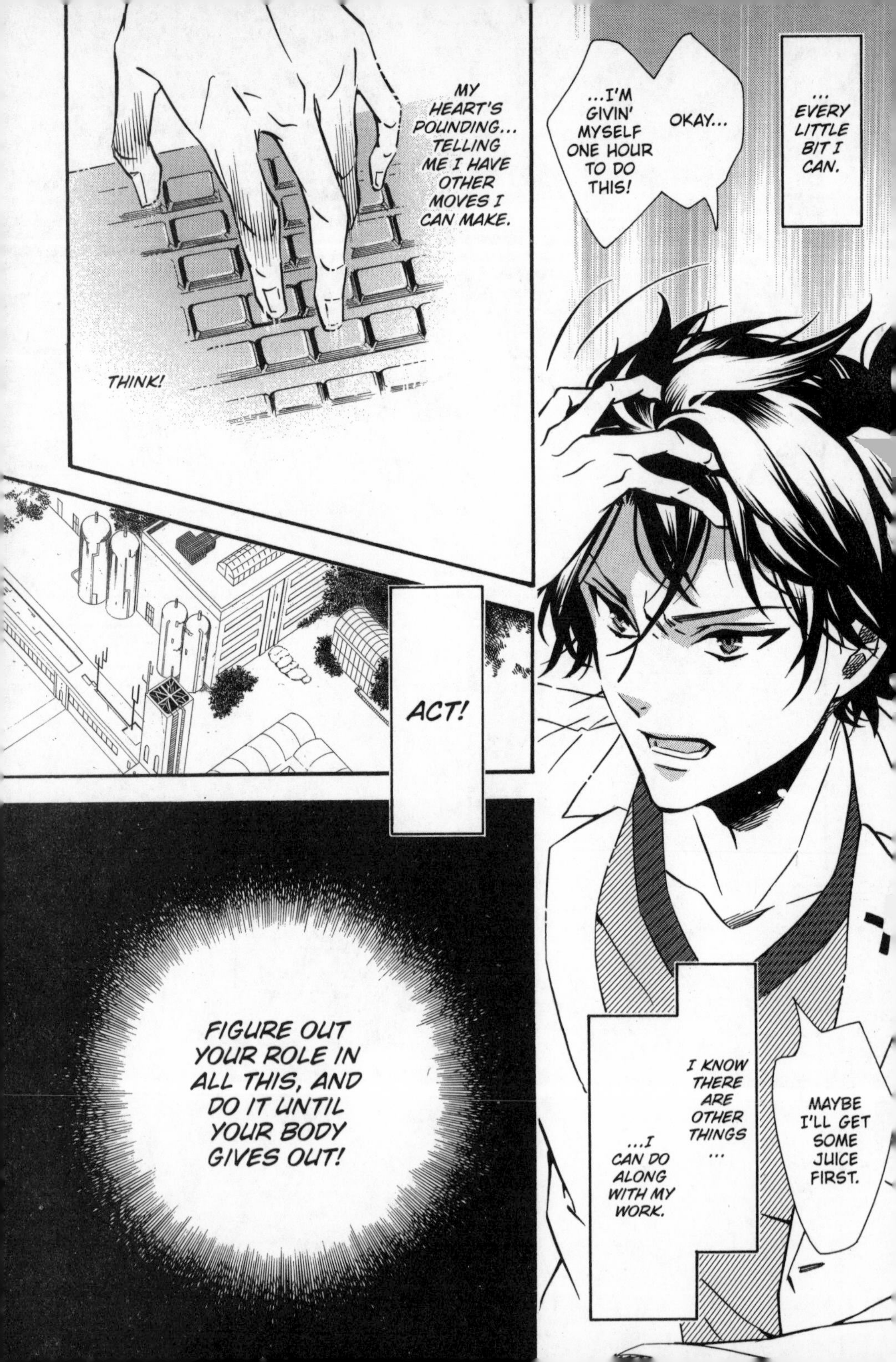
...EVERY LITTLE BIT I CAN.
OKAY...
...I'M GIVIN' MYSELF ONE HOUR TO DO THIS!
MAYBE I'LL GET SOME JUICE FIRST.
I KNOW THERE ARE OTHER THINGS ...
...I CAN DO ALONG WITH MY WORK.
MY HEART'S POUNDING... TELLING ME I HAVE OTHER MOVES I CAN MAKE.
THINK!
ACT!
FIGURE OUT YOUR ROLE IN ALL THIS, AND DO IT UNTIL YOUR BODY GIVES OUT!

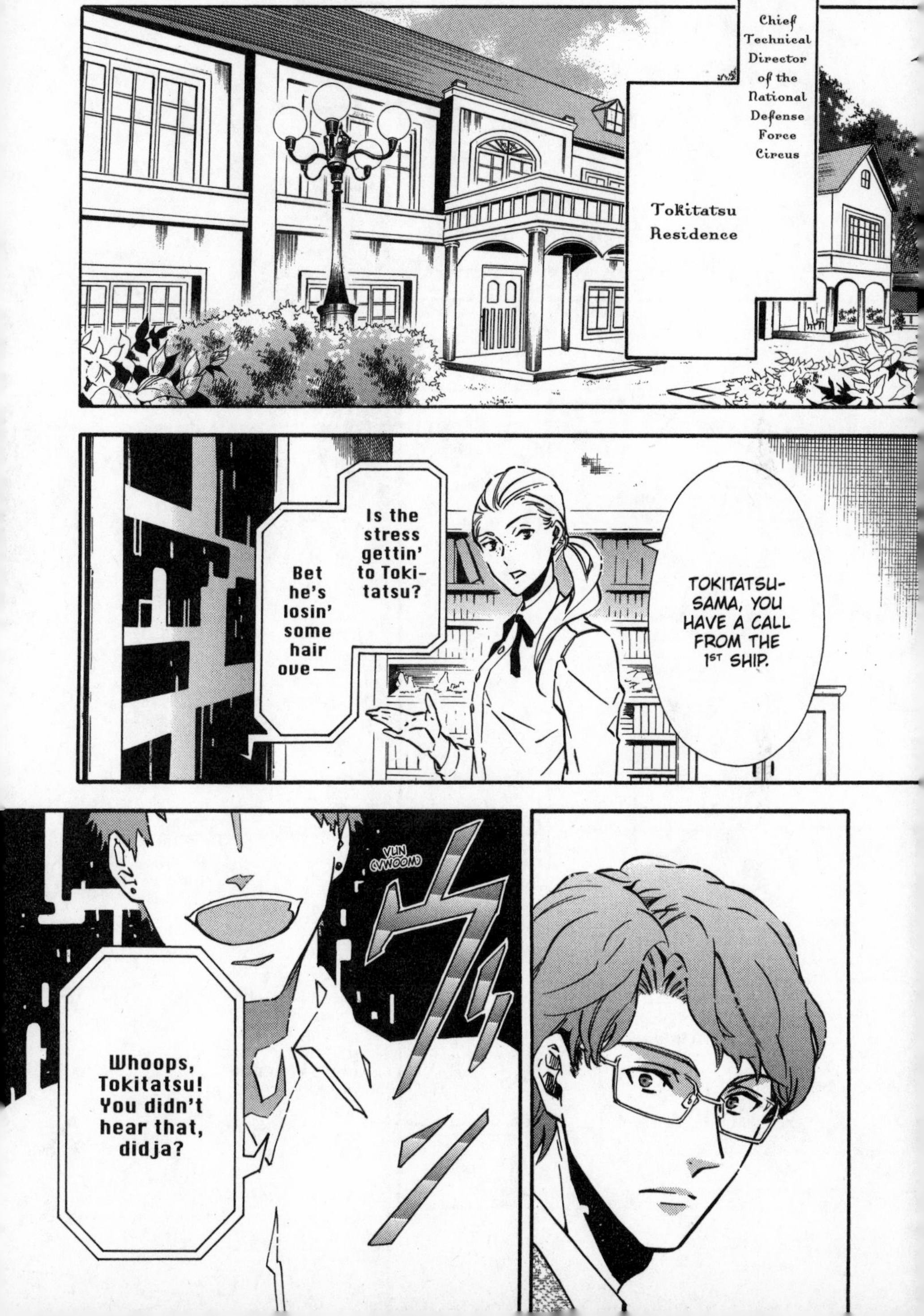
Chief Technical Director of the National Defense Force Circus
Tokitatsu Residence
TOKITATSU-SAMA, YOU HAVE A CALL FROM THE 1ST SHIP.
Is the stress gettin' to Toki-tatsu? Bet he's losin' some hair ove—
VUN (VWOOM)
Whoops, Tokitatsu! You didn't hear that, didja?

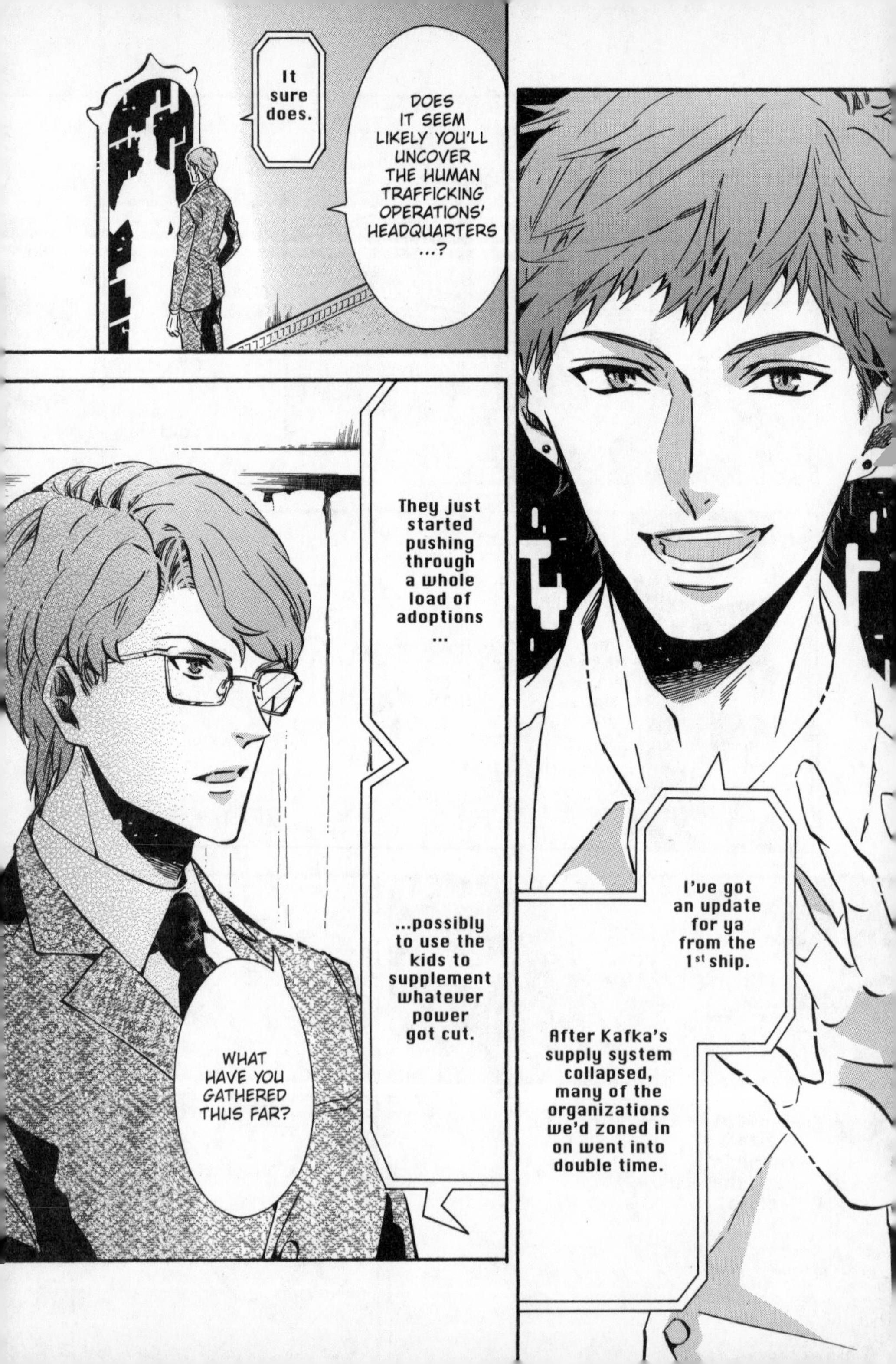
I've got an update for ya from the 1st ship.
After Kafka's supply system collapsed, many of the organizations we'd zoned in on went into double time.
DOES IT SEEM LIKELY YOU'LL UNCOVER THE HUMAN TRAFFICKING OPERATIONS' HEADQUARTERS ...?
It sure does.
They just started pushing through a whole load of adoptions ...
...possibly to use the kids to supplement whatever power got cut.
WHAT HAVE YOU GATHERED THUS FAR?

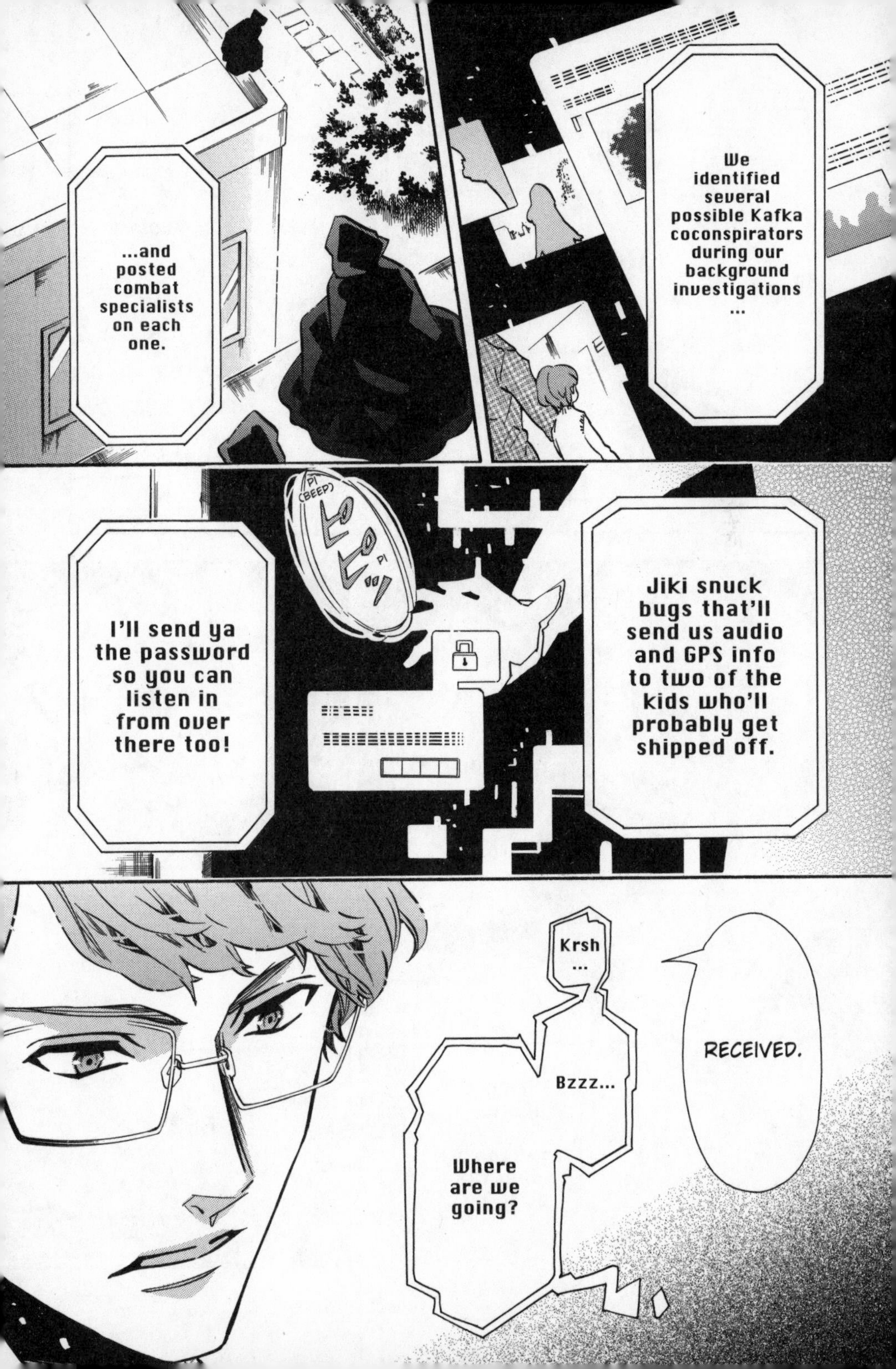
We identified several possible Kafka coconspirators during our background investigations ...
...and posted combat specialists on each one.
Jiki snuck bugs that'll send us audio and GPS info to two of the kids who'll probably get shipped off.
PI (BEEP)
PI
I'll send ya the password so you can listen in from over there too!
RECEIVED.
Krsh ...
Bzzz...
Where are we going?

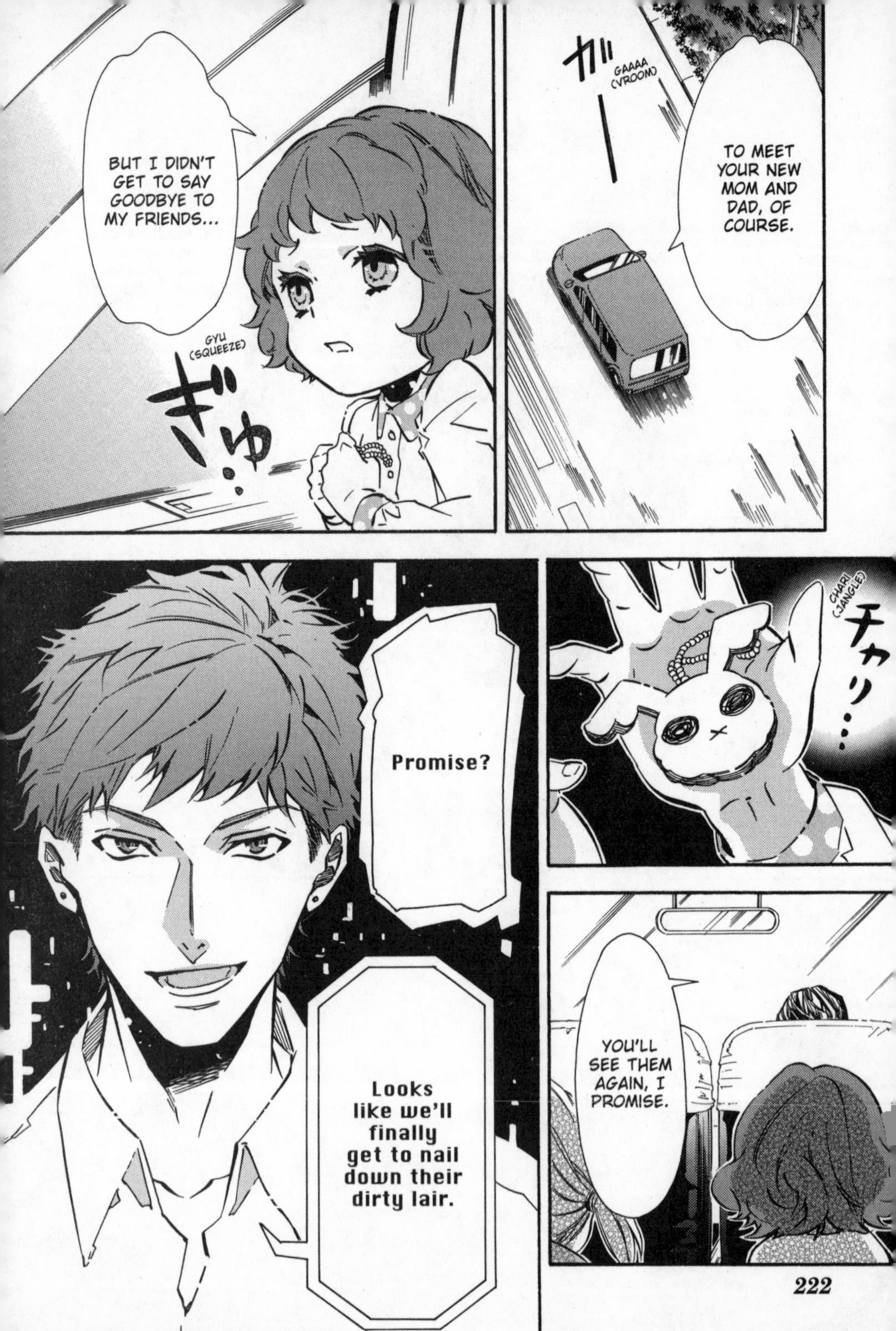
GAAAA (VROOM)
TO MEET YOUR NEW MOM AND DAD, OF COURSE.
BUT I DIDN'T GET TO SAY GOODBYE TO MY FRIENDS...
GYU (SQUEEZE)
CHARI (JANGLE)
YOU'LL SEE THEM AGAIN, I PROMISE.
Promise?
Looks like we'll finally get to nail down their dirty lair.

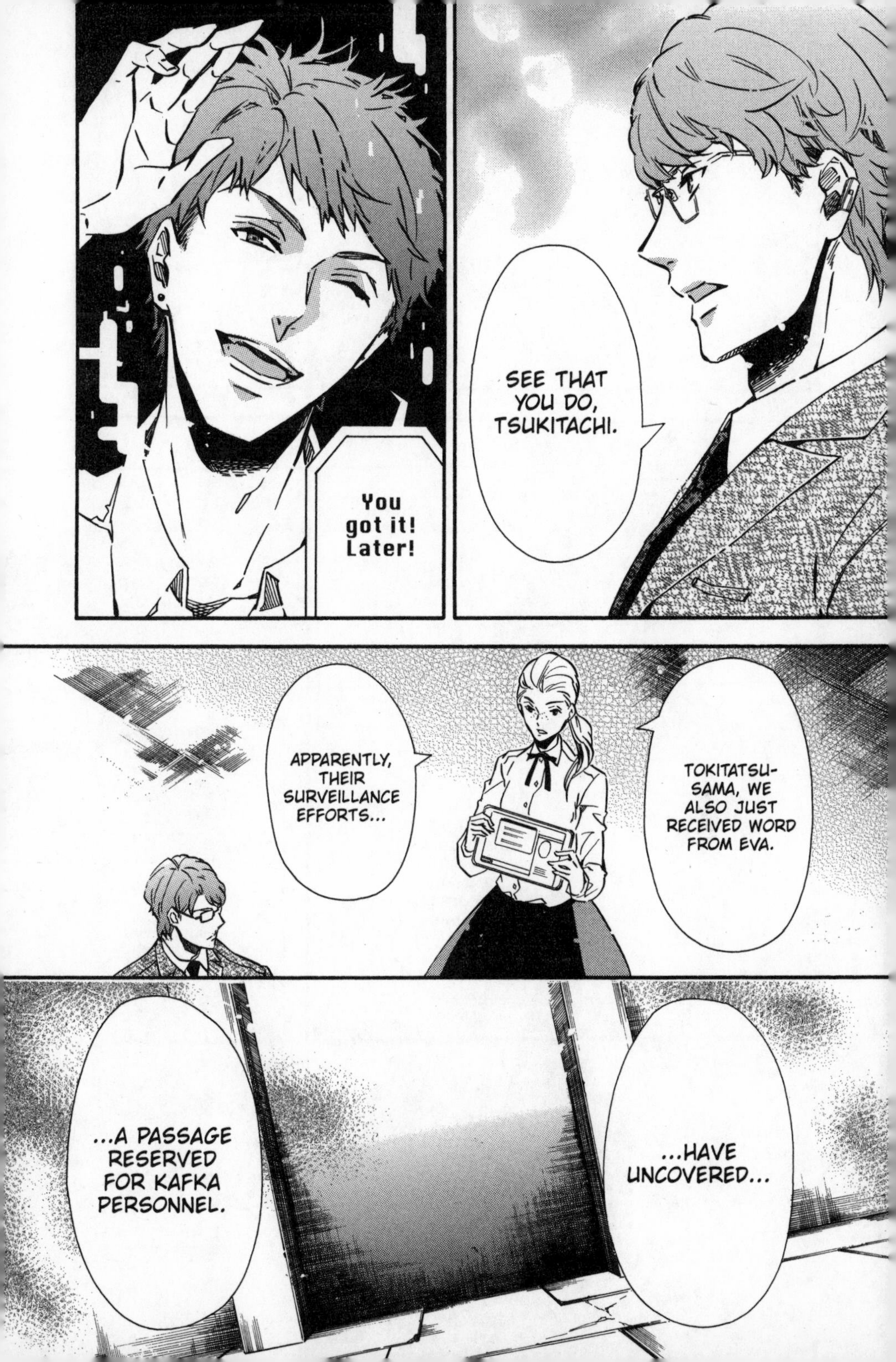
SEE THAT YOU DO, TSUKITACHI.
You got it! Later!
TOKITATSU-SAMA, WE ALSO JUST RECEIVED WORD FROM EVA.
APPARENTLY, THEIR SURVEILLANCE EFFORTS...
...HAVE UNCOVERED...
...A PASSAGE RESERVED FOR KAFKA PERSONNEL.

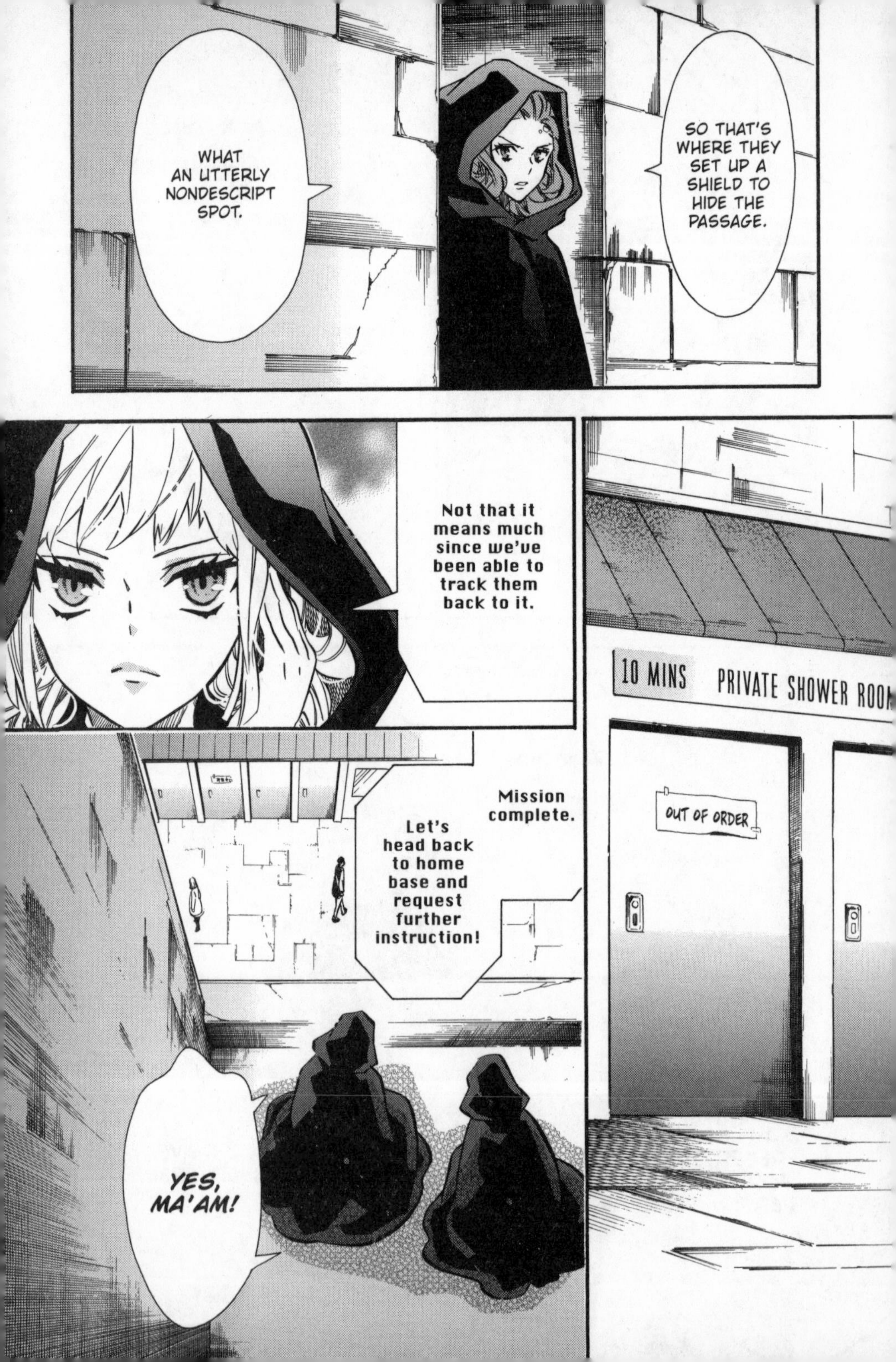
SO THAT'S WHERE THEY SET UP A SHIELD TO HIDE THE PASSAGE.
WHAT AN UTTERLY NONDESCRIPT SPOT.
10 MINS
PRIVATE SHOWER ROOM
OUT OF ORDER
Not that it means much since we've been able to track them back to it.
Mission complete.
Let's head back to home base and request further instruction!
YES, MA'AM!

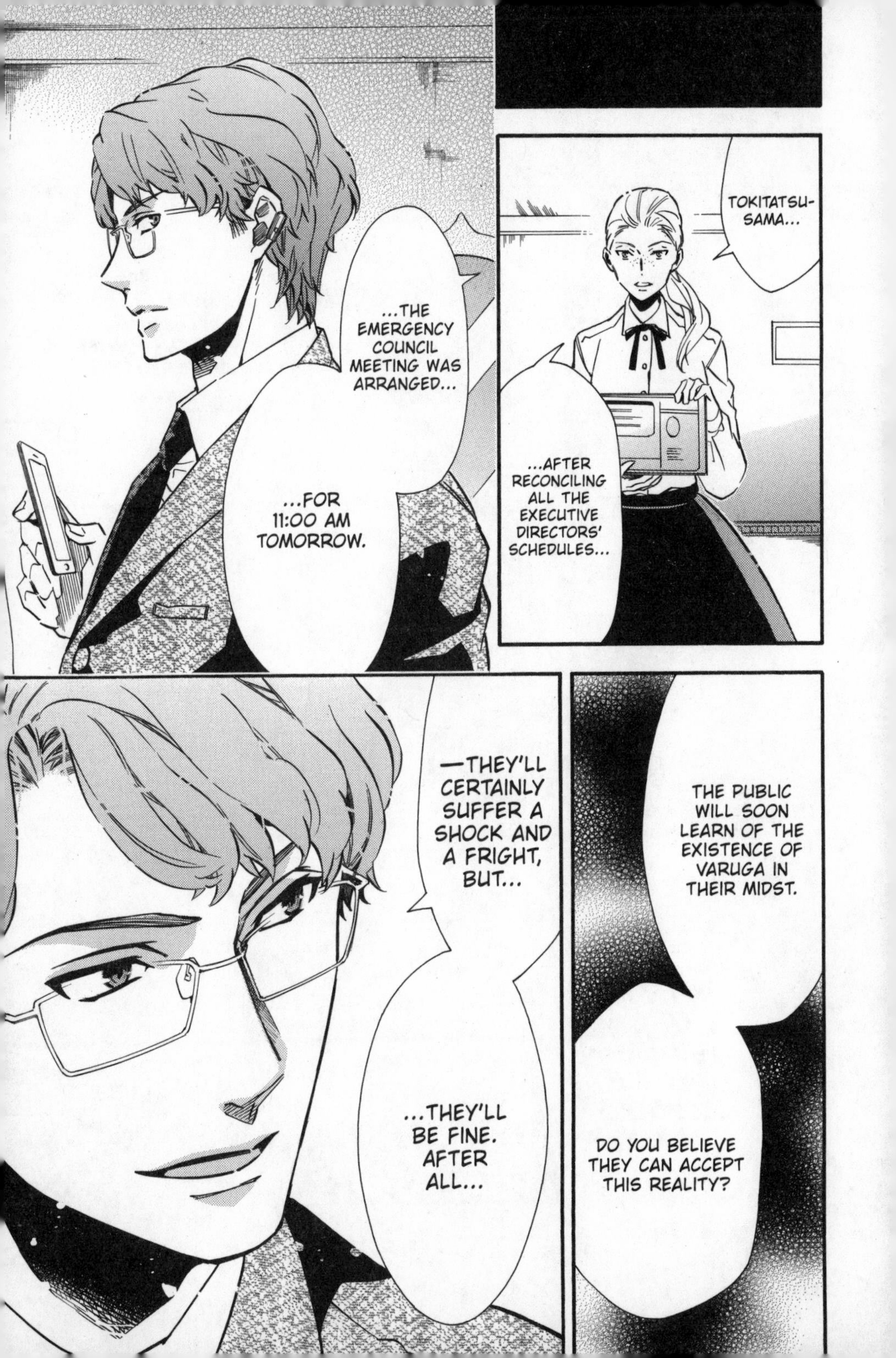
TOKITATSU-SAMA...
...AFTER RECONCILING ALL THE EXECUTIVE DIRECTORS' SCHEDULES...
...THE EMERGENCY COUNCIL MEETING WAS ARRANGED...
...FOR 11:00 AM TOMORROW.
THE PUBLIC WILL SOON LEARN OF THE EXISTENCE OF VARUGA IN THEIR MIDST.
DO YOU BELIEVE THEY CAN ACCEPT THIS REALITY?
—THEY'LL CERTAINLY SUFFER A SHOCK AND A FRIGHT, BUT...
...THEY'LL BE FINE. AFTER ALL...

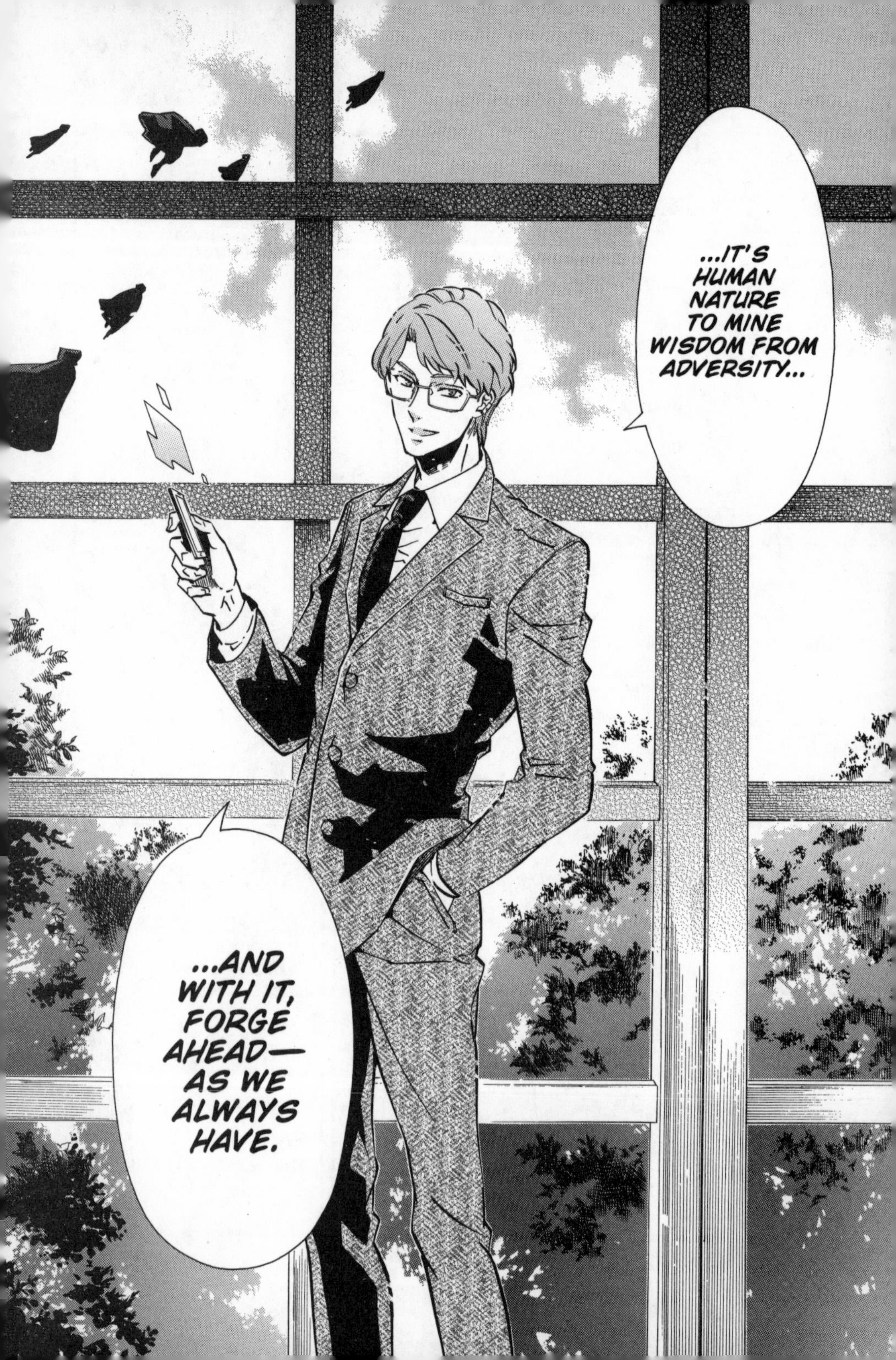
...IT'S HUMAN NATURE TO MINE WISDOM FROM ADVERSITY...
...AND WITH IT, FORGE AHEAD— AS WE ALWAYS HAVE.

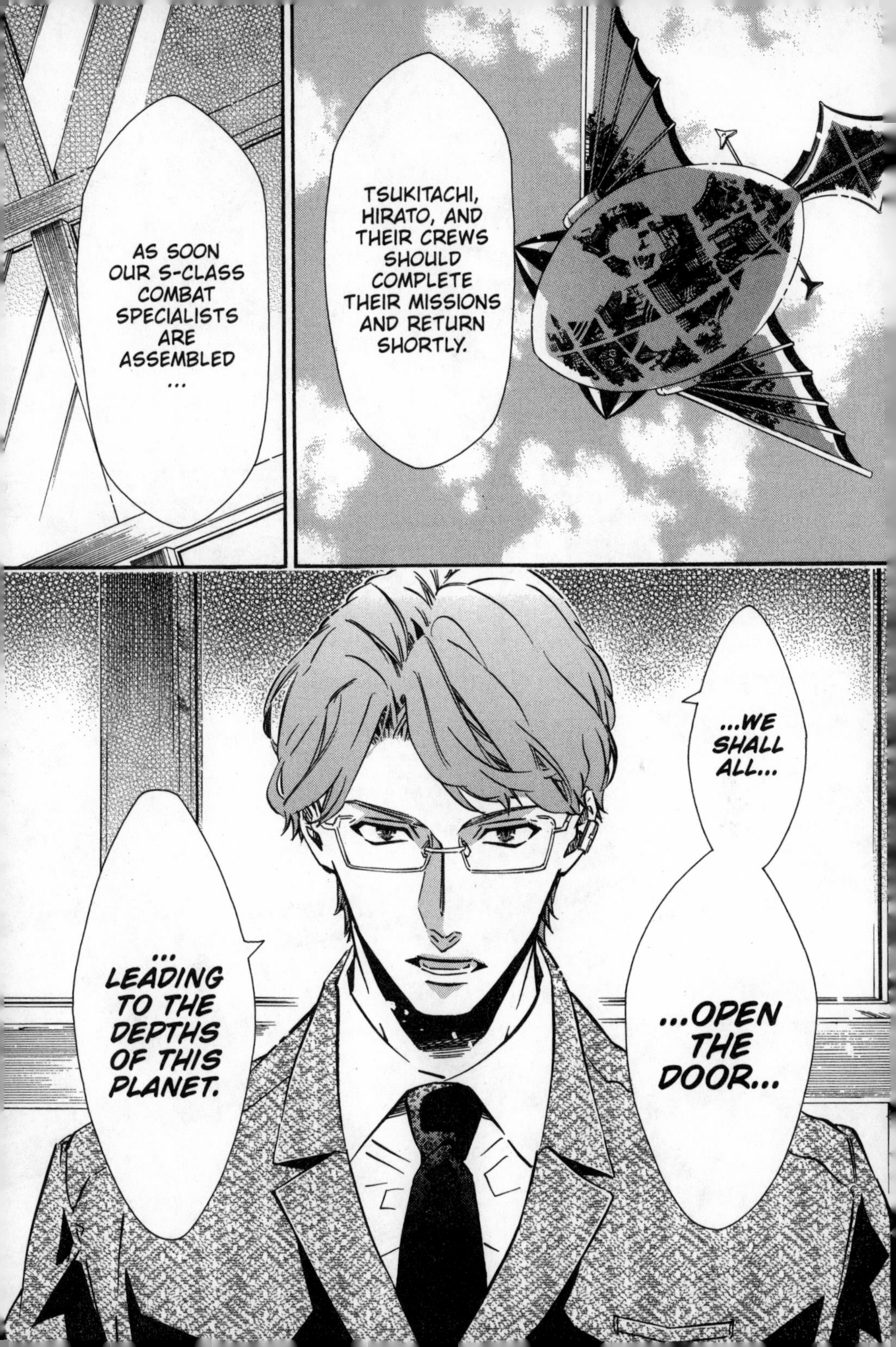
TSUKITACHI, HIRATO, AND THEIR CREWS SHOULD COMPLETE THEIR MISSIONS AND RETURN SHORTLY.
AS SOON OUR S-CLASS COMBAT SPECIALISTS ARE ASSEMBLED ...
...WE SHALL ALL...
...OPEN THE DOOR...
... LEADING TO THE DEPTHS OF THIS PLANET.

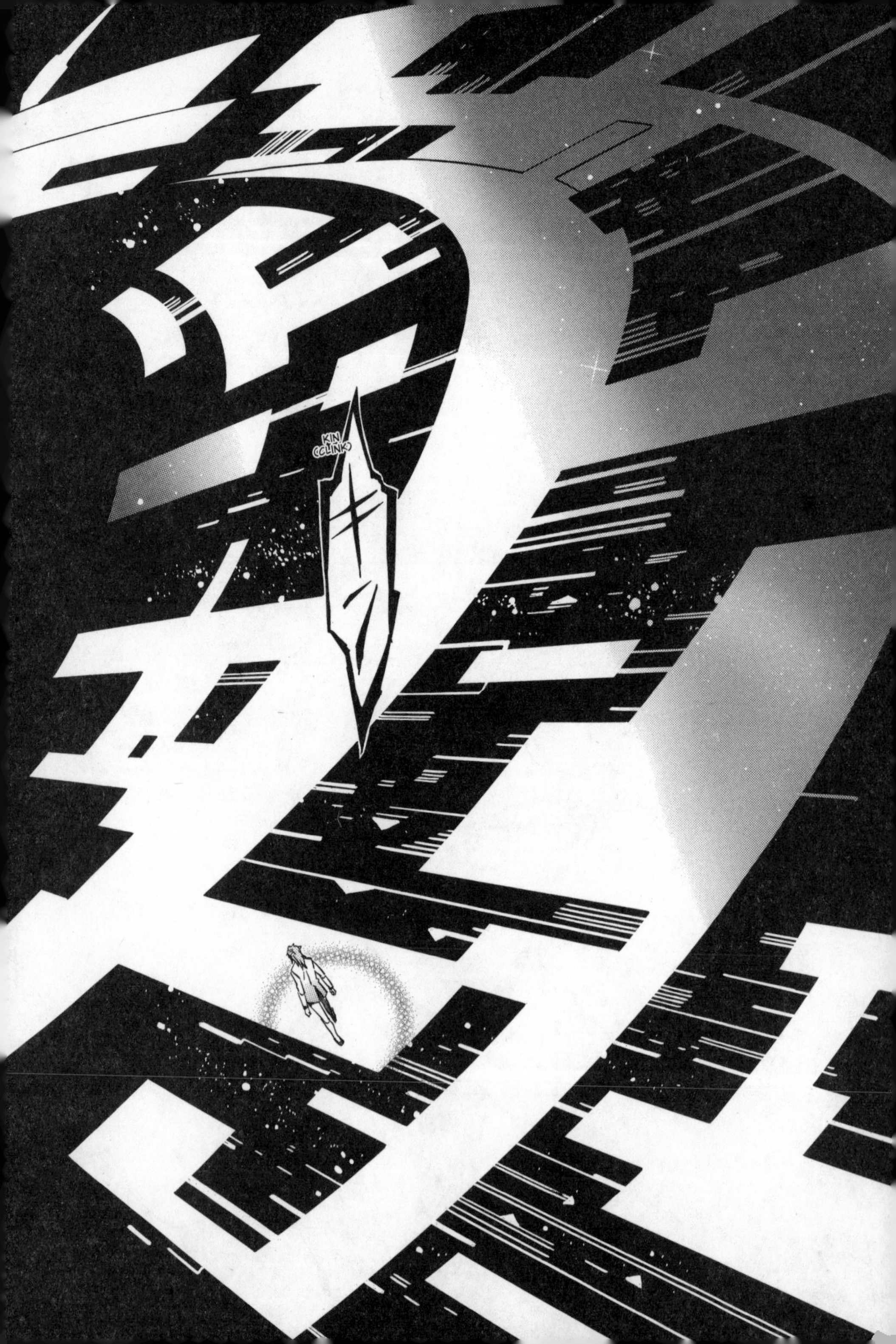
KIN
(CLINK)

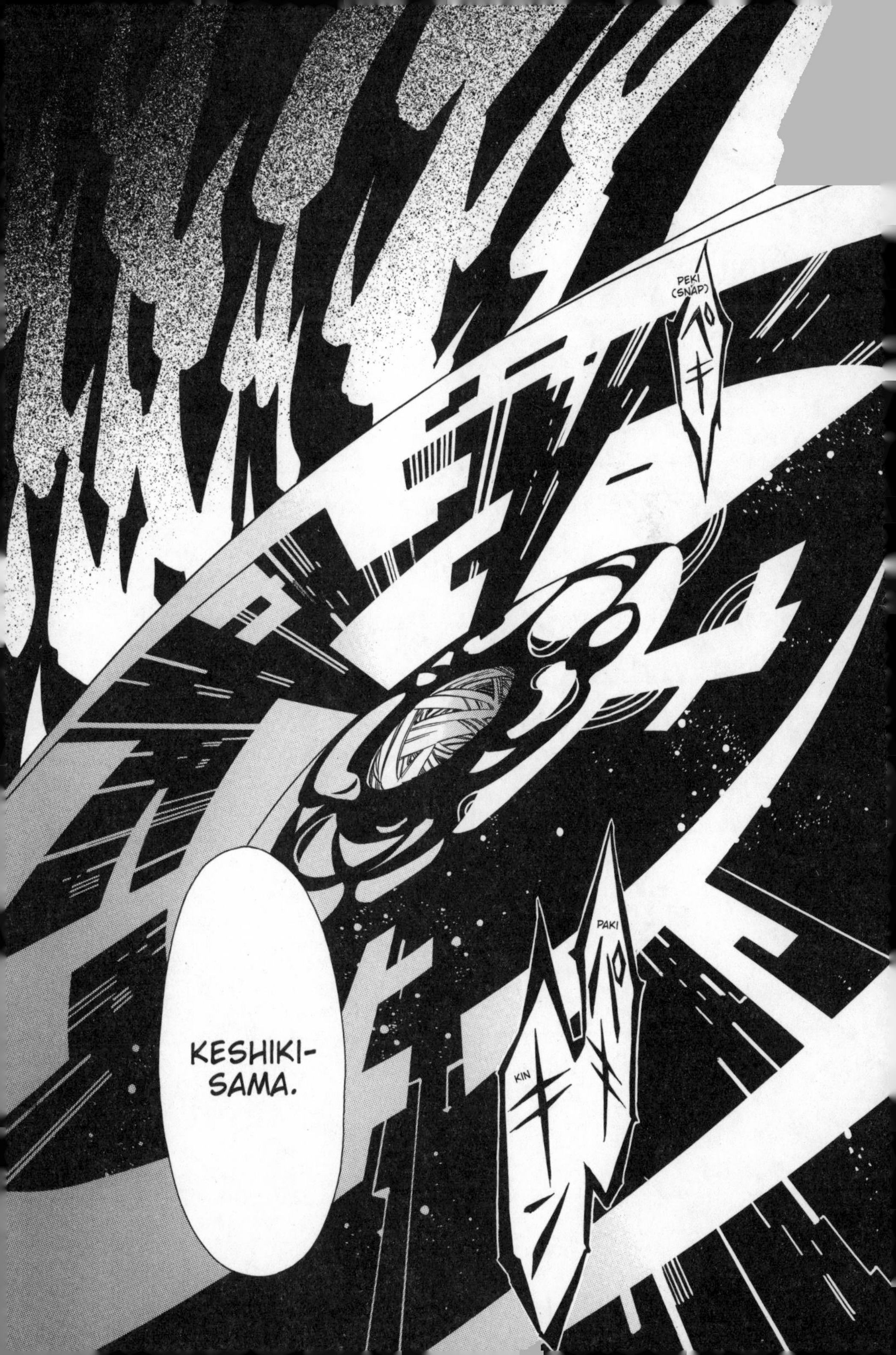
PEKI (SNAP)
PAKI
KIN
KESHIKI-SAMA.

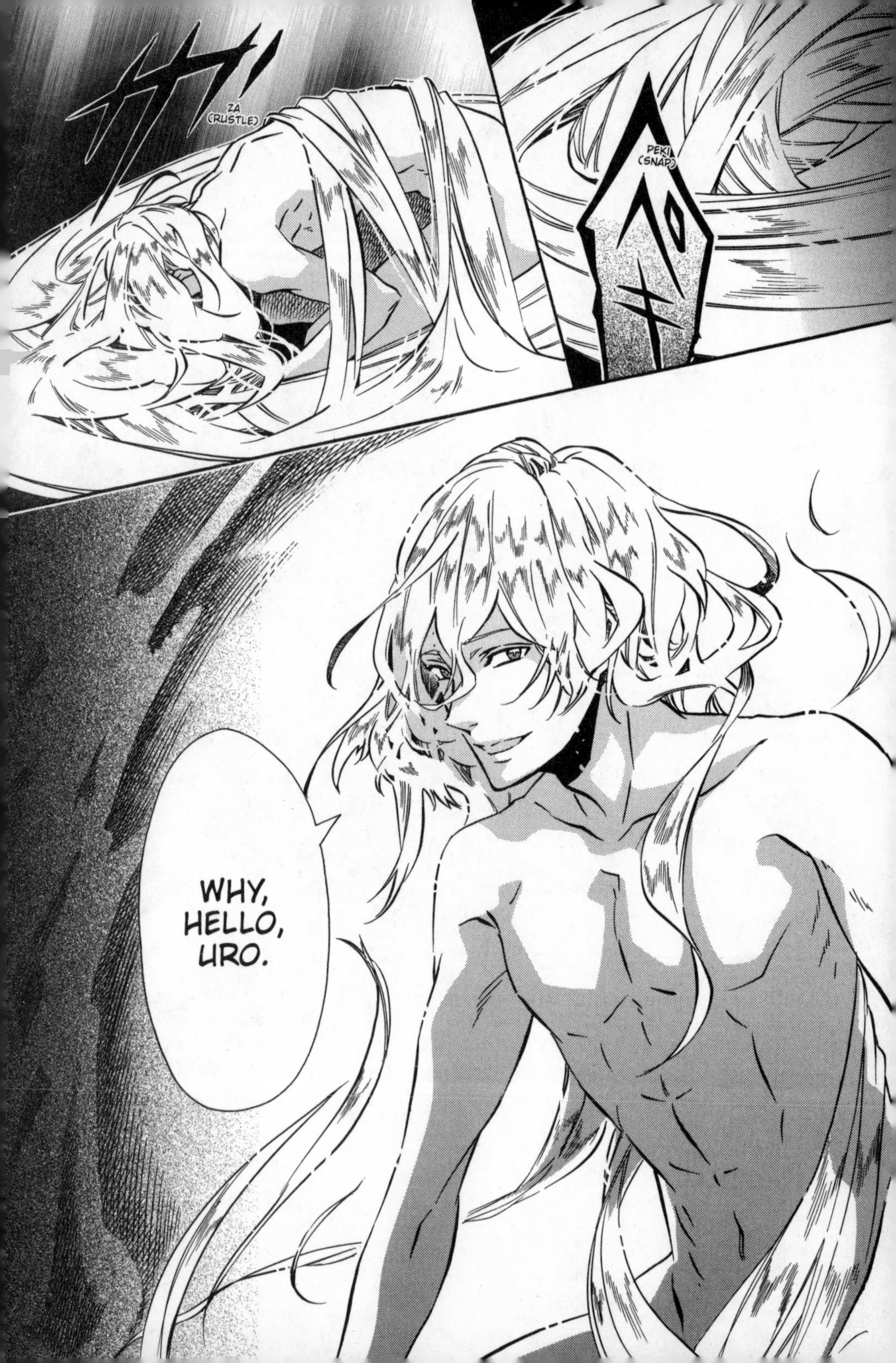
PEKI (SNAP)
ZA (RUSTLE)
WHY, HELLO, URO.

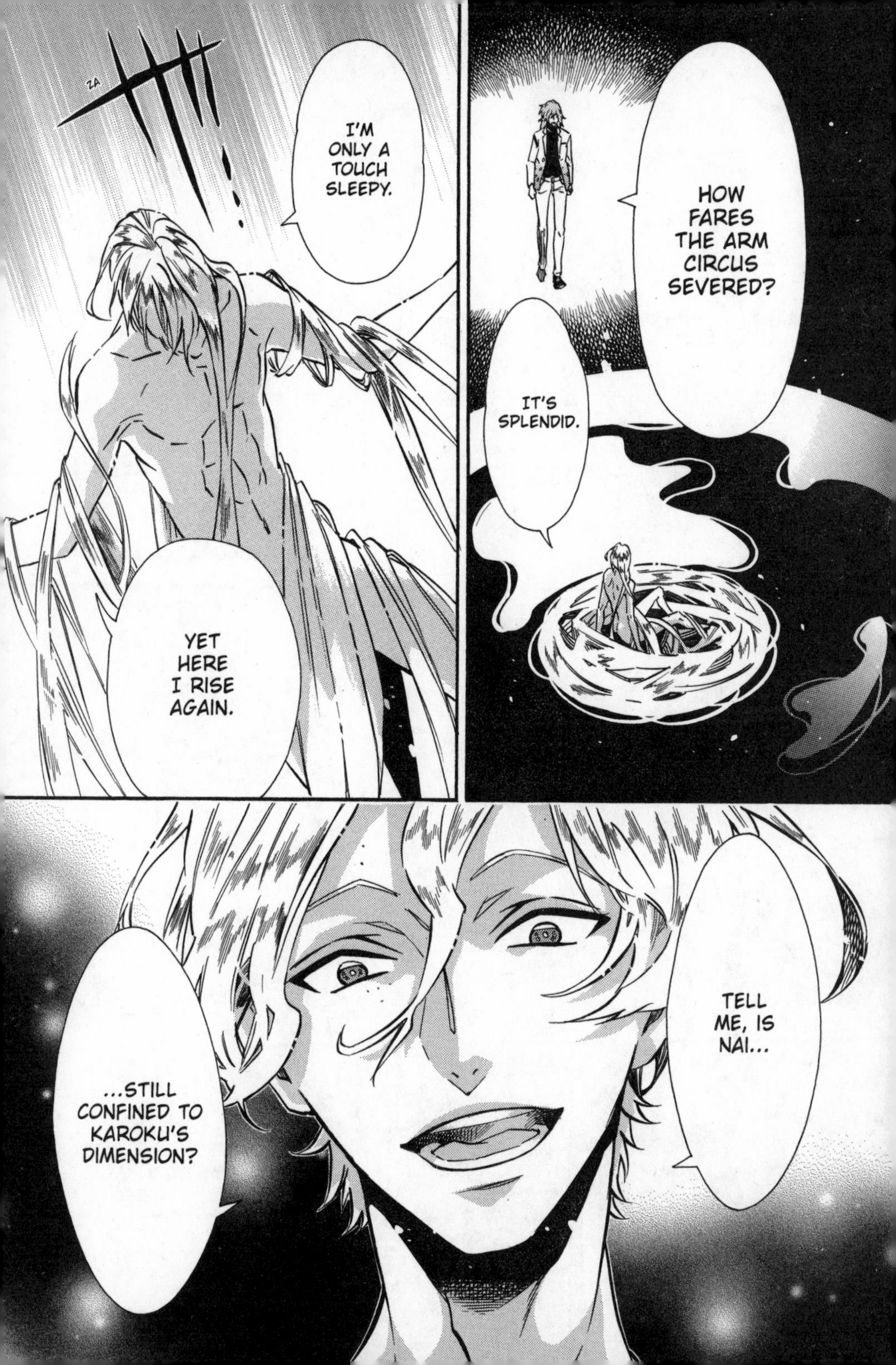
HOW FARES THE ARM CIRCUS SEVERED?
IT'S SPLENDID.
ZA
I'M ONLY A TOUCH SLEEPY.
YET HERE I RISE AGAIN.
TELL ME, IS NAI...
...STILL CONFINED TO KAROKU'S DIMENSION?

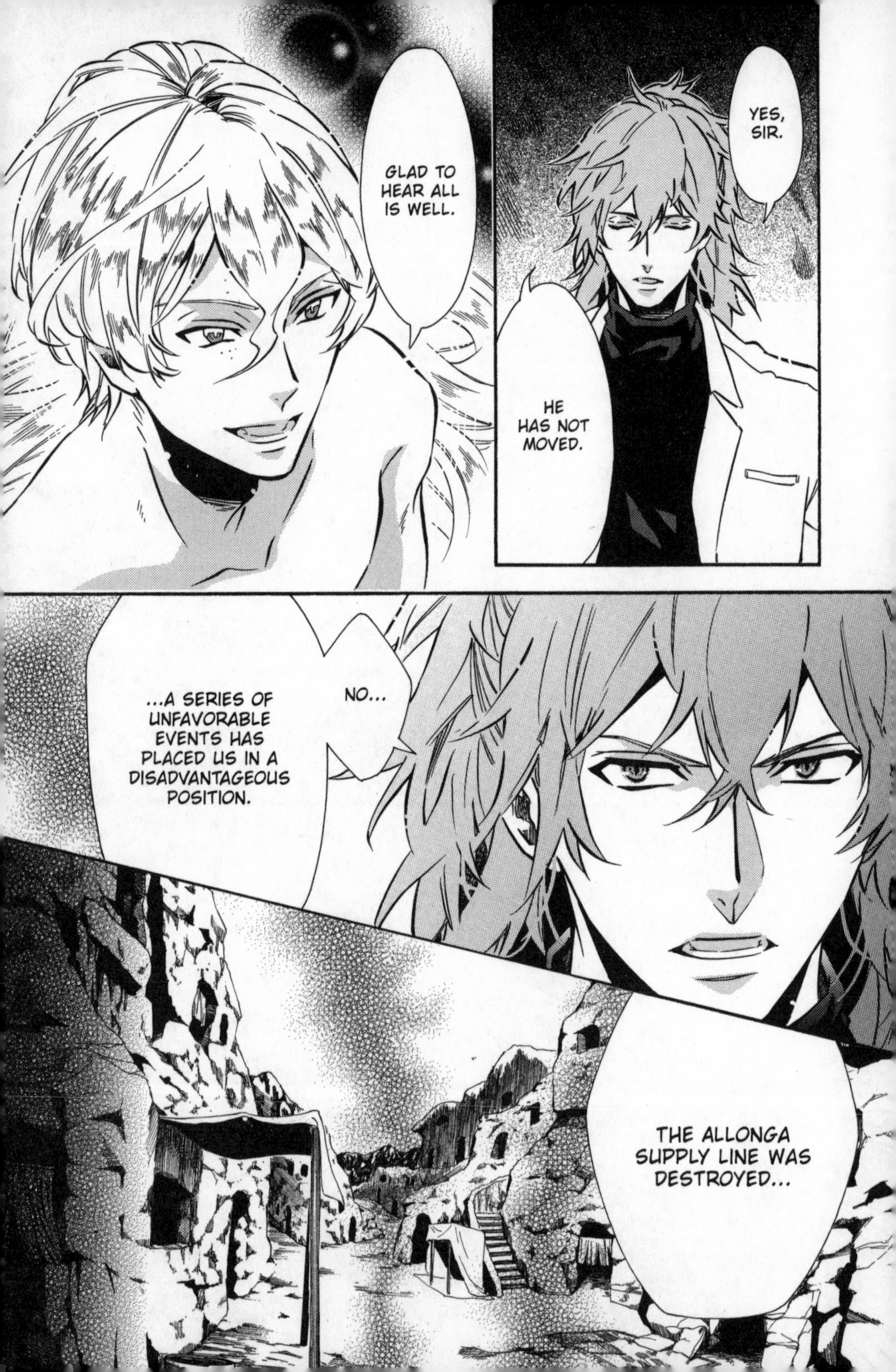
YES, SIR.
HE HAS NOT MOVED.
GLAD TO HEAR ALL IS WELL.
NO...
...A SERIES OF UNFAVORABLE EVENTS HAS PLACED US IN A DISADVANTAGEOUS POSITION.
THE ALLONGA SUPPLY LINE WAS DESTROYED...

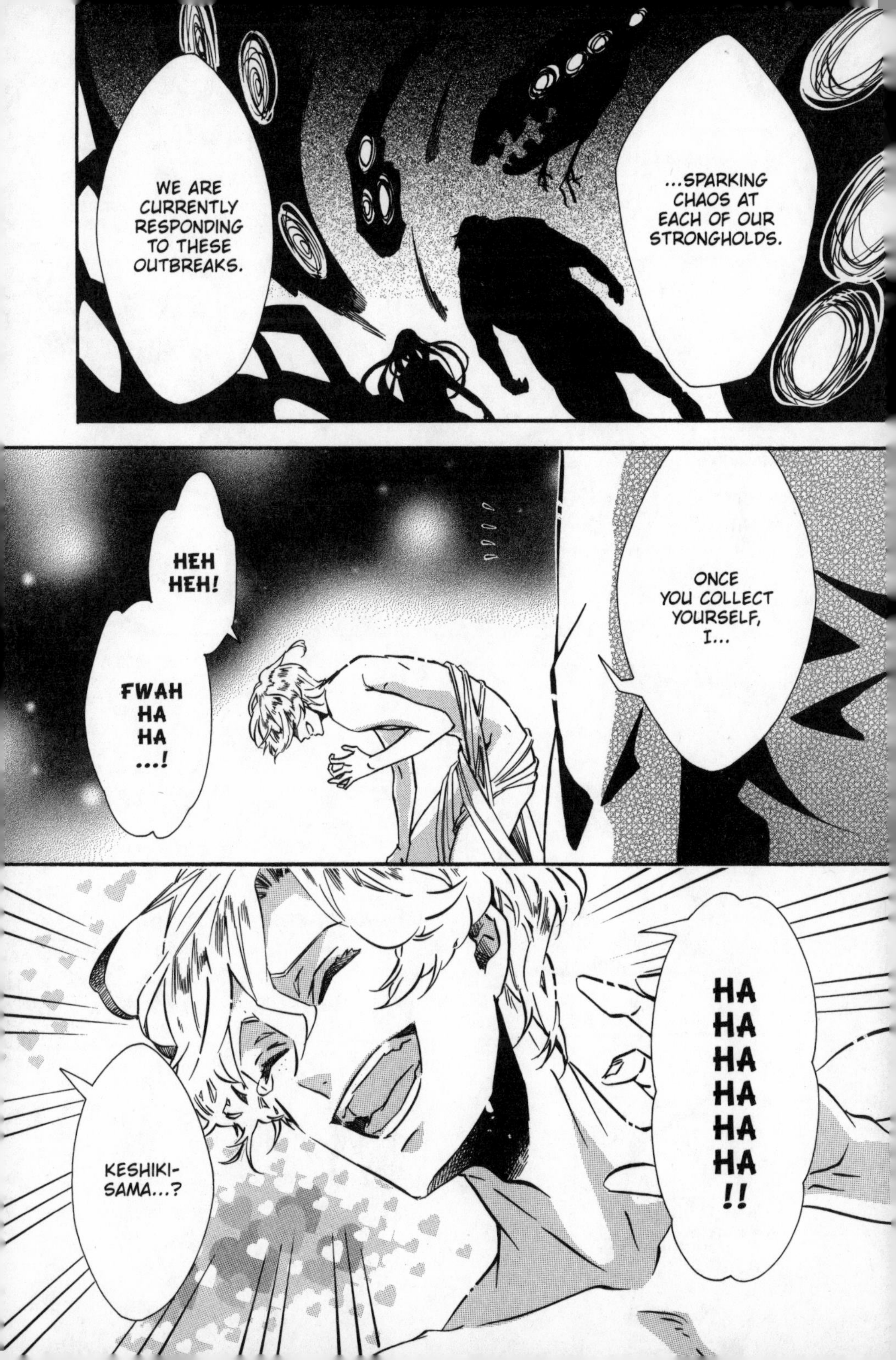
...SPARKING CHAOS AT EACH OF OUR STRONGHOLDS.
WE ARE CURRENTLY RESPONDING TO THESE OUTBREAKS.
ONCE YOU COLLECT YOURSELF, I...
HEH HEH!
FWAH HA HA ...!
HA HA HA HA HA HA HA !!
KESHIKI-SAMA...?

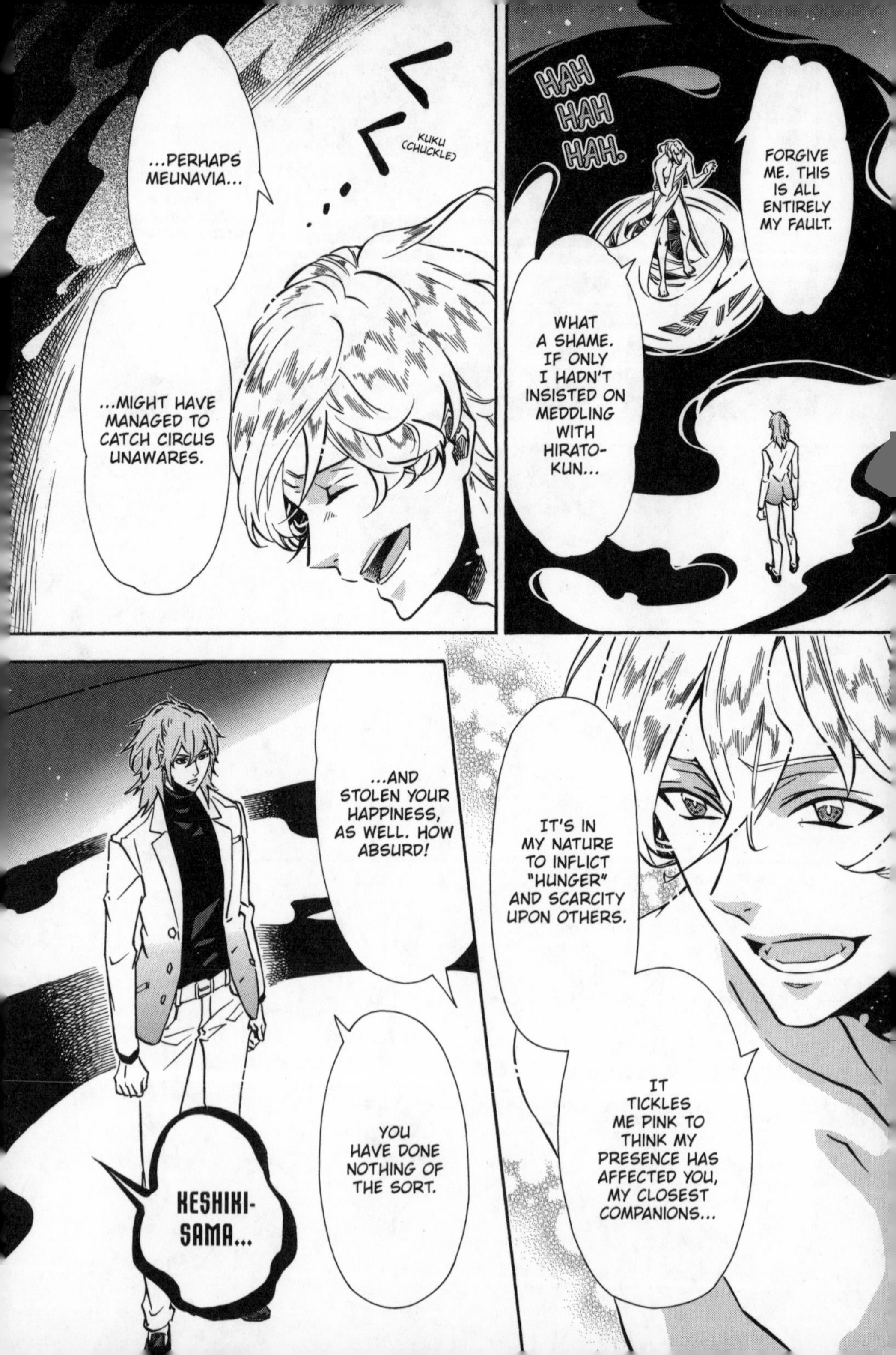
FORGIVE ME. THIS IS ALL ENTIRELY MY FAULT.
HAH HAH HAH.
WHAT A SHAME. IF ONLY I HADN'T INSISTED ON MEDDLING WITH HIRATO-KUN...
KUKU (CHUCKLE)
...PERHAPS MEUNAVIA...
...MIGHT HAVE MANAGED TO CATCH CIRCUS UNAWARES.
IT'S IN MY NATURE TO INFLICT "HUNGER" AND SCARCITY UPON OTHERS.
IT TICKLES ME PINK TO THINK MY PRESENCE HAS AFFECTED YOU, MY CLOSEST COMPANIONS...
...AND STOLEN YOUR HAPPINESS, AS WELL. HOW ABSURD!
YOU HAVE DONE NOTHING OF THE SORT.
KESHIKI-SAMA...

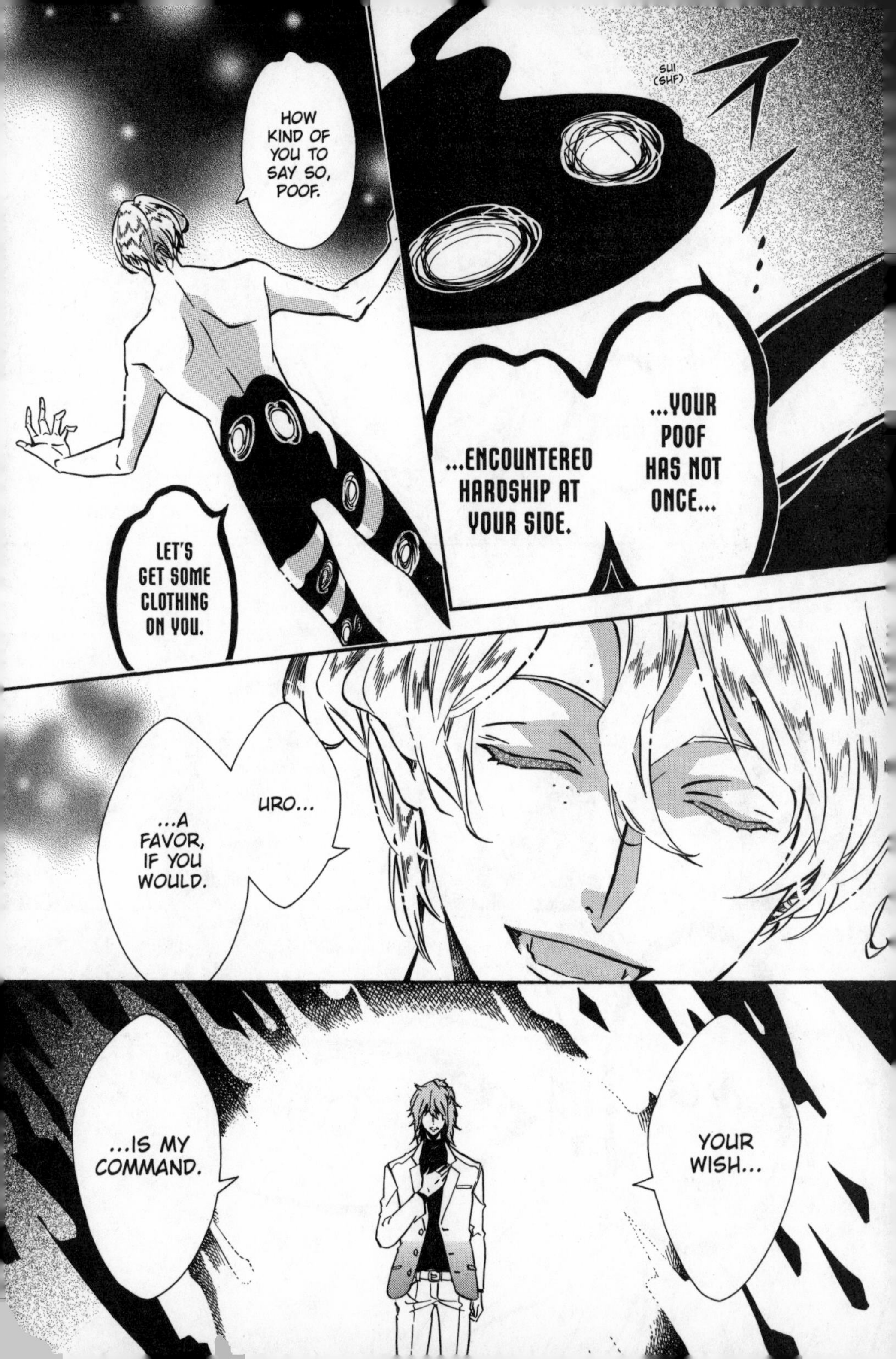
SUI (SHF)
...YOUR POOF HAS NOT ONCE...
...ENCOUNTERED HARDSHIP AT YOUR SIDE.
HOW KIND OF YOU TO SAY SO, POOF.
LET'S GET SOME CLOTHING ON YOU.
URO...
...A FAVOR, IF YOU WOULD.
YOUR WISH...
...IS MY COMMAND.

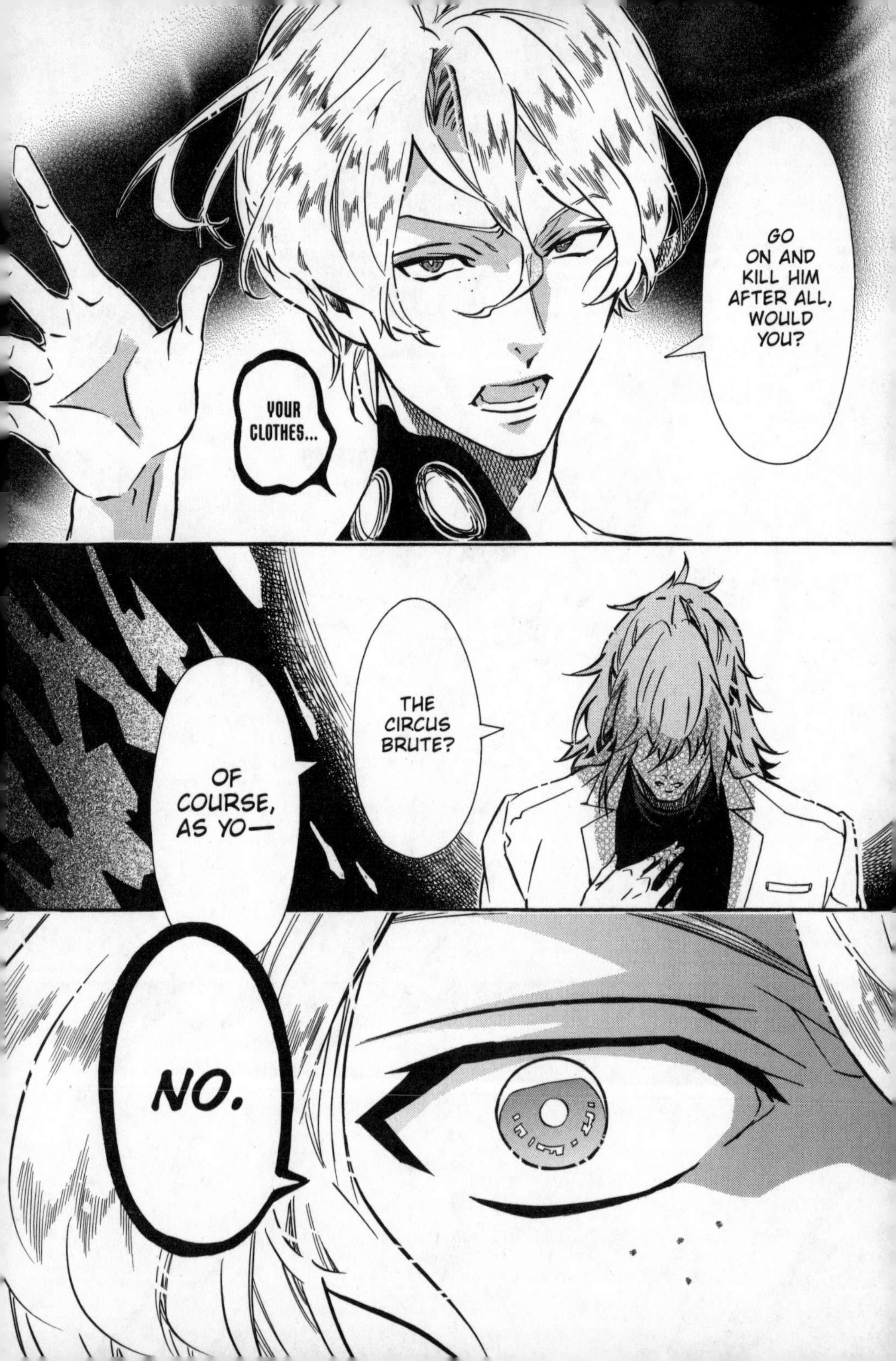
GO ON AND KILL HIM AFTER ALL, WOULD YOU?
YOUR CLOTHES...
THE CIRCUS BRUTE?
OF COURSE, AS YO—
NO.

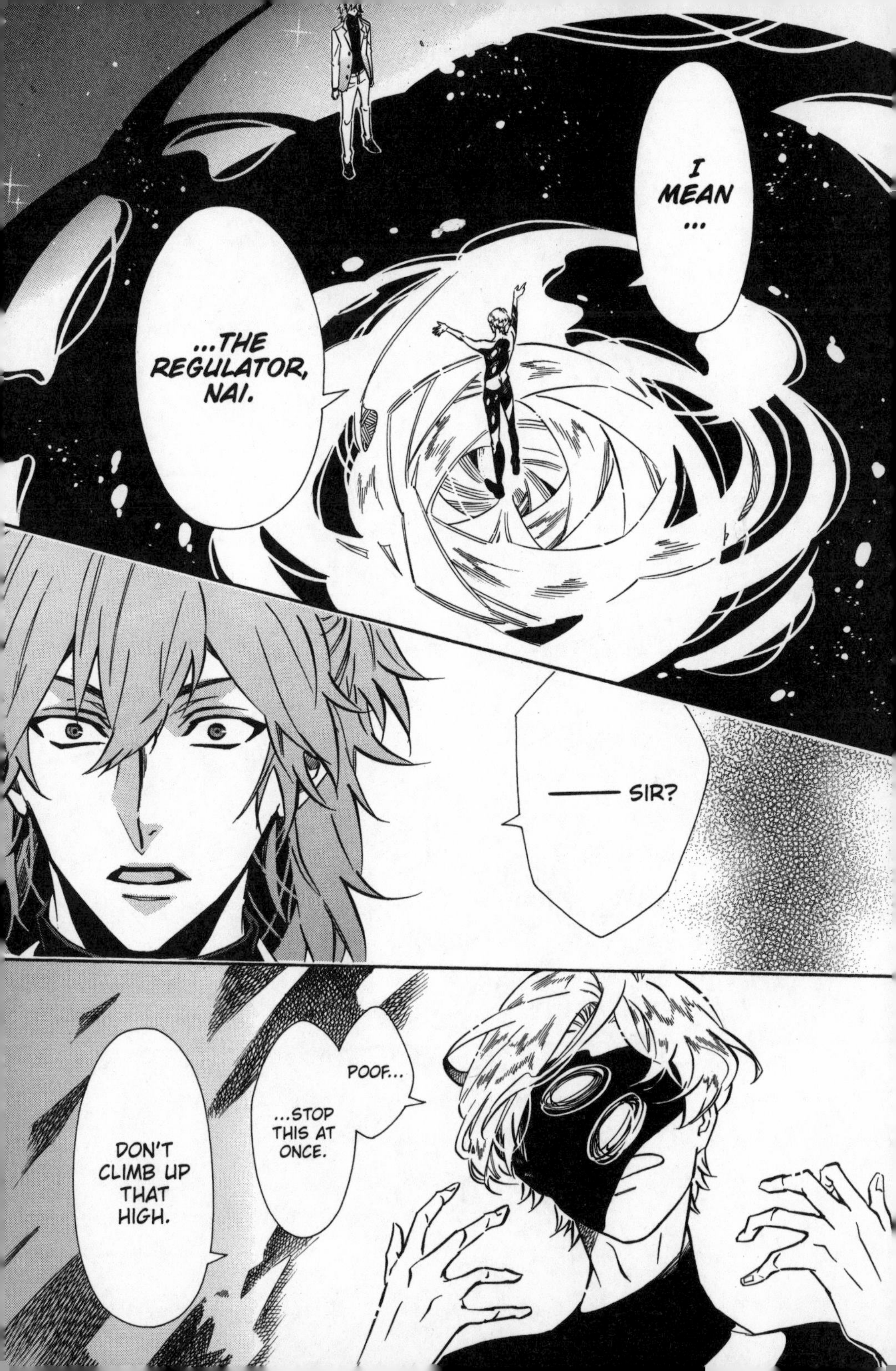
I MEAN ...
...THE REGULATOR, NAI.
—— SIR?
POOF...
...STOP THIS AT ONCE.
DON'T CLIMB UP THAT HIGH.

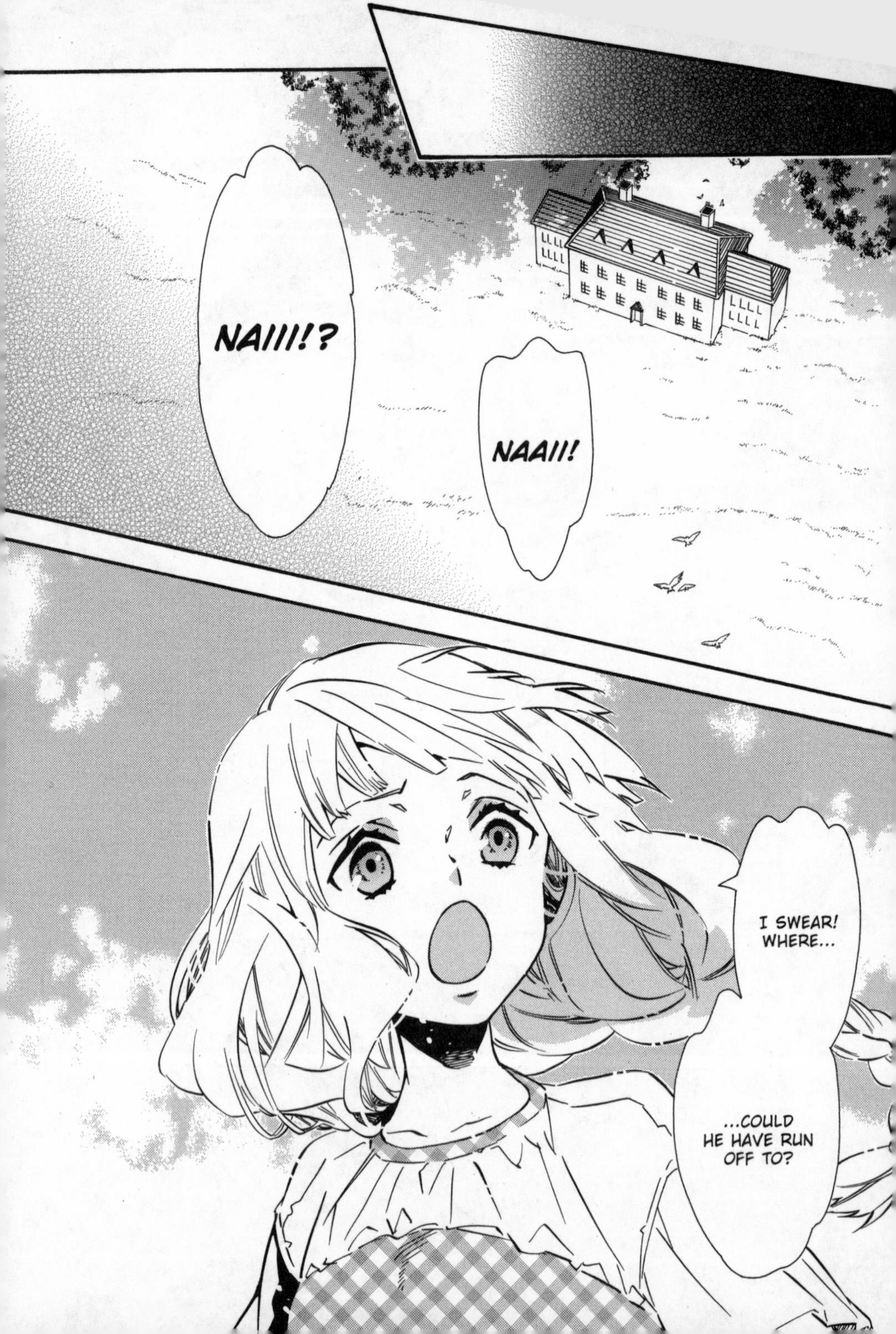
NAAII!
NAIII!?
I SWEAR! WHERE...
...COULD HE HAVE RUN OFF TO?

KARNEVAL

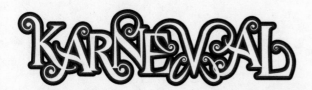

KARNEVAL

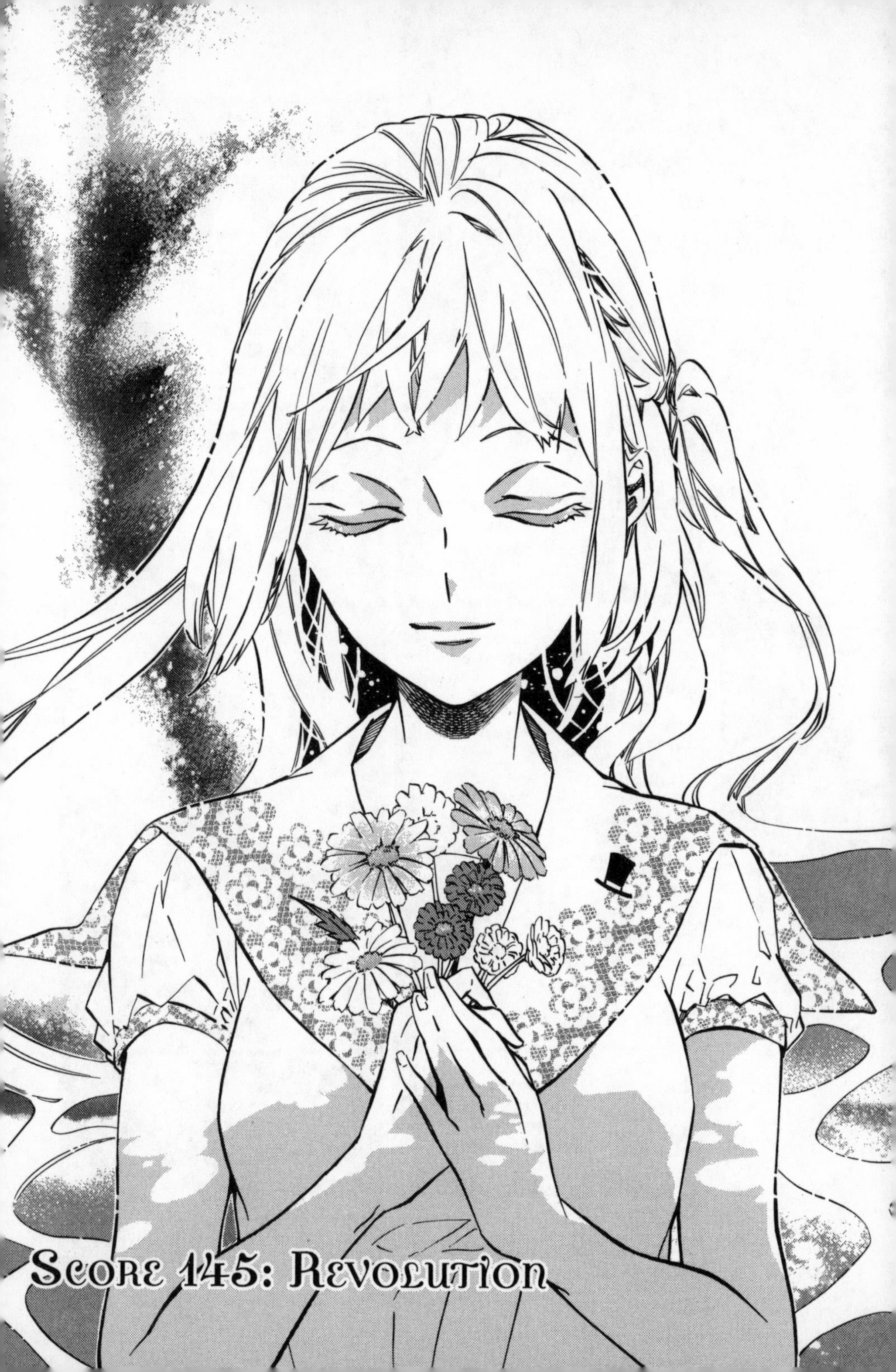
Score 145: Revolution

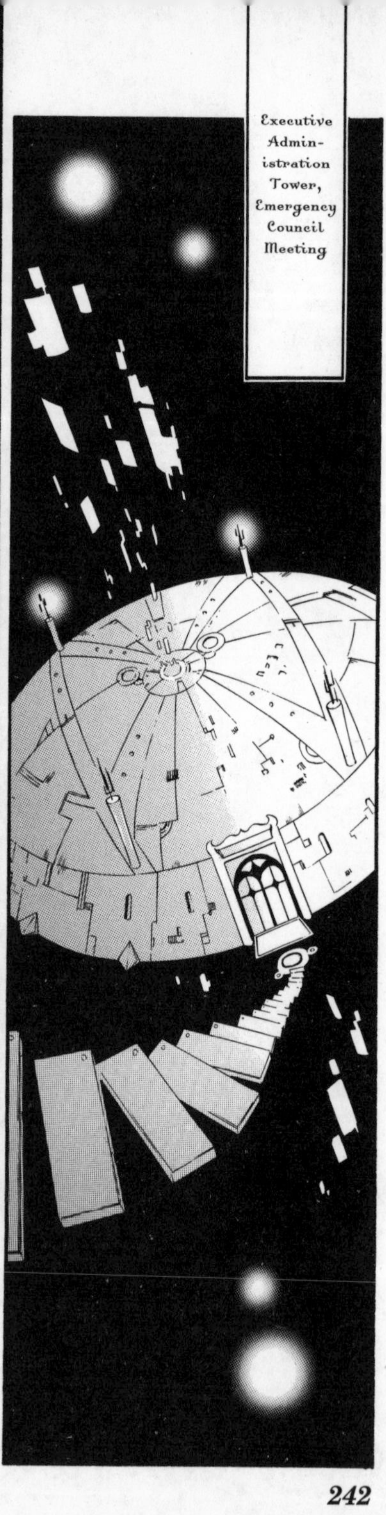
Executive Administration Tower, Emergency Council Meeting

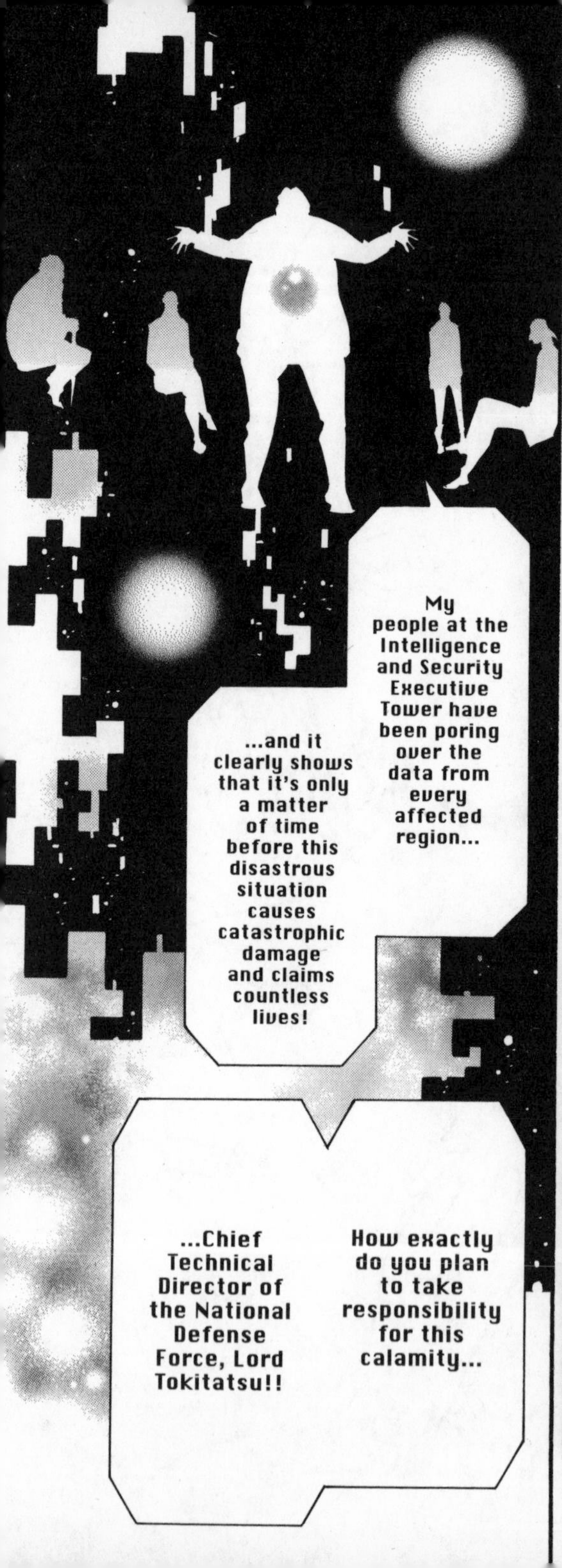
My people at the Intelligence and Security Executive Tower have been poring over the data from every affected region...
...and it clearly shows that it's only a matter of time before this disastrous situation causes catastrophic damage and claims countless lives!
How exactly do you plan to take responsibility for this calamity...
...Chief Technical Director of the National Defense Force, Lord Tokitatsu!!

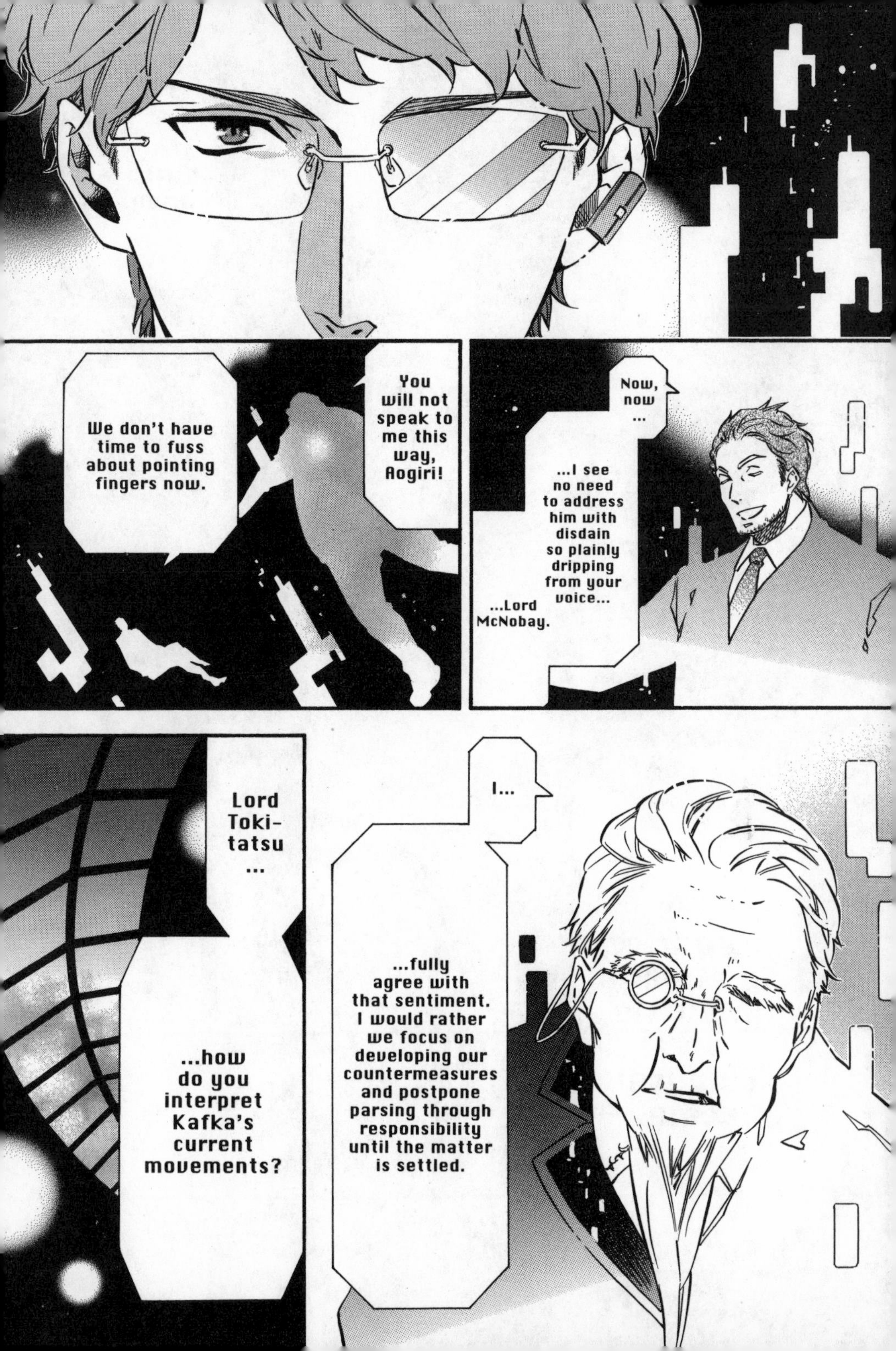
Now, now...
...I see no need to address him with disdain so plainly dripping from your voice...
...Lord McNobay.
You will not speak to me this way, Aogiri!
We don't have time to fuss about pointing fingers now.
I...
...fully agree with that sentiment. I would rather we focus on developing our countermeasures and postpone parsing through responsibility until the matter is settled.
Lord Toki-tatsu...
...how do you interpret Kafka's current movements?

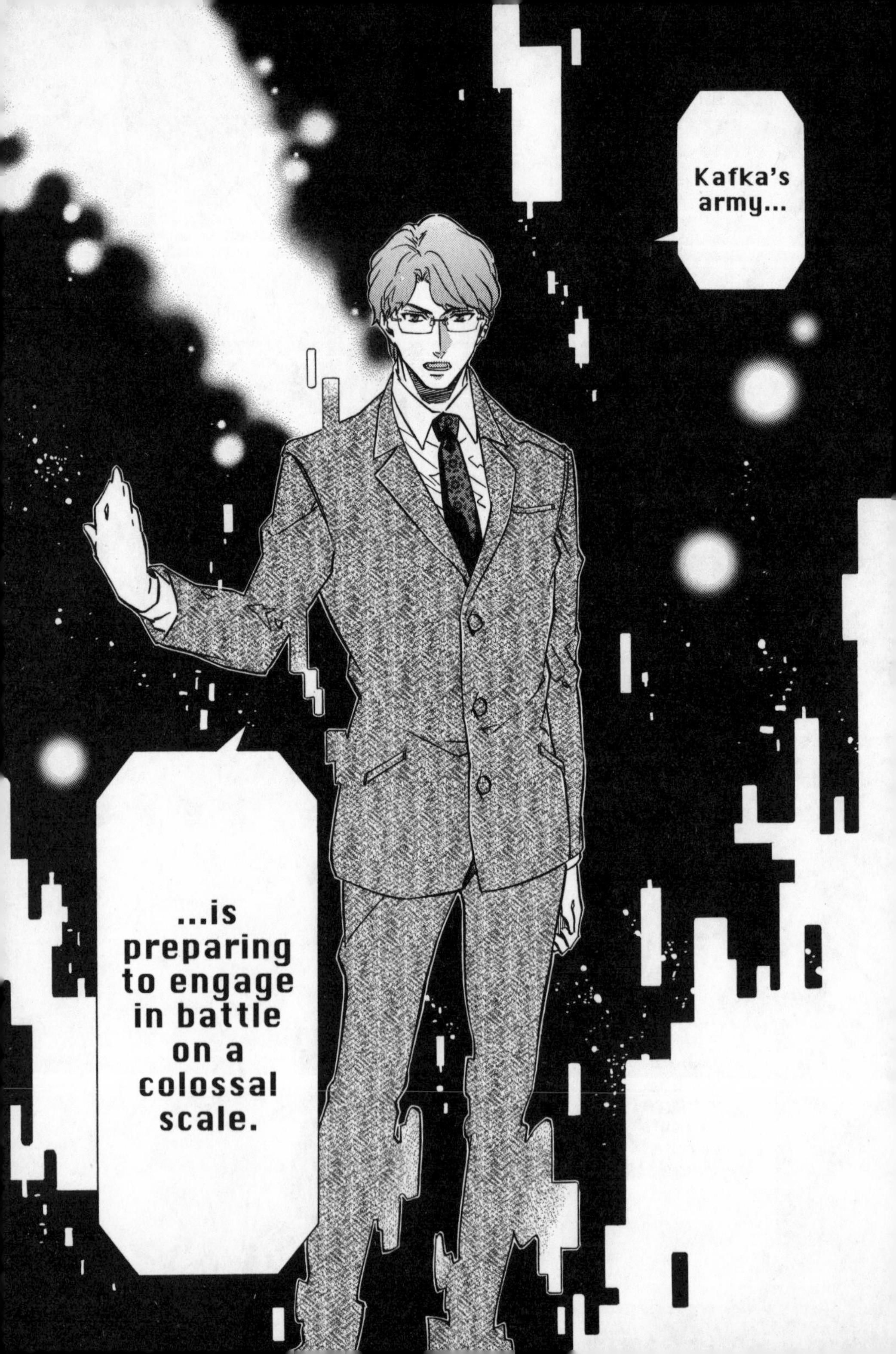
Kafka's army...
...is preparing to engage in battle on a colossal scale.

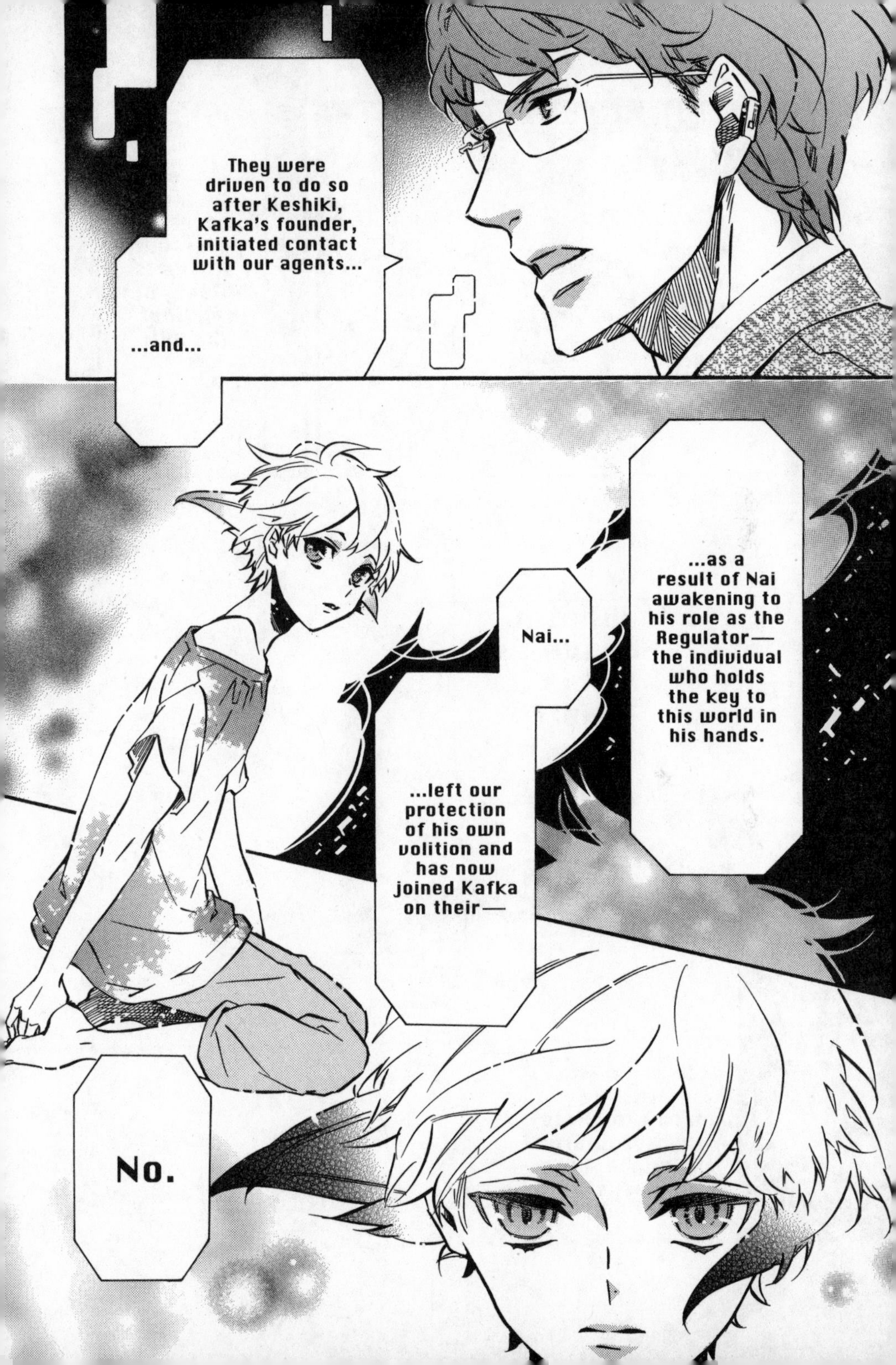
They were driven to do so after Keshiki, Kafka's founder, initiated contact with our agents...
...and...
...as a result of Nai awakening to his role as the Regulator—the individual who holds the key to this world in his hands.
Nai...
...left our protection of his own volition and has now joined Kafka on their—
No.

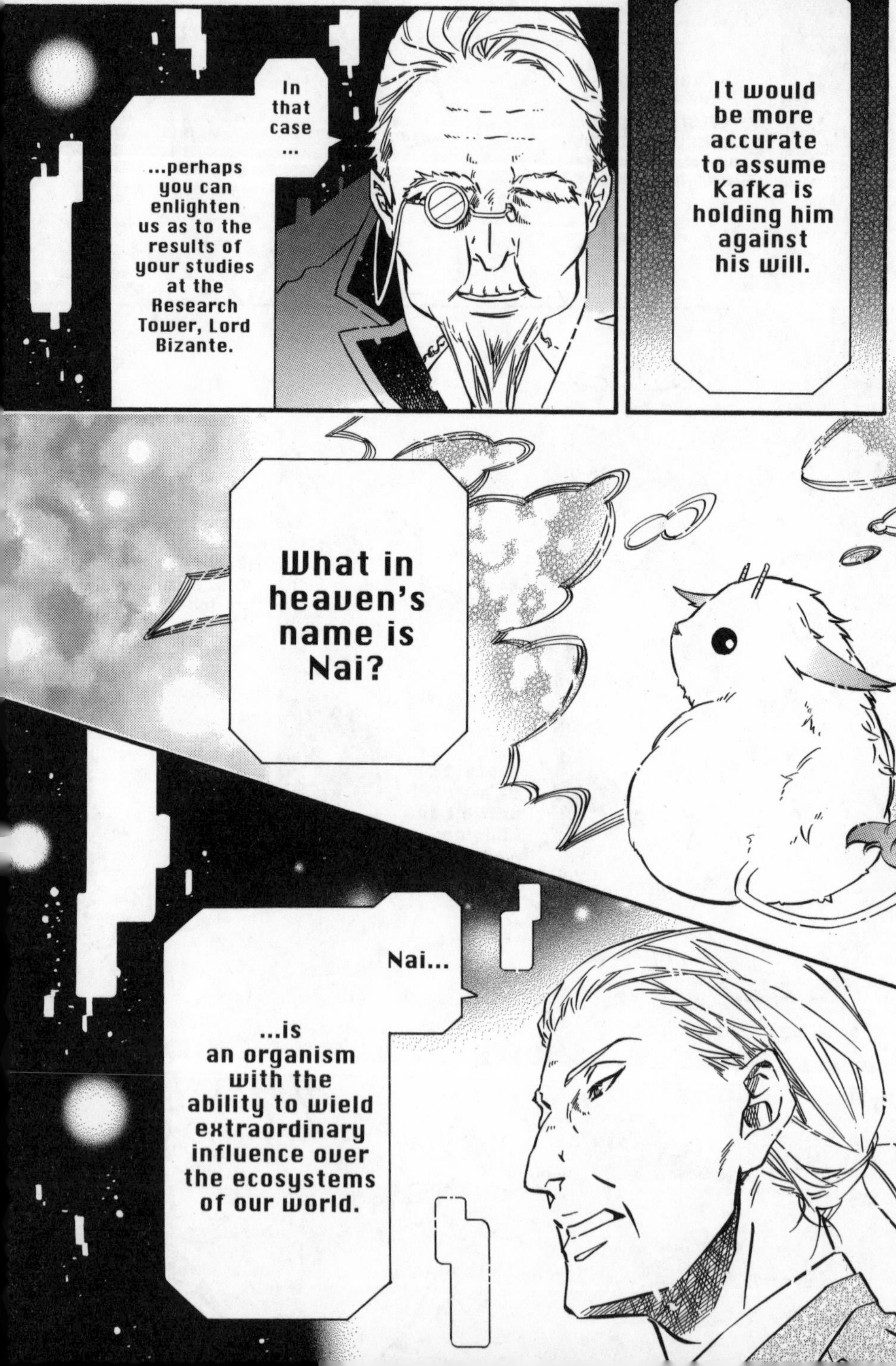
It would be more accurate to assume Kafka is holding him against his will.
In that case...
...perhaps you can enlighten us as to the results of your studies at the Research Tower, Lord Bizante.
What in heaven's name is Nai?
Nai...
...is an organism with the ability to wield extraordinary influence over the ecosystems of our world.

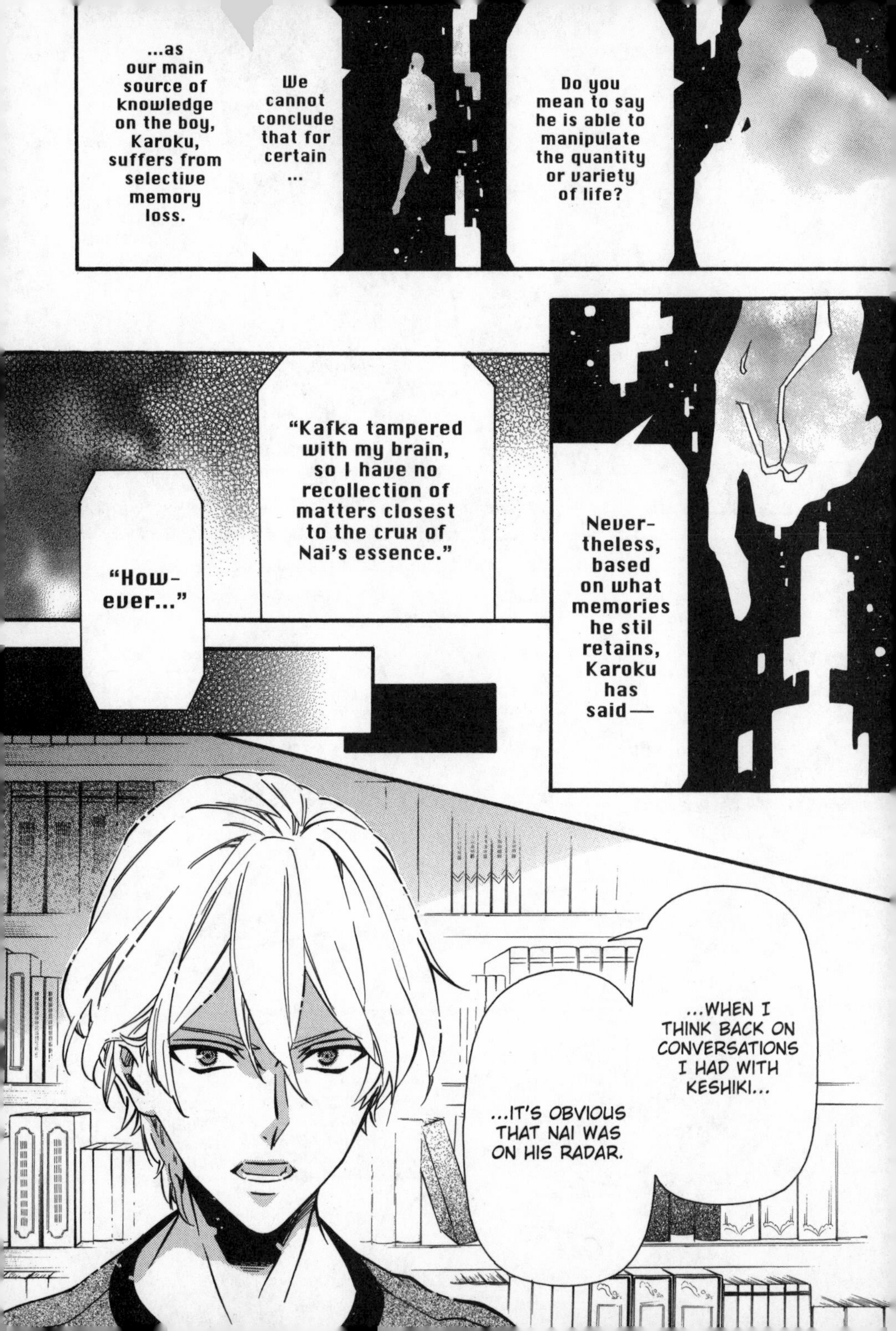
Do you mean to say he is able to manipulate the quantity or variety of life?
We cannot conclude that for certain ...
...as our main source of knowledge on the boy, Karoku, suffers from selective memory loss.
Never-theless, based on what memories he stil retains, Karoku has said—
"Kafka tampered with my brain, so I have no recollection of matters closest to the crux of Nai's essence."
"How-ever..."
...WHEN I THINK BACK ON CONVERSATIONS I HAD WITH KESHIKI...
...IT'S OBVIOUS THAT NAI WAS ON HIS RADAR.

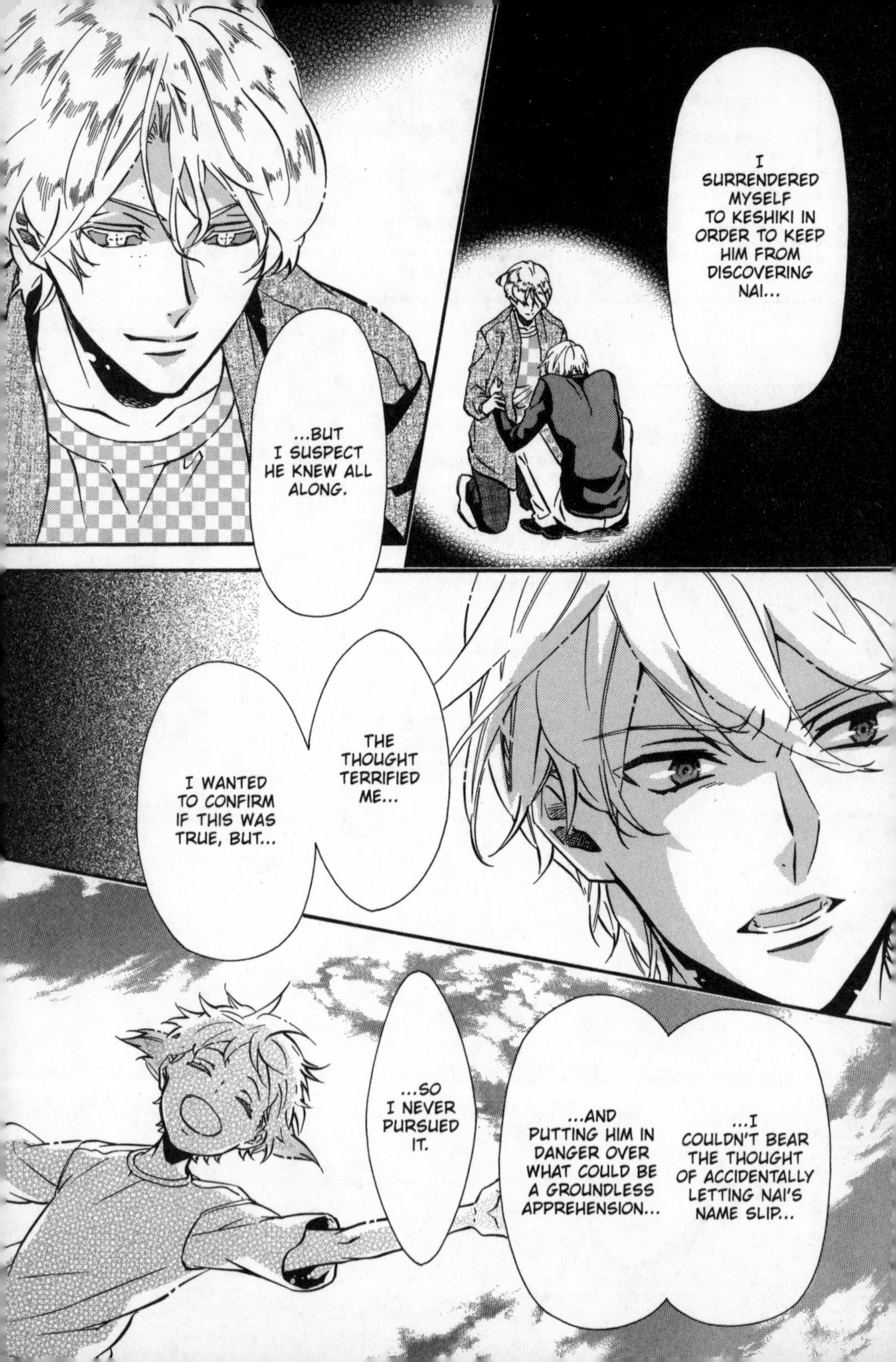
I SURRENDERED MYSELF TO KESHIKI IN ORDER TO KEEP HIM FROM DISCOVERING NAI...
...BUT I SUSPECT HE KNEW ALL ALONG.
THE THOUGHT TERRIFIED ME...
I WANTED TO CONFIRM IF THIS WAS TRUE, BUT...
...I COULDN'T BEAR THE THOUGHT OF ACCIDENTALLY LETTING NAI'S NAME SLIP...
...AND PUTTING HIM IN DANGER OVER WHAT COULD BE A GROUNDLESS APPREHENSION...
...SO I NEVER PURSUED IT.

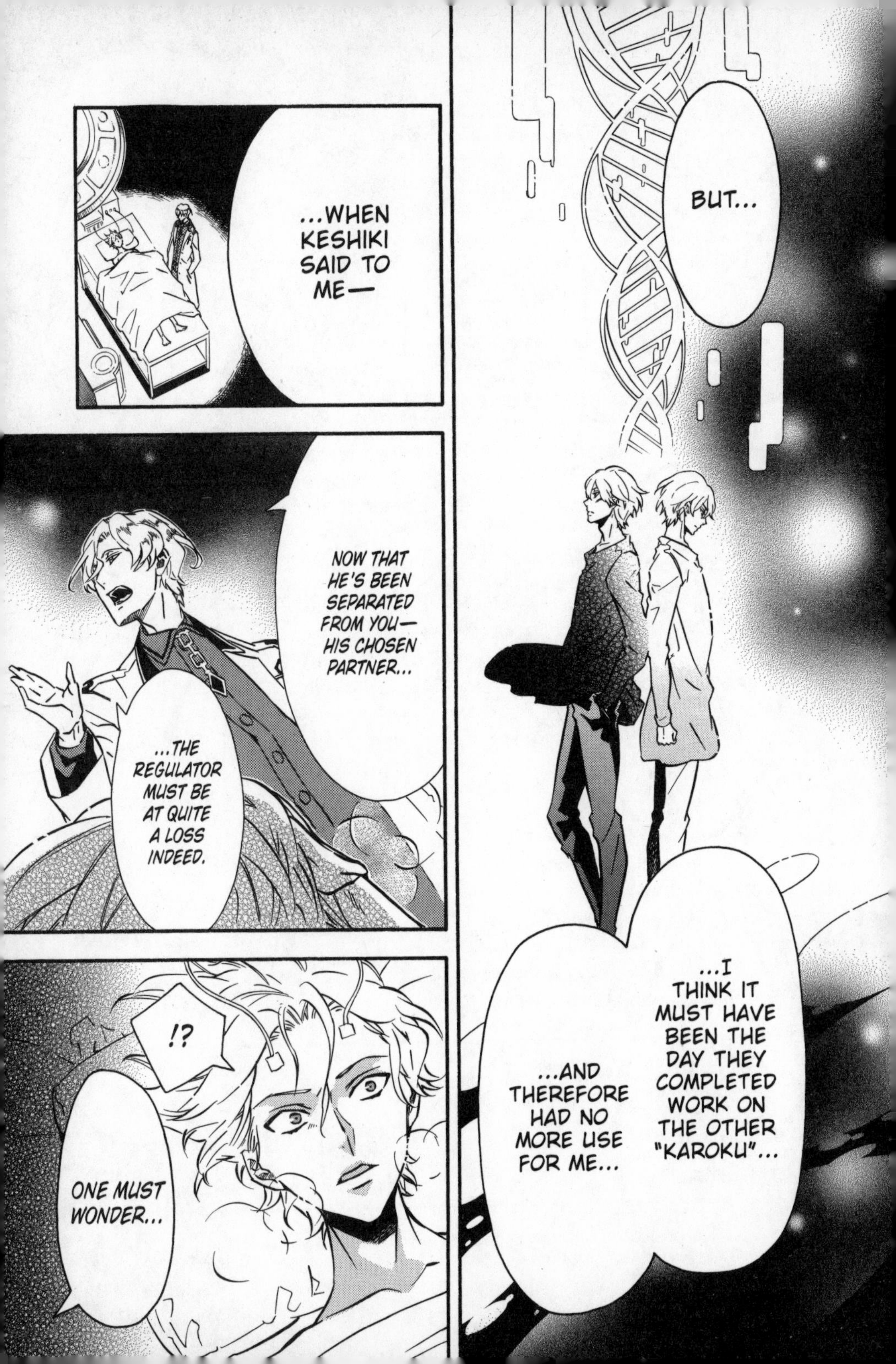
BUT...
...I THINK IT MUST HAVE BEEN THE DAY THEY COMPLETED WORK ON THE OTHER "KAROKU"...
...AND THEREFORE HAD NO MORE USE FOR ME...
...WHEN KESHIKI SAID TO ME—
NOW THAT HE'S BEEN SEPARATED FROM YOU—HIS CHOSEN PARTNER...
...THE REGULATOR MUST BE AT QUITE A LOSS INDEED.
!?
ONE MUST WONDER...

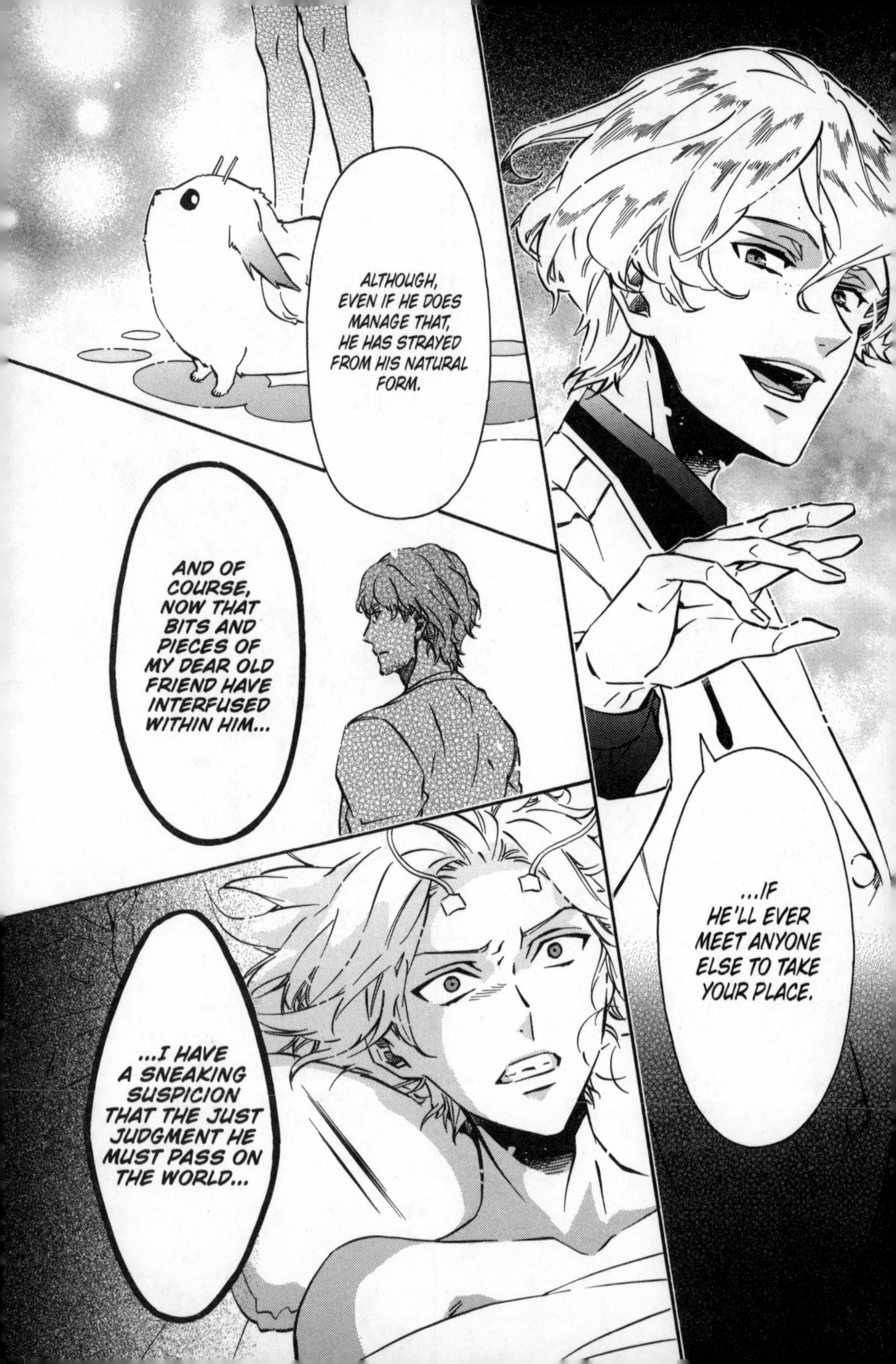
ALTHOUGH, EVEN IF HE DOES MANAGE THAT, HE HAS STRAYED FROM HIS NATURAL FORM.
AND OF COURSE, NOW THAT BITS AND PIECES OF MY DEAR OLD FRIEND HAVE INTERFUSED WITHIN HIM...
...I HAVE A SNEAKING SUSPICION THAT THE JUST JUDGMENT HE MUST PASS ON THE WORLD...
...IF HE'LL EVER MEET ANYONE ELSE TO TAKE YOUR PLACE.

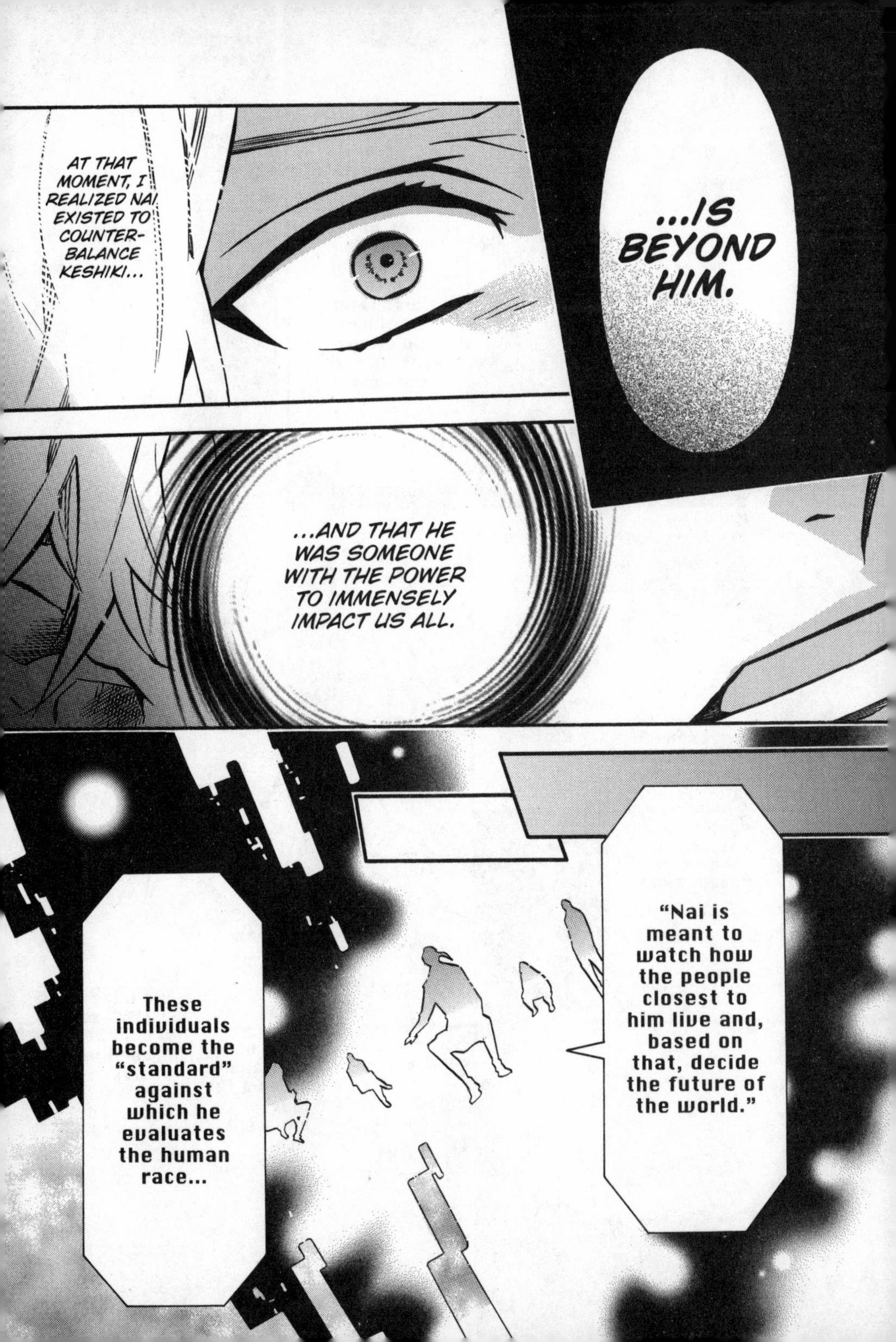
...IS BEYOND HIM.
AT THAT MOMENT, I REALIZED NAI EXISTED TO COUNTER-BALANCE KESHIKI...
...AND THAT HE WAS SOMEONE WITH THE POWER TO IMMENSELY IMPACT US ALL.
"Nai is meant to watch how the people closest to him live and, based on that, decide the future of the world."
These individuals become the "standard" against which he evaluates the human race...

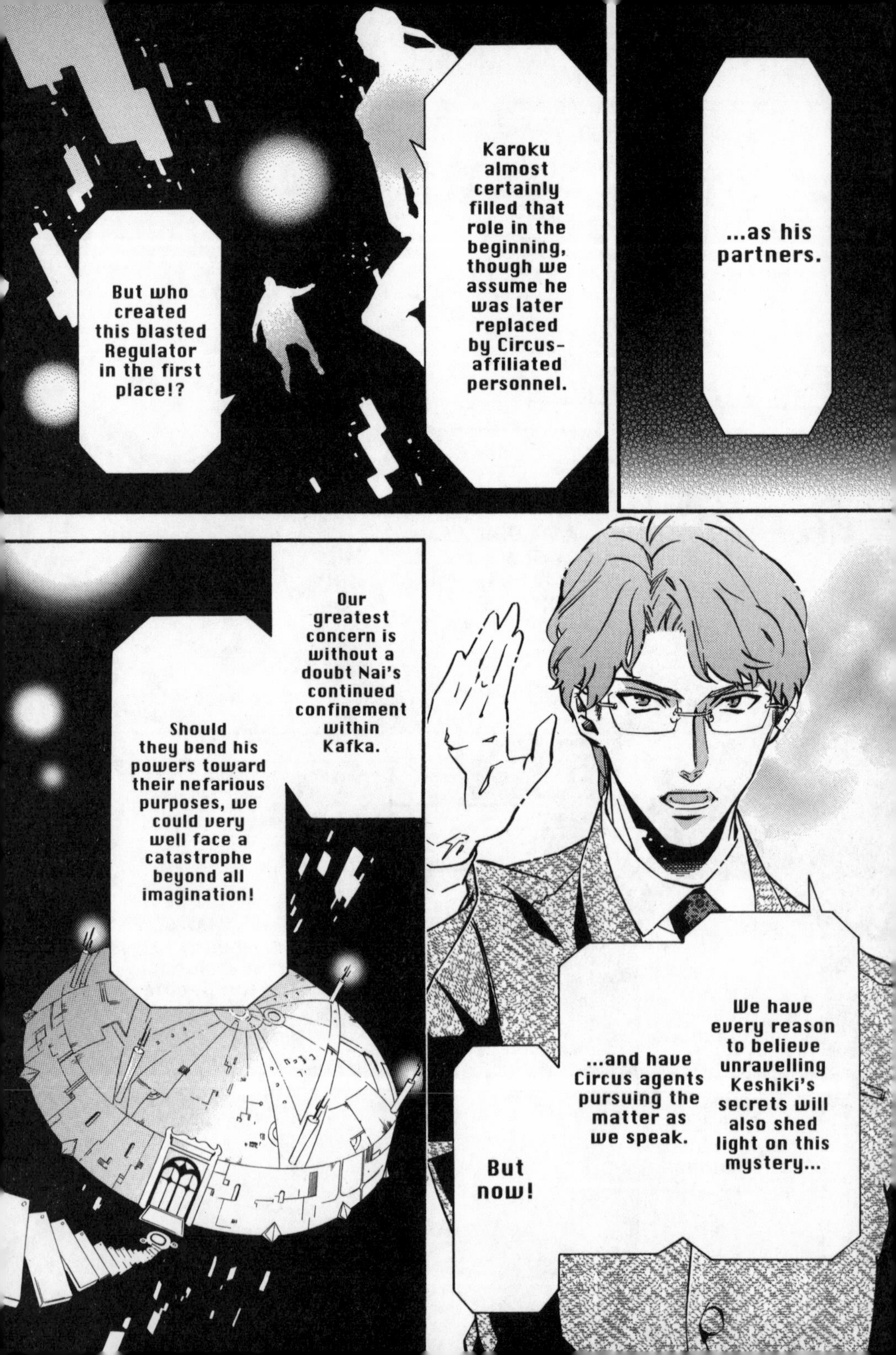

...as his partners.
Karoku almost certainly filled that role in the beginning, though we assume he was later replaced by Circus-affiliated personnel.
But who created this blasted Regulator in the first place!?
We have every reason to believe unravelling Keshiki's secrets will also shed light on this mystery...
...and have Circus agents pursuing the matter as we speak.
But now!
Our greatest concern is without a doubt Nai's continued confinement within Kafka.
Should they bend his powers toward their nefarious purposes, we could very well face a catastrophe beyond all imagination!

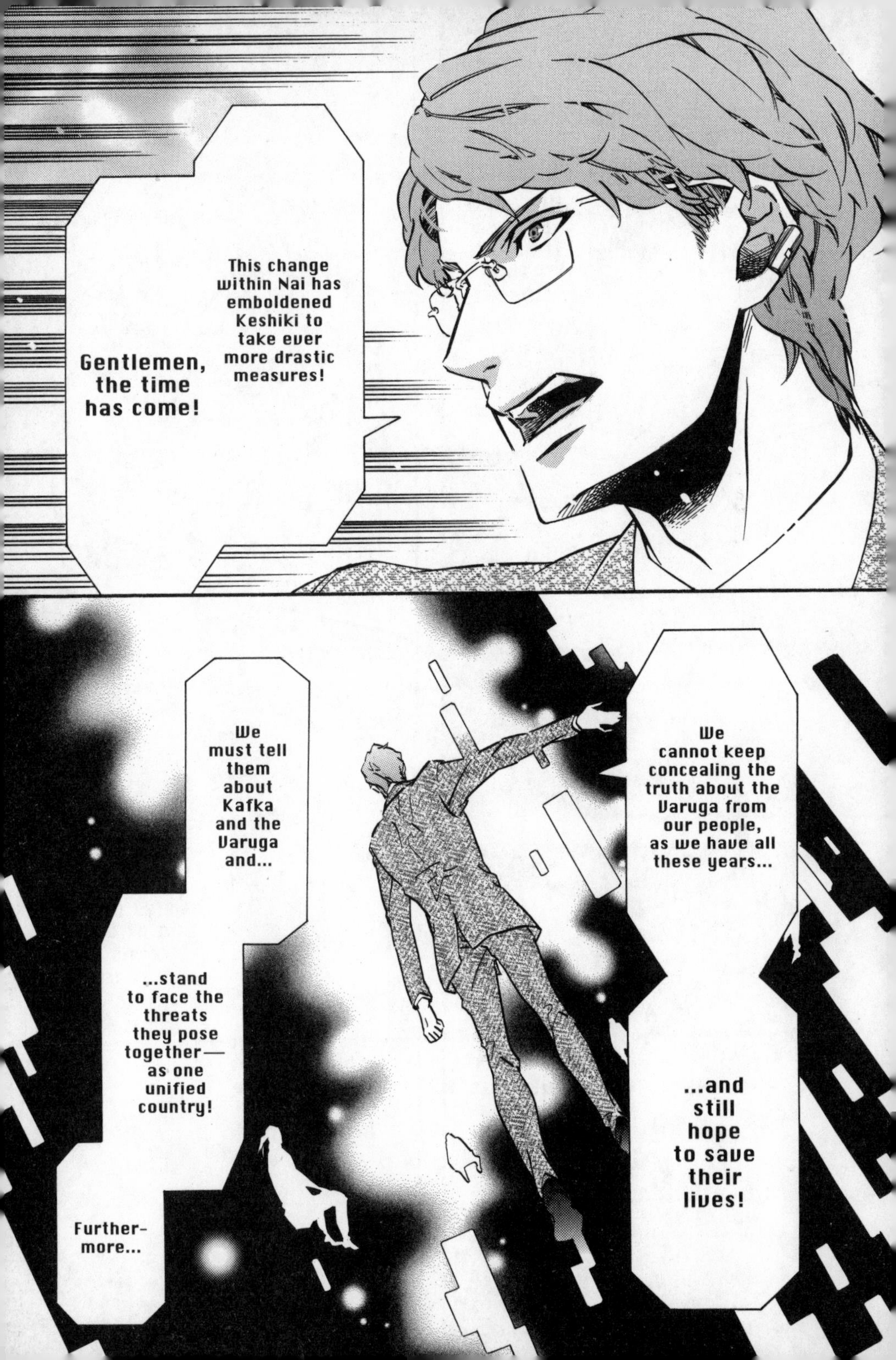
This change within Nai has emboldened Keshiki to take ever more drastic measures!
Gentlemen, the time has come!
We cannot keep concealing the truth about the Varuga from our people, as we have all these years...
...and still hope to save their lives!
We must tell them about Kafka and the Varuga and...
...stand to face the threats they pose together—as one unified country!
Further-more...

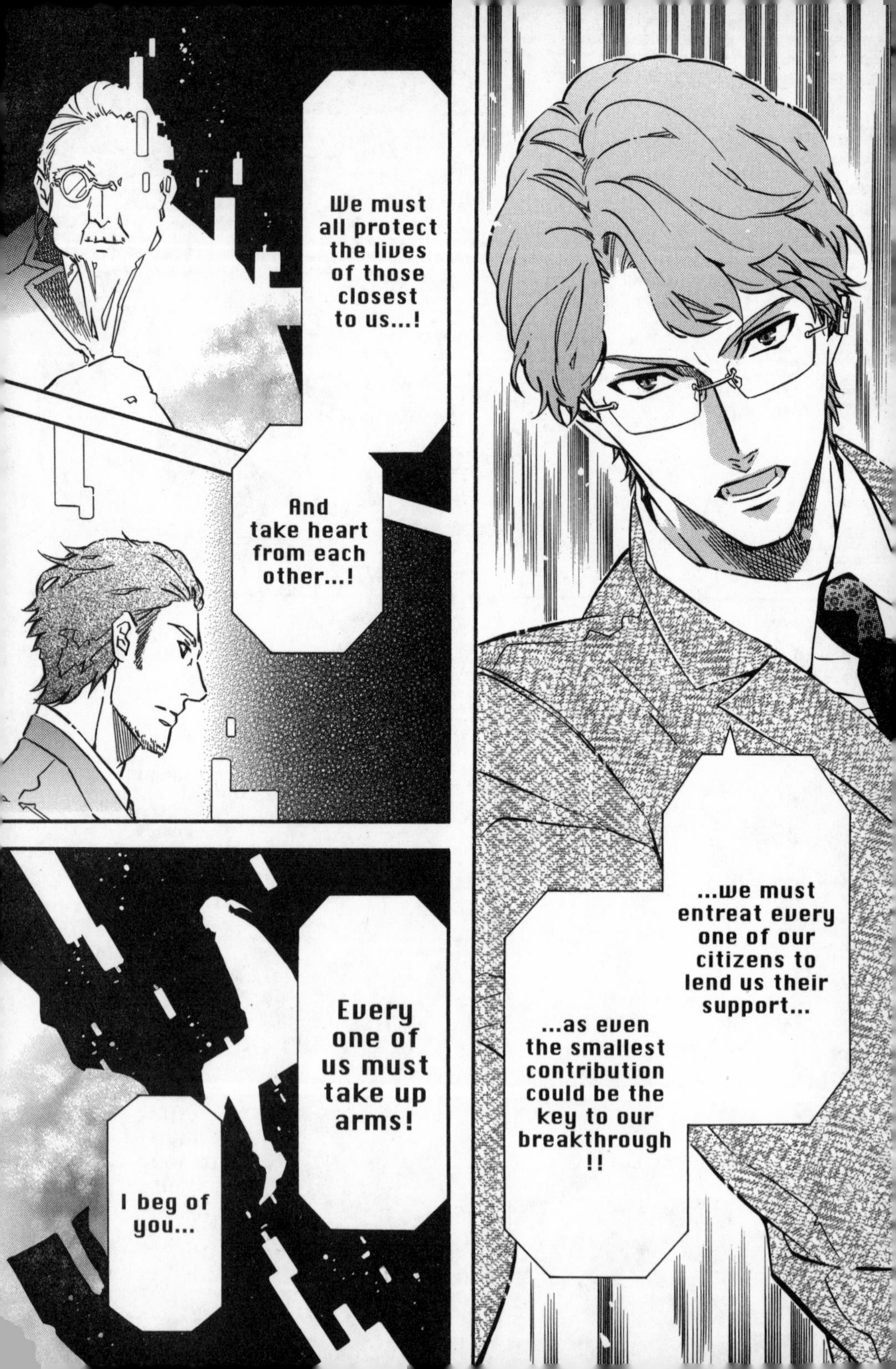
...we must entreat every one of our citizens to lend us their support...
...as even the smallest contribution could be the key to our breakthrough !!
We must all protect the lives of those closest to us...!
And take heart from each other...!
Every one of us must take up arms!
I beg of you...

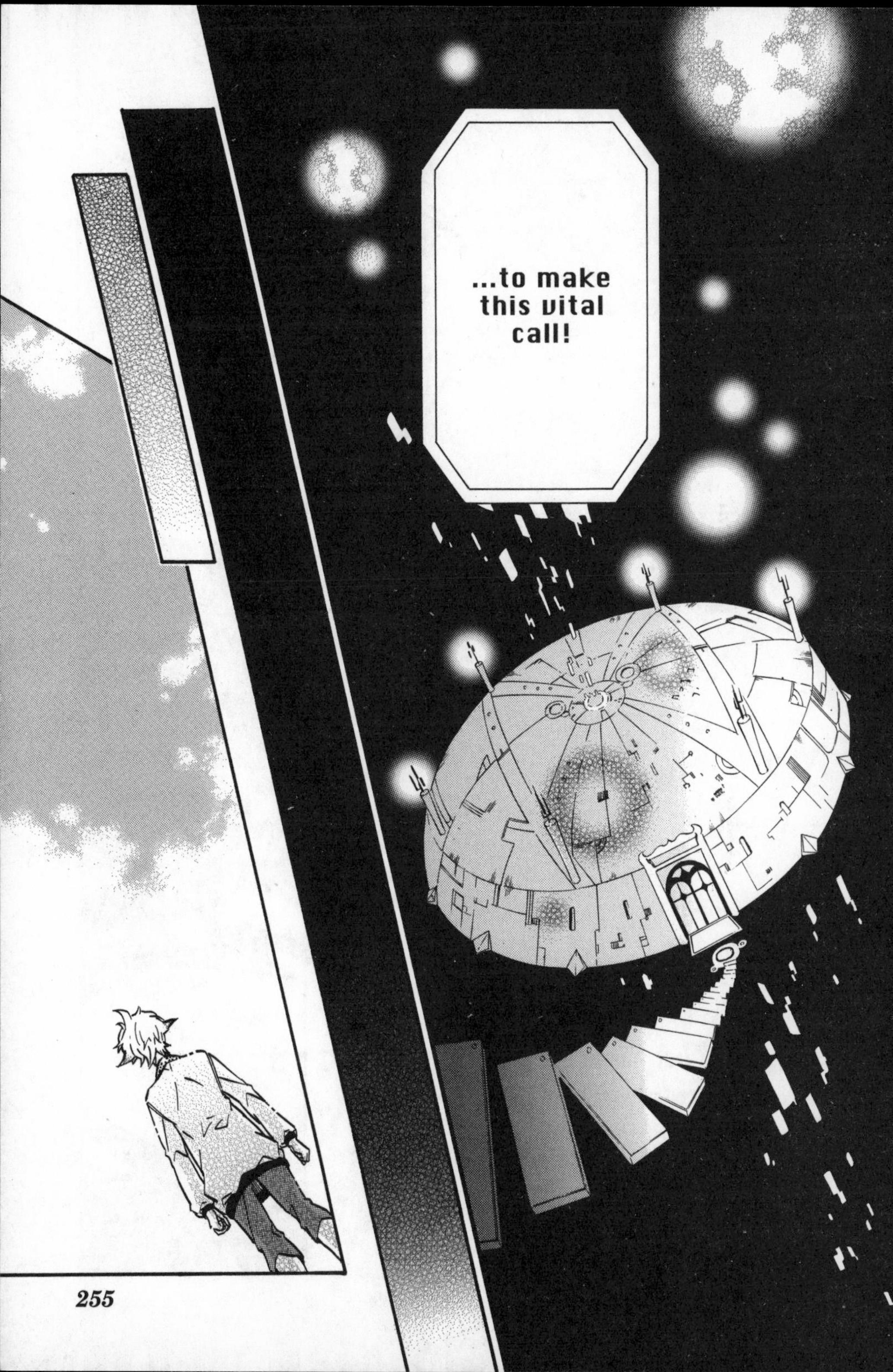
...to make
this vital
call!

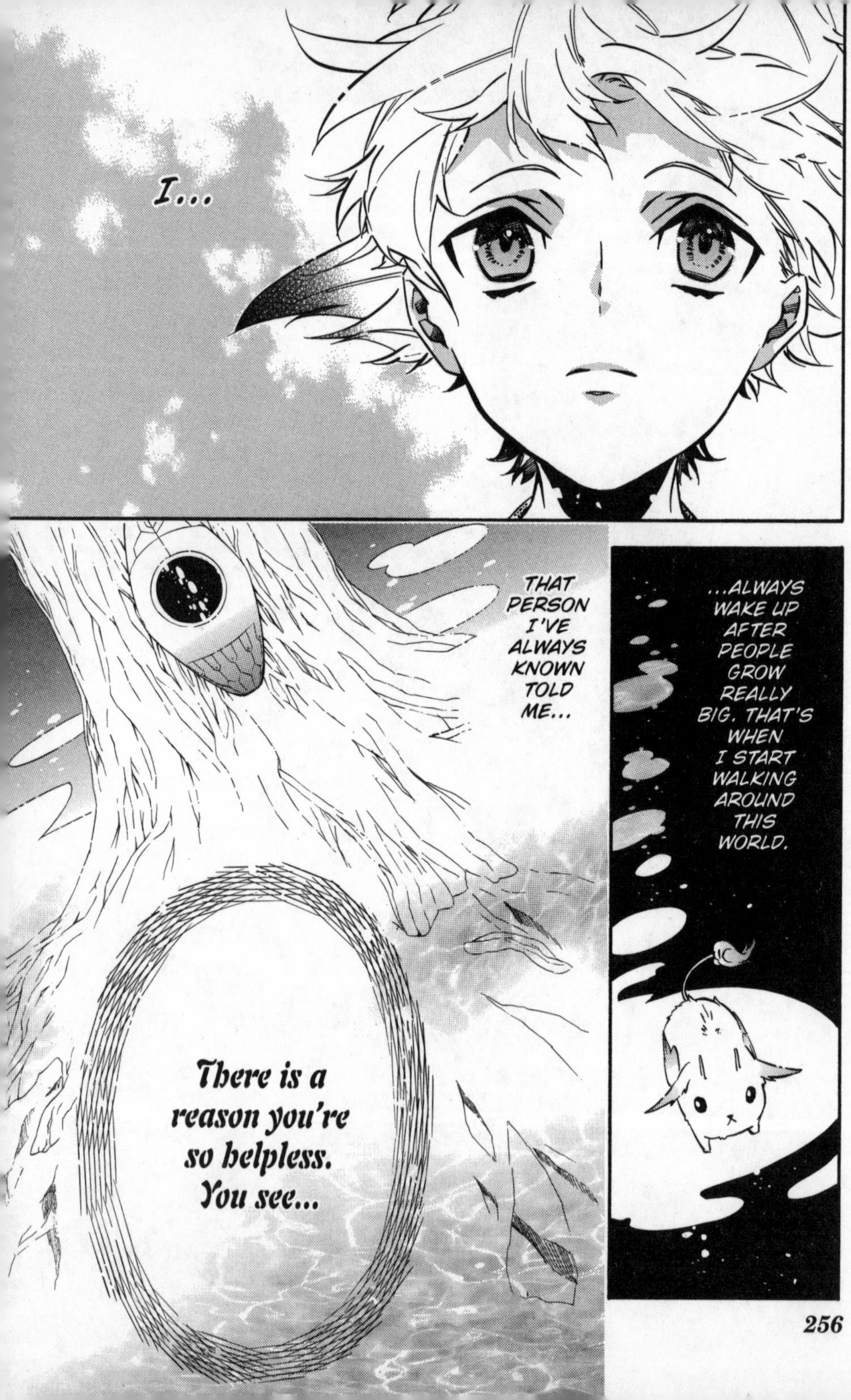
I...
...ALWAYS WAKE UP AFTER PEOPLE GROW REALLY BIG. THAT'S WHEN I START WALKING AROUND THIS WORLD.
THAT PERSON I'VE ALWAYS KNOWN TOLD ME...
There is a reason you're so helpless. You see...

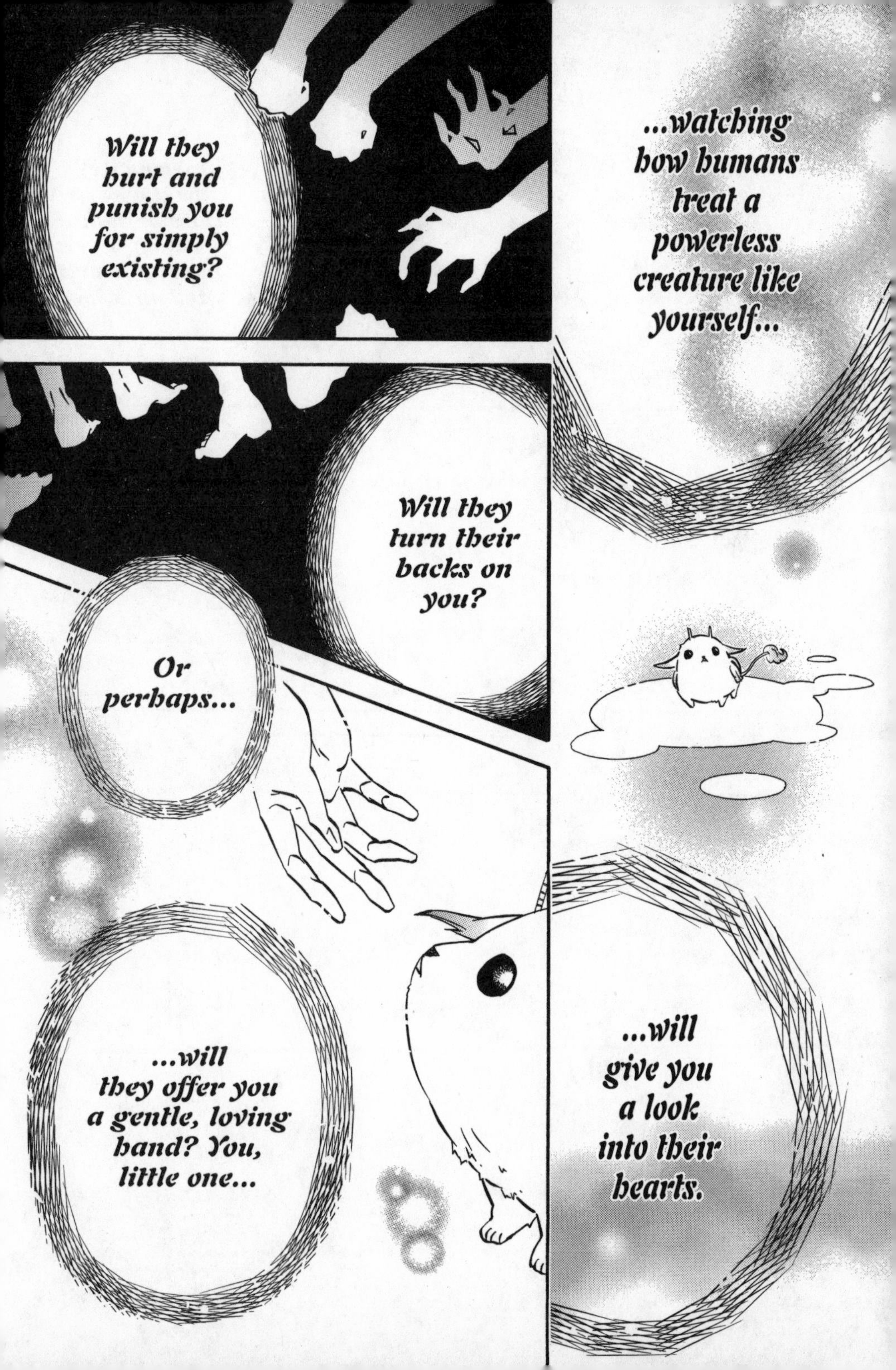
Will they hurt and punish you for simply existing?
Will they turn their backs on you?
Or perhaps...
...will they offer you a gentle, loving hand? You, little one...
...watching how humans treat a powerless creature like yourself...
...will give you a look into their hearts.

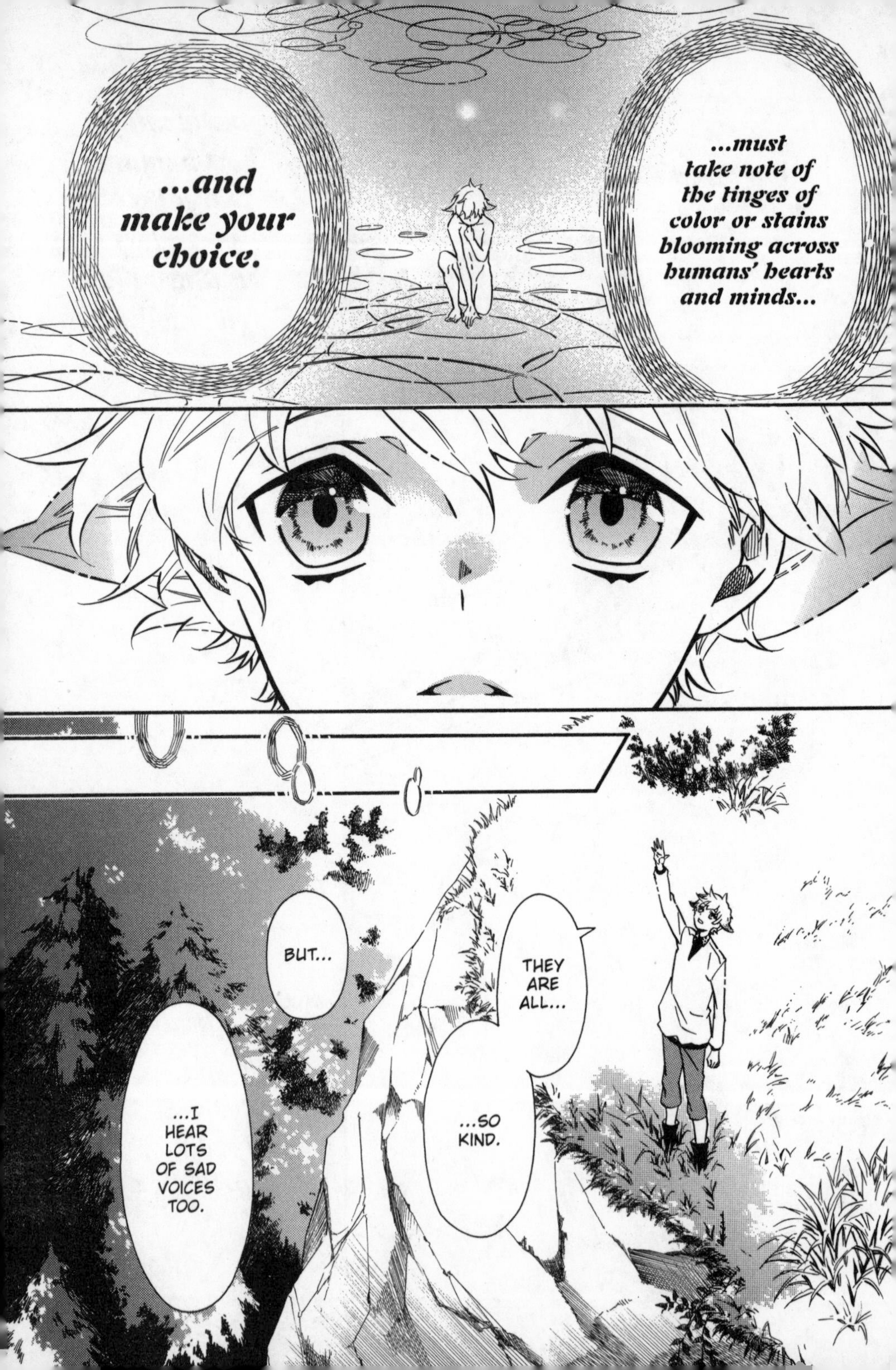
...must take note of the tinges of color or stains blooming across humans' hearts and minds...
...and make your choice.
THEY ARE ALL...
...SO KIND.
BUT...
...I HEAR LOTS OF SAD VOICES TOO.

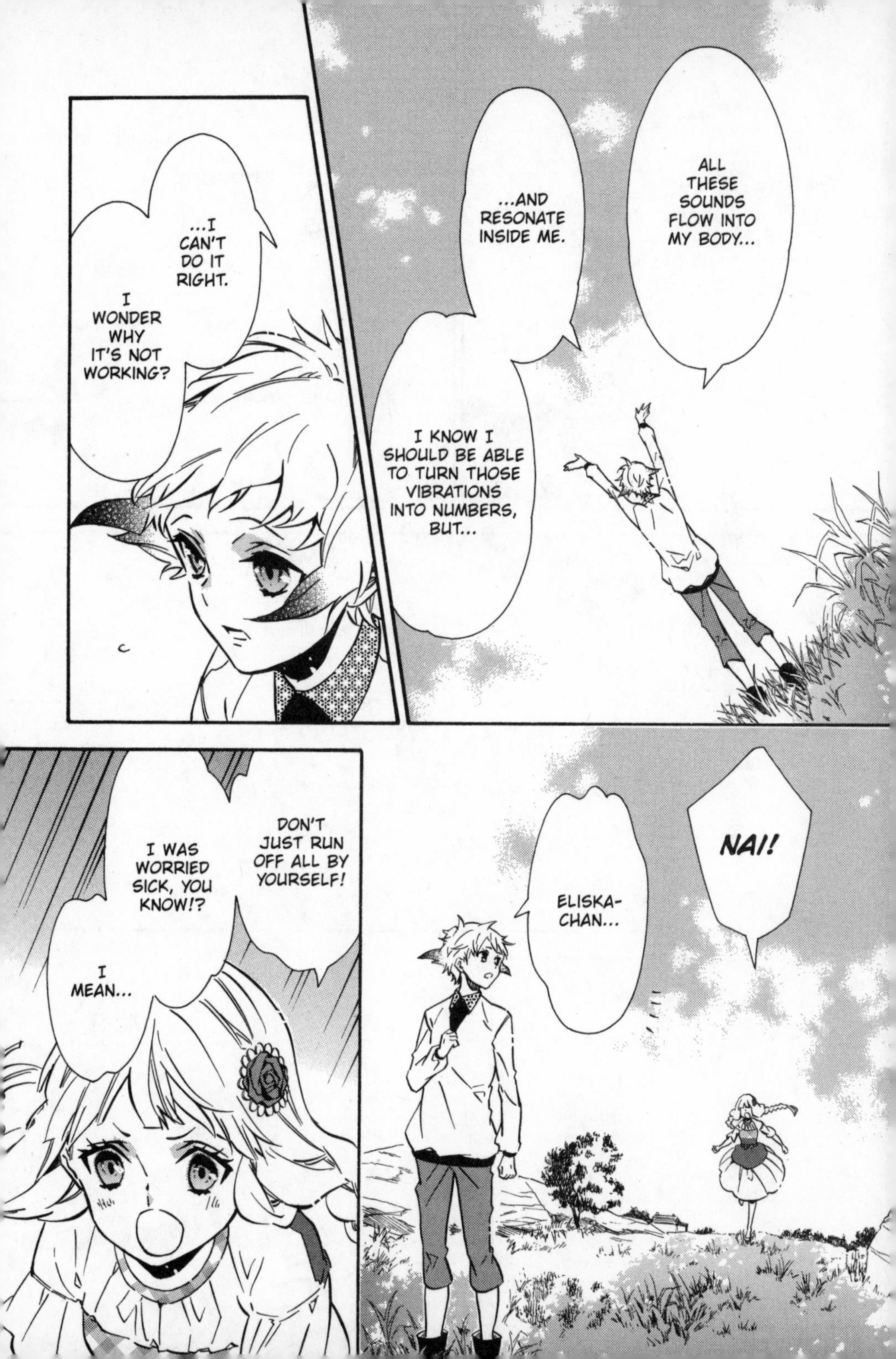
ALL THESE SOUNDS FLOW INTO MY BODY...
...AND RESONATE INSIDE ME.
I KNOW I SHOULD BE ABLE TO TURN THOSE VIBRATIONS INTO NUMBERS, BUT...
...I CAN'T DO IT RIGHT.
I WONDER WHY IT'S NOT WORKING?
NAI!
ELISKA-CHAN...
DON'T JUST RUN OFF ALL BY YOURSELF!
I WAS WORRIED SICK, YOU KNOW!?
I MEAN...

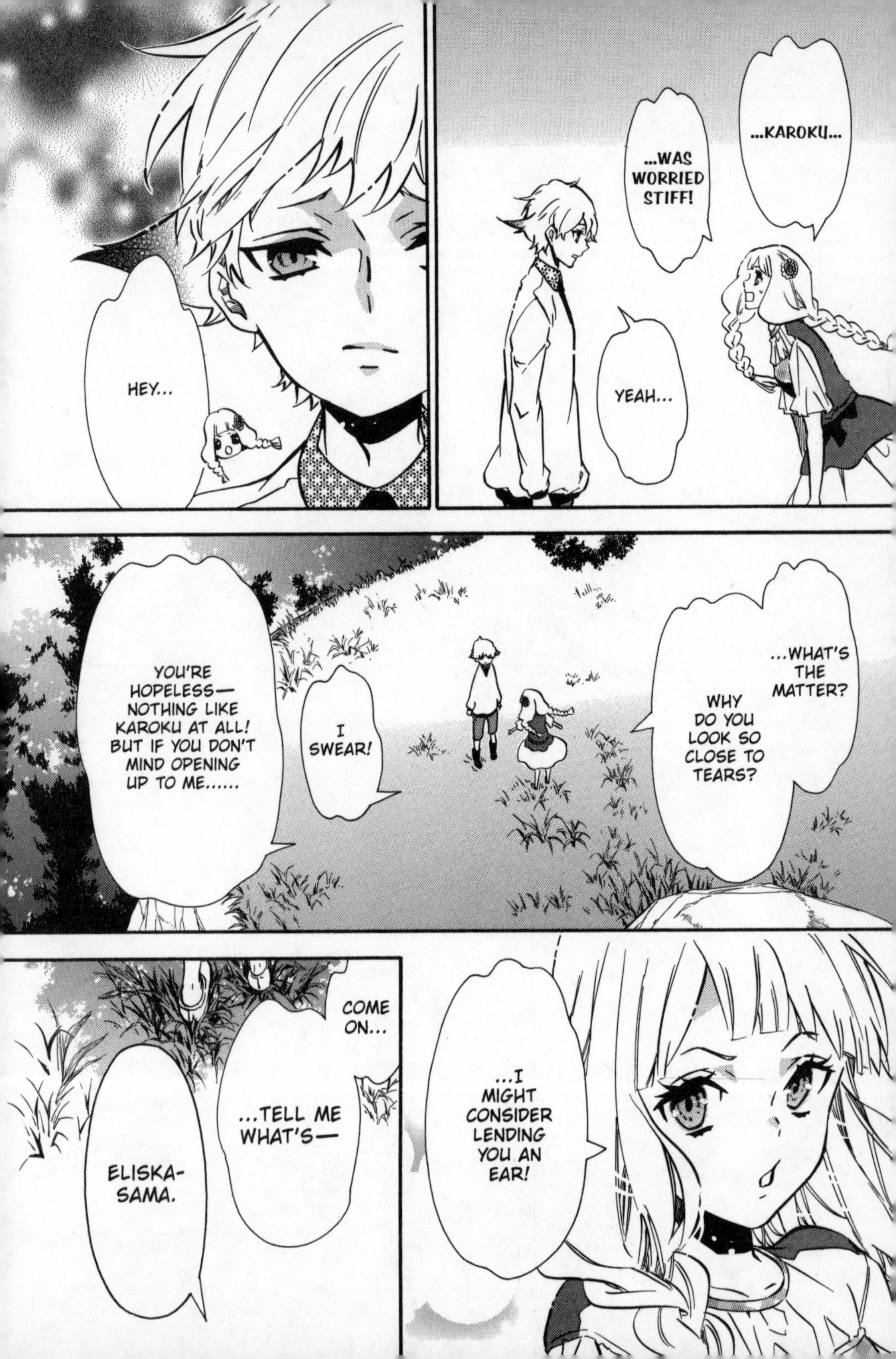
...KAROKU...
...WAS WORRIED STIFF!
YEAH...
HEY...
...WHAT'S THE MATTER?
WHY DO YOU LOOK SO CLOSE TO TEARS?
I SWEAR!
YOU'RE HOPELESS—NOTHING LIKE KAROKU AT ALL! BUT IF YOU DON'T MIND OPENING UP TO ME......
...I MIGHT CONSIDER LENDING YOU AN EAR!
COME ON...
...TELL ME WHAT'S—
ELISKA-SAMA.

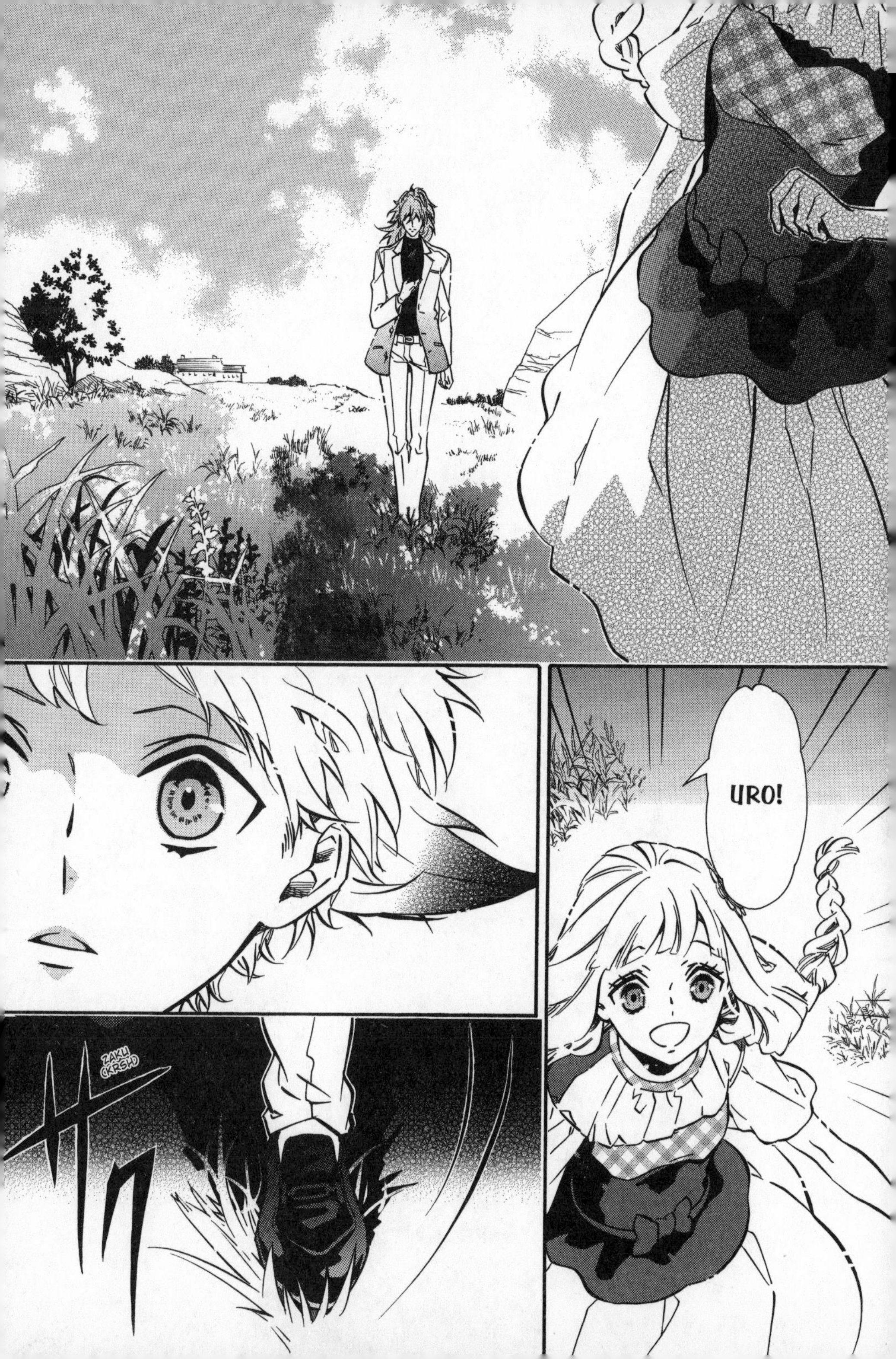
URO!
ZAKU (KRSH)

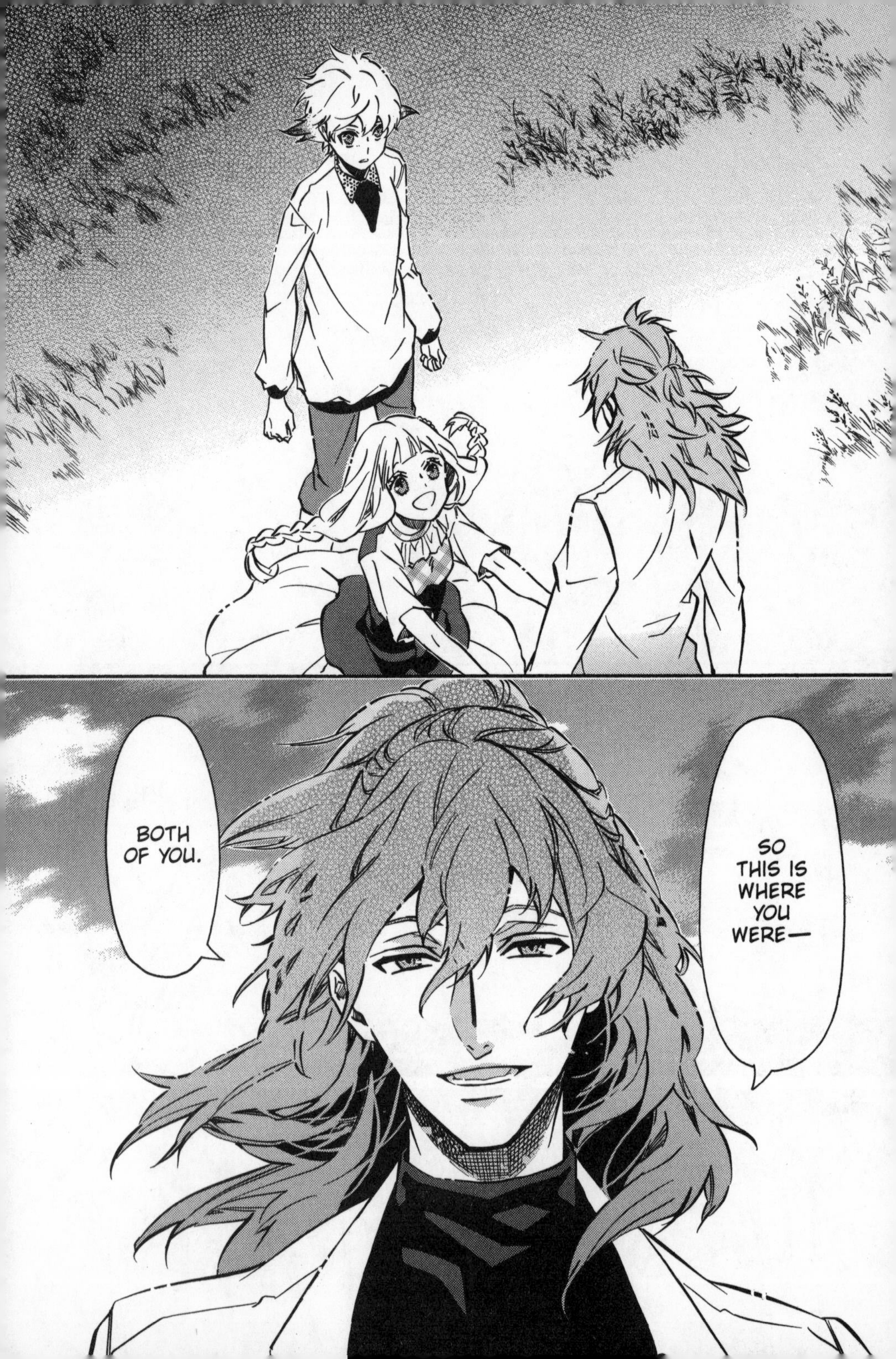
SO THIS IS WHERE YOU WERE—
BOTH OF YOU.

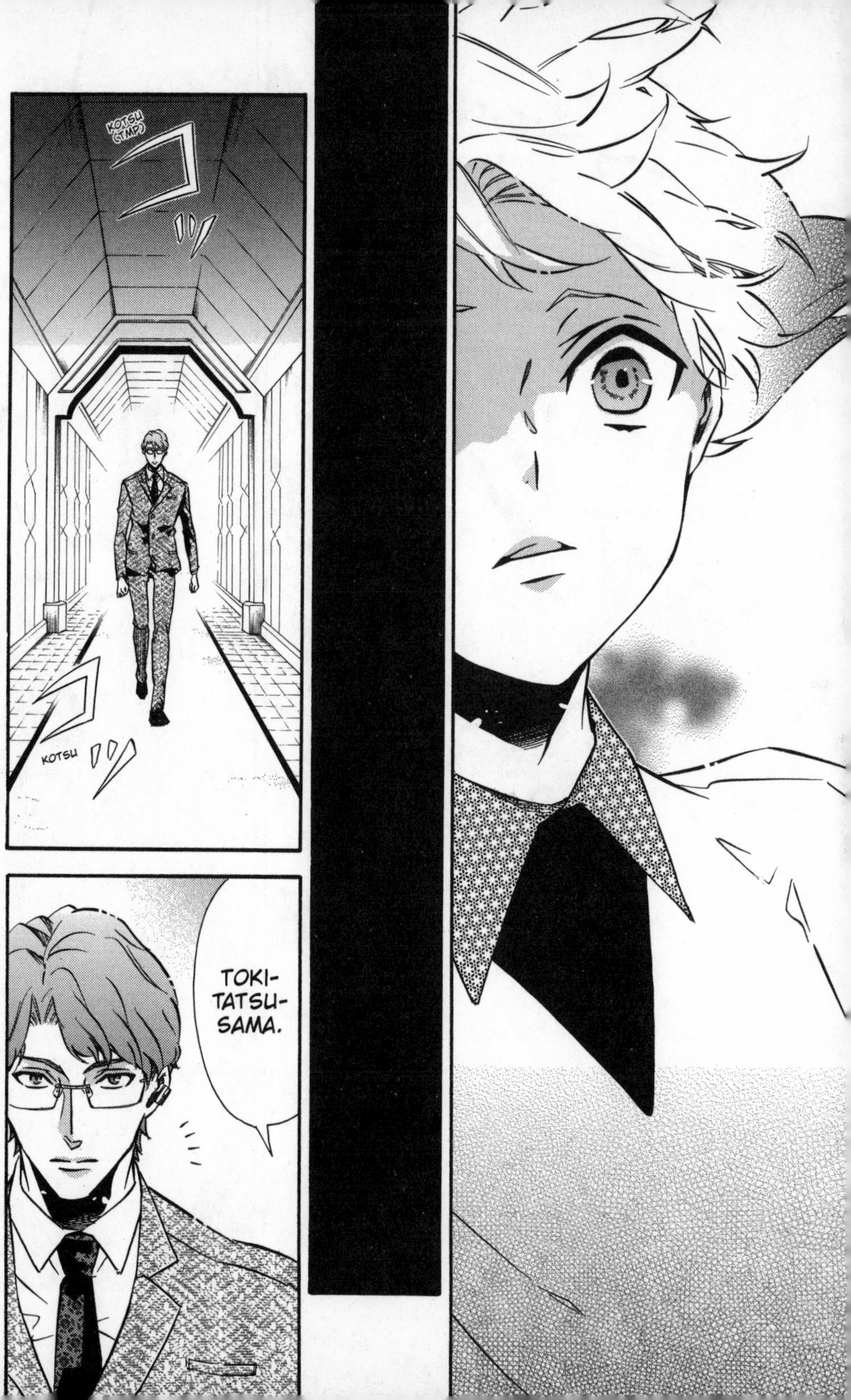
KOTSU (TMP)
KOTSU
TOKI-TATSU-SAMA.

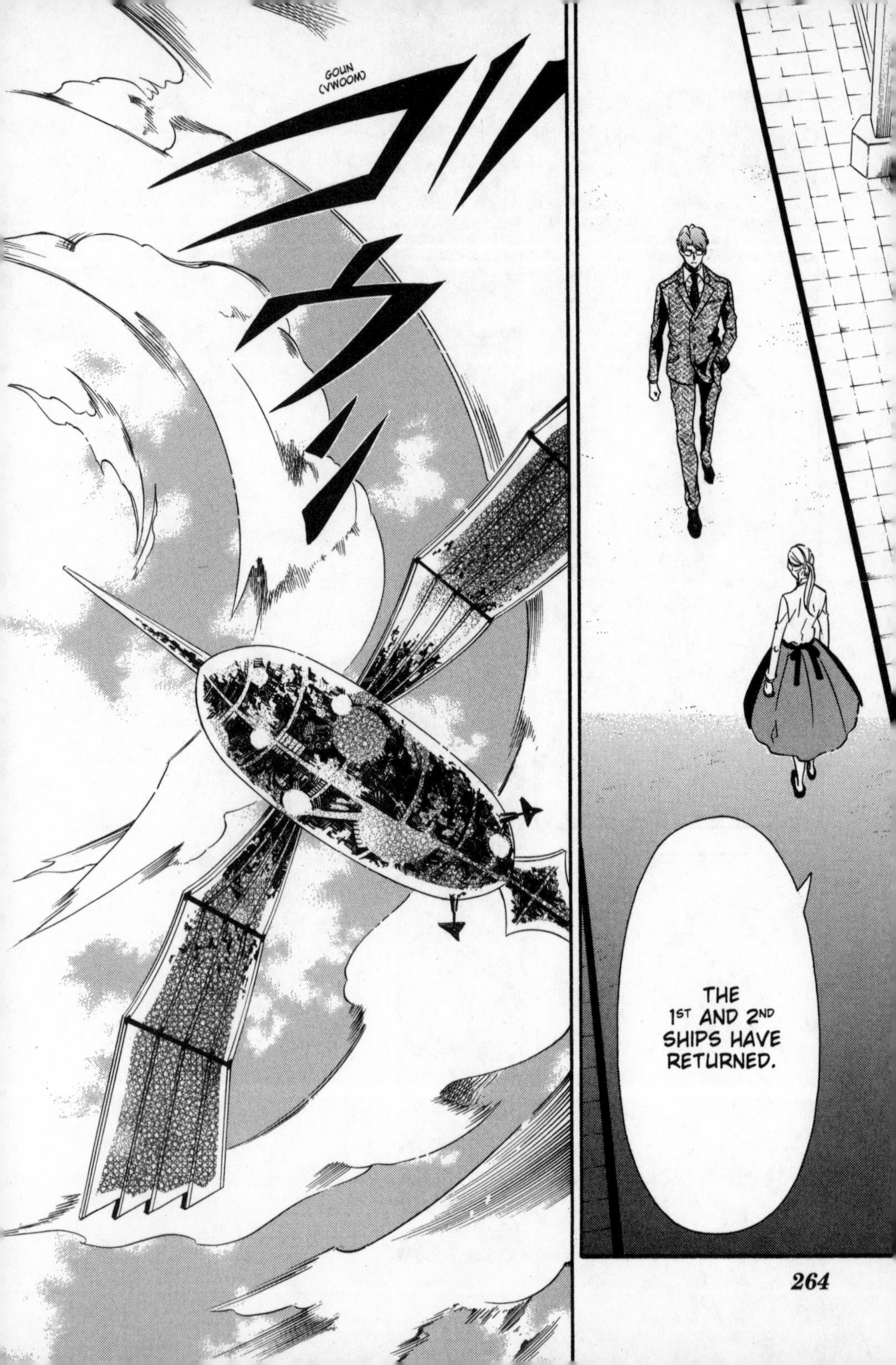
THE 1ST AND 2ND SHIPS HAVE RETURNED.
GOUN (VWOOM)

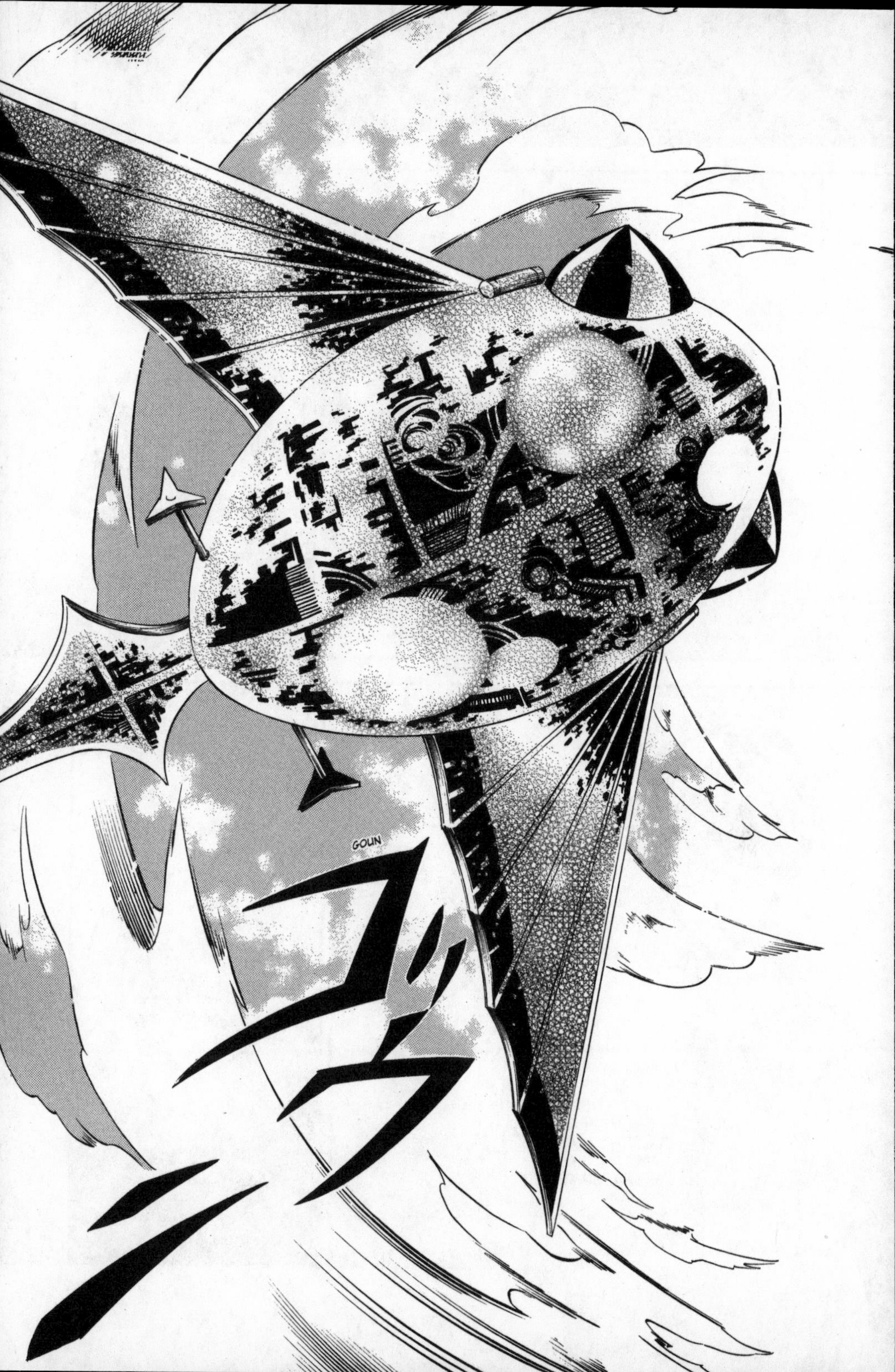
GOUN

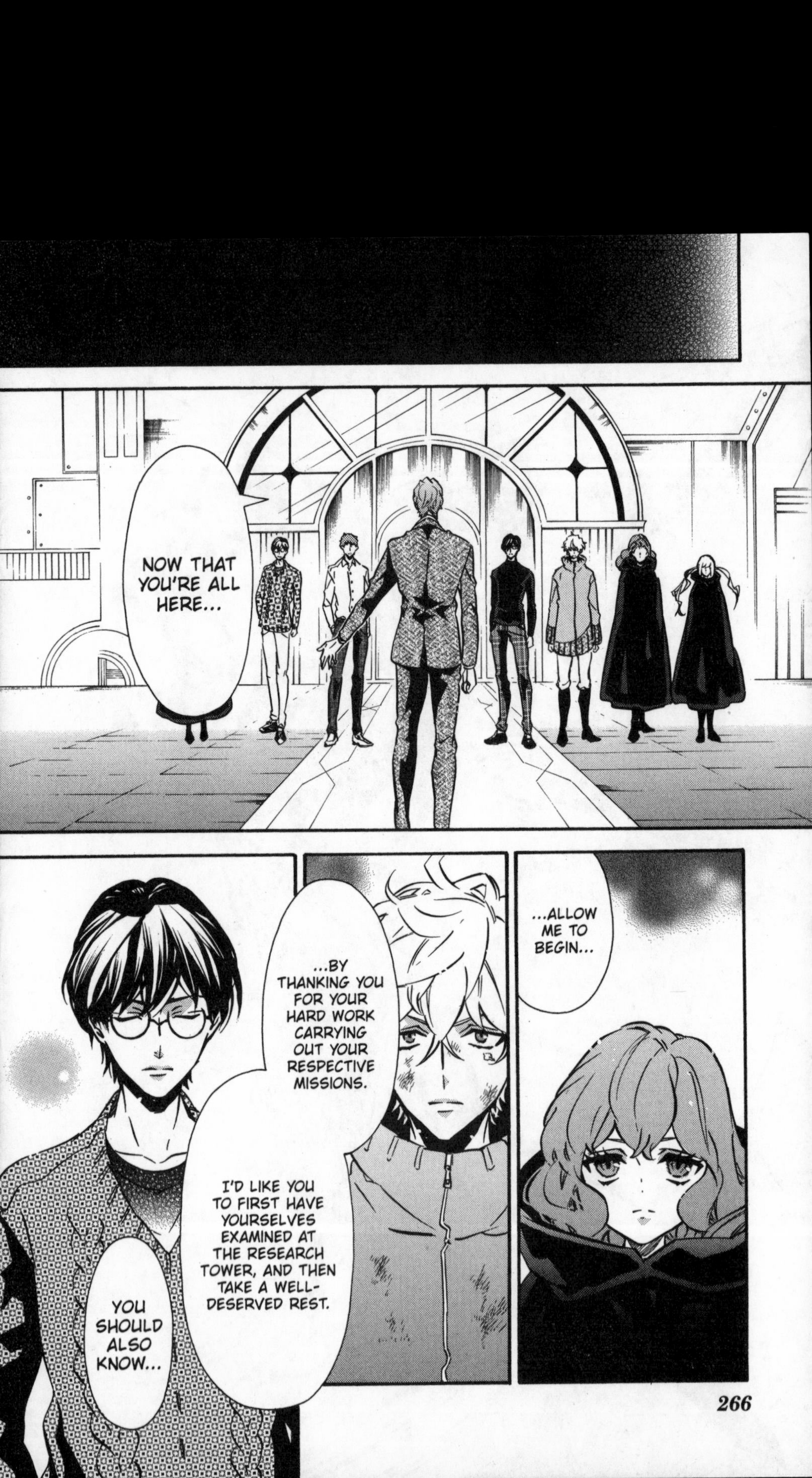
NOW THAT YOU'RE ALL HERE...
...ALLOW ME TO BEGIN...
...BY THANKING YOU FOR YOUR HARD WORK CARRYING OUT YOUR RESPECTIVE MISSIONS.
I'D LIKE YOU TO FIRST HAVE YOURSELVES EXAMINED AT THE RESEARCH TOWER, AND THEN TAKE A WELL-DESERVED REST.
YOU SHOULD ALSO KNOW...

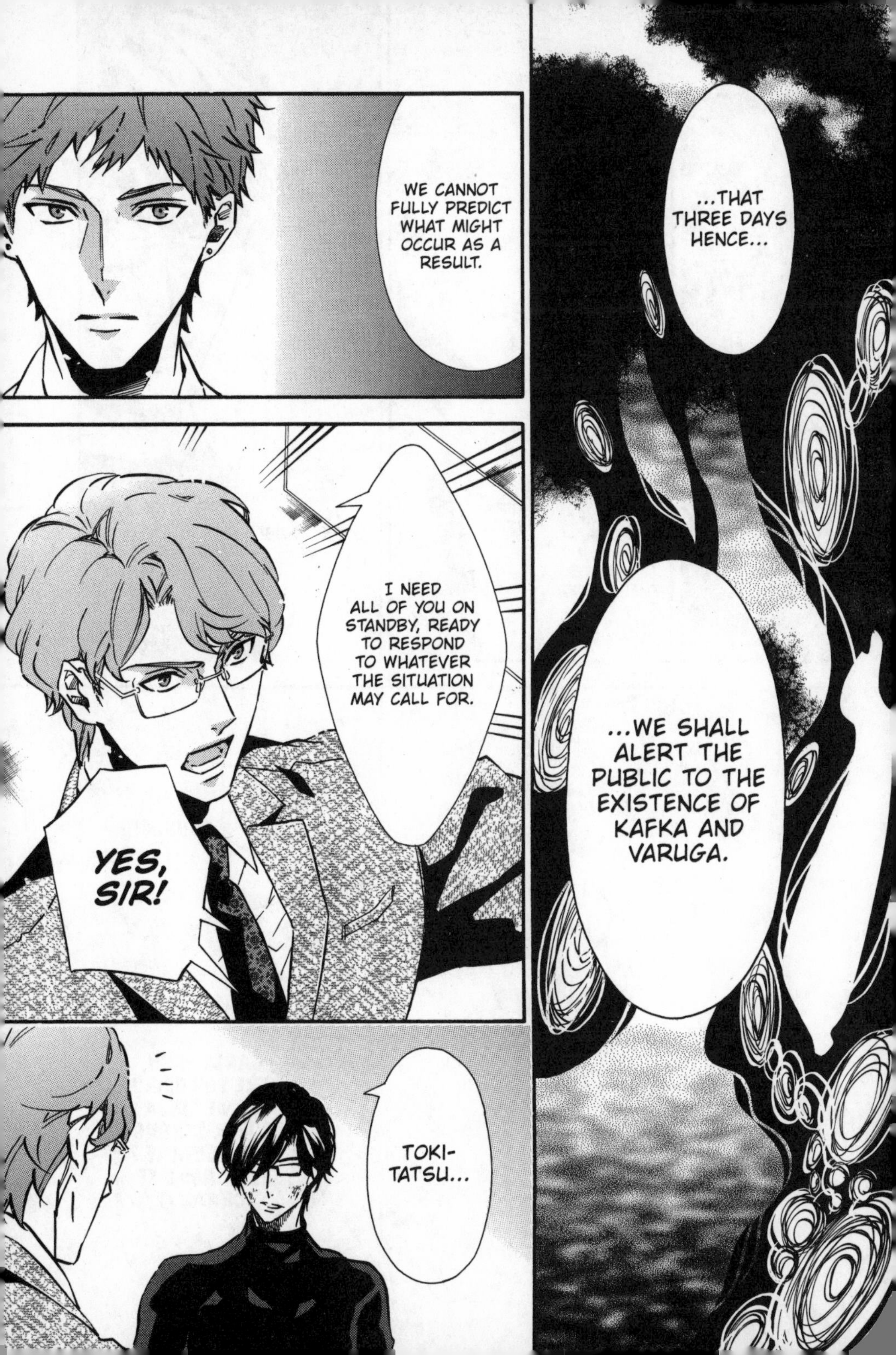
...THAT THREE DAYS HENCE...
...WE SHALL ALERT THE PUBLIC TO THE EXISTENCE OF KAFKA AND VARUGA.
WE CANNOT FULLY PREDICT WHAT MIGHT OCCUR AS A RESULT.
I NEED ALL OF YOU ON STANDBY, READY TO RESPOND TO WHATEVER THE SITUATION MAY CALL FOR.
YES, SIR!
TOKI-TATSU...

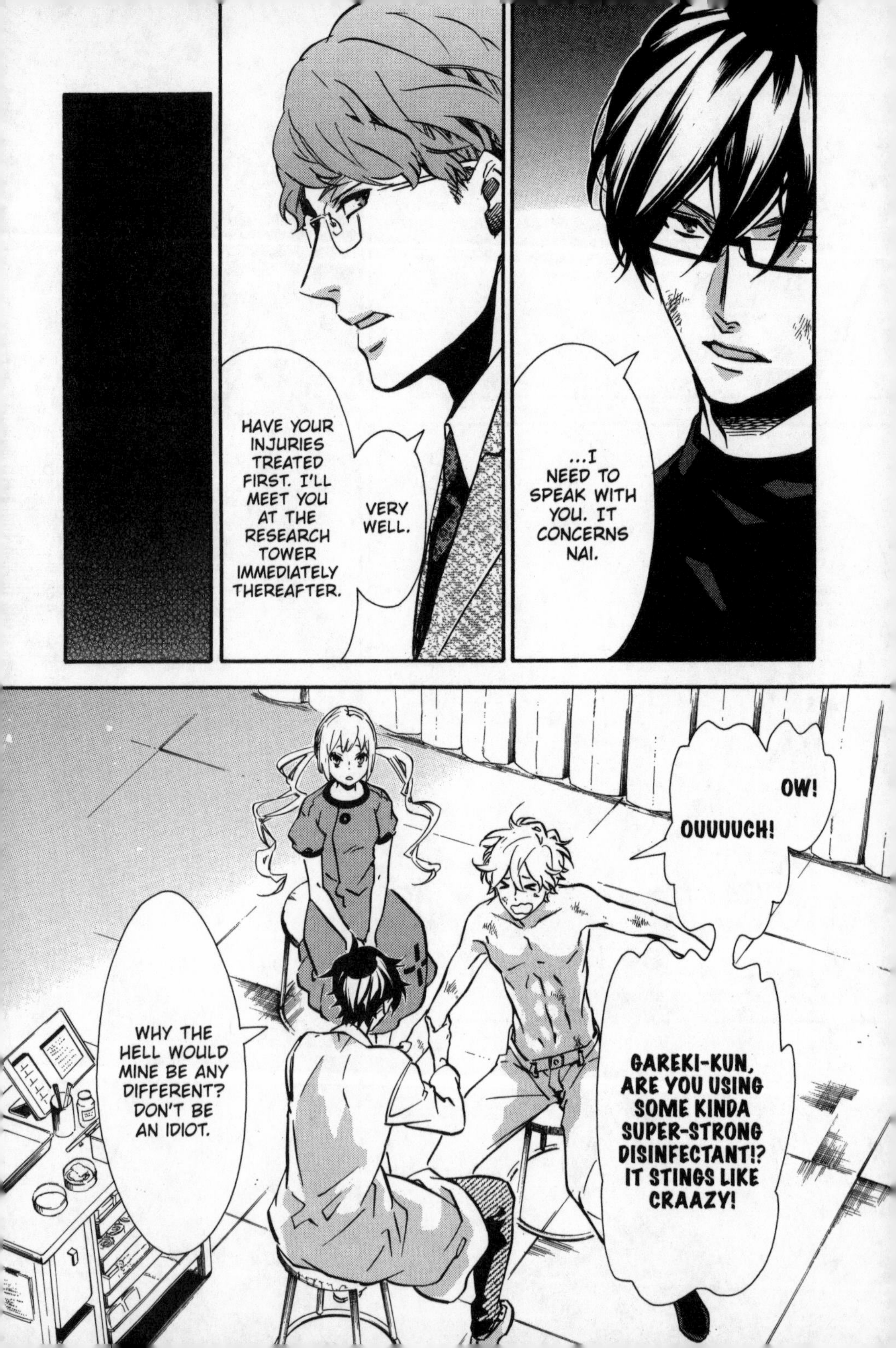
...I NEED TO SPEAK WITH YOU. IT CONCERNS NAI.
VERY WELL.
HAVE YOUR INJURIES TREATED FIRST. I'LL MEET YOU AT THE RESEARCH TOWER IMMEDIATELY THEREAFTER.
OW!
OUUUUCH!
GAREKI-KUN, ARE YOU USING SOME KINDA SUPER-STRONG DISINFECTANT!? IT STINGS LIKE CRAAZY!
WHY THE HELL WOULD MINE BE ANY DIFFERENT? DON'T BE AN IDIOT.

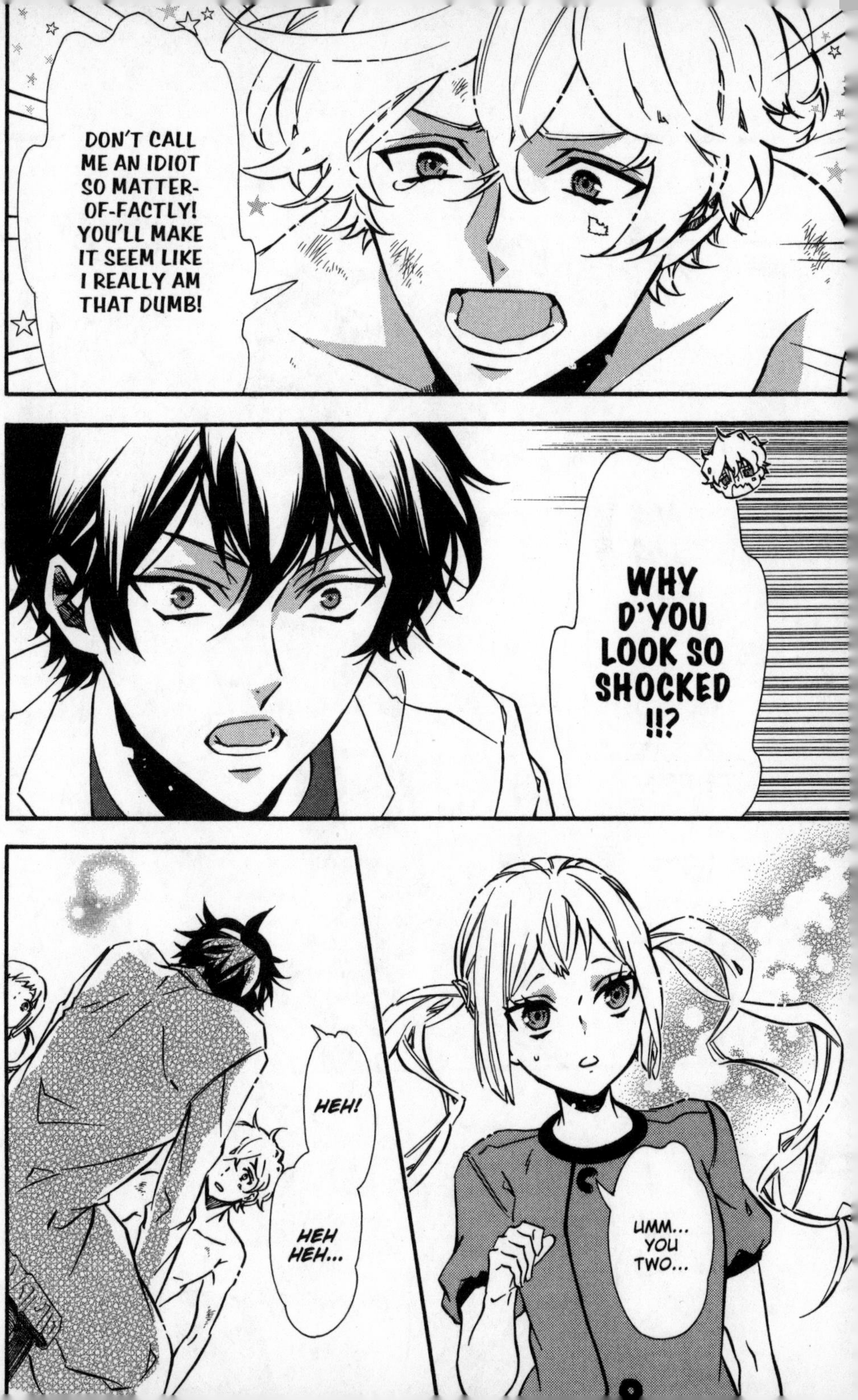
DON'T CALL ME AN IDIOT SO MATTER-OF-FACTLY! YOU'LL MAKE IT SEEM LIKE I REALLY AM THAT DUMB!
WHY D'YOU LOOK SO SHOCKED !!?
UMM... YOU TWO...
HEH!
HEH HEH...

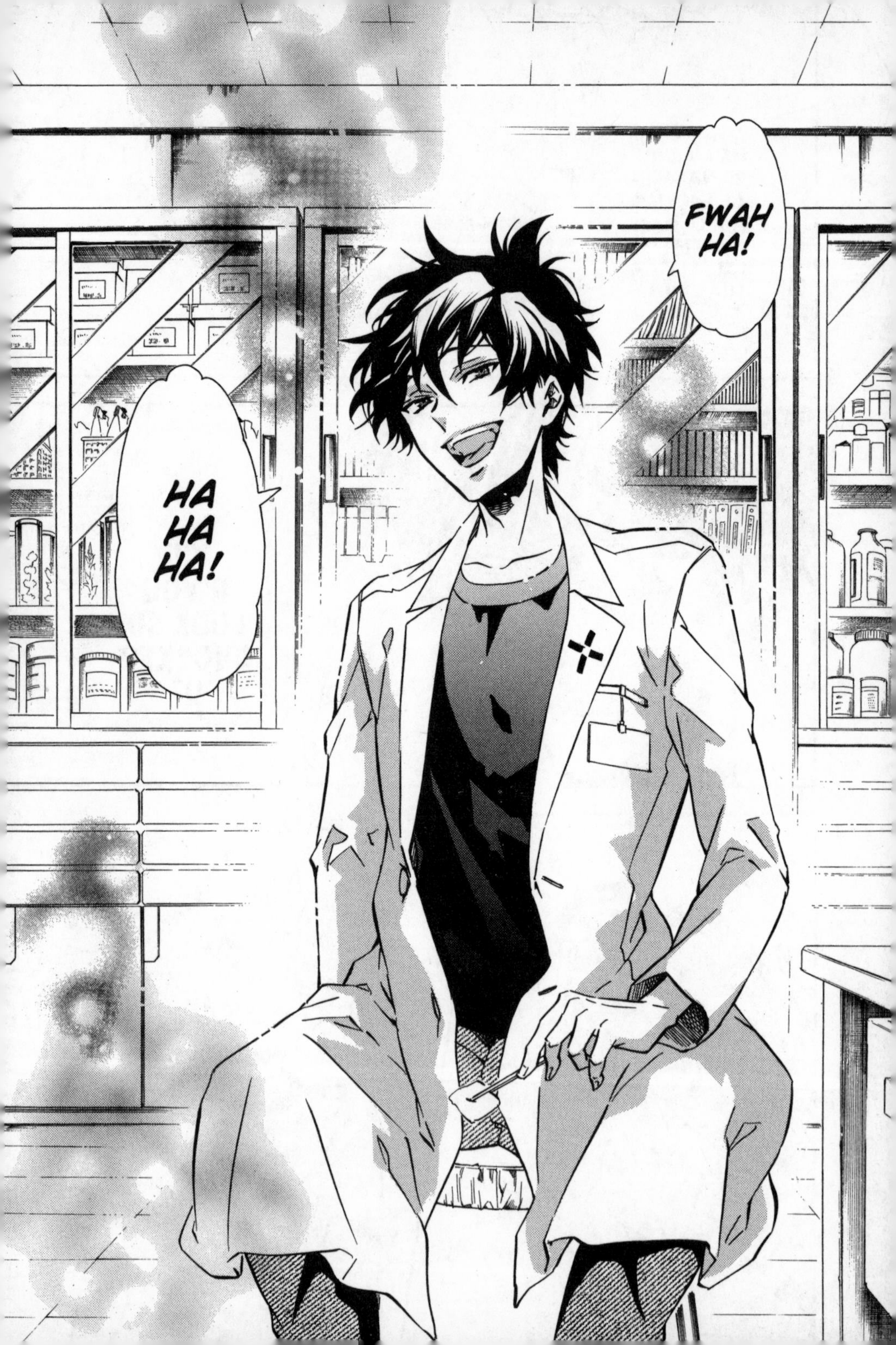
FWAH HA!
HA HA HA!

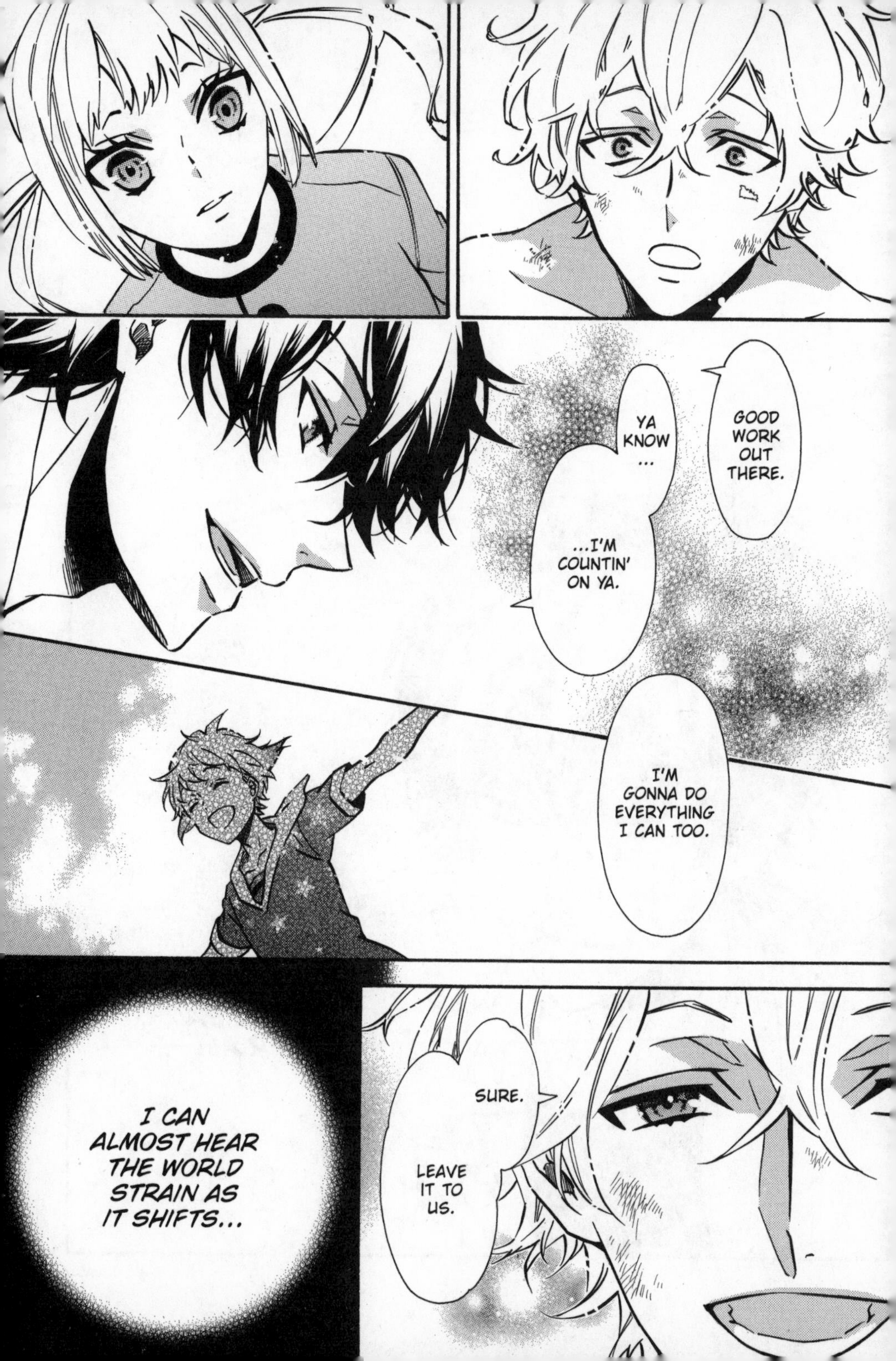
GOOD WORK OUT THERE.
YA KNOW ...
...I'M COUNTIN' ON YA.
I'M GONNA DO EVERYTHING I CAN TOO.
SURE.
LEAVE IT TO US.
I CAN ALMOST HEAR THE WORLD STRAIN AS IT SHIFTS...

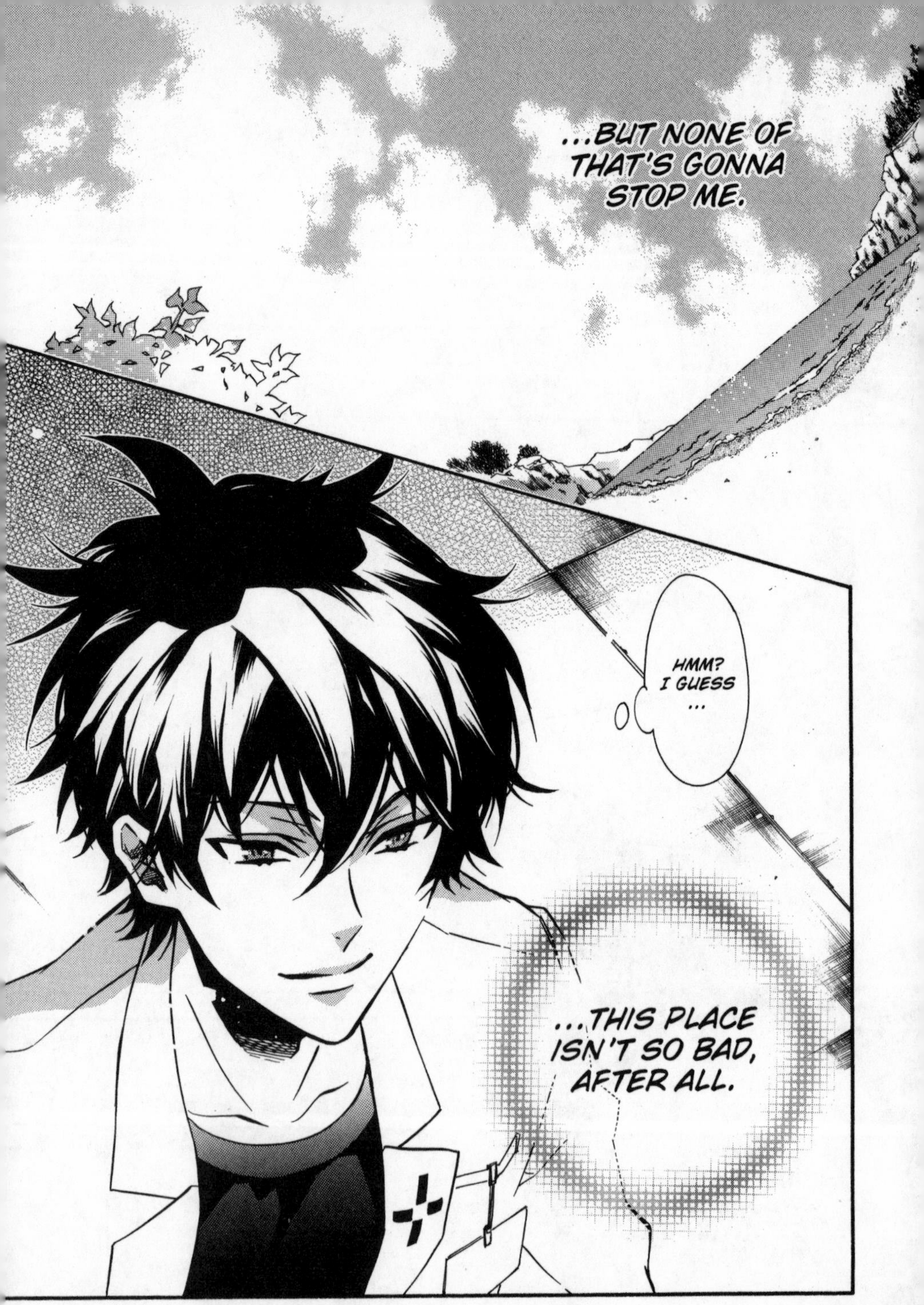
...BUT NONE OF THAT'S GONNA STOP ME.
HMM? I GUESS ...
...THIS PLACE ISN'T SO BAD, AFTER ALL.

KARNEVAL

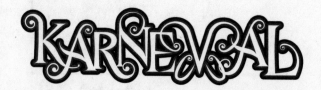

KARNEVAL

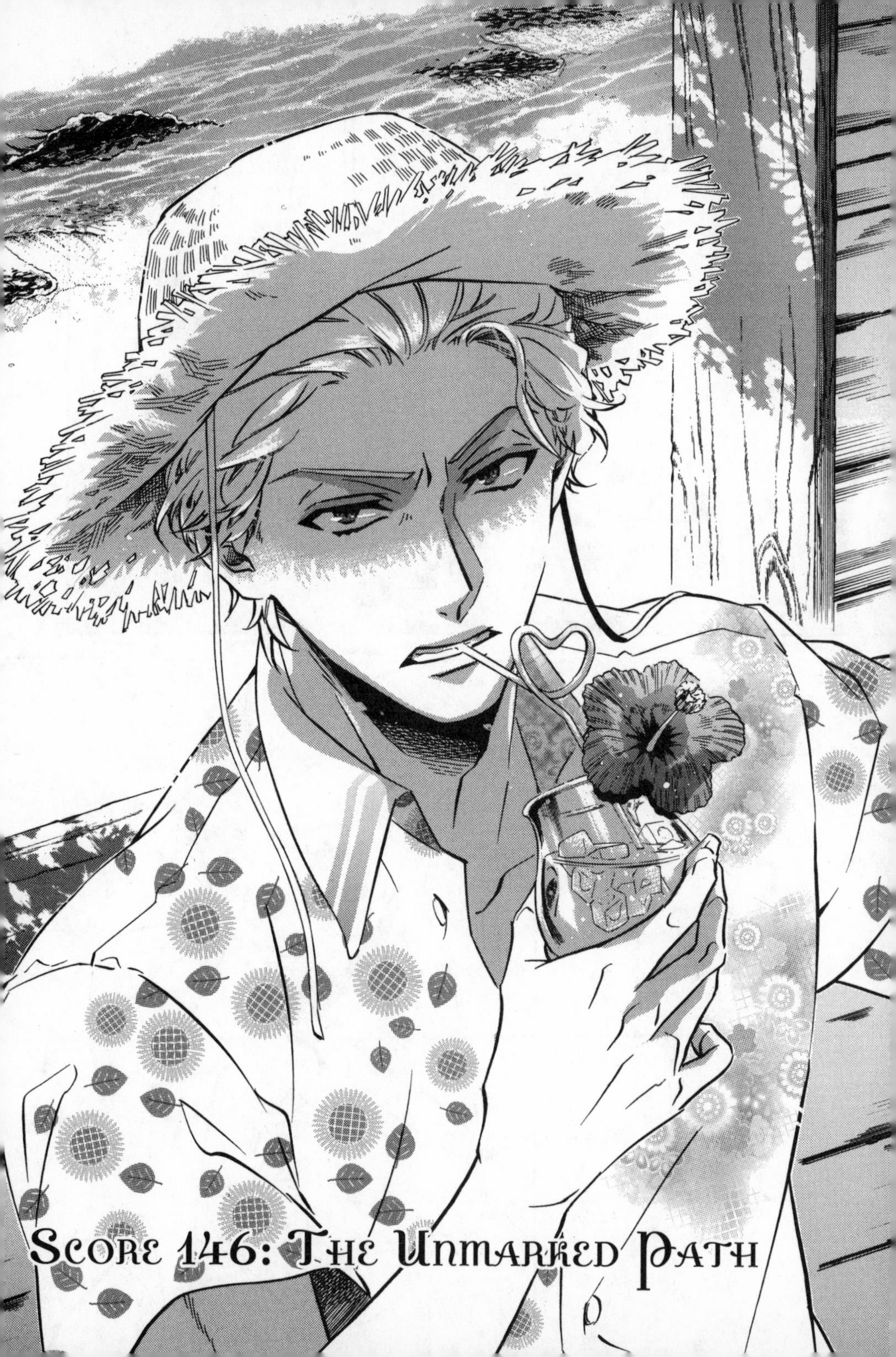
Score 146: The Unmarked Path

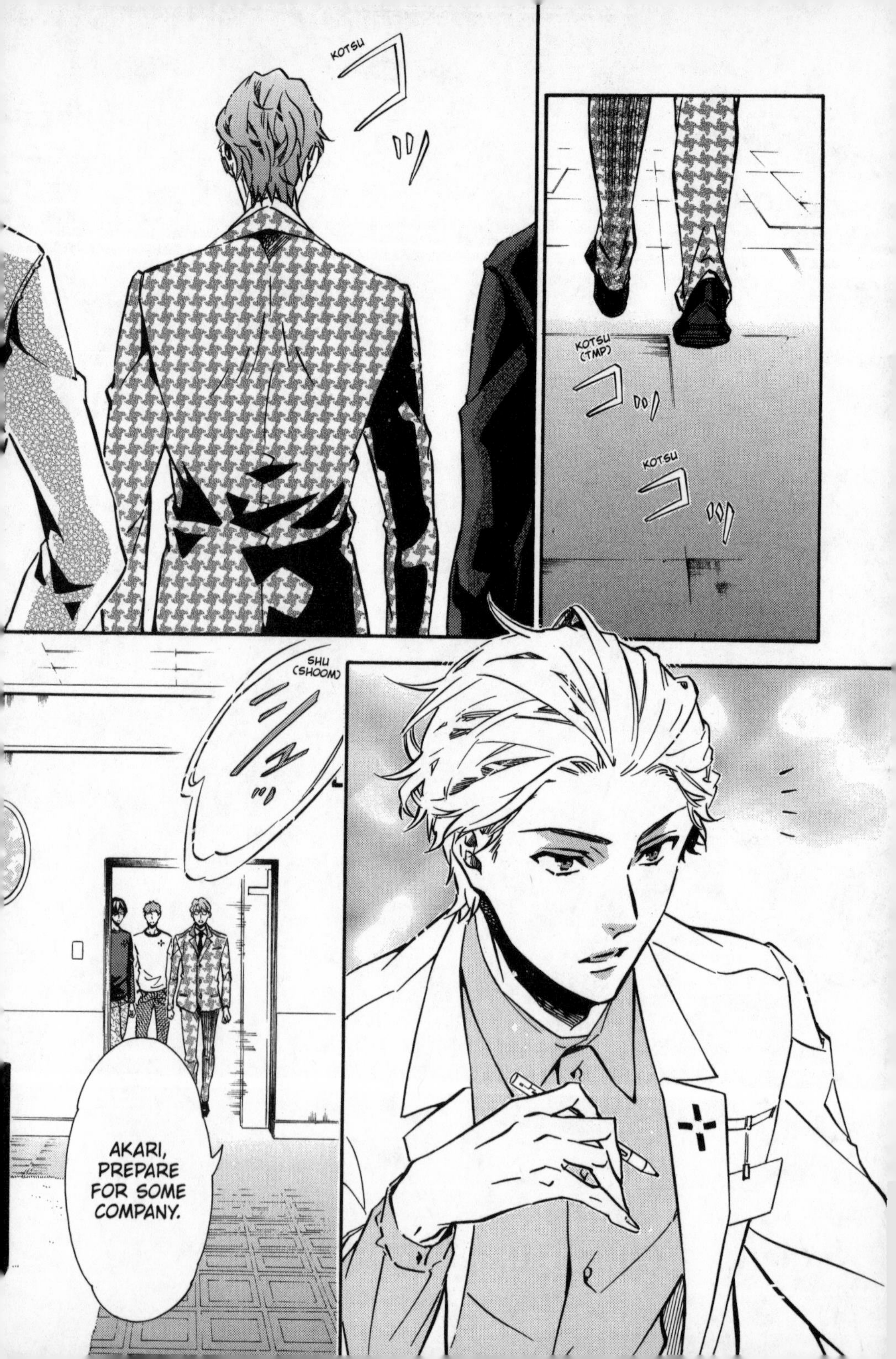
KOTSU (TMP)
KOTSU
KOTSU
SHU (SHOOM)
AKARI, PREPARE FOR SOME COMPANY.

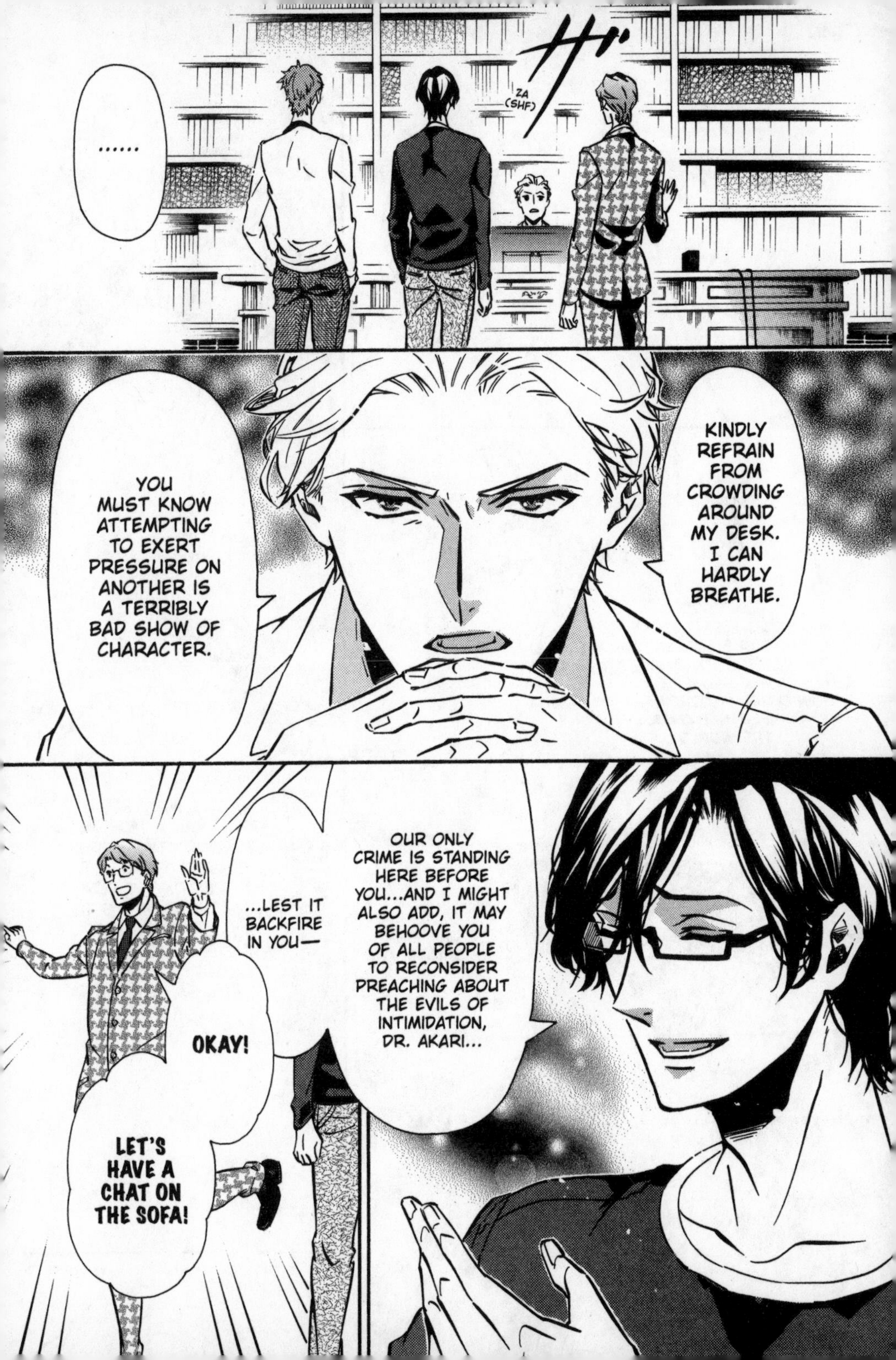

ZA (SHF)
......
KINDLY REFRAIN FROM CROWDING AROUND MY DESK. I CAN HARDLY BREATHE.
YOU MUST KNOW ATTEMPTING TO EXERT PRESSURE ON ANOTHER IS A TERRIBLY BAD SHOW OF CHARACTER.
OUR ONLY CRIME IS STANDING HERE BEFORE YOU...AND I MIGHT ALSO ADD, IT MAY BEHOOVE YOU OF ALL PEOPLE TO RECONSIDER PREACHING ABOUT THE EVILS OF INTIMIDATION, DR. AKARI...
...LEST IT BACKFIRE IN YOU—
OKAY!
LET'S HAVE A CHAT ON THE SOFA!

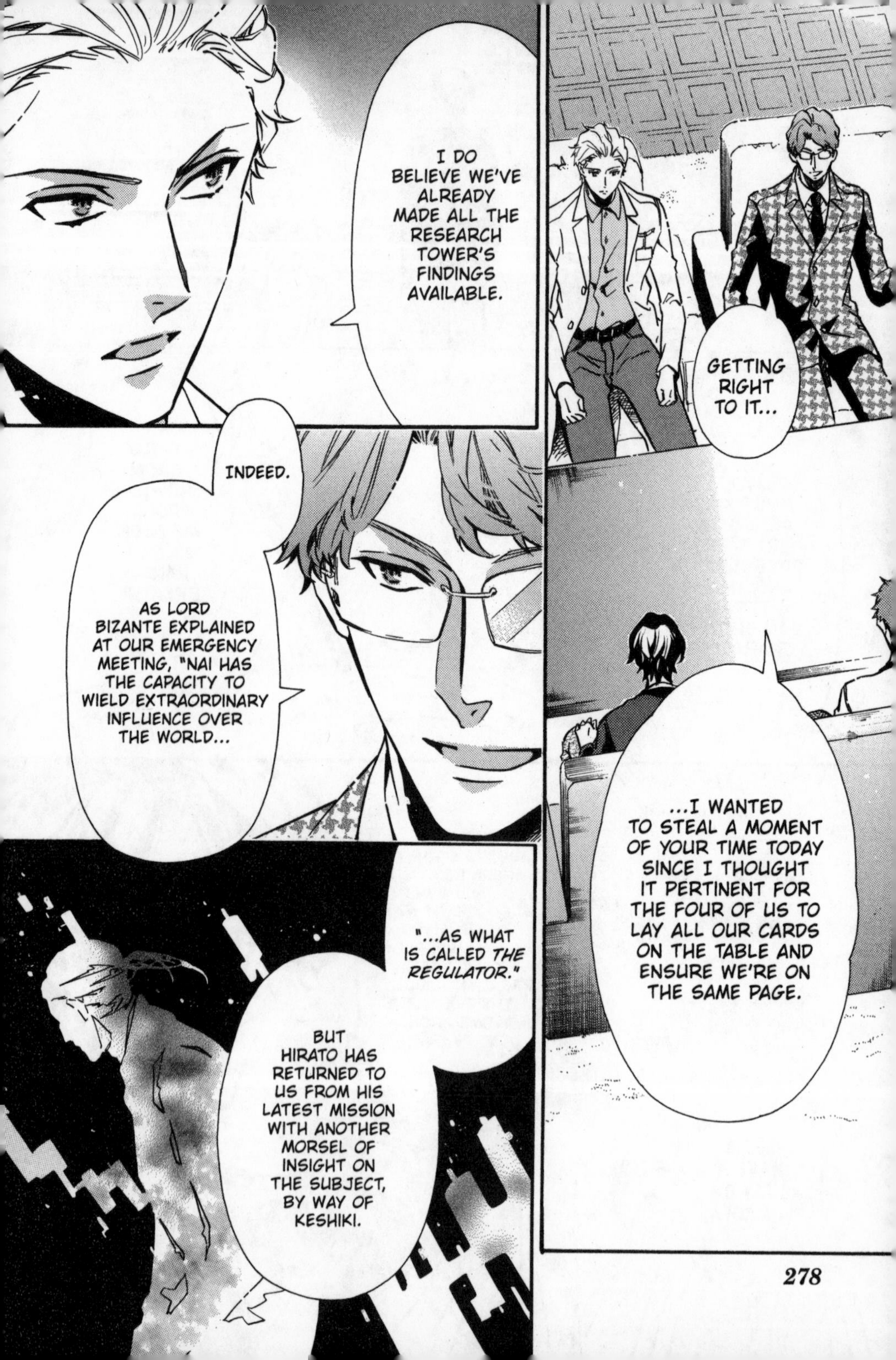
GETTING RIGHT TO IT...
I DO BELIEVE WE'VE ALREADY MADE ALL THE RESEARCH TOWER'S FINDINGS AVAILABLE.
...I WANTED TO STEAL A MOMENT OF YOUR TIME TODAY SINCE I THOUGHT IT PERTINENT FOR THE FOUR OF US TO LAY ALL OUR CARDS ON THE TABLE AND ENSURE WE'RE ON THE SAME PAGE.
INDEED.
AS LORD BIZANTE EXPLAINED AT OUR EMERGENCY MEETING, "NAI HAS THE CAPACITY TO WIELD EXTRAORDINARY INFLUENCE OVER THE WORLD...
"...AS WHAT IS CALLED *THE REGULATOR.*"
BUT HIRATO HAS RETURNED TO US FROM HIS LATEST MISSION WITH ANOTHER MORSEL OF INSIGHT ON THE SUBJECT, BY WAY OF KESHIKI.

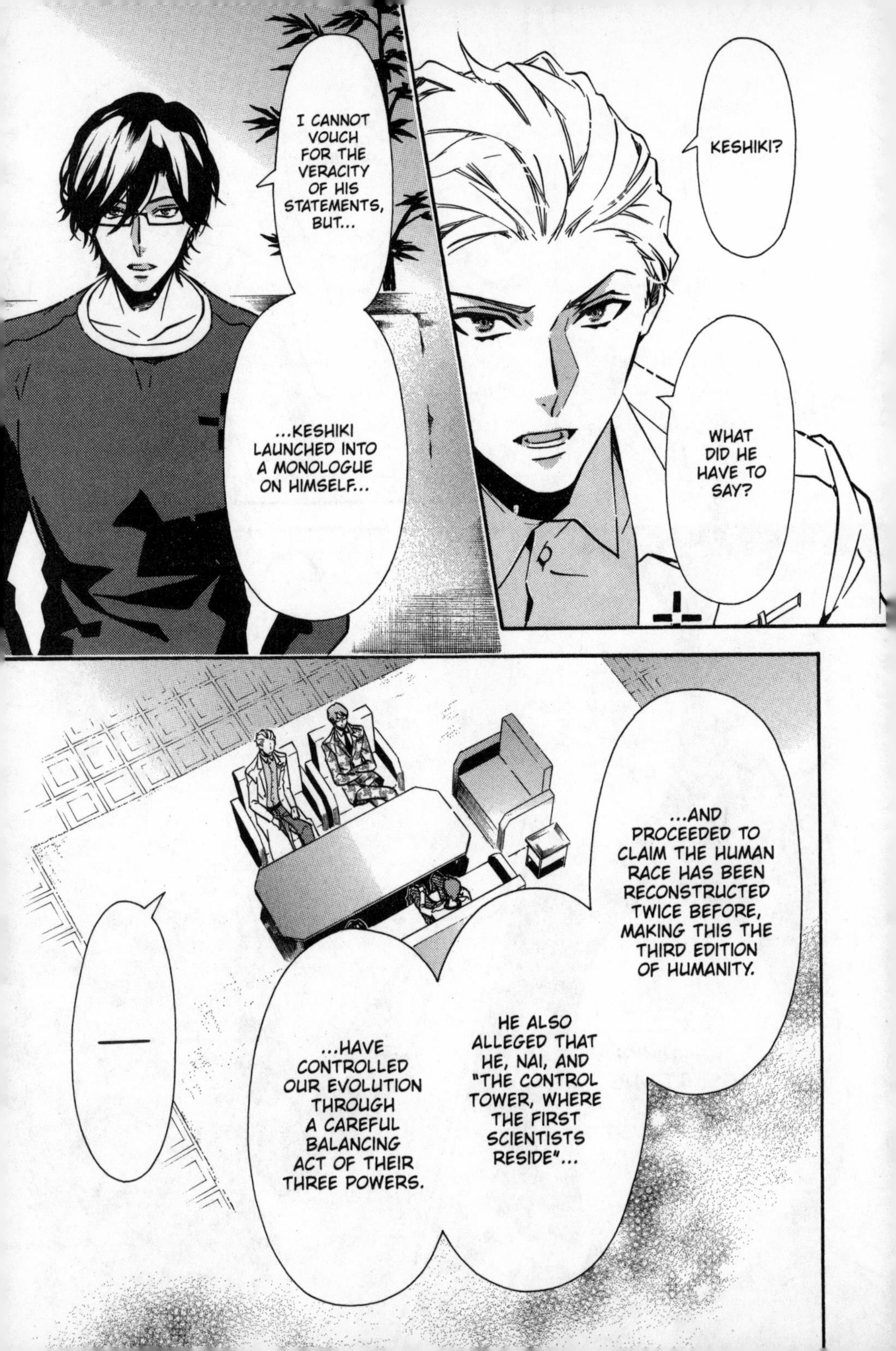
KESHIKI?
WHAT DID HE HAVE TO SAY?
I CANNOT VOUCH FOR THE VERACITY OF HIS STATEMENTS, BUT...
...KESHIKI LAUNCHED INTO A MONOLOGUE ON HIMSELF...
...AND PROCEEDED TO CLAIM THE HUMAN RACE HAS BEEN RECONSTRUCTED TWICE BEFORE, MAKING THIS THE THIRD EDITION OF HUMANITY.
HE ALSO ALLEGED THAT HE, NAI, AND "THE CONTROL TOWER, WHERE THE FIRST SCIENTISTS RESIDE"...
...HAVE CONTROLLED OUR EVOLUTION THROUGH A CAREFUL BALANCING ACT OF THEIR THREE POWERS.
—

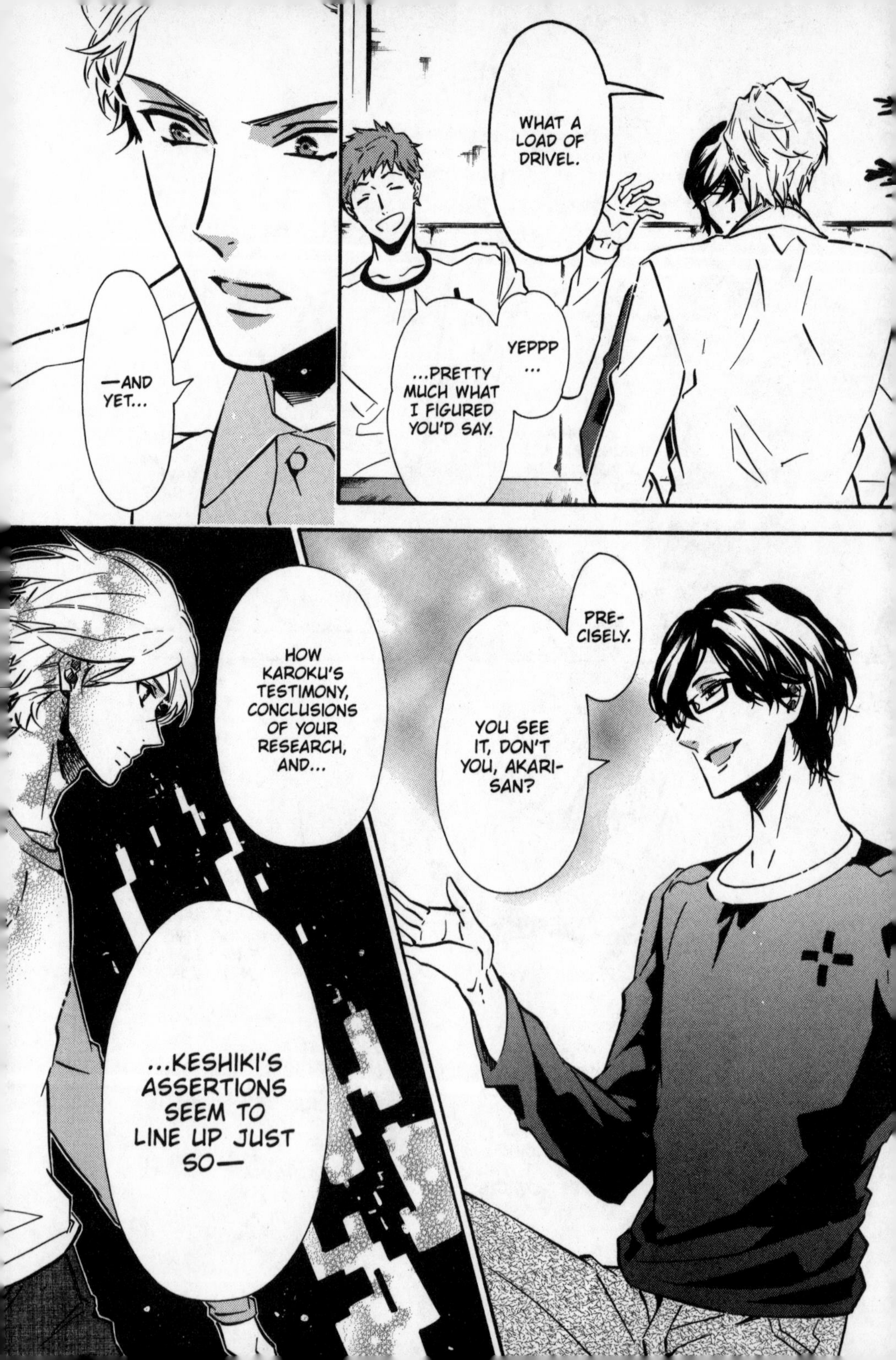
WHAT A LOAD OF DRIVEL.
YEPPP...
...PRETTY MUCH WHAT I FIGURED YOU'D SAY.
—AND YET...
PRE-CISELY.
YOU SEE IT, DON'T YOU, AKARI-SAN?
HOW KAROKU'S TESTIMONY, CONCLUSIONS OF YOUR RESEARCH, AND...
...KESHIKI'S ASSERTIONS SEEM TO LINE UP JUST SO—

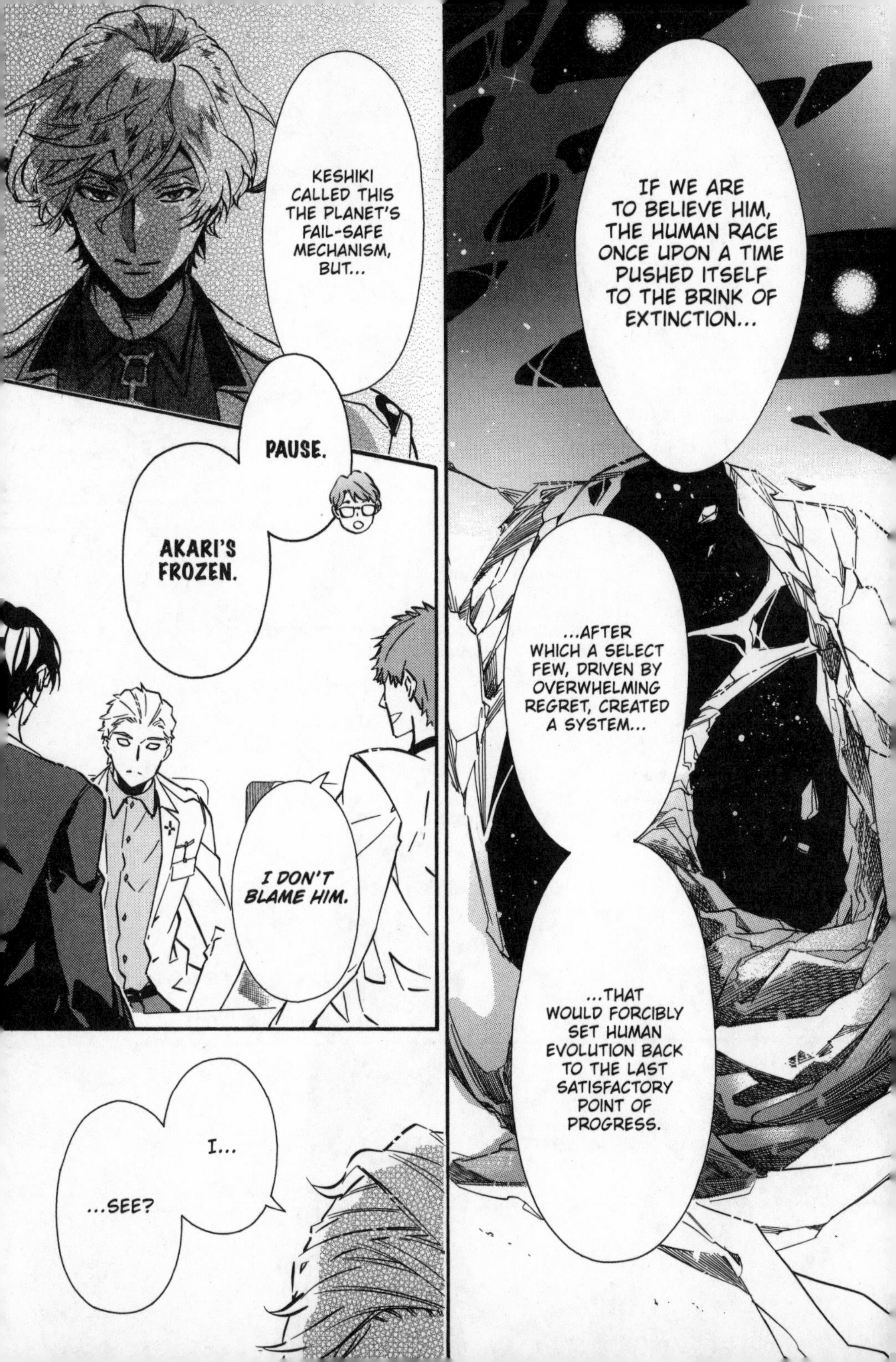
IF WE ARE TO BELIEVE HIM, THE HUMAN RACE ONCE UPON A TIME PUSHED ITSELF TO THE BRINK OF EXTINCTION...
...AFTER WHICH A SELECT FEW, DRIVEN BY OVERWHELMING REGRET, CREATED A SYSTEM...
...THAT WOULD FORCIBLY SET HUMAN EVOLUTION BACK TO THE LAST SATISFACTORY POINT OF PROGRESS.
KESHIKI CALLED THIS THE PLANET'S FAIL-SAFE MECHANISM, BUT...
PAUSE.
AKARI'S FROZEN.
I DON'T BLAME HIM.
I...
...SEE?

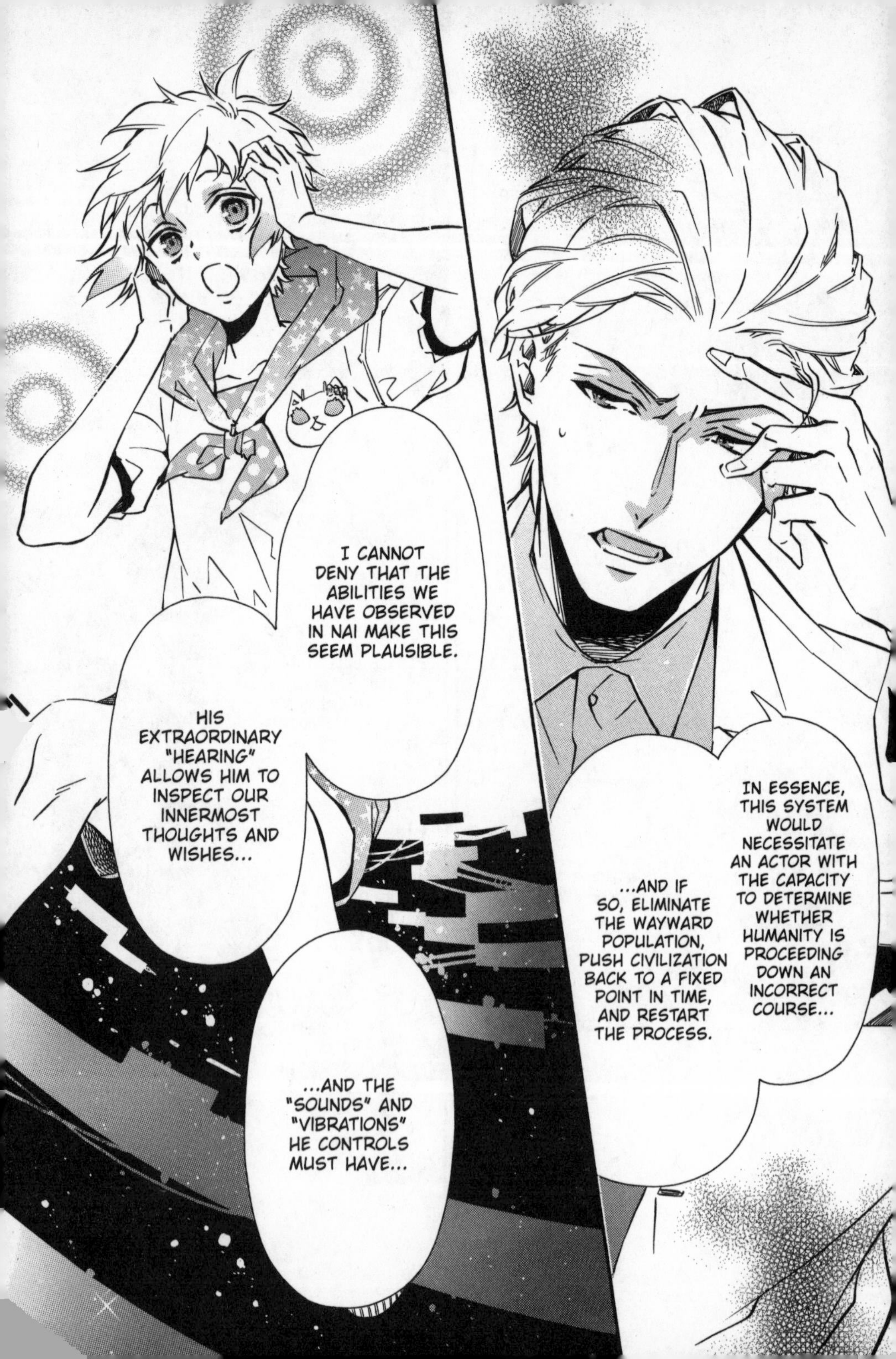
IN ESSENCE, THIS SYSTEM WOULD NECESSITATE AN ACTOR WITH THE CAPACITY TO DETERMINE WHETHER HUMANITY IS PROCEEDING DOWN AN INCORRECT COURSE...
...AND IF SO, ELIMINATE THE WAYWARD POPULATION, PUSH CIVILIZATION BACK TO A FIXED POINT IN TIME, AND RESTART THE PROCESS.
I CANNOT DENY THAT THE ABILITIES WE HAVE OBSERVED IN NAI MAKE THIS SEEM PLAUSIBLE.
HIS EXTRAORDINARY "HEARING" ALLOWS HIM TO INSPECT OUR INNERMOST THOUGHTS AND WISHES...
...AND THE "SOUNDS" AND "VIBRATIONS" HE CONTROLS MUST HAVE...

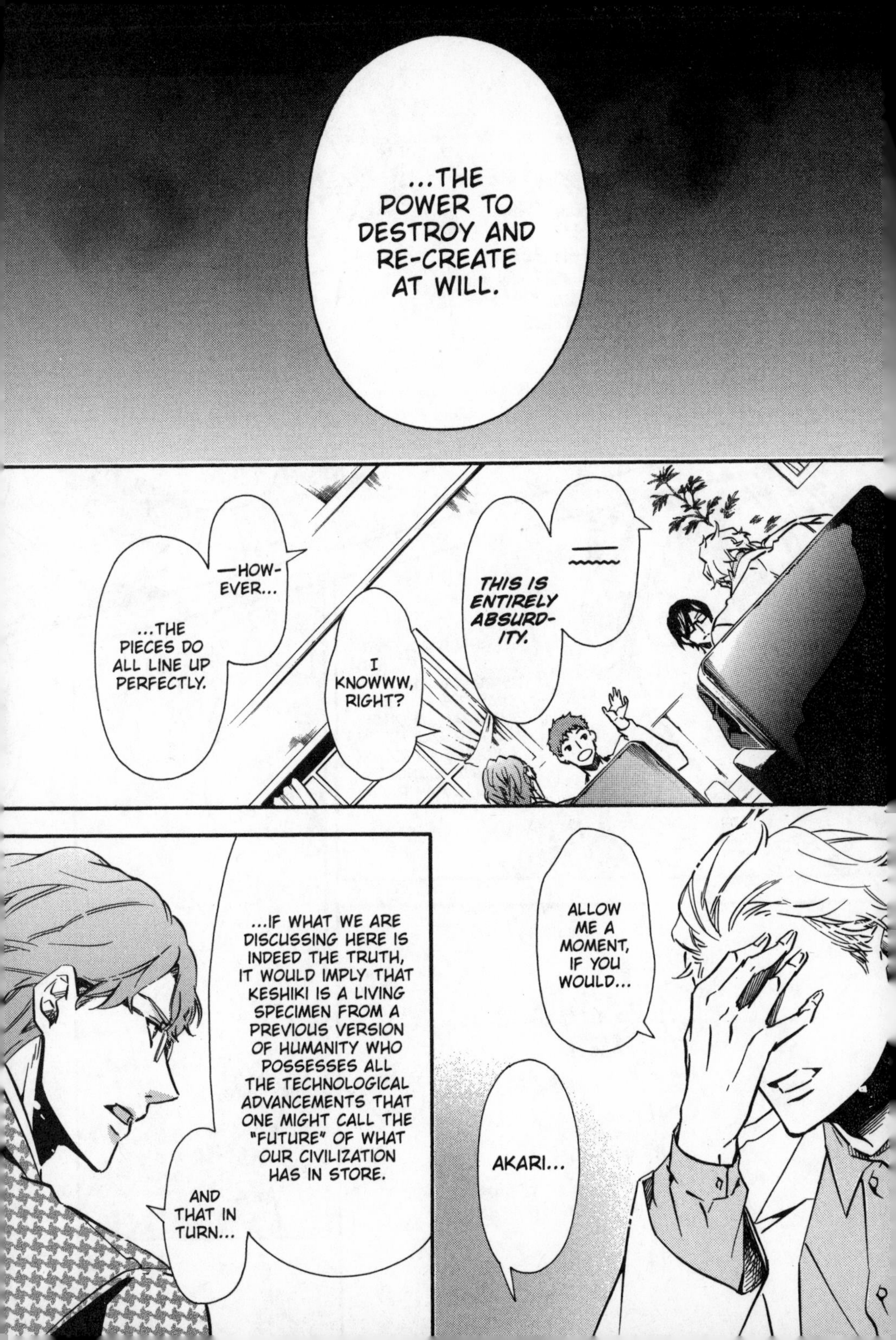
...THE POWER TO DESTROY AND RE-CREATE AT WILL.
—— THIS IS ENTIRELY ABSURDITY.
I KNOWWW, RIGHT?
—HOWEVER... ...THE PIECES DO ALL LINE UP PERFECTLY.
ALLOW ME A MOMENT, IF YOU WOULD...
AKARI...
...IF WHAT WE ARE DISCUSSING HERE IS INDEED THE TRUTH, IT WOULD IMPLY THAT KESHIKI IS A LIVING SPECIMEN FROM A PREVIOUS VERSION OF HUMANITY WHO POSSESSES ALL THE TECHNOLOGICAL ADVANCEMENTS THAT ONE MIGHT CALL THE "FUTURE" OF WHAT OUR CIVILIZATION HAS IN STORE.
AND THAT IN TURN...

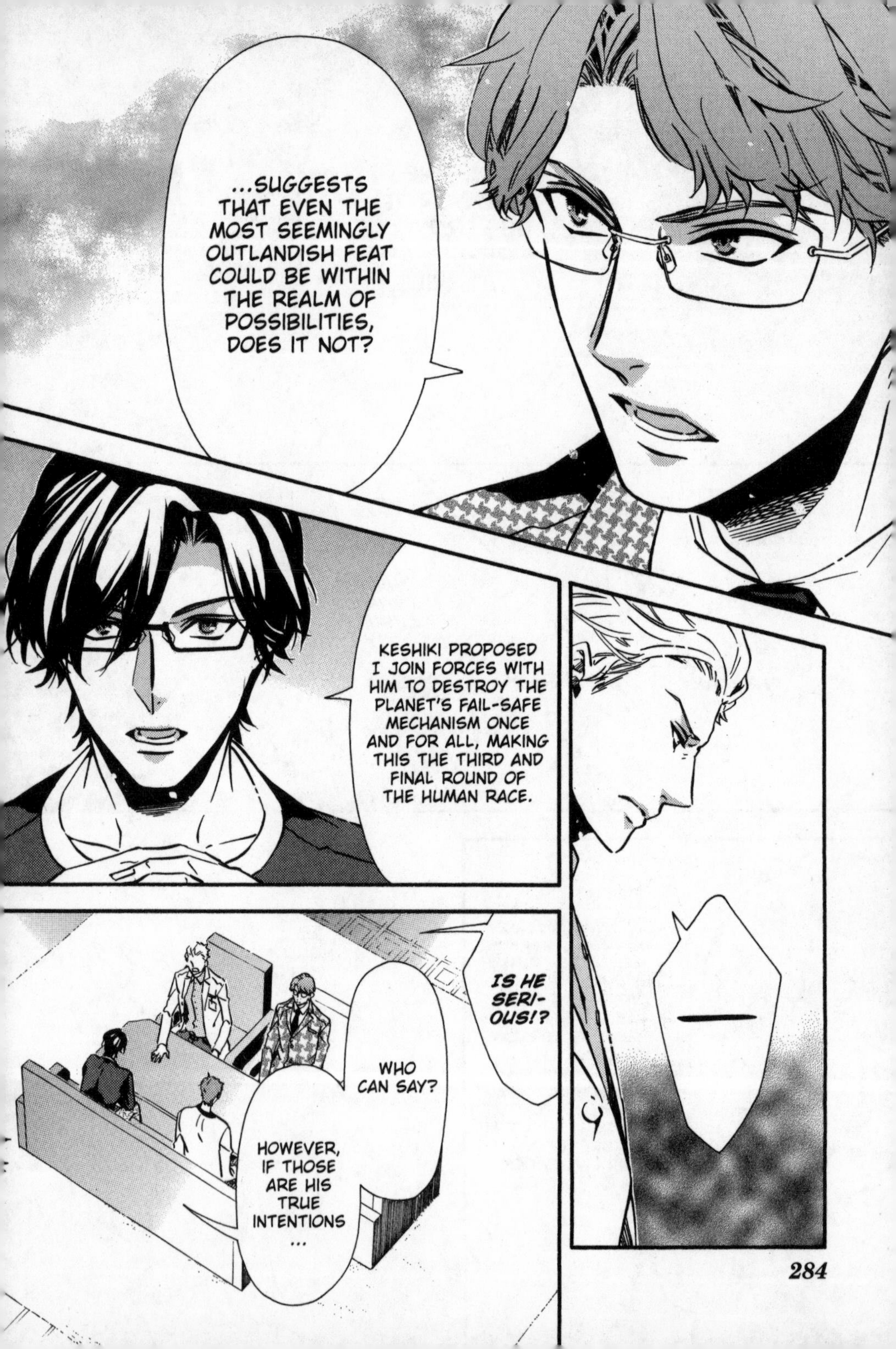
...SUGGESTS THAT EVEN THE MOST SEEMINGLY OUTLANDISH FEAT COULD BE WITHIN THE REALM OF POSSIBILITIES, DOES IT NOT?
—
KESHIKI PROPOSED I JOIN FORCES WITH HIM TO DESTROY THE PLANET'S FAIL-SAFE MECHANISM ONCE AND FOR ALL, MAKING THIS THE THIRD AND FINAL ROUND OF THE HUMAN RACE.
IS HE SERI-OUS!?
WHO CAN SAY?
HOWEVER, IF THOSE ARE HIS TRUE INTENTIONS ...

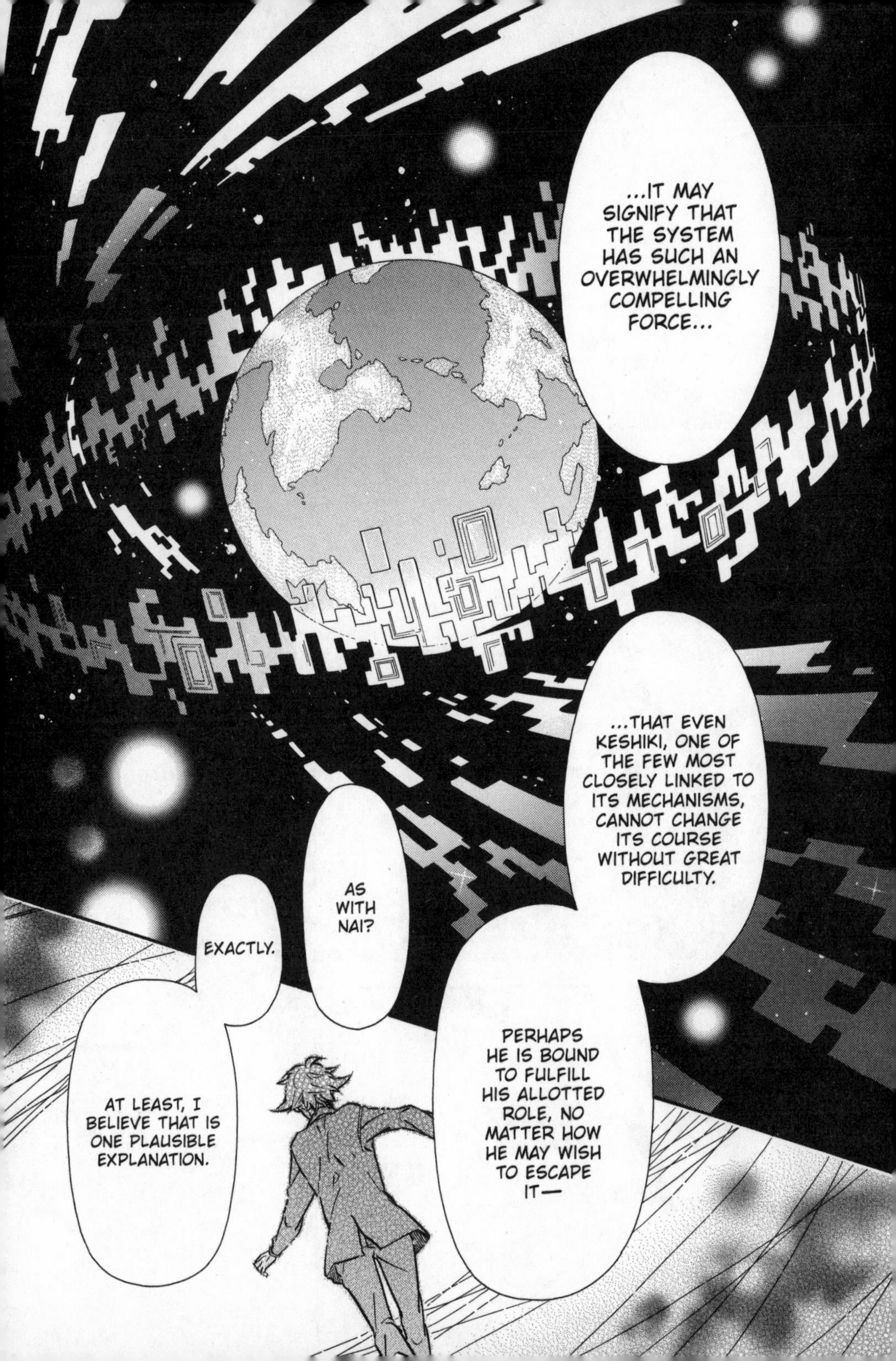
...IT MAY SIGNIFY THAT THE SYSTEM HAS SUCH AN OVERWHELMINGLY COMPELLING FORCE...
...THAT EVEN KESHIKI, ONE OF THE FEW MOST CLOSELY LINKED TO ITS MECHANISMS, CANNOT CHANGE ITS COURSE WITHOUT GREAT DIFFICULTY.
PERHAPS HE IS BOUND TO FULFILL HIS ALLOTTED ROLE, NO MATTER HOW HE MAY WISH TO ESCAPE IT—
AS WITH NAI?
EXACTLY.
AT LEAST, I BELIEVE THAT IS ONE PLAUSIBLE EXPLANATION.

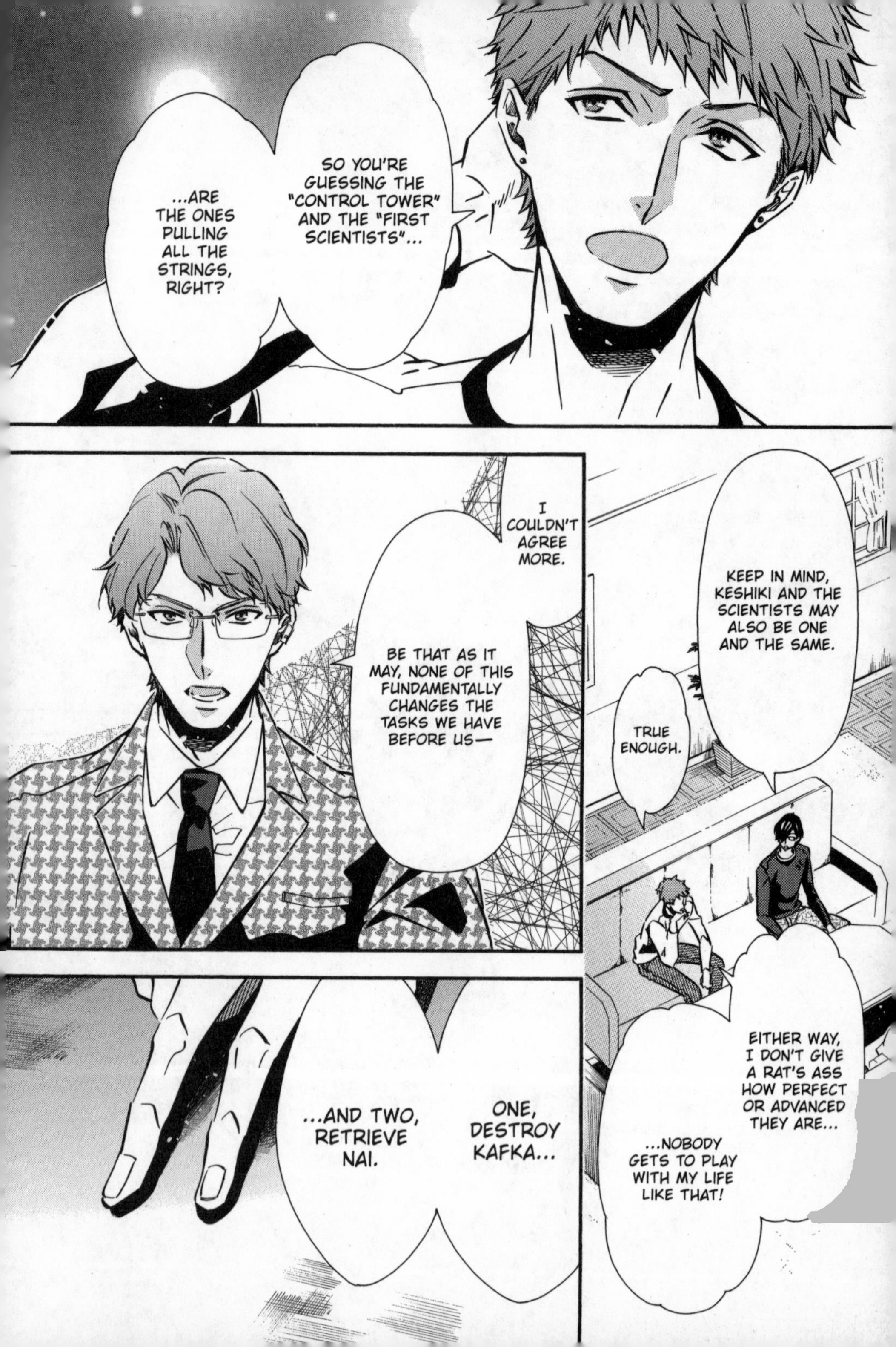
SO YOU'RE GUESSING THE "CONTROL TOWER" AND THE "FIRST SCIENTISTS"...
...ARE THE ONES PULLING ALL THE STRINGS, RIGHT?
KEEP IN MIND, KESHIKI AND THE SCIENTISTS MAY ALSO BE ONE AND THE SAME.
TRUE ENOUGH.
EITHER WAY, I DON'T GIVE A RAT'S ASS HOW PERFECT OR ADVANCED THEY ARE...
...NOBODY GETS TO PLAY WITH MY LIFE LIKE THAT!
I COULDN'T AGREE MORE.
BE THAT AS IT MAY, NONE OF THIS FUNDAMENTALLY CHANGES THE TASKS WE HAVE BEFORE US—
ONE, DESTROY KAFKA...
...AND TWO, RETRIEVE NAI.

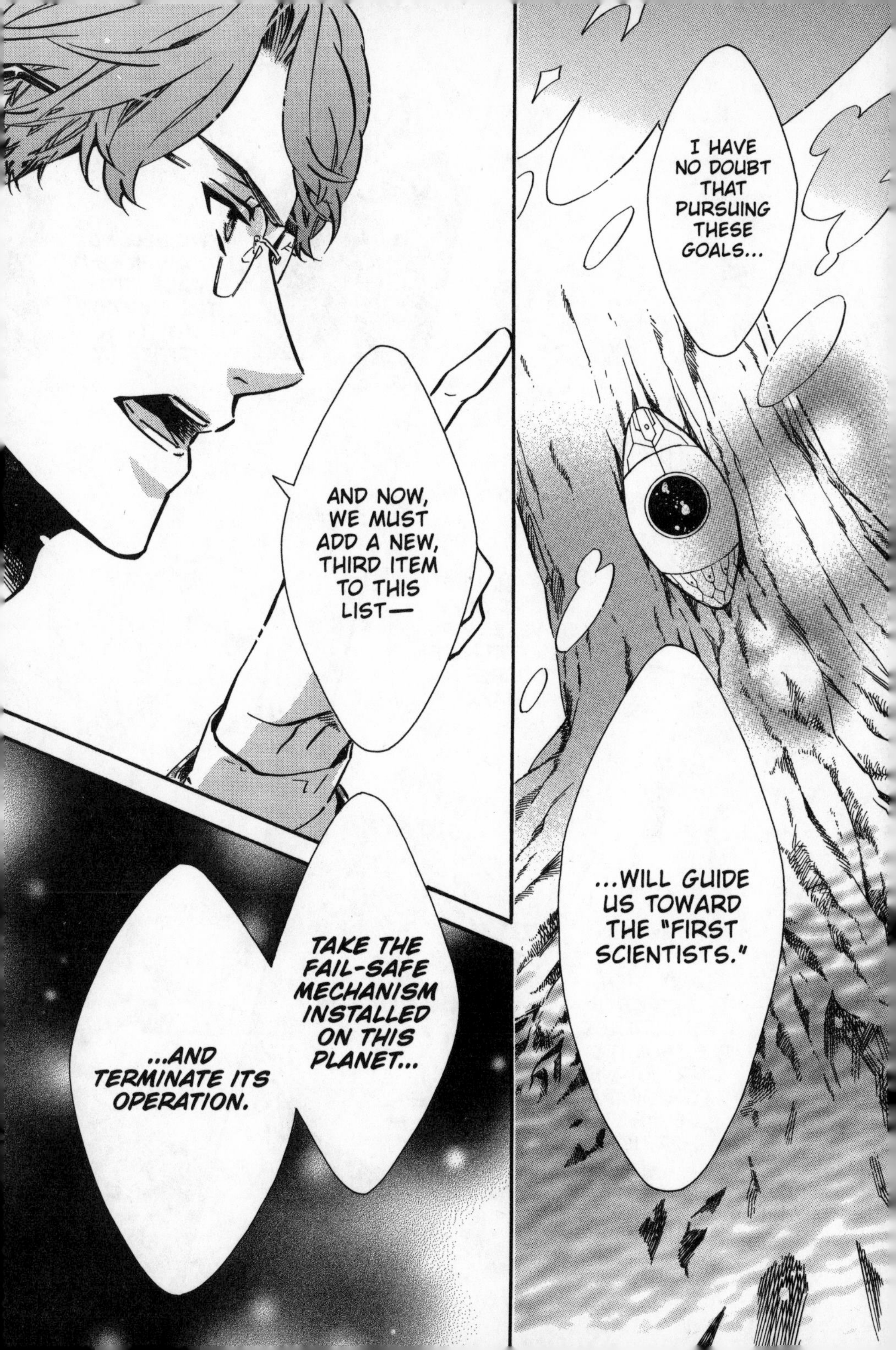
I HAVE NO DOUBT THAT PURSUING THESE GOALS...
...WILL GUIDE US TOWARD THE "FIRST SCIENTISTS."
AND NOW, WE MUST ADD A NEW, THIRD ITEM TO THIS LIST—
TAKE THE FAIL-SAFE MECHANISM INSTALLED ON THIS PLANET...
...AND TERMINATE ITS OPERATION.

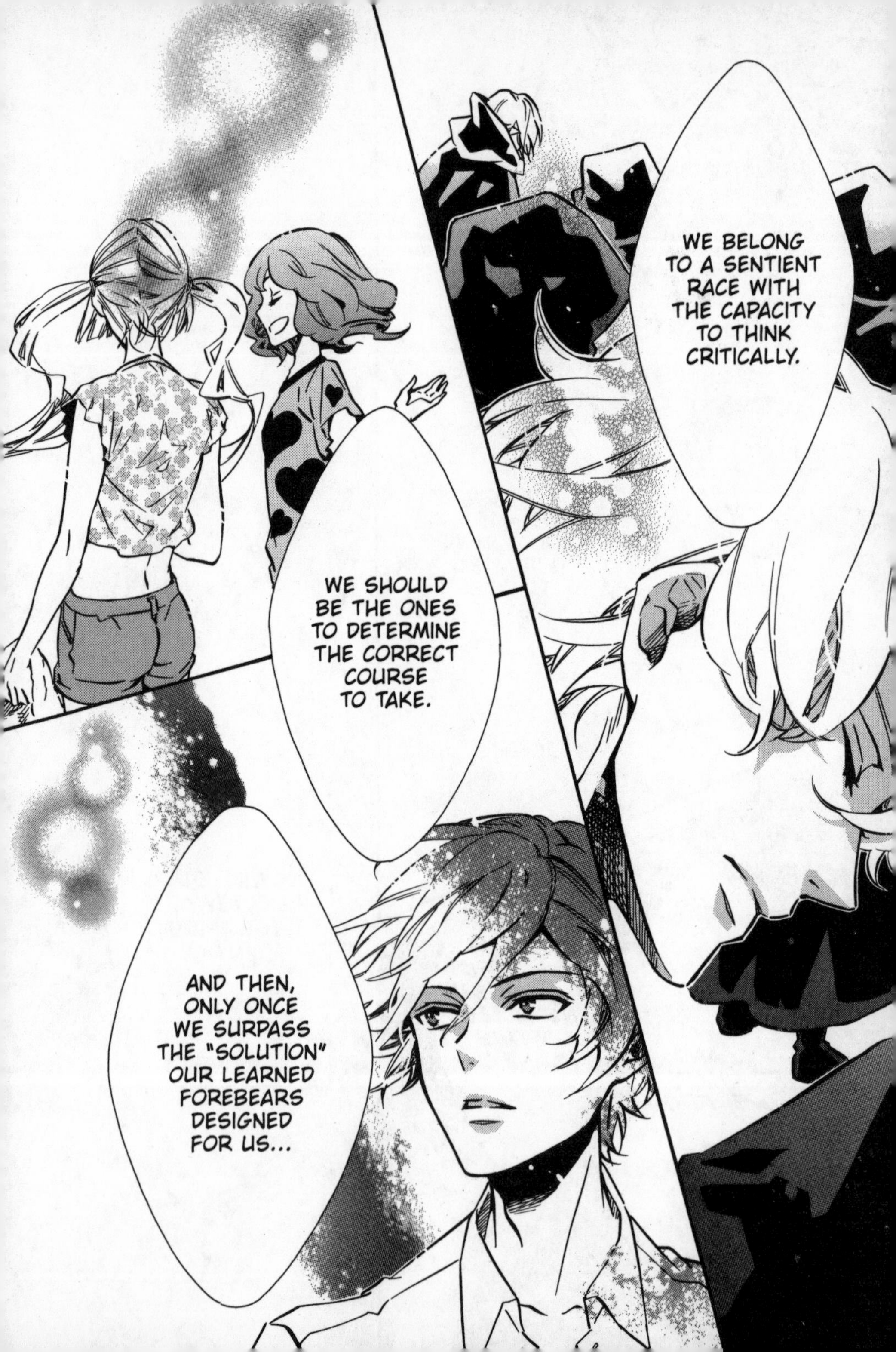
WE BELONG TO A SENTIENT RACE WITH THE CAPACITY TO THINK CRITICALLY.
WE SHOULD BE THE ONES TO DETERMINE THE CORRECT COURSE TO TAKE.
AND THEN, ONLY ONCE WE SURPASS THE "SOLUTION" OUR LEARNED FOREBEARS DESIGNED FOR US...

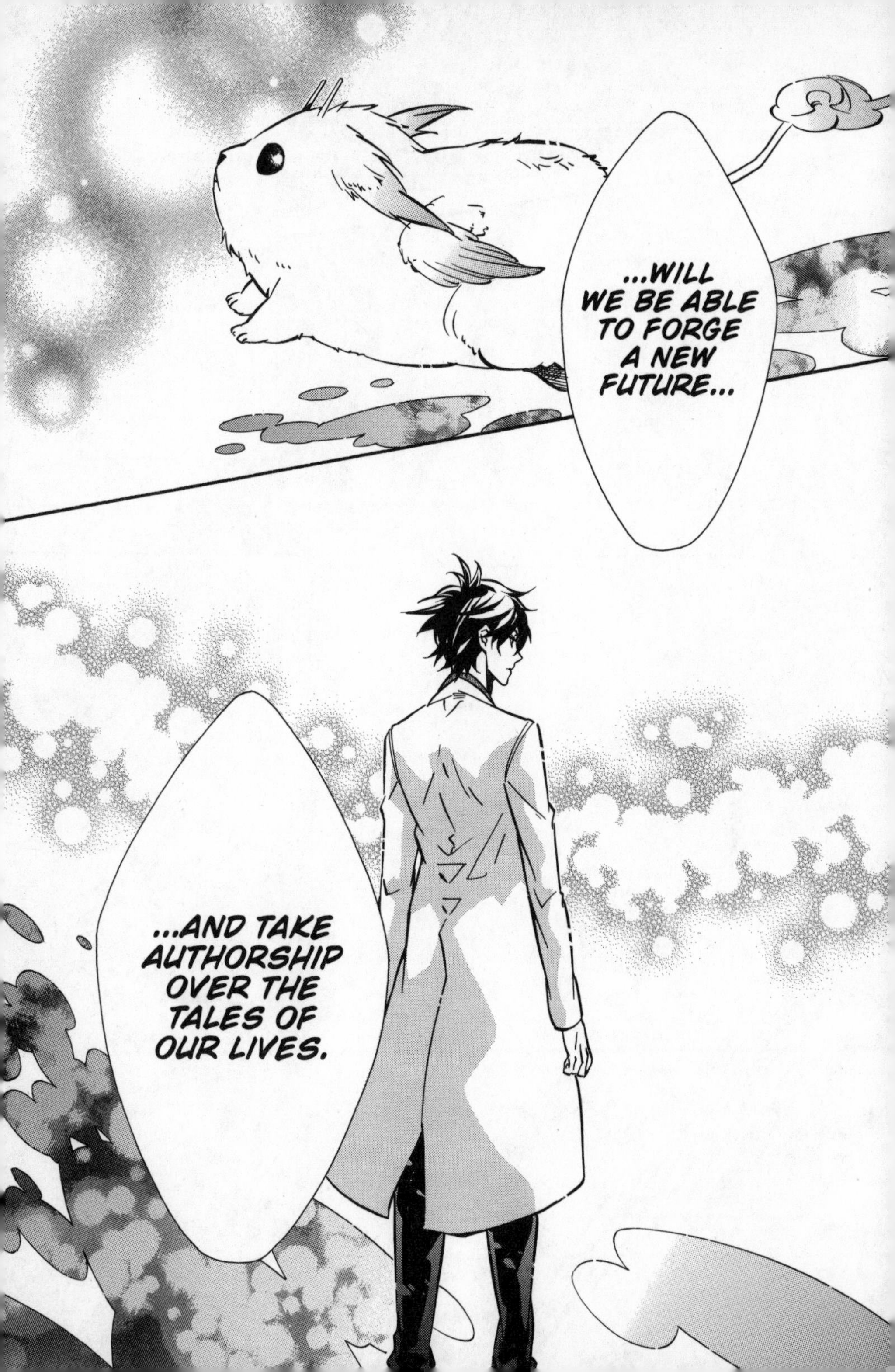
...WILL WE BE ABLE TO FORGE A NEW FUTURE...
...AND TAKE AUTHORSHIP OVER THE TALES OF OUR LIVES.

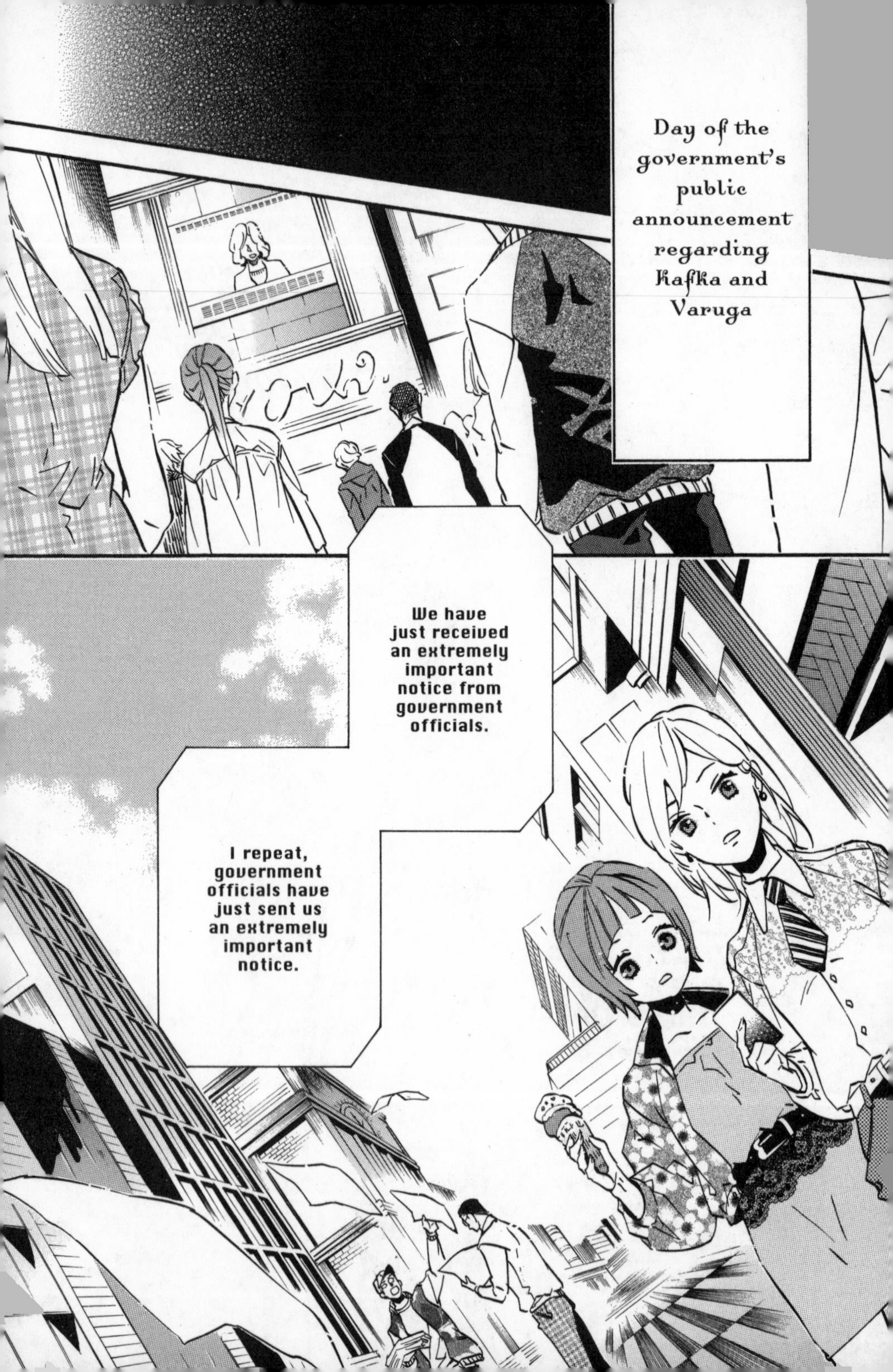
Day of the government's public announcement regarding Kafka and Varuga
We have just received an extremely important notice from government officials.
I repeat, government officials have just sent us an extremely important notice.

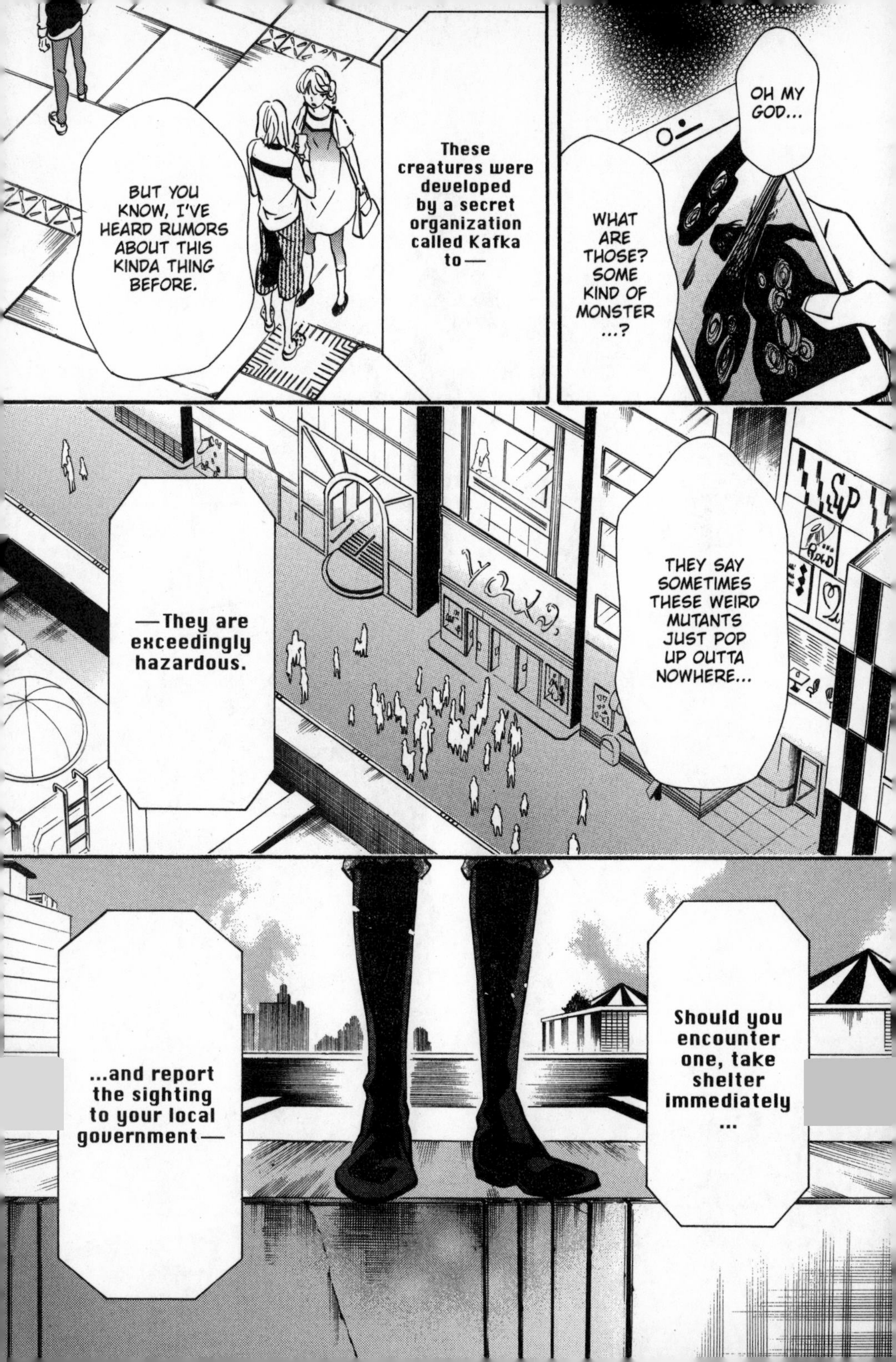
OH MY GOD...
WHAT ARE THOSE? SOME KIND OF MONSTER ...?
These creatures were developed by a secret organization called Kafka to—
BUT YOU KNOW, I'VE HEARD RUMORS ABOUT THIS KINDA THING BEFORE.
THEY SAY SOMETIMES THESE WEIRD MUTANTS JUST POP UP OUTTA NOWHERE...
—They are exceedingly hazardous.
Should you encounter one, take shelter immediately ...
...and report the sighting to your local government—

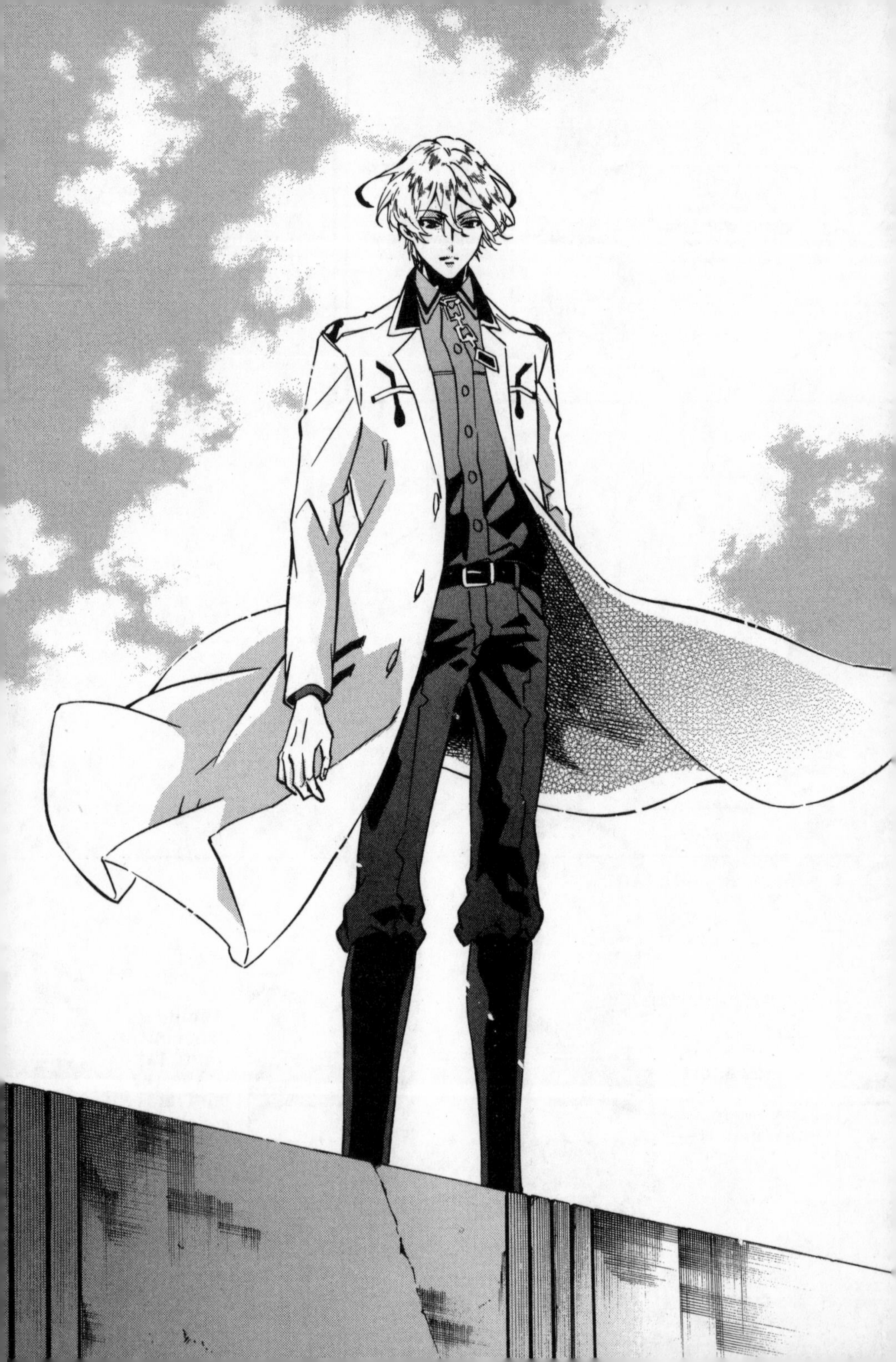

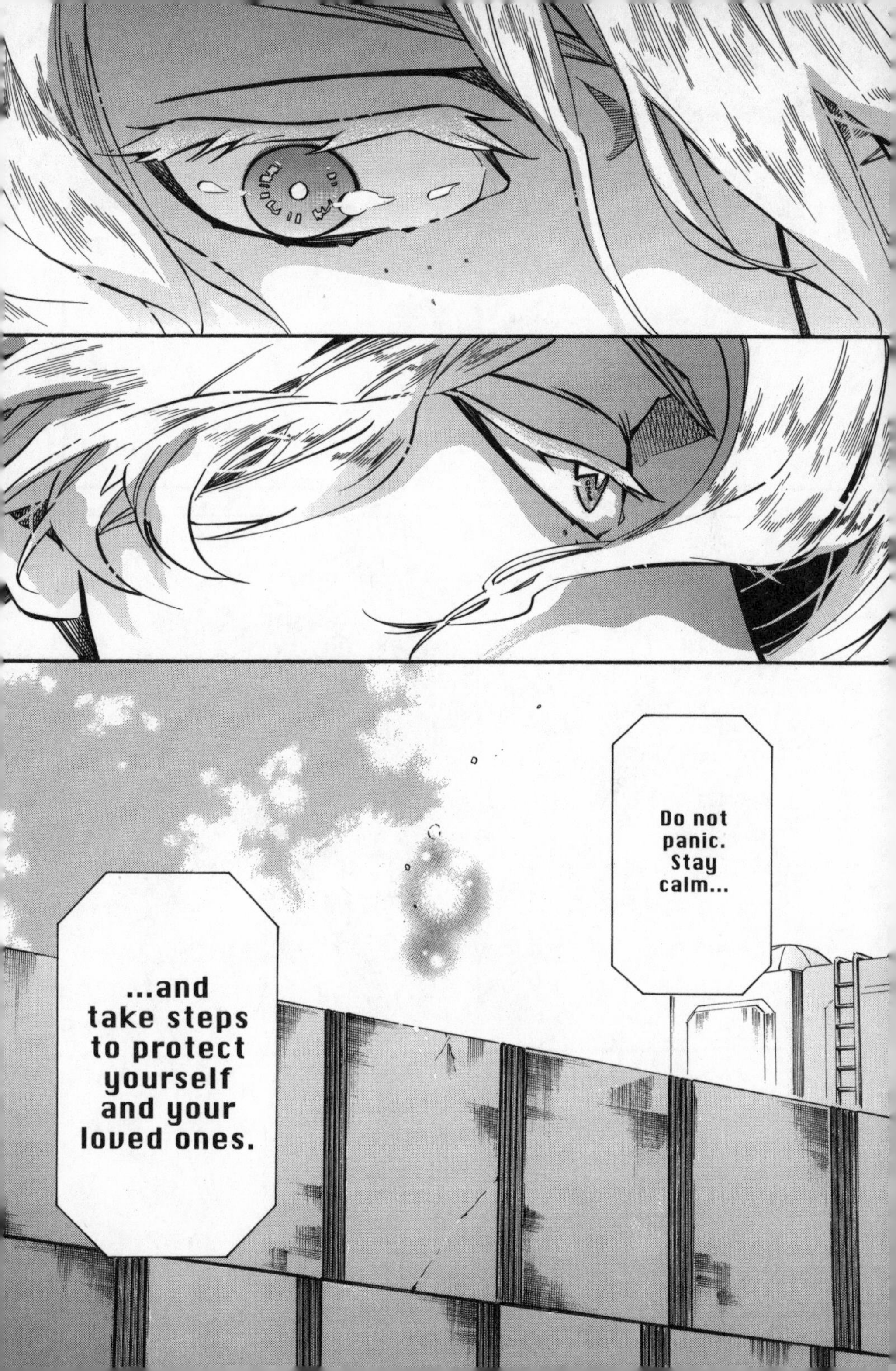
Do not panic. Stay calm...
...and take steps to protect yourself and your loved ones.

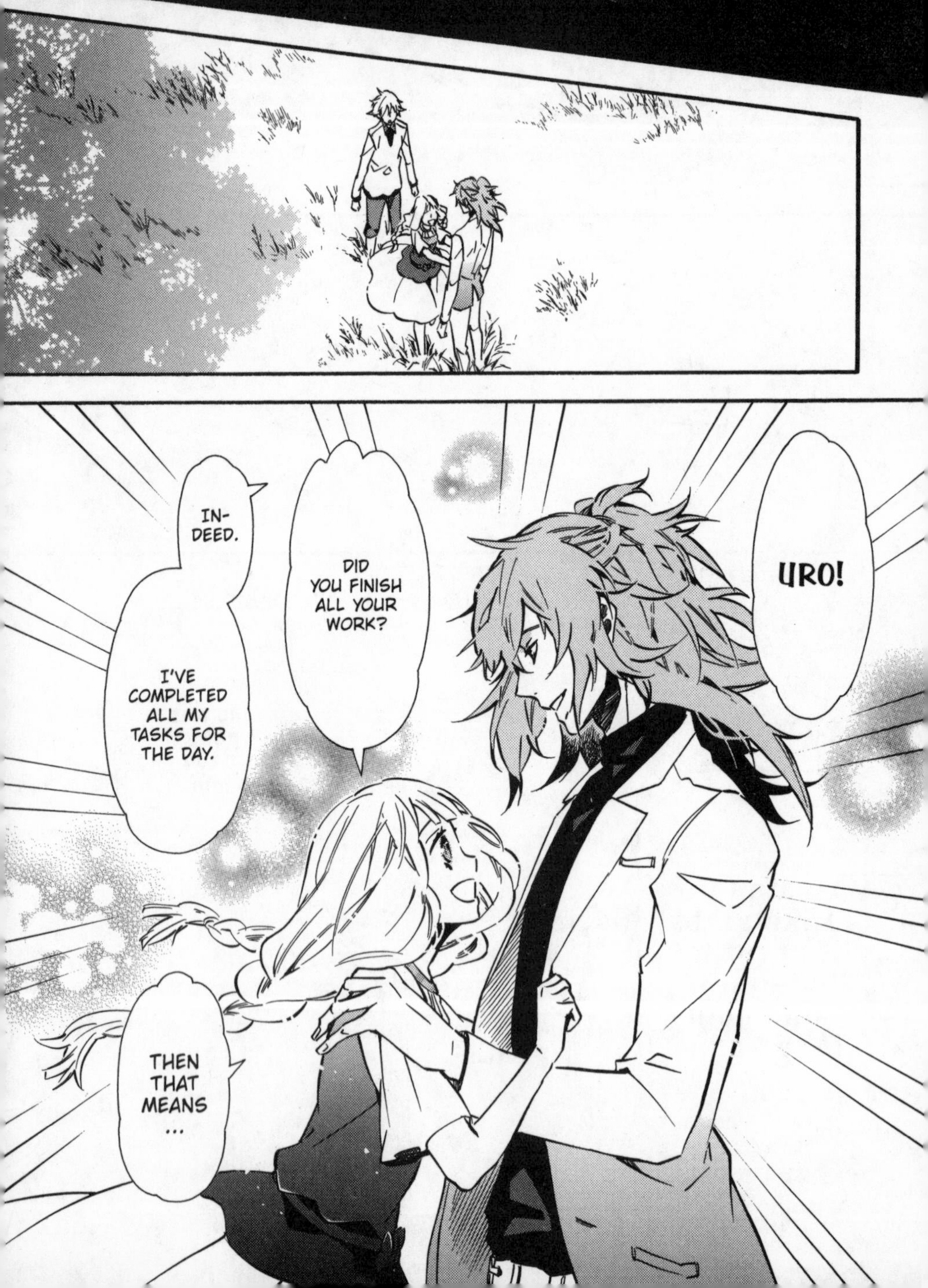
URO!
DID YOU FINISH ALL YOUR WORK?
IN-DEED.
I'VE COMPLETED ALL MY TASKS FOR THE DAY.
THEN THAT MEANS ...

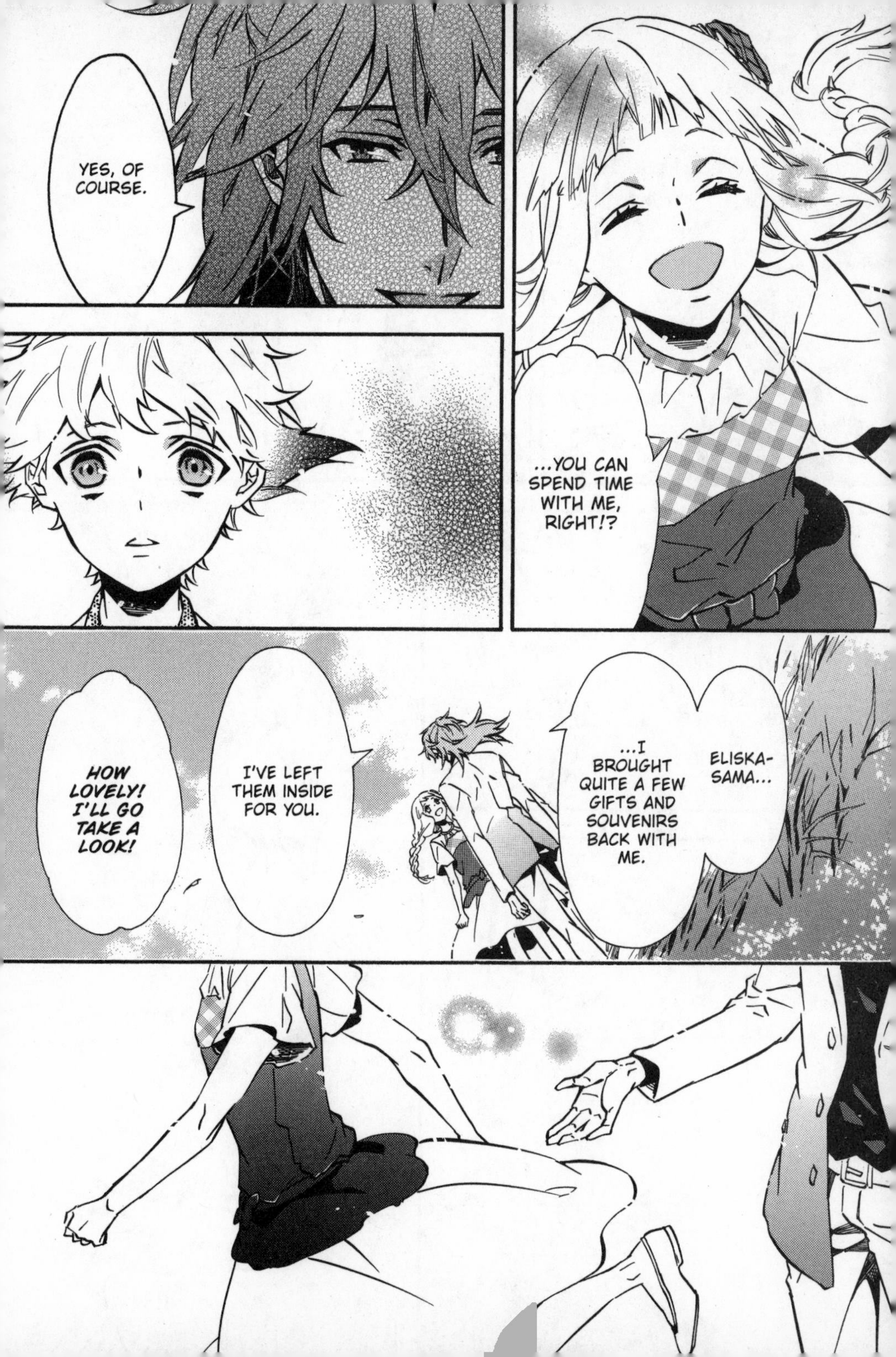
...YOU CAN SPEND TIME WITH ME, RIGHT!?
YES, OF COURSE.
ELISKA-SAMA...
...I BROUGHT QUITE A FEW GIFTS AND SOUVENIRS BACK WITH ME.
I'VE LEFT THEM INSIDE FOR YOU.
HOW LOVELY! I'LL GO TAKE A LOOK!

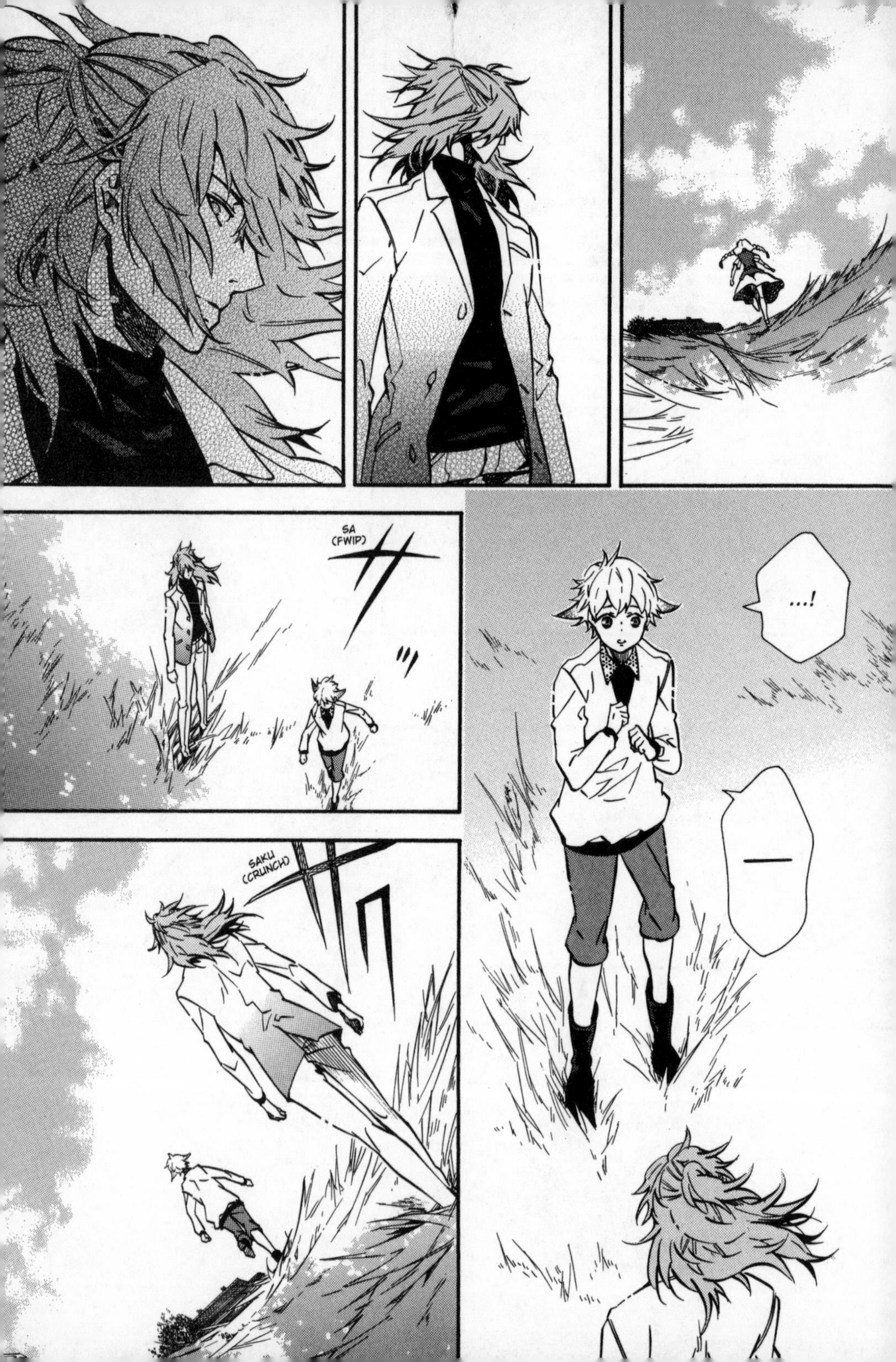
...!
—
SA (FWIP)
SAKU (CRUNCH)

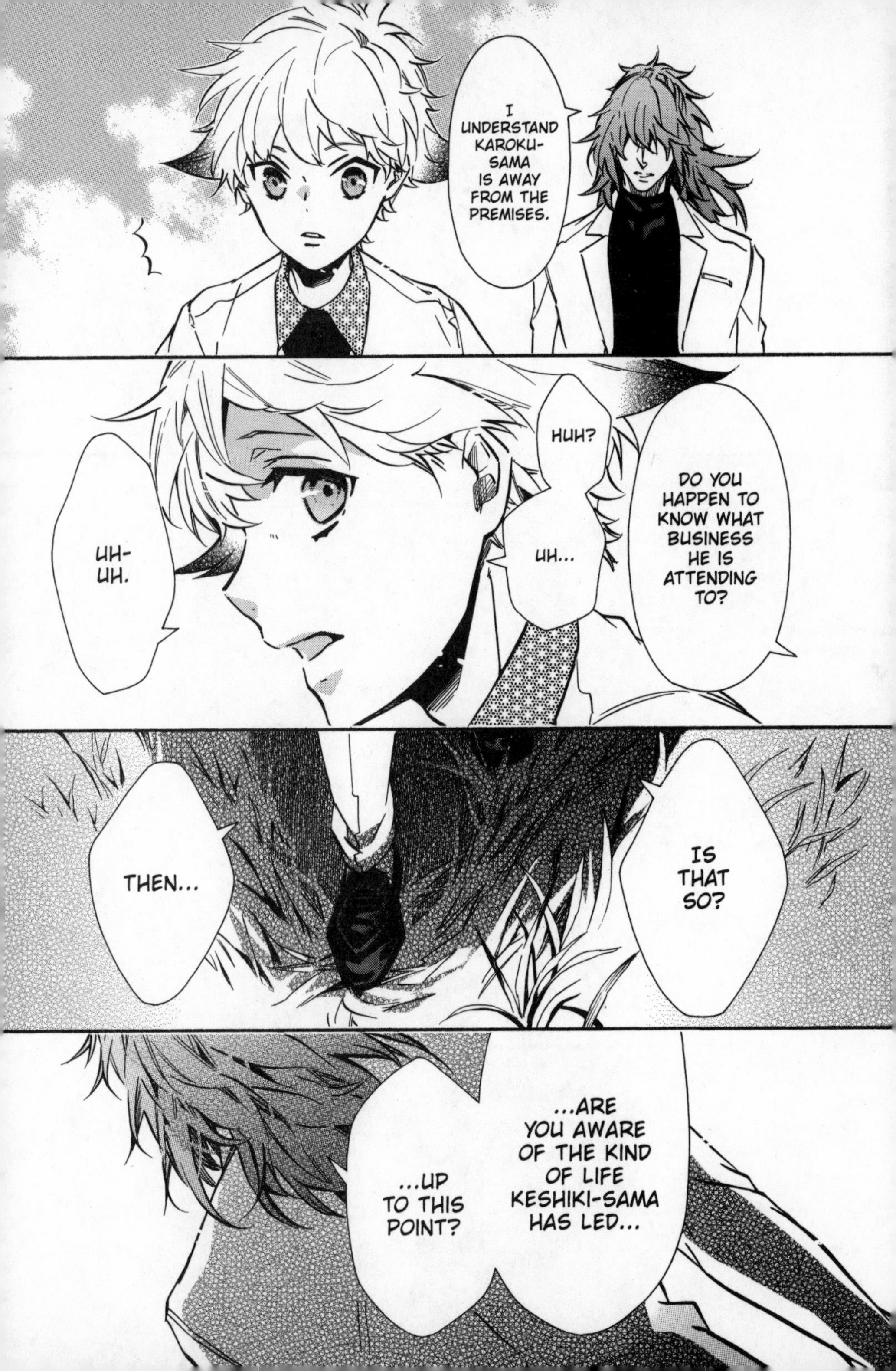
I UNDERSTAND KAROKU-SAMA IS AWAY FROM THE PREMISES.
DO YOU HAPPEN TO KNOW WHAT BUSINESS HE IS ATTENDING TO?
HUH?
UH...
UH-UH.
IS THAT SO?
THEN...
...ARE YOU AWARE OF THE KIND OF LIFE KESHIKI-SAMA HAS LED...
...UP TO THIS POINT?

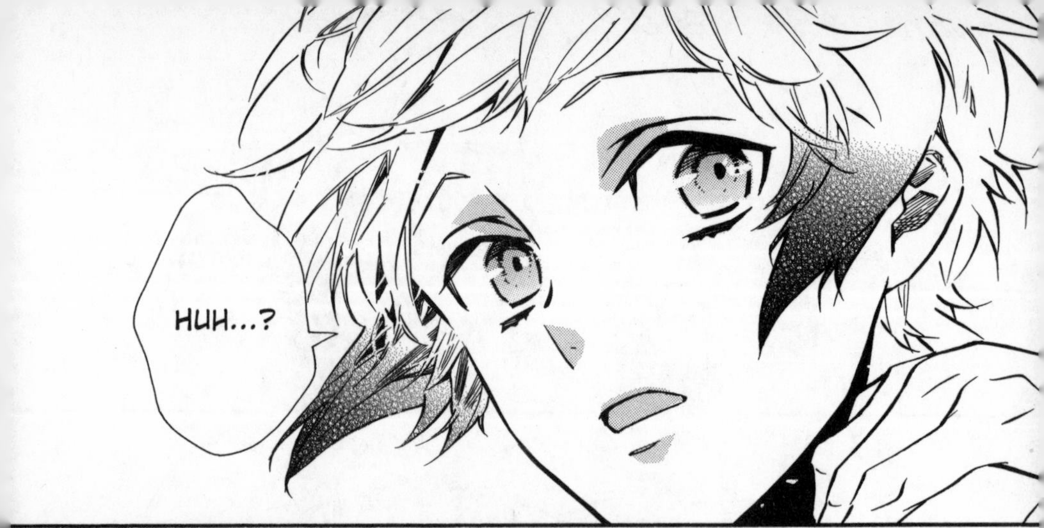
HUH...?
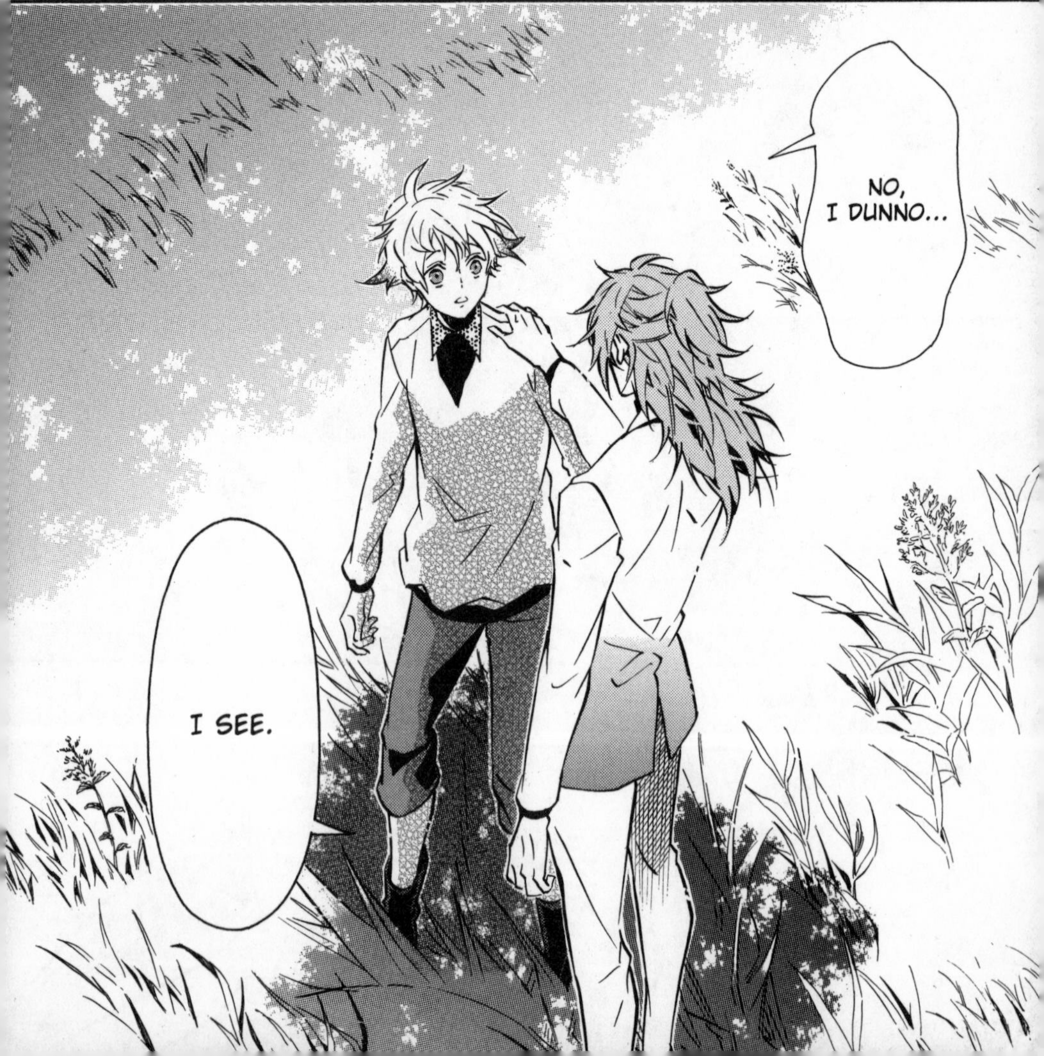
NO, I DUNNO...
I SEE.

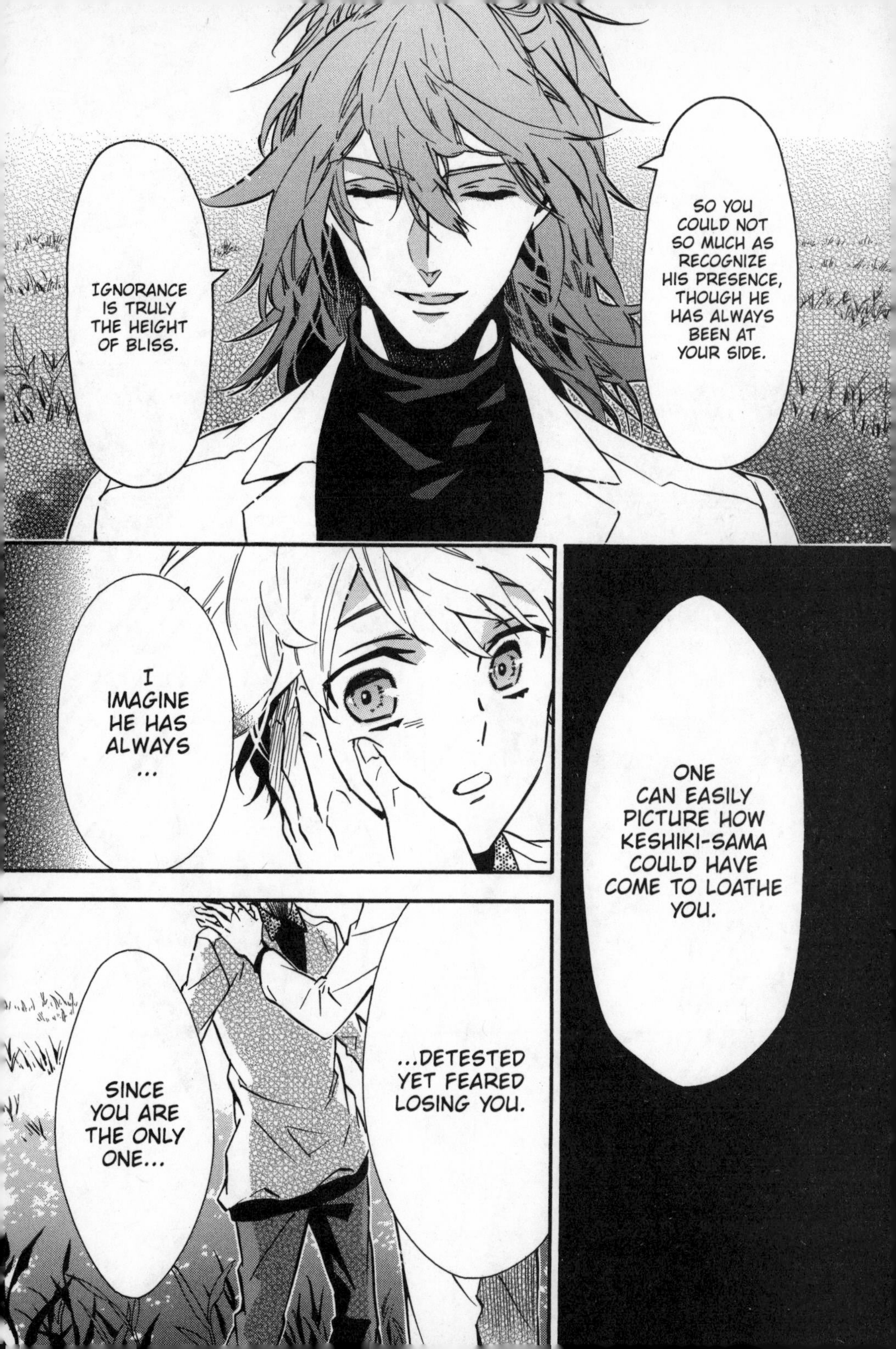
SO YOU COULD NOT SO MUCH AS RECOGNIZE HIS PRESENCE, THOUGH HE HAS ALWAYS BEEN AT YOUR SIDE.
IGNORANCE IS TRULY THE HEIGHT OF BLISS.
ONE CAN EASILY PICTURE HOW KESHIKI-SAMA COULD HAVE COME TO LOATHE YOU.
I IMAGINE HE HAS ALWAYS ...
...DETESTED YET FEARED LOSING YOU.
SINCE YOU ARE THE ONLY ONE...

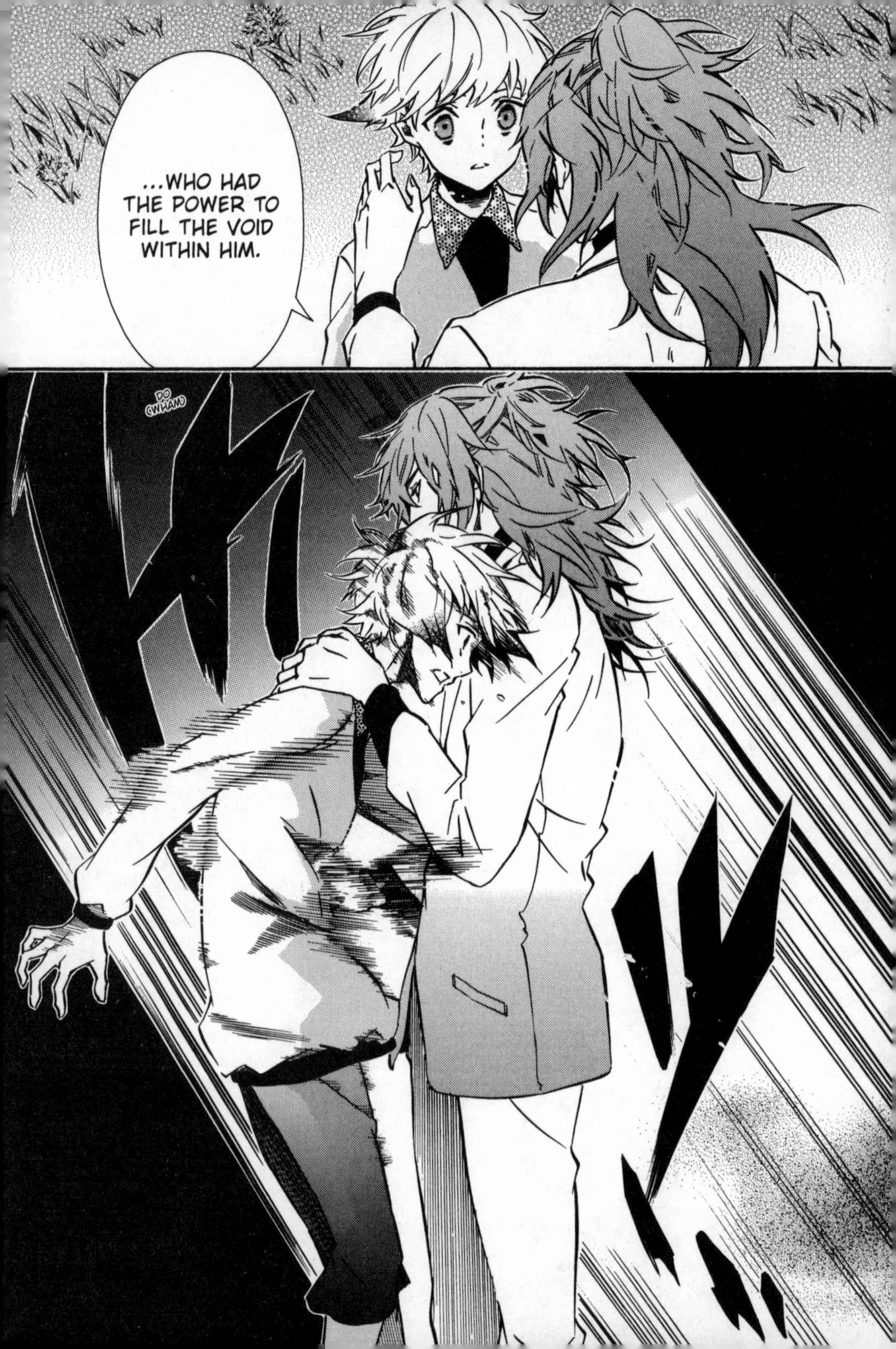
...WHO HAD THE POWER TO FILL THE VOID WITHIN HIM.
DO
(WHAM)

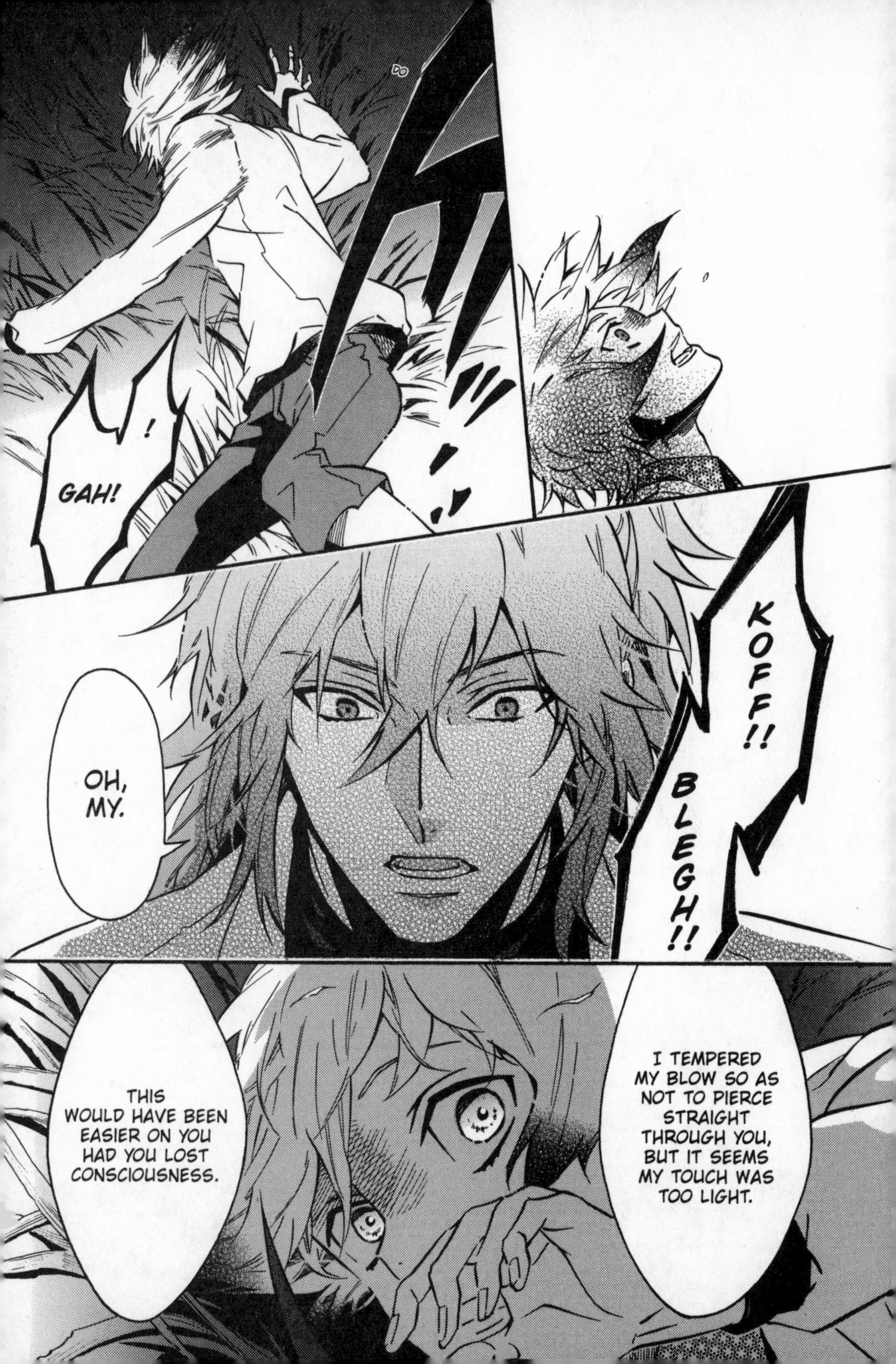
DO
!
GAH!
KOFF!!
BLEGH!!
OH, MY.
I TEMPERED MY BLOW SO AS NOT TO PIERCE STRAIGHT THROUGH YOU, BUT IT SEEMS MY TOUCH WAS TOO LIGHT.
THIS WOULD HAVE BEEN EASIER ON YOU HAD YOU LOST CONSCIOUSNESS.

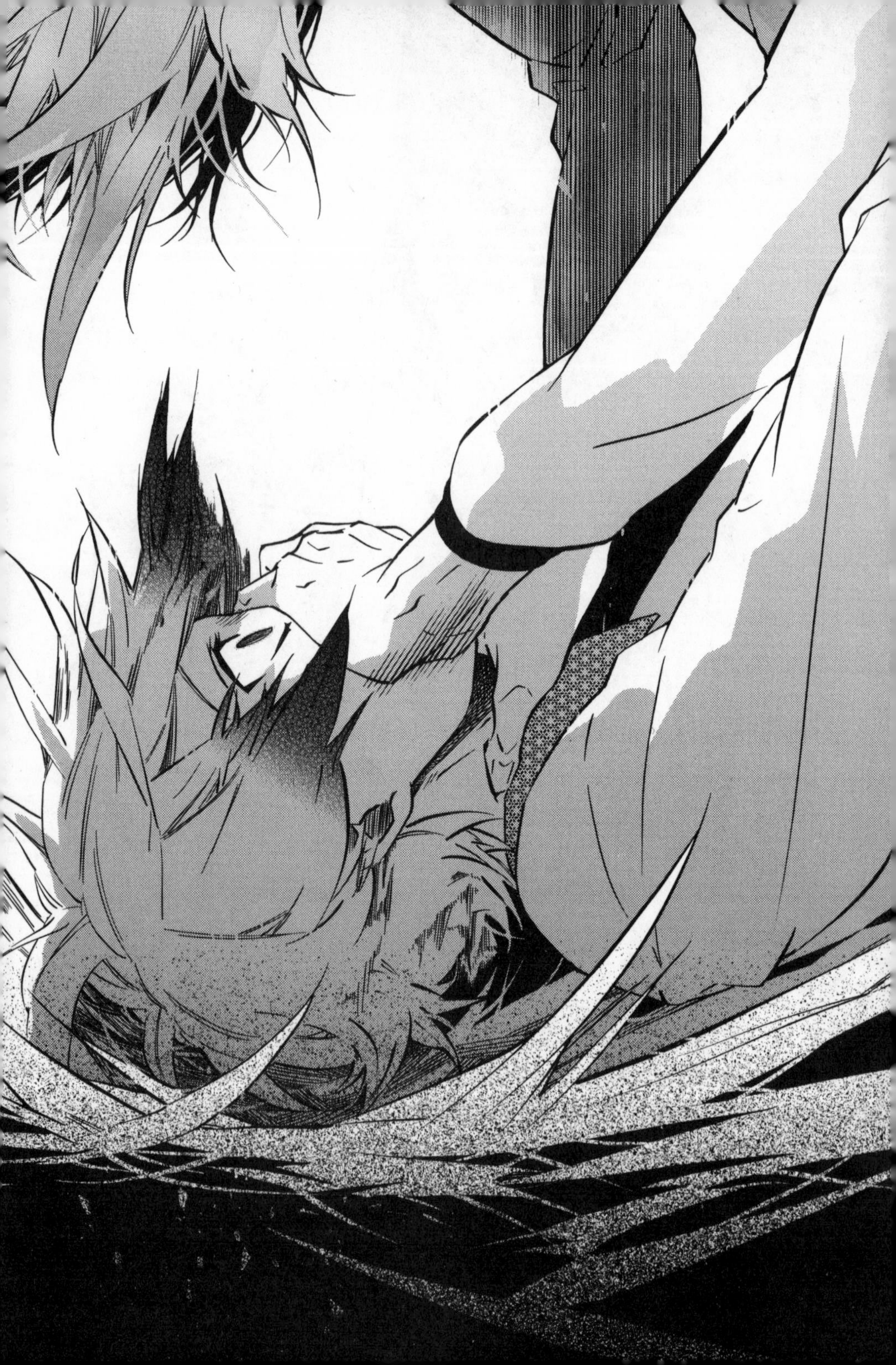

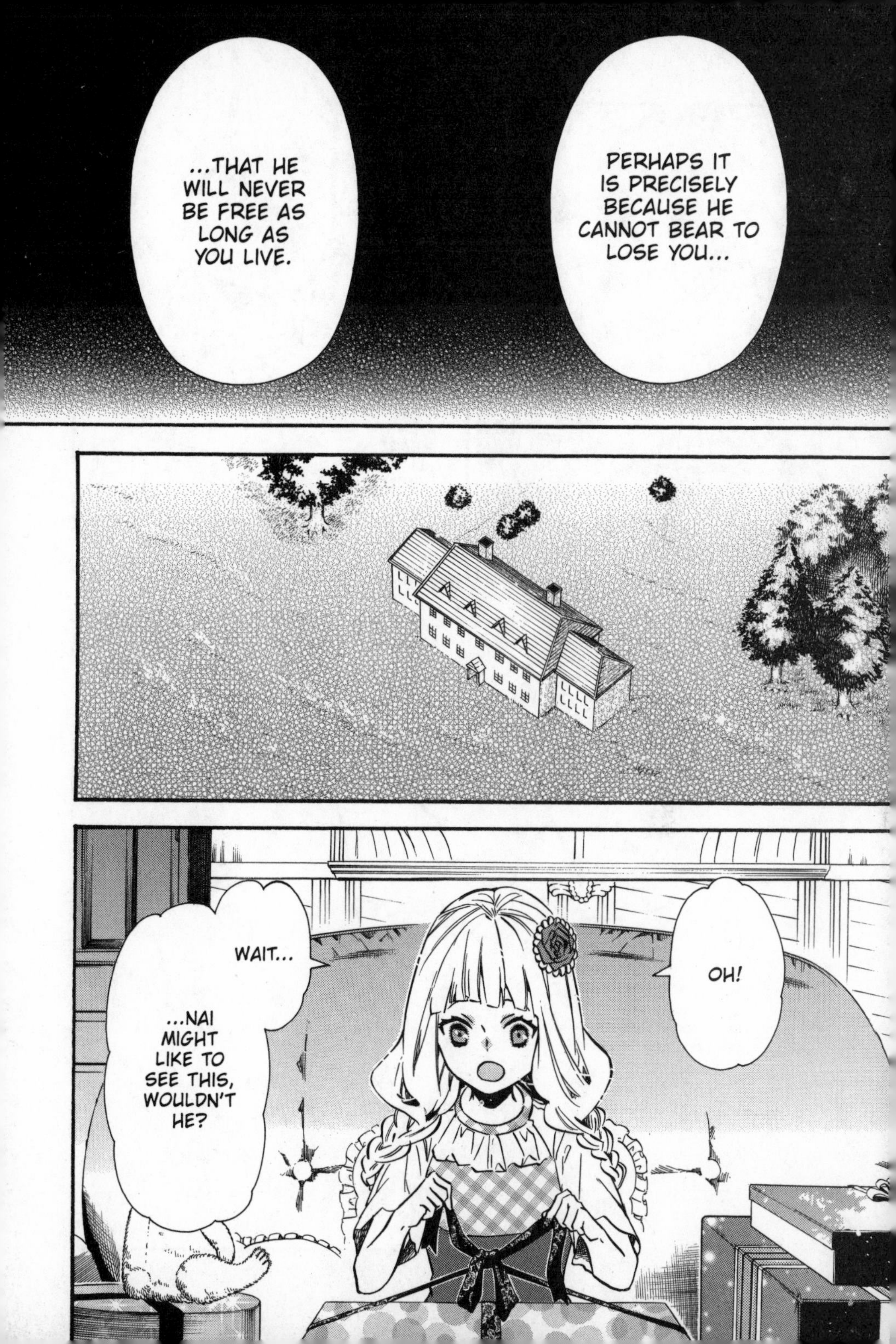
PERHAPS IT IS PRECISELY BECAUSE HE CANNOT BEAR TO LOSE YOU...
...THAT HE WILL NEVER BE FREE AS LONG AS YOU LIVE.
OH!
WAIT...
...NAI MIGHT LIKE TO SEE THIS, WOULDN'T HE?

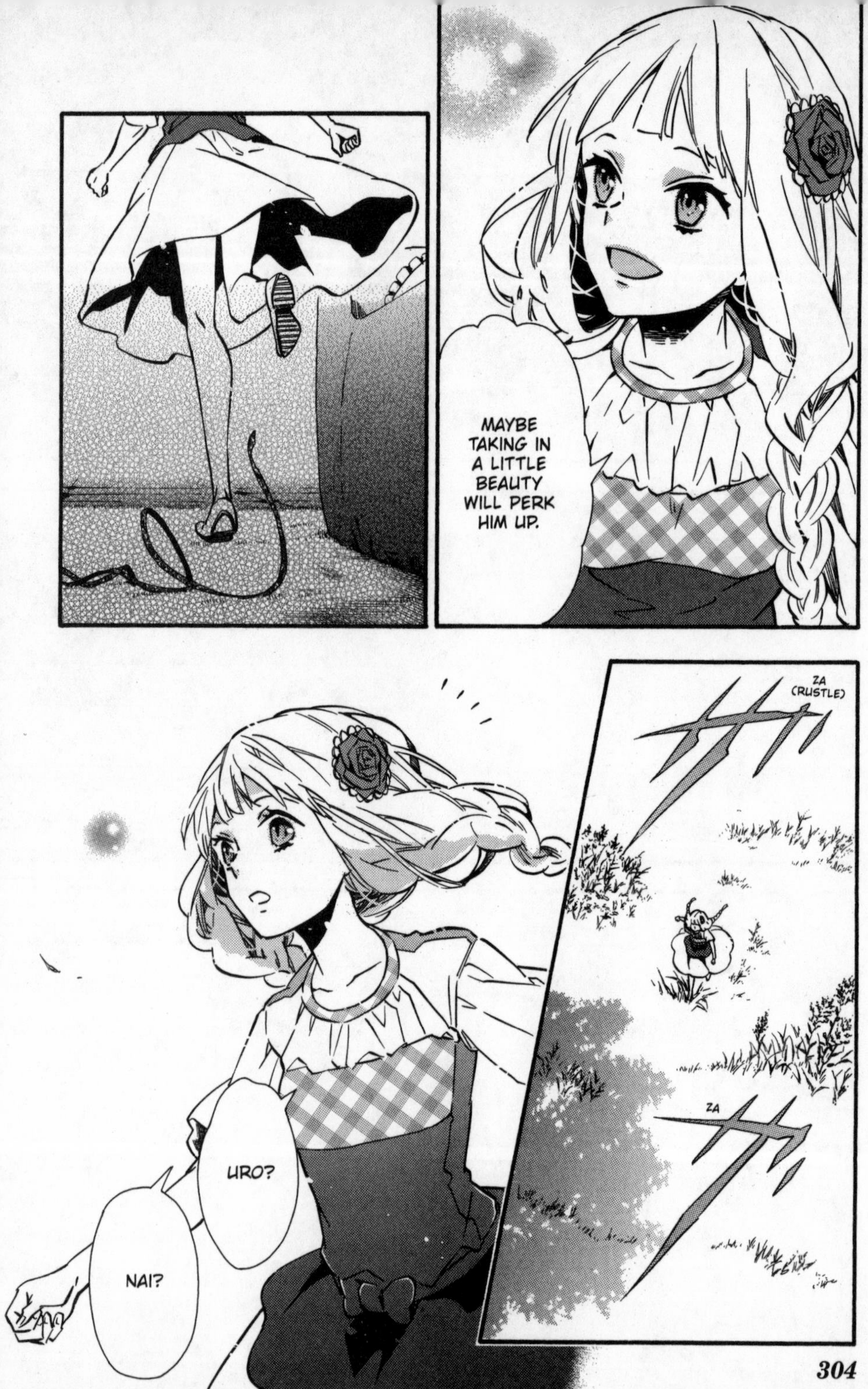
MAYBE TAKING IN A LITTLE BEAUTY WILL PERK HIM UP.
ZA (RUSTLE)
ZA
URO?
NAI?

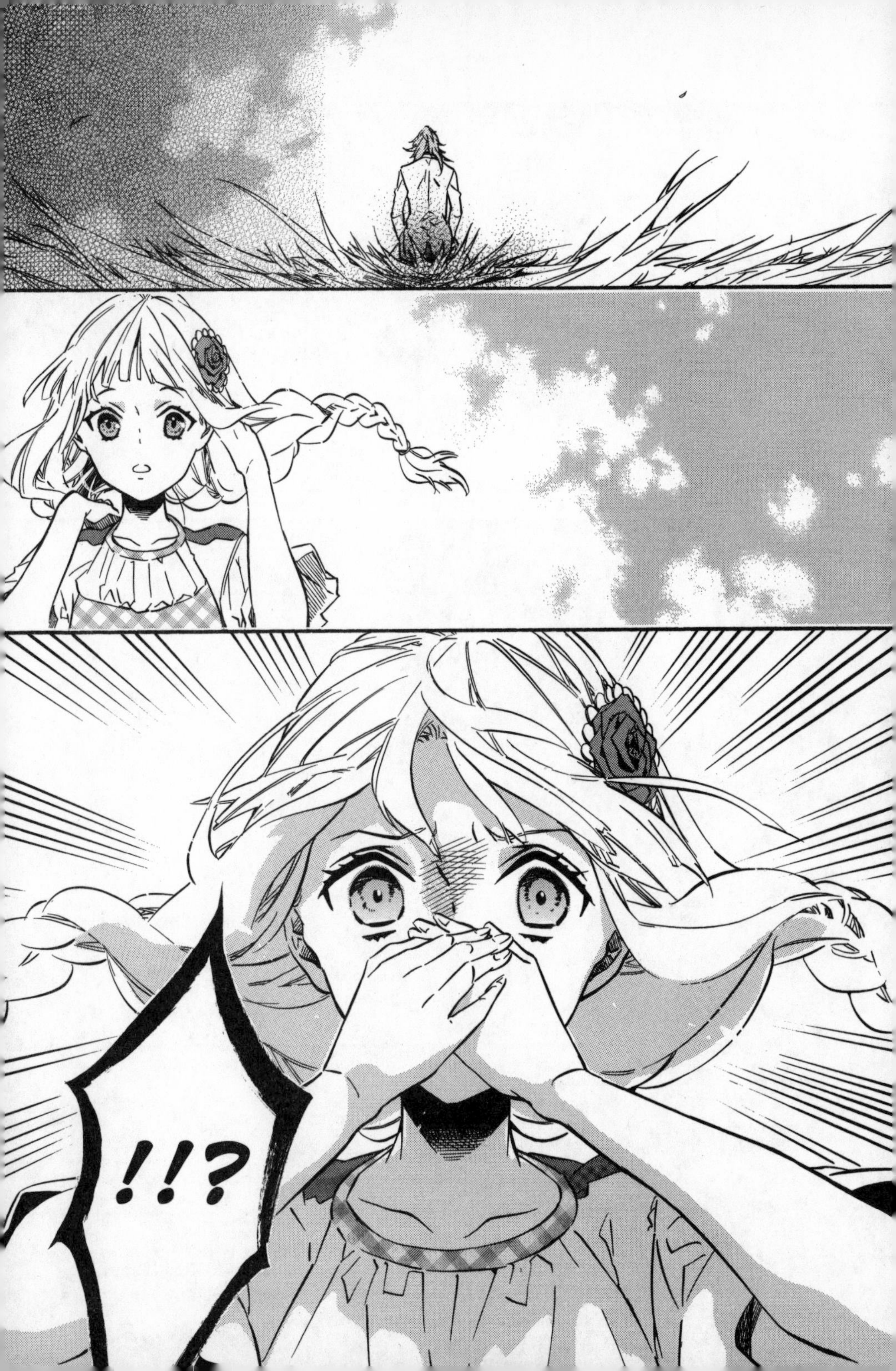
!!?

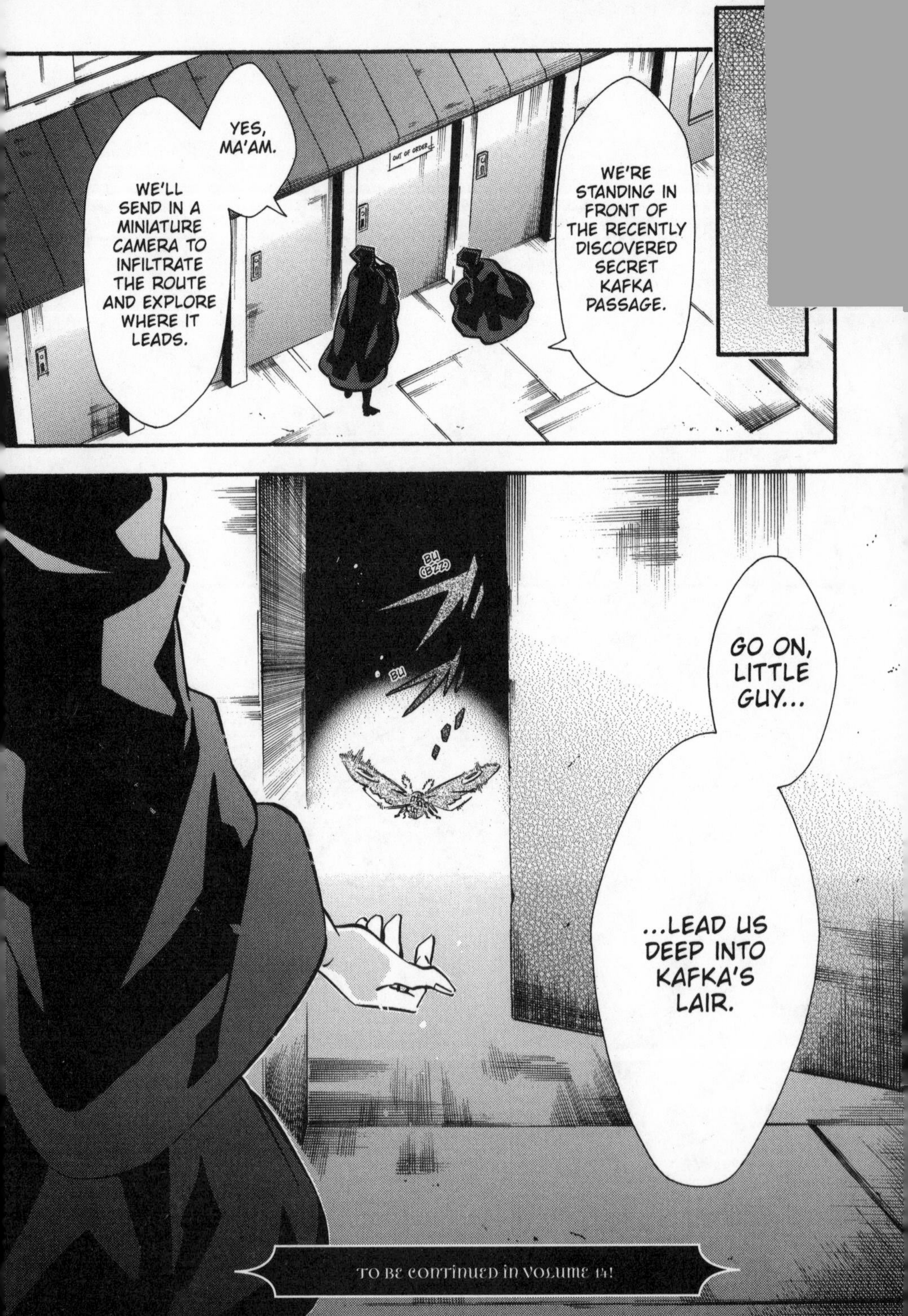
WE'RE STANDING IN FRONT OF THE RECENTLY DISCOVERED SECRET KAFKA PASSAGE.
OUT OF ORDER
YES, MA'AM.
WE'LL SEND IN A MINIATURE CAMERA TO INFILTRATE THE ROUTE AND EXPLORE WHERE IT LEADS.
BU (BZZ)
BU
GO ON, LITTLE GUY...
...LEAD US DEEP INTO KAFKA'S LAIR.
TO BE CONTINUED IN VOLUME 14!

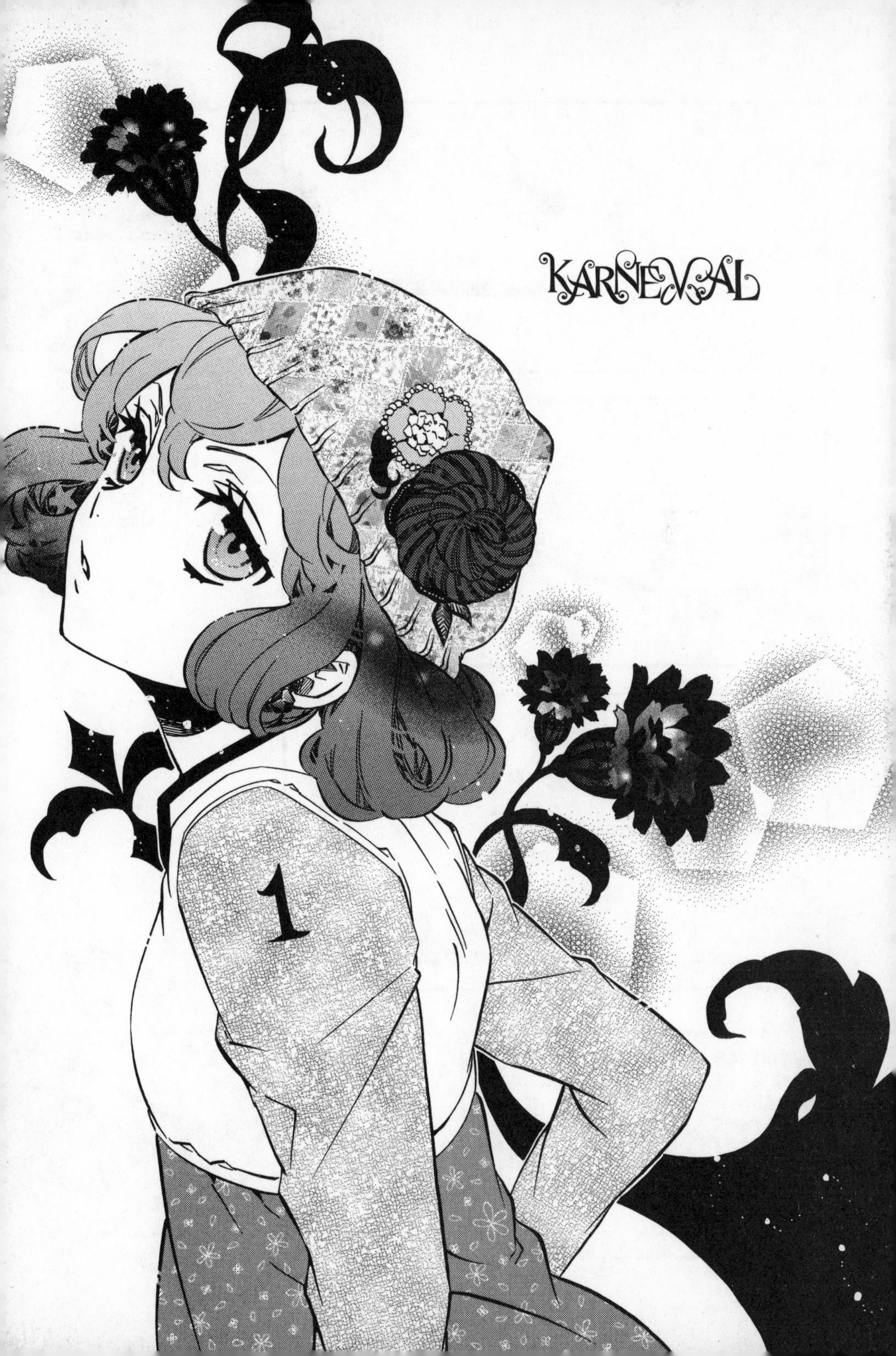
KARNEVAL
1

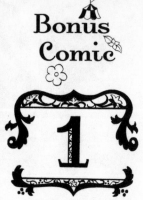

Bonus Comic 1

Innocent Eyes

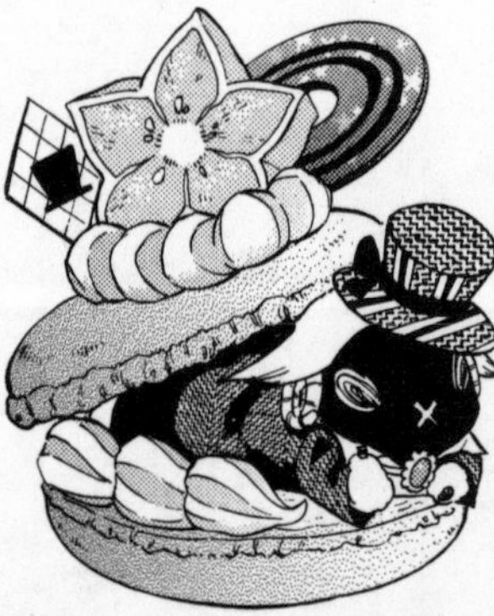

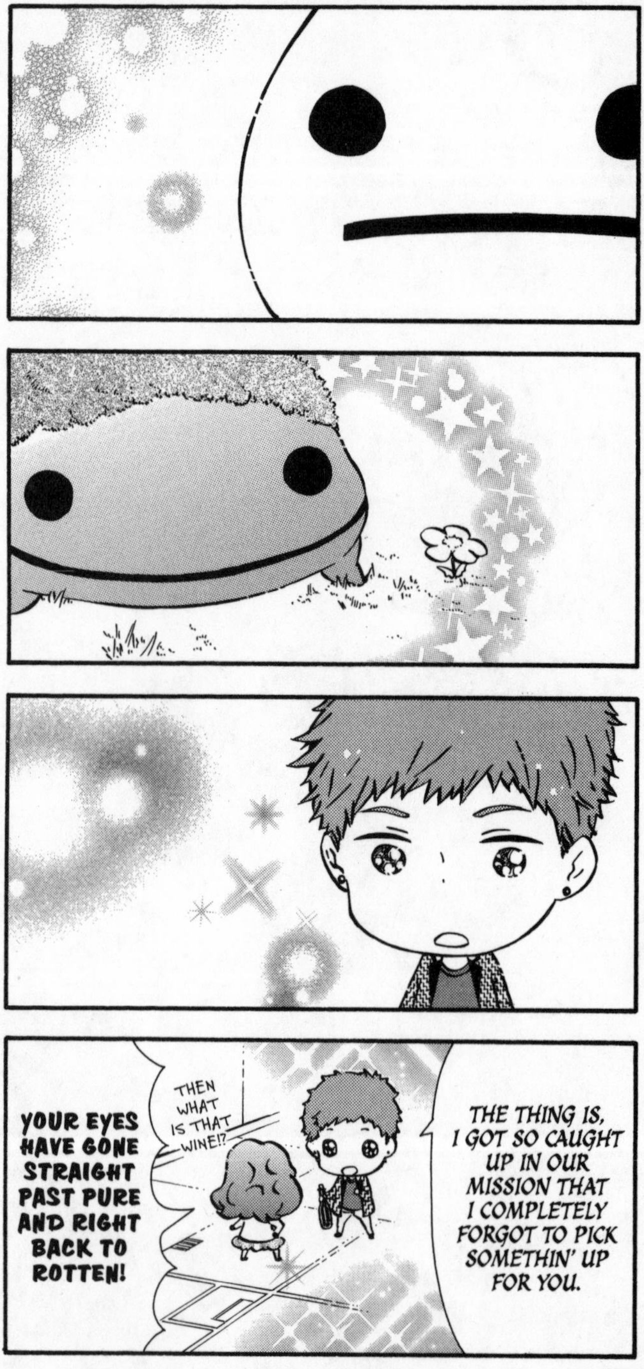
THE THING IS, I GOT SO CAUGHT UP IN OUR MISSION THAT I COMPLETELY FORGOT TO PICK SOMETHIN' UP FOR YOU.
THEN WHAT IS THAT WINE!?
YOUR EYES HAVE GONE STRAIGHT PAST PURE AND RIGHT BACK TO ROTTEN!

Bonus Comic 2

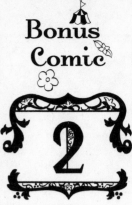

One Therapy Session, Please.

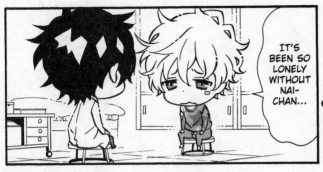

IT'S BEEN SO LONELY WITHOUT NAI-CHAN...
I BORROWED THE MOSS LIZARD PLUSHIE HE LEFT AND HUG IT WHILE I SLEEP, BUT IT'S NOT ENOUGH...
WHOA.
THAT'S REAL BAD.
YOU'RE A GROWN-ASS MAN, AND YOU STILL SLEEP WITH STUFFED ANIMALS? YOU'VE GOTTA DO SOMETHING ABOUT THAT BEFORE ANYTHING ELSE.
FROM NOW ON, DON'T TAKE ANY MORE PLUSHIES WITH YOU TO SLEEP.
BU—
BUT IF I'M ALL ALONE ON THAT HUGE BED...!
I'LL NEVER GET TO SLEEEEEP!
NOT WITHOUT MY NYANPERONAAAAS!
YOGI'S... CLINGING TO HIS SAFETY GAREKI-KUN AGAIN...

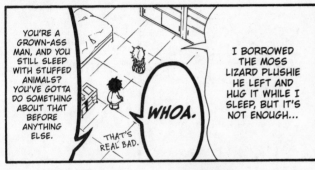

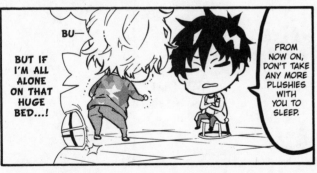

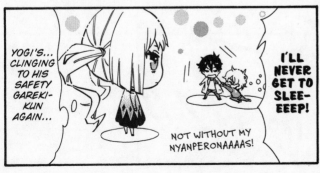

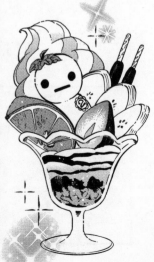

Bonus Comic

3

What Might This Be?

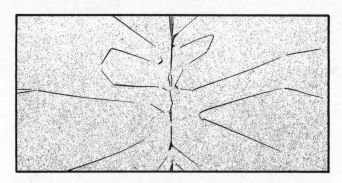

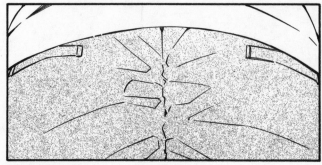

OOH-LA-LA!

IT'S MY BUTT CRACK!

SEE YOU-BUN! ♪

GA (WHACK)

OOOOOW! YOU RIPPED MY—

AFTERWORD

THANK YOU SO MUCH FOR READING THE SECOND HALF OF KARNEVAL OMNIBUS 13. I HOPE YOU ENJOYED IT. AS I WRITE TO YOU NOW, A BEAUTIFUL FULL MOON IS PERCHED HIGH IN THE SKY. I'VE ALWAYS LOVED STARING UP AT THE SKY AND LIKE TO STARGAZE FOR A BIT BEFORE GOING TO BED. ALL TOO OFTEN I'D GET CURIOUS ABOUT THE BRIGHTER ONES THAT CAUGHT MY EYE AND FALL ASLEEP WITHOUT ANY ANSWERS, SO I RECENTLY DOWNLOADED AN APP WITH A CONSTELLATION MAP AND AM HAVING FUN LEARNING ALL THE DIFFERENT NAMES. SOME NIGHTS THERE'LL BE THUNDER BOOMING OFF IN THE DISTANCE. I LOVE WATCHING LIGHTNING TOO, SO I'LL SOMETIMES TURN MY CAMERA TOWARD THE STORM AND SHOOT A LITTLE VIDEO, GUSHING OVER HOW COOL IT IS ALL THE WHILE. IT'S SO BEAUTIFUL TO SEE A STREAK OF LIGHT APPEAR IN ONE PLACE, THEN RUSH OVER AN ENORMOUS EXPANSE WITH INCREDIBLE FORCE, OR WATCH A LIGHTNING BOLT RACE DOWN AND EXPLODE IN A FLASH. I PRAY YOU ALL HAVE LOVELY DAYS AND NIGHTS AHEAD OF YOU!

Touya Mikanagi

Special Thanks

MOTSU-SAN, SUAMA-SAN, (・‿・)-SAN,
MY EDITOR OOHASHI-SAN,
EVERYONE AT ICHIJINSHA PUBLISHING,
ALL THE COLLABORATORS AND
EVERYONE AT OUR AFFILIATED
COMPANIES, MY FRIENDS, MY FAMILY,

and to you!

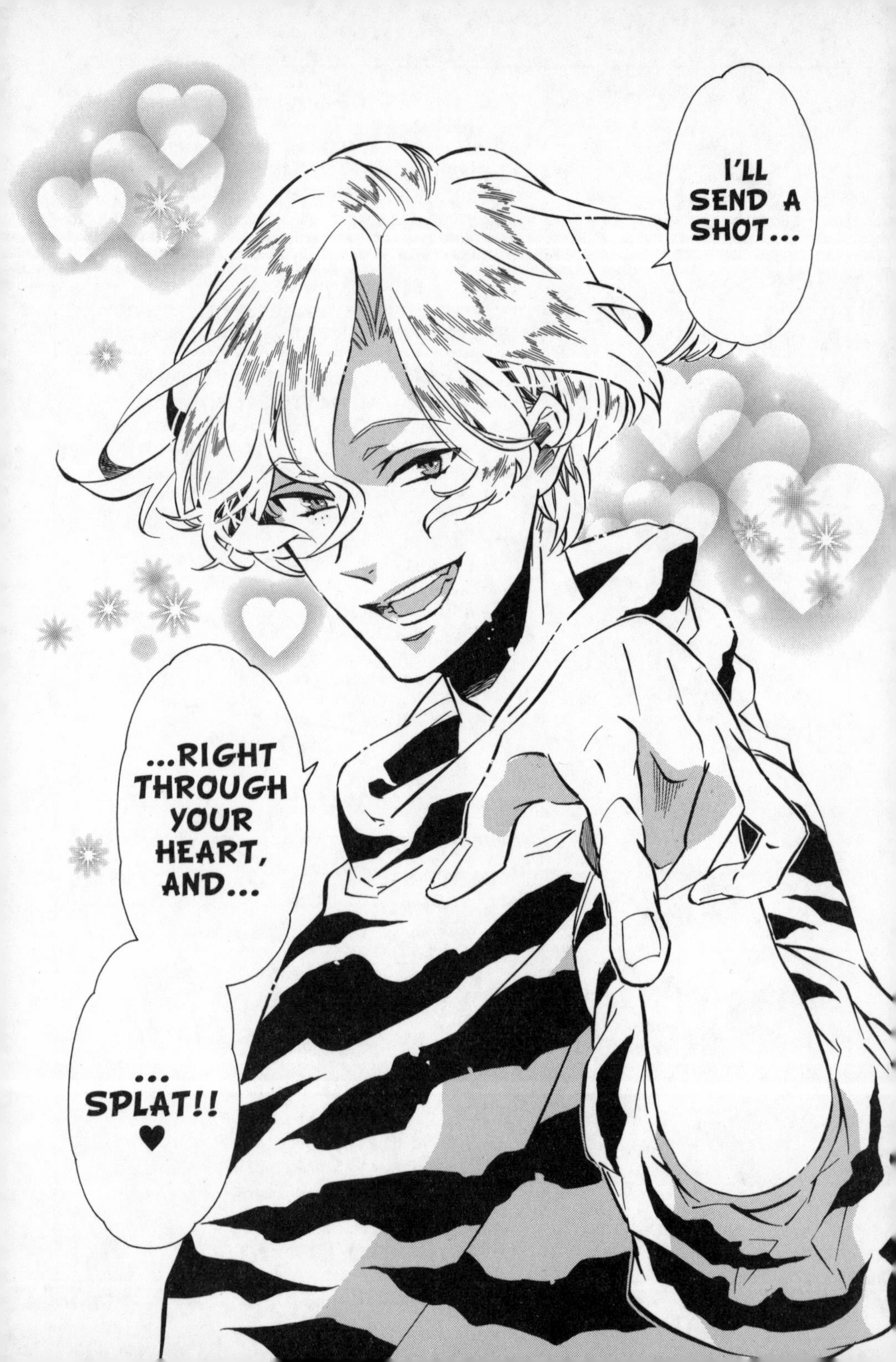
I'LL SEND A SHOT...
...RIGHT THROUGH YOUR HEART, AND...
...SPLAT!! ♥

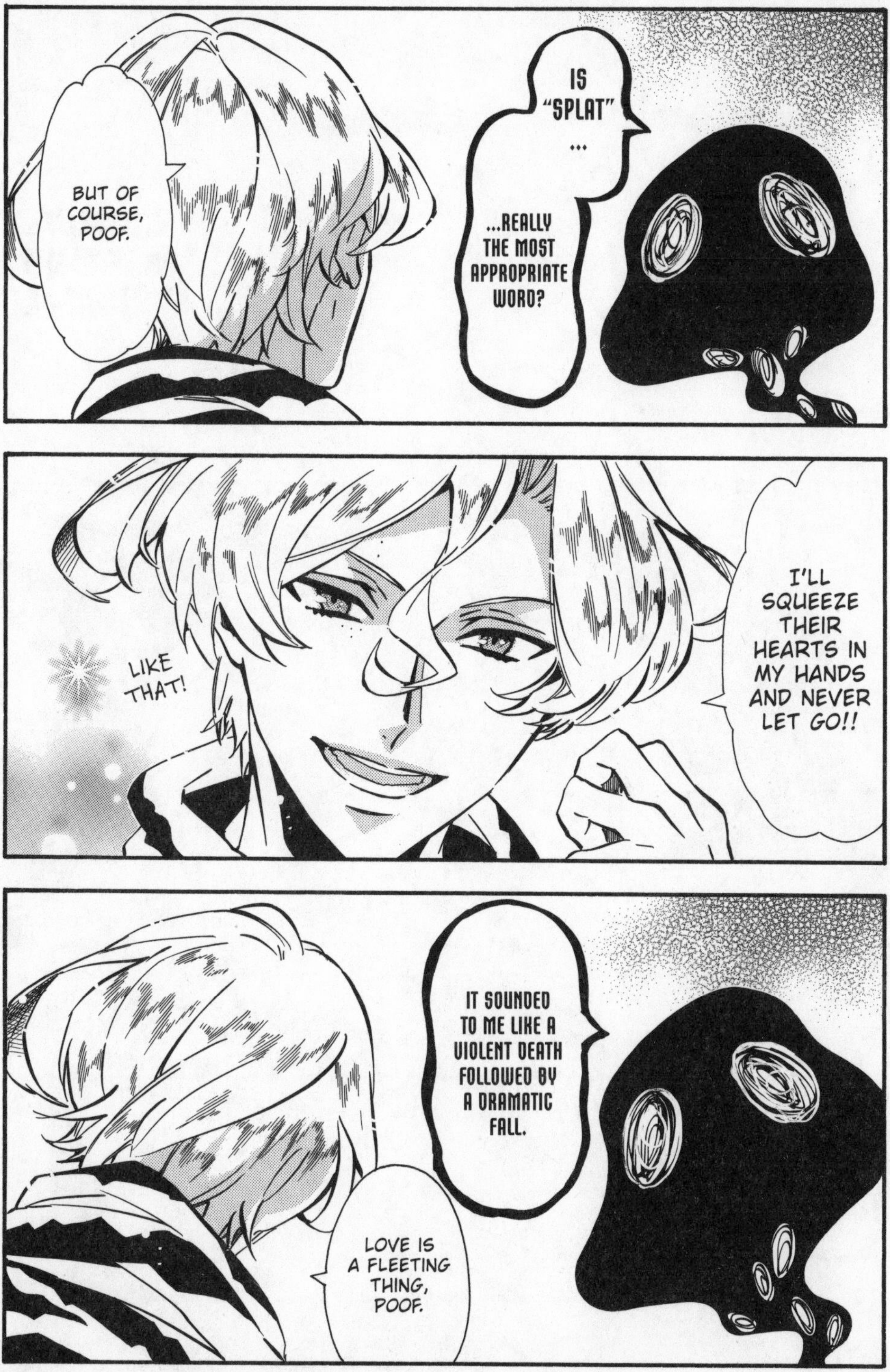
IS "SPLAT" ... ...REALLY THE MOST APPROPRIATE WORD?
BUT OF COURSE, POOF.
I'LL SQUEEZE THEIR HEARTS IN MY HANDS AND NEVER LET GO!!
LIKE THAT!
IT SOUNDED TO ME LIKE A VIOLENT DEATH FOLLOWED BY A DRAMATIC FALL.
LOVE IS A FLEETING THING, POOF.

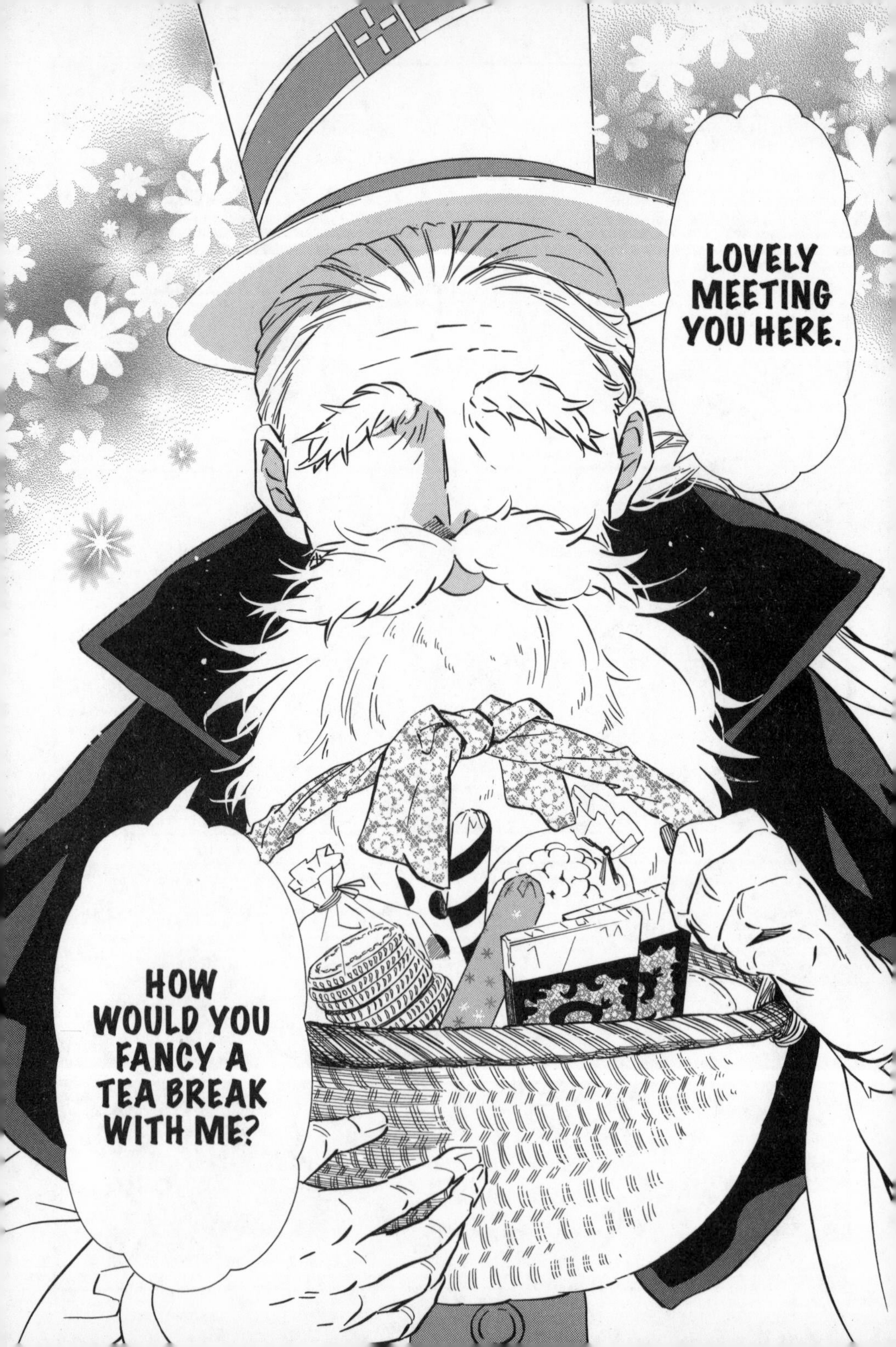
LOVELY MEETING YOU HERE.
HOW WOULD YOU FANCY A TEA BREAK WITH ME?

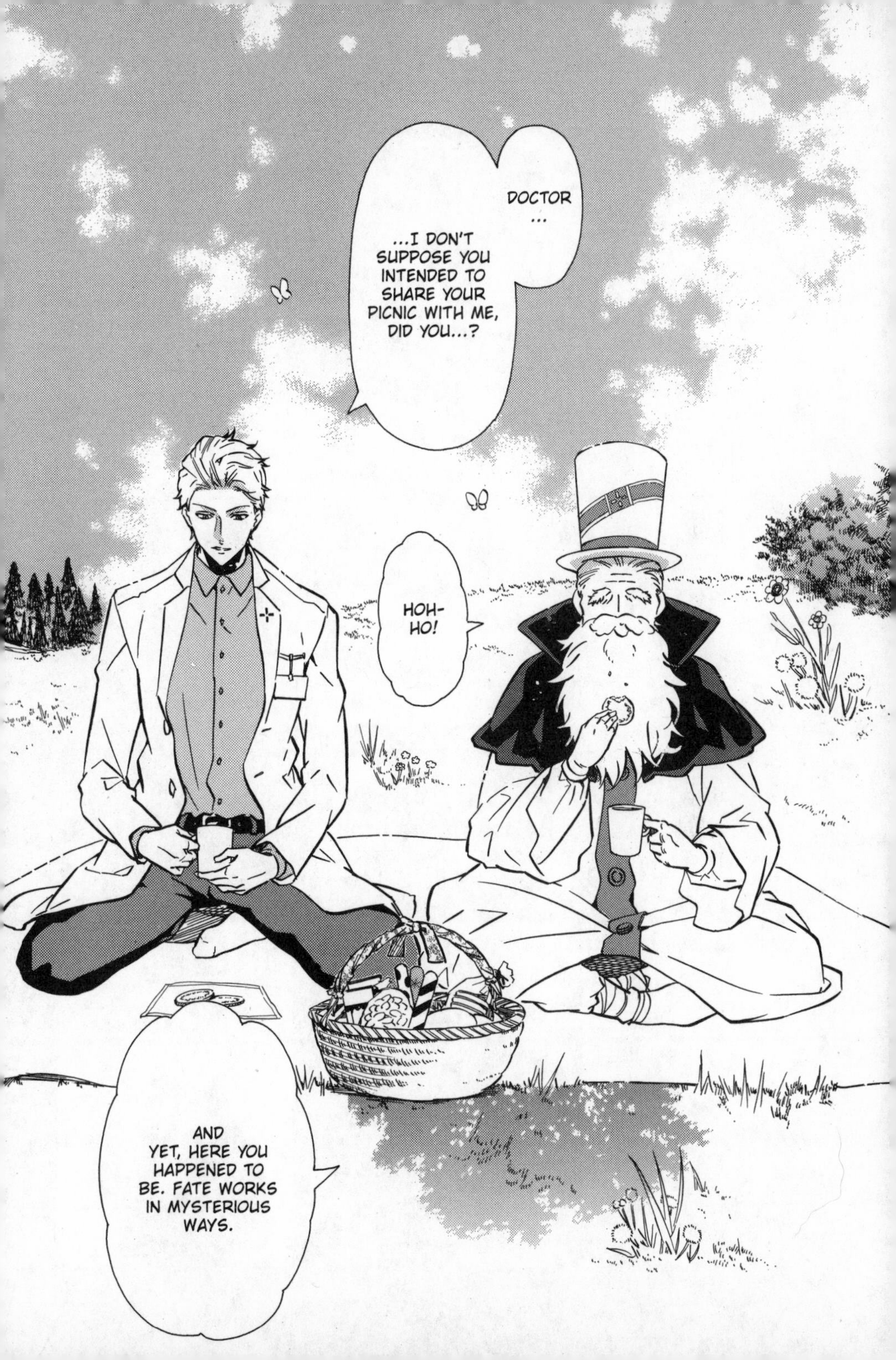
DOCTOR ...
...I DON'T SUPPOSE YOU INTENDED TO SHARE YOUR PICNIC WITH ME, DID YOU...?
HOH-HO!
AND YET, HERE YOU HAPPENED TO BE. FATE WORKS IN MYSTERIOUS WAYS.

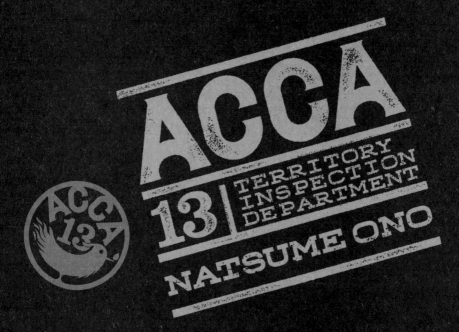

ACCA 13 | TERRITORY INSPECTION DEPARTMENT

NATSUME ONO

Complete in six volumes!
On sale now to rave reviews!!

With the world divided up into thirteen districts, ACCA is the
massive organization that unifies them all. ACCA Headquarters
Inspection Department Vice-Chairman Jean Otus—also known
as "Jean the cigarette peddler"—is a pretty shrewd man.
But he finds himself caught in a web of intrigue as rumors
spread within the organization of a coup d'état. Words, eyes,
invitations follow him everywhere. The secret machinations
of the entire world reach out to trap Jean!!

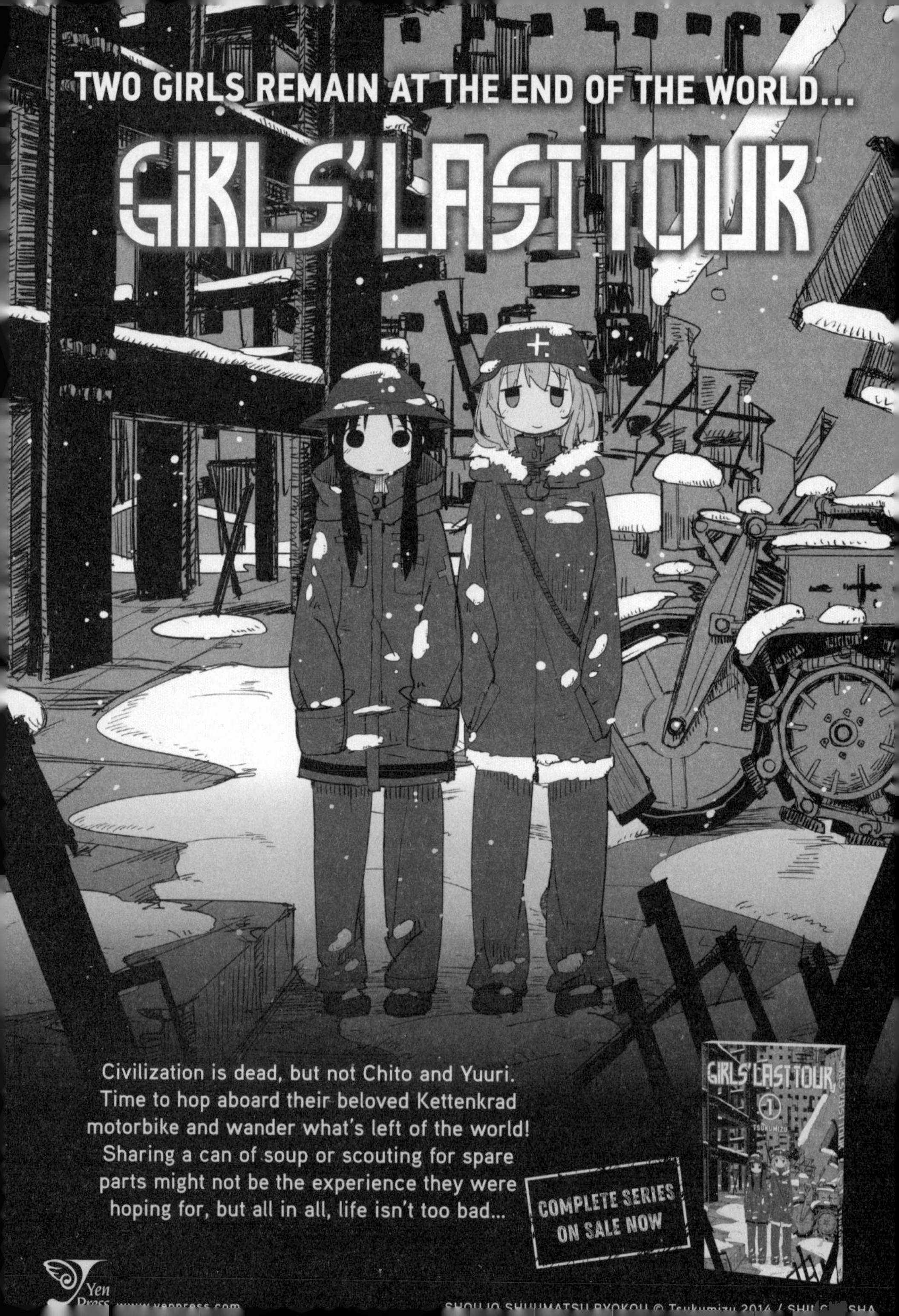
TWO GIRLS REMAIN AT THE END OF THE WORLD...
GIRLS' LAST TOUR
Civilization is dead, but not Chito and Yuuri. Time to hop aboard their beloved Kettenkrad motorbike and wander what's left of the world! Sharing a can of soup or scouting for spare parts might not be the experience they were hoping for, but all in all, life isn't too bad...
COMPLETE SERIES ON SALE NOW
GIRLS' LAST TOUR
1
TSUKUMIZU
Yen Press
www.yenpress.com
SHOUJO SHUUMATSU RYOKOU © Tsukumizu 2014 / SHINCHOSHA

The Detective Is Already Dead

When the story begins without its hero

Kimihiko Kimizuka has always been a magnet for trouble and intrigue. For as long as he can remember, he's been stumbling across murder scenes or receiving mysterious attaché cases to transport. When he met Siesta, a brilliant detective fighting a secret war against an organization of pseudohumans, he couldn't resist the call to become her assistant and join her on an epic journey across the world.

...Until a year ago, that is. Now he's returned to a relatively normal and tepid life, knowing the adventure must be over. After all, the detective is already dead.

Volume 1 available wherever books are sold!

YenPress.com

TANTEI HA MO, SHINDEIRU. Vol. 1
©nigozyu 2019
Illustration: Umibouzu
KADOKAWA CORPORATION

©Aidalro/SQUARE ENIX

VOLUMES 1-14 IN STORES NOW!

VOLUMES 1-16 AVAILABLE DIGITALLY!

Toilet-bound Hanako-Kun

At Kamome Academy, rumors abound about the school's Seven Mysteries, one of which is Hanako-san. Said to occupy the third stall of the third floor girls' bathroom in the old school building, Hanako-san grants any wish when summoned. Nene Yashiro, an occult-loving high school girl who dreams of romance, ventures into this haunted bathroom...but the Hanako-san she meets there is nothing like she imagined! Kamome Academy's

©Makoto Morishita/SQUARE ENIX

VOLUMES 1-11 IN STORES NOW! »»

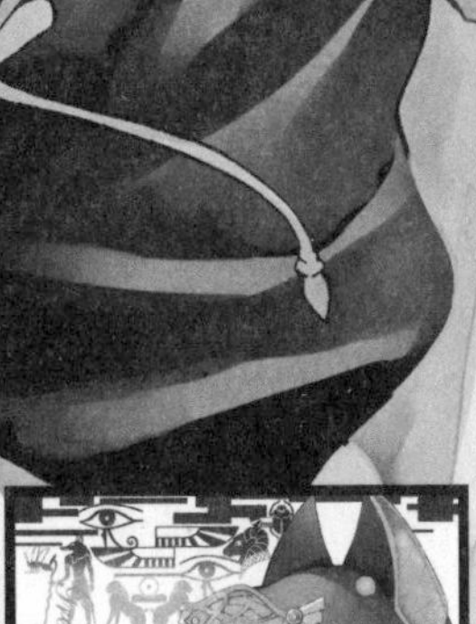

From the sands of ancient Egypt to the streets of modern Japan, being displaced by thousands of miles and years won't distract the newly resurrected Great Priest Imhotep from his hunt for the Magai, devious beings who impersonate the gods and have an appetite for destruction! When schoolgirl Hinome crosses paths with this illustrious ancient, is her loner lifestyle about to change for the better...or the worse?!

For more information visit www.yenpress.com

BUNGO
STRAY DOGS

Volumes 1-21
available now

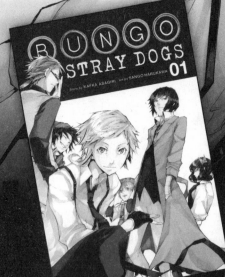

**If you've already seen
the anime, it's time to
read the manga!**

Having been kicked out of the
orphanage, Atsushi Nakajima rescues
a strange man from a suicide attempt—
Osamu Dazai. Turns out that Dazai is
part of a detective agency staffed by
individuals whose supernatural powers
take on a literary bent!

BUNGO STRAY DOGS © Kafka Asagiri 2013
© Sango Harukawa 2013
KADOKAWA CORPORATION

www.yenpress.com

 Yen
Press

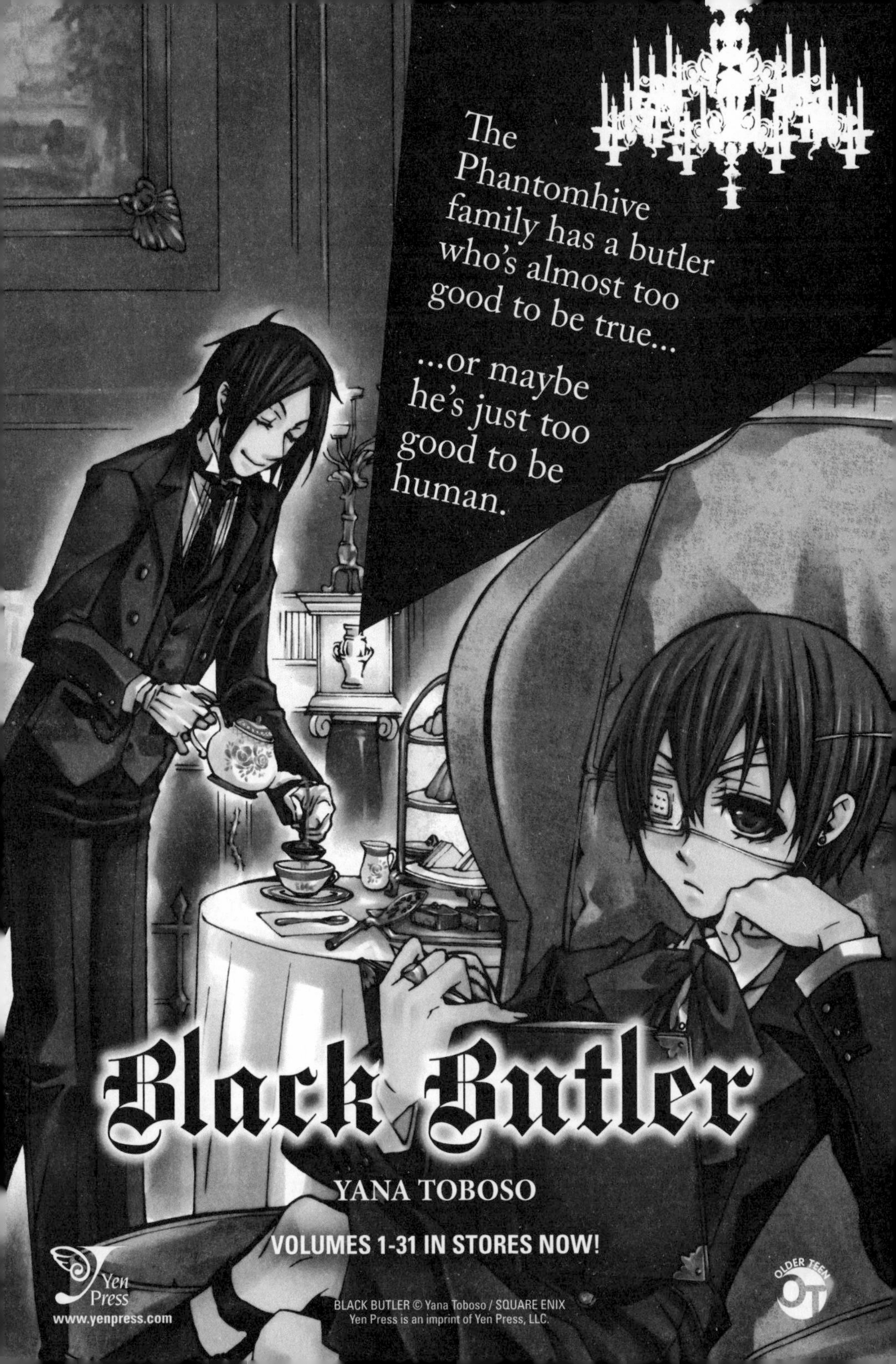
The Phantomhive family has a butler who's almost too good to be true...
...or maybe he's just too good to be human.
Black Butler
YANA TOBOSO
VOLUMES 1-31 IN STORES NOW!
Yen Press
www.yenpress.com
BLACK BUTLER © Yana Toboso / SQUARE ENIX
Yen Press is an imprint of Yen Press, LLC.
OLDER TEEN
OT

So I'm a Spider, So What?

I'M GONNA SURVIVE—JUST WATCH ME!

I was your average, everyday high school girl, but now I've been reborn in a magical world...as a spider?! How am I supposed to survive in this big, scary dungeon as one of the weakest monsters? I gotta figure out the rules to this QUICK, or I'll be kissing my short second life good-bye...

MANGA VOL. 1-10   **LIGHT NOVEL VOL. 1-13**

AVAILABLE NOW!

YOU CAN ALSO KEEP UP WITH THE MANGA SIMUL-PUB EVERY MONTH ONLINE!

KUMO DESUGA, NANIKA? © Asahiro Kakashi 2016 ©Okina Baba, Tsukasa Kiryu 2016
KADOKAWA CORPORATION

KUMO DESUGA, NANIKA? ©Okina Baba, Tsukasa Kiryu 2015 KADOKAWA CORPORATION

YenPress.com

PRESENTING THE LATEST SERIES FROM
JUN MOCHIZUKI

THE CASE STUDY OF
VANITAS

**READ THE CHAPTERS AT
THE SAME TIME AS JAPAN!**

**AVAILABLE NOW WORLDWIDE
WHEREVER E-BOOKS ARE SOLD!**

©Jun Mochizuki/SQUARE ENIX CO., LTD.

www.yenpress.com

KARNEVAL 13

Touya Mikanagi

Translation: Alexandra McCullough-Garcia   Lettering: Phil Christie

This book is a work of fiction. Names, characters, places, and incidents are the product of the author's imagination or are used fictitiously. Any resemblance to actual events, locales, or persons, living or dead, is coincidental.

Karneval vols. 25-26 © 2020 by Touya Mikanagi. All rights reserved. First published in Japan in 2020 by Ichijinsha Inc. Tokyo. Publication rights for this English edition arranged through Kodansha Ltd., Tokyo.

English translation © 2022 by Yen Press, LLC

Yen Press, LLC supports the right to free expression and the value of copyright. The purpose of copyright is to encourage writers and artists to produce the creative works that enrich our culture.

The scanning, uploading, and distribution of this book without permission is a theft of the author's intellectual property. If you would like permission to use material from the book (other than for review purposes), please contact the publisher. Thank you for your support of the author's rights.

Yen Press
150 West 30th Street, 19th Floor
New York, NY 10001

Visit us at yenpress.com • facebook.com/yenpress • twitter.com/yenpress • yenpress.tumblr.com • instagram.com/yenpress

First Yen Press Edition: May 2022

Yen Press is an imprint of Yen Press, LLC.
The Yen Press name and logo are trademarks of Yen Press, LLC.

The publisher is not responsible for websites (or their content) that are not owned by the publisher.

Library of Congress Control Number: 2016936531

ISBNs: 978-1-9753-3715-5 (paperback)
978-1-9753-3716-2 (ebook)

10 9 8 7 6 5 4 3 2 1

WOR

Printed in the United States of America